International Handbook of Technology Education
Reviewing the Past Twenty Years

INTERNATIONAL TECHNOLOGY EDUCATION STUDIES

Scope
Technology Education has gone through a lot of changes in the past decades. It has developed from a craft oriented school subject to a learning area in which the meaning of technology as an important part of our contemporary culture is explored, both by the learning of theoretical concepts and through practical activities. This development has been accompanied by educational research. The output of research studies is published mostly as articles in scholarly Technology Education and Science Education journals. There is a need, however, for more than that. The field still lacks an international book series that is entirely dedicated to Technology Education. *The International Technology Education Studies* aim at providing the opportunity to publish more extensive texts than in journal articles, or to publish coherent collections of articles/chapters that focus on a certain theme. In this book series monographs and edited volumes will be published. The books will be peer reviewed in order to assure the quality of the texts.

International Handbook of Technology Education
Reviewing the Past Twenty Years

Marc J. de Vries

Eindhoven University of Technology, Eindhoven, The Netherlands

Ilja Mottier

PATT Foundation, Leiden, The Netherlands

SENSE PUBLISHERS
ROTTERDAM / TAIPEI

A C.I.P. record for this book is available from the Library of Congress.

ISBN 90-77874-12-7 (Hardback)
ISBN 90-77874-06-2 (Paperback)

Published by: Sense Publishers,
P.O. Box 21858, 3001 AW
Rotterdam, The Netherlands

Printed on acid-free paper

Contents

PREFACE

This Handbook in a way is the outcome of a jubilee. Its chapters were originally written as papers for the 15th International PATT Conference that was held in Haarlem, the Netherlands, April 18-22, 2005. This conference marked 20 years of PATT conferences. PATT started out as a research into Pupils Attitudes Towards Technology (hence the acronym PATT). A national survey in the Netherlands produced outcomes that were intriguing enough to give rise to interest in other countries. As the original Dutch survey started to be replicated in other countries, a first workshop was held in 1985 to bring together the people that were involved in these efforts to discuss methods and outcomes of PATT-studies. This PATT-workshop was to be the first of a still continuing series. At that time we did not yet envision that PATT conferences were to become a long-standing series, and for that reason there was no '1' added to the name of the workshop: it was just PATT, not PATT-1. But later on it appeared that PATT-1 would have been appropriate after all. In the course of time, the scope of PATT conferences broadened. Not only the PATT-studies were discussed, but also consequences for and relationships with all other aspects of technology education: curriculum development, teacher education, education for entrepreneurship, environment, industry, assessment of technology education, impacts of technology education, etcetera. Most of the PATT conferences were held in the Netherlands, but later on PATT conferences were also held in other countries: Kenya, Poland, South Africa, and Scotland. An agreement with ITEA, moderated by Dr. Kendall Starkweather, led to a series of biannual PATT conferences that were embedded in the ITEA Annual Conferences programs.

As PATT-15 had a sort of jubilee character it was decided to use that opportunity to invite people to submit papers in which retrospective views on 20 years of technology education were presented. This appeared to be a good decision, as many colleagues expressed an interest to see what progress had been made in the past two decades. The PATT-15 conference provided a useful platform for discussing these developments and for obtaining a truly worldwide perspective, as countries from all continents were represented. It was our opinion that such a unique opportunity to get an impression of what 20 years of continued efforts in technology education have brought should be opened to those who could not participate as well. It was about that same time that Peter de Liefde came up with the idea to start a new series of books that was to be entirely dedicated to technology education (contrary to series with 'Science Education and Technology Education' that in fact deal with science education primarily). It seemed to be a good idea to start this new series for Sense Publishers with what is now the 'Handbook 20 Years of Technology Education'.

The editors of this book have made a selection of the PATT-15 papers and all of them went through a review process. We want to thank those colleagues who were willing to review papers: *Frank Banks (UK), Rod Custer (USA), John Dakers (UK), Jacques Ginestié (France), Chak-Yin Tang (Hong Kong), John Williams (Australia).* Thanks to their efforts the quality of this book has been guarded carefully. Special thanks to John Dakers and Wendy Dow for the work they did on language editing some papers written bij non-native speakers.

Contrary to many other thematic books we have not strived for uniformity in the papers. This does justice to reality. The situation in different countries varies so widely that the stores of two decades of technology education can take quite different shapes. For some countries we have several expensive papers each of which focus on a different aspect of technology education; for other one short paper is the most efficient way to describe what has happened in 20 years. Some papers are based on empirical research findings; for other countries such data for the description do not exist (yet). This may give the Handbook a somewhat unorthodox appearance, but in our view this is the best way to deal with the global reality of technology education.

We want to thank Peter de Liefde for his initiative to publish this Handbook as the first of the new series '*International Technology Education Studies*'. The technology education community already owes a lot to Peter because of his efforts with respect to the International Journal of Technology & Design Education in the time that he still worked for Kluwer Academic Publishers (now Springer). We wish him all the best with his young publishing company, and we are well aware that its success will be of great value to the field of technology education internationally.

Papendrecht/Leiden, Fall 2005

Marc de Vries and Ilja Mottier
Board of the PATT-Foundation

Part A General introductions

MARC J. DE VRIES

1. TWO DECADES OF TECHNOLOGY EDUCATION IN RETROSPECT

WHY LOOK BACK IF YOU NEED TO MOVE FORWARD?

This handbook offers a fairly unique collection of articles, each of which looks back at a 20 year period of technology education. The collection is truly international. But why bother to write all those retrospective texts? One is tempted to answer: because you can learn from the past how to act in the future. That is certainly not an answer that everyone will take for granted. Some sources say that Henri Ford, the famous car manufacturer, once made the following remark: "history is bunk". Ford was a practical man. His main concern was how to improve the production process of his model-T cars by using the concept of mass production. Studying the past for him did not seem to be a useful way to spend his time. Another quote in the same realm is: "the only thing we learn from history is that we do not learn anything from history" (source unknown). According to this quote it does not matter what the past tells us, because we will not listen anyway. We make the same mistakes over and over. Yet, it may well be that we do unwise by ignoring the past. Here is a third quote: "history teaches nothing, but only punishes for not learning its lessons". This quote takes a different point of view: it may seem that history is a random collection of facts, but once we have concluded from that there nothing can be learnt from history and acted accordingly, we find out to our misfortune that we could have avoided mistakes by taking into account what history after all did appear to tell.

In the development of a school subject or learning area, a period of 20 years is relatively short. Most school subjects have developed in the course of a process that took perhaps even several ages (depending on what one counts as the true starting point of the development). For technology education, it has been a turbulent period, even though indeed it was 'just' 20 years. That makes it even more difficult to draw conclusions from it. Still a retrospective view on the past two decades of technology education may be a useful exercise. In the first place it tells us how we got where we are now. Understanding the current situation can be enriched by insights about how technology education has become what we know it is now. Various questions about why we do the things the way we do them can be answered at least partially by information about the paths that led to the position we take now. In the second place it may help us decide about future steps. 'May' because there is no simple one-to-one relationship between what was in the past

M.J. de Vries, I. Mottier (eds.), International Handbook of Technology Education, 3–11.

and what will be in the future. In that respect the idea that we can simply copy the successful acts from the past into the future does not hold. Too many things change over time and all of those play a part in the failure or success of our acts. Yet is helps to take into account as many as those 'background variables' as we can identify when we try to draw some careful conclusions from the past about what is wise and what is unwise to do. Even then we hesitate to be too firm in our answers, but even if our understanding is only partial, it is still better than knowing nothing.

WHAT CAN HAPPEN IN 20 YEARS?

The articles in this Handbook reveal the diversity in 'histories of technology education' in various countries in the world. Certainly there a common themes and concerns that reoccur in nearly all countries, but the actual process of technology education evolutions differs from one country to the other. Some patterns can be identified. In some cases it seems that there has not been much movement at all. In some countries, technology education was a craft-oriented school subject 20 years ago and it still is. Some of the Scandinavian countries are in that category, but also Switzerland and Austria. One seldom meets people from those countries in (international) technology education conferences, not do we find publications about those countries in our scholarly journals. In other countries the situation of technology education looks very much the same as the situation of 20 years ago, but rather than stability there was a period of back-and-forth movement, or, if one prefers to phrase it differently, a period of circular movement. Changes have been made and have been made undone in the same short 20-year period. Malta, and in some respects Scotland, are examples of that. It can be a very frustrating experience to be involved in such a movement. Fortunately in a third category of countries real and lasting progress has been made. Country size does not seem be play a vital part in that, because both a large country such as the USA, and a much smaller country such as New Zealand can be counted among the countries in this category. Evidently the secret of success is not in being small or being large, but in other factors that are worth identifying because they might yield important information about what works and what does not (again: we have to be careful here and take into account the many peculiarities and 'background variables'). Fourthly and finally, there are countries in which developments in the past 20 years have led to a point of decision. In those 20 years fundamental changes have been made in the teaching about technology in schools, and now the politicians want to see results. In many cases it is difficult to anticipate what kind of results they see as valuable. But in any case politicians are not patient people. In spite of what educationalists say, twenty years is a long rather than a short period for them. Money has been invested and they want to harvest now. Educationalists will see that as unfair, but it is social reality and just the way things are. In countries such as France and the Netherlands we see this happening: governments push to decisions: do we want to keep technology education as a distinct entity in the curriculum, do we integrate it with better-established entities such as science education, or do we want to do away with it totally? Of course one can not reasonably expect a new or drastically reformed school subject to result in concrete evidence of success in just 20 years. Yet, for several countries the fate of technology education depends on that.

The picture sketched above is a simplification for countries that consist of states each of which has a certain degree of autonomy in educational matters. Canada and Germany are examples of that. Different states in those countries have taken different routes in the past 20 years and with different outcomes. In the case of Germany the variety makes it virtually impossible to write an article on '20 years of technology education in Germany'. For Canada an effort has been made to write such an article, but here we see at least some movement towards a common approach between states. Such a movement is possible, as the examples of the USA and Australia show us. Those countries started our 20 year period with a very diversified situations, but in that period quite serious efforts have been made to reach agreements among the various states. It is clear that there are advantages of scale in that. Practice also reveals that agreements at a high level of management do not immediately result in changes at the 'work floor level'. Policy and practice can be quite different things.

AREAS OF PROGRESS

In spite of all the frustrations that people go through in several of the countries that are represented in this Handbook, the overall impression is that there are at least some areas where real progress has been made in the past 20 years. In this section the most important ones will be described. For all of those it needs to be emphasized that none of them guarantees the survival of technology education. The examples of France and the Netherlands show that technology education has come under serious threat in spite of the fact that substantial progress has been made in several of the areas that will be described here. In particular the New Zealand case shows that it is only when a combination of areas of progress in is place, the position of technology education in the curriculum flourishes.

A first area of progress is in the philosophical basis for technology education. Two types of progress are visible here. The first one is the evolution of the philosophy of technology as a disciplinary field. In the past 20 years the existing 'Continental' philosophy of technology ('Continental' thereby referring to the fact that most philosophers of this kind of 'the big questions' philosophy lived and worked on the European Continent), became accompanied by a more analytically-oriented kind of philosophy of technology. Analytical philosophy originally was mainly Wittgenstein-oriented and positivist philosophy, but now it is much broader. In general one can say that a stream of philosophers has grown that are interested in analyzing technology 'from inside' rather than only making normative statements about the 'impacts' or 'effects' of technology on humans and on society. Debates about 'the big questions' according to those philosophers would benefit greatly from careful analyses about what technology actually is and how themes such as technical artifacts, technological knowledge, design processes can be conceptualized properly. A second progress is that technology educators in the past two decades have become more and more interested into studying the field of philosophy of technology. Perhaps they had good reasons to do that not until recently. Many of the Continental philosophers wrote fairly critically about technology without showing evidence of a real understanding of what engineers do and think (and perhaps even without showing evidence of a genuine interest to get to know that). That can be a reason for people involved in teaching technology to keep distance from those philosophers in whose eyes technology can only do harm. Many of the analytical philosophers of technology have an engineering background themselves. That makes them more attractive for technology educators as references in the process of establishing a conceptual framework for technology education. The need for having such a framework is becoming more and more evident, in particular in those countries in which the position of technology education in the curriculum is under threat now. If in such a situation neither teachers, nor teacher educators, nor curriculum developers can give a proper and convincing answer to the question "what is your subject about?", then one can expect serious trouble.

A second area of progress is the scope of the content of technology education in the school curriculum. Here a movement has taken place from a position in which technology education has a narrow focus, being mainly about craft skills, towards a situation in which teaching about technology also takes into account the social aspects of technology and the more cognitive, conceptual and epistemic aspects of technology. It is interesting to see that this broadening of scope has led to different changes in the definition of the content of technology education at the policy level. In some countries the widening of scope has resulted in the insight that it is simply impossible and fruitless to try to capture each and every topic in the curriculum by working with a detailed description of the subject content. In such countries, like the UK and South Africa, the content description at policy level has become less detailed, thus leaving ample opportunity for schools to make their own widening of scope according to their local needs. In other countries, such as the USA, the broadening in scope resulted in a more detailed description of standards for technology education. The idea behind doing that is the experience that schools will not broaden the scope of technology education unless that get clear directions about what new aspects to include. It is difficult to say which of these two approaches (becoming less detailed or more detailed) works best and probably this is an example of where one must take into account all the 'background variables' of a country when assessing what can be learnt from it.

The broadening in content scope has gone hand in hand with a pedagogical development. In the early phases of technology education there was a strong focus on learning specific skills in a sort of guilds tradition. The master would show how to do it and the pupil would copy the act. Nowadays pupils are expected to develop their own ideas about technology, thereby starting from intuitive ideas towards ideas that have been learnt in authentic situations (as far as educational settings allow for realizing those, of course). In this respect technology education has been in the fortunate position that there were many newly gained insights in science education. Terms as 'cognitive apprenticeship', 'authentic learning', and 'constructivist approach' could all be borrowed from science education. That, of course, does not mean that technology education could skip all the years of struggle that science education went through to get grips on these issues, but it surely helped technology education mature in a much shorter period. Such struggles can be seen for example in the way design projects have been conducted in the UK in earlier years. Pupils were then guided to fairly prescribed processes that sometimes almost got the character of 'rituals'. Pupils were forced to come up with more than one possible design solution, merely for the fact that the design process flowchart demanded so. No one seemed to be concerned about the fact that pupils did this only to immediately reject the options in which they has never believed anyway but that they had produced only for the sake of obeying the teacher's flowchart. So clearly, struggles have been there in finding a good pedagogy for technology education even given the possibilities of transfer from science education pedagogy.

A fourth area of progress in the overall development of technology education worldwide is educational research. Twenty years ago for publishing research output there were only science education journals available for people conducting technology education research. Now we have several scholarly journals, one of which is published by a well-respected commercial academic publisher. The existence of such journals is a precious thing. It guarantees that technology education research can be published, also in cases where there is no direct relationship with science education. But those journals need content, and therefore it is important that technology education research is done and will continue to be done. In the past 20 years the research agenda has certainly made progress. In earlier years, most technology education research dealt with desired curriculum content. If at all these studies were of an empirical nature, they were surveys among experts to ask their opinions about what should be taught and learnt in technology education. This was certainly a necessary part of the research agenda, and to some extent it will always remain to be that. But gradually a new type of study emerged: empirical studies into classroom practice. Such studies were extremely useful, for example for revealing the 'ritual' character of many design projects. Also an interest emerged in getting to know what pupils, students and teachers think about technology and about technology education. This type of research, though, still today is only a small minority of all research studies, in spite of the fact that it seems to have an evident relevance for teaching about technology.

A fifth area in which undeniable progress has been made is the assessment of technology education. It must be remarked right away, though, that this is at the same time an area in which there is still a tremendous lot of work to be done. As for studies into people's ideas about technology, for assessment studies too it seems totally needless to defend the relevance of such studies. And yet, for a long time there have been scarcely any developments there. Testing cognitive aspects of technology by means of paper-and-pencil tests was taken for granted as well as testing craft skills by letting pupils make simple (and useless) objects. That creative and problem solving skills also needed to be evaluated, and that this was a very complicated matter, was not recognized until recently. It is only since recent years that we begin to understand the need for developing more sophisticated and varied instruments for assessing the various cognitive, affective and psychomotor aspects of technology. Much work has been done in portfolio type of assessments, in particular in the UK. Also in terms of research methodology undeniably progress has been made. In earlier years only quantitative research methods were taken seriously. But more recently, qualitative research methods have become real sources of insights, even though some methodological difficulties still linger on. In the meantime, educational research is certainly one of the areas that is under serious threat at the same time. The number of research centers for technology education worldwide seems to decrease rather than to increase. This has an impact, of course, on the flow of articles that go into scholarly journals for technology education. It also has an impact on the number and quality of project proposals that agencies such as the Technical Foundation of America receive. There is certainly no reason to sit back and enjoy the results of success.

The sixth area of progress is the international communication and cooperation in technology education. The past two decades have shown the emergence of a number of series of international conferences and projects. One of the long-term ones is the series of PATT conferences (PATT is the acronym for: Pupils' Attitudes Towards Technology). Such conferences and projects are no longer temporary exchanges of ideas, but they are more and more influencing the development of technology education in various countries. Finland is a good example of that. Key persons in technology education participated in international activities and implemented ideas from that into their national curriculum. Another example is South Africa, where the original UK influence was increasingly mixed with ideas from other countries. Another indication for the internationalization of technology education is the increasing ambition of the USA's main teachers' association ITEA (International Association for Technology Education) to give international support to technology educators in various ways (for instance, by hosting the Technology Education Research Forum, in which major trends in technology education are identified and debated by people from all over the world). It may well be that these international contacts will become of crucial importance for the survival of technology education. In South Africa it had almost been decided to remove technology education as such from the curriculum, but the South African technology educators were able to convince their government that this would put South Africa in an isolated position internationally. Likewise, referring to developments in other countries may help technology educators in countries where technology education is under threat.

A TIME OF DECISION

As it has been remarked before, in a number of countries it seems the hour of truth has come. Governments question the relevance of technology education in their national curriculum, given the unclear status and results it still has. Several of the articles in this Handbook testify about decreasing numbers of hours for technology education in the schools' timetables, decreasing numbers of available teachers and of teachers-in-training, and decreasing budgets for technology teachers and for technology education research. In a number of countries the solution that governments envision is to integrate technology into science education. That is not an unreasonable thought. Technology, or at least modern technology, and science are closely intertwined. But the combination of technology education and science education is a mixed blessing for technology. Certainly there are positive aspects to this: technology will gain from the status of science educations, once linked to it more closely. Also there is gain in terms of content: a good understanding of the nature of technology necessarily entails an understanding of the relationship between science and technology. But there is a reverse side. Teaching the nature of technology as such may easily get lost once it is in the hand of science educators, many of whom still work with the old 'technology as applied science' paradigm. In the philosophy of science and of technology this paradigm has been abandoned almost entirely, but in education it still hangs around. In that paradigm technological topics are used in science education to motivate pupils to learn science content, or to show the 'application' of science in devices and systems. But the process that leads from science knowledge (and a whole lot of other factors) toward the products that we see around us remains hidden in that approach. And is not that process in the very heart of technology?

Yet, there is hope. The articles in this Handbook that tell us about serious threats to technology education are balanced by other articles that present cases of success. The survival of technology education in South Africa has been mentioned already before, as well as the success of the introduction of technology education in New Zealand. Also we read about enthusiastic teachers and pupils in countries such as Israel and Chile. This enthusiastic atmosphere is sometimes so evident that it can not be ignored by policy makers. That enthusiasm perhaps in the end is the best proof that something has been gained, even though it can not yet be expressed and calculated in terms of increased numbers of students in engineering, improved national economies, better results in industries or whatever 'objective' variable one would like to use as an indicated for the success of technology education.

HOW THEN TO PROCEED?

There is one thing one can be sure about: enthusiastic teachers and pupils will not be there unless we continue our efforts to build up a sound technology education theory and practice. Both these sides need to be covered. There is a continuous need to get clarity about the nature of technology and of technology education. At the same time we need to work on a technology education practice that convinces governments, school administrators and school boards, teachers, parents, and pupils, that teaching and learning about technology is not only fun but also a necessary component of every (future) citizen's general education. The fact that these efforts have shown not to be sufficient for guaranteeing the survival of technology education should never hold us back from continuing these efforts. At the same time we need to improve in sophistication in our dealing with the political process that in the end is decisive for technology education in schools. Often this process is a mystic sort of alchemy to us. We have great difficulties to estimate what is important in the eyes of those who decide about the position of technology education in a country's educational system. Perhaps it would be worthwhile for technology educators to invest in gaining a better understanding of this process. It may not be the most interesting issue from an academic point of view, but it could well be of crucial importance for the decision about whether or not ultimately there will be any other activity for those involved technology education. Seeking international support has already been mentioned as a possible success factor in the survival of technology education in the coming decades.

THE STRUCTURE OF THE HANDBOOK

Two options for structuring the content of this Handbook have been considered. In the first option the content is present thematically. Such an approach would lead to sections on standards and curriculum content, on teacher education, on the use of media, on assessment, and on educational research, just to mention a couple of possible themes. We have chosen the alternative option of presenting the developments in technology education of the past two decades country-wise. The various themes in the development of technology education are so closely intertwined that describing national developments in terms of separated themes would seriously hurt the validity of that description. Therefore we have asked people to write about 20 years of technology education in their countries in a more comprehensive way. At the same time, for a number of countries articles have been written that do have a certain focus on specific issues, to enrich the more overall description of the country's technology education evolution. The series of national surveys of 20 years of technology education are preceded by a small number of papers of a more general scope, namely about (the nature of) comparative studies and about trends in research methodologies. These articles are meant to guide us in our appreciation of the nationally oriented part of the Handbook. The order of the countries in this part is not related in any respect to the importance of those countries or to the success or failure of developments. We have only grouped countries in larger regions or continents. Even that is already more than one can really justify. The variety in approaches of technology education in Europe is already so large that the sense of taking Europe as one region is questionable. Yet, for other 'regions' (North America, for instance) there is more justification in presenting developments in that way.

This editors' choice has resulted in the following structure of the Handbook. This introductory chapter is followed by two papers of a more general nature: Starkweather's article on the relevance of technology education and for studying developments in technology education, Pavlova's article on comparative studies, Dagan's article as a concrete example of such a study, and Middleton's article on international trends in technology education research methodologies. Then follow a number of sections that contain studies on specific countries. We start with a section on North-American developments. The set of articles about the USA have some different focuses: standards (Dugger), elementary education (Engstrom), state-level developments (Hoepfl), research (Ritz and Reed), and funding (Martin). For Canada we have three accounts: one that describes the overall situation in Canada (Hill), one that focuses on one of the Canadian states (Haché) and one that focuses on sustainability as an issue in Canadian technology education (Elshof). Next region is the Australasian part of the world. Here we find UK influences, but blended with elements from many other approaches. Countries represented in this section are Australia (Williams), New Zealand (Jones), Hong Kong (Volk) and Japan (Matsuda and Mita). Can we identify differences in this region, the next region, Europe, shows even more variation. The UK is described most extensively here, and for good reasons because it has the longest and richest tradition in teaching about technology. Papers about the England and Wales have different focuses: specific projects (Barlex), design (Lawler), food technology (Rutland), relationships with science (Banks and McCormick), and assessment (Stables and Kimbell). Scotland is part of the UK, but has an educational approach that is distinct from the England and Wales educational system. Two papers describe developments in Scotland (Dakers and Doherty/Canavan; the two papers reveal differences between policy and practice). Other countries in this section are Belgium (Van de Velde and Hantson), France (Ginestié and Verillon; the latter with a specific focus on cognition research), Germany (Höpken), Malta (Purchase), Finland (Kananoja and Rasinen; the latter with a focus on gender) and the Central and Eastern European countries (Novakova). Given the fact that Israel has many connections with Europe, both politically and in its educational orientation, we have included this country in the Europe section (Barak and Kipperman; the latter with a focus on relationships with science). Finally we have Chile and South Africa, two countries in different parts of the southern hemisphere. Chile is a relative newcomer in technology education, but progress is quite impressive (Elton). A general survey of South Africa (Stevens) is accompanied by one that focuses on rural areas (Potgieter), a particular challenge to technology education in all African countries.

Although this selection leaves many countries not represented here, the editors claim that all relevant developments in technology education of the past two decades are described in this Handbook. The collection shows that those two decades have brought both growth and maturing, and also serious threats for the future. What will become of technology education worldwide is by no means evident at this moment. The survey of developments that is presented in this Handbook may serve a role in helping technology educators in different countries strengthen the position and practice of teaching about technology. The fact that technology is so important for our whole world, and is one of the main factors in the globalization of today, justifies that technology should be taught for all citizens. In that respect we agree with a remark, made by Dugger, when he said something like this: "now we work on a project 'Technology for All Americans'. The next step should be: Technology for All".

KENDALL N. STARKWEATHER

2. A RETROSPECTIVE LOOK AT WHAT WAS ESSENTIAL FOR TECHNOLOGY EDUCATION DURING THE PAST 20 YEARS

In our closets back in our homes, our youth hangs in between old winter coats and forlorn ties, waiting for the new, maybe revised, or just different "us" to emerge. For as human beings, we know that we will progress in some fashion, good or bad, and make adjustments to what we wear, do, and how we think about things. What was essential before may not be essential now or in the future. All that we can predict is that change will happen. We do know that we will look different physically, think different mentally, and change in what is important to us.

Focusing on "what was essential" rather than "what changed" during the past years causes us to ground our speculation in hope. What is essential to us is the same as what gives meaning to our lives, work, and world community.

Factors in society cause changes in what we consider essential. Political decisions are made. Natural and technological events happen that shake the world. It has been said that life is 10% what happens to you and 90% what you do about it. The natural human reaction is to make adjustments and move forward to the best of our ability.

A retrospective look at the many events that have occurred either intentionally or as a result of a series of events is a humbling task. Few worldwide efforts in our field have exceeded the amount of research and collaboration that have come from 20 years of technology education.

World leaders in technology, innovation, design, and engineering (TIDE) education have found this effort to be beneficial in advancing thought and practice. Leaders from many countries have been influenced by this effort. The number and names of those leaders are too numerous to count or identify. However, I would be remiss if I did not note the pioneering work of Dr. Jan Raat as a central figure who made a difference to many who followed him. He was a true gentleman, outstanding educator, and leader in our profession.

Historians tell us that it is important to look to our past so that we will not make the same mistakes in the future. We have so much to learn if we properly identify that which was important or essential to take forward in our work and lives. One would think that looking back 20 years would be easy for everything is unchangeable. However, we cannot look back without also looking to the present or future. We need a sense of continuity or perspective about the period in time.

We know that what was essential in the past may be of little importance in the future. In the end, the particulars of what people think about what happened in the last 20 years and what might be essential in the next 20 will matter less than the

M.J.de Vries,I. Mottier (eds.), International Handbook of Technology Education, 13–17.

exercise of pondering the question. Still, it is comforting from time to time to work backward, from the anxieties and ambiguous portents of daily life to the basics.

The following are questions to ponder when thinking about two decades of constant work.

- What was essential to our field in the last 20 years?
- Just as important, what was done about it?
- Are we proud of what we did?
- What led us to think in the direction(s) that we took?
- How did the events fit into the longer continuum of time relating to before and after the last 20 years?
- Did we make a difference?

We know that even 15 years ago, most of us did not have the use of desktop or portable computers as a part of our daily work routine. Laptops and portable phones were rare and unwieldy luxuries or were considered non-essential. We saw the Cold War come to an end. Four years later, the post war was shattered by acts of terrorism. Today, the language of the future has a dark edge.

The following selected events happened around the world since 1985. Around the World Timeline 1985-2005:

1985 New Zealand is declared a nuclear free zone
1985 Discovery of virus that causes AIDS is announced
1986 Partial meltdown at Soviet nuclear power plant (Chernobyl in Ukraine)
1986 U.S. space shuttle Challenger explodes after launch
1988 Pan American 747 explodes from terrorist bomb over Scotland
1989 Tanker Valdez spills 11 million gallons of crude oil into Alaskan Sound
1989 After 28 years, Berlin Wall opens to the West
1990 Hubble Space Telescope is boosted into orbit
1991 World Wide Web starts
1994 English Channel Tunnel between England & France is formally opened
1995 DVD Digital Video Disc becomes a consumer product
1997 Mars Pathfinder lands
2001 World Trade Center in New York City is leveled by terrorist
2004 Taipei 101, World's Tallest building opens in Taiwan
2005 Tsunami devastates India Ocean region causing destruction unparalleled in history
(Boorstin, 1977)

It would be easy for each of us to add another 15 events to this list that relate to our home country. During this same time, the number of inventions and discoveries related to science and technology has been enormous. For example, the advent of the Internet and all of the inventions related to its use has considerably changed the financial, educational, political, and religious institutions in our society. Other advances relate to artificial intelligence, genetics, biotechnologies, nano-technologies and more. We have been a busy world of creators, inventors, designers, and innovators - reflecting what has become a very highly sophisticated, technological society with no end in sight.

Have we been able to keep up as a profession that professes to have content and methodology reflecting such an innovative society? What have we done during this same time? The following listing outlines what we have accomplished over the last 20 years.

TIDE Progress- 1985-2005; TIDE educators have-

- Adjusted their respective national curriculum thrusts to stay in the mainstream of efforts to advance education.
- Addressed changes relating to narrowing curriculum, enhancing achievement, and increased testing.
- Concentrated on student achievement at all levels (low-to-high ability levels).
- Adjusted definitions (i.e.-technology) as events in society have caused changes in their meaning.
- Created standards or similar criteria to be used in determining what students should know, be able to do, or value.
- Produced assessments in the quest to measure student performance.
- Advanced the technical content of the subject area to reflect the changes evolving from new technological disciplines.
- Advanced research on teaching and learning, professional and curriculum development, and teacher education and training.
- Explored new delivery methods as electronic advances have created new opportunities.

A closer examination of this list reveals that the items are timeless and essential for any subject area or discipline to advance during a given period of time. However, they are even more important to a subject area that changes as technology changes.

TIDE educators have also-

- Continued advocacy with policy makers, decision makers, and stakeholders to better position the field.
- Advanced new ideas on ways of thinking about TIDE.
- Built relationships with new communities, coalitions, and other subject areas to better position themselves within the education community.
- Fought for creditability such as the thrust in selected countries to become one of the basic or core school subjects.

- Shared successes and opportunities with colleagues from around the world.
- Closely examined the place in the school curriculum that the subject should be offered.
- Fought traditional thinking that placed the subject in training or skills curriculum rather than general education curriculum.
- Worked to position technology (TIDE) as a parallel subject in the curriculum with its mathematics and science partners.
- Looked at new borders for the subject area to include science/technology, engineering/technology, or science/technology/engineering/mathematics (STEM) resulting from technological advances and the latest curriculum thrusts.
- Served as the primary advocates from and for the educational community seeking to gain the proper role for this subject in an innovation oriented society.

As educators, we have been very busy. We have not been big in number when compared to our mathematics and science colleagues in our schools. However, we have carved an important position for our subject based on simple logic or reasoning. In short, what we teach is essential for a country to thrive in a world of challenge and change. The needs of a country to be innovative are as follows.

Educate next-generation innovators
Deepen science and engineering skills
Explore knowledge intersections
Equip workers for change
Support collaborative creativity
Energize entrepreneurship
Reward long-term strategy
Build world-class infrastructure
Invest in frontier research
Attract global talent
Create high-wage jobs
(Council on Competitiveness, 2004)

These characteristics require the expertise of the economic, political, corporate, and educational institutions of a country all working together to achieve success. They require school subjects that allow experiences with technology, design, invention, and engineering.

Educators in our field have made adjustments, as fast as their resources would allow. One goal has been to create societal members who are in tune with technological innovations. We know that innovation improves the quality of lives in countless ways. Therefore, we have been and will continue to strive to:

- Enable achievement of dramatically higher levels of health.
- Develop product options for the aging population
- Find plentiful, affordable, environmentally friendly sources of energy
- Improve products and services by making them more affordable
- Expand access to knowledge
- Offer new forms of convenience, customization, and entertainment
- Solve the great challenges facing society

With these thoughts, we know that we will have an educational role in the years ahead. The intersection of invention and insight that creates innovation begins with strong and meaningful experiences related to technology, design, and engineering.

Asking the question- What was essential? started this presentation. We have attempted to put meaning into our lives and the lives of our students through activities designed to improve our profession. This work has been accomplished with optimism so fundamental to life that we hardly notice its presence, an optimism of essentials.

It is easy to answer this kind of question, which demands equal parts contemplation and speculation. And, the question itself- What is essential?- is ultimately an elegant rephrasing of the most basic question- What is the meaning of our lives? But, we ask it now because we are at a point in history filled with anxiety and nothing allays fear like getting back to the basics.

We hoard and plan as we muddle on regardless of a world that gives us little reassurance about our future! We have entered a time not just of known unknowns, but also of unknown unknowns! We are mortal beings, which struggle in the world to raise families, stay healthy, satisfy curiosity, amuse ourselves, and leave behind a record of who and what we were doing during our allotted time on the planet.

We did make a difference! You all are to be congratulated on your efforts during the past 20 years for doing your part to further discussion and advance ideas that made a difference. We changed the clothes in our professional closets and continued wearing those that were of importance. We advanced learning during our time to promote the ideals of our profession. In the end, the prime essential for our field will be to raise successful children with just values to be positive contributors to the complex, demanding, and fulfilling future that we anticipate with optimism.

REFERENCES

Boorstin, D. (1977) *National geographic atlas of world history*. Washington, DC: National Geographic Society.

Council on Competitiveness. (2004). *Innovate America: National innovation initiative report*. Washington, DC: Author.

MARGARITA PAVLOVA

3. COMPARING PERSPECTIVES: COMPARATIVE RESEARCH IN TECHNOLOGY EDUCATION

INTRODUCTION

Retrospective analysis of what has been happening in a particular area over a particular period of time can provide a valuable reflection on how a phenomenon is being developed, what issues have been addressed and how it is possible to proceed in the future. This paper reflects on a number of different ways by which comparative research in technology education has been undertaken over the last 20 years. It is possible to identify three major periods in the process of its development. When technology education was established as a learning area a comparison had been made at the level of curriculum documents, syllabi and State Orders. People involved in this process were looking around the world for ideas.

The second stage of development of comparative research in technology education could be characterised by a great number of published or presented papers that described the situation in a particular country (Ajeyalemi, 1990; Putnam, 1992; Middleton, 1996; etc). Even though comparison, as such, was not used in this research, the underlying assumption was that it should inform the research community on different approaches towards the development of technology education and that it would be beneficial for the field.

The third stage involved comparison between two or more countries about one or more specific aspects of technology education. These include the meaning of the major concepts, teaching methods, goals, the balance between the global trends and local specificities, etc. (Lewis, 1996; Gradwell, 1996; Pavlova, 1998). This represented a movement from a somewhat superficial to a more systematic comparison, from comparison as a natural way of learning to comparison as a research method.

Histories of any field are collected and reflected on through the histories of individuals who are involved in the development of the field. The development of comparative education research is reflected in the biographical history of the author's professional development. In 1988-1991 that research aimed at analysing English approaches to technology education and was conducted with the goal of informing and influencing the process of policy development in Russia. In 1997 – 2001 the research was focused on a particular issue – knowledge in technology education, with the aim to analyse it across several countries and to develop a framework for its conceptualisation. Writing about Russian technology education was also being undertaken in parallel with this.

M.J. de Vries, I. Mottier (eds.), International Handbook of Technology Education, 19–32.

Thus the paper will reflect on these stages and personal history of research and propose a way for the further development of comparative research in technology education, the way that can provide a framework for a better understanding of the role of technology education and its contribution towards students' development and learning.

STAGE ONE – HELP ME TO ESTABLISH TECHNOLOGY EDUCATION

From the very early days of establishing technology education, comparative research played a significant role in its development. Technology education as a field of study was widely recognised by the end of the 1980s although the debate on including *Technology* in school curriculum started much earlier. By the end of the 1980s education, coupled with market reforms, became the dominant position in educational policy. Education has been seen as the source of responsiveness to technological change. A close association between education and the economy brought technology education as an important area of discussion in many reports undertaken by educational authorities in different countries. Changes in educational policy and the existence of different practical courses in school curriculum became the background for including technology education in the curriculum of comprehensive schools internationally.

In particular the assumption was made about the goals of technology education - to be relevant to the economic needs of the nation and to prepare students for work and life in society. Technology education was seen as a means for developing knowledge, skills, attitudes and values which allow students to maximize their flexibility and adaptability to their future employment, mainly, and to other aspects of life as well. In the UK, the former Secretary of State for Education, Kenneth Baker, announced that Technology as a subject was considered to be "of great significance for the economic well-being of this country" (cited in Barnett, 1992, p. 85). *A Statement on Technology for Australian Schools* explained: "Technology programs prepare students for living and working in an increasingly technological world and equip them for innovative and productive activity" (Curriculum Corporation, 1997, p. 4). In the USA it was announced that technology education was "vital to human welfare and economic prosperity" (ITEA, 1996, p.1).

This was the first stage in the development of comparative research in technology education. A comparison had been made at the level of curriculum documents, syllabi and State Orders. People involved in the development of technology education were looking around the world for ideas. During this first stage, approaches to the analysis were not very systematic. Every team that started work on the Syllabus for a particular country looked at the international experience, in many cases by going to other countries as published works were not available.

Similar research had been done at the national level in countries where the educational system was not centralised. For example in Australia this type of research examined developments in Australian schools in the area of technology education in different states. A report of this study the *K-12 Technology Curriculum Map* was published in 1991. It stated that there was no generally accepted definition of technology education. A variety of roles designated for technology education highlight the absence of a common way of providing it in schools. Understanding of technological courses varied dramatically between applied science, informational technology, industrial technology and trade subjects. Technology education programs were focused on:

- the translation of scientific principles and ideas into tangible outcomes (Technology Studies);
- particular crafts (Practical Studies);
- natural phenomena (Science Studies);
- socio-cultural matters (Humanities Studies) (AEC, 1991).

However, the 1991 study identified a shift from an emphasis on physical and practical skills towards the inclusion of the more intellectually demanding processes of identifying needs, designing, problem-solving and appraising.

The results of this study highlighted the need to develop a common rationale for technology education across Australia to provide the different states with a common ground for school education in that area. It was established in 1994, through the National *Statement* and *Profiles*. This comparative research is a typical example of the first stage research. Its main goal was to inform the development of educational policy in the area.

Table 1. Comparison of the formal parameters.

	Australia (QLD)	France	Russia
Level on which the Syllabus is approved	State	National	National
Subject/learning area	Learning area	Subject	Subject
Compulsory	Y1-Y10	Y1 – Y8	Y1 – Y 9
Number of hour, per week	1 - 2	1 - 2	2 (in Y9 – 1hour)
How is it presented	On 6 levels and beyond via 4 strands	Through the 3 cycles and scenarios	3 levels and 11 content modules

Sometimes the superficial comparisons of this period were not able to provide many insights into what was really happening and why it might be appropriate or not for particular settings. Comparison of formal parameters such as those presented in Table 1 provides some data but its usefulness was limited.

Comparative research at this stage was associated with one feature of the process of globalisation: the international circulation of ideas through social and political networks bringing common elements to curriculum documents of different countries. Compression of the world (Robertson, 1995) provided an opportunity to have a look at the 'universal' elements of technology education, and they had been explored through the supranational connections. The author's research was searching for the 'universal' elements in the English Syllabus that could improve Russian technology education (Pavlova, 1993). One of the elements was a design-based approach to curriculum development.

STAGE TWO – LET ME TELL YOU WHAT'S HAPPENING IN MY COUNTRY

Stage two in comparative research in technology education is related to another feature of globalisation: development of specific, conceptualised characteristics and emphasis on the realisation of policy in specific national settings. By the end of 1990s an issue of universalism versus cultural diversity became the main methodological challenge in comparative education research (Mitter 1997; Masemann, 1997). An argument had been made that the context of the particular country should be extensively analysed so that comparison can happen. Although there was little discussion of comparative methodology in technology education a large number of articles were published in the International Journal of Technology and Design Education (e.g. Potgieter, 2004; Jones, Harlow, Cowie, 2004; Wilson, and Harris, 2004; Compton, Harwood, 2003; Jones, 2003; Ginestié, 2002; Turnbull, 2002; Verner, Betzer, 2001; Given, Barlex, 2001; Volk, Yip, and Lo, 2003; Jones, and Moreland, 2002) as well as papers presented at international conferences (e.g. Huang, 2002; Compton and Harwood, 2002; Molwane, 2001, Lebeaume, 2003) that describe technology education (or particular issues) relevant to a particular country.

This research outlined what was specific for particular countries and how common ideas were being implemented. There were no comparative elements as such in this type of research. However, the underlying idea was that the cross-national comparison should have happened in the minds of academics. A lot of publications had a very descriptive nature that was not really helpful in moving the field forward. Particular contexts were described but it was not framed by the broader context that provides links or shared starting points for further analysis (universal side was not explored).

The author's personal history of this stage relates to the analysis and description of technology education in Russia. The issues addressed included general description, analysis of the process of change, approaches towards teaching, design as a new concept, etc. For example, a number of limitations had been identified in interpretation and use of a design-based approach towards teaching technology. These were mainly caused by traditional perceptions of the educational process as a systematic approach to teaching based on theory (Pavlova and Pitt, 2000; Pavlova, 2002a).

STAGE THREE – THIS IS AN ISSUE, LET'S COMPARE

The dominant approach in comparative education by the end of 1990s was a cross-national comparison. It had been challenged by a number of researchers in comparative education (Welch, 1993; Cowen, 1996). As a result, an important methodological problem was raised: what are the appropriate units for comparative analysis. This challenge was addressed in technology education research by choosing a particular issue (unit of analysis) such as problem solving, students' attitudes, activities and comparing it across a number of countries (e.g. Banks, Barlex, Jarvinen, O'Sullivan, Owen-Jackson, Rutland, 2004; Graube, Dyrenfurth, and Theuerkauf (Eds.), 2004; Rasinen, 2003; Hill, Anning, 2001). Although, the global-local problematic has not been particularly explored, this type of analysis was useful for a number of reasons. Firstly it demonstrated an attempt to focus on a particular issue and to find better solutions that would be appropriate for particular contexts. Secondly, it represented a systematic approach towards comparison using comparison as a method of research. All three stages in the history of comparative education are closely interrelated, each provides knowledge and understanding required for the next stage.

Reflection on research done by the author, on knowledge in technology education provides an example of the study relevant to Stage three. A comparative analysis of educational documents that were directly connected to the policy in technology education was a part of that research. Consistency in choosing documents and their position (the statutory status or the consultative nature of the document) were considered as important issues in achieving a systematic approach towards comparison (Pavlova, 1998, Pavlova, 2001). For example, the date of publication of the documents analysed (before April 1999) was among the factors employed to provide a measure of consistency in the analysis. Multi-level analysis framed by the global –local considerations provided an appropriate methodology for this comparison. Results of the analysis that related to knowledge in technology education documents is summarised in Table 2.

This summary highlights that only declarative/conceptual knowledge was stated in the curriculum documents of Russia, the UK and the USA. In those countries procedural knowledge could be implicitly seen through the description of what students should be able to do or skills required. In the latest version of the Australian *Statement* declarative knowledge was not separately specified. The assumption was made that through the specified activities students develop the 'required' knowledge. Thus, the emphasis was on procedural knowledge.

Required knowledge was explicitly described in the UK and the USA documents. In the UK document a list of knowledge was specified from the very first document and then gradually developed throughout the analysed period. In the USA the nature of knowledge in technology had been explored and then used as content for the *Standards*. Through the analysed period a shift had been made from considering technology as a body of knowledge to limiting its place as a part of the structure of technology. Nevertheless, knowledge *per se* remained in a very important place in the USA document.

Table 2. Understanding knowledge in curriculum documents - comparison between four countries

	Australia	**UK**	**USA**	**Russia**
Definition of knowledge	Non-explicit: Information is knowledge generated and used in everyday life	Not stated	Knowledge is interpreted information that can be put to use	Not stated
Source of knowledge for technology education	Not clear, Knowledge is not explicitly stated, the required activities are specified	*Terms of Reference* stated knowledge which students need to have to achieve technological capability	Place and nature of knowledge in technology	Non-justified selection of knowledge – what students have to learn to achieve the aims of the subject
What knowledge is stated?	Technical knowledge about information, systems, materials and process of designing, making, appraising + value judgments connected to those issues	Technical knowledge about materials, systems, structures, products, etc.	Technological knowledge; emphasise on the relationship between technology and society and vice versa	Technical knowledge or particular knowledge (legislation, for example)
Relationship knowledge/ understanding	Not stated	Not stated	Understanding is knowledge synthesised into new insights	Not stated
Structure	Boundaries are not clear	Boundaries are not clear	It is possible to set up boundaries	Boundaries are clear
Is the selected approach justified?	No	Several assumptions have been made, no theoretical justification	Yes	No theoretical justification

Technological knowledge is seen as having clear boundaries in the USA and Russia, and without clear boundaries in the UK and Australia. At the end of the analysed period, in the UK the emphasis was on technical knowledge, although values were considered as playing an important role in technology. In Russian documents technical knowledge was seen as important to achieve the aims of technology education and was described in the content modules. In the USA, the philosophical/sociological aspects of the relationship between technology and society were stated as important.

The forms of knowledge and levels of its generalisation (using Mitcham's approach) were used to some extent in the USA documents. In Australia, Russia, and the UK documents they were not discussed. In Australia and the UK the main emphasis was on lower levels of generalisation (artisan skills and technical maxims). In Russia and the USA the higher levels of knowledge were also involved (technological theories and descriptive laws). Knowledge *about* technology (as a general phenomenon) was included in the USA *Standards* and to a very limited extent - in the Australian *Statement*.

These results together with analysis done on the other levels (academic discourse, academic perceptions) provided a basis for the development of a conceptual model of knowledge in technology education that incorporated universal-context-dependant elements.

This research also demonstrates that a different approach towards comparison is required to understand better the nature of technology education in different contexts. There is a need to have a framework that would allow an understanding of technology education not only on the level of educational policy, curriculum theories, and academics' perceptions but also on the level of school practice.

Comparison on the basis of two ideological beliefs about the purposes of general education is proposed as a way forward in developing comparative research in technology education. These beliefs are: whether education is designed to broaden minds and develop all students in the creation of a better society or is it really about training students to live and work in a market-oriented state, to be 'productive' in seizing the opportunities of the market. These two approaches summarize an important issue that divides different social theories in their views on the role of education in society.

STAGE FOUR – COMPARE TO ESTABLISH A BETTER SOCIETY

The comparative research presented in stages 1-3 above was focussed mainly on providing information and increasing awareness of what is happening around the globe. Here it is argued that comparative research in technology education can serve another purpose – it can help to establish a better society. In the proposed approach a comparison is made between two different rationales, thus cross-national comparison is overwritten by comparison that crosses country borders. In all societies it is possible to identify two major groups of technology educators who have different answers for the question: what is the nature of technology education? Is it instrumental or developmental? Two issues will be used to demonstrate the utility of the proposed approach to comparative research. They are: values in technology education and education for sustainable development.

VALUES IN TECHNOLOGY EDUCATION

The necessity of exploring values in technology education has been argued by a number of authors (Layton, 1991; Barlex, 1993; Prime, 1993; McLaren, 1997; Breckon, 1998; Holdsworth and Conway, 1999) to be a vital aspect of a comprehensive technology curriculum. These researchers highlight the potential of a technology curriculum in enriching students' awareness and appreciation of their responsibility as members of a technological society. Further development of research in this area (Pavlova, 2002b) proposed a framework for addressing values in technology education based on the ideas drawn from philosophy (e.g. Habemas, 1974/1963) and psychology (e.g. Oser, 1994) and related to the notion of the hierarchical order of values (Schwartz, 1992 cited in Prime, 1993; Rokeach, 1973).

Among technology teachers, values related to competence (technical, economic) have a priority compared to moral values (Holdsworth and Conway, 1999). However, as stated by Habermas (1974/1963) rationality (defined as efficiency and economy) "cannot itself be placed on the *same* level with all the other values"(p.259) or prevail above them. He cited Hans Albert who made the suggestion:

to place in the foreground ... in the establishment of a criterion for the validity of ethical systems, the satisfaction of human needs, the fulfillment of human desires, the avoidance of unnecessary human suffering. Such a criterion would have to be discovered and established, just as this is true for the criteria of scientific thought. (Habermas,1974/1963, p.280)

Thus, rationality and effectiveness must be framed by moral considerations. Moral values constitute a part of the person's value system. According to Rokeach (1973) moral values refer to those "that have an interpersonal focus which, when violated, arouse pangs of conscience or feeling of guilt for wrongdoing" (p.8). They refer mainly to modes of behaviour and "do not necessarily include values that concern end-states of existence"(p.8). The moral (morality) is considered as an aspect of the ethical, "namely that which particularly concentrates on obligation, the ought and ought-not, on duty and conscience and human virtues, where the ethical will also include consideration of the good life, happiness, well-being, admirable conduct over and above the call of duty"(Jarrett, 1991, p.14).

Moral values of both students and teachers should be addressed in technology education. In relation to the professional morality of the teacher a concern similar to that expressed by Habermas provides a basis for the theory that starts from the assumption that no professional action should be guided only by "functional criteria of means and end relations under the perspective of functional success" (Oser, 1994, p.60). As argued by Oser (1994)

A responsible professional action must be informed by a structure of moral values that enables the actor to estimate positive and negative consequences that concern human beings immediately or indirectly. The relationship between success and care in regard to consequences is the core criterion of this theory. (p.60)

Thus, moral values should be at the top of the teachers' hierarchy of values. It was suggested (Pavlova, 2002b) that in order to provide adequate learning experiences to students, technology teachers need to consider the relationship between effectiveness and responsibility as a starting point for approaching value analysis. The regulative model of professional morality, which 'limiting the aspects of effectiveness by the aspect of responsibility', was proposed as a framework for the development of an appropriate classroom environment in technology education. Teachers should view the classroom environment and the process of designing and making primarily as "a moral enterprise but as serving functional purposes"(Oser, 1994, p.103). It is important that teachers' attention is being focused on moral values and on the inclusion of students as real discourse partners in discussion of ethically problematic situations.

Classroom environments that cultivate responsibility will stimulate students to put moral values first that would not be considered as one category of values among the others but as a reference point for all design decisions. The nature of technology education provides a rich context that can be easily moved beyond the concept of effectiveness. To deal with values effectively the teacher has to develop an appropriate classroom environment that will

- help students to recognise a situation as being ethically problematic,
- enable students to have a voice and express their feelings and thoughts, and
- find a solution that serves the best interests of all parties involved.

Thus, it was suggested that discussion of *values* presented in technology education literature at the moment, should be replaced by discussion of *moral values*. Also three components of values have to be taken into account:

- Cognitive component provides the awareness of different values and demonstrates reasons to put moral values first.
- Affective component establishes links between the technological task and students feeling by putting technology into a meaningful context.
- Behaviour component gives students an opportunity to act in accordance with their moral values.

The third component of values, a behavioral one, is not explicitly presented in technology education literature. However, it is analyzed in the psychological research as an important component of values that may lead to action (Rokeach, 1973).

Thus an argument about moral values that provides a frame for all technological activities strongly supports the importance of 'developmental' rationale for technology education.

EDUCATION FOR SUSTAINABLE DEVELOPMENT

The notion of developing students so they are capable of being involved in the creation of a better society, by developing their responsibility is closely related to the concept of sustainability that is concerned about the future of humanity and the quality of life for the further generations. "Education not only provides the scientific and technical skills required, it also provides the motivation, justification, and social support for pursuing and applying them. Education increases the capacities of people to transform their visions of society into operational realities" (UNESCO, 2001a, p.1)

Education for sustainable development (ESD) has gradually become an important issue for many educators internationally. UNESCO, for example, specifies that since Rio, there has been increasing recognition of the critical role of education in promoting sustainable life patterns in order to "change attitudes and behaviour of people as individuals, including as producers and consumers, and as citizens carrying out their collective activities" (UNESCO, 2001b, p.3).

Technology education as a part of general education can play an important role in promoting sustainable production and consumption. When the concept of sustainability is discussed within technology education it is focused mainly on the ethical aspects of the decisions that students make during design processes and on the sustainable design of products, with a major emphasis on the environmental impacts of these products (Elshof, 2003; Martin, 2003). These impacts can be assessed using such methodologies as Life Cycle Analysis (LCA) (http://www.pre.nl/life_cycle_assessment/default.htm) and Design for Environment (DfE) (http://www.pre.nl/ecodesign/default.htm).

A number of documents were developed to address the issue of education for sustainable development (ESD) at the national/state levels. For example, in the UK, in 2002 the Qualifications and Curriculum Authority produced a curriculum guidance document for schools, identifying the main concepts relating to ESD which provide opportunities to students to learn about ESD (referred to in Office for Standards in Education, 2003). In Australia, different states are developing their vision on ESD (Wooltorton, 2002). However the role of technology education in ESD has not been fully elaborated.

For example, a reference to appropriateness is made in the Queensland Syllabus. Appropriate technologies can be interpreted as 'technologies with a human face' aimed to enable people to earn a sustainable living. Although the 'right' statements are made in the content of technology education for Queensland schools, they are not included in the description of outcomes. Thus no assessment mechanism is proposed to measure to what extent teachers include these concepts in their practice and to what extent students will consider these issues when they are making judgments. In addition, a number of in-service materials have been printed to facilitate the implementation of technology education. However, examples (case studies) that are included in the Source book demonstrate that the meaning of appropriateness is very limited. Appropriateness is considered in terms of the particular local context and only within the current situation (not oriented towards the future). The 'right' examples of design projects do not include the description of how appropriateness/sustainability can be taught.

Thus there are a number of problems in the representation of ESD in technology education. Not all aspects of sustainability (environmental, social, economic, ethical) have been conceptualised within technology education and as a result, guidance for technology education teachers concerning what to teach, how to teach and how to assess student learning is not coherent and comprehensive. Recent research on these issues (Pavlova, 2004) proposed a systematic representation of ESD for technology education and a framework for planning learning activities that can be a useful tool in facilitating discussion.

Although further research is required in developing ESD via technology education, its importance has been clearly stated. Together with an emphasis on moral values these highlight the importance of developing responsibility in technology education students that, in turn, relates to an identifiable rationale for technology education and teaching practice. Understanding of what rationale for technology education is used, instrumental or developmental, can provide a clear understanding of what technology education is about in a particular setting. Thus this framework for comparative research will help to gain a deeper understanding of technology education on both theoretical and practical levels and to see universal and contextualised elements in approaching the area.

CONCLUSION

This paper reflects on the history of comparative education research in technology education. Three stages of its development has been identified and analysed using some samples of research done in this area as well as some sample from personal professional history. Two important methodological issues: global trends – local specificities, and appropriate units of analysis were discussed to highlight different approaches adapted at different stages. A move towards the next stage in the development of comparative research in technology education has been argued as essential in moving research forward. Comparison on the basis of two ideological beliefs about the purposes of general education: whether education is designed to broaden minds and develop all students in the creation of a better society or is it really about training students to live and work in a market oriented state, to be 'productive' in seizing the opportunities of the market, was argued as an effective way of gaining an understanding of technology education in a particular setting. The importance of this new framework has been justified through discussion of two research issues – values in technology education and education for sustainable development.

REFERENCES

Ajeyalemi, D.(Ed.) (1990). *Science and technology education in Africa: Focus on seven Sub-Saharan countries.* Lagos, Nigeria: University of Lagos.

Ankiewicz, P., van Rensburg, S., Myburgh, C. (2001). Assessing the attitudinal technology profile of South African learners: A pilot study. *International Journal of Technology and Design Education* 11(2) pp. 93-109.

Australian Educational Council (1991). *K-12 Technology curriculum map: A report to the Australian Education Council, August 1990*. Carlton, Victoria: Curriculum Corporation.

Banks, F., Barlex, D., Jarvinen, E.-M., O'Sullivan, G., Owen-Jackson, G., Rutland, M. (2004). DEPTH – Developing professional thinking for technology teachers: An international study. *International Journal of Technology and Design Education*, 14(2), pp. 141-157.

Barlex, D. (1993). The Nuffield approach to values in design and technology. *Design and Technology Teaching*, vol. 26, no.1, pp. 42-45.

Barnett, M. (1992). Technology, within the National Curriculum and elsewhere. In J. Beynon & H. Mackay (Eds.), *Technological literacy and the curriculum* (pp. 84-104). London: Falmer Press.

Becker, K. H. and Maunsaiyat, S. (2002). *Thai Students' Attitudes and Concepts of Technology*. *Journal of Technology Education* 13(2) 6-20.

Breckon, A. (1998). National curriculum review in design and technology for the Year 2000. *The Journal of Design and Technology Education*, vol. 3, no.2, pp. 101-105.

Compton, V., Harwood, C. (2003). Enhancing technological practice: An assessment framework for technology education in New Zealand. *International Journal of Technology and Design Education*, 13(1) pp. 1-26.

Compton, V. and Harwood, C. (2002). Making progress: Progression and technology education in New Zealand. In H Middleton, M. Pavlova and D. Roebuck (Ed), *Learning in technology education: Challenges for the 21ˢᵗ century* (pp. 62-70). Brisbane: Griffith University.

Cowen, R. (1996). Editorial. *Comparative Education, 32* (2), 149-150.

Curriculum Corporation. (1997). *A statement on technology for Australian schools*. Carlton, Victoria: Author.

Elshof, L. (2003). Teacher's interpretation of sustainable development. In J. Dakers and M.J. de Vries (Eds.) *PATT-13 International conference on design and technology educational research* (pp. 45-51). Glasgow, UK: Faculty of Education University of Glasgow.

Ginestié, J. (2002). The industrial project method in French industry and in French schools. *International Journal of Technology and Design Education*, 12(2), pp. 99-122.

Given, N., Barlex, D. (2001) The role of published materials in curriculum development and implementation for secondary school design and technology in England and Wales. *International Journal of Technology and Design Education*, 11(2), pp. 137-161.

Gradwell, J. B. (1996). Philosophical and practical differences in the approaches taken to technology education in England, France and the United States. *International Journal of Technology and Design Education*, 6 (3), 239-262.

Graube, G., Dyrenfurth, M.J. and Theuerkauf, W.E. (Eds.) (2004). *Technology education: International concepts and perspectives*. Frankfurt am Main: Peter Lang.

Habermas, J. (1974). *Theory and practice* (J. Viertel, Trans.). Boston: Beacon. (Original work published 1963).

Holdsworth, I. & Conway, B. (1999). Investigating Values in Secondary Design and Technology Education. *The Journal of Design and Technology Education*, vol. 4, no.3, pp. 205-214.

Hill, A.M., Anning, A. (2001) Comparisons and contrasts between elementary/primary 'school situated design' and 'workplace design' in Canada and England. *International Journal of Technology and Design Education*, 11(2), pp. 111-136.

Huang, C.-S.J. (2002). Educational reform and the technology education curriculum in Taiwan's primary schools. In H Middleton, M. Pavlova and D. Roebuck (Ed), *Learning in technology education: Challenges for the 21ˢᵗ Century* (pp. 211-220). Brisbane: Griffith University.

International Technology Education Association (1996). *Technology for all Americans. A rational and structure for the study of technology*. Reston, Virginia: Author.

Jarrett, J I. (1991). *The teaching of values: caring and appreciation*. London: Routledge.

Järvinen, E-M., Twyford, J. (2000). The influences of socio-cultural interaction upon children's thinking and actions in prescribed and open-ended problem solving situations (An investigation involving design and technology lessons in English and Finnish primary schools). *International Journal of Technology and Design Education* 10(1) pp. 21-41.

Jones, A. (2003) The development of a national curriculum in technology for New Zealand. *International Journal of Technology and Design Education* 13(1) pp. 83-99.

Jones, A. and Moreland, J. (2002) Technology education in New Zealand, *Journal of Technology Studies* 28(1/2)130-134.

Jones, A., Harlow, A., Cowie, B. (2004) New Zealand teachers' experiences in implementing the technology curriculum. *International Journal of Technology and Design Education* 14(2), pp. 101-119.

Layton, D. (1991). *Aspects of national curriculum: Design and technology.* York: NCC.

Lebeaume, J. (2003). The place of technology education in the curriculum: The French example of main issues for the middle school. In J. Dakers and M.J. de Vries (Eds) *PATT-13 International conference on design and technology educational research* (pp. 41-44). Glasgow, UK: Faculty of Education University of Glasgow.

Lewis, T. (1996). Comparing technology education in the U.S. and UK *International Journal of Technology and Design Education,* 6 (3), 221-238.

Martin, M. (2003). Significance of sustainability issues for design and technology education: rhetoric, reality and resources. In J. Dakers and M.J. de Vries (Eds) *PATT-13 International conference on design and technology educational research* (pp. 165-169). Glasgow, UK: Faculty of Education University of Glasgow.

Masemann, V. L. (1997). Recent directions in comparative education. In C. Kodron (Ed.), *Comparative education: Challenges - intermediation - practice; Essays in honour of Wolfgang Mitter on the occasion of his 70th birthday* (Vol.1, pp. 127-134). Köln: Böhlau Verlag.

McLaren, S. (1997). Value judgements: Evaluating design - A Scottish perspective on a global issue. *International Journal of Technology and Design Education,* vol. 3, no.3, pp. 259-278.

Middleton, P. (1996) The development of a technology short course in South Africa. *Journal of Design and Technology education,* 1(2), 130-135.

Mitter, W. (1997). Challenges to comparative education. Between retrospect and expectation. *International Review of Education,* 43 (5-6), 401-412.

Molwane, O.B. (2001). Establishing trends in design and technology teachers' approaches in Botswana. In E.W.L. Norman and P.H. Roberts (Eds.), *IDATER 2001 International conference on design and technology education research and curriculum development* (pp.84 - 91). Loughborough, UK: Department of Design and Technology, Loughborough University.

Office for Standards in Education (2003). *Taking the first step forward...towards an education for sustainable development: Good practice in primary and secondary schools.* London: the Author.

Oser, F. K. (1994). Moral perspectives on teaching. In L. Darling –Hammond, *Review of Research in Education,* vol. 20 (pp. 57 – 127). Washington, DC: American Educational Research Association.

Pavlova, M. (1993). *Technology - a new subject at school.* St. Petersburg : Libra.

Pavlova, M. (1998). Concept of knowledge in technology education: a cross-cultural perspective. In J. J. Smith and E.W.L. Norman (Eds.), *IDATER 98 International conference on design and technology education research and curriculum development* (pp. 237- 243). Loughborough, UK: Department of Design and Technology, Loughborough University.

Pavlova, M. and Pitt, J. (2000). A design-based approach to technology education - is it acceptable practice in Russia? In P.H. Roberts and E.W.L. Norman (Eds.), *IDATER 2000 International conference on design and technology education research and curriculum development* (pp. 147 - 154). Loughborough, UK: Department of Design and Technology, Loughborough University.

Pavlova, M. (2001). *Theorizing knowledge in technology education: policy analysis of four countries.* Unpublished PhD thesis. Melbourne: La Trobe University.

Pavlova, M. (2002a). Technology education in Russia: socio-cultural limitations to design- approach. *Science in Vocational and Technical Education,* 15, 15 -39.

Pavlova, M. (2002b)."Teaching" values in technology education: a critical approach for the theoretical framework. In H Middleton, M. Pavlova and D. Roebuck (Ed), *Learning in technology education: Challenges for the 21st century* (pp.96 –102). Brisbane: Griffith University.

Pavlova, M (2004) Sustainability: towards systematic approach for its conceptualisation in technology education. Paper for the international conference on *Purposes and assessments within technology education,* Paris, March 2004, http://membres.lycos.fr/aeet/

Potgieter, C. (2004). The impact of the implementation of technology education on in-service teacher education in South Africa (Impact of technology education in the RSA), *International Journal of Technology and Design Education* 14(3) pp. 205-218.

Prime, G. M. (1993). Values in technology: An approach to learning. *Design and Technology Teaching,* 26(1), pp. 30-36.

Putnam, A.R. (1992). Technology education in the United States: A national comparison of philosophy, implementation, and organisation, *Journal of Epsilon Pi Tau,* 18(1), 38-44.

Rasinen, A. (2003) An analysis of the technology education curriculum of six countries. *Journal of Technology Education,* 15(1), 31 –47.

Robertson, R. (1995). Glocalization: Time-space and homogeneity - heterogeneity. In M. Featherstone, S. Lash, & R. Robertson (Eds.), *Global modernities* (pp. 25-44). London: SAGE.

Rokeach, M. (1973). *The nature of human values,* Free Press, New York.

Schwartz, S. H. (1992). Universals in the content and structure of values: theoretical advances and empirical tests in 20 countries, *Advances in Experimental Social psychology,* Vol.25, Academic Press.

Turnbull, W. (2002). The Place of Authenticity in Technology in the New Zealand Curriculum *International Journal of Technology and Design Education* 12 (1) pp. 23-40.

UNESCO(2001a).Education-Key to a viable future www.unesco.org/education/esd/english/education/role.shtml

UNESCO(2001b).Beyond basic education to education for sustainable development, www.unesco. org/education/esd/english/education/beyond.shtml

Verner, I. M., Betzer, N. (2001). Machine control – A design and technology discipline in Israel's senior high schools. *International Journal of Technology and Design Education,* 11(3), pp. 263-272

Volk, K., Yip, W.M. and Lo, T. K. (2003). Hong Kong pupils' attitudes toward technology: The impact of design and technology programs. *Journal of Technology Education,* 15(1), 48-63.

Welch, A. R. (1993). Class, culture and the state in comparative education: Problems, perspectives and prospects. *Comparative Education,* 29 (1), 7-28.

Williams J. P. and Keirl, S. (2001). The status of teaching and learning of technology in primary and secondary schools in Australia. In E.W.L. Norman and P.H. Roberts (Eds.), *IDATER 2001 International conference on design and technology education rsearch and curriculum development* (pp.153 - 162). Loughborough, UK: Department of Design and Technology, Loughborough University.

Wilson, V. and Harris, M. (2004).Creating change? A review of the impact of design and technology in schools in England. *Journal of Technology Education,* 15(2), 46-65.

Woooltorton, S. (2002). *Education for sustainability: A background paper prepared for the state sustainability strategy.* Perth: Edith Cowan University.

ALEJANDRO E. FERRARI, MARCOS BERLATZKY, MARIO CWI, LUIS PEREZ, DOV KIPPERMAN, SERGEY GORINSKIY AND OSNAT DAGAN

4. IS THE WHOLE MORE THAN THE SUM OF ITS COMPONENTS? AN ANALYSIS OF TECHNOLOGY EDUCATION IN ORT SCHOOLS AROUND THE WORLD

INTRODUCTION – WHAT IS WORLD ORT?

ORT, the largest non-governmental international Jewish education network, provides technology education and training all over the world. Its global network now teaches over 270,000 students in five continents (as detailed in table 1) with highly-acclaimed, cutting-edge technology training . One of ORT's main aims is to promote technology education in its schools, as a means to its ultimate goal of providing its students with economic self-sufficiency.

In every country, each ORT school follows the requirements of the local National Curriculum. Within their countries, these schools are technology education leaders. However, as part of a global organization, ORT schools play an important role as leaders of innovation in technology studies. World ORT supports the development and translation of instructional materials and collaboration with colleagues through seminars, e-forums and in-house publications, which in turn enables it to promote technology education its own ORT schools and, moreover, to contribute on a national and international level.

During the past twenty years, new concepts of technology literacy, such as Design and System Approach, have become accepted in many countries. ORT schools implement this process (moving from "Hands on" towards "Minds on") as an integral part of their educational system.

In this paper we will describe the processes of change and development in technology education that have taken place during the last twenty years in each of the three ORT centers (Argentina, Israel and Russia) and relate them to the changes that have occurred in technology education within those countries.

We are going to focus on identifying the changes in technology education that have occurred since 1985 in the three countries' ORT schools, and we would like to show the advantages of belonging to a worldwide educational network such as World ORT.

M.J. de Vries, I. Mottier (eds.), International Handbook of Technology Education, 33-51

Table 1: The number of young and adult students in ORT schools all over the world (Dec. 2003)

	Young Students (up to age 18)	Adult Students (aged 18+)	Total
Argentina	4787	1951	6738
Brazil	291	48	339
Bulgaria	652	0	652
Chile	1493	0	1493
Cuba	95	311	406
France	2740	2181	4921
Hungary	0	1700	1700
India	309	64	373
Israel	74863	18749	93612
Italy	990	152	1142
Mexico	2974	1229	4203
South Africa	120	1157	1277
Switzerland (IC*)	10920	31100	42020
USA	16357	2648	19005
USA (IC*)	9555	43900	53455
UK	1137	833	1970
Uruguay	192	7078	7270
Venezuela	1769	1203	2972
Russia	6678	10039	16717
Kyrgyzstan	73	0	73
Ukraine	4316	4091	8407
Belarus	583	1348	1931
Moldova	499	144	643
Latvia	365	240	605
Lithuania	290	130	420
Total	142048	130296	272344

IC = International Cooperation

THE CHANGES IN TECHNOLOGY EDUCATION IN ORT SCHOOLS IN ARGENTINA, ISRAEL AND RUSSIA

The changes in technology education at the ORT school in Argentina

1. The Argentine education system: structural changes during the 1990s

In order to analyze what has happened in technology education during the last twenty years, it is necessary to mention the implementation of a new Federal Law on Education which, since 1995, has modified both the Educative National System structure and the teaching contents. Until that moment, except for a few pilot projects, technology as a subject only existed at Technical Schools (for children aged 13 to 18 years) and their goal was to train technicians in various paths (electronics, building, chemistry, computing science, etc.) in order to prepare them to enter the workplace. In all other schools, which produced graduates in arts, humanities, sciences or business orientation, technology was almost absent. Furthermore, there was no technological component to the curriculum of compulsory education at primary level (up to 12 years old). There were some subjects, such as hands-on activities, which were geared towards the development of manual abilities.

The new law regarding Education Reform had resulted in 10 years of compulsory education, starting at Elementary Level (i.e. aged five – preschool) and nine years of Basic General Education. Amongst the changes in the curriculum, the topic of technology, also called Technology Education, was integrated into the general education for every student.

High school and secondary school curricula also changed according to this Law. Following international trends, specialized training is given in the last three (non-compulsory) years of school, known as "Polymodal", for those students who elect to stay on. Students choose one orientation from several options: humanistic, health, technical, artistic, etc. Technology is given its own place and every orientation, be it technical or humanistic, has technological aspects to its curriculum. Of course in technical orientations where the focus is on the training of future technicians, technology is therefore taught for a greater proportion of the week (as described in table 2).

Table 2: The technology education structure before and after the new Federal Law

Before 1995			After 1995		
			Age 5	Pre school	
Compulsory	Primary School	Age 6-12	First Cycle Age 6-8 Second Cycle Age 9-11	Basic General Education	Compulsory
	Secondary School	Age 13-17	Third Cycle Age 12-14		
			Age 15-17	Polymodal	

How the State facilitated the integration of technology subjects

Within the Federal Law, the desire is declared to integrate "socially meaningful knowledge" to schools, which includes technology and informatics.
There is a list of basic common technology contents that have to be taught at schools all over the country. Each province authority has the responsibility to decide on the instructional methods of those contents and whether they should have a specific curricular space, or even whether to integrate these contents across the curriculum in different subjects.

There is no National Curriculum on technology or indeed on any other subject. Every province develops its own curriculum, on the basis of these basic common contents, and thus the level of implementation of technology education varies widely. There are some provinces where technology is entirely absent from the classroom, due to lack of teacher training or lack of curriculum materials. In places where technology is taught, there is a tension between the various curricular approaches: teaching technology concepts versus teaching hands-on activities.
We would like to present two examples of possible ways to implement technology education:

- The province of Buenos Aires (more than 30% of the total population) took the decision that the technology content would appear across the curriculum, in every subject. There are no specific curriculum materials for technology education, but there are some elements of technology within other subjects. Moreover, there is no specific teacher training, but teachers of other subjects are taught how to teach the technology contents. We can say that, apart from some minor activities, the teaching of technology is absent in that province.

From 2003 on, as a pilot project, some schools have been chosen to dedicate a few hours to teaching technology as a specific field to children aged 12 to 14 years old.

- The city of Buenos Aires, the capital city of Argentina, decided that technology should be part of an integrated subject called "Knowledge of the World", in the curriculum for 6- to 8-year-olds. The technology aspects are the responsibility of a special teacher (formerly the skilled handcraft teacher), who has to plan the teaching in cooperation with the Social Studies teacher. The local authority produces the curriculum materials and the training for both types of teacher.

For children aged 9 to 12 years old, technology has its own space, with a trained teacher (also a skilled handcraft teacher). For this, it is necessary to have a teacher with a higher level of technical training. Therefore, there are teacher training sessions whose goal is to fill some of the gaps in the knowledge in this subject. Most of the technology teachers are women, upon whom this change has been imposed, assuming they would teach something that they were not trained for. The main problem was the shift from hands-on activities to design and innovation activities. The training, which was intensive and initially compulsory, has now become optional, as a support to the teachers' task.

Integrating technology into the school curriculum

The proposal to include technology subjects into the school curriculum was not an isolated process, but rather was part of the structure of curriculum changes that were being implemented throughout the National Education system.

Each school community (parents, students, teachers and head-teachers) has different perceptions about technology education. These various perceptions can generate many varying expectations from a new subject which is only in its infancy.

Today, interest and enthusiasm are decreasing and we are witnessing a new stage, where technology holds a more critical, logical and considered place within schools.

At the national level of technical education, or the training for the labor market, the technical education reforms are currently being critically analyzed. Technicians are perceived as not fulfilling the expectations of society or of the market. The debate is whether it is necessary to go back to traditional technical education, or if it would be possible to improve the model of technician-training that has been proposed by the reform.

2. Technology at the ORT school in Argentina

The ORT Technical School is one of the most important technical schools in the country. It was established in 1943 by World ORT with the mission of giving assistance to Jewish immigrants, most of them countrymen from Europe, through the teaching of arts and manual trades.

By the beginning of the 1980s, the school had a curricular structure similar to the rest of the technical schools in the country:

- three years of Secondary School, when science and humanities were taught and some practical abilities were developed through workshops oriented towards technical training in many subjects including electrics, mechanics and carpentry;
- three years of High School, designed to impart techniques in different paths (for example: electronics, construction and chemistry).

At that time, the ORT school was considered highly innovative, due to its structure, and the teaching of informatics as both a medium for training technicians and as a didactic resource for teaching other curriculum subjects.

The new curricular space called Science Workshop was created with the aim of finding answers to certain questions: Do we provide students with situations involving the design and analysis of technological devices? Will they achieve a better understanding of some scientific abstract concepts?

From these experiences, teachers realized that the knowledge put into practice by students does not come only from the field of science. There appear to be different kinds of knowledge, processes and thinking in relation to the activity of design. The Science Workshop therefore changed its name and it is now called the Science & Technology Workshop. Two main routes emerged – "the process of design" and "the system approach". The design activities focus on the building of technological devices such as scales, bridges, or articulated arms; the system analysis activities focus on hydraulic systems and the "black box". All these activities were focused on the developing of general skills of design and analysis.

In parallel, students continued learning about technologies in workshops on many subjects including electrics, carpentry and mechanics. These traditional workshops were built around the teaching of concepts, techniques and procedures from "expert management".

Thus, in the new school, the independent field of "Technology Education" has arisen, with the primary aim of integrating system analysis skills development with knowledge of specific technologies, e.g. teaching Electricity during the same workshop as Design, or teaching Electricity and Mechanics with a system approach. The system approach is also used to find a set of general concepts, which relate to energy, materials and information.

Landmark

During 1989, the donation of didactic materials from World ORT was an important milestone in the development of Technology subject matter at the ORT school. These didactic materials were appointed for training professionals in subjects such as automation and robotics, and could be adapted to students aged 14 years old. These materials were considered an innovating factor in the development of system analysis and technological problem-solving. So, cultural adaptations were made (in addition to the translation to Spanish), and student work guides, teacher guides and software, hardware and didactic kits were designed.

This Project had a large impact beyond its pedagogical goals in two aspects: Firstly, it increased students' motivation, which had a direct positive influence on the quality and the quantity of learning. Secondly, the prestige of technology as a curriculum subject increased, both within the school and outside in the educative community, official bodies and government ministries.

The chance of seeing such young children solving technological problems related to artificial vision systems, logical and programming controllers, robotic arms, flexible production cells or exploring robots, became a very good reason to visit ORT schools and take an interest in technology education. As a result, requests and demands came from schools and public bodies for external counseling. There is now a new challenge: to transfer the model and the strategies to other contexts.

3. Sharing our expertise

During the last twenty years, different organizations and private institutions have recognized the expertise of the ORT Technical School in technology education, and requested their advice while considering implementation themselves – e.g., in pilot projects on a small scale, using curriculum materials developed at ORT School; some ORT technology teachers began writing and planning programs in collaboration with teams from the National Ministry of Education at provincial level. Over the years there has been a cooperation agreement between the ORT Argentina Association and certain local government officials, whereby these administrative bodies can benefit from ORT's capacity and potential in design, and implement, manage and control training planning and curriculum development in technology education. For example, in an agreement between the province of Buenos Aires, the local Ministry of Education, and the ORT Argentina Association, it was decided that ORT Argentina specialists would work on a project paid for by the World Bank about the extension of school hours for children ages 12 to 14 in 200 schools, technology education being one of the chosen subjects. In addition, specialists from ORT Argentina are spearheading a process to change the subject of technology at "polymodal" level (i.e. for 14-17 year-olds).

Changes in technology education at an ORT school in Israel

1. An Overall View of the Technology Education Frameworks in Israel

Technological studies in Israel take place in two frameworks (as described in figure 1): 1. Technology literacy for all (in elementary, secondary high school and in higher education) and 2. Technical and vocational tracks in high school and higher education.

In 1993, the Israeli government established a commission, chaired by Professor Harari of the Weizman Institute. The resulting report declared:
"We call upon the Government of Israel to announce a national program for strengthening, deepening and improving the study of mathematics, natural science and technology in all sections of the education system, in order to prepare the next generation of citizens of Israel for life in a scientific-technological era."
With regard to Science & Technology, the report recommended:
"Combining science and technology in secondary school (grades 7-9) into one subject, namely Science & Technology, which will be studied at least six hours per week over three years."

Based on these recommendations, new national curricula were developed and implemented. The secondary school Science & Technology curriculum (created in 1996) consists of seven main subjects: Materials, Energy, Technological Systems and Products, Information & Communication, Earth and Universe, Creatures and Life, and Ecological Systems.

Figure 1: The education system in Israel *Technological literacy for all*

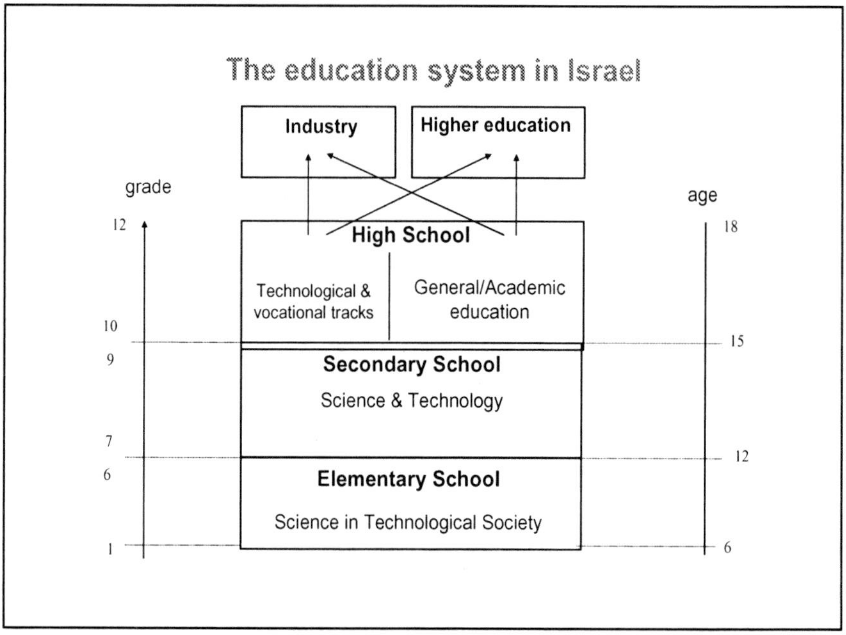

Technical and vocational education in high school (grades 10-12)

The aim of technology education in Israeli high schools is to prepare students who specialize in technology/pre-engineering related disciplines for employment and for further higher education.
One third of all Israeli high school students are studying within this framework. A technology-based matriculation is needed in order to pursue a degree in Engineering.
About 20% of students who study technology in grades 10 to 12 either go on to higher education in colleges for technicians (grade 13) and practical engineers (grade 14), or to university faculties of technology (which entails four years of study).

2. Changes that have been made in terms of curriculum rationale and content in Israeli schools

Technological literacy for all

In the last two decades, three new national curricula have been developed and implemented, from elementary school ("Science in Technology Society", 1985) to secondary school ("Science & Technology",1996), up to high school ("Technology Sciences", 2000: "Science & Technology in Society, 2000).

Two main trends characterize the changes in these curricula:
   a) Emphasizing the system approach and problem solving (design processes) as central concepts in the curriculum (as is done in other countries);
   b) Those new curricula focus on the relationships (coordination/ collaboration/integration) between science and technology within a social context (which is a different approach to that adopted by most countries).

Technical and vocational education in high school (grades 10-12)

In the last four years, the Israeli Ministry of Education and ORT Israel have focused on developing and implementing new innovative science and technology/pre-engineering disciplines and subjects, such as:
- Mechatronics,
- Engineering Sciences,
- Biotechnology,
- Environmental Sciences
- Bio-medical Engineering.

3. The Status of Technology Education in Israel

Technology literacy for all

From a technology education point of view, the new curriculum was a milestone. It served as a lever to enable a shift from technical education (industrial art and hands-on activities) to technology education which emphasizes thinking skills such problem solving and a system approach.

On the other hand, on the way to becoming more "academic" by focusing on thinking skills and less using of practical skills (such as sketching), we might risk losing some of the significant instructional features of technology education. In the last four years, due to the declining hours devoted to science and technology in secondary schools, a situation has arisen where although the science & technology is compulsory, some schools don't have a technology department; and in some other schools, technology is taught by science teachers.

Technology Education in High Schools

The current status of Technology Education in high school can be characterized by the following features:

- a variety of disciplines – from "low tech" disciplines (e.g. tourism) through traditional discipline (e.g. mechanics and electronics) up to "high-tech" disciplines (e.g. biotechnology and software engineering).
    - the technology education system provides a solution for students according with varying interests and abilities, in that different diplomas can be obtained, from vocational diplomas and partial matriculation right up to full matriculation.

However, uniting all the disciplines together under the umbrella of "technology education", combined with the poor image of technology education in the eyes of many students and parents (compared to science) does not help to promote technology education as something that provides important skills for life, as well as being a vehicle for a future career.

Technology Education provision in high school is under public criticism – with some even questioning whether we need to teach technology in high school at all. The criticisms that are leveled include:

- the lack of clarity between various disciplines within technology education.
- the high cost, compared to other subjects (e.g. social studies and even science).
- technology education does not relate to real life.

Curriculum programs are not often updated; however, were they to be, on a regular basis, many teachers would not able to cope with the reforms that would consequently need to be implemented.

4. ORT Israel within the educational framework

Technology education in ORT schools

ORT Israel is the largest non governmental educational network in Israel, with more than 150 schools all over the country (including secondary, high schools, industrial colleges and academic colleges). It serves 11% of all the secondary-school students in the country. Figure 2 indicates the importance of technology education within ORT schools compared to other schools in the country.

Figure 2: Distribution of Students in ORT secondary schools

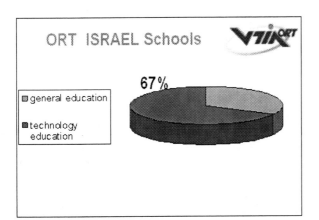

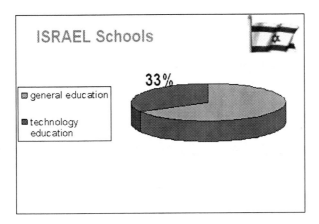

R&D Center

The ORT Israel Moshinsky R&D and Training Center in Tel Aviv fulfils a number of functions:

- ORT Israel plays a leading role in developing curriculum materials (e.g. textbooks, websites, lab activities and multimedia CDs) for all secondary schools in Israel, focusing on the technology aspects of the unified curriculum for Science and Technology (Dagan & Kipperman, 2001).

Each school is allocated a tutor to work with the science and technology teachers, helping them to implement the new curriculum and its materials (Shemla & Soffer, 2000).

43

- In the last four years, the Israeli Ministry of Education and ORT Israel have focused on developing and implementing new science and technology/pre-engineering curricula, in order to attract more capable students (especially females) to the technology education framework, and to update and adapt new technologies from industry to the school curriculum.

The main concepts driving the development of the new technology curriculum are:

- inter-relationships between science and technology
- inter-disciplinary and multi-disciplinary topics
- attractiveness generally, and to female students in particular
- creating a learning community, i.e. students and teachers
- project-based learning

The series of new science and technology curricula based on the rationale above, previously listed in this report, was in fact developed at the ORT Israel Moshinsky R&D Center.

Changes in technology education in the ORT network of schools in Russia

1. Technology education in Russian school

The twenty-year period chosen by the editors of this book for review was a very significant time for Russia and the other countries of the former Soviet Union. Twenty years ago, great changes emerged in these countries; the evolving educational system reflected the transformations in economics and society. The change from focusing solely on traditional and old-fashioned "labor education" towards integrating technology education was a prominent feature of the educational reform.

Early Technology Curriculum

In 1993 a new educational topic appeared in the Russian National Curriculum, entitled "Technology". This field included three subjects: Labor Education, Graphics (Technical Drawing) and Technology. Altogether, 808 compulsory hours of technology were taught in all Russian schools from the academic year of 1993.

According to the national "compulsory minimum content" there were several compulsory items, which all school students in Russia had to study (known as the "General Technology Component"):

- Technology in modern society

- Technological culture and its components
- Culture of labour: organization of work process, and preparation for the work place.
- Modern energy saving and material saving technologies
- Graphical modelling
- Artisan handicraft and home-craft
- Impact of technology on society and environment
- Social needs
- Design
- Entrepreneurship
- Budgeting
- Advertising

In addition to the "general technology component", each school could teach a special technology component in a particular "direction" or "area" of labour.

The optional directions included:

- Technology of materials
- Manual and machine manufacturing
- Art work with materials
- Textile manufacturing and food production or domestic culture
- Agricultural technologies

Within these optional areas were:
- industry
- economics
- education
- medicine
- building
- transport
- office work
- informational technologies
- applied art
- agriculture
- cattle breeding
- the service sector.

After meeting the demands of the national curricula, regional and school educational authorities could then introduce their own technology items.

"What is to be done?" – This long-standing question for the Russian intelligentsia appeared again before technology educators and teachers. Most schools continued to teach woodwork to the boys and domestic science to the girls;

some decided to replace engineering tools with computers. The rest simply removed technology from the school timetable. But in general, no technology revolution took place in school.

At the same time there was one innovation – *design* as a core idea, which allowed the new subject "Technology" to be distinguished from the old topic of "Labour". Students continued making the same chairs and pies that their grandfathers and grandmothers had, but now they did it as part of the design process. The idea of needs analysis as the start of the *design circle* had been brought from English and Wales's concept of *Design and Technology*, and was successfully applied in many Russian schools. But we have to acknowledge that the first decade of "Technology" at school did not fully justify society's hopes.

New Technology Curriculum

After several years of experimentation, new educational standards and national curricula were designed in 2004, which included three curriculum components:
- national (which must take up at least 75% of the total teaching time),
- regional (to be taught in not less than 10% of total teaching time)
- the school's own (which must be taught in not less than 10% of total teaching time).

The national component now accounts for <u>only 448 academic hours of compulsory teaching technology from grades 1 to 8.</u> There is the option to choose technology education from grades 9 to 11. In elementary school (grades from 1 to 9) "compulsory minimum content" takes into consideration students' interests and abilities, the school's capabilities, and local social and economical circumstances. It can be studied in 1 of 3 trends:

1. Technology as a Technical skill.
2. Technology in the Service sector.
3. Technology in Agricultural.

After 8 years of education, in grade 9 the school can add technology as a "taster", prior to students committing to specific subjects for matriculation. In high school (in grades 10-11) technology is not a compulsory subject within the national component. It can be studied for 70 - 280 hours at matriculation level. In addition to general subjects, students can select one area for special technology training. While comparing the two technology curricula, we can see that technology as a school subject became more flexible and less restrictive.

2. Technology education in ORT Russia

Established in Russia 125 years ago, ORT returned to its origins after a fifty-year absence in 1991. The opening of the ORT Technology School in Moscow, inaugurated in 1995, was quickly followed by other schools and technology centres in Moscow, St. Petersburg, Kiev and other cities of the former Soviet Union. In the current academic year 2004-2005, thirteen ORT school and technology centres are operating in Russia, Ukraine, Moldova, Belarus, Latvia and Lithuania.

In general, ORT technology curricula correspond with National Curriculum requirements, but are based on different principles, with the concepts of design and technological literacy as a system approach being the core for teaching technology in ORT's technology centres.

Bearing in mind the National Curriculum, ORT suggested a three-step structure for its "Technology for All" program (Gorinskiy, 2003):

- In grade 5, pupils study the module "Introduction to Technology" that deals with the questions: What is the purpose of technology? In the future, what will be the influence of technology on the environment and on society? And what are the social aspects of technological development? Pupils study several applications of technology, e.g. telecommunications, transportation and food technology. One of the most important parts in the 5th grade technology curriculum is the introduction to technological modelling based on LEGO Dacta "Simple Mechanisms" sets.
- In grades 6-9, pupils study Technology Education modules and ICT supporting materials, based on the system approach. The main modules are Design Process, Technological Systems, Materials and Products, and Energy and Information.
- In grades 10-11 some high schools give their pupils elements of initial vocational training in certain technological domains (e.g. ICT, CNC and Video Technology).

Technology courses are studied in parallel with ICT, which is used from the first year of the program (grade 5, age 10) as a practical tool for studying technology. Since 2003, ORT students have had the option of studying specialized technology courses using ORT's e-learning system. As it embarked upon technology education programs, ORT Russia faced a problem concerning its teachers: most pedagogical university graduates do not have enough experience to teach technology according to the technology literacy paradigm. ORT invited not only professional teachers to its schools, but also a number of engineers and scientists. In order to prepare teachers with different backgrounds to teach technology, ORT has developed its *continual professional development* (CPD) system. Teacher training is an important element of this system and includes periodical teacher training seminars as well as other formal and informal activities.

III. COMPARISON AND CONCLUSIONS

Comparison:

In this part of the paper, we would like to compare the Technology Education in ORT schools in Argentina, Israel and Russia over the last 20 years, specifically in the following aspects:
1. the changes in terms of curriculum rationale and content.
2. the changes in the role of teachers.
3. the formal status of technology education.

Firstly, we have to point out that in Argentina there are two ORT schools, each featuring both a secondary and a high school; in Russia there are 13 technology centers (grades 5 to 11) and in Israel there are 40 secondary schools (grade 7-9) and 65 high schools (grade 10-12).

1. The changes in terms of curriculum rationale and content

In the early 1990s, reform took place in all of the three countries (Russia and Israel in 1993, and Argentina in 1995); in Russia there was further reform in 2004.

In the 1990s reforms, we see that each of the countries decided to add some element of technology education to their curriculum; since the second reform occurred in Russia, we see acceptance in all three countries of technology as a literacy. However, there are differences in their aims, their subject matter, their level of importance and their significance. In Israel, this reform led to the National Curriculum including Science and Technology as a compulsory subject matter (as literacy for k-12); in Argentina this reform led to certain compulsory concepts (even though it is not included in every region and province); in Russia, technology education is compulsory and has been taught over many hours, but prior to the last change (in 2004) most of it was "hands on" manual activities.

Whilst noting the differences in what had developed in the ORT schools in these countries, we can see there are also wide similarities. Around the same year, the ORT schools in the three countries had separately (but after some collaboration) reached the conclusion that technology literacy had to be taught based on two main concepts: Design Process and System Approach.

Curriculum materials were therefore developed for these two main subjects. There was contact between the three centers, and exchanges of knowledge, with World ORT providing both leadership and funding.

Even if there are similarities of Design and System Approach in the main concepts and in technology knowledge in secondary schools (material, energy and information) in the ORT schools of the three countries, there are disparities in the instructional methods which reflect their cultural differences. If we compare technology knowledge aspects of the ORT high school in Argentina for example, we would be looking at professional technical education such as electronics, computer science, biotechnology, chemistry, design, musical production, mass media communication, business administration and master building (all of them leading to a technical degree). In Israel there are two paths: technology sciences (at literacy level), and biotechnology, engineering sciences, environmental sciences and bio-medical engineering as vocational paths/tracks. In Russia, it is professional training.

All of the three ORT centers had led the way within their own country in technology literacy (or "technology for all", as it is called in Russia). In Israel, the ORT R&D center developed the curriculum materials for the Israeli Ministry of Education; the Argentinean team cooperates with the Ministry of Education and influences the curriculum of the province of Buenos Aires among others; the Russian Centers, who work with institutes of higher education and local authorities, are considered to be the best technology centers in Russia.

2. The changes in role of teachers

From the beginning of the 1990s, when the technology curricula were changed in all three countries from "hands on" to an integrating thinking process for problem solving, design process and system approach, teachers' roles began to change too.

There was a lack of suitable teachers in all three of these countries. In Argentina and Israel, most of the teachers were not included in the process of change, and consequently it was difficult for them to become accustomed to it. In Russia the teachers had no literacy knowledge at all. ORT Argentina, ORT Israel and ORT Russia introduced wide-scale teacher training programs in order to teach them the new concepts and to help them along the instructional process, through seminars and personal tutoring. International seminars for technology teachers from ORT school around the world take place in London every year (e.g. the Hatter Technology Seminar and the Wingate IT Seminar), with the goal of sharing new concepts and new teaching methods.

3. The formal status of technology education

We all feel that in the school community (teachers, principles, students and parents) the word 'technology' can generate many interpretations, explanations and expectations, which in turn can create an element of confusion in defining what technology is. This lack of clarity can cause further difficulties when it comes to actually teaching the subject.

Technology education does not enjoy a particularly high status in the countries we have discussed. In Israel, when they combine technology with science, one hopes that the status of technology education will become equal to that of science; and indeed, for a few years, it was. In the last two years there has been a reduction in the number of teaching hours and, due to the low status of technology as a subject, these teachers were the first to be dismissed.

In Russia, most parents and students are not especially conscious of "technology" at school and continue to think in terms of traditional "labor". As a result, the status of both the subject and its teachers is very low. But in ORT Russia schools, students can study technology as a modern subject that is connected to the hi-tech world. Thus, technology has evolved into one of the students' favorite subjects.

Generally, there are more similarities than differences in most of the compared aspects between the three ORT centers. Some of these similarities are a result of the cooperation over the last eight years between the teachers and the curriculum developers, where ideas, concepts and knowledge have been exchanged between the various countries.

Conclusions on the main role of World ORT

Being part of a worldwide educational network such as World ORT enables us to exchange ideas, methods, knowledge, curriculum materials and experience from all over the world. These collaborations take place in a number of ways:

During 1999, World ORT organized a delegation of Israeli developers to Argentina, and Russian teachers and developers delegation to Israel, whilst ORT Israel's curriculum materials were being translated to other languages and being used as the basis for teacher training.

During recent years, World ORT has organized seminars for teachers and developers in technology education (Hatter Technology Seminar). In these seminars, teachers share their knowledge, studying with and learning from their colleagues from around the globe and learning from expert guest speakers. Above all, these seminars have established a community of technology educators, resulting in strong professional and personal relationships. These relationships have formed the basis for cooperation and sharing knowledge, and have led to consultations and the translation of teaching materials.

A multi-lingual website for technology education is now being developed. This website will contain all the abstracts of curriculum materials that have been developed in ORT centers all across the world, as well as recording the teachers' in-class experiences. There will also be forums to discuss technology teaching dilemmas and for sharing knowledge; competitions; and the facility to request and provide guidance where it is needed. This website will be the technology resource, forum and virtual meeting place for ORT technology educators.

The World ORT "Design for Sustainability" competition has been organized and was recently launched. Its aim is to enhance the teaching and studying of design by integrating the focus on environmental and sustainability aspects at different ages, across ORT schools around the world.

World ORT, as a large education network that emphasises technology education, does a lot in order to promote this subject in its schools around the world; however, it could do even more by facilitating further collaboration between curriculum developers and teachers – for example, through jointly developing curriculum materials, and by researching the parallels and differences between ORT schools. Nonetheless, we can see that affiliation to the World ORT network is vital for ORT schools and centres worldwide. Not only is every component of technology education in these three countries well structured, productive, and contributory to ORT's students and the World ORT organization; but furthermore, the whole system is much more than the sum of all its parts.

REFERENCES

Dagan, O., & Kipperman, D. (2001). Systems in action: A multimedia environment for learning technology systems. *PATT-11 conference proceedings*, 59-66.

Gorinskiy S. (2003). ORT's Approaches to teaching technology in the countries of the former Soviet Union: Goals, implementation and results. *PATT-13 conference proceedings*, 178-184.

Kipperman, D. (2003). The Noise around us – A problem-based learning and collaboration between science & technology. *PATT-13 conference proceedings*, 97-102.

Shemela, A. & Sofer, R. (2000). Diffusion of the STS curriculum in ORT Israel junior high schools. *PATT-10 conference proceedings*, 91-102.

HOWARD MIDDLETON

5. CHANGING PRACTICE AND CHANGING LENSES: THE EVOLUTION OF WAYS OF RESEARCHING TECHNOLOGY EDUCATION

INTRODUCTION

A person standing under a street lamp looking for his keys at night is asked by an observer where he lost them. He replies, "over there" (in the dark) when asked why he is looking where he is when the keys are somewhere else he replies "the light's better here" (anonymous contribution)

The quote above was originally used to ridicule quantitative research by suggesting that this form of research sought to examine that which was easy to examine but in the process failed to examine anything that was worth examining. I will argue that there is a degree of truth in the joke in terms of technology education research twenty years ago. I think there is evidence to suggest that maybe we were looking in the wrong places, for the wrong things and drawing the wrong conclusions.

A LITTLE HISTORICAL CONTEXT

In many countries, technology education grew out of a variety of earlier studies including, industrial arts, crafts, Sloyd and industrial or manual training to name a few. These earlier programs tended to evolve as practice-based practical studies. In many countries the preparation of teachers for these subjects was undertaken in institutions whose focus was teaching rather than research. As a consequence, practice evolved and was shaped through the influence of entities such as professional associations, curriculum advisors and departments of education. I need to say at the outset, however, that some of the generalisations I make hold up for much of the world but not for the USA. For example, technology education departments (Industrial arts) in the USA had strong research outputs from early in the 20th century, and this appears to have declined during the course of the last thirty years. The first PhD in the area in the USA was awarded during the 19th century, whereas in Australia, for example, the first was awarded during the 1990's. That being said, the general thrust of the argument I will develop holds true for most countries.

M.J. de Vries, I. Mottier (eds.), International Handbook of Technology Education, 53–61

In developing the argument presented in this paper I am drawing on papers examining research in technology education that together span the period since 1985. The papers comprise works by De Vries, (2000), Petrina (1998), and Zuga (1997). While drawing on these papers, my purpose is singular and different from that of the authors of the papers. De Vries sought to establish the match between the outputs of technology education research and the needs and priorities of teachers. Petrina examined the papers published in the Journal of Technology Education (JTE) to establish the kinds of research being published as a way of informing what should be published in the future while Zuga examined technology education in the USA through journal articles and dissertations to draw some conclusions about what kinds of research had been done and what needs to be done.

In this paper I am arguing that the kinds of research methodologies that have been employed over the last twenty years are evolving in ways that are making them more suitable for researching the things that need to be researched about technology education. I am not arguing that all research in technology education is compatible with this evolution but that there is evidence that it is happening. My purpose in doing so is based on the belief that using the correct research tools is as important to achieving the research aims for technology education as researching the right topics. Further, some research tools are necessary for the conduct of certain research so that availability of tools can, to some degree, determine what is researched, and what we are able to discover. Lastly, evolution can be ordered or entropic. To ensure that research provides outcome that allow technology education to evolve in an ordered and positive way it is important to highlight positive developments in research methodologies as well as research findings.

DESPERATELY SEEKING SCIENTIFIC (RESPECTABILITY) THROUGH SAMENESS

Twenty years ago much of the research in technology education was either highly quantitative, highly descriptive or both. In her 1997 analysis, Zuga indicates that during the period 1987 to 1993, 62% of studies in the USA were descriptive studies of the current status of technology and 38% about curriculum developments. Zuga cites only three studies that provide critical analyses of, for example, how teachers implement curriculum (Cox, 1991; Scarborough, 1993; Zuga, 1987). Zuga goes on to conclude that most of the studies used Delphi methods but restricted those surveyed to state supervisors and teacher educators, rather than teachers or students.

Why were we doing these kinds of studies using only these methodologies? I would argue that one of the reasons was that we were still suffering from the inferiority complex that the social sciences and the humanities had finally thrown off. That is, we were still desperate to achieve academic respectability. We reasoned that the best way to do that was to do our best to replicate the methods of science. We were asking questions in very measured but limited ways, and often they were not the right questions and not asked in the right ways.

In addition, I think it is arguable that we were suffering from what I would call a belief in the stratification of human ways of knowing. That is, the idea that different ways of representing knowledge should be accorded different status. In this hierarchy, knowledge represented by numeric symbols is accorded highest status, knowledge represented by language or language-like representations are accorded the next highest level, knowledge represented in images next and knowledge represented by action last. Everyone has seen cartoons with Einstein with $E = MC^2$ in the text balloon. The implicit assumption taken from Einstein's work is that he, along with other great scientists and inventors, thought predominately in abstractions, despite the plentiful evidence indicating that many eminent people in these fields used images or the manipulation of concrete objects to develop ideas (Weber & Perkins, 1992). The translation of these ideas into abstract representations occurred, in Einstein's case, after the initial imaginal representation of the idea (Holton, 1971/72).

At the other end of the spectrum, until the work of Polanyi (1983) on tacit knowledge became widely known and it's veracity acknowledged (for example, Sternberg, 2000), the idea that knowledge might reside in a representation that we could not describe using symbols was new and contested. It still is but less often now.

WHAT WAS THE EFFECT?

To examine the effects of these studies and the methodologies used to conduct them some context is required. In the period leading up to and during the early 1980s newly created (re-created) technology education, or design and technology education programs were appearing. Technology teachers, researchers and curriculum and pedagogy specialists were looking at different ways by which teachers might teach and students might learn. The proposed teaching methods represented a significant pedagogical change, which at its simplest could be described as a move from teacher-directed to student-centred learning or at another level described in terms of a move from didactics to constructivist theories (Von Glaserfield, 1987) about learning.

The kinds of research projects and the methodologies being used during that period were not suitable for illuminating such questions as how students solve ill-defined problems or how students generate new ideas, or how teachers provide appropriate scaffolding to students engaged in developing design solutions. Illumination would not come about through isolating single variables or quantifying collective opinions, however, eminent or considered they might be. More importantly, research outcomes that might inform practice were not being produced. As a technology curriculum consultant at around 1985 I was often asked questions like "what do I do if a student tells me they have read the brief, done some research and can't think of anything"

The effect of the concentration on quantitative, descriptive research, was that little real help was provided to practitioners in working out how this new way of teaching and learning might happen. Where practitioners worked it out for themselves, research was often unable to provide the analysis of what was happening and why. These would have been useful things to have done because when you examine documents about the introduction of new curricula in the early 1980s the documents often spelled out a list of hopes and expectations without any research to support what was intended.

I think it is arguable that the limitations in the early research hindered our understanding of the new pedagogies and, as a consequence, the successful introduction of new technology education programs. They weren't bad, they were just limited in what they could tell us and how, what they did tell us, related to what we needed to know. In turn, our capacity to argue the merits of the new technology education programs was limited by this lack of suitable research findings. Practitioners were left making statements of belief rather than being able to argue on the basis of evidence. In many cases teachers rejected design approaches as unworkable because their background didn't provide a suitable preparation and research wasn't filling the gap. My own Masters degree (Middleton, 1993), illustrates the point I make. It examined whether design based high school industrial arts courses developed creativity in students more than traditional courses. I used the Torrance Test of Creative Thinking (1972) and established that, yes, design based industrial arts courses did develop creative thinking abilities in students more than traditional courses. However, the quantitative methodology provided no examination of why that might be so.

COMFORTABLY CORNERING CLARITY THROUGH EXPLORATIONS OF UNIQUENESS

I want to move now to more recent times. What one sees emerging is research in technology education that has some distinctly different characteristics to earlier research. The characteristics can be categorised as involving new methodologies, attempts to interpret rather than only describe or quantify, and the greater use of mixed methodologies to answer the why as well as the what, and existing methodologies not previously used in technology education research. What was the motivation for the change?

The introduction of problem-solving into technology programs was probably one motivating factor. During the early 90's we were discovering differences between technological problem-solving and the existing research on problem-solving (Newell & Simon, 1972). Technological or design problems couldn't be explained by the existing theoretical models that were derived from research in mathematics and puzzles (Schon, 1992). Design problems didn't have the clearly defined starting points of mathematics and the solutions were anything but clear (at the outset). In addition, it was usually the case that the voyage from problem to solution was not restricted to a limited range of options (Middleton, 1998; 2003).

The socially constructed, hierarchical view of knowledge, dominant in the early 1980s, was being seriously challenged during the later period. For example, in the early period, Pylyshyn (1973, 1981) argued that mental images as representations of knowledge simply didn't exist. The later work of Kosslyn (1994+) provided physiological evidence via the use of new technology (Positron Emission Tomography) to verify the existence of both imaginal and symbolic modes of mental representation in human beings. Moreover, other researchers (Weber et al, 1990) attempting to explain the thinking processes of contemporary inventors found that mental images were used for quite complex processing and in fact, were more efficient for processing certain kinds of information.

An examination of historical evidence suggests that mental imagery is an important representation for the processes of discovery and invention (Perkins, 1992). So, rather than being a representation that is at the bottom end of the hierarchy in terms of importance as a way of representing information in problem-solving and learning, the more recent literature suggests it deserves a higher status.

Similarly, tacit knowledge is being re-evaluated and seen in a new light (Sternberg et al, 2000). Tacit knowledge is regarded as a key feature that distinguishes the expert from the merely very good in areas as diverse as motor racing and surgery. That is, the feature that puts Michael Schumacher ahead of the next-ranked Formula One driver is not superior conceptual or procedural knowledge but superior tacit knowledge. We still don't know enough about tacit knowledge but it is a feature of technological activity and therefore a reason to look for ways to examine its role in learning. Moreover, it is an area where research in technology education might reveal more general insights into this important aspect of human knowledge.

The move to design based technology program is probably one of the prime motivators for the change in research methodologies. Quantitative methods can tell us if a particular process in a directed or competency-based learning approach is more efficient that another in imparting highly specified learning. The task of unpacking what is happening in a design laboratory requires more sophisticated methods. An extension of this is the introduction of technology education programs in primary schools. What kinds of technological problems are appropriate for students at particular stages and how are they thinking and responding to those problems requires innovative research approaches, providing another motivator for looking at new ways to examine human phenomena.

Finally, technology educators are coming out of their cosy cocoons. Many technology educators felt secure in what they did, even if their laboratories were seen by school administrators as dumping grounds for less able or disruptive (usually male) students. If technology departments in schools had a secure future, then so did departments in universities. The closing down of technology education departments in schools in a number of countries across the globe and the axing of university programs at institutions such as the University Maryland and Sydney University, sent some alarm bells ringing. Protestations that what we were doing was good had ceased to be compelling in a world that wanted hard evidence.

WHAT IS BEING DONE?

I will touch on a few examples of recent work to illustrate the change in research in technology education. We are using new methodologies and discovering new things. In 1994 Lloyd and Scott examined the conventional wisdom that images in the form of drawings and sketches did not contribute anything new to verbal protocols. The conventional view was that the sketches were simply mirror images of the verbal data. Lloyd and Scott tested the assumption by videorecording design activity using protocol analysis procedures where subjects verbalise anything that comes into their head, produced transcripts of the verbal activity and removed the sound track from the videorecording. They then asked people to view the transcripts and describe the images they would expect to find. Another group were given soundless video to view and asked to predict the dialogue that would accompany the images. The degree to which people could do this was about 20%. The new method was able to disprove a long-held view and one that was not positive for technology education.

We are making greater use of research findings and methodologies from other disciplines not previously used in technology education, and we are utilising theory to provide frameworks for analysing research. The Walmsley study (2004) drew on Cognitive theory (Anderson, 1983), Setting theory (Barker, 1972) and activity theory (Engestrom, 1987) to provide the framework for analysing data about what students thought about their learning environment. The data consisted of a questionnaire, and videotape data of the students engaging in technological learning. Similarly, the Banks et al (2004) study drew on curriculum theory (Shulman (1986), cognitive theory (Gardner, 1983, 1991) and the European tradition of didactics and pedagogy (Verret, 1975; Chevellard, 1991, in Banks, 2004), to devise tools for technology teachers to reflect on professional knowledge.

WHAT IS THE EFFECT?

We are developing a more complex understanding of what is involved in teaching and learning in technology education. In addition, we are learning more about how to do technology education better. Our increased understanding of the thinking processes students engage in when solving technological problems, the kinds of psychological blocks that tend to get in the way of them finding solutions, and the kinds of teaching strategies that can be used to overcome these are areas where we now know more and more importantly, have a better understanding of where we need further research.

We are also learning more about how to learn more about what we are doing. That is, we are finding the most appropriate ways to examine the particular characteristics of technology education. Ways that acknowledge its multi-modal characteristics and the particular kinds of problem-solving involved when students are presented with a design brief and required to come up with a solution.

We are engaging more with the wider educational research community. At the technology education research conference hosted by the American Association for the Advancement of Science (AAAS) in Washington in 2001, presenters included cognitive theorists, science researchers, information technology researchers and curriculum research specialists, in addition to technology education researchers.

We are verifying, quantifying and qualifying some long-held beliefs. The research by Walmsley (2001) confirmed, albeit in a limited way, that providing a design-based learning environment did encourage technology students to engage in higher-order thinking more than was the case with a directed learning environment. Research by Purcell and Gero (1996) is quantifying the effects of fixation in the design process and research by Middleton (1998) is qualifying the previous understanding of problems as they apply to design problems.

We are contributing to knowledge more generally and by challenging some firmly entrenched assumptions about what is important in terms of how knowledge is represented in thinking and of how people solve problems most efficiently. The research by Lloyd and Scott, Walmsley and Gero and Purcell all challenge existing assumptions.

DOES IT MATTER ANYWAY?

The changes in the kinds of research technology education researchers have been engaging in during more recent years are significant in a number of ways beyond those mentioned already. I would argue that the research output from many of these more recent studies have been important because increasingly we need to justify the existence of technology education programs in ways that are credible to general education decision-makers. Findings that eminent technology educators think that technology education programs are important (Newcombe, 2004), while heart-warming, are probably less useful in convincing educational administrators of the value of technology education programs than studies that verify important learning outcomes from those programs using measures verified elsewhere (Walmsley, 2001).

WHAT CAN ONE CONCLUDE?

There are a number of conclusions to be drawn from this paper. Over a twenty year period research in technology education has evolved from the use of reasonably simple methodologies to the use of methods that are better suited to the complex nature of many aspects of technology education, and of what we need to find out. We are finally able to verify some long held beliefs about the nature of learning in technology education classes and disprove other views about knowledge that have not supported the value of technology education. We need to continue with these studies so that we can: develop a better understanding of the discipline; contribute to knowledge in general; and for purposes of advocacy.

REFERENCES

Anderson, J. R. (1982). Acquisition of cognitive skills. *Psychological Review*, 89, (4), 369-406.
Banks, F., Barlex, D., Jarvinen, E., O'Sullivan, G., Owen-Jackson, G., & Rutland, M. (2004). DEPTH – developing professional thinking for technology teachers: an international study. *International Journal of Technology and Design Education*, 14, 141-157.

Barker, R. G. (1978). Theory of behaviour settings. In R. G. Barker and Associates, *Habitats, environments and human behaviour*. San Francisco: Jossey Bass.

Cox, D. W. (1991). A study of the impact of the technology education movement on industrial arts programs in two Ohio middle schools, *Dissertation Abstracts International*.

Engestrom, Y. (1987). *Learning by expanding: an activity-theoretical approach to developmental research*. Helsinki: Orienta-Konsultit Oy.

Gardner, H. (1983). *Frames of mind: the theory of multiple intelligences*. New York: Basic Books.

Gardner, H. (1991). *The unschooled mind*, New York: Basic Books.

Holton, G. (1971/72). On trying to understand scientific genius. *American Scholar*, 41, 95-110.

Kosslyn, S. (1994). *Image and brain: the resolution of the imagery debate*. Cambridge Mass: Bradford Books.

Lloyd, P., & Scott, P. (1994). Discovering the design problem. *Design Studies*, 17, (4), 435-449.

Middleton, H. E. (2002). Complex problem solving in a workplace setting, *International Journal of Educational Research*, 37, 67-84.

Middleton, H. E. (1998). *The role of visual mental imagery in solving complex problems in design*. Unpublished PhD thesis. Brisbane: Griffith University.

Middleton, H. E. (1983). *Creative thinking abilities and an industrial design course*. Unpublished master of education dissertation. Canberra College of Advanced Education. The Evolution of Ways of Researching 63.

Newcombe, J. (2000). *Conceptualising technology education for general education: A Delphi study*. Unpublished honours dissertation, Brisbane: Griffith University.

Newell, A., & Simon, H. A. (1972). *Human problem solving*. New Jersey: Englewood Cliffs.

Perkins, D. N. (1992). The topography of invention. In R. J. Weber & D. N. Perkins (Eds.), *Inventive minds*. New York: Oxford University Press.

Petrina, S. (1998). The politics of research in technology education: A critical content and discourse analysis of the Journal of Technology Education, Volumes 1-8. *Journal of Technology Education*, 10, (1), 27-57.

Polanyi, M. (1983). *The tacit dimension*. NY: Doubleday and Co.

Purcell, A. T., & Gero, J. S. (1996). Design and other types of fixation. *Design Studies*, 17, (4), 363-383.

Pylyshyn, Z. W. (1981). The imagery debate: analogue media versus tacit knowledge. *Psychological Review*, 88, (1), 16-45.

Pylyshyn, Z. W. (1973). What the mind's eye tells the mind's brain: a critique of mental imagery. *Psychological Bulletin*, 80, (1), 1-24.

Scarborough, J. D. (1993). 'Phys-ma-tech: Operating strategies, barriers, and attitudes' *The Technology Teacher*, 52, (6). 35-38.

Schon, D. A. (1992). The design process. In V. A. Howard (Ed.), *Varieties of thinking: essays from Harvard's philosophy of education research center*. New York: Routledge.

Shulman, L. S. (1986). Those who understand: knowledge growth in teaching, *Educational Research Review*, 57, 1-22.

Sternberg, R. G. (2000). *Practical intelligence in everyday life*. Cambridge: Cambridge University Press.

Torrance. E. P. (1972). *Torrance test of creative thinking: Norms technical manual*. Lexington Mass: Ginn & Co.

Von Glaserfield, E. (1987). Learning as a constructive activity. In C. Janvier (Ed.), *Problems of representation in the teaching and learning of mathematics*, Hillsdale New Jersey: Earlbaum, 3-17.

Walmsley, B. (2001). *Technology education learning environments and higher-order thinking*. Unpublished Honours dissertation. Griffith University.

Weber, R. J., Moder, C. L., & Solie, J. B. (1990). Invention heuristics and mental processes underlying the development of a patent for the application of herbicides. *New Ideas in Psychology*, 3, 321-336.

Weber, R. J., & Perkins, D. N. (1989). How to invent artefacts and ideas. *New Ideas in Psychology*, &, 49-72.

Zuga, K. (1997). An analysis of technology education in the United States based upon an historical overview and review of contemporary curriculum research. *International Journal of Technology and Design Education*. 7, 203-217.

Zuga, K. (1987). *Industrial arts reform: trapped in a technocratic ideology*. Eric document ED282 994.

Part B Country studies

WILLIAM E. DUGGER, JR.

6. TWENTY YEARS OF EDUCATIONAL STANDARDS FOR TECHNOLOGY EDUCATION IN THE UNITED STATES

INTRODUCTION

Educational reform in the United States over the past decade and a half has been driven by educational standards. All major subject matter areas (approximately 15) have developed educational standards at the national level. Also, every one of the 50 states as well as some local school districts have developed standards. This paper will present a historical overview of all of the educational standards developed and implemented in technology education in the United States over the past quarter of a century.

IN THE BEGINNING

Our profession created its first set of *Standards for Industrial Arts Programs* (Virginia Tech, 1981), made possible through a grant from the U.S. Department of Education. This was later revised to reflect a more contemporary focus in 1985 as *Standards for Technology Education Programs* (International Technology Education Association, 1985). The later revision was funded by the Technical Foundation of America (TFA) and distributed by ITEA. These were program standards and they provided criteria for such topics as philosophy (of the program), instructional program (curriculum), student population served, instructional staff, administration and supervision, support systems, instructional strategies (methods), public relations, safety and health, and the evaluation process.

In the late 1980s and early 1990s, there were major national efforts evolving in this country to develop educational standards in a number of subject areas in K–12 schools. This began with the National Council of Teachers of Mathematics (NCTM) publishing *Curriculum and Evaluation Standards for School Mathematics* (NCTM, 1989). This was subsequently followed by *Professional Standards for Teaching Mathematics* (NCTM, 1991) and *Assessment Standards for School Mathematics* (NCTM, 1995).

In 1990, the American Association for the Advancement of Science (AAAS) printed a visionary document on the rationale and need for science literacy in the U.S. schools titled, *Science for All Americans* (AAAS, 1990). It was followed by *Benchmarks for Science Literacy* (AAAS, 1993). The National Research Council produced a parallel set of science standards in 1995 in the document titled, *National Science Education Standards* (NRC, 1995).

M.J. de Vries, I. Mottier (eds.), International Handbook of Technology Education, 65–81.

In the last half of the 1990s, there were numerous other subject matter standards created and published in social studies, history, geography, art, English, physical education, business education, and others.

CREATING A VISION FOR WHAT STANDARDS FOR TECHNOLOGICAL LITERACY SHOULD BE

In the first funded phase of TfAAP, ITEA wanted to develop a document that would discuss the power and promise of technology in our lives today. It wanted to also establish a universal need of technological literacy for all people. This was very important since the study of technology in America's schools was a relatively new educational effort. ITEA did this in a two-year project from 1994 to 1996 through the publication of *Technology for All Americans: A Rationale and Structure for the Study of Technology (R&S)* (ITEA, 1996). This document provided a structure for what the content in the study of technology could be in the future.

In retrospect, the development of *R&S* was a very valuable tool in grounding the profession in what every student should know and be able to do in order to be technologically literate. The *R&S* document was prepared through assistance from project staff and a group of writing consultants made up from a 25-member National Commission for Technology Education. In developing the various drafts of the document, hundreds of practitioners of technology, engineering, science, mathematics, and other areas served as reviewers of this material.

STANDARDS FOR TECHNOLOGICAL LITERACY: CONTENT FOR THE STUDY OF TECHNOLOGY

From 1996 to 2000, *Standards for Technological Literacy: Content for the Study of Technology (STL)* was developed, reviewed, published, and disseminated. *STL* sets forth the vision that all students can and should become technologically literate. Four groups advised and provided input to TfAAP during the development of *STL*—(1) the Advisory Group, (2) the Standards Team, (3) a committee of the National Research Council of the National Academy of Sciences, and (4) a focus group from the National Academy of Engineering. The Advisory Group advised ITEA in the best practice for standards development and determined ways for the study of technology to be integrated within the total school curriculum. Key representatives of the National Council of Teachers of Mathematics (NCTM), the National Science Teachers Association (NSTA), the American Association for the Advancement of Science (AAAS) Project 2061, the National Research Council (NRC) that developed the *National Science Standards*, the National Academy of Engineering (NAE), ITEA, and the Foundation for Technology Education formed the Advisory Group for TfAAP. They met semiannually to provide specific advice on the development of the standards, and how technology education could be integrated with other fields of study, especially science and mathematics.

The Standards Team proposed, evaluated, and recommended the content of the standards. TfAAP used a 27-member Standards Team comprised of 3 subteams with 9 people each (one team for Grades K-5, one team for Grades 6-8, and one team for Grades 9-12) to provide input to TfAAP staff who were responsible for the writing, generating, and consensus-building process of the standards. The team was made of classroom teachers, supervisors, and teacher educators from technology education as well as elementary administrators and representatives from science, mathematics, and engineering.

In 1999 and 2000, the NRC of the National Academy of Sciences (NAS) and a special focus group of engineers from the NAE were also involved in the formal review of *STL*. In mid December 1999, the NRC committee issued a final report stating that ITEA/TfAAP had "successfully completed the review process established by the NRC." In early 2000, the NAE committee issued a public statement in support of *STL*. Additionally, the project received funding from the Technical Foundation of America in the development of three standards-related implementation publications for the elementary, middle, and high schools.

Overview of the Standards Document

The document begins with a preface that sets the stage for the publication. Chapter 1 provides a broad perspective on preparing students for a technological world. Chapter 2 contains the overview of the features of *STL*, as well as its format. Chapter 2 also provides a section that deals with the primary users of the standards, as well as recommendations for using the standards for curriculum development. Lastly, Chapter 2 lists administrator guidelines for resources based on *STL*. Chapters 3 through 7 contain major categories under which the standards were developed. Lastly, Chapter 8 is a call to action regarding how ITEA can acquire help from others within and outside of the profession to adopt implementing *STL*. The document also has an appendix, which includes the history of the project, a compendium that provides a quick overview of the standards and related benchmarks, and an articulated curriculum example for Grades K–12, as well as references, acknowledgements, a glossary, and an index.

Features of STL

Standards for Technological Literacy: Content for the Study of Technology (*STL*) represents the collective view of hundreds of people regarding what should be the content for the study of technology in Grades K–12. In order to be as broadly valuable as possible, *STL* was created with the following basic features:

- It offers a common set of expectations for what students in technology should learn.
- It offers specific details about what every student should learn about technology.

- It is developmentally appropriate for students.
- It provides a basis for developing meaningful, relevant, and articulated curricula at the local and state/provincial levels.
- It promotes content connections with other fields of study in Grades K–12.

STL is not a curriculum. A curriculum provides the specific details of how the content (*STL*) is to be delivered, including organization, balance, and the various ways of presenting the content in the classroom, while standards describe what the content should be. Curriculum developers, teachers, and others should use *STL* as a guide for developing appropriate curricula, but the standards do not specify what should go on in the classroom.

In laying out the essentials for the study of technology, *STL* represents a recommendation from educators, engineers, scientists, mathematicians, and parents about what skills and knowledge are needed in order to become technologically literate. It is not, however, a federal policy or mandate. Nor does *STL* prescribe an assessment process for determining how well students are meeting the standards, although it does provide criteria for this assessment.

Format of STL

The individual standards presented in *STL* are organized into five major categories:

- The Nature of Technology (Chapter 3)
- Technology and Society (Chapter 4)
- Design (Chapter 5)
- Abilities for a Technological World (Chapter 6)
- The Designed World (Chapter 7)

Under the five major categories, there are 20 standards. See Figure 1 for a listing of the categories and standards.

Figure 1. Listing of Standards for Technological Literacy
Taken from International Technology Education Association. (2000). *Standards for technological literacy: Content for the study of technology.* Reston, VA: Author.
The Nature of Technology Standard 1.   Students will develop an understanding of the characteristics and scope of technology. Standard 2.   Students will develop an understanding of the core concepts of technology. Standard 3.   Students will develop an understanding of the relationships among

technologies and the connections between technology and other fields of study.

Technology and Society

Standard 4.　　　Students will develop an understanding of the cultural, social, economic, and political effects of technology.

Standard 5.　　　Students will develop an understanding of the effects of technology on the environment.

Standard 6.　　　Students will develop an understanding of the role of society in the development and use of technology.

Standard 7.　　　Students will develop an understanding of the influence of technology on history.

Design

Standard 8.　　　Students will develop an understanding of the attributes of design.

Standard 9.　　　Students will develop an understanding of engineering design.

Standard 10.　　　Students will develop an understanding of the role of troubleshooting, research and development, invention and innovation, and experimentation in problem solving.

Abilities for a Technological World

Standard 11.　　　Students will develop the abilities to apply the design process.

Standard 12.　　　Students will develop the abilities to use and maintain technological products and systems.

Standard 13.　　　Students will develop the abilities to assess the impact of products and systems.

The Designed World

Standard 14.　　　Students will develop an understanding of and be able to select and use medical technologies.

Standard 15.　　　Students will develop an understanding of and be able to select and use　agricultural and related biotechnologies.

Standard 16.　　　Students will develop an understanding of and be able to select and use energy and power technologies.

Standard 17.　　　Students will develop an understanding of and be able to select and use　information and communication technologies.

Standard 18.　　　Students will develop an understanding of and be able to select and use　transportation technologies.

Standard 19.　　　Students will develop an understanding of and be able to select and use　manufacturing technologies.

Standard 20.　　　Students will develop an understanding of and be able to select and use　construction technologies.

Standards

Standards for Technological Literacy: Content for the Study of Technology (*STL*) has written statements about what is valued in the study of technology that can be used for judging quality. The document specifies what every student should know and be able to do in order to be technologically literate and offers criteria to judge progress toward a vision of technological literacy for all students. *STL* contains requirements for students to become technologically literate as a result of their education from kindergarten through Grade 12. These standards set forth goals to be met in five major categories of technology. (See Figure 1.)

Benchmarks in STL

Benchmarks play a vital role in *STL*. They provide the necessary elaboration of the broadly stated standards. Benchmarks, which are statements that enable students to meet a given standard, are provided for each of the 20 standards at the K-2, 3-5, 6-8, and 9-12 grade levels. (See Figure 2 for a sample of the benchmarks.) The benchmarks are followed by supporting sentences that provide further detail, clarity, and examples. Like the standards, the benchmarks are required for students to meet the standards. Teachers should feel free to add to the benchmarks to further enhance the ability of the student to meet a given standard.

Figure 2. A Representative Standard and Benchmarks

Standard 8 – Students will develop an understanding of the attributes of design.

In order to realize the attributes of design, students in grades 3-5 should learn that

    C. The design process is a purposeful method of planning practical solutions to problems. The design process helps convert ideas into products and systems. The process is intuitive and includes such things as creating ideas, putting the ideas on paper, using words and sketches, building models of the design, testing out the design, and evaluating the solution.

D. Requirements for a design include such factors as the desired elements and features of a product or system or the limits that are placed on the design. Technological designs typically have to meet requirements to be successful. These requirements usually relate to the purpose or function of the product or system. Other requirements, such as size and cost, describe the limits of a design.

From research in education, it has been found that if previously learned knowledge is tapped and built upon, it is likely that children will acquire a more coherent and thorough understanding of these processes than if they are taught them as isolated abstractions (NRC, 1999). With this in mind, the benchmarks are articulated or "ramped" from Grades K–12 to progress from very basic ideas at the early elementary school level to the more complex and comprehensive ideas at the high school level. Certain content "concepts," such as systems, resources, requirements, optimization, and trade-offs, processes, and controls, are found in the benchmarks, which extend across various levels to ensure continual learning of an important topic related to a standard.

Advancing Excellence in Technological Literacy: Student Assessment, Professional Development, and Program Standards

In March 2003, the International Technology Education Association (ITEA) released *Advancing Excellence in Technological Literacy: Student Assessment, Professional Development, and Program Standards* (*AETL*) at its 65th annual conference in Nashville, Tennessee. *AETL* is based on *Standards for Technological Literacy: Content for the Study of Technology* (*STL*) and is designed as a companion to *STL*. *AETL* was developed by TfAAP from 2000 to 2003.

The three sets of standards in *AETL* support *STL*. *AETL* provides standards and guidelines that address student assessment, professional development, and program enhancement. The primary goal of all the standards is to help students achieve technological literacy. The eleven-person TfAAP Advisory Group provided valuable counsel in the best practice of standards development to the project. They met annually in Washington, DC.

The TfAAP Standards Writing Team was made up of 27 people (three teams of nine). They provided detailed input in fashioning the initial draft of *AETL*, and their continued review and input have added strength and quality to the final document. The development and refinement of *AETL* took place over three years (2000-2003) and involved hundreds of educators and experts in the fields of technology, mathematics, science, engineering, and other disciplines. Their input was attained through various methods, including hearings, Web-based electronic document review, and individual reviews through the mail and in person. Three formal drafts of *AETL* were developed and reviewed before the final draft was prepared in autumn 2002.

Overview of AETL

Chapters 1 and 2 of *AETL* provide valuable introductory material. Chapter 1 is an overview that presents the rationale of need and conceptually introduces Chapters 3, 4, and 5. Chapter 2 discusses relevant principles and definitions.

AETL consists of three separate but interrelated sets of standards.

- Student Assessment Standards (Chapter 3)
- Professional Development Standards (Chapter 4)
- Program Standards (Chapter 5)

The standards in *AETL* are based upon *STL*. To fully and effectively implement the content standards in *STL*, all of the *AETL* standards presented in Chapters 3, 4, and 5 must be met through the guidelines. While *AETL* is designed to leave specific curricular decisions to educators, teachers, professional development providers, and administrators should use *STL* and *AETL* as guides for advancing technological literacy for all students. And finally, Chapter 6 of *AETL* invites users to participate in the visionary basis of *STL* and *AETL*.

Student Assessment Standards (Chapter 3)

The definition for student assessment presented in *AETL* is "the systematic, multi-step process of collecting evidence on student learning, understanding, and abilities and using that information to inform instruction and provide feedback to the learner, thereby enhancing student learning." The primary audience for the student assessment standards is teachers. It is important to note that the standards are applicable to those who educate students on any aspect of technology.

The five organizational topics for the student assessment standards are:

- Consistency with *STL*
- Intended Purpose
- Research-Based Assessment Principles
- Practical Contexts
- Data Collection

While the student assessment standards (see Figure 3) define how assessment of technological literacy should be designed and implemented, Chapter 3 does not provide a test, quiz, or other handy instrument to be photocopied and used in the laboratory-classroom. This task is left—as it should be—to individual teachers and others.

Figure 3. Student Assessment Standards

A-1. Assessment of student learning will be consistent with *Standards for Technological Literacy: Content for the Study of Technology* (*STL*).

A-2. Assessment of student learning will be explicitly matched to the intended purpose.

A-3. Assessment of student learning will be systematic and derived from research-based assessment principles.

A-4. Assessment of student learning will reflect practical contexts consistent with the nature of technology.

A-5. Assessment of student learning will incorporate data collection for accountability, professional development, and program enhancement.

Users of the student assessment standards should recognize that student assessment should be *formative* (ongoing) as well as *summative* (occurring at the end). Further, users should recognize that the assessment process should be *informative*, that is, it should inform students and teachers about progress toward technological literacy and provide data on the effectiveness of instruction and the program. Teachers should use student assessment data to improve classroom practices, plan curricula, develop self-directed learners, report student progress, and research teaching practices.

Professional Development Standards (Chapter 4)

Chapter 4 presents criteria for professional development providers (including teacher educators, supervisors, and administrators) to use in planning professional development. Professional development includes a continuous process of lifelong learning and growth that begins early in life, continues through the undergraduate, pre-service experience, and extends through the in-service years.

The standards are applicable to those who prepare teachers on any aspect of technology, including teachers whose primary focus may be another subject area.

The seven organizational topics for the professional development standards are:

1. Consistency with *STL*
2. Students as Learners
3. Curricula and Programs
4. Instructional Strategies
5. Learning Environments
6. Continued Professional Growth
7. Pre-Service and In-Service

See Figure 4 for a listing of the professional development standards.

Users of this document should focus on preparing teachers to continue to pursue professional development to keep up with changing technologies and current research on how students learn. The necessity to address issues of technological literacy is pertinent to all programs that prepare teachers of every grade level, including K-5 elementary teachers and teachers of science, mathematics, social studies, language arts, and other content areas. Therefore, faculty members in every teacher preparation program can use *STL* and *AETL* to determine how the technological literacy of teacher candidates can be enhanced.

As defined in *AETL*, the program refers to everything that affects student learning, including content, professional development, curricula, instruction, student assessment, and the learning environment implemented across grade levels. The system-wide technology program manages the study of technology in technology laboratory-classrooms as well as in other content area classrooms. The primary audience for the program standards is twofold: (1) teachers and (2) administrators (including supervisors). As a result of this, the guidelines are divided for addressing these two audiences.

Figure 4. Professional Development Standards

PD-1.   Professional development will provide teachers with knowledge, abilities, and understanding consistent with *Standards for Technological Literacy: Content for the Study of Technology* (*STL*).

PD-2.   Professional development will provide teachers with educational perspectives on students as learners of technology.

PD-3.   Professional development will prepare teachers to design and evaluate technology curricula and programs.

PD-4.   Professional development will prepare teachers to use instructional strategies and enhance technology teaching, student learning, and student assessment.

PD-5.   Professional development will prepare teachers to design and manage learning environments that promote technological literacy.

PD-6.   Professional development will prepare teachers to be responsible for their own continued professional growth.

PD-7.   Professional development providers will plan, implement, and evaluate the pre-service and in-service education of teachers.

Program Standards (Chapter 5)

Chapter 5 presents criteria for teachers and administrators (including supervisors) responsible for the technology program and system-wide technology program. The standards are applicable to those who organize the learning of students on any aspect of technology. The five organizational topics for the program standards are:

- Consistency with *STL*
- Implementation
- Evaluation
- Learning Environments
- Management

Users of the program standards should recognize that thoughtful design and implementation of technology programs at school levels and of system-wide technology programs at district levels are necessary to provide comprehensive and coordinated experiences for all students across grade levels and disciplines, including science, mathematics, social studies, language arts, and other content areas. The program standards (see Figure 5) call for extending technology programs beyond the domain of the school. Technology programs should, for example, involve parents, the community, business and industry, school-to-work programs, and higher education as well as professionals in engineering and other careers related to technology. And finally, it is essential that adequate support for professional development be provided by administrators to ensure that teachers remain current with the evolving fields of technology and educational research.

Figure 5. Program Standards

P-1. Technology program development will be consistent with *Standards for Technological Literacy: Content for the Study of Technology* (*STL*).

P-2. Technology program implementation will facilitate technological literacy for all students.

P-3. Technology program evaluation will ensure and facilitate technological literacy for all students.

P-4. Technology program learning environments will facilitate technological literacy for all students.

P-5. Technology program management will be provided by designated personnel at the school, school district, and state/provincial/regional levels.

Guidelines, Enablers to Meet the Standards

Guidelines play a vital role in *AETL*. Under each standard a number of guidelines are presented and must be addressed to enable the user to meet a given standard. ITEA does not recommend that users eliminate any of the guidelines; however, users may add to the guidelines if there is a need to accommodate local differences. A sample standard (A-4) with related guidelines is presented in Figure 6.

Figure 6. Standard A-4 with Related Guidelines

Standard A-4: Assessment of student learning will reflect practical contexts consistent with the nature of technology.

Guidelines for meeting Standard A-4 require that teachers consistently:

A. Incorporate technological problem solving.
B. Include variety in technological content and performance-based methods.
C. Facilitate critical thinking and decision making.
D. Accommodate for modification to student assessment.
E. Utilize authentic assessment.

New Technology Standards-Based Addenda

Educational standards provide criteria for learning and ensure quality in educational programs. Standards-based technology programs can deliver technological literacy. ITEA offers two published standards documents for technological literacy: *Standards for Technological Literacy: Content for the Study of Technology* (*STL*) (ITEA, 2000/2002) and *Advancing Excellence in Technological Literacy: Student Assessment, Professional Development, and*

Program Standards (*AETL*) (ITEA, 2003). The purpose of these documents is to advance the technological literacy of all students. Together, they identify a vision for developing a technologically literate citizenry.

The ITEA Addenda series (to *STL* and *AETL*) is part of the standards package for technological literacy. They were produced by the TfAAP staff with special assistance from ITEA's Center to Advance the Teaching of Technology and Science (CATTS). These addenda are based on the standards but include concrete processes or suggestions for incorporating national, state, and/or local technological literacy standards into the programs of all students throughout Grades K–12. Additionally, all of the documents contain worksheets for educators to use to make changes specific to their locality and situation. The new addenda series marks another pioneering effort in educational reform, as it provides a supplement to educational standards that focuses on the entire picture of program reformation rather than concentrating solely on curricula. The new addenda are:

- **Student Assessment**

Measuring Progress: A Guide to Assessing Students for Technological Literacy (ITEA, 2004)

- **Programs**

Realizing Excellence: Structuring Technology Programs (ITEA, 2005)

- **Curricula**

Planning Learning: Developing Technology Curricula (ITEA, 2005)

- **Professional Development**

Developing Professionals: Preparing Technology Teachers (ITEA, 2005)

STL, *AETL*, and the four addenda are available for viewing at ITEA's website (www.iteaconnect.org).

OTHER RESEARCH

The International Technology Education Association's (ITEA) Technology for All Americans Project (TfAAP) has been the longest and most comprehensive research effort in the history of the profession. In addition to the years of developmental research guided by ITEA's TfAAP in developing, reviewing, validating, and finalizing *R&S*, *STL*, and *AETL*, the project has been involved in other formal research on people's knowledge of and beliefs about technology.

In 2001, ITEA commissioned the Gallup Organization from Princeton, New Jersey to conduct a nationwide survey of 1,000 homes to assess what Americans know about technology. This research was funded by NSF and NASA. Three years later, in 2004, ITEA's TfAAP revisited this effort and hired the Gallup Organization to conduct a second poll. In the second research effort, five questions from the original poll were carried over to the 2004 instrument and eleven new questions were generated by a committee to complete the instrument. A report of both the 2001 and 2004 ITEA/Gallup polls can be found at the ITEA's website (www.iteaconnect.org).

The 2001 and 2004 ITEA/Gallup polls were designed to determine how the public views technological literacy and the importance of technology in their daily lives. The opportunity to do a second study in 2004 so closely following the first has resulted in adding to, reinforcing, and augmenting the understandings gained in the earlier study. Given the accumulation of data, conclusions can be drawn with confidence.

The three conclusions drawn in the earlier study are both reinforced and extended by the additional data reported in the 2004 ITEA/Gallup poll. They are repeated and slightly revised in the following:

- The public understands the importance of technology in our everyday lives and understands and supports the need for maximizing technological literacy.
- There is a definitional difference in which the public thinks first of computers when technology is mentioned, while experts in the field assign the word a meaning that encompasses almost everything we do in our everyday lives.
- The public wants and expects the development of technological literacy to be a priority for K–12 schools.
- Men and women are in general agreement on the importance of being able to understand and use technology and on the need to include technological literacy as part of the schools' curriculum.

The cumulative weight of the two studies justifies additional conclusions that add to our understanding.

- People translate their feelings regarding the importance of technology into a desire to know how technologies work, with emphasis on those technologies that impact their daily lives.
- Attitudes toward technology and technological applications are directly related to age. In general, younger people assign a greater importance to knowing how technologies work and feel they have more influence in decisions related to technological applications.

IMPLEMENTATION OF STL AND AETL

The ITEA's TfAAP staff has conducted numerous workshops, hearings, presentations, and program development activities around the country since 1994. In the summer of 2000, the TfAAP staff conducted workshops at 11 NASA centers around the U.S. There were approximately 250 participants from 38 states who received an orientation to *STL*.

In the early fall of 2000, a group of six Standards Specialists nationwide were formed to help implement *STL* and *AETL*. They have conducted approximately 70 workshops and presentations involving over 2,300 individuals in the U.S.,

Thailand, and Canada on *STL* and *AETL*. These Standards Specialists will continue to offer implementation assistance after the TfAAP project finishes.

The TfAAP staff has undertaken many public relations efforts to inform others about *STL* and *AETL*. Numerous articles in technology education periodicals and journals have been written. A new website to inform the public about the importance of technological literacy has been created by TfAAP. It is www.iteaconnect.org/ACT/. Suggestions and input to the ACT website are welcome; please send correspondence to ITEA (www.iteaconnect.org). Sessions at the ITEA Conference have been conducted on how to develop an effective public relations program.

HOW WELL ARE THE STANDARDS BEING USED IN THE UNITED STATES?

Educational reform in the United States over the past decade has been centered around educational standards. The nationally-developed standards in all of the major subject matter areas have had considerable influence on all the states' educational standards. The content found in the nationally-developed standards has provided direction and ingredients for most of the 50 states' educational standards. Additionally, some local school districts that have developed their own standards were greatly influenced by the nationally-developed standards.

In 2004, a survey of state supervisors in technology education was conducted by ITEA's TfAAP staff, Shelli Meade and William Dugger. In response to the question, "Is *Standards for Technological Literacy: Content for the Study of Technology (STL)* used in your state," there were 41 states that reported using *STL* either at the state level or at the local level (Meade & Dugger, p. 29). Additionally, the state supervisors reported that *AETL* was being used in 22 states (which, at the time, was very good since *AETL* had only been published less than a year) (See Table 1).

Question: Is *STL* and *AETL* used in your state?

	STL Used in Your State? 2004	*AETL* Used in Your State? 2004
Yes	41	22
No	7	23
Unknown	2	5
No Response	1	1
No Answer	1	1

Table 1: Summary of 2004 ITEA-TfAAP study on the usage of national technological literacy standards in the 50 states in the U.S.

Jill Russell, the Third Party Evaluator for TfAAP, has conducted surveys on the implementation progress of *STL* and *AETL*.

In 2003, an e-mail survey was sent to 410 randomly selected members of ITEA who were teachers, department chairs, or state supervisors. Sixty individuals completed and returned the survey. Of the respondents, 75% were teachers, 13% were department chairs (most of who also taught), and 12% were state supervisors. Thus, the responses heavily reflect the classroom teacher perspective.

When asked the extent to which they were familiar with ITEA's *Standards for Technological Literacy* document, most of this group had, at a minimum, looked through the standards. In fact, over half had compared the standards with their own curriculum, and a third had even participated in training.

Almost everyone (93%) who completed the survey thought the standards were important. The remaining few said they were not sure. Many reasons were offered in justification for the importance of the standards. The primary themes offered were that *Standards for Technological Literacy*:

1. Helps to validate the profession.
2. Gives direction to the curriculum.
3. Facilitates movement toward more standardization of technology education across the country.
4. Provides for a better understanding of expectations and goals.
5. Identifies the essential content that students need to learn.
6. Provides a vision for technological literacy.

The respondents also offered their opinions on the quality of the standards. About 87% indicated they believed the quality of the standards to be either excellent or very good. Another 13% said the standards were good.

The respondents were asked to rate their expectations regarding the impact of the standards upon technology education, and on grades K–12 in general.

1. Over 60% expected a significant impact on technology education, with another 33% predicting some impact. Four percent expected very little impact.
2. Forty percent expected a significant impact on grades K–12, and another 51% expected some impact. Nine percent thought there would be very little impact on grades K–12. (Russell, 2003)

Overall, *STL* and *AETL* have been very well accepted and implemented in the U.S. Still a continuous effort needs to be made to keep this momentum going so that every child is technologically literate in the future.

CHALLENGES FOR THE FUTURE

ITEA's TfAAP and its work to generate *STL*, *AETL*, and other related materials does not represent an end, but a beginning. We would like to thank all of the hundreds of people who have contributed to and gave input to us. In other fields of study, developing standards has often proven to be the easiest step in a long, arduous process. Therefore, getting these technology standards accepted and implemented in Grades K–12 in every school will be far more difficult and daunting than developing them has been. Only through the combined efforts of educational decision makers everywhere will we be able to ensure that all students develop higher levels of technological literacy.

REFERENCES

American Association for the Advancement of Science, Project 2061. (1990). *Science for all Americans.* New York: Oxford University Press.

American Association for the Advancement of Science, Project 2061. (1993). *Benchmarks for science literacy.* New York: Oxford University Press.

Dugger, W.E., Jr., Bame, A.E., Pinder, C.A., & Miller, D.C. (1981). *Standards for industrial arts programs.* Blacksburg, VA: Industrial Arts Program, Virginia Tech.

Dugger, W.E., Jr., Bame, A.E., Pinder, C.A., & Miller, D.C. (1985). *Standards for technology education programs.* Reston, VA: International Technology Education Association.

Dyrenfurth, M.J., & Kozak, M.R. (Eds.). (1991). *Technological literacy.* 40th Yearbook Council of Technology Teacher Education. Peoria, IL: Macmillan-McGraw.

Geography Education Standards Project. (1994). *Geography for life: National geography standards.* Washington, DC: National Geographic Society.

International Society for Technology in Education. (2000). *National educational technology standards for students: Connecting curriculum and technology.* Retrieved November 7, 2002 from http://cnets.iste.org/.

International Technology Education Association. (1985). *Technology education: A perspective on implementation.* Reston, VA: Author.

International Technology Education Association. (1988). *Technology: A national imperative.* Reston, VA: Author.

International Technology Education Association. (1996). *Technology for all Americans: A rationale and structure for the study of technology.* Reston, VA: Author.

International Technology Education Association. (2000/2002). *Standards for technological literacy: Content for the study of technology.* Reston, VA: Author.

International Technology Education Association. (2003). *Advancing excellence in technological literacy: Student assessment, professional development, and program standards.* Reston, VA: Author.

International Technology Education Association. (2004). *Measuring progress: Assessing students for technological literacy.* Reston, VA: Author.

International Technology Education Association. (2005). *Realizing excellence: Structuring technology programs.* Reston, VA: Author.

International Technology Education Association. (2005). *Developing professionals: Preparing technology teachers.* Reston, VA: Author.

International Technology Education Association. (2005). *Planning learning: Developing technology curricula.* Reston, VA: Author.

Meade, S., & Dugger, W.E. (2004). Reporting the status of technology education in the U.S. *The Technology Teacher, 64* (2), 29-33.

Music Educators National Conference. (1994). *National standards for arts education.* Reston, VA: Author.

Music Educators National Conference. (1994). *The vision for arts education in the 21st century.* Reston, VA: Author.

National Academy of Engineering & National Research Council. (2002). *Technically speaking: Why all Americans need to know more about technology.* (A. Pearson & T. Young, Eds.). Washington, DC: National Academy Press.

National Business Education Association. (2000). *Assessment in business education, Yearbook 38.* Reston, VA: Author.

National Council for History Standards. (1996). *National standards for history.* Los Angeles, CA: National Center for History in the Schools.

National Council for the Social Studies. (1994). *Curriculum standards for social studies: Expectations of excellence*. Washington, DC: Author.

National Council of Teachers of English. (1996). *Standards for the English language arts*. Urbana, IL: International Reading Association and the National Council of Teachers of English.

National Council of Teachers of Mathematics. (1989). *Curriculum and evaluation standards for school mathematics*. Reston, VA: Author.

National Council of Teachers of Mathematics. (1991). *Professional standards for teaching mathematics*. Reston, VA: Author.

National Council of Teachers of Mathematics. (1995). *Assessment standards for school mathematics*. Reston, VA: Author.

National Council of Teachers of Mathematics. (2000). *Principles and standards for school mathematics*. Reston, VA: Author.

National Research Council. (1996). *National science education standards*. Washington, DC: National Academy Press.

National Research Council. (2001). *Knowing what students know: The science and design of educational assessment*. (J. Pellegrino, N. Chudowsky, & R. Glaser, Eds.). Washington, DC: National Academy Press.

National Research Council. (2002). *Investigating the influence of standards: A framework for research in mathematics, science, and technology education*. (I.R. Weiss, M.S. Knapp, K.S. Hollweg, & G. Burill, Eds.). Washington, DC: National Academy Press.

Ravitch, D. (1995). *National standards in American education*. Washington, DC: The Brookings Institution.

Russell, J.F. (2003). Standards for technological literacy: Views from the field. *The Technology Teacher, 64* (4), 29-31.

Snyder, J.F., & Hales, J.A. (Eds.). (1981). *Jackson's Mill industrial arts curriculum theory*. Reston, VA: International Technology Education Association.

Waetjen, W.B. (1989). *Technological problem solving: A proposal*. Reston, VA: International Technology Education Association.

Waetjen, W.B. (1990). *Technology and human behavior*. Reston, VA: International Technology Education Association.

Watjen, W.B. (1992). Shaping the future of the profession. Critical issues in technology education, *Camelback symposium. A compilation of papers*. Reston, VA: International Technology Education Association.

DANIEL E. ENGSTROM

7. CHANGES AND PROGRESS IN ELEMENTARY TECHNOLOGY EDUCATION

INTRODUCTION

For the past 20 years the field of technology education, in the United States, has made significant strides at the middle and high school levels. Standards are available in most states for grades K-12 and many states and private agencies have developed curricular frameworks for technology education at the secondary level. At the elementary school, there has not been the plethora of curriculum, resource availability, and especially research about elementary technology education experience. This paper will trace some of the historical trends in elementary technology education by examining four separate aspects of it. Part one will briefly discuss characteristics of successful programs in elementary school technology education (ESTE). Part two will show a compilation of data from state standards projects specific to grades K-5 in technology education and how they align to the *Standards for Technological Literacy* (ITEA, 2000). The third section will examine approaches that teacher preparation institutions have made to deliver elementary technology education. Finally, the fourth section will provide an overview of major-funded research studies related to elementary technology education.

PART I: CHARACTERISTICS OF SUCCESSFUL ELEMENTARY TECHNOLOGY EDUCATION

For an ESTE program to be successful, it must begin with the teacher. A variety of models have been presented in the literature over the past 20 years to implement successful ESTE. Each of these models require well-trained, energetic, and creative classroom teachers who desire to learn and deliver a new curriculum and processes and an administration that is willing to take some risks (Kirkwood, 2000).

In 1997 Foster reported the results of a study that identified three predominant classifications of philosophies toward ESTE. These three included content, process, and method. Content is defined as students gaining and understanding of the knowledge about technology. Foster indicted that "To these writers, technology (or alternatively, technology education) is a discipline" (p. 22). Content based teachers would tend to focus on the study of the seven facets of the designed world as identified in the *Standards for Technological Literacy* (ITEA, 2000). Teachers who prefer to deliver ESTE through a process fall into one of two arenas: design as a process or a problem solving process. Finally, proponents of ESTE delivery as a method indicate that there is already too much material to be covered in the

M.J. de Vries, I. Mottier (eds.), International Handbook of Technology Education, 83–93
© *2006 Sense Publishers. All rights reserved.*

classroom and that technology can not be a separate subject and should be seamlessly integrated into the regular curriculum.

Many elementary teachers currently use some type of "hands-on" activities within their classroom, although this type of activity does not necessarily qualify as an ESTE activity. Kieft (1997) indicated that "One survey of exemplary elementary school programs indicated that just about every elementary school teacher at every grade level implemented some type of hands-on activity each day (p. 254). This does indicate that students desire to and learn better in a setting where active learning is present (see also Foster, 1997). It is important to note that technology education, at any level, is more than just "hands-on" activities, but involves the development of technological literacy: The ability to use, manage, understand, and assess technology (ITEA, 2000).

PART II: STANDARDS IN ELEMENTARY TECHNOLOGY EDUCATION

There continues to be confusion between technology education and educational technology standards. In 1998 The International Standards on Technology in Education (ISTE) developed standards entitled National Educational Technology Standards for Students (NETS*S). These standards were designed to produce technology capable students, specifically in communication and information technologies. As of May 2004, "At the state level, 49 of the 51 states have adopted, adapted, aligned with, or otherwise referenced at least one set of standards in their state technology plans, certification, licensure, curriculum plans, assessment plans, or other official state documents" (Use of NETS by States, 2002). The NETS*S standards focus on the development of computer technology skills in six areas including:

1. Technology Communication Tool
2. Technology Problem Solving and Decision-Making Tools
3. Technology Productivity Tools
4. Technology Research Tools
5. Social, Ethical, and Human Issues
6. Basic Operations and Concepts (Thomas & Knezek, 2002, p. 4)

The authors of this manuscript conducted a general survey to determine the extent to which states have published standards for ESTE. To conduct the survey, each state department of education website was searched and reviewed to determine if such standards existed for ESTE. Throughout the process it was important to differentiate between standards for computer literacy (NEST*S) and those that are more closely aligned with the *Standards for Technological Literacy* (ITEA, 2000). It should also be noted that many states have a technology education curriculum framework that may include ESTE concepts. Curricular frameworks usually provide a philosophic background and suggested learning outcomes, course outlines/descriptions, and suggested activities, but unlike standards they are usually neither legislatively enacted nor required for implementation. There are many states that are currently working on developing state standards for ESTE, although they were not considered unless they appeared in published form. For example, the state of Maryland does not have specified content standards for ESTE, but does have a suggested technology education framework. Furthermore, technology education teachers in Maryland are certified in grades 7-12 and thereby would not be certified for elementary school levels as a specialty area. Of the 50 states, 12 have published standards in technology education for elementary school. The breakdown can be found in Table 1.

	Connecticut	Maine	Michigan	Nevada	New Jersey	New York	Ohio	Pennsylvania	Vermont	Wisconsin
Materials, Tools, and Processes	X		X	X	X	X	X	X	X	X
Technological Impacts and Consequences	X	X	X	X	X	X	X	X		X
Career Awareness	X		X	X						X
Problem Solving	X	X	X	X	X	X	X	X	X	X
Technological/Engineering Design	X		X		X	X	X	X	X	X
Information Systems	X	X	X		X	X	X	X		
Production Systems	X				X	X		X		
Transportation Systems	X				X					
Biotechnology Systems							X	X		
Technological Systems				X		X	X	X	X	
History of Technology	X	X	X		X	X	X			X
Human Ingenuity & Endeavors		X						X	X	X

Table 1: ESTE State Standards

From the data provided in the Table 1, it reveals that the use of materials, tools, and processes, technological impacts and consequences, problem solving, history of technology, and technological/engineering design are most consistently listed as standards for ESTE. It also shows that for ESTE to begin to take hold, more states need to adopt standards for technology education at the elementary level.

PART III: TEACHER PREPARATION IN ELEMENTARY TECHNOLOGY EDUCATION

"There is no complete record of the number of elementary teachers in the U.S. certified to teach technology education or incorporate technology education concepts and principles into their curriculum throughout the school year" (Newberry, 2001, p. 11). Changing the way ESTE is delivered in the class has been a monumental problem. With a shortage of certified technology education teachers for middle and high school program, it is somewhat unrealistic to think that full-time elementary technology education teachers would be available. For ESTE to take make an impact on the technological literacy development there must be a consistent effort to train teachers to deliver contemporary standards-based technology programs. This training may take the form of university courses, in-service training, or special workshops.

Linnell (2000) reported only 15 technology education teacher preparation schools in the United States offered a course in ESTE. Of those 15, "it appears that only five universities in the United States offer technology concepts courses for elementary education and technology education majors throughout the academic year" (p. 96). The remaining 10 universities indicated that the course was not offered on a consistent basis or only during the summer. One year later Newberry reported that a survey conducted of the status of technology education in each state revealed that only 14 teacher education programs in the United States prepare teacher to deliver ESTE (2001).

In 2002, Flowers and Kirkwood reported that Ball State University piloted an online ESTE course entitled *Practicum for Technology Education for the Elementary Grades*. The course focused on the importance of integrating technology education into the classroom with "strategies related to classroom organization, physical planning, and tool and material acquisition" (p. 9). In a recent phone conversation with Dr. Jim Flowers, the Online Technology Education Coordinator for Ball State, online course has been offered three during three summers. Since the course is not a requirement of degree seeking graduate students, he indicated that only a handful of students have enrolled in the course each offering.

To determine the extent to which an ESTE course for elementary students was effective, Kirkwood reported the results of a study of 492 teachers who took a two-credit-hour course entitled "Technology Education for Elementary Grades" (2000). The course was delivered in 1995 and 1996 for elementary education majors and taught by a technology education faculty member. The results of the study showed that 82 (48%) of the respondents indicated an understanding of ESTE and were using it in their classroom. The study goes on to show that "only 35% of all respondents ... benefited significantly from, or even remembered, a class that was required of all or nearly all of them" (p. 14). The author indicated that this result was disappointing and indicated that a two-credit-hour course was not enough time to adequately prepare elementary teachers to teach ESTE.

PART IV: RESEARCH FINDINGS IN ELEMENTARY TECHNOLOGY EDUCATION

The final section of this paper will summarize five projects and publications that received funding for or are nationally recognized in the development and implementation of ESTE. Each project has a national scope and was begun after 1985. Of the projects listed, four were funded by the National Science Foundation. Dr. Gerhard Salinger, current program officer at NSF indicated in 2002 that NSF has "been funding projects that provide guidance for achieving technological literacy and demonstration of particular implementation strategies" (¶ 2). This effort was thought to also make more students aware of the career choices in the field of engineering and possibly improve the number of students going into that field.

In 1996 the International Technology Education Association released its first issue of *Technology and Children*. The journal was started to "provide a point of communications between children and their teachers in elementary classrooms across the country" (Botrill, 1996, p. 1). The emphasis of the journal has always been the integration of technology education into the elementary classroom by providing relevant articles, design briefs, school showcases and relevant information. This journal is published four times each year and is available for a subscription cost of $25.00 per year for ITEA members. Each issue of *T&C* is "packed with practical, innovative, and creative articles and activities for the elementary teacher. Interdisciplinary learning program successes and other current issues are addressed." (Technology and Children, 1996, p. 21) This is the only journal that specifically focuses on ESTE, although other publications including *T.I.E.S.*, *Tech Directions*, *Journal of Industrial Teacher Education*, and *Journal of Technology Education* also include ESTE related articles.

A World in Motion (AWIM)
Funding Agencies: Society of Automotive Engineers Foundation (Challenges 1 & 4) & National Science Foundation (Challenge 2 & 3)
Dates: 1990 – current
Director: Kathleen O'Connor
Institution: Society of Automotive Engineers
Contact Information: http://www.sae.org/foundation/awim/

In 1990 the Society of Automotive Engineers developed a curriculum for students in grades 4-6 entitled *A World in Motion*. This curriculum offered students an opportunity to experience authentic engineering design challenges, increase their interest in mathematics and science, develop a more competitive workforce, and eventually reverse the decline of students entering the field of engineering. Each challenge is designed to take approximately 3 weeks. Challenge I contains three different activities (Skimmer, JetToy, and Steel Can Rover) and is written specifically for grades 4 through 6. These three activities cover topics such as friction, forces, design, creativity, and basic engineering principles. With support from the National Science Foundation, in 1996 and 1998 *AWIM* released Challenge 2 and Challenge 3 for grades 7 and 8 respectively (AWIM 2004).

AWIM provides the initial curriculum and supplies for a class of 27 to 32 students at no cost. Teachers are expected to partner with a local engineer to deliver the curriculum. Since the inception of the program almost 15 years ago, *AWIM* estimates that over 20,000 schools and 2 million students in grades 4-10 have experienced the curriculum. The curriculum continues to grow and has recently added a fourth challenge entitled *Electricity and Electronics*. This challenge is CD-ROM based and geared for students in grades 4-10.

Children Designing and Engineering (CD&E)
Funding Agency: National Science Foundation
Dates: 1998 – current
Director: Pat Hutchinson
Institutions: The College of New Jersey and New Jersey Chamber of Commerce
Contact Information: http://www.childrendesigning.org/

The Children Designing and Engineering (CD&E) project developed 12 thematic units that are given in Table 2. Each unit "draws on research from a wide range of current educational orientations… [including] contextual learning and problem-based learning" Hutchinson, 2003, p. 2). All 12 units are intended to be four to six weeks in length and begin with a design brief that engages the students in the learning situation. The design problem is presented in either a video format, a game, a book, or in interactive story. This introduction of a problem, through the design brief, is meant to stimulate the student's thinking early on in learning process. As students begin to solve the presented challenge they follow a design loop that helps students better plan and make their solution.

Grades K-2	Grades 3-5	Partner Company
Opening Day at the Safari Park	Camp Koala	Six Flags Wild Safari
Bright Ideas Playhouse	Say It with Light, Inc.	Lucent Technologies
Earth-Friendly Greetings	Paper Products: You Be the Judge	Marcal Paper
Waterworks for Watertown	--	Elizabethtown Water Company
--	Solar-powered Energy Savers	Public Service Electric & Gas Company
Cranberry Harvest Festival	Juice Caboose	Ocean Spray Cranberry Products
Germbusters & Co.	Suds Shop	Johnson & Johnson

Table 2: CD&E Thematic Units

Preliminary results from the study show that students had a high degree of understanding, especially of science concepts and that research and presentation skills, collaboration, self-confidence and problem-solving abilities improved. In addition, teachers indicated that they generally enthusiastic about the units and that although the units may take more time the learning is more lasting. (Hutchinson, 2002, p. 20).

Integrating Mathematics, Science, and Technology in the Elementary Schools (MSTe)
Funding Agency: National Science Foundation
Dates: 1997 - 2002

Directors: Michael Hacker, David Burghardt, & Thomas Liao
Institution: Hofstra University & Stony Brook University
Contact Information: http://www.hofstra.edu/mste

The mission of the MSTe Project is "to provide expertise, inspiration, support and means to all elementary teachers in the participating schools so that they might better construct and sustain learner-centered environments where curriculum, instruction and assessment are guided by contemporary pedagogical practices and matched to MST learning standards" (Hacker, 2002, p. 1). Six goals were developed to carry out this mission and are given below from the MSTe website.

GOAL 1. To equip a group of leadership teachers in three-person MSTe teams with enhanced pedagogical, content, and leadership skills in order that they might reflect upon and improve their own practice, conduct exemplary inservice programs for other teachers, and become regional MST leaders.

GOAL 2. To provide 1,320 NYS elementary school teachers with the ability to use inquiry and design as mechanisms to connect MST in their classrooms; to enhance their MST skills; and to encourage them to engage in reflective practice.

GOAL 3. To develop a substantial and significant infrastructure of MST capability within the MSTe Project schools.

GOAL 4. To enhance the mathematical, scientific, and technological capabilities of elementary school students through instruction that interconnects MST.

GOAL 5. To support systemic change by enhancing the scale-up efforts of the NYSSI and NYCUSI and bring the lessons learned to MSTe Project participants.

GOAL 6. To develop an Implementation and Resource Guide as a planning and decision-making tool for MSTe teams. (MSTe, n.d., p. 1).

Overall the project exceeded its intended outcomes by training 126 state team leaders and 1282 trained participants for a total of 1408, exceeding the target of 1200 teachers by over 200 individuals. The major findings of this project include:

1. Teachers are quite receptive to integrating design and technology into classroom activities in mathematics and science.
2. There is a need for continual professional development for a project of this magnitude to be sustained.
3. State mandated standardized tests constrain the possibilities of an inquiry and design based teaching process.
4. Mentoring teachers is important for change to occur.
5. Strong support from administration is critical to allow teachers to take risks in their teaching.
6. Priority and care needs to be given to reform activities since schools can handle only so many reform projects at a time.

Invention, Innovation, and Inquiry: Units for Technological Literacy, Grades 5 & 6
Funding Agency: National Science Foundation
Dates: 2001 – current

Directors: Daniel E. Engstrom, Kendall Starkweather
Institution: International Technology Education Association
Contact Information: http://www.iteawww.org/i3

Invention, Innovation, and Inquiry (I³) is so named because invention and innovation are the hallmarks of technological thinking and action as inquiry is for science. Project activities include designing 8-10 day units that develop technological literacy in students, grades 5-6; developing teaching and learning resources based on selected technological and science literacy standards; and disseminating the units to teachers. Each unit has standards-based content, suggested teaching approaches, and detailed learning activities including brainstorming, visualizing, testing, refining, and assessing technological designs. Specific attention will be given to how inventions, innovations, and systems are created and how technology becomes part of people's lives. The engineering design process is at the heart of each unit along with the integration of mathematics and science concepts.

All units are developed through a rigorous process of writing, expert reviewing, and pilot and field-testing. Each unit is developed using the Understanding By Design approach (Wiggins and McTighe, 1999). All the units were pilot tested by technology education teachers in 5th and 6th grade classrooms. In the final phase units are field tested by general education 5th and 6th grade teachers. After each review, extensive revisions are made resulting in teacher-friendly units that focus on student learning of technological capabilities and understandings.

Both pilot teachers and field test teachers have given very positive reviews of the units and the student learning they engender. Through focus groups, site visits, and written reviews these teachers have reported that students expanded their understanding of technology, used the engineering design process to solve problems, developed basic design skills, and related mathematics and science to real-world situations. One teacher noted that because of the I³ units her students "can claim a much broader understanding of technological literacy, innovation, inspiration, and invention."

The ten units being developed include:
1. Invention: The Invention Crusade
2. Innovation: Inches, Feet, & Hands
3. Communication: Communicating School Spirit
4. Manufacturing: The Fudgeville Crisis
5. Transportation: Across the United States
6. Construction: Beaming Support
7. Power and Energy: The Whispers of Willing Wind
8. Design: Toying with Technology
9. Inquiry: The Ultimate School Bag
10. Technological Systems: Creating Mechanical Toys

Mission 21
Funding Agency: National Aeronautics & Space Administration (NASA)

Dates: 1987 - 1992
Directors –
Institution – Virginia Tech
Contact Information: http://teched.vt.edu/TE/html/ResM21.html

Mission 21 is designed to launch science and technology across the elementary curriculum. The project sought to help "elementary school teachers introduce the concept of technology education into the classroom through meaningful activities that are suitable for integration into the curriculum" (Brusic, Dunlap, Dugger, & LaPorte, 1988, pp. 23-24). The core value of the Mission 21 project is "the application of the problem-solving process to a variety of technological problems, thereby increasing students' technological literacy" (p. 23). The cooperative effort created the teacher resource guides which show teachers how to integrate technological concepts into their existing programs. The materials of the program are divided into three levels. Level one is for grades one and two, level two is for grades three and four and level three is for grades five and six. *Mission 21* is an ongoing project and funding support shows future technology education research efforts.

Stuff that Works!
Funding Agency: National Science Foundation
Dates: 1997 – current
Directors: Gary Benenson and James Neujahr
Institution: City College of New York
Contact Information: http://citytechnology.ccny.cuny.edu

The primary goal of *Stuff that Works* is to research and develop a professional development model that supports the wide-scale integration of technology education into the elementary grades. The project developed a series of five guides that are given in Table 3. Each guide provides five sections that allow teachers to deliver the concepts presented in the guide including:

Appetizers are short activities that the teacher can do to become familiar with the topics.

Concepts provide an overview of the main concepts of the guide and how it relates to mathematics, science, technology, and other subjects.

Activities include a variety of classroom projects and units that students can complete that are related to the topic.

Stories provide documented commentaries from teachers who have field tested the guides. These help to further understand the concepts by providing photos, samples of students work, and children dialog.

Resources is a framework to support implementation including a bibliography and discussion about assessment.

About Standards relates that content to national standards.

Title	Overview
Designed Environments	Uses an engaging approach to teaching how the process of design makes environments work.
Mapping Ideas	Uses an engaging approach to teaching how space is organized and use and how maps express meaning about space.
Mechanisms and Other Systems	Uses an engaging approach to teaching how and why basic technologies work – those devices, systems procedures, and environments that improve people's lives.
Packaging Ideas	Uses an engaging approach to teaching how and why bags, boxes, cartons, and bottles work to contain, protect, and dispense and display products.
Signs Symbols & Codes	Uses an engaging approach to teaching different methods for representing information.

Table 3: Stuff that Works Publication Series

In all five guides, the authors reported some summary field test results. These results indicated that these materials helped students to:

- ✓ Observe and describe phenomena in detail;
- ✓ Explore real objects and situations by creating models and other representations;
- ✓ Identify salient aspect of problems;
- ✓ Use evidence-based reasoning;
- ✓ Apply the scientific method;
- ✓ Ask thoughtful questions (beyond the yes or no variety)
- ✓ Communicate in oral, written and graphic form;
- ✓ Collaborate effectively with others. (Benenson & Neujahr, 2002, p. 2)

CONCLUSIONS

This article sought to elaborate on some trends in ESTE in the United States by examining standards and national projects in ESTE. It is clear from the information that there still is a significant lack of understanding of how children learn about technology and design skills. Many of the projects showed that children do learn more when content is integrated with technological concepts, but failed to show how that learning takes place. It is the hopes of the authors that research in this area will continue to be funded by organizations such as NSF and NASA.

REFERENCES

AWIM (2004). *A world in motion: Talking points*. Warrendale, PA: Author.
Benenson, G. & Neujahr, J. L. (2002). *Packaging and other structures*. Portsmouth, NH: Heinemann.
Bottrill, P. (1996). Preview of a new journal. *Technology and Children, 1*(1), 1-2.

Brusic, S. A., DunlapD., D., Dugger W. E., & LaPorte J. E. (1988, December). Launching technology education into elementary classrooms. *The Technology Teacher*, 23-25.

Flowers, J. & Kirkwood, J. (2002). Now on the web: Elementary technology education for teachers. *Technology and Children, 6*(1), 9-10.

Foster, P. N. (1997). Classifying approaches to and philosophies of elementary-school technology education. *Journal of Technology Education, 8*(2), 21-34.

Hacker, M. (2002, Winter). Final issue farewell. *MSTe, Visions for Change, 5*(1). Retrieved from http://www.hofstra.edu/pdf/MSTe_visions.pdf

Hutchinson, P. (2002, Spring). Children designing and engineering: Contextual learning units in primary design and technology. *Journal of Industrial Teacher Education. 39*(3), Retrieved March 17, 2005, from http://scholar.lib.vt.edu/ejournals/JITE/v39n3/

International Technology Education Association. (2000). *Standards for technological literacy: Content for the study of technology*. Reston, VA: Author.

Kieft, L. D. (1997). Teacher education. In J. J. Kirkwood & P. N. Foster (Eds.), *Elementary School Technology Education: The 46th yearbook of the Council on Technology Teacher Education*. New York: Glencoe.

Kirkwood, J. J. (2000, Spring). The status of technology education in elementary schools as reported by beginning teachers. *Journal of Industrial Teacher Education. 37*(3), Retrieved March 17, 2005, from http://scholar.lib.vt.edu/ejournals/JITE/v37n3/

Linnell, C. C. (2000). Identifying institutions that prepare elementary teacher to teach technology education: Promoting ESTE awareness. *Journal of Industrial Teacher Education. 38*(1), 91-102.

MSTe: Mission, Goals, and Accomplishments. (n.d.). Retrieved March 17, 2005 from http://www.hofstra.edu/Academics/SOEAHS/TEC/MSTE/MSTe_Goals.cfm

Newberry, P. B. (2001). Technology education in the US: A status report. *The Technology Teacher, 61*(1), 8-12.

Salinger, G. (2002, Spring). Foreword. *Journal of Industrial Teacher Education, 39*(3), Retrieved March 17, 2005, from http://scholar.lib.vt.edu/ejournals/JITE/v39n3/

Technology and Children. (1996). The new journal: Technology and children. *Technology and Children, 1*(1), 21.

Thomas, L. G. & Knezek, D. G. (2002, Summer). Standards for technology-supported learning environment [Electronic Version]. *The State Education Standard*, 4.

Use of NETS by States (2004, May). Retrieved March 1, 2005, from http://cnets.iste.org/docs/States_using_NETS.pdf

Wiggins, G. and McTighe, J. (1999) *Understanding by design*. Alexandria VA: Association for Supervision and Curriculum Development.

MARIE HOEPFL

8. THE EVOLUTION OF TECHNOLOGY EDUCATION IN THE UNITED STATES: THE CASE OF NORTH CAROLINA

NATIONAL TRENDS IN TECHNOLOGY EDUCATION

Much has been written over the years about the curriculum change process from industrial arts to technology education. This topic has been examined from the perspective of philosophical rationales for change; teacher resistance to change; strategies for facilitating change; degree to which change has occurred; and so on (see, for example, Akmal, Oaks, & Barker, 2002; Dyrenfurth, et.al, 1993; Lauda & McCrory, 1986; LaPorte, 1990; Linnell, 1994; McCade & Litowitz, 1990; and Oaks, 1991). The purpose of this paper is to conduct a personalized reflection on the curriculum change process, using one state as a case study to illustrate key features of the change process, both good and bad.

It's always fascinating to read historical accounts of some of the seminal theorists in technology education. Consider the following quote (with which some liberties have been taken):

[Technology education] is a study of the evolution of industry, showing how the complex factory system with organized capital, organized labor, and highly specialized machine production has grown from the simplest beginnings; it [is] a practical study of design—of the principles of design in relationship to their appropriate usage in specific products—as design is used today and as it has developed among participation through the making of many projects. (adapted from Bonser, 1913, as cited in Herschbach, McPherson, & Latimer, 1982, p. 36)

Bonser and his contemporaries Mossman, Dewey, and others were in the first decades of the twentieth century writing about industrial arts in much the same way that we write about technology education today. They promoted the study of industry as being a critical element of the education of all children, because such study reflected the world in which the children lived. They were concerned not just with students learning about the details of industrial processes, but also with learning about how industrial processes shaped society, the economy, and the environment. Furthermore, they recognized that learning by doing provided opportunities for children to learn about the world in ways that were more meaningful and appropriate for some, if not all, children—learning that could engage them in ways that book learning alone could not.

Then as now, however, the theoretical and philosophical goals of the study of industry/technology had to compete with the more pragmatic (or perhaps just easier to define) aspects of technical study. The goals of economic development,

M.J. de Vries, I. Mottier (eds.), International Handbook of Technology Education, 95–111.

preparation for the world of work, and acquisition of the mechanics of technical expertise struggled for dominance over the more illusory, high-minded goals of education for more effective, informed, and responsible citizenship.

A 1999 nationwide study conducted by Sanders (2001) provides some evidence of the disparate nature of a curriculum with competing goals. This study uncovered some positive trends in technology education in the United States, such as increased numbers of female students and teachers, an increased emphasis on problem-solving skills, and a decreased emphasis on developing skills in the use of tools and machines. On the other hand, a professed lack of emphasis among survey respondents on goals such as "evaluate the positive and negative consequences of technological ventures," and "understand technical culture" (Sanders, 2001, p. 46) suggests a lack of commitment to the "softer" side of technological literacy. Similarly, an examination of the most popular course titles in 1999 suggests an inconsistency in curricular approaches (Table 1). Once beyond the top-ranked "general tech ed" courses, we see an array of traditionally-titled course categories, such as wood technology and drafting.

Table 1. *The Ten Most-Taught Course Categories in Technology Education/Industrial Arts*

Rank	1999 [1]	1979 [2]	1963 [3]
1	General Tech Ed	General Woods	General IA
2	Drafting/CAD	General Metals	Woodworking
3	Wood Technology	Mechanical Drawing	Drafting
4	Metal Technology	Drafting	Metalworking
5	Arch Draw/Arch Draft	General Industrial Arts	Graphic Arts
6	Electricity/Electronics	Architectural Drafting	Electricity/Electronics
7	Manufacturing	Graphic Arts	Crafts
8	Communications	Auto Mechanics	Power Mechanics
9	Automotives	Electricity	Home Mechanics
10	Graphic Communication	Woodworking	Photography

[1]From Sanders (2001); [2]From Dugger et.al (1980); [3]From Schmitt & Pelley (1966).
Source: Sanders, 2001, p. 50.

Establishing Curriculum Standards

The *Standards for Technological Literacy (SfTL)* (International Technology Education Association [ITEA], 2000) provide a rallying point for curriculum development efforts in technology education. The emphasis on understanding the nature of technology and the use of design under constraint illustrates that technological literacy requires going beyond the use of tools and machines. There is still ample room in the curriculum for traditional material processing kinds of activities, but no longer is the curriculum bound by the technological "systems" defined by the *Jackson's Mill Industrial Arts Curriculum Theory* (Snyder & Hales, 1981). As project leaders for the *SfTL* project have consistently pointed out, however, standards do not equal curricula, and the long process of interpretation, implementation, and evaluation is still underway.

Walking the Tightrope

Some of the most influential curriculum theorists throughout the last century have called for variations on the theme of the study of technology for its social/political implications (what might be termed the literacy approach). This has been balanced by an equal emphasis by others on the use and development of tools and systems to accomplish specific goals (what might be termed the pragmatic approach). Education that emphasizes career development, acquisition of skills in the use of technology, and education for "a more competitive economy"—to borrow an often-used rationale—is an education that can be easier to sell and easier to teach, for it focuses on a straightforward, nut-and-bolts kind of content. A patina of discussion laid over top that examines socio-cultural impacts is just that: superficial coverage of the heart of what technological literacy might be said to be about. At the same time, a meaningful engagement with technological issues and the search for solutions to societal needs requires a certain level of technical understanding and expertise; expertise that can only be built through exposure, time, and active engagement. Effective study of technology, then, takes time—a commodity not often available to technology education programs that must take their place among the crowded, fragmented curriculum.

PROGRESS AND QUESTIONABLE OUTCOMES: THE CASE OF NORTH CAROLINA

The issues that have played out on the national scale are reflected to varying degrees on the state level. There is, however, considerable diversity in the way that technology education is defined and supported from one state to the next. For example, in North Carolina technology education and trade and industry (T&I) courses and teacher licensure were separated a number of years ago. Drafting, woods, construction, auto mechanics, and similar trade skill courses are distinct from the technology education curriculum. In many states, this is not the case. Some states, such as Connecticut, include technology education under the same state jurisdiction as science and mathematics. North Carolina includes technology education under the umbrella of career and technical (vocational) education (CTE). A number of states require some exposure to technology education, particularly at the middle school level. North Carolina has no such requirement. In spite of these differences, the challenges of curriculum reform in technology education remain the same.

Course Offerings

In the nearly 20 years since 1987, technology education in North Carolina has undergone some significant curricular changes. At that time, the state scope and sequence model included 22 technology education courses (Table 2). Most of these could be offered for either a semester or full year. In addition, districts in the state have always been able to adopt specialized courses as "local options." The courses in place in 1987 made use of curriculum models developed in other states, including the applied physics courses called "Principles of Technology." These courses were developed by the Center for Occupational Research and Development in Texas, and have enjoyed small but steady enrollments in North Carolina since their adoption. It was not until 1992 that the state created its own guides for technology courses.

Change over the past twenty years has been marked, though not revolutionary. The systems approach promoted in Jackson's Mill (Snyder & Hales, 1981) remains clearly evident to this day. However, by 1992 the number of state-supported course offerings had dropped considerably, to a total of 13 courses (Table 3). During that curriculum adoption cycle, teams of teachers and teacher educators were engaged to write course frameworks and support guides, a practice that continues for all CTE courses in the state. With the benefit of federal funding via the Carl D. Perkins vocational education legislation, the state has been able to support curriculum revision cycles on a roughly five-year basis. That is, each course in the state-adopted sequence model has been revised on a rotating basis approximately every five years.

By 1996, the state supported the adoption of a specialty course, Scientific and Technical Visualization, which was developed by Dr. Aaron Clark and colleagues at North Carolina State University (Table 4). This course seeks to integrate science and technology content, specifically focusing on the use of computer-based imaging tools.

In 2002, a new sequence of specialty courses came on the scene (Table 5). Project Lead the Way (PLTW) has launched an aggressive nationwide campaign for adoption of its pre-engineering course sequence. One North Carolina school came on board in 2001, and to date there are a total of five schools statewide that have become part of the PLTW network (Project Lead the Way, 2005a). A determination was made by officials at the state's Department of Public Instruction to include PLTW within the technology education scope and sequence. However, like Principles of Technology, the curriculum was developed by outside entities and is, in a sense, outside of the control of state officials and teachers. In particular, PLTW requires schools to sign adoption agreements and to meet certification requirements established by the parent organization (Project Lead the Way, 2005b).

Table 2. *Technology Education Scope and Sequence, 1987*

Grade 7	Grade 8	Grades 9-10	Grades 11-12	Grade 12
Exploring Technology	Contemporary Technology	Communication Systems	Graphic Communication Systems	Technology Research and Development
			Electronic Communication Systems	Industrial Enterprise
			Media Communication Systems	Pilot Course
		Construction Systems	Structures and Systems	
			Construction Planning and Design	
			Electro/Mechanical Systems and Services	
		Manufacturing Systems	Manufacturing Materials and Processes	
			Product and Production System Design	
			Designing Products	
		Transportation Systems	Technical Elements of Transportation	
			Planning and Designing Transportation Systems	
			Human and Product Transportation Systems	
		Principles of Technology I	Principles of Technology II	

Table 3. *Technology Education Scope and Sequence, 1992*

Grades 7-8	Grades 9-12	Grades 9-12	Grades 10-12	Grade 12
Exploring Technology Systems	Fundamentals of Technology			Technology Studies
		Communication Systems	Advanced Communication Systems	
		Manufacturing Systems	Advanced Manufacturing Systems	
		Structural Systems	Advanced Structural Systems	
		Transportation Systems	Advanced Transportation Systems	
			Principles of Technology I	Principles of Technology II

Table 4. *Technology Education Scope and Sequence, 1996*

Middle Grades	Level I	Level II	Level III	Level IV
Exploring Technology Systems	Fundamentals of Technology			Technology Studies
		Communication Systems		
		Manufacturing Systems		
		Structural Systems		
		Transportation Systems		
		Scientific & Technical Visualization I	Scientific & Technical Visualization II	
			Principles of Technology I	Principles of Technology II

Table 5. *Technology Education Scope and Sequence, 2002*

Middle Grades	Level I	Level II	Level III	Level IV
Exploring Technology Systems	Fundamentals of Technology			Advanced Studies
		Communication Systems		
		Manufacturing Systems		
		Structural Systems		
		Transportation Systems		
		Principles of Technology I	Principles of Technology II	
		Scientific & Technical Visualization I	Scientific & Technical Visualization II	
		Project Lead the Way I	Project Lead the Way II	

Another item worth noting is the structure of the Level IV course, which by 2002 was called "Advanced Studies." A version of this course has been offered since at least 1987. It is designed as a senior capstone course in which students identify and work on research and development projects under the mentorship of a technology instructor. By 2002, all CTE program areas in the state had adopted a similar course within their own sequence of courses, precipitating use of the more generic course title.

Samples of the state's technology education course descriptions and curriculum guides can be viewed at: http://www.dpi.state.nc.us/workforce_development/technology/course-descriptions.html. The technology education course guides currently in place all provide comprehensive resource materials for teachers, including sample lesson plans, PowerPoint lecture notes, and content narratives for each unit. These guides are now offered in CD format in which related sections are hyperlinked throughout the document to facilitate ease of use by classroom teachers.

Since 1992, the technology education curriculum in place in North Carolina has been characterized by several recurring elements. One is the use of a simplified problem-solving strategy known as the "DEAL" model (Define, Explore, Act,

Look Back and Evaluate). Second, a focus on use of the systems model to organize curriculum content has prevailed. Third, some attention is paid in all courses to the concept of the impacts of technology. Fourth, teamwork skills, including things like the parliamentary procedure used in running student organizations, are part of all courses. Finally, in addition to a focus on aspects of the technical content found in each "systems" area, there is typically a final, extended unit that emphasizes the application of this content to the design and construction of related systems.

In these regards, North Carolina's curriculum is certainly similar to technology education curricula across the United States (that is, among those states that have actually moved beyond a traditional industrial arts curriculum approach). Where the state differs from many others is in the fact that it has adopted prescriptive, detailed curriculum models for state-approved technology education courses. These models are supported, and in a sense enforced, by the statewide accountability system that was adopted along with the curriculum models.

Curriculum Accountability

All CTE program areas in North Carolina make use of what is known as the VOCATS accountability system. Much like the series of standards and end-of-grade/course tests that govern the core curriculum courses, CTE courses have "blueprints" that identify the major outcomes for each course. There are associated, secured-item test banks that are administered to all students upon completion of each course. Tests are monitored by teachers from other areas, so theoretically the technology teacher will never know what questions will be asked on the end-of-course test, aside from what can be gleaned from the practice tests that are made available. Most districts stipulate that the end-of-course VOCATS test count for 20-25% of the final course grade. These test scores are also reported in the aggregate to the state department, which compiles the data. Some districts monitor scores and work with individual teachers to identify areas of needed improvement, but this is not a widespread practice.

Unlike test scores for the core academic subjects, which are linked to teacher bonus pay, VOCATS scores do not carry punitive measures for teachers with low-achieving students. They can have some repercussions within the district, however, and the VOCATS system represents a fairly effective measure for ensuring that teachers follow the state-approved course blueprints. Like most such tests, they also lead to an increased likelihood that teachers will teach for coverage, and can have a detrimental impact on innovation, particularly among inexperienced teachers. This year, the state is pilot testing the use of performance assessments, but it is too soon to determine whether these will be adopted or not.

Enrollment Trends

During the 1999-2000 school year, a total of 65,700 students were enrolled in technology education courses in North Carolina (rounded up to the nearest hundred). At the high school level, 17,600 boys and 3,600 girls enrolled in technology education courses; at the middle school level, 28,600 boys and 15,900 girls (North Carolina Department of Public Instruction, 2000). By 2004, the total number of students enrolled in technology education courses in grades 7-12 had risen 25%, to 81,900 students. By far the largest number of students was enrolled in the middle grades Exploring Technology course. A look at the numbers of students enrolled in the high school course offerings is more telling (Table 6).

Table 6. *Total Enrollment in Technology Education Courses, 2001-2004*

Course	2000-2001	2002-2002	2002-2003	2003-2004
Advanced Studies	1,312	1,152	1,372	1,321
Principles of Technology I	2,774	2,291	2,779	3,141
Principles of Technology II	730	630	749	904
Exploring Technology Systems	47,275	45,427	55,881	56,641
Fundamentals of Technology	10,681	10,265	12,175	12,366
Manufacturing Systems	993	714	634	832
Communication Systems	2,290	1,578	1,993	1,878
Transportation Systems	407	473	666	917
Structural Systems	748	766	889	904
Local Option	199	262	465	2,807

Source: North Carolina Department of Public Instruction (2004a)

It's evident from this data that two courses dominate the field in terms of overall enrollments: the middle grades Exploring Technology and the high school "gateway" course Fundamentals of Technology. Once beyond these two survey courses, enrollment numbers drop precipitously. The disparity between male and female student enrollment numbers at the high school level is also troubling, and the trend persisted through 2004, with a 6:1 ratio of male to female students enrolled (nearly 18,000 to 3,000 students, respectively). Finally, a comparison of overall enrollments in technology education compared to enrollments in other CTE areas suggests another worrisome trend. In 2004, high school enrollments in Family and Consumer Sciences courses were 90,600 compared to 21,700 in technology education. Business Education high school enrollments were 161,134; Trade and Industry enrollments were 82,900; even Health Occupations enrollments surpassed technology education, at 30,800 students (North Carolina Department of Public Instruction, 2004b). If technology education proposes to influence the technological literacy of all students, then we have a long way to go, indeed, to reach those students.

Revising the Scope and Sequence Model: 2005 and Beyond

Partly in response to the troubling enrollment numbers in advanced-level courses in technology education, but primarily in response to larger efforts like the *SfTL,* a scope and sequence revision process was launched in September, 2004. A team of classroom teachers, teacher educators, business leaders, engineering educators, and others was brought together to create a new conceptual framework for technology education. There were several "givens" moving into the process: (1) Principles of Technology, Scientific Visualization, and Project Lead the Way had to remain part of the scope and sequence in their present form; (2) new courses could not be labeled "pre-engineering" courses, because PLTW had been sanctioned by the state to fulfill that role; (3) there had to be an integrative thread spiraling through all courses; and (4) courses had to be appropriate for all types of learners, not just the college bound.

Discussions among the group have been lively and have focused on issues such as marketing, market forces (what kinds of courses will attract talented students?), access (should there be single or multiple gateway courses at the high school level?), and resource demands (realistically, how many courses can a lone technology teacher at one school deliver to reach the greatest number of students?). The resulting conceptual model (Figure 1), although still in the formative stages, has taken on greater flexibility but is more streamlined than the model currently in place.

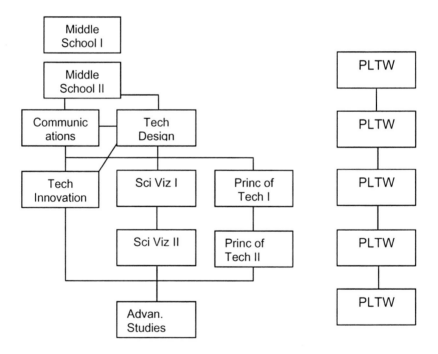

Figure 1. Draft revised scope and sequence model for technology education

In this model, there will be two middle-level courses compared with the current one course. There will be multiple "gateway" courses at the high school level. The number of state-developed high school technology education courses will be reduced to only four, and these will focus on issues, processes, and tools within "designed world" contexts. There will be a greater emphasis on how technology education courses interact with other courses, including skill-development courses in T&I education and beyond. Project Lead the Way, which currently includes a five-course sequence, will exist as a separate and distinct pathway for those students who plan to pursue engineering careers.

Questions remain about what the specifics of the course content will be, how and whether classroom teachers will accept the proposed model, what kinds of professional development will be needed, whether the new approach will be more appealing to a broader audience, what changes will be required in teacher education programs, and more.

CHALLENGES TO PROGRESS

The Faustian Bargain: Can We Afford Perkins?

North Carolina, like many other states, includes technology education under the CTE funding umbrella provided by the Carl D. Perkins Vocational-Technical Education Act of 1998 (PL 105-332). This alliance has proven to be both a blessing and a curse. Although technology education has long attempted to distance itself philosophically from the rest of vocational education, we have gladly shared in the riches offered by Perkins, money that pays for professional development of teachers, equipment and supplies, and teaching positions. The trade-off for this share of the wealth is a continuing difficulty in trying to position "technology education as general education," and an ongoing share of the worry that policy makers will abandon their support of this funding, as is currently the case. Dr. Susan Sclafani, Assistant Secretary for the U.S. Department of Education's Office of Adult and Vocational Education, defends President Bush's 2006 budget proposal (in which he proposes a complete halt to Perkins funding), in this way:
The President's 2006 budget proposal includes $1.5 billion for a new High School Initiative and an additional $323 million for other activities that will strengthen secondary school education, but requests no funding for Vocational Education or for the Smaller Learning Communities programs. Despite decades of federal investment, the Vocational Education program has produced little evidence of improved academic outcomes for students. On the most recent NAEP assessments, less than 10% of vocational students scored at or above proficiency in mathematics (2000) and only 29% scored at or above proficiency in reading (1998). The most recent National Assessment of Vocational Education (NAVE) found no evidence that high school vocational courses contribute to academic achievement or postsecondary enrollment.... Also, the NAVE found that high school students, on average, earn more credits in vocational education (4.2) than in math (3.5) or science (3.2). But the most telling data come from employers—according to a February 2005 Achieve, Inc. survey employers estimate that 39 percent of high

school graduates, who have no further education, are not prepared for their current job and that 45 percent are unprepared for advancement. (Sclafani, 2005, ¶ 3)

A critical examination of this testimony reveals several flaws: first, in relating NAEP scores of vocational students, Sclafani does not offer comparisons with data from previous NAEP assessments. The mere fact that the average high school student has taken more CTE than mathematics course work is being offered as prima facie evidence that this student's education was substandard. And the data from employers does not appear to distinguish between vocational student completers and high school graduates in general.

At the same time, Bush's budget request for fiscal year 2006 calls for a 73% increase to expand the availability of Advanced Placement and International Baccalaureate programs in high-poverty schools (Spellings, 2005). The United States is clearly in the throes of a "back to the basics" focus on the "core academic subjects," and anything associated with vocational education is in a state of disfavor. As rumors of the demise of Perkins funding have circulated, school districts are bracing for change. One large district in North Carolina has preemptively closed its middle grades technology education programs, under the assumption that there will be no federal funding for these programs next year.

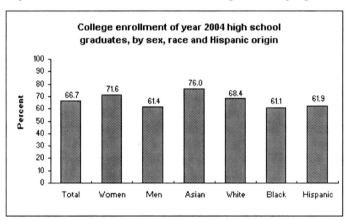

Figure 2. College enrollment data in the United States.
Source: United States Department of Labor (2005).

Clearly, a more detailed analysis of the issues is in order. Figure 2 shows the percentage of high school graduates in the U.S. who enrolled in college programs in 2004. Among 2003 CTE graduates in North Carolina, 80% are enrolled in some form of continuing education (North Carolina Department of Public Instruction, 2005). This suggests that participation in CTE programs does not deter students from pursuing postsecondary education, and may in fact promote it. According to data from the National Assessment of Vocational Education, in 1998 96% of public high school students earned one or more CTE credits; 44% earned three or more CTE credits; and 19% earned three or more credits in more than one CTE program area (United States Department of Education, n.d.). There is obviously an audience for CTE course work. What will be the effects on student retention, promotion, and enrollment in postsecondary education programs if funding for CTE is discontinued?

There is a secondary pressure in place as well. At the same time as CTE is being de-emphasized, testing requirements in the core subjects have been increased through the *No Child Left Behind* federal education legislation. If federal funding flows in non-earmarked block grants to school districts, they will do what strapped districts have always done: devote as much money as possible to those subjects and requirements that "count." Any tendencies at the local level to devote money to CTE programs including, in some cases, technology education, will face enormous challenges.

As a final note on the issue of funding, continued reliance on Perkins has the potential to delay the adoption of technological studies at the elementary level. Because Perkins is, at its core, a workforce development initiative, distribution of these monies for programs below grade 7 is usually prohibited. In the minds of many technology educators, the study of technology will only reach its full potential and legitimacy when it is reflected throughout the K-12 experience and beyond.

Adopting the Vision: Who's Carrying the Torch?

The type of curriculum promoted by the *SfTL* is a complex one, requiring a multitude of skills and conceptual understandings to deliver effectively. Findings such as the one noted by Sanders (2001), that there do not appear to be large numbers of unlicensed technology teachers, can be misleading. The increase in the use of alternative routes to licensure means that some "fully licensed" teachers may have received minimal focused training in the delivery of the technology curriculum. For example, in North Carolina an individual who holds a bachelor's degree in a technical field (such as construction technology) qualifies for the provisional route to licensure. He or she would be required, at most, to complete 18 hours of course work, only six of which would be categorized as pedagogy or methods courses. In the absence of focused training, teachers rely on a handful of measures to familiarize themselves with the curriculum: they remember their own experiences years ago in what was probably a shop class; they ask for advice from school administrators who, in many instances, are just as ill-informed about the curricular goals of technology education; or they follow the lead of fellow teachers, in the rare cases where more than one technology teacher is housed at a school, some of whom may not be desirable tutors. In the best-case scenario, these teachers become active in their state's professional organization, and learn through association with other, experienced technology teachers. Detailed curriculum guides, while extremely helpful, cannot on their own provide the level of understanding and expertise needed for skillful planning and delivery.

This is not meant to downplay the contributions made by the many excellent technology teachers in schools across the state and nation. However, the importance of how the study of technology is promoted and perceived at the classroom level cannot be overemphasized: perception is reality, and technology education on the whole will only be as desirable as the accumulated evidence of effective learning experiences in thousands of classrooms.

The Allure of STEM: Do We Know Who Our Friends Are?

Recent attention by funding agencies such as the National Science Foundation (NSF), the *National Science Education Standards* (National Research Council, 1996), the National Academy (Pearson & Young, 2002), and, to a lesser degree, organizations like the Institute of Electrical and Electronic Engineers (IEEE) has produced a flurry of optimism that technology education will experience enhanced recognition and status. There are good reasons to expect that widespread calls for greater technological literacy will, indeed, have positive impacts on technology education. This movement toward alliance with the science and engineering communities in particular has precedence and is therefore logical to pursue. By most accounts (see, for example, Pearson and Young, 2002), technological literacy is a goal that will only be achieved through focused attention on several fronts. And, as Lewis (2004) demonstrates, the deep historical connections between technology and engineering are clear. Such alliances are expected to have strategic benefits, not the least of which is being associated with perceived high-value fields (rather than the often problematic vocational education), thus making the study of technology more appealing to high school students of all ability levels (Lewis, 2004).

Yet vigilance is in order for those who wish to preserve the broader social goals that have long been promoted for technology education (and, before it, industrial arts). In most presentations this author has heard in recent years on the subject of pre-engineering at the K-12 level, there is evidence of a clear agenda: placing students in the pipeline toward engineering careers. This agenda is sometimes couched in the broader language of technological literacy, but not always; movements like Project Lead the Way are unabashed about their goal of producing future engineers. Lewis (2004) sums it up this way:

...the essential notion remains, that study of technology education ought to lead to multiple ends. This very important fact is a caution that while the subject may derive from engineering, the many roads that could lead from it are a strong argument against it becoming pre-anything. (p. 35)

Another problematic aspect of positioning technology education as the face of applied science and engineering is that technology teachers will need to possess the mathematical and science backgrounds to fulfill this role. Certainly, through well-planned preparation programs this can occur, and this could be a real benefit of a shift toward a greater STEM emphasis. But such changes take time, and at present few technology teacher education programs require more than a minimal amount of science or math as part of their preparation programs (McAlister, 2004).

There is an almost unavoidable sense of turf battle inherent in alliances with stronger partners like science and engineering which technology educators will have to come to terms with for mutually beneficial partnerships to occur. What seems to be at stake is that technology education may come to be seen as superfluous, if we promote our existence solely on the basis of being able to support other subjects, but are perceived as not being able to deliver on that promise. Many technology educators believe that there are unique contributions made by technology education and that it should therefore be justified in its own right, but these contributions must be demonstrated clearly, in terms that are meaningful to the larger community, in order for technology to hold equal status in the quadripartite STEM collaboration.

Strangled by Obscurity: What's in a Name?

A group of technology educators came together at the 2004 conference of the International Technology Education Association (ITEA) to offer their versions of what was dubbed "the elevator talk." This referred to the ongoing problem many face of trying to explain what technology education is in a succinct, clear way that does not involve use of the word "shop." Although the session was somewhat tongue in cheek, there was nothing humorous about the fact that, without exception, a large group of long-time professionals in the field could relate directly to the necessity of having to *explain* to nearly everyone just exactly what it is they do. Appropriately or not, the word technology has assumed a narrow meaning in the popular lexicon, and this presents what is probably an insurmountable challenge to the identity of technology education. A new brand identity is needed, which accurately captures what occurs in programs and leaves no doubt in people's minds what is being referred to.

In North Carolina, this problem of identity is compounded by the fact that business education (a separate field of teacher licensure) has adopted the name "business technology education." And pre-service teachers in the state are all required to create a "technology portfolio" that aligns with the International Society for Technology in Education (ISTE) National Educational Technology Standards for Teachers (the so-called NETS-T). These portfolios are compilations of artifacts that demonstrate ability to use information technology tools in educational settings. Who can blame people with no direct exposure to technology education programs for being confused about its goals and purposes?

The Curriculum Conundrum: When Does Everything Equal Nothing?

Technology education has been touted as an "integrator" that "reinforces and complements the material that students learn in other classes" (ITEA, 2002, p. 6). Once technology education is viewed as the place where all other subjects can be applied and made sense of, it's tempting to start imagining all sorts of scenarios for ways that students can, through the study of technology, create a "conceptual framework for the study of everything" (Brady, 2004, p. 276).

Technological studies ... have a critical role to perform in helping children learn content in other subjects within the school environment. That is, it has a strong and powerful role as an integrator of knowledge by reinforcing and complementing material students learn in other school subjects....Subject matter integration helps not only to develop connections among different subject areas but also to appreciate that all knowledge is interconnected. (Martin, 2002, p. 54)

Literacy for a technological age is a large goal, requiring several types of knowledge: the capacity to understand and use complex technical systems; the capacity to grasp the social, cultural, environmental, and economic ramifications of their use; and the capacity to engage in modifying technical systems effectively based on this larger understanding. Echoing the curricular aims espoused by Dewey, Mossman, and Bonser nearly a century ago, we are still seeking a curriculum that helps achieve the "main task of educating," which is "to help students make more sense of the world, themselves, and others" (Brady, 2004, p. 277).

By laying stakes on the slippery high ground of integration, however appealing the notion, we set ourselves up for failure. This is because we either must prepare all technology teachers to be able to be effective integrators themselves, or we must convince other teachers to become active collaborators. In the first instance there is simply too much that must be taught; in the second, we rely on the time and commitment of others, a situation bound to disappoint. At best we have models such as the ImaST curriculum for middle grades, which actively prepares math, science, and technology teachers to deliver an integrated curriculum, or materials that have been carefully prepared to include content from multiple subject areas (such as the College of New Jersey's *Children Designing and Engineering* materials).

Does this mean that the goal of integration should be abandoned? The study of technology does provide myriad, rich contexts for investigation that *must* involve integration from a variety of disciplines, including math and science. However, to focus too keenly on integration as a deliverable of the technology education curriculum applies a similarly unnecessary pressure like that which stems from promoting technology through its capacity to help achievement in other areas. By trying to be too many things to too many people, we risk becoming…nothing.

REFERENCES

Akmal, T., Oaks, M., & Barker, R. (2002). The status of technology education: A national report on the state of the profession. *Journal of Industrial Teacher Education, 39*(4), 6-25.

Brady, M. (2004). Thinking big: A conceptual framework for the study of everything. *Phi Delta Kappan, 86*(4), 276-281.

Dyrenfurth, M., Custer, R., Loepp, F., Barnes, J., Iley, J., & Boyt, D. (1993). A model for assessing the extent of transition to technology education. *Journal of Industrial Teacher Education, 31*(1), 57-83.

Herschbach, D., McPherson, W., & Latimer, T. (1982). *Industrial arts: A historical perspective.* Reston, VA: American Industrial Arts Association.

International Technology Education Association. (2000). *Standards for technological literacy: Content for the study of technology.* Reston, VA: Author.

Lauda, D., & McCrory, D. (1986). A rationale for technology education. In R.E. Jones & J.R. Wright (Eds.), *Implementing Technology Education, ACIATE 35ᵗʰ Yearbook* (pp. 15-46). Encino, CA: Glencoe Publishing Company.

Lewis, T. (2004). A turn to engineering: The continuing struggle of technology education for legitimization as a school subject. *Journal of Technology Education, 16*(1), 21-39.

Linnell, C. (1994). Facilitating curriculum change: Teacher concerns as a factor. *Journal of Industrial Teacher Education, 31*(3), 93-96.

Martin, G. (2002). Rationale and structure for *Standards for Technological Literacy*. In Ritz, Dugger, and Israel (Eds.), *Standards for technological literacy: The role of teacher education* (pp. 47-58). Council on Technology Teacher Education 51st Yearbook. New York, NY: Glencoe McGraw-Hill.

McCade, J., & Litowitz, L. (1990). Technology education demands a balanced curriculum. *The Technology Teacher, 49*(8), 6-8.

McAlister, B. (2004). *Are technology education teachers prepared to teach engineering design and analytical methods?* Paper presented at the annual meeting of the Mississippi Valley Technology Teacher Education Conference, Chicago, IL.

National Research Council. (1996). *National science education standards*. Washington, DC: National Academy Press.

North Carolina Department of Public Instruction. (2005). *2004 Consolidated annual performance report*. Retrieved March 20, 2005 from: http://www.dpi.state.nc.us/workforce_development/publications/cap_report/cap_report_2004.pdf.

North Carolina Department of Public Instruction. (2004a). *Technology education status report*. Raleigh, NC: Author.

North Carolina Department of Public Instruction. (2004b). *2004 Numbers report for career-technical education*. Retrieved March 30, 2005 from: http://www.ncpublicschools.org/workforce_development/publications/numbers/2004_cte_numbers.pdf.

North Carolina Department of Public Instruction. (2000). *2000 Numbers report for Workforce Development Education*. Retrieved March 20, 2005 from: http://www.dpi.state.nc.us/workforce_development/publications/exec_summary/summary_99.pdf.

Oaks, M. (1991). A progress report on the transition from industrial arts to technology education. *Journal of Industrial Teacher Education, 28*(2), 61-72.

Pearson, G., & Young, T. (2002). *Technically speaking: Why all Americans need to know more about technology*. Washington, DC: National Academy Press.

Project Lead the Way. (2005a). *Schools in the PLTW network in NC*. Retrieved April 1, 2005 from: http://www.pltw.org/schoollist.asp?toSelect=NC.

Project Lead the Way. (2005b). *Project Lead the Way certifications*. Retrieved April 1, 2005 from: http://www.pltw.org/certifications.shtml.

Sanders, M. (2001). New paradigm or old wine? The status of technology education practice in the United States. *Journal of Technology Education, 12*(2), 35-55.

Sclafani, S. (2005). *Statement by Susan Sclafani, Assistant Secretary for Vocational and Adult Education*. Testimony before the House Subcommittee on Labor/HHS/Education Appropriations on the FY 2006 budget request for high school reform, high quality teachers and school leadership. Retrieved April 1, 2005 from: http://www.ed.gov/news/speeches/2005/03/03182005a.html.

Snyder, J. & Hales, J. (Eds.). (1981). *Jackson's Mill industrial arts curriculum theory*. Charleston, WV: West Virginia Department of Education.

Spellings, M. (2005). *Expanding the promise, continuing the progress*. Senate Testimony before the Senate Labor, Health and Human Services, Education, and Related Agencies Appropriations Subcommittee, March 2, 2005. Retrieved April 1, 2005 from: http://www.ed.gov/news/speeches/2005/03/03022005.html.

United States Department of Education. (n.d.). *Charting a new course for career and technical education*. High School Leadership Summit Issue Paper. Retrieved March 18, 2005 from: http://www.ed.gov/about/offices/list/ovae/pi/hsinit/papers/cte.pdf.

United States Department of Labor, Bureau of Labor Statistics. (2005). *College enrollment of 2004 high school grads*. Retrieved April 8, 2005 from: http://www.bls.gov/opub/ted/2005/mar/wk4/art02.htm.

JOHN RITZ AND PHILIPS REED

9. TECHNOLOGY EDUCATION AND THE INFLUENCES OF RESEARCH

A United States Perspective, 1985-2005

Technology education has progressed well through its development in the U.S. over the past two decades. Enrollments in grade levels 6-12 have reached an all time high. Major research projects have provided direction for curricular change. The curriculum has moved forward to keep abreast of emerging technologies. Distance learning has assisted teachers in their professional development. With progress, challenges have been encountered in meeting teacher demand and maintaining curricular focus.

The past 20 plus years of curriculum re-design in technology education in the U.S. has resulted from both internal research and best practices of other nations. Today curriculum designers are influenced by federally funded research projects undertaken in the 1960s and then undertaken by individuals, states, foundations, and associations during the 1970s, 1980s, and 1990s, which brought to the forefronts the study of the systems of technology (variously configured as communication, construction, manufacturing, and transportation), *Standards for Technological Literacy* (ITEA, 2000), and current movements that included design (as exemplified by our colleagues from other countries) and engineering processes. Besides these research-based prospects, there have been outside influences to the technology teaching profession from companies who provided technology study modules, textbooks, and computer software.

Moves from shop work to the study of industry and technology began in the U.S. in the 1960s. This reform was stimulated by government-funded research to support the race to space and support national defense. Major curricular changes included the study of industry and the technologies of industry. For example, the American Industry Project (Face & Flug, 1967) focused on the study of the elements of industry (i.e., finance, management, communication, materials, etc.) and the Industrial Arts Curriculum Project (Towers, Lux, & Ray, 1966) studied the systems of industrial technology (i.e., The World of Manufacturing and The World of Construction). These programs had major impacts on the curriculum reform that occurred in secondary schools and universities during the 1970-1980s. Courses such as American Industry and the World of Manufacturing and the World of Construction were high school courses, complete with teaching resources.

DeVore and graduate students at West Virginia University researched technology as a discipline and established a structure for the study of technology

M.J. de Vries, I. Mottier (eds.), International Handbook of Technology Education, 113–123.

(DeVore, 1964). The results were school-based research projects that showed how the study of technology could be undertaken. Graduate assistants worked with teachers at demonstration sites. Their impact was a major influence on technology education curriculum design, which caused technology to be studied through the systems of production, communication, and transportation.

During the late 1970s and early 1980s, the content for the U.S. study of technology was solidified through the *Jackson's Mill Curriculum Theory* which designated that the curriculum for technology education include the study of communication, construction and manufacturing (production), transportation, and the impact these technologies have on individuals, society, and the environment (Snyder & Hales, 1981). In the 1980s, the U.S. study of technology was also influenced by the study of design, which was brought to the U.S. by Ron Todd and others from Great Britain and the Netherlands (Todd, 1985).

National Council for the Accreditation of Teacher Education (NCATE), in conjunction with International Technology Education Association and Council for Technology Teacher Education, established guidelines for the preparation of technology teachers. Early guidelines were based on the study of systems of technology - communication, construction, manufacturing, and transportation (ITEA, 1987). This was the most powerful instrument for change in teacher preparation – gaining national accreditation. Federal vocational funding was also removed from universities' teacher education programs and retained at the state department of education levels during the 1990s. From the early 1970s through the early 1990s, universities provided curriculum development and teacher inservice on integrating technological systems, design, and technology and culture into the curriculum. After vocational funding centralization, limited projects have been undertaken through the contractual method with universities in their states.

These efforts caused name and curricular changes in the U.S. The International Technology Education Association name was born in 1985. Individual states changed their association and school subject names in the years to follow. Teacher licensure requirements were also changed to include courses in the systems of technology and technology and culture.

In the early 1990s some individual U.S. states began to include design in their curriculum, i.e., design and technology. Modular technology, based on the latest technological developments grew steadily in the U.S. Teacher education curriculum expanded to include the systems and new technologies, i.e., automation, biotechnology, digital communications, etc.

In the mid-1990s, the Technology for All Americans Project stimulated research, which resulted in *Standards for Technological Literacy* (ITEA, 2000). The implementation of the standards are receiving mixed acceptance in the first decade of the 21st century. State departments of education and local school systems, driven through university collaboration, are making the biggest implementation changes. National Council on the Accreditation of Teacher Education, in conjunction with International Technology Education Association and Council on Technology Teacher Education, has accreditation standards that direct the preparation of technology teachers. These accreditation guidelines now parallel the *Standards for Technological Literacy* (ITEA, 2000) and include the foundations of teacher preparation – curriculum, instructional strategies, learning environments, students, and professional growth (ITEA, 2003a).

The latest trend to influence the content for the study of technology education in the U.S. has been the engineering process. Some states have included engineering courses in their curriculum formats because of our technological relationship with the profession of engineering. U.S. high school students continue to enroll in drafting and design courses offered through technology education because they feel these courses will aid them as they pursue engineering careers. The technology education profession knew that engineering was much more than drafting, so they planned more appropriate programs.

Since the U.S. has more demand than the number of graduates who are completing engineering programs, the engineering profession has come to the technology education profession to seek assistance in marketing engineering professions. Since some outsiders believed that technology education continues to be shop work, they set about to create an engineering program that is not rooted in the technology education profession. The most prominent example was developed in the late 1980s and is known as *Project Lead the Way* (PLTW) (2005). This program is sponsored in each state by an engineering university. However, PLTW relies on technology education teachers to get trained and implement the engineering courses associated with Project Lead the Way. It will be interesting to watch these programs and relationships mature.

To truly understand the content development for technology education that has occurred in the past twenty years in the U.S., one must also look at the influences that educational vendors have had on shaping the delivery of technology education instruction. One arena to view is that of the textbook publishers. This group has been supportive of the technology education program change movement. The publishers are in business to make a profit, so they pay close attention to curricular trends. They hire professionals who understand curriculum movements and these are usually the curriculum leaders in the U.S. Another group of vendors that has shaped the instructional programs have been those who have developed instructional modules. With new technologies emerging, they have figured ways to education people about these technologies. The companies often hire engineers to design instructional trainers on the new technologies. They have developed self-contained instructional materials and activities that are packed with equipment. Vendors often use what materials are available with little integration of curriculum.

Many schools have developed their middle schools' programs to consist of a number of self-contained modules, which students rotate through (Brusic & LaPorte, 2000). Examples would include modules on bridge building, rockets, electronics, CAD, etc. Other vendors have developed software packages that either support instruction or educational modules. Sim-City^{TM} and Car Builder^{TM} software, as well as, electronic circuit boards are examples of commercially available products. Some in the U.S. profession see these as extensions of the older shop work programs, bringing them to a high-tech realm, while others see them as great public relations ventures for technology education (see Petrina, 1993;

Gloeckner & Adamson, 1996; Pullias, 1997; Starkweather, 1997; Rogers, 1998). The major shortcomings are that they usually do not include the social cultural aspects that should be included in a technology education program and that they offer a vendor's perception of the technology education curriculum.

Change in the content for technology education in the U.S. has been in the control of various agents. One of the key groups has been the university faculty who train the teachers for these instructional programs. Teacher preparation has led and reacted to the above curricular changes. Because of collaboration through educational accreditation agencies, many of these curriculum changes have been brought to reality in teacher preparation. For example, the systems of technology have been transformed into the systems of the designed world as outlined in *Standards for Technological Literacy* (ITEA, 2000). Design and technology and technology and culture have become integral components of teacher preparation. All have been pushed by research, best practice, and *Standards for Technological Literacy* (ITEA, 2000). In addition, distance-learning techniques have added to the preparation of teachers through initial licensure, continued professional development, and master degree completion (Ndahi & Ritz, 2002). This has allowed university programs to have a broader impact on the general university curriculum by positioning technological literacy as an outcome of university general education. Offerings have included science and technology goals, computer literacy skills, and technology and society perspectives within university coursework requirements (Todd & Karsnitz, 1999).

Accreditation is important to programs at leading U.S. universities. If the programs are not judged to be worthy by outside evaluation bodies, the programs do not receive financial support or are discontinued. There are over 200 programs in the U.S. that can prepare technology teachers. However, only 39 are accredited by the National Council for the Accreditation of Teacher Education, in conjunction with ITEA and CTTE (CTTE, 2005). Others are accredited by NCATE through a state partnership program. The key to accreditation is that the accrediting body establishes the standards that the teacher preparation institution has to meet. Since the 1980s, the Council on Technology Teacher Education has worked to set the standards of judgment. The technical content to be taught and the methods of preparing professional teachers has always been the basis for these standards. Early standards' technical contents (e.g., *Standards for technology education programs*) (Dugger, Bame, & Pinder, 1985) were based on the curriculum structure that resulted from the Jackson's Mill Curriculum Theory (Snyder & Hales, 1981). After the *Standards for Technological Literacy* (ITEA, 2000) were established, the Council on Technology Teacher Education re-designed the accreditation standards (ITEA, 2003a) to be based on the standards for technological literacy. In both the old and newer standards, research and best practice served as the basis for making teacher preparation judgments. Teacher preparation programs are re-designing themselves as they prepare for accreditation. The newest knowledge that is emerging in the preparation of teachers is design and technology and although not new, technology and culture. The benchmarks in the *Standards for Technological*

Literacy (ITEA, 2000) are self explanatory in the knowledge that teachers of technology education need to master.

Another thread that is being woven into teacher preparation in the U.S. is distributed delivery of instruction through various electronic means - television, web, and CD formats (Ndahi & Ritz, 1999, 2002; Turner & Reed, 2005). Many programs have used these means for the advanced preparation of teachers through the M.S. degree; most notably, Old Dominion University and Ball State University. They have also been found useful for updating teachers to the elements that make-up technological literacy. Few programs are providing distance learning for initial teacher preparation. The two drawbacks are providing for laboratory/technical instruction and the distance the candidates would have to travel to a common site for laboratory instruction to take place (Hobbs, Moon, & Banks, 1997). It is hoped that developments in delivery technologies will improve so that laboratory courses can be taught from a distance.

Because of the universality of technology and culture knowledge and courses needed for the preparation of technology teachers, some faculties have found ways to included some of their courses in the general education (liberal arts) curriculum of their universities (Todd & Karsnitz, 1999). Common courses that can be found are introduction courses and technology and society courses. These offerings get faculty working with others in the university's general education programs and add to the importance of technology education to the campus. As we get teachers better qualified to deliver technology education in U.S. schools, the school-based programs are also improving. New teachers are taking leadership roles within their state as they redefine the technology education curriculum.

U.S. student programs have taught technology mainly at the secondary level, grades 6-12. Limited work has been undertaken at the elementary level; what has been taught has been exemplary. Many U.S. states have made technology education a requirement in the middle grades (6-8), with few states having a high school mandate. Academic standards have taken the main stage in American education; test taking has been mandated through the federal legislation of *No Child Left Behind* (U.S. Department of Education, 2001). Middle and high school programs have retained the systems approach to the study of technology in their curriculum frameworks. Vendor prepared modules and software appear to drive much of what has occurred in classrooms and laboratories. State associations have been providing much of the educational classroom materials and the professional development of teachers. State departments of education have been developing frameworks to show how technology courses reinforce the academic core competencies. These have appeared to be subject survival techniques. Engineering as a profession has been explored as content/process for study in some states and through funded projects. Technology education has been valued by school administrators as alternative learning pathways for various student populations. Business and industry has seen technology education as a pathway into the workforce. Much work had gone into the development of the school-based curriculum for technology education. There were curriculum frameworks, outcome lists for student achievement per course, and instructional materials developed by state departments of education (see Virginia Department of Education, 2005). Much of this work was contracted to universities and their faculties. However, with the redirecting of federal funds that flowed to the universities through the states, the funds have been limited to the technology education specialists at the state levels. Of the funds that have remained, they have been used to update outcome lists, but they have not been used to develop much instructional materials. With the *No Child Left Behind* federal legislation (U.S. Department of Education, 2001), the academic standards have become the ruling force in American schools. State departments of education have been using their limited funding to show how technology education and other workforce education curriculum can be used to better prepare students to master the core academic subjects. As a result, school systems have been relying on vendors of modules, software, and textbooks for their instructional guidance. State technology education professional associations have taken over in providing the professional development of teachers and are also providing instructional materials for their members (see GITEA, 2005). Seeing the need for the development of curriculum and instructional support for technology education, the International Technology Education Association, through its Center to Advance the Teaching of Technology and Science (CATTS) division, has set up a curriculum and research arm to help move states ahead in implementing technology education. CATTS has developed curriculum materials in conjunction with states and technology education curriculum developers. To become a consortium member and received the ITEA materials for its teachers, states must pay a fee to the association. In addition to CATTS, the International Technology Education Association has developed outstanding resource materials to assist teachers in implementing technology education. Examples include the Humans Innovating Technology Series (HITS) and Kids Innovating Technology Series (KITS). Engineering programs are also being sought by school systems to include in their offerings to students. Again, this is a result of relationships with engineering professionals and a way to establish a better image for technology education. For the technology education research community, the federal government, through the National Science Foundation, has supported some of the research for preparing curriculum which will engage learners that want to become engineers (Pearson, 2004). School administrators support having traditional technology education shop work classes in their schools for their non-academic populations. These administrators believe that weaker versions of technology education can capture the interests of the non-academic students, keep them in school, and possibly provided some skills which will assist them in entering the workplace. Although this is not the major focus of technology literacy programs, these beliefs provide support for some teachers not to change their programs. Employers also support these beliefs. Consequently, change does not occur as technology education professionals would like.

There are a lot of job-training programs in American schools (see the twelve divisions of the Association for Career and Technical Education [ACTE], http://www.acteonline.org/). However, many of these programs, referred to as trade

118

and industrial programs, usually require the student population to leave their high school for half day and be bussed to a career and technical education center. Students are resistant to leave their high school and peers, so many do not choose this type of education. Other schools systems are turning their in-house technology education programs into trade type programs where students earn specialized certificates while in high school. These certificates are set on industrial standards, so teachers believe they are doing the right thing to teach trade specific skills such as computer networking, computer assisted design, and computer operations. Obtaining a certificate often requires a student to be a program completer, which means he or she must complete a sequence of two or more courses in a program (Frederick County Public Schools, 2005).

Because of a lack of leadership, technology education in the U.S. is taking several pathways. Much of this lack of leadership can be blamed on the downsizing of institutions at various levels (Volk, 1997). Many technology education personnel are overworked with other system tasks and cannot provide the leadership to its core missions. For example, one of the major issues facing the U.S. is getting a sufficient supply of teachers to cover the existing programs (Ritz, 1999).

Teacher corps preparation for technology education has not been able to meet U.S. teacher demands. Projections have shown through two five-year studies that the U.S. lacks about 1,000 qualified teachers each year (Weston, 1997). For this reason, technology education is identified as a critical shortage teaching area in most states. A great number of students enter programs as internal university transfer students. These have been the traditional aged college students who go to college as undecided majors and then transfer into technology education. Current technology education majors usually bring their friends into programs. Alternative teacher preparation has grown over the past 15 years. Many second career candidates (military is a large segment) have entered the profession through traditional teacher preparation routes (Ritz, 1999). Some universities have created alternative programs that grant credit for prior training and work experience. Career switchers are another teacher preparation route that has emerged. It is a fast track program where entrants need a B.S. degree for admissions. The career switchers program usually takes a summer for preparation. However, shortages of qualified technology education teachers persist in the U.S. A small percent of the teacher work force in technology education have been female, although 79% of U.S. teachers have been female (Ornstein & Hunkins, 1998). In an attempt to make all U.S. teachers highly qualified (term from *No Child Left Behind* legislation), tests have become a benchmark within the U.S. educational system. No matter which track technology education candidates take to become a teacher, most states have qualifying tests. States commonly use an academic skills test for admittance such as the Praxis I developed by Educational Testing Services. States vary with their acceptable score. For program completion, candidates must also pass a content knowledge test, usually Praxis II, Technology Education. If a program is designed using the CTTE/NCATE standards, their candidates can easily obtain passing scores on Praxis II. However, if the teacher preparation program does not have a standards-based curriculum, then program completers have problems obtaining passing scores on this instrument. Although Praxis II exists for technology education, the test has not been updated to include the *Standards for Technological Literacy* (ITEA, 2000). It continues to measure knowledge of professional education and the systems of communication, construction, manufacturing, and transportation.

Although the technology education profession has made great strides forward in moving from shop work to technological literacy, threats to technology education exist in American schools. The biggest threat to the vitality of this school subject is to continue to have a qualified pool of teachers (Weston, 1997). Although the shortage of teachers is a known factor, many young people are not choosing teaching as a career. If a qualified teacher does not exist, school administrators are closing programs and converting the facilities to academic classrooms. Federal and state law mandates that students must pass certain academic courses and earn a set number of academic credits to graduate. A large group of U.S. students are disenchanted with their high school academics. However, the federal government is requiring that extra resources be used to engage these students to pass the federal and state endorsed accountability tests. This compounds the teacher shortage problem, because technology is required in most middle schools, grades 6-8. Few U.S. states require technology education at the high school level. Limits in leadership are another threat to technology education in the U.S. People are not as professionally involved in their careers as in past decades. It is hard to find individuals to run for office in their state and national technology education professional associations. Lack of commitment does not provide strength to counteract threats. People feel safe when they should be preparing to defend their professions. Technology education has not had the resources to improve its image with the public. Some still consider our subject as shop work. Technology education has the research-based content that needs to be taught to move our society into the future, but the profession does not have the know-how and resources to move us beyond an elective in the schools. Training and investment needs to be made in public relations agendas and actions. Time constraints and resource limits prohibit the U.S. from making further gains for the school subject of technology education. Due to operating costs and low enrollments, many university teacher preparation programs have been downsized or eliminated (Volk, 1997). During the past three years there have been announcements to hire 45, 60, and 75 technology education and/or industrial technology university faculty. However, the numbers prepared each year hovers around 10 [1]. Where are the replacements going to come from in the future? Without teacher educators, where will the teachers be prepared and who will provide for professional leadership? The number of graduate students spiked in the 1970's but is on a downward trend (Reed, 2001). These are daunting problems facing technology education in the U.S.

SUMMARY

Technology education research and investment have been found throughout the U.S. educational systems. Exemplary technology education programs exist. However, outside threats have persisted due to poor school performance of students in the academic subject areas and the threat to closing programs due to lack of qualified teachers. Leadership gaps and limited public relations efforts have been found to be detrimental to long-term health of technology education in the U.S.

While there is solid evidence to suggest technology education is still in a state of flux after twenty years (Sanders, 2001), there are several very positive trends. First, the *Standards for Technological Literacy* (ITEA, 2000) and *Advancing Excellence in Technological Literacy* (ITEA, 2003b) have had a significant impact on the profession. These materials have been widely accepted by the profession and endorsed by outside organizations. Additionally, these materials are making state curriculums, textbooks, vendor materials, and teacher preparation programs more relevant and rigorous.

Secondly, despite the closing of teacher preparation institutions, most notably at land grant universities, distance learning is helping to reach more students than ever before. Programs at Old Dominion University, Ball State University, and Valley City State University are using various techniques to reach more professionals (Flowers, 2001; Ndahi & Ritz, 1999, 2002; Mugan, Boe, & Edland, 2004; Turner & Reed, 2005).

A third significant trend in the United States is the political climate. Organizations such as the National Academy of Engineering, The National Research Council, and the National Science Foundation have endorsed technology education in various ways. The National Academy of Engineering was a significant supporter for the creation of *Standards for Technological Literacy* (ITEA, 2000) and continues to be a vocal ally. The National Research Council joined the National Academy of Engineering to host several conferences and thoroughly articulated the national implications for technological literacy in *Technically speaking: Why all Americans need to know more about technology* (Pearson & Young, 2002). The National Science Foundation continues to fund projects for secondary engineering programs and science, technology, engineering, and mathematics (STEM) initiatives.

The support is very clear for technological literacy in the United States. We are on the verge of seeing the hard work of the past two decades come to fruition. There is public support (ITEA, 2001 & 2004) and support from national organizations outside the profession. We must maintain our uniform vision, provide leadership, and stay on the course of progress.

[1]Reed, P. A. & Ritz, J. M. (2005). Doctoral program supply and demand. Unpublished research paper based on Schmidt, K. (2004) and faculty position postings in professional journals, listservs, and mailings. Norfolk, VA: Old Dominion University, Department of Occupational and Technical Studies

REFERENCES

Brusic, S. A. & LaPorte, J. E. (2000). *The status of modular technology education in Virginia*. Retrieved March 31, 2005 from http://scholar.lib.vt.edu/ejournals/JITE/v38n1/brusic.html.

Council on Technology Teacher Education (CTTE). (2005). *Programs nationally recognized by NCATE*. Retrieved February 1, 2005 from http://teched.edtl.vt.edu/CTTE/HTML/NCATE1.html#ApprovedPrograms.

DeVore, P. W. (1964). Technology: A structure for industrial arts content. In *New Directions for Industrial Arts: Addresses & Proceedings of the 26th Annual Convention of the American Industrial Arts Association* (pp. 78-80). Reston, VA: American Industrial Arts Association.

Dugger, W.E., Bame, E. A., & Pinder, C. A. (1985). *Standards for technology education programs*. South Holland, IL: Goodheart-Willcox Company, Inc.

Face, W., & Flug, E. (1967). *The establishment of American industry as a traditional subject between general and vocational education*. Menominee, WI: Stout State University, American Industry Project.

Flowers, J. (2001). Online learning needs in technology education. *Journal of Technology Education, 13*(1), 17-30.

Frederick County Public Schools. (2005). *A guide to industry certification, licensure, & verified credits*. Winchester, Virginia: Author.

Georgia Industrial Technology Education Association (GITEA). (2005). *Educational resources*. Retrieved February 2, 2005 from http://www.gitea.org/cookbook_files/cookbook.htm

Gloeckner, G. & Adamson, G. (1996). Modular technology education: A Wild West point of view. *The Technology Teacher*, September, 16-19.

Hobbs, S., Moon, B. and Banks, F. (1997) *Open and Distance Education, New Technologies and the Development of Teacher Education in Europe: A Handbook*. Milton Keynes: The Open University. ISBN 0 7492 7554 5.

International Technology Education Association (ITEA). (2004). *The Second Installment of the ITEA/Gallup Poll and What It Reveals as to How Americans Think About Technology*. Reston, VA: Author.

International Technology Education Association (ITEA). (2003a). *ITEA/CTTE/NCATE. Curriculum Standards: Initial Programs in Technology Teacher Education*. Reston, VA: Author.

International Technology Education Association (ITEA). (2003b). *Advancing Excellence in Technological Literacy: Student Assessment, Professional Development, and Program Standards*. Reston, VA: Author.

International Technology Education Association (ITEA). (2001). *ITEA/Gallup poll reveals what Americans think about technology*. Reston, VA: Author.

International Technology Education Association (ITEA). (2000). *Standards for technological literacy: Content for the study of technology*. Reston, VA: Author.

International Technology Education Association (ITEA). (1987). *ITEA/CTTE/NCATE. Curriculum Standards*. Reston, VA: Author.

Mugan, D., Boe, J., & Edland, M. (2004). Standards-based technology teacher education online: An innovative new program at Valley City State University. *The Technology Teacher*, 64(1), 25-29.

Ndahi, H. (1999). Utilization of distance learning technology among industrial and technical teacher education faculty. *Journal of Industrial Teacher Education, 36*(4), 21-37.

Ndahi, H., & Ritz, J. M. (2002). Distance learning in industrial teacher education programs. *Journal of Technology Studies, 28*(1), 64-69.

Ornstein, A. & Hunkins, F. (1998). *Curriculum foundations, principles and theory*. Boston: Allyn and Bacon.

Pearson, G. (2004). *Collaboration conundrum*. Retrieved March 31, 2005 from http://scholar.lib.vt.edu/ejournals/JTE/v15n2/pearson.html

Pearson, G., & Young, A.T. (Eds.). (2002). *Technically speaking: Why all Americans need to know more about technology*. Washington, DC: National Academy Press. Retrieved from http://www.nae.edu/techlit.

Petrina, S. (1993). Under the corporate thumb: Troubles with our MATE (Modular Approach to Technology Education), *Journal of Technology Education*, 5(1), 72-80.

Project Lead the Way (PLTW). (2005). *About Project Lead the Way*. Retrieved February 2, 2005 from http://www.pltw.org/AUHistory.shtml.

Pullias, D. (1997). The future is... Beyond modular. *The Technology Teacher*, April, 28-29.

Reed, P. A. [Ed.]. (2001). The technology education graduate research database: 1892-2000. Council on Technology Teacher Education Monograph #17. Retrieved February 1, 2005 from http://teched.vt.edu/ctte/HTML/Monographs1.html.

Ritz, J. M. (1999). Addressing the shortage of technology education teaching professionals: Everyone's business. *The Technology* Teacher, 59(1), 8-12.

Rogers, G. (1998). Concerns about technology education laboratories, *Journal of Industrial Teacher Education*, 35(3), 93-95.

Sanders, M. E. (2001). New Paradigm or Old Wine? The Status of Technology Education Practice in the United States. Journal of Technology Education, 12(2), 35-55.

Schmidt, K. [Ed.]. 2004. *Industrial teacher education Directory, 42nd Edition*. National Association of Industrial and Technical Teacher Educators and Council on Technology Teacher Education.

Snyder, J. F., & Hales, J. A. (1981). *Jackson's Mill industrial arts curriculum theory*. Charleston, WV: West Virginia Department of Education.

Starkweather, K. (1997). Are we thinking to achieve? *The Technology Teacher*, 57(2), 5-6.

Todd, R. D. & Karsnitz, J. R. (1999). Identifying and solving professional problems. In Gilberti, A. F., and Rouch, D. L., Eds., *Advancing professionalism in technology education* (pp. 139-164). Peoria, IL: Glencoe/McGraw-Hill.

Todd, R. D. (1985). Technology Education: An international perspective. In *Technology Education: A perspective on implementation*. Reston, VA: International Technology Education Association.

Towers, E. R., Lux, D. G., & Ray, W. E. (1966). *A rationale and structure for industrial arts subject matter*. Columbus OH: Ohio State University.

Turner, J. E. & Reed, P. A. (2005). Creation of a Faculty Task List for Teaching in a Televised Distance Learning Environment. *Journal of Industrial Teacher Education, 41*(2), 5-20.

U.S. Department of Education. (2001). *A guide to education and No Child Left Behind*. Retrieved February 1, 2005 from http://www.ed.gov/nclb/overview/intro/guide/index.html.

Virginia Department of Education. (2005). *Virginia's CTE resource center*. Retrieved February 1, 2005 from http://www.cteresource.org/.

Vork, K. (1997). Going, going, gone? Recent trends in technology teacher education programs. Retrieved March 31, 2005 from http://scholar.lib.vt.edu/ejournals/JTE/v8n2/Volk.jte-v8n2.html .

Weston, S. (1997). Teacher shortage- Supply and demand. *The Technology Teacher, 57*(1), 6-9.

GENE MARTIN

10. FROM IDEAS TO FRUITION – EXTERNAL FUNDING AND ITS IMPACT ON TECHNOLOGY EDUCATION

The genesis for technology education today throughout the world is often traced to the foresight of a select few individuals who believed there was a need for a new area of study within the school curriculum. Some of the individuals who provided the initial major impetus for technology education worked in isolation from their colleagues, while others worked in tandem. Regardless of their sometime unique, often cumbersome, and even unorthodox approaches to bring about change, however, great progress has been made in the last 20 years throughout the world by a host of individuals and organizations who sought to further the goals of technology education.

In the United States, one organization that has made a very significant impact on the advancement of technology education is the Technical Foundation of America. Since its inception, the foundation has funded several hundred projects that advanced the goals of education programs in the United States and throughout the world. Many of these funded projects were in technology education.

During the early years of the foundation's existence, grant seekers sought funds to develop new curricula. The curricula often reflected individuals' best thinking of the time in what technology education was suppose to look and be like throughout the remainder of the 20th century. Later, as the profession's members became more accustomed and even sophisticated in teaching technology, the foundation hosted symposia that brought together leaders in the field to discuss and often debate issues associated with the different movements taking place in technology education. In addition, the foundation hosted leadership conferences, retreats for leaders of professional organizations, and "comparative" issues conferences; and it helped establish a technology education center at a major university. And, while all of these activities were occurring, the foundation funded proposals that represented the special research interests of technology education faculty in the United States and abroad.

The world has changed throughout the past 20 years and change is no more apparent than in the different types of grant proposals the foundation receives today as compared to that which it received 10 to 20 years ago. Change, for example, is evident in (a) the number of proposals it receives each year requesting funding; (b) the quality of the proposals; (c) the subject matter emphasis of the proposals; and (d) the creative nature of the content and methodology of the proposals. Today, for whatever reason, technology educators are less aggressive in

M.J. de Vries, I. Mottier (eds.), International Handbook of Technology Education, 125–131.

seeking grant funds. Maybe the lack of grant seeking activity is a reflection of the declining number of technology educators and the declining number of technology education programs in the United States; and maybe it's a reflection of the greater societal demands being placed on individuals within the teaching profession. It is the premise of this paper that the major events in technology education in the United States over the past 20 years closely parallel the grant and program funding patterns of the foundation. The goal, therefore, is to identify and describe a select few of these grants and programs.

MISSION

How does the foundation establish priorities when deciding where to focus its resources to further the goals of the technology education profession? What is the procedure for applying for a grant? And, what is the process by which decisions are made on which proposals are funded and which proposals are not funded? Before any one of these three questions may be answered, however, the foundation's mission must first be explored. The mission of the foundation is as follows: "The foundation exists to effect change in technology education; serve as an advocate for the profession; and act as a catalyst to generate ideas, identify issues, and stimulate critical thinking." The overriding principles in the mission statement are in the action words of "effect change," "advocate," "catalyst," "identify," and "stimulate." These principles have guided the foundation since its inception when making funding decisions for all of its grants and programs.

Establishing Priorities. As it relates to the first question, every 12 to 18 months, the foundation brings together a group of leaders (classroom teachers, supervisors, and teacher educators) in the profession who serve as an advisory group. In their advisory capacity, the participants discuss with the foundation's trustees (a) the direction they foresee the profession moving over the next decade, (b) identify targets of opportunity the foundation should consider, and (c) suggest possible programs that should be conducted.

Application. The procedure to apply for a grant is rather simple, at least when compared to other philanthropic foundations. Grant guidelines require the grant seeker to provide an executive summary with accompanying details that address a documented need for the project and, of course, a budget. Above all else, however, the proposal must document that the proposed activity supports the foundation's mission.

Review Process. As it relates to the third question, each year the foundation sends copies of the proposals it receives to an independent jury of professional educators in the field. Jury members work independently of one another throughout the proposal review process. Jury members identify the strengths and weaknesses of each proposal and inform the foundation whether a proposal meets the foundation's mission.

CURRICULUM DEVELOPMENT INITIATIVES

One of the earliest projects (*circa* 1980) that received funding from the foundation was the Jackson's Mill Industrial Arts Curriculum Theory project. In the United States, many people in the profession regard the Jackson's Mill project as the major and most significant event that gave birth to "modern" day technology education. The Project's organizers (James Hales and James Snyder of West Virginia) incorporated a modified Delphi technique to select its participants, who represented classroom teachers, supervisors, teacher educators, and professional organization executives. The participants were widely recognized as a Who's Who in technology education in the United States.

As originally conceived by the Jackson's Mill project organizers, participants were to attend a series of meetings with an open mind and with an infectious desire and spirit to bring about significant and meaningful change in the profession. The organizers believed, and the belief was shared by the participants, that the profession had become stagnant and that it needed a new focus and a new direction if it was ever to have a major impact on education throughout the remaining years of the 20th century. Some people in the profession at the time feared that the profession would not survive unless meaningful and purposeful change occurred.

The Jackson's Mill project provided just what the profession needed. The outcomes of the Project were timely and they were printed in paperback and distributed nationally and internationally. The paperback went through several reprints as it was a very popular piece of scholarly literature. The paperback was used by faculty and students in almost every undergraduate and graduate professional education class in the United States. During the 1980s, the Project was probably the most often quoted document in the profession's literature and it is still quoted even today; and it was a topic of discussion at almost every professional meeting of technology educators. The foundation provided the Project's organizers funds to host some of their meetings. The foundation's trustees believed, like the Project's organizers, that significant and meaningful change needed to occur in the profession if teaching technology was to ever become a reality in the schools of the United States.

A major curriculum effort funded from 1982 to 1984 was the Industry and Technology Education Curriculum Development project. Nationally, the project was designed to extend the work of the Jackson's Mill project and it was the first major curriculum development effort by technology educators in the United States immediately following the Jackson's Mill project. The project's investigators (R. Thomas Wright of Ball State University and Leonard Sterry of the University of Wisconsin-Stout) developed a guide that contained technology education program structures for small-, medium-, and large-sized schools. It was the profession's first attempt at identifying technology education for school enrollments of all sizes. The guide also included course outlines for the various course content offerings. Several hundred guides were printed and made available to technology educators. The guide was used by key school stakeholders throughout the 1980s.

Another initiative funded by the foundation that was also a follow up to the Jackson's Mill project resulted in a project and publication entitled *A Conceptual Framework for Technology Education*. Among the many topics covered in the publication was a description of the technological method. The publication covered bio-related, communication, production, and transportation technologies. Today, the publication is available through the International Technology Education Association.

CENTER FOR INDUSTRIAL TECHNOLOGY EDUCATION

The foundation assisted Ball State University in establishing its Center for Industrial Technology Education (CITE) in the mid-1980s. The CITE project, funded over a five year time period, developed a series of technology education activity packets that assisted classroom teachers in making the transition from industrial arts to technology education. Each packet contained 10 activities that were deemed appropriate for students in the 6th through 12th grades. Several hundred packets were developed by the CITE project team. Today, the packets continue to be distributed in limited quantities by the International Technology Education Association.

PROFESSIONAL ASSOCIATION INITIATIVES

The lifeblood of any profession is often the role that professional associations serve in meeting the goals, ideals, and ambitions of its members. Since 1980, the foundation has contributed funds to several different professional associations. In the early years, for example, some organizations needed funds just to sustain themselves as the size of their memberships was small; while others sought funds to carry out new and/or innovative projects that would further the goals of their associations. Arguably, some associations would not be in existence today if the foundation had not provided funds during a critical time of need. The foundation has provided funds to assist associations in supporting and conducting membership drives, hosting in-service workshops, establishing and supporting advisory councils, hosting strategic planning sessions, hosting major conferences, underwriting costs associated with conference speakers, supporting students to attend and participate in conferences, developing leadership development kits, conducting public relations campaigns, hosting teleconferences, conducting demonstration projects, hosting roundtables, developing professional improvement plans, developing competitive events guides, supporting teacher recruitment, videotaping interviews of technology education leaders, and supporting program enhancements. Associations that have benefited directly from the foundation's philanthropy include the International Technology Education Association, the Technology Student Association, the Technology Education Collegiate Association, over 30 state technology education associations in the United States, World Council of Associations for Technology Education, SkillsUSA – VICA, the

National Association of Industrial and Technical Teacher Education, and the National Association of Trade and Industrial Education.

PROFESSIONAL DEVELOPMENT CONFERENCES

Starting in the late 1970s and moving through the mid-1980s, a series of technology education symposia were held in various locations throughout the United States. Often, but not always, each symposium was hosted by a university that also had a technology education department and faculty. The symposia provided a forum that could not be provided by any of the professional organizations and the symposia were conducted so they would not be in conflict with the annual meetings of the professional associations. While each symposium had a rather unique theme and accompanying program, a symposium's format provided a platform that allowed and encouraged an open discussion of ideas related to designing, developing, and implementing technology education. Participants exited the symposia with new knowledge, new skills, and new dispositions about the role of technology education in schools. Several of the symposia that were funded by the foundation included those hosted by University of Wisconsin-Stout, Ball State University, Illinois State University, The Ohio State University, and Northern Illinois University.

Throughout its existence, the foundation hosted a number of seminars and conferences that focused on topics that were deemed critical to the technology education profession at the time and they were topics that needed to be addressed by a representative population of the profession's members. In the early 1980s, for example, the theme for one of the conferences was, "Are We Prepared for a Technological Future." In the early 1990s, the foundation demonstrated its support to the profession by hosting a group of national and international leaders in technology education in a series of critical issues conferences. In 2003, the foundation co-hosted a conference with Griffith University (Australia) that focused on comparative initiatives in technology education between Australia and the United States. Prior to any of these conferences, however, the foundation would bring together a group of technology education leaders to develop the conferences' programs. It was another way the foundation demonstrated to the profession that it wanted the profession's members and not the foundation to establish the conferences' agendas.

One of the most widely acclaimed foundation-sponsored issues' conferences was held in Scottsdale, Arizona in the early 1990s. This conference became known as the Camelback Symposium because it was held in a conference facility that was located at the base of Camelback Mountain. Camelback Symposium papers were printed in a softbound book and the book was widely distributed throughout the profession by the International Technology Education Association. More important than a published book, however, was the message that the Camelback Symposium communicated to the profession: a research base and research agenda needed to be established by the profession's members before the profession could ever expect to make a meaningful impact in schools. The Camelback Symposium helped to plant a seed for the nationally and internationally acclaimed Technology for All Americans project of the 1990s.

PARTICIPANTS

Throughout its existence, the foundation has made every effort to reach out to technology educators at all levels of education while recognizing the unique positions they hold in their local school environments. Technology education classroom teachers have benefited directly from the foundation's program of work. The foundation's funded curriculum efforts of the 1980s and 1990s later became part of the content for the study of technology in many elementary and secondary schools throughout the United States. Classroom teachers, supervisors, and teacher educators are considered as equals by the foundation and each has benefited immensely from the foundation's program of work. In the late 1990s and on two different occasions, for example, the foundation hosted study abroad programs for technology education classroom teachers. These teachers, along with a mentor from each of their states, were invited to participate in a study abroad program in the United Kingdom to learn about design and technology. The study abroad programs were hosted by the Centre for Design and Technology Education at the University of Wolverhampton. Today, many of these classroom teachers have incorporated design and technology into their school's curriculum; and on an annual basis, several of these same classroom teachers attend International Technology Education Association and state level conferences and give presentations on what they are doing in the classroom as a result of studying design and technology in the United Kingdom. The content and instructional strategies learned in the United Kingdom have impacted technology education, including classroom teachers and their students, in selected technology education programs throughout the United States.

RESEARCH INITIATIVES

In addition to developing new curricula and providing support for hosting conferences, symposia, and seminars, the foundation funded several research proposals that were emanating from the work of a select group of technology teacher educators in the United States and abroad. Regretfully, however, the "flow" of research proposals submitted to the foundation has been limited and each year the number of research proposals the foundation receives continues to decline. For whatever reason, it does not appear that the technology education profession has established research as an important part of its agenda. Successful research grant seekers have focused their energies on the following topics: measuring student competencies in technology education; development of exit examinations; developing assessment criteria for technology teacher education; identifying criteria for hiring first-time technology education teachers; stimulating continuing research; identifying the processes of a technologist; learning effects of modular curriculum design; technology education status studies; and using cognitive holding power concepts and activity theory to develop student thinking in technology education. Within just the past few years, the foundation funded a project at Illinois State University that encourages undergraduates to become active in conducting research and seeking grants.

RETROSPECT AND PROSPECT

Technology education has undergone many changes over the past 20 years. Many of these changes were initiated by individuals while other changes were initiated by professional associations and organizations. The Technical Foundation of America, through its funding of grants and programs, has served as an advocate and catalyst to effect change. Its efforts have helped the profession's members generate ideas, identify issues, and stimulate critical thinking on a range of topics. Arguably, its impact has been significant and long lasting. Fortunately, over the past 20 years, other organizations and agencies have also stepped to the forefront to assist the technology education profession. Most noticeably among these groups have been the National Science Foundation and the National Aeronautics and Space Administration.

In retrospect, there have been several defining moments in the history of technology education over the past 20 years. Arguably, not one of these moments appears to be more important than the critical role philanthropy has played in providing funding for worthy projects and programs. If a mosaic of technology education's future was to be created, it would surely include philanthropic organizations as one of the key stakeholders. In prospect, philanthropy will play an even greater role in technology education's future by assisting individuals and associations in bringing about purposeful and meaningful change. More important, however, future initiatives in technology education will be influenced by the grant seeking motivations and ambitions of the profession's members.

ANN MARIE HILL

11. REFLECTIONS ON TWENTY YEARS OF WANDERING THROUGH THE PATHWAYS AND FOREST OF TECHNOLOGICAL EDUCATION IN ONTARIO, CANADA

ENTERING THE ONTARIO FOREST

In 1987, by accepting a university position at Queen's University in Kingston, Ontario, the wanderer left the Québec Technical/Vocational Education forest and entered the forest of Technological Studies in Ontario. The Ontario forest seemed familiar as there were many similarities with Québec. Both Canadian provinces had two educational paths for the study of technology: Industrial Arts that began in senior elementary school (Grades 7 and 8) and continued in various degrees at the secondary school level, and Technical/Vocational Education (Québec) or Technological Studies (Ontario) that was offered throughout secondary school (Grades 9 through 12/13).

The similarities between the two paths were apparent: both were electives or non-compulsory courses, and both had little, if any, female enrolment. The cover page of the August 1972 issue (Vol. 14, No. 2) of the Canadian Vocational Journal (see Figure 1) portrays class composition and a teacher that are accurate even 15 years later. But there were also differences between the two paths: Industrial Arts was an interest course typically taken by academically oriented children, and the Technical/Vocational and Technological Studies routes were comprised of a variety of courses related to the world-of-work. These latter courses were typically taken by students who had an interest in a particular workplace or professional career immediately after secondary school, and who potentially would enter post-secondary education at some later date. Also, these courses were taken by students who had academic challenges and did not intend to pursue postsecondary academic studies.

TECHNOLOGICAL STUDIES IN ONTARIO: 1985 TO 1987 REVISIONS

Ontario is geographically the largest Canadian province and it is also the most populated, industrialized province (Hill, 2003). In the early 1980s, Ontario's 1960s curriculum for the study of technology was still in use and it reflected a curriculum that was primarily related to employment opportunities in the workplace. The mere titles of these 1960 curriculum guidelines reflect this intention: for the Intermediate Division of secondary school (Grades 9 and 10) the Ministry of Education's

M.J. de Vries, I. Mottier (eds.), International Handbook of Technology Education, 133–169.

(OME) document was titled, *Technical Subjects RP-27, 1963* (OME, 1963a) and for the Senior Division of secondary school (Grades 11to 13) the document was titled, *Curriculum RP-35 (Occupational, Practical Subjects), 1962* (OME, 1962). The curriculum documents portray a variety of discrete technical courses, but all courses were unified under a program umbrella called Technological Studies. The main focus was on course content, not the learner, and as such skill acquisition and mastery learning were paramount. Also, there existed a second path for the study of technology, an Industrial Arts path, for students who wanted an interest course in technology. Here the guiding curriculum document was titled, *Industrial Arts, I.19 and S19, 1963* (OME, 1963b).

Figure 1. The 1970s Image of Technological Studies Continues Into the 1980s

In 1985, a revision process for the Ontario curriculum guidelines for Technological Studies began. In the end, the program and its numerous courses again focused primarily on technical content and technical skills, but the technical subjects were aligned to changing needs: "It reflects the changing skill requirements of business and industry" (OME, 1985a, p. 1). Another change in the curriculum documents was the formal attention given to the learner, something that was not explicit in earlier documents, and to alternative enrolment routes for the secondary school courses in this program: "It also suggests instructional strategies and programs for assisting students in making a transition from school to work" (OME, 1985a, p. 1). As with all other subject area curriculum guidelines, Technological Studies curriculum was aligned with Ontario's curriculum framework represented in a document titled, *Ontario Schools: Intermediate and Senior Divisions* (**OS:IS**) (OME, 1984).

In this educational revision period, the publication of new curriculum guidelines began in 1985 and continued to 1987. By 1987 there were three parts to the revised Technological Studies curriculum guidelines: (1) *Technological Studies Intermediate and Senior Divisions. Part A: Policy for Program Planning* (OME, 1985a), an overview document providing a program framework; (2) *Technological Studies Intermediate and Senior Divisions. Part B* that actually consisted of 10 different curriculum guidelines, each representing courses for a technical area by categorizing them into Subject Groupings. These 10 curriculum guidelines in turn housed the specific courses for each subject grouping, Grades 9 through 12; and (3) *Technological Studies Intermediate and Senior Divisions. Part C: Ontario Academic Courses* (OME, 1987b), or the Grade 13 curriculum guideline for university bound students. Figure 2 displays the relationship of OS:IS to the three parts of Technological Studies curriculum guidelines.

ONTARIO SCHOOLS: INTERMEDIATE AND SENIOR DIVISIONS – (OS:IS)		
TECHNOLOGICAL STUDIES		
PART A	PART B – Subject Groupings	Part C – OAC (Grade 13)
Policy for Program Planning (OME, 1985a)	1. Transportation Grouping (OME, 1986a) 2. Construction Grouping (OME, 1986b) 3. Electrical Grouping (OME, 1985b) 4. Food Services Grouping (OME, 1986c) 5. Graphics Grouping (OME, 1986d) 6. Horticultural Grouping (OME, 1987a) 7. Materials, Processes, & Design Grouping (n/d) 8. Manufacturing Grouping (OME, 1986e) 9. Personal Services Grouping (OME, 1986f) 10.Textiles Grouping (OME, 1986g)	Ontario Academic Courses (OAC) (OME, 1987b) • Computer Technology - Interfacing • Analog & Digital Electronics • Fluid Power & Control

Figure 2. Ontario Technological Studies – 1985 to 1987 Revisions

Each of the above 10 subject groupings housed a number of different courses and outlined which were to be offered at different grade levels. An example of course listings in a subject grouping curriculum guideline is illustrated in Figure 3.

This Graphics grouping provided a series of varied courses from Grade 9 through to Grade 12, but no Grade 13 or Ontario Academic Courses existed in this grouping.

Subject Grouping	Course	Division	Approved Course Levels			Course Code
Graphics Grouping	Drafting	Intermediate	Basic	General	Advanced	TDR
	Drafting-Architectural	Senior		General	Advanced	TDA
	Drafting-Electrical	Senior		General	Advanced	TDE
	Drafting-Mechanical	Senior		General	Advanced	TDM
	Drafting-Comprehensive	Senior	Basic	General	Advanced	TDG
	Blueprint Reading and Sketching	Intermediate	Basic	General	Advanced	TDB
	Blueprint Reading and Sketching	Senior	Basic	General	Advanced	TDB
	Graphic Communications	Intermediate	Basic	General	Advanced	TGR
	Graphic Communications	Senior	Basic	General	Advanced	TGR
	Photography	Intermediate	Basic	General	Advanced	TGP
	Photography	Senior	Basic	General	Advanced	TGP
	Vocational Art	Intermediate	Basic	General	Advanced	TGV
	Vocational Art	Senior	Basic	General	Advanced	TGV

Figure 3. A Subject Grouping Example: Graphics Grouping

In the Technological Studies curriculum guidelines of 1985 to 1987, courses were categorized not only by subject groupings, but also by Intermediate Division (Grades 9 and 10) and Senior Division (Grades 11 to 13), and by Course Levels (Basic, General or Advanced). Generally, Intermediate Division courses were designated as exploratory courses: "In all cases, exploratory courses must offer students an opportunity to learn about career possibilities and alternative training routes" (OME, 1985a, p. 11). Senior Division courses expanded "the core knowledge, skills, and concepts outlined for the Intermediate Division (OME, 1985a, p. 12)....Emphasis in Senior Division courses should be placed on problem-solving and on student's ability to work independently" (OME, 1985a, p. 13).

While not explicit in the curriculum guidelines, Course Levels (Basic, General or Advanced) really referred to student ability level. Basic-level courses were aimed at students with academic difficulties, General-level courses were directed at students who wanted an interest or exploratory course and whose grades were average, and Advanced-level courses were for students who intended to continue on to post-secondary studies. Figure 4 describes the three levels of difficulty. This three level system became known as "streaming" as it streamed students into ability groupings. An examination of the subject groupings and corresponding courses A reveals that not all subject groupings had Advanced-level courses.

Basic Level	General Level	Advanced Level
Basic-level courses are designed to focus on the development of personal skills, social understanding, self-confidence, and preparation for the world of work. The academic work and related skills should be perceived by the students as being personally useful. Such courses will assist students to prepare for a successful, independent home and working life, to manage personal financial resources, to communicate effectively, and to develop attitudes that foster respect for the environment, good health and fitness, and a positive attitude towards work and leisure. These courses should serve the needs of the student who may not participate in post-secondary education and provide a good preparation for direct entry into employment. (OME, 1984, p. 16)	General-level courses should be considered as appropriate preparation for employment, careers, or further education in certain programs in the colleges of applied arts and technology and other non-degree granting post-secondary educational institutions... (OME, 1984, p. 16)	Advanced-level course should focus on the development of academic skills and prepare students for entry into university or to certain programs of the colleges of applied arts and technology. Such courses should be designed to assist students to understand theoretical principles, practical applications, and substantive content of a subject...(OME, 1984, p. 16)

Figure 4. Levels of Difficulty

Another dimension of the courses was delivery. At the Intermediate level, a broad approach was intended for Grade 9 courses through two different approaches: (1) an integrated approach and (2) a general or interdisciplinary approach.

The integrated approach, as described in the curriculum guideline, was seen as "possible in an industrial arts or other multi-disciplinary shop or laboratory that has, in the same room, equipment related to three or more subject fields. The role of the individual teacher is to relate the various subject activities and skill developments to one another, while simultaneously allowing each subject to be explored separately" (OME, 1985a, p. 12). The interdisciplinary approach required "planning by a group of teachers and focuses on a group of compatible subjects that can be explored usefully in combination. The groupings can be based on three of four subjects selected from any one of the nine subject groupings in Part B... (excluding the Materials, Processing, and Design subject grouping)" (OME, 1985a, p. 12).

The text in parenthesis is significant; the integrated approach represented the old industrial arts subject that no longer existed in the 1985 to 1987 curriculum revision. Industrial arts in this curriculum era was replaced with the Materials, Processing, and Design subject grouping under the Technological Studies umbrella (and which, curiously, was the only subject grouping for which the curriculum guideline was never completed, published or implemented). In contrast, the interdisciplinary approach used the nine subject groupings for which all curriculum guidelines were completed, published and implemented. In Grade 10, courses were categorized under the same nine subject groupings as in the Grade 9 interdisciplinary approach. Grade 10 courses were to "allow students to explore in greater depth the particular subject area in which they were interested" (OME, 1985a, p. 12).

At the Senior Division, courses in Grades 11, 12 and 13 (OAC) could be offered in typical classrooms, workshop or laboratory settings in schools, or through alternative approaches such as school-related and community-related packages, co-operative education, work experience or the Linkage program. These terms are defined below:

- "The term *school-related package* refers to a particular set of courses planned by the school to provide a curricular emphasis for students who have a specific educational goal. Such a goal could include postsecondary education or training in a particular field, direct entry into employment in a specific vocational field, or general education in a particular area of study" (OME, 1985a, p. 13). In essence, this was an interdisciplinary approach where teachers worked together to offer a number of courses in an educational package (OME, 1985a, p. 13).
- "The term *community-related package* refers to a set of courses planned by the school and the community to provide students with a curricular emphasis related to a major economic base in the community" (OME, 1985a, p. 13).

- "**Co-operative education** can provide all students with valuable experiences in career exploration and skill development. It also provides a viable alternative fro students who have difficulty coping with the regular school environment." (OME, 1985a, pp. 13-14). Out-of school components of co-operative education were built into a student's timetable.
- "**Work experience** is an integral part of a specific course. As a component of the student's course, work experience gives the student opportunities to exercise and reinforce the technical skills and knowledge acquired in school. It also provides an orientation to the workplace and opportunities for additional career exploration through discussion with experienced workers" (OME, 1985a, p. 14) and was seen as beneficial to students in their third and fourth year of secondary school.
- "**The Linkage program** aligns subject content in certain secondary school programs with training programs outlined by the Ministry of Colleges and Universities for the postsecondary level....The alignment o f the curriculum allows secondary school students enrolled in technological studies courses...to continue their theoretical training after graduation, with minimum overlap" (OME, 1985a, p. 14) in content. In curriculum theory, this is known as articulation and continuity of the curriculum.

In retrospect, there were four significant developments in Technological Studies that occurred due to the revisions of 1985 to 1987. The first was the idea of interdisciplinarity; connecting discrete knowledge and subject grouping knowledge when possible. This was a departure from the idea of disconnected discrete technical knowledge in the 1960 curriculum guidelines. The second was an increased focus on problem-solving as a learning strategy for technical content. The third was that Industrial Arts was placed under the umbrella of Technological Studies. The fourth was what happened to the Industrial Arts curriculum within the Technological Studies framework. In the Ministry document titled, *Technological Studies Intermediate and Senior Divisions. Part A: Policy for Program Planning* (OME, 1985a) the Intermediate Division is described as exploratory. The document reads:

The present industrial arts programs in Grades 7 and 8 provide the first opportunity for students to explore technological studies. It is important at this level to provide an overview of secondary school opportunities in the various fields of technological studies and postsecondary career opportunities. The program provides a basic introduction through practical experiences to the identification and use of hand tools, the aesthetic appreciation and design of various projects, the qualities and uses of various materials, power machinery, and basic problem-solving skills. Along with these basic skills and knowledge, stress should be placed on safe working practices and on the concept that technological studies courses are equally for girls and boys. In Grades 9 and 10, further refinement and development of basic skills and knowledge should continue, with an increasing emphasis on creative problem-solving. (p. 11)

This excerpt depicts that in the 1985-1987 curriculum reform period, Industrial Arts was envisioned to be the foundation for Technological Studies. In addition, the 'Preface' of this same Ministry document clearly stated that the new curricular document series (Parts A, B and C) "supersedes and replaces *Industrial Arts, I.19 and S19, 1963*, the subjects authorized by *Curriculum RP-35 (Occupational, Practical Subjects), 1962* and the Intermediate Division (Grades 9 and 10) courses outlined in *Technical Subjects RP-27, 1963*" (OME, 1985a, p. 1). For Industrial Arts, a new curriculum was envisioned as one of the 10 subject groupings of the Technological Education *Part B* series. The subject grouping was called 'Materials, Processes, and Design' and the curriculum document was to be titled, *Technological Studies Intermediate and Senior Divisions. Part B: 7. Materials, Processes, and Design Subject Grouping*. What actually happened was that this one subject grouping's curriculum guideline never advanced past the Draft stage by 1987.

An analysis of the draft curriculum document sheds light on this situation. The attempted draft curriculum guideline (OME, 1987) did not 'fit' with the curriculum framework that was used for the other nine curriculum guidelines in Technological Studies. Authors, who were industrial arts teachers, continued to see 'it' as a subject that began in elementary school and continued to Grade 12. They had difficulty redefining their subject area within the context of the new curriculum framework. The draft document of 1987, titled, *Technological Studies Intermediate and Senior Divisions. Part B: 7. Materials, Processes, and Design Subject Grouping, Draft* listed the following courses and grades:

- Industrial Arts (Grades 7-10)
- Industrial Arts (Grades 11-12)
- Design Studies (Grades 9-12)
- Elements of Technology (Grades 9-12)

As this draft document was problematic, it was not approved by the Ministry of Education. Unfortunately, it went beyond the mandate of Grades 9-12, and it did not clarify the essence of this subject grouping; neither its purpose or its identity in the context of the reform. It tried to be all things — its past industrial arts curriculum, the American curriculum (Elements of Technology) and a curriculum influenced by the United Kingdom (Design Studies). As such, it missed the mark and the opportunity to advance this subject grouping. All other nine subject groupings in Technological Studies had been developed, printed, distributed to schools and implemented by 1987. And provincial government elections were nearing.

In the end, there was a change in government at election time—from a Conservative to a Liberal government. The newly elected Liberal provincial government put education under the microscope. In 1989 it published its draft document titled, *Action Plan 1989-94, Restructuring the Education System. A*

Framework for Consultation, Draft. (OME, 1989). This document set into action a restructuring of the Ontario education system:

In the April 1989 Speech from the Throne, the Government announced a major set of initiatives to improve the quality of education in Ontario. These initiatives will restructure the education system into four major components:

- The Early Years (junior and senior kindergarten)
- The Formative Years (grades 1 to 6)
- The Transition Years (grades 7 to 9)
- The Specialization years (grades 10-12)

A priority in the Specialization years will be the revitalization of Technological Education. (OME, 1989, p. 1)

Revitalization meant reform, and reform was no stranger to Technological Studies. Because Technological Studies was intrinsically connected to changing technology in the world outside school, and the jargon at that time was that the world was 'rapidly changing' around us, this subject area had already experienced curriculum revision in 1985-1897 while other subject areas did not. Because of the focus of this reform period on Technological Studies, a consultation process specifically for this subject area—and a name change from Technological Studies to Technological Education—was approved. This process lead to a document titled, *Technological Education: Consultation Paper* (OME, 1990). Together, this document and the *Action Plan* (OME, 1989) paved the path for significant revisions to Technological Education in Ontario.

Alongside these developments, and in an attempt to remedy the situation of a failed curriculum document and to regain public appeal, the organization that represented the industrial arts teachers in Ontario changed their name to Design and Technology. They then proceeded to write a second draft curriculum document titled, *Design and Technology, Draft* (OME, 1989). This document listed the following courses and grades:

- Design and Technology (Grades 7-12)
- Design Studies (Grades 9-12)
- Elements of Technology (Grades 9-12)

With this draft document, the design and technology teachers (new name) attempted to regain a separate place in the curriculum. This second attempt also failed as the draft again was situated itself outside of the Ontario curriculum framework and the Technological Education umbrella. In an attempt to clarify the confused situation of Design and Technology, Hill and Salter (1991) wrote a document titled, *A New Definition for Technological Education in Ontario: A Position.* The authors posited that Design and Technology should be offered in the elementary school curriculum and that its role was to be foundational for Technological Education in the secondary school. In the secondary school curriculum, it should exist within the reform framework, that is, under the umbrella of Technological Education, as one of 10 subject groupings; materials, processes, and design.

TECHNOLOGICAL EDUCATION IN ONTARIO: 1995 REFORM

The *Action Plan* (OME, 1989) outlined a five-year, year-by-year plan. During this time period, Ontario seemed to have a pattern of political party change at election time every five years, and education always seemed to be on the political agenda. This resulted in educational change when government changed. The election cycle saw 1990 as the next election year, so the Liberal Party moved quickly to ensure implementation of the 1989
Action Plan. When an election was called in 1990, the New Democratic Party (NDP) defeated the Liberals with a majority government. To some degree, the NDP continued the initiatives set out in the *Action Plan* and in addition, in May 1993, established a Royal Commission on Learning.
The Commission's report titled, *For the Love of Learning* (OME, 1994) was released after one and a half years of consultation and consolidation of findings. The report suggested a vision and an action plan to guide the reform of elementary and secondary education in Ontario and offered 167 recommendations. Recommendation number 11 in 'Chapter 8: The Learner from Age 6 to 15' (Grades 1 to 9) states:
11. That curriculum guidelines be developed in each subject taught within the common curriculum, to assist teachers in designing programs that will help students achieve the learning outcomes in The Common Curriculum. These guidelines should include concrete suggestions on how teachers can share with parents ways to help their children at home;
(http://www.edu.gov.on.ca/eng/general/abcs/rcom/full/volume2/chapter8.pdf, page 36)
This recommendation put forward the idea that all previous subject guidelines for elementary school education should be compiled into only one curriculum guideline. This recommendation was adopted and lead to one curriculum guideline of 112 pages in length for the elementary school titled, *The Common Curriculum* (OME, 1995a). Another recommendation of the Royal Commission was that elementary school should be from Grades 1 to 9 instead of Grades 1 to 8. In addition, in a section of the report on core subjects, the study of technology in the elementary school was highlighted:
Technology (broad-based)
Like art, broad-based technological studies, which challenge students to apply mathematics and science to materials and processes - to design and develop objects and techniques as ways to solve problems - are extremely important, and it makes good sense to include them in the elementary curriculum, from the early years onward. Broad-based technologies include: communications, construction, technological design, hospitality services, manufacturing, personal services, and transportation.

As part of the core curriculum, technology offers all students the opportunity to apply the problem-solving and reasoning strategies they acquire in math, science, and language to concrete problems of design and use of tools and materials. All students need a basic understanding of how physical materials and processes are produced and applied, and many learn best when they are given frequent opportunities to make the abstract concrete. This is most obvious for young learners (through Grade 6), but even students mature enough to deal with abstraction benefit some very strongly - from testing their knowledge concretely and appropriately.

Students whose way of learning is more spatial than linguistic benefit especially from the inclusion of technological education in the core curriculum. But it is also true that technological education helps to develop literacy skills, in an applied and immediately relevant way, because it requires the student to read manuals, make lists, write requisitions, and give and follow oral and written instructions. (http://www.edu.gov.on.ca/eng/general/abcs/rcom/full/volume2/chapter8.pdf, pages 24-25)

Note in the first paragraph above, that the subject grouping names for broad-based technology that guided the secondary school reform were used for the elementary (primary) school as well. We will return to this point later.

One of the most significant outcomes of the Royal Commission's report was an educational shift from a focus on subject content and some attention to the learner, to a focus on the learner, on student learning and on learning through process instead of learning content. This is evident in the last paragraph of the above quotation and in the title of their report, *For the Love of Learning*. The NDP government based policy and curriculum guideline revisions on research findings, for example, research in learning styles and multiple intelligences and research in student learning and learning theories. This was indeed a new approach to education in Ontario.

At the secondary school level, The Royal Commission's report took into consideration the recommendation of an earlier report by Radwanski (OME, 1987c) to replace streaming (Basic, General and Advance levels) with a "a single and undifferentiated high-quality educational stream for all students". But the Ministry of Education wanted 'destreaming' only in the first and second years of secondary school, that is, Grades 9 and 10. Recommendations 16 to 18 in 'Chapter 9: The Learner from Age 15 to 18' outlines the vision for this change:

16. That secondary school be defined as a three-year program [Grades 10, 11, 12- no Grade 13]…;

17. That only two, not three, differentiated types of courses should exist;

18. That some courses, (to be called Ontario Academic Courses, or OAcCs) be offered with an academic emphasis; that others (to be called Ontario Applied Courses, or OApCs) be offered, with an emphasis on application; and that still others be presented as common courses, blending academic and applied approaches, and with no special designation;

In the early 1990s, while the Royal Commission was conducting its research and the Ministry of Education was engaged in a Consultation Process with educators and the public regarding curriculum reform, the study of technology also was being developed at a grassroots level by educators in collaboration with the Ministry. Boards of Education, not the Ministry of Education, sent teams to Europe to examine how technology was studied in different European countries, from elementary through to secondary school. These individuals returned to their Boards of Education to develop courses and consulted with the Ministry of Education on the curriculum guideline for the study of technology. In a way, it was a time when the technology educators directed the Ministry of Education. While this was an interesting bottom-up experiment, and in some ways refreshing, it was also problematic. Competing special interest groups vied for Ministry of Education attention and the opportunity for input. Politically, the Ministry of Education could not listen to one group over another – it had opened the floodgate and the water entered.

Curriculum revisions in Industrial Arts and Technological Studies have always been more political than other subject areas in Ontario. To name a few reasons, (a) there is an extensive amount of content that could be included in a curriculum but not everything can be included, so there are competing interests, and (b) forces outside of education itself have always attempted to bare influence on this subject area. The late 1980s and early 1990s was a time of political tensions amongst educators of Technological Studies and Industrial Arts, and the Ministry of Education tried to please both sides. In this regard, there seemed to be a lack of strong leadership from the Ministry of Education. What existed was a period of curriculum development that shifted frequently – depending on who was being heard by and had influence over the Ministry at that moment in time. Accordingly, the development of the curriculum guidelines for the study of technology changed frequently and was very unsettled.

In the 1985 curriculum revision, as mentioned earlier, Industrial Arts had been placed within the Technological Studies umbrella and renamed. As mentioned earlier, by 1987 the draft curriculum document for this subject grouping, 'Materials, Processes, and Design', was not approved by the Ministry of Education during the Liberal government. A second attempted draft curriculum document titled, *Design and Technology, Draft* was not approved by the next government either (NDP). It did not align with the NDP government's vision of one elementary school curriculum document, or with the new secondary school document that was envisioned for Broad-based Technological Education.

In the end, the final elementary school curriculum document that was approved by the NDP government titled, *The Common Curriculum* (OME, 1995a), listed only four curricular groupings for content in the elementary school:

- The Arts
- Languages
- Mathematics, Science, and Technology
- Personal and Social Studies: Self and Society

This curriculum guideline outlined all learning outcomes for each of the above curricular groupings. The use of the term learning outcomes instead of goals and objectives was another significant change in the curriculum reform of this period. Learning outcomes were seen as reinforcing a focus on the learner and "observable and/or measurable knowledge, skills, and values that students are expected to have developed at certain key stages of their schooling" (OME, 1995a, p. 9). Key stages were at Grades 3, 6 and 9. Learning outcomes were proclaimed to be the antithesis of goals and objectives that were seen as content driven and focused on teacher intent rather than on student learning.

The section in *The Common Curriculum* (OME, 1995a) for Mathematics, Science, and Technology outlines the purpose of each of these three content areas. For technology, the document states:

In technological education, students develop the ability to use a variety of methods and processes to solve problems. They develop skills in design and fabrication and the use of tools (including the computer), acquire understanding of various technological systems such as manufacturing and agriculture, and learn to evaluate the impact of technology on people and the environment.

Technological education is important for learning in many subject areas and is appropriate at all grade levels. Younger students learn about technology by exploring through play. In later grades, students use technology to solve problems. Activities should involve real-life applications in all subject areas....
(OME, 1995a, p. 71)

One significant result of curricular decisions represented in *The Common Curriculum* was that all elementary school students learned about technology. This required elementary school teachers to teach technology, in addition to the school subjects that they had traditionally taught. In the end, this turned out to be quite problematic because most elementary teachers were female and did not have experience in teaching technology. Ministry of Education documents were drafted (OME, 1992a, 1992b, 1992c, 1994) to shed light on both discussion and policy for the study of technology in elementary schools, and Boards of Education quickly focused on professional development for technology at the elementary school level. This was a very awkward time, as schools had adopted and were implementing the study of technology at the elementary school level before any curriculum guidelines were approved, and in the end, none of the draft documents (OME, 1992a, 1992b, 1992c, 1994) were approved before government changed once again, a discussion that we return to later in this paper.

During the curriculum reform of this period there were also significant changes to secondary school curriculum documents. In Technological Studies, this umbrella term was changed in name to Technological Education, and the previous curriculum guidelines (Parts A, B and C) were replaced with one guideline of 139 pages titled, *Broad-based Technological Education: Grades 10, 11, and 12* (OME, 1995). The focus of this document was on the learner and learning processes at the expense of content; however, the role of Technological Education within these new contexts was still blended with previous workplace concerns:

As "job descriptions" become broader and more general, workers will need to be competent in a number of different areas, and be able and willing to learn about and use new procedures and emerging technologies. In short, workers increasingly need both a commitment to lifelong learning and a variety of "transferable skills" – skills that will allow them to respond to changing conditions by using their existing knowledge and expertise in new ways. (OME, 1995, p. 4)

But this was about the only similarity with the past curriculum guidelines. The new guideline was very different and represented significant changes to the study of technology in secondary schools. For example, it:

- described new names and a new vision for different content areas; these were broad-based –
  - o Communications Technology
  - o Construction Technology
  - o Hospitality Services
  - o Manufacturing Technology
  - o Personal Services
  - o Technological Design
  - o Transportation;
- was almost void of technical content for each of the above content areas;
- focused on invention and other design and production procedures (higher order thinking skills);
- focused on process and technological activities within a problem solving framework;
- focused on interactions between technology, society and the environment;
- focused on common main components, open-ended problem solving and the design process across the seven broad-based technological education content areas;
- was based on the premise that "students may have begun to use some type of design process as early as Junior Kindergarten. All students should be familiar with and understand the process by the time they reach Grade 10" (OME, 1995, p. 9); and
- re-defined secondary school from Grade 10 to Grade 12 with a view to dismantle Grade 13 (OAC).

These significant changes were described as key features in the secondary school curriculum guideline. Key features posited that programs must:

- promote integrated learning. That is, they should help students to see how their learning in one area is connected to their learning in another and to conditions in the real world...

- emphasize problem solving, with a focus on problems that lend themselves to more than one type of solution, or that may require novel types of solutions. Through this type of "open-ended" problem solving, students gain valuable experience in identifying, analysing, defining, and solving many different types of problems. The "open-ended" aspect is important to reflect conditions in the real world, where the problems students are likely to encounter will not always be clear-cut...
- emphasize the process of problem solving as well as the product or solution. In order to solve problems, students must use a number of basic problem-solving techniques. Taken together, these techniques add up to a "process" that can be used consistently to find solutions to many different types of problems. The ability to use a particular process or group of techniques to solve problems is a valuable "transferable skill" – one that can be used in many different situations and for a variety of purposes...
- use projects, and the activities and tasks required to complete them, as the primary means through which students learn the subject matter and reach the expected outcomes for the course or program...
- emphasize learning by doing. That is, the students should acquire knowledge and skills primarily through doing the specific tasks required to complete a project, rather than from texts or teacher instruction. Students understand concepts and procedures more readily when they encounter them first through concrete examples.
- emphasize independent and small-group learning activities. Programs that use this approach are called "student centered". The purpose of using a student-centered format... (pp. 5-6)

In addition to the key features, the new curriculum guideline outlined three main components of Broad-based Technological Education: "physical products, human processes, and environmental systems. Each of these areas must be studied within the framework of the ten concepts used in technological education.... As well, the teaching-learning approaches employed must emphasize open-ended problem solving and the use of a variety of design processes" (OME, 1995, p. 7). The focus on human processes, environmental systems and the impact of technology on society and the environment fundamentally shifted the philosophical underpinnings of Technological Education in Ontario. Hill (1994, 1997) described this shift as one from realism to pragmatism and reconstructionism. In addition to philosophical shifts, the framework of the curriculum shifted as well. This framework was based on ten concepts. They were:

1. Structure
The essential physical or conceptual parts of a product, process, or system, including the way in which the parts are constructed or organized.
2. Material
The substance or information from which the structure is made.

3. Fabrication
The act or process of forming and assembling materials and structures.
4. Mechanism
The parts of a structure that allow it to work or function.
5. Power and energy
The resource that enables a mechanism to perform work.
6. Controls
The means by which a mechanism is activated and regulated.
7. Systems
Combinations of interrelated parts (structures and/or mechanisms) that make up a whole and that may be connected with other systems.
8. Function
The use for which a product, process, or system is developed.
9. Aesthetics
The aspects of a product, process, or system that make it pleasing to the human senses.
10. Ergonomics
The aspects of a product, process, or system that allow people to use it efficiently – that is, with minimal waste of time or energy. (OME, 1995, p. 8)

While the use of a variety of design processes was encouraged, this curriculum guideline provided a five-step design process model: (1) Developing a Focus; (2) Developing a Framework; (3) Choosing the Best Solution, (4) Implementing a Plan; and (5) Reflecting on the Process and Product (see OME, 1995, pp. 9-10). The guideline also stated that:
A design process includes all the stages in the development of a product or process. Designing is not necessarily a linear activity, however, but may require the student to reformulate or restate the problem, or revise the plan for solving it, or both. Although the process may have distinct stages, those stages will not necessarily be followed in a rigid sequence. (p. 9)

Ontario had adopted an understanding of design process as the entire design loop – in brief, seen as design, production and testing – that was non-linear in nature and practice. The relationship between problem-solving and design was described as follows: "design processes are used as a problem-solving model in all technological education programs" (OME, 1995, p. 9). As such, problem-solving was the umbrella under which design was one method.
As this new curriculum was implemented in Ontario, many design and technology teachers began teaching Broad-based Technological Education (especially Technological Design). Many of these teachers implemented design as a fairly rigid process with teacher selected projects. Here, students produced variations on a teacher-made design brief. This understanding and practice was based on past draft documents; documents that had not been approved by the Ministry of Education of several governments. The spirit of the new Broad-based

Technological Education curriculum was quite different than teacher assigned design briefs.

Research was conducted to document how some schools were implementing the new curriculum and incorporating the societal and environmental concerns into problem-solving and projects at the secondary school level. Hill (1998) reported on case study research in Ontario where Broad-based Technological Education classrooms adopted problem-solving in real-world contexts. Lewis, Petrina and Hill (1998) posited taking problem solving one step further to involve students in problem posing first. To examine both of these approaches, problem posing and problem solving, enacted in an Ontario secondary school, Hill and Smith (1998) conducted research and began to document authentic learning in Technological Education. In this curriculum reform era, Ontario's approach to Technological Education was quite different than countries that developed design and technology curriculum as 'design' and 'make' (for example, England and Wales, and Australia); a curriculum that seemingly separated the mind and hand, while some researchers of these countries supported the opposite (e.g., the work of Richard Kimball). Ontario's curriculum was more similar in nature to that of New Zealand's Technology Education; a curriculum that also was positioned in a framework of problem-solving in real-life contexts.

The philosophical underpinnings of Ontario's new Broad-based Technological Education had shifted this content area in an ambitious and significant way. The Ministry of Education realized that financial support was needed to create learning environments in schools to support the new curriculum. Therefore, a special fund of 60 million dollars (Technological Education Program Equipment Renewal Fund - TEPERF) was established to assist schools in renewing their programs and classroom equipment to align with the new curriculum. To receive TEPERF, schools had to contribute matching funds for facilities renovation.

While the implementation of Broad-based Technological Education was somewhat successful, over time cracks began to show. The new curriculum document focused on process not content. As a result, many teachers floundered for technical content upon which to base the process. In this curriculum reform and with TEPERF, professional development for teachers had not been part of the reform and renewal processes, and as such, some teachers referred to past documents for assistance in identifying content information. This situation resulted in many diversions from the intended curriculum. But diversion from the intended curriculum was prevalent across all content areas at both the elementary and secondary school levels. In the end, the substantial changes in school policy and curriculum without professional development and without additional funding (except for TEPERF) left school teachers and the Ontario school system confused and exhausted. In addition, just as Ontario's new curriculum framework and guidelines officially entered the school systems in 1995, Ontario held elections.

TECHNOLOGICAL EDUCATION IN ONTARIO: 1999/2000

In the election campaign of 1995, the leader of the Conservative Party made educational reform a priority. The Conservative Party won the election with a majority government and education underwent significant reform once again. This government immediately began reform by returning elementary school to Grades 1 to 8, secondary school to Grades 9 to 12 and by producing a plan to phase out Grade 13 (OAC). They also returned to a subject-based approach to curriculum and returned to the idea of curriculum documents for each subject area at both the elementary and secondary school levels. The focus of this curriculum reform era shifted from the learner and what research found about student learning, to a focus on content for each subject and on progression of each subject in a grade-by-grade approach. This was a government that adopted the international testing movement. It advocated back-to-the basics and implemented provincial testing in language arts and mathematics at Grades 3 and 6, and an English literacy test in Grade 10. This latter was required for high school graduation. It also focused on teacher and school accountability, student assessment and evaluation, learning expectations (instead of outcomes), parental involvement in the school system, a curriculum reform process that would produce new curriculum policy documents (not guidelines – a significant semantic difference) and a plan for a five-year curriculum revision cycle for the policy documents they were to produce.

In this reform, curriculum policy documents for elementary schools were developed first. They were released from 1997 to 1998. The curriculum policy documents for secondary schools were developed thereafter, and released from 1999 to 2000. The study of technology at the elementary school level was included in the policy document titled, *The Ontario Curriculum, Grades 1-8. Science and Technology* (MOE, 1998). Graham Orpwood of York University, Ontario and this author wrote the introductory sections of the document. Here, technology was described as including:

…much more than the knowledge and skills related to computers and their applications. Technology is both a form of knowledge that uses concepts and skills from other disciplines (including science) and the application of this knowledge to meet an identified need or solve a specific problem using materials, energy, and tools (including computers). The method of technology consists of inventing or modifying devices, structures, systems, or processes. (p. 3)

Further,

Technology is also "a way of knowing" and a process of exploration and experimentation. Technological investigation involves the application of methods known as design processes, which in turn involve the use of concepts and procedures such as the identification of a need or problem and the selection of a best solution. (p. 4)

This document also posited that "students see science and technology in this wider context, social and economic [sic] – as endeavours with important consequences for people – and that they learn to relate their knowledge of science and technology to the world beyond the school" (p. 4).

This policy document also described goals for science and technology in Grades 1 to 8 and a framework of strands and topics for content organization.

The goals are intended to ensure that all students acquire a basic scientific literacy and technological capability before entering secondary school. The goals for students are:

- to understand the basic concepts of science and technology;
- to develop the skills, strategies, and habits of mind required for scientific inquiry and technological design; and
- to relate scientific and technological knowledge to each other and to the world outside the school. (p. 4)

This progression of content, grade-by-grade, was repeated in all other curriculum policy documents for Grades 1 to 8 (The Arts, French, Health and Physical Education, Language, Mathematics, Native Languages, Social Studies, and History and Geography).

As schools began to implement this new curriculum, researchers (Hill & Anning, 2001a, 2001b) were concerned that elementary school level technological design, within a science and technology framework, was not connected to the world outside school with regard to contexts for design activities and the design process that was used. Hill and Anning (2001a, 2001b) found that school technological design was quite independent of how designers in the real world carried out this creative activity, and that teacher-designated design tasks and design process were generally quite rigid. Welch and Lim (2000) found that novice untutored Grade 7 students had varied ways to go about design and brought to class tacit design knowledge. Thus, they cautioned teachers about the use of rigid design process models. Other researchers (Gardner & Hill, 1995 a, 1995b) were concerned that technology would be subsumed by science and understood as science. In the end, for the most part, the study of technology in Ontario elementary schools has been subsumed by science. This is not surprising as science is the comfort zone of most elementary school teachers, technology was a new component of the curriculum and once again professional development was not part of the reform process for the new policy documents.

At the secondary school level, two curriculum policy documents were created during this reform era. One policy document was for Grades 9 and 10 (MOE, 1999) and the other was for Grades 11 and 12 (MOE, 2000). Each of these two documents, once again, represented significant changes for Technological Education but at the same time retained the idea of Broad-based Technology courses in Grades 10-12. Key changes were:

- the creation of an introductory course for Technological Education in Grade 9 named Integrated Technologies that would be taught by teachers with any one of the seven Broad-based Technology teacher qualifications;
- Computer Studies was placed under the Technological Education curriculum umbrella – Technological Education policy

documents now consisted of Integrated Technologies, Broad-based Technology and Computer Science, but entry to teacher education programs and teacher qualifications for each were different;

- a shift from a focus on process and student learning;
- a renewed curricular focus on content with expectations of what students will know or be able to do at the end of each course
- a shift from learning outcomes to learning expectations;
- a focus on teacher accountability and student assessment and evaluation and to this end, the adoption of the use of a four-level rubric as the preferred instrument of assessment;
- a return to a more traditional understanding of the Broad-based Technologies, described in course expectations (this has resulted in fewer non-traditional female students in both teacher education and secondary school programs);
- a transfer of some past Technological Education course into Computer Studies;
- a return to the concept of 'streaming' in Grades 11 and 12, now renamed Destinations instead of Levels, with three Destinations – Workplace, College, University/College;
- a retention of the idea of 'Open' courses in Grades 9 and 10; and
- a curriculum framework for all Technological Education courses, from Grade 9 to Grade 12, that retained the ten technological concepts but added the three stands for the organization of expectations – (1) Theory and Foundations, (2) Skills and Processes, and (3) Impact and Consequences.

Both curriculum policy documents, *The Ontario Curriculum, Grades 9 and 10. Technological Education* (MOE, 1999) and *The Ontario Curriculum, Grades 11 and 12. Technological Education* (MOE, 2000), similarly describe the place of Technological Education in the curriculum:

The power of technology, its pervasiveness, and its continual advances demand a rigorous curriculum and the commitment of educators to understand it, promote its responsible use, and enable students to become problem solvers who are self-sufficient, entrepreneurial, and technologically literate. Students must acquire the technological skills and knowledge required to participate in a competitive, global economy. They must become critical and innovative thinkers, able to question, understand, and respond to the implications of technological innovation, as well as to find solutions and develop products.

Technological education focuses on developing students' ability to work creatively and competently with technologies that are central to their lives. Their development as technologically literate individuals throughout elementary and secondary school enhances their success in postsecondary studies and in the workplace....

Technological education promotes the integration of learning across subject disciplines...Similarly, technology supports students' work in other subjects. It develops research skills, supports development in literacy and mathematics, and fosters creativity, critical thinking, and problem solving. In addition, it promotes global citizenship and environmental awareness.

Technological education contributes to learning in other areas of the curriculum by providing practical contexts and applications for the knowledge and skills acquired...(OME, 1999, pp. 2-3; OME, 2000, pp. 3-4)

In addition, both of these new curriculum policy documents kept course organization around seven Broad-based Technologies, but some names were changed:

- Communications Technology
- Construction Technology
- Health and Personal Services
- Hospitality and Tourism
- Manufacturing Technology
- Technological Design
- Transportation

Both documents used expectations to detail course content. Expectations "describe the knowledge and skills that students are expected to develop and demonstrate in their class work, on tests, and in various other activities on which their achievement is assessed and evaluated" (OME, 1999, p. 6; OME, 2000, p. 12). In both documents, the curricular framework changed. While the framework kept the ten technological concepts from the previous curriculum guideline, strands were added to the framework to organize expectations. There were three strands:

Theory and foundation. The key ideas about concepts, components and systems, materials, services, and products.

Skills and processes. The technological skills and processes required for responding to a variety of practical challenges.

Impact and consequences. Safety-related issues, career opportunities, and the implications of technology. (OME, 1999, p. 7; OME, 2000, p. 13)

Both of the new curriculum policy documents continued the educational approach of the past curriculum guideline; a focus that was student-centered, activity-based, and project-driven. "The philosophy that underlies the teaching of broad-based technology is that students learn best by doing. The curriculum in this area takes an activity-based, project-driven approach to learning that provides students with knowledge, skills, and experiences..." (OME, 1999, p. 4; OME, 2000, p. 5). The documents also describe teaching approaches:

Technological education involves knowing, doing, testing, designing and building, and evaluating. Teaching and learning approaches should address all of these areas. Students should use projects as a major means of achieving these expectations, and they should be provided with a combination of information and experience that will prepare them to make informed choices about the use of

153

various technologies, to use technology wisely and well, and to solve technological problems. Students will be involved in:

- investigating technological products, systems, and processes;
- gaining knowledge of the principles and processes of technology;
- exploring needs that can be met through technology;
- creating and evaluating alternatives and modifications in relation to these needs;
- developing safe and efficient work habits;
- making products that satisfy defined specifications and standards of quality and safety;
- making connections between technology and society (past, present, and future);
- assessing related career opportunities and requirements;
- developing confidence to contribute to a technological society. (MOE, 1999, p. 6; OME, 2000, p. 12)

The curriculum described above for this reform era made some effort to inform curriculum on research findings about student learning, and cognitive and higher order thinking domains situated in problem solving processes. However, the main focus was on the reintroduction of the psychomotor domain – technical skills and knowledge, within a problem solving context. As mentioned earlier in this paper, the lack of technical content in the past curriculum document was problematic for teachers and programs, and the Conservative government lost no time acting on this information. It fit their agenda to use Technological Education to focus on skills shortages rather than on the educational benefits of this content area. The new curriculum policy documents also supported varied avenues for course delivery:

courses that emphasize a particular area or that exceed 110 hours of scheduled instructional time to allow students to prepare for certification, apprenticeship programs, or school-work transition programs, the content and the skills and processes related to the area of emphasis and/or the additional practice should reflect current industry practices and standards. (OME, 2000, p. 7)

Research during this curricular period was conducted and found educational support for Technological Education within the secondary school educational system. Hill (1999) documented that linking the world in school to the world outside school through community-based projects created relevant learning environments for students and that these opportunities benefited students in positive ways. Hill and Smith (In press, a) further articulated their theory of authentic learning that emerged from research in Technological Education classrooms in Ontario. Smith, Hill, Lang, Sinnott, & Zigman (2004) provided classroom detail for authentic learning. This research also has caught the attention of science educators (Hill & Smith, in press, b), and as such, provides an example where research in Technological Education contributes to science education. Other research (Elshof, 2003) has focused on issues of teacher's views of sustainability within the Technological Education curriculum and their own practice.

TECHNOLOGICAL EDUCATION IN ONTARIO IN 2005 AND THE FUTURE

All curricula from the 1999/2000 reform have now been in place for 5 to 6 years. During this time, Ontario has once again changed government, electing a Liberal government in 2003. This Liberal government also made education part of its election platform, but has wisely kept the curriculum policy documents and the five-year cycle plan for revision of the previous government. As such, the Technological Education policy documents are in line for the revision process in 2005.

In addition to research conduced by researchers in Technological Education, social scientists (e.g., the work of Allen King) have documented the overall impact of the 1999/2000 curricular reform. Generally, all curricula, not just Technological Education, have been found to be heavily charged with content, and that:
students are struggling. Recent research by Professor Alan King of Queen's University estimates that, of those students who began Grade 9 in Ontario in 1999, at least 25 per cent (40,000 students) will leave school without graduating. Students enrolled in the Grade 9 Applied Math program continue to struggle. The 2002-2003 province wide Grade 9 math assessments reveal that about 20 per cent of students in the Applied program met the provincial standard. Other research indicates that youth who drop out have reading skills that average a full level below those who stay in school or graduate. (MOE, 2004, April 29)

To address the problem of school retention, a Ministry of Education news release of June 8, 2004 posited:
Minister of Education Gerard Kennedy today announced a new consolidated program to lower drop-out rates in Ontario high schools. Under the Student Success program, curriculum issues will be fixed, technical education programs will be improved and additional alternatives will be provided for struggling students.
"Ontario needs every high school student to get a good outcome from their public education," said Kennedy. "By making sure that struggling students get the help they need, we'll keep more kids in school and better prepare them for their future, whether that be college, university or the workforce."
Today's announcement is the first step in creating a new role for public high schools. Success for students will move beyond college and university to include apprenticeships and skilled job placements. Future steps include raising the school leaving age to 18 and creating an alternative diploma combining work experience and academic accomplishment. (MOE, 2004, June 8)

This same news release describes the Student Success program:
The student success program is the first installment for a new role for publicly funded education. The first phase of the program will be targeted at creating new

opportunities for student success -- whether that is an apprenticeship, a job placement with skills or college or university. Success will go beyond traditional academic achievement and include excellence in alternative high school programs. The result will be fewer students dropping out, less uncertainty about career choices and more meaningful outcomes for every student. Future phases of the program will include raising the school leaving age to 18 and creating an alternative diploma combining work experience and academic accomplishment.

It continues, and highlights Technological Education:

To ensure that students are properly prepared for the workforce, the government is investing $20 million – an increase of $12 million – to update dilapidated high school technology so that students are training with appropriate equipment. This is for students in technological education and vocational programs including: construction, health and personal services, hospitality and tourism, manufacturing and transportation.

The concern about student retention has significant implications for Technological Education. Ontario has had a blended approach to Technological Education curriculum over the past two decades, that is, both academic and vocational in nature. Its role has been seen as a program that: responds to multiple ways of student knowing and learning and that offers alternative learning environments; attracts students with varied goals – from continuing on to university, to going immediately to work after secondary school; and meets the needs of students who are at risk of not completing secondary school.

Recent research, presently being written for publication, has found that enrolment in Workplace destination courses in Ontario is very low. Most students, who enroll in Technological Education in Ontario, enroll in the College or University/College destination courses (Dr. Allen King, personal communication, March 2005). This is a very interesting turn of events for Technological Education. It is anticipated that these findings will bring with them recommendations for pilot projects where secondary school in Ontario can be completed in a college environment, not only in a secondary school environment. The logic is that if a secondary school is not conducive to learning for students who have been labeled at-risk, then learning environments outside of secondary schools could assist these students to graduate and to continue on to further education. Presently, adult learning centers exist for this purpose, but their curriculum does not articulate with that of college programs.

A recent policy report outlining recommendations for postsecondary education in Ontario (Rae, 2005) stated the following:

High School Credits
More boldly, a pilot program should be established to give selected colleges authority and funding to offer high school credits and diplomas to students who want to complete their high school diploma in a college environment, with a vocational focus and a direct link to further college study. (p. 46)

This report was submitted to the Premier of Ontario and to the Minister of Training, Colleges and Universities. It is expected to be influential. Such recommendations, if widely adopted, could result in lower enrolment in secondary school Technological Education Programs and the need for fewer teachers, or it could change the nature of Technological Education in the secondary school environment. Because Technological Education is an elective course in secondary schools and not a requirement for graduation, enrolment is always a key concern.

Finally, the existing Grades 1 to 8 Science and Technology and Grades 9 to 12 Technological Education curriculum policy documents are presently in the five-year cycle plan for revision. The first stage of the revision plan is the authoring of research papers upon which to base future decisions and curricula. The present government requires that policy and decisions be informed by research and evidence. This author has been contracted to write the research paper for Technological Education, Grades 9 to 12. Findings from this research will be combined and analysed within an Ontario context to generate the research paper and to provide recommendations for revisions to Ontario's Technological Education curriculum, a curriculum that will serve the next five years.

REFERENCES

Elshof, L. (2003). Teacher's interpretation of sustainable development. In J. R. Dakers & M. J. de Vries (Eds.), *Pupils Attitudes toward technology: Thirteenth international conference on design and technology* (pp. 45-51). Glasgow, UK: University of Glasgow Faculty of Education. see http://www.iteawww.org/PATT13/PATT13.pdf.

Gardner, P. & Hill, A.M. (1999a). Technology education in Ontario: Evolution, achievements, critique and challenges. Part 1. *International Journal of Technology and Design Education, 9*, 103-136.

Gardner, P. & Hill, A.M. (1999b). Technology education in Ontario: Evolution, achievements, critique and challenges. Part 2. *International Journal of Technology and Design Education, 9*, 201-239.

Hill, A.M. (1994). Perspectives on philosophical shifts in vocational education: From realism to pragmatism and reconstructionism. *Journal of Vocational and Technical Education*, 10(2), 37-45.

Hill, A.M. (1997). Reconstructionism in technology education. *International Journal of Technology and Design Education* , 7(1-2), 121-139.

Hill, A.M. (1998). Problem solving in real-life contexts: Alternatives for design in technology education. *International Journal of Technology and Design Education, 8*(3), 203-220.

Hill, A.M. (1999). Community-based projects in technology education: An approach for relevant learning. In W.E. Theuerkauf, & M.J. Dyrenfurth (Eds.), *International perspectives on technological education: Outcomes and futures* (pp.285-298). Braunschweig/Ames.

Hill, A.M. (2003). Technology and its study in Canadian secondary schools. *Canadian Journal of Science, Mathematics, and Technology Education, Special Issue on Technology Education, (3)*1, 5-16.

Hill, A.M., & Anning, A. (2001a). Comparisons and contrasts between elementary/primary 'school situated design' and 'workplace design' in Canada and England. *International Journal of Technology and Design Education, 11(2)*, 111-136.

Hill, A.M. & Anning, A. (2001b). Elementary/primary teachers' and students' understanding of 'school situated design' in Canada and England. *Research in Science Education. Special Issue, 31*, 117-135.

Hill, A.M., & Salter, H. (1991). *A new definition for technological education in Ontario. A position.* Kingston, ON: Faculty of Education, Queen's University.

Hill, A.M., & Smith, H.A. (1998). Practice meets theory in technological education: A case of authentic learning in the high school setting. *Journal of Technology Education, 9*(1), 29-41. http://scholar.lib.vt.edu/ejournals/JTE/v9n2/hill.html.

Hill, A. M., & Smith, H. A. (In press, a). Many paths to meaning: Research support for the study of technology in secondary school curriculum, *International Journal of Technology and Design Education.*

Hill, A. M., & Smith, H. A. (In press, b). Problem-based contextualized learning. In S. Alsop, L.Bencze, & E. Pedretti (Eds.), *Analysing exemplary science teaching: Theoretical lenses and a spectrum of possibilities for education* (pp. 136-145, plus references. 15 pages). Maidenhead, UK: Open University Press.

Lewis, T., Petrina, S., & Hill, A.M. (1998). Problem posing—Adding a creative increment to technological problem solving. *Journal of Industrial Teacher Education, 36*(1), 6-36.

Ontario Ministry of Education. (1962). *Curriculum RP-35 (occupational, practical subjects), 1962.* Toronto, ON: Queen's Printer for Ontario.

Ontario Ministry of Education. (1963a). *Technical subjects RP-27, 1963.* Toronto, ON: Queen's Printer for Ontario.

Ontario Ministry of Education. (1963b). *Curriculum industrial arts, 1.19 and S19, 1963.* Toronto, ON: Queen's Printer for Ontario.

Ontario Ministry of Education. (1984). *Ontario schools: Intermediate and senior divisions* (OS:IS). Toronto, ON: Queen's Printer for Ontario.

Ontario Ministry of Education. (1985a). *Technological studies intermediate and senior divisions. part A: policy for program planning.* Toronto, ON: Queen's Printer for Ontario.

Ontario Ministry of Education. (1985b). *Technological Studies Intermediate and Senior Divisions. part B: 3. electrical Grouping.* Toronto, ON: Queen's Printer for Ontario.

Ontario Ministry of Education. (1986a). *Technological studies intermediate and senior divisions. part B: 1. transportation grouping.* Toronto, ON: Queen's Printer for Ontario.

Ontario Ministry of Education. (1986b). *Technological Studies Intermediate and Senior Divisions. part B:2. construction Grouping.* Toronto, ON: Queen's Printer for Ontario.

Ontario Ministry of Education. (1986c). *Technological studies intermediate and senior divisions. part B: 4. food services grouping.* Toronto, ON: Queen's Printer for Ontario.

Ontario Ministry of Education. (1986d). *Technological studies intermediate and senior divisions. part B: 5. graphics Grouping.* Toronto, ON: Queen's Printer for Ontario.

Ontario Ministry of Education. (1986e). *Technological studies intermediate and senior divisions. part B: 8. manufacturing grouping.* Toronto, ON: Queen's Printer for Ontario.

Ontario Ministry of Education. (1986f). *Technological studies intermediate and senior divisions. part B: 9. Personal Services Grouping.* Toronto, ON: Queen's Printer for Ontario.

Ontario Ministry of Education. (1986g). *Technological studies intermediate and senior divisions. Part B: 10. Textiles Grouping.* Toronto, ON: Queen's Printer for Ontario.

Ontario Ministry of Education. (1987a). *Technological studies intermediate and senior divisions. part B: 7. horticultural grouping.* Toronto, ON: Queen's Printer for Ontario.

Ontario Ministry of Education. (1987b). *Technological studies intermediate and senior divisions. part C: Ontario academic courses.* Toronto, ON: Queen's Printer for Ontario.

Ontario Ministry of Education. (1987c). *Ontario study of the relevance of education, and the issue of dropouts.* Prepared by George Radwanski. Toronto,ON: Queens Printer for Ontario.

Ontario Ministry of Education. (1989). *Action plan 1989-94, Restructuring the education system. A framework for consultation. Draft.* Toronto, ON: Author.

Ontario Ministry of Education. (1992a). *Technological education. Early years to specialization years. Internal discussion paper. Draft.* Toronto, ON: Author.

Ontario Ministry of Education. (1992b). *Support document, design processes in technology. Draft excerpts preview document.* Toronto, ON: Author.

Ontario Ministry of Education. (1992c). *Curriculum guideline, design processes in technology. draft preview document.* Toronto, ON: Author.

Ontario Ministry of Education. (1994). *Technological education: A policy overview for technological education, JK to Graduation. Draft.* Toronto, ON: Author.

Ontario Ministry of Education. (1995). *For the love of learning. Report of the royal commission on learning.* Toronto, ON: Queen's Printer for Ontario.
http://www.edu.gov.on.ca/eng/general/abcs/rcom/full/index.html

Ontario Ministry of Education and Training. (1995a). *The Common Curriculum. Policies and Outcomes. Grades 1-9.* Toronto, ON: Queen's Printer for Ontario.

Ontario Ministry of Education and Training. (1995b). *Broad-based technological education. Grades 10, 11, and 12, 1995.* Toronto, ON: Queen's Printer for Ontario. http://www.edu.gov.on.ca/eng/document/curricul/bbtech/b-beng.html]

Ontario Ministry of Education. (1998). *The Ontario curriculum, grades 1-8. Science and technology.* Toronto, ON: Queen's Printer for Ontario. http://www.edu.gov.on.ca/eng/document/curricul/scientec/scientec.html

Ontario Ministry of Education. (1999). *The Ontario curriculum, grades 9 and 10. Technological education.* Toronto, ON: Queen's Printer for Ontario. [see http://www.edu.gov.on.ca/eng/document/curricul/secondary/techno/techful.html]

Ontario Ministry of Education. (2000). *The Ontario curriculum, grades 11 and 12. Technological education.* Toronto, ON: Queen's Printer for Ontario. http://www.edu.gov.on.ca/eng/document/curricul/secondary/grade1112/tech/tech.html

Ontario Ministry of Education. (2004, April 29). Building the Ontario education advantage: student achievement. *Ontario Education. Excellence for All*, v.3. Toronto, ON: Author. http://www.edu.gov.on.ca/eng/document/nr/04.03/building.pdf

Ontario Ministry of Education. (2004, June 8). *Struggling high school students get new bridge to success.* http://ogov.newswire.ca/ontario/GONE/2004/06/08/c2345.html?lmatch=&lang=_e.html]

Rae, B. (2005). *Ontario: A leader in learning. Report & recommendations.* Toronto, ON: Queen's Printer for Ontario. http://www.raereview.on.ca/en/report/default.asp?loc1=report

Smith, H. A., Hill, A. M., Lang, J., Sinnott, J., & Zigman, J. (2004, May). *Many paths to meaning: A close look at authentic learning.* Symposium presented at the meeting of the Canadian Society for the Study of Education, Winnipeg, MB.

Welch, M., & Lim, H. S. (2000). The strategic thinking of novice designers: Discontinuity between theory and practice. *The Journal of Technology Education*, 26(1). http://scholar.lib.vt.edu/ejournals/JOTS/Summer-Fall-2000/welch.html

APPENDIX A

Appendix Courses in Technological Studies (by Subject Grouping)

*Courses identified with this symbol will continue for the time being to be based in part on existing Senior Division guidelines, such as the *Elements of Technology* series and particular Grade 11 and 12 outlines in *Technical Subjects RP-27, 1963.*

Course	Div	Approved Course Levels			Course Code
1. Transportation Grouping	Automotive Mechanics	Int	Basic	General	Advanced	TAM
	Automotive Mechanics*	Sr	Basic	General	Advanced	TAM
	Auto Body Repair	Int	Basic	General		TAB
	Auto Body Repair*	Sr	Basic	General		TAB
	Small Engines	Int	Basic	General		TAE
	Small Engines*	Sr	Basic	General		TAE
	Service Station Attendant	Int	Basic			TAS
	Service Station Attendant	Sr	Basic			TAS
	Agricultural Equipment Servicing	Int	Basic	General		TAG
	Agricultural Equipment Servicing	Sr	Basic	General		TAG
2. Construction Grouping	Woodwork	Int	Basic	General	Advanced	TCW
	Construction Technology*	Sr	Basic	General	Advanced	TCY
	Carpentry*	Sr	Basic	General		TCC
	Industrial Woodwork*	Sr	Basic	General		TML
	Masonry and Trowel Trades	Int	Basic	General		TCT
	Masonry and Trowel Trades	Sr	Basic	General		TCT
	Heating, Refrigeration, and Air Conditioning	Int	Basic	General	Advanced	TCH
	Heating, Refrigeration, and Air Conditioning*	Sr	Basic	General	Advanced	TCH
	Plumbing and Pipefitting	Int	Basic	General		TCP
	Plumbing and Pipefitting*	Sr	Basic	General		TCP
	Building and Equipment Maintenance	Int	Basic	General		TCM
	Building and Equipment Maintenance	Sr	Basic	General		TCM
	Custodial Services	Int	Basic			TCS
	Custodial Services	Sr	Basic			TCS
	Painting and Decorating	Int	Basic	General		TCD
	Painting and Decorating	Sr	Basic	General		TCD

	Course	Div	Approved Course Levels			Course Code
3. Electrical Grouping	Applied Electricity	Int	Basic	General	Advanced	TEA
	Electrical Technology*	Sr	Basic	General	Advanced	TEY
	Electronics	Int		General	Advanced	TEL
	Electronics*	Sr		General	Advanced	TEL
	Electrical Appliance Repair	Int	Basic	General		TER
	Electrical Appliance Repair	Sr	Basic	General		TER
	Computer Technology*	Sr		General	Advanced	TEC
4. Food Services Grouping	Baking	Int	Basic	General		TFB
	Baking	Sr	Basic	General		TFB
	Food Preparation — Commercial	Int	Basic	General		TFC
	Food Preparation — Commercial	Sr	Basic	General		TFC
	Food Preparation — Domestic	Int	Basic	General		TFD
	Food Preparation — Domestic	Sr	Basic	General		TFD
	Restaurant Services	Int	Basic	General		TFR
	Restaurant Services	Sr	Basic	General		TFR
5. Graphics Grouping	Drafting	Int	Basic	General	Advanced	TDR
	Drafting — Architectural*	Sr		General	Advanced	TDA
	Drafting — Electrical*	Sr		General	Advanced	TDE
	Drafting — Mechanical*	Sr		General	Advanced	TDM
	Drafting — Comprehensive*	Sr	Basic	General	Advanced	TDG
	Blueprint Reading and Sketching	Int	Basic	General	Advanced	TDB
	Blueprint Reading and Sketching	Sr	Basic	General	Advanced	TDB
	Graphic Communications	Int	Basic	General	Advanced	TGR
	Graphic Communications*	Sr	Basic	General	Advanced	TGR
	Photography	Int	Basic	General	Advanced	TGP
	Photography	Sr	Basic	General	Advanced	TGP
	Vocational Art*	Int	Basic	General	Advanced	TGV
	Vocational Art*	Sr	Basic	General	Advanced	TGV

	Course	Div	Approved Course Levels			Course Code
6. Horticulture Grouping	General Horticulture	Int	Basic	General	Advanced	THO
	General Horticulture	Sr	Basic	General	Advanced	THO
	Landscape Design and Maintenance	Int	Basic	General		THL
	Landscape Design and Maintenance	Sr	Basic	General		THL
	Nursery Production	Int	Basic	General		THN
	Nursery Production	Sr	Basic	General		THN
	Greenhouse Production	Int	Basic	General		THG
	Greenhouse Production	Sr	Basic	General		THG
	Floral Design	Int	Basic	General		THD
	Floral Design	Sr	Basic	General		THD
7. Materials, Processes, and Design Grouping	Industrial Arts, Grades 7 and 8	Int	----	----	----	----
	Industrial Arts, Grades 9 and 10	Int	Basic	General	Advanced	TIN
	Industrial Arts	Sr	Basic	General	Advanced	TIN
	Design Studies	Int	Basic	General	Advanced	TID
	Design Studies	Sr	Basic	General	Advanced	TID
	Elements of Technology*	Int	Basic	General	Advanced	TIE
	Elements of Technology*	Sr	Basic	General	Advanced	TIE
8. Manufacturing Grouping	Machine Shop Practice	Int	Basic	General	Advanced	TMS
	General Machinist*	Sr	Basic	General	Advanced	TMS
	Millwright*	Sr		General	Advanced	TMM
	Mechanical Technology*	Sr		General	Advanced	TMY
	Sheet Metal Practice	Int	Basic	General	Advanced	TMT
	Sheet Metal Practice*	Sr	Basic	General	Advanced	TMT
	Welding	Int	Basic	General		TMW
	Welding*	Sr	Basic	General		TMW
	Foundry Practice	Int	Basic	General		TMF
	Foundry Practice*	Sr	Basic	General		TMF
	Power Transmission and Control	Int		General	Advanced	TMC
	Industrial Control – Power and Processes*	Sr		General	Advanced	TMC
	Hydraulics and Pneumatics*	Sr		General	Advanced	TMH
	Instrumentation*	Sr		General	Advanced	TMI
	Principles of Technology*	Sr		General	Advanced	TMP

	Course	Div	Approved Course Levels		Course Code
9. Personal Services Grouping	Cosmetology	Int	Basic	General	TPC
	Cosmetology	Sr	Basic	General	TPC
	Guiding and Tourist Services	Int	Basic	General	TPG
	Guiding and Tourist Services	Sr	Basic	General	TPG
	Home Nursing, Child Care, and Health Care Services	Int	Basic	General	TPH
	Home Nursing, Child Care, and Health Care Services	Sr	Basic	General	TPH
10. Textiles Grouping	Sewing and Clothing Construction	Int	Basic	General	TXS
	Sewing and Clothing Construction	Sr	Basic	General	TXS
	Textile Maintenance and Servicing	Int	Basic	General	TXM
	Textile Maintenance and Servicing	Sr	Basic	General	TXM
	Upholstery	Int	Basic	General	TXU
	Upholstery	Sr	Basic	General	TXU

APPENDIX B

Table 1. Strands and Topics: Science and Technology, Grades 1-8				
Strand	**Life Systems**	**Matter and Materials**	**Energy and Control**	**Structures and Mechanisms**	**Earth and Space Systems**
Grade 1	Characteristics and Needs of Living Things	Characteristics of Objects and Properties of Materials	Energy in Our Lives	Everyday Structures	Daily and Seasonal Cycles
Grade 2	Growth and Changes in Animals	Properties of Liquids and Solids	Energy From Wind and Moving Water	Movement	Air and Water in the Environment
Grade 3	Growth and Changes in Plants	Magnetic and Charged Materials	Forces and Movement	Stability	Soils in the Environment
Grade 4	Habitats and Communities	Materials That Transmit, Reflect, or Absorb Light or Sound	Light and Sound Energy	Pulleys and Gears	Rocks, Minerals, and Erosion
Grade 5	Human Organ Systems	Properties of and Changes in Matter	Conservation of Energy	Forces Acting on Structures and Mechanisms	Weather
Grade 6	Diversity of Living Things	Properties of Air and Characteristics of Flight	Electricity	Motion	Space
Grade 7	Interactions Within Ecosystems	Pure Substances and Mixtures	Heat	Structural Strength and Stability	The Earth's Crust
Grade 8	Cells, Tissues, Organs, and Systems	Fluids	Optics	Mechanical Efficiency	Water Systems

Available from http://www.edu.gov.on.ca/eng/document/curricul/scientec/scientec.html

APPENDIX C

Achievement Chart – Grades 11 and 12, Technological Education				
Categories	50-59% (Level 1)	60-69% (Level 2)	70-79% (Level 3)	80-100% (Level 4)
Knowledge/ Understanding	**The student:**			
knowledge of facts, technical terminology, procedures, and standards	demonstrates limited knowledge of facts, technical terminology, procedures, and standards	demonstrates some knowledge of facts, technical terminology, procedures, and standards	demonstrates considerable knowledge of facts, technical terminology, procedures, and standards	demonstrates thorough knowledge of facts, technical terminology, procedures, and standards
understanding of concepts (e.g., uses of computer operating systems)	demonstrates limited understanding of concepts	demonstrates some understanding of concepts	demonstrates considerable understanding of concepts	demonstrates thorough and insightful understanding of concepts
understanding of relationships between concepts (e.g., energy conservation and manufacturing processes)	demonstrates limited understanding of relationships between concepts	demonstrates some understanding of relationships between concepts	demonstrates considerable understanding of relationships between concepts	demonstrates thorough and insightful understanding of relationships between concepts
Thinking/ Inquiry	**The student:**			
thinking skills (e.g., evaluating professional practices and principles)	uses thinking skills with limited effectiveness	uses thinking skills with moderate effectiveness	uses thinking skills with considerable effectiveness	uses thinking skills with a high degree of effectiveness
inquiry/design skills (e.g., identifying the problem; formulating questions; planning; selecting strategies and resources; analysing and interpreting	applies few of the skills involved in an inquiry/design process	applies some of the skills involved in an inquiry/design process	applies most of the skills involved in an inquiry/design process	applies all or almost all of the skills involved in an inquiry/design process

information; forming conclusions)				
Communication	**The student:**			
communication of information (e.g., computer and technical specifications)	communicates information with limited clarity	communicates information with moderate clarity	communicates information with considerable clarity	communicates information with a high degree of clarity, and with confidence
use of language, symbols, and visuals (e.g., computer programming and technical drawing)	uses language, symbols, and visuals with limited accuracy and effectiveness	uses language, symbols, and visuals with some accuracy and effectiveness	uses language, symbols, and visuals with considerable accuracy and effectiveness	uses language, symbols, and visuals with a high degree of accuracy and effectiveness
communication for different audiences and purposes (e.g., tourism, construction)	communicates with a limited sense of audience and purpose	communicates with some sense of audience and purpose	communicates with a clear sense of audience and purpose	communicates with a strong sense of audience and purpose
use of various forms of communication (e.g., presentation software, technical reports)	demonstrates limited command of the various forms	demonstrates moderate command of the various forms	demonstrates considerable command of the various forms	demonstrates extensive command of the various forms
Application	**The student:**			
application of ideas and skills in familiar contexts (e.g., demonstrating good customer service practices)	applies ideas and skills in familiar contexts with limited effectiveness	applies ideas and skills in familiar contexts with moderate effectiveness	applies ideas and skills in familiar contexts with considerable effectiveness	applies ideas and skills in familiar contexts with a high degree of effectiveness
transfer of concepts, skills, and procedures to new contexts (e.g., applying scientific principles to health care and personal services)	transfers concepts, skills, and procedures to new contexts with limited effectiveness	transfers concepts, skills, and procedures to new contexts with moderate effectiveness	transfers concepts, skills, and procedures to new contexts with considerable effectiveness	transfers concepts, skills, and procedures to new contexts with a high degree of effectiveness

application of procedures, equipment, and technology (e.g., use of design instruments, machine and hand tools)	uses procedures, equipment, and technology safely and correctly only with supervision	uses procedures, equipment, and technology safely and correctly with some supervision	uses procedures, equipment, and technology safely and correctly	demonstrates and promotes the safe and correct use of procedures, equipment, and technology
making connections, (e.g., between personal experiences and the subject, between subjects, between subjects and the world outside the school)	makes connections with limited effectiveness	makes connections with moderate effectiveness	makes connections with considerable effectiveness	makes connections with a high degree of effectiveness

Note: A student whose achievement is below 50% at the end of a course will not obtain a credit for the course.

Available from:
http://www.edu.gov.on.ca/eng/document/curricul/secondary/grade1112/tech/tech.html#program

167

APPENDIX D

Prerequisite Charts for Technological Education, Grades 9–12
Part A: Broad-Based Technology

These charts map out all the courses in the discipline and show the links between courses and the possible prerequisites for them. They do not attempt to depict all possible movements from course to course.

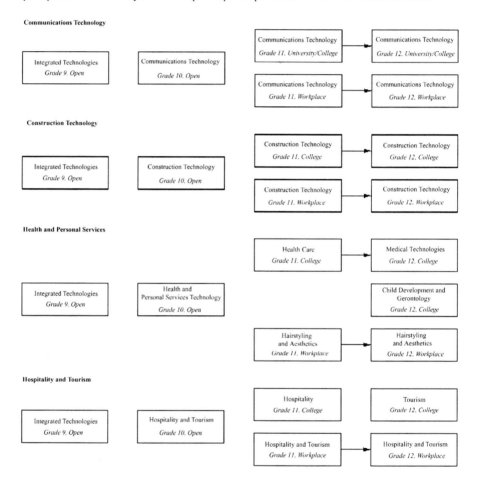

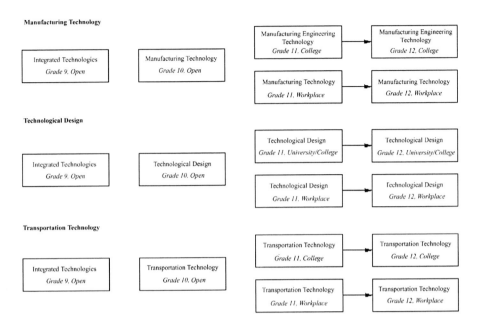

Part B: Computer Studies

These charts map out all the courses in the discipline and show the links between courses and the possible prerequisites for them. They do not attempt to depict all possible movements from course to course.

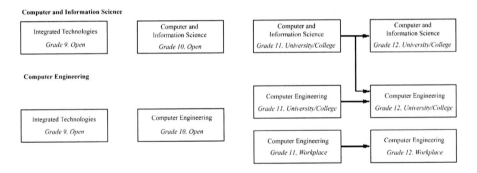

Available from:
http://www.edu.gov.on.ca/eng/document/curricul/secondary/grade1112/tech/tech.html#program

GEORGE J. HACHÉ

12. DEVELOPMENTS IN TECHNOLOGY EDUCATION IN CANADA

HISTORICAL FOUNDATION

There has never been a strong federal presence in promoting a common technology education program as a specific curricular area of study in Canadian k-12 schools and this has been largely due of the non-existence of legislation that would provide for this. The British North of 1867 that separated the powers of Federal and Provincial governments clearly recognized the responsibility for establishing school system as resting with each of the Canadian Provinces (Maton, 2004).

In spite of this, similar curriculum offerings evolved in Canadian schools and by the mid 1960s all Provinces offered similar industrial arts and/or craft type programs. However, when the "technology education movement" surfaced with diverging views on how to best introduce technology into schools, each Province turned to different approaches. Among these, and most notable, were the technology education views of the Canadian pioneer of technology education, Henry Ziel, who precipitated changes in the Province of Alberta schools (Evans, 1998, Fardo, 2005). Although the "Ziel Philosophy" was the focus of much debate, it only influence minor changes in the manner the Province of Prince Edward Island developed their Technology Education Program. The Province of Ontario adapted a British style design-technology program and the American based "Material and Manufacturing" style of technology education became the focus for inclusion in New Brunswick middle schools. The other Provinces were slower in adopting changes. Throughout the 70s and 80s other Provinces generally endorsed the name of Technology Education, or some derivation of it, but continued to offer Industrial Arts programs with minor technological enhancing modification. Those Provinces that had Vocational Education like offering for their senior high schools generally retained their programs.

INFLUENCES THAT PROMOTED TECHNOLOGY OFFERINGS IN SCHOOLS

A need to offer more technology to young Canadians, though school activity, became apparent throughout the 80s and the decades that followed. The type of technology, and the manner in which it was incorporated in schools, was largely mitigated by local budgets and the availability of teachers qualified as technology teachers (Hache and Sharpe, 1992). More importantly, and by the mid 1980s, a new movement had materialized to over shadow the slow changes occurring within the organized Technology Education models that existed in each of the Provinces.

M.J. de Vries, I. Mottier (eds.), International Handbook of Technology Education, 171–177.
© 2006 Sense Publishers. All rights reserved.

Computers, and their allied components, were introduced into school subjects and quickly became perceived as the type of technology most needed, largely underpinned by their rapid growth in all segments of the Canadian economy (Milton, 2005). This emerging trend featured a base for technology activity and a growing information provision and was readily adopted throughout Canada in deference to the ongoing, if not slower, developing curricular areas of Technology Education.

Throughout the 1980s the only consensus that prevailed among Technology Education professionals on how to view this curriculum existed only within Provinces by proponents of Technology Education. Difference and diverse views of how to organize Technology Education continued to be national norm (Sharpe and Hache, 1992). A closer look, however, reveals that two fundamentally different approaches had emerged. On one front were the views that promoted Technology Education as founded in skill attainment, career selection, problem solving with the use of tools and acquire familiarity with technological processes. Not uncommon in the profession at large, these were seen as largely based in industry and rationalized with popular imperatives that the advancing technological economy in Canada required enhanced skill. Chinien, Oaks & Boutine conducted a national survey and queried whether there was consensus on these views among educators (2002). They reported that schools based technological literacy was evident, empowering and rooted in essential skill development needed by any advancing economy. They also indicated that the base for any technology program was not unrelated to technological literacy, and provided a strong rationale for replacing the traditional Industrial Arts programs with modern Technology Education. However they also noted a "low priority in retraining of teachers for new technology"

On the second front, deployment computers as a learning tool became evident and increasingly regarded as a viable technology-type offering. In 1992 Sharp observed increasing interest in modernizing Technology Education but cautioned that the trend risked "… overemphasizing the use of computer technology in the curriculum, …" (Sharpe, 1994). Sharp's caution had already gripped Canadian view of what constituted technology education as the computer movement continued to grow and impact school.

By the end of the 1990's Hill and Smith observed that vocational education courses that prepared students for industry were less prominent in secondary schools then they had been in previous decades, but were strengthened in post-secondary schools, both private and public (1998). In another article Hill described a view of constructivism as a vital element for emerging Technology Education programs (1997). Her views also appear to support a de-industrialization type of technological offering that were characteristic of the ad-hoc computer activities continued to thrive in any number of courses in schools where they appeared.

Increasingly, reports appeared to recommend an expansion of technology use in Canadian schools, but few recognized Technology Education as a means to convey the technology (Canadian Education Association, 2001, Industry Canada, 2005). Rather, they recommended creation of incentives for teachers to integrate technology, usually computer learning type of technology. More advisory than prescriptive, and with greater emphasis developing a learning type of technology offering, the reports served to stimulate, if not endorse, the ad-hoc computer based advancement occurring in school curricula. Industry Canada, and others, would follow-up with the means to develop and distribute resources and information that would become useful for all teachers who wished to integrate technology into their courses. Canadian teachers, themselves became partners in the production of technological information and this featured on many present day Internet sites. The general movement to include computers in all aspects of schooling was readily supported by school administrators who found computers could easily be viewed as a tenable technology offering and an attractive alternative to the Technology Education programs that were typically laden with industrial type equipment and simulations that were often outdated, more expensive to purchase and sustain, and required hard to find qualified teachers to service such programs (Hache, 1996). The result of all of this was greater deployment of computer-based offerings in consort with, or in lieu of, Technology Education programs (Hache, 1997).

PROVINCIAL DOCUMENTS AND REVITALIZING TECHNOLOGY EDUCATION

When looking for an all encompassing definition for the term Technology Education in Canada one can quickly recognizes a diversity of needs prevail and need to be accommodated (Hache and Sharpe, 1991, Hache, 1997). Today diversity is the standard for Technology Education as the programs continue to be deployed differently in all Provinces (Yamansaki and Savage, 1998). A thorough description of the differences is, however, well beyond the scope of this paper. Nevertheless, the reader is encouraged to review the many programs that exist and explore the differences. To enable this each Province was contacted for current documentation that best describe their offering. As all provide easy-to-access Internet sites that contain information to describe their technology offering.

- Newfoundland and Labrador http://www.ed.gov.nl.ca/edu/sp/techedu.htm
- Nova Scotia http://ednet.ns.ca/action.php?sid=865172598&url=http://www.ednet.ns.ca/pdfdocs/outcomes/by_subject/tech_ed_7-9.pdf&action=go&id=1341
- Prince Edward Island http://www.edu.pe.ca/curriculum/elem-march13-02.pdf
- New Brunswick http://ltt.nbed.nb.ca/tve.asp
- Québec http://www.meq.gouv.qc.ca/DGFJ/dp/programmes_etudes/secondaire/technoa.htm
- Nunavut http://www.gov.nu.ca/education/eng/css/progstudies7_12.htm
- Ontario http://www.edu.gov.on.ca/eng/document/curricul/secondary/techno/techful.html
- Manitoba http://www.edu.gov.mb.ca/ks4/cur/teched/ http://www.edu.gov.mb.ca/ks4/docs/support/tfs/

- Saskatchewan http://www.sasked.gov.sk.ca/docs/policy/cels/index.html
- Alberta http://www.education.gov.ab.ca/k_12/curriculum/bySubject/cts/
- Yukon http://www.education.gov.yk.ca/general/services.html
- British Columbia http://www.bced.gov.bc.ca/irp/tech_ed/tetoc.htm
- Northwest Territories
  http://www.ece.gov.nt.ca/Divisions/kindergarten_g12/indexK12.htm

A review of the information contained in the above show that crafts, industrial art, industrial arts combined with technological education, technological education (design technology), computer technology education, science and technology, technology integration in a host of curricular areas, technology and vocational education hybrid, and vocational type education with technological enhancement continue to exist in Canadian schools.

Also evident in the above information is indication of a movement to establish commonality for a Technology Education offering that could be applied in eastern Canadian Provinces, defying the long standing practice of maintaining non-similarity (Atlantic Canada Education Foundation, 2005).

NON "TECHNOLOGY EDUCATION" TECHNOLOGY OFFERINGS IN THE CURRICULUM

The second front described earlier in this article, that which revolves around the introduction of computer and its allied technology in all aspects of curriculum, and at all levels in schools, has largely been integrative in nature (Industry Canada 2003). Computer technology has appeared in any number of hybrid, ad-hoc and formalized courses. Communications technology, agricultural technology, space technology, technology in music, and a host of others are examples. They have been largely deployed in the form of student activities, projects, guidelines, and general technology related information that can be easily integrated into existing or stand-alone courses. Teacher and student generated home page sites, information bases, and blogs compliment those offered by a host of agencies representing a cross section of Canadian interests. They are readily available to anyone accessing the Internet to profile this movement. Below are a small of the many technology offerings that are utilized in Canadian schools on this ad hoc front. Accessing these will provide ample evidence of the manner that technological information is entering Canadian schools.

- Canada Skills Net http://www.skillnet.ca/pub/index.html?iin.lang=en
- Industry Canada School Net http://www.schoolnet.ca/home/e/help/faq.asp promotes the effective use of information and communications technologies (ICT) in learning.
- Magnet School Programs in Ontario and British Columbia http://www.vansd.org/vocweb/magnet.html
- Canada School Net http://www.schoolnet.ca/home/e/
- National Education Portal BELLE http://www.findarticles.com/p/articles/mi_m3563/is_8_17/ai_75508078

- Science and Technology in Ontario
  http://www.edu.gov.on.ca/eng/document/curricul/scientec/scientec.html
- CanTech http://www.canteach.ca/links/linktechdict.html
- Learning Science and Technology http://www.fas.org/learn/index.html
- School net computer and technology information
  http://www.schoolnet.ca/home/e/resources/browse_results.asp?LangID=1
  &SECTION=0&SUBJECT=16
- Marc Garneau School http://schools.tdsb.on.ca/marcgarneau/
- Super Blog Community http://edublog.infopop.cc/6/ubb.x
- Industry Canada Collaborative Projects
  http://www.schoolnet.ca/alasource/e/project.centre/gr2/project-search.asp
- Media awareness network http://www.media-
  awareness.ca/english/index.cfm
- Technology Education Resources for Teachers
  http://www.intel.com/ca/education/resource.htm
- Virtual Teacher Center
  http://www.virtualteachercentre.ca/pd/welcome.aspx
- Typical Elementary School Page http://www.cdli.ca/CITE/themes.html
- Learn Canada Professional Development http://www.learncanada.ca/

After a review of some of the above links one can easily see that an ability to find, collect, review, and contextualize the information has become the main challenge for teachers who integrate technology in their teaching. But these are not unfamiliar skills for Canadian teachers who have been encouraged by increasing access to professional development, high-speed internet access, computers and allied learning technology, and general popular support, all elements that are even accessible on-line though a number of the above links.

CONCLUSION

In writing this article, this author recognized that what might constitute a legitimate description of Technology Education in Canada is arguable at best, as it has taken on a number of interpretations and directions in recent years in Canada. He also noted that it is in keeping with the historically pattern of evoking diversity in scholastic matters, largely in direct response to local differences that exist. What was most apparent in the information and programs that were was that continue to be closely tied to local conditions. Older crafts and industrial arts programs are still sustained in communities where the is a perceived need to feature such program while programs that have industry as their central theme thrive in centers in locations where industry dominates the regional economy. Technology Education, its derivatives, and technology entering schools cloaked in computers with all its allied components are also viewed as reflecting the diverse economy that prevails throughout the Canadian landscape. Although Provincial governments provide a basis for technology education that can fit into their setting, they do so differently to allow local interpretations. Computers have made major inroads as the technology of choice in many small communities where formal technology programs had not been previously available or affordable and are even viewed as technology education in many settings. Accordingly they have also grown prominently in urban school, where formal Technology Education programs exist to add strength to these programs and in other subjects that had previously not accessed technology.

Canadian teachers themselves are the agents of technology change in Canada. They have conjured a variety technology-based learning experiences in spite of the barriers they face. Their intuitions have extended the boundaries of what Canadian teachers see as constituting a viable technology education, both in organized curriculum efforts and a host of ad-hoc applications. In era of rapid expansion of technology teachers have found diversity and decentralization, at the core for all technology, are vital notion when it comes to technology education. In accepting diversity and change they continue to provide more opportunity, for more folks, to do more technological things, in any number of different settings than had previously been the case.

REFERENCES

Atlantic Canada Education Foundation (2005) Foundations for Atlantic Canada technology education curriculum. Unpublished interprovincial curriculum document, Provinces of Newfoundland and Labrador, Prince Edward Island, New Brunswick, and Nova Scotia. Retrieved March 24, 2005 from
www.gov.nf.ca/edu/sp/foundations/tech_edu/te_found_nf-lab_full.pdf

Canadian Education Association (2001). Summit on Technology in Education 2001. Retrieved March 24, 2005 from http://64.233.167.104/search?q=cache:sEZrUV79sncJ:www.cea-ace.ca/media/en/Tech_Summit_Final_Report.pdf+need+for+technology+in+education+canada&hl=en&ie=UTF-8

Chinien, C., Oaks, M. & Boutine, F. (2002) A national consensus on technology education in Canada. *Journal of Industrial Teacher Education*, 32, 2. Retrieved March 24, 2005 from http://scholar.lib.vt.edu/ejournals/JITE/v32n2/chinien.html

Ertl, H & Plante, J. (2004). Connectivity and Learning in Canadian Schools. Science, Innovation and Electronic Information Division of Statistics Canada. Retrieved March 24, 2005 from http://www.statcan.ca/cgi-bin/downpub/listpub.cgi?catno=56F0004MIE2004011

Evans, R. (1998). A challenge. *Journal of Industrial Teacher Education*, 36, 2. Retrieved March 24, 2005 from http://scholar.lib.vt.edu/ejournals/JITE/v36n2/evans.html

Fardo, S. (2005). Foundations of technical education. Internal document, Department of Technology Eastern Kentucky University. Retrieved March 24, 2005 from http://www.technology.eku.edu/facstaff/FARDO/TTE261/UPDATED/Lesson9.htm

Hache, G. (1996). Taking a hard look at technology education. *Prospects*, 3, 2. Retrieved March 24, 2005 from http://www.cdli.ca/Community/Prospects/v2n3/techeduc.htm

Hache, G. (1997). Shaping the way we learn new technology. *Prospects*, 4, 1. Retrieved March 24, 2005 from http://www.cdli.ca/Community/Prospects/v4n1/te.html

Hache, G, & Sharpe, D. (1991). Technology education: the rural context factor. *Technology in School and Industry: Emerging didactics for Human Resource Development*. NATO ASI Series. Springer-Verlag Pubs. 146-157.

Hill, A. (1997). Reconstructism in technology education. *International Journal of Design and Technology Education*. 7, 2. Retrieved March 24, 2005 from http://www.springerlink.com/app/home/contribution.asp?wasp=55e6c4b40cf44da1a76add1f

9e3ca574&referrer=parent&backto=issue,12,15;journal,24,24;linkingpublicationresults,1:102912,1

Hill, A. & Smith, H. (1998). Practice meets theory in technology education: a case for authentic learning in high school. *Journal of Technology Education.* 9, 2. Retrieved March 24, 2005 from http://scholar.lib.vt.edu/ejournals/JTE/v9n2/pdf/hill.pdf

Industry Canada (2005). *Allan Rock minister of industry names leading schools in the integration of information technology.* Retrieved March 24, 2005 from http://www.ic.gc.ca/cmb/welcomeic.nsf/558d636590992942852564880052155b/85256a5d006b972085256dc20050a14f!OpenDocument

Industry Canada (2001). Summit on Technology in Education 2001. Retrieved March 24, 2005 from http://64.233.167.104/search?q=cache:sEZrUV79sncJ:www.ceaace.ca/media/en/Tech_Summit_Final_Report.pdf+need+for+technology+in+education+canada&hl=en&ie=UTF-8

Looker, D. & Thiesessen,V. (2003). Growth of information technology: the digital divides in Canadian schools. Retrieved March 24, 2005 from http://www.statcan.ca/cgi-bin/downpub/listpub.cgi?catno=81-597-XIE2003001

Maton, W. F. (2004). The constitution act, 1876. Retrieved March 24, 2005 from http://www.solon.org/Constitutions/Canada/English/ca_1867.html

Milton, P. (2005) Trends in the integration of itc and learning in k-12 system. Canadian Education Association Toronto Ontario. Retrieved March 24, 2005 from http://www.cea-ace.ca/media/en/Trends_ICT_Integration.pdf

Sharpe, D. (1994). Perspectives on technology education from across the pond. *IDATER,* Loughborough Department of Design and Technology. Retrieved March 24, 2005 from http://www.lboro.ac.uk/departments/cd/docs_dandt/idater/database/sharpe94.html

Sharpe, D. & Hache, G. (1992). Diverse approaches to technology education in Canadian schools. *A Comparative Analysis In Technological Literacy, Competence and Innovation in Human Resource Development.* Proceedings of the First International Conference on Technology Education, Weimar, 239-246.

Yamanski, S. & Savage, E. (1998). Views of technology education in Canada and the united kingdom. *Journal of Technology Studies.* Retrieved March 24, 2005 from http://scholar.lib.vt.edu/ejournals/JOTS/Winter-Spring-1998/yamazaki.html

An electronic version of this chapter that incorporates active hot links is available from ghache@mun.ca

LEO ELSHOF

13. TECHNOLOGICAL EDUCATION AND ENVIRONMENTAL SUSTAINABILITY, A CRITICAL EXAMINATION OF TWENTY YEARS OF CANADIAN PRACTICES AND POLICIES

It has been almost 35 years since initial UNESCO call for an international 'Earth Day' to draw attention to the human impact on the planet Earth. Over a decade has passed since the first Rio 'Earth Summit' and over fifteen years since the Brundtland Report first injected 'sustainable development' into the popular consciousness. The last twenty years has witnessed the emergence of environmental sustainability as a prominent theme in public policy throughout the world. The 2002 Johannesburg World Summit on Sustainable Development (WSSD) identified the need to educate young people from developed countries about issues such as Life-Cycle Analysis (LCA) as well as unsustainable patterns of consumption and production (United Nations, 2002:14). Despite ample evidence that environmentally unsustainable methods and levels of production and consumption in rich developed countries lie at the heart of the sustainable development conundrum (Meadows, 2004; Speth 2004), there are few indications that a sustainability discourse has emerged from the Canadian technology education community.

This paper will look at the last twenty years of technological education in Canada through a 'sustainability' lens. Technological education has a central role to play in helping young people develop the skills, knowledge and attitudes required to transform the term 'sustainable development' beyond mere policy rhetoric to one of embodied reality. The transformation of our built environment, our patterns and modes of consumption, transportation and energy use are all necessary in order to slow down and halt the degradation of the Biosphere. This paper will not only take a retrospective look at the relationship between technological education and the environment in Canada, but will also offer a number of recommendations for transforming technological education to meet the global sustainability challenge. Some of the questions which will be addressed include:

- Over the last twenty years have we really made substantive progress in technology education to address critical dimensions of the relationship between technology and sustainability?
- How should concepts such as eco-efficiency, industrial ecology, sustainable entrepreneurship, cleaner production, product service systems and Life-Cycle thinking inform technology teacher education programs and classrooms?

M.J. de Vries, I. Mottier (eds.), International Handbook of Technology Education, 179–182.

This analysis will identify and contrast the changes which have occurred in a number of provincial technology education curricula with the emergence of a broader public sustainability discourse within Canada over the past twenty years. Comparisons will also be drawn to the Government of Canada's (2002) consensus report "*A Framework for Environmental Learning and Sustainability in Canada*" and the 'broadly transferable sustainable development skills' Chinien (2003) has identified as critical for the Canadian workforce. Although education in Canada is a provincial responsibility, the paper will argue that a new Pan-Canadian 'Eco-tech' initiative is required to ensure that both teachers and their students acquire the knowledge, skills, and attitudes needed to transform traditional technological practices and attitudes into more sustainable ones.

In terms of environmental sustainability Canada is falling behind other countries (Dion, 2004; Boyd, 2004; Statistics Canada, 2004). Although Canadians like to consider themselves 'environmental leaders' the actual performance of Canada on the environmental front is quite another story. North Americans have the highest regional ecological footprint on the planet (WWF, UNEP, 2004) and in aggregate at least, model an unsustainable consumer lifestyle lived at full throttle. Canadians have the eighth largest ecological footprint per capita on the planet, surpassed in North America only by the United States which has the second largest global footprint (WWF, 2004; Wackernagel, 2002). Canadians are also the second largest consumers of water in the world, and its emissions of CO_2 and other key air pollutants on a per unit GDP and per capita basis are among the highest in the OECD (Dion, 2004). In a recent study by the Conference Board of Canada which looked at the environmental performance of 23 OECD countries, Canada dropped from a twelfth place ranking to sixteenth in 2003 (Commissioner of the Environment and Sustainable Development, 2004:2). However the global market and a demand for higher environmental performance in goods and services is forcing Canadian business and industry to: embrace environmental/ sustainability reporting, environmental design and management processes, meet Kyoto climate accord commitments, and to attend to concerns surrounding eco-efficiency, supply chain stewardship and the link between environment and value creation (Conference Board of Canada, 2003). As well, Canada has recently ratified the Kyoto Climate Accord on greenhouse gas emissions, and widespread technological and social innovation will be necessary if Canada is to keep its Kyoto commitments and avoid an 'ingenuity gap' (Homer-Dixon, 2000). Enlightened thinking about the nature of waste and pollution in product design and manufacturing have moved beyond 'end-of-pipe' considerations in which pollution is considered as an afterthought, toward proactive *'Design-for-the Environment'* (DfE) and 'restorative' (Cunningham, 2002) approaches in which life-cycle costs are thoroughly considered in design. Proactive approaches to technological thinking related to sustainable production and consumption, and product systems, has been more advanced in the EU than in North America, and the Canadian Minister of the Environment has warned that Canadians risk their quality of life if they ignore the imperative of a sustainability transformation within Canadian industry. He emphasizes that what he terms the "new industrial revolution"…as "one of the most important issues for our nation today" (Dion, 2004:2). Unfortunately Canadian technology education curricula over the last twenty years have reflected at best, a tepid response to the sustainability crisis. In a number of provinces it remains out of step with the Canadian Government's industrial strategy which is guided by a vision of Canada as: "*a leader in the development, commercialization and adoption of innovative sustainable development tools, practices and technologies throughout the economy*" (Industry Canada, 2003:viii).

Petrina (2000) has argued that the conventional design, problem solving and technological methods employed in technological education embody an unsustainable technocentric political ecology. A neoliberal political ecology which emphasizes efficient production and consumption of globalized product forms at the expense of environmental and social justice remains for the most part unexamined and unchallenged within technology education. In fact, evidence suggests that technology curricula over the last twenty years in Canada has uncritically incorporated a number of business and industry imperatives related to efficient 'just-in-time' skills, themes situated in "competitive supremacy and conservative politics" (Petrina, 2000). Technology education is losing ground to traditional industrial education in British Columbia (Petrina & Dalley, 2003) and some evidence indicates that in Ontario with what its 'vocational orientation' (Gardner & Hill,1999a;b) in the senior secondary years, is following suit.

REFERENCES

Boyd, D. R. (2004). *Sustainability within a generation. A New Vision for Canada.* Vancouver, David Suzuki Foundation.

Chinien, C. (2003). *Skills to last- broadly transferable sustainable development skills for the Canadian workforce.* A Technical Research Report Human Resources Development Canada. Winnipeg, National Centre for Workforce Development.

Commissioner of the Environment and Sustainable Development. (2004). *Report of the commissioner of the environment and sustainable development to the House of Commons.* Ottawa, Office of the Auditor General of Canada.

Conference Board of Canada. (2003). *Environmental practice and performance of Canadian business and industry.* Ottawa, Conference Board of Canada.

Cunningham, S. (2002). *The restoration economy.* San Francisco, Berrett-Koehler.

Dion, S. (2004). *Environmental action for economic competitiveness: Will Canada lead the new industrial revolution?* A speech delivered to the Calgary Chamber of Commerce September 10, 2004. Ottawa, Environment Canada.

Gardner, P. L. and A. M. Hill (1999a). Technology Education in Ontario: Evolution, Achievements, Critiques and Challenges Part 1: The Context. *International Journal of Technology and Design Education* 9: 103–136.

Gardner, P. L. and A. M. Hill (1999b). Technology Education in Ontario: Evolution, Achievements, Critiques and Challenges Part 2: Implementation and Evaluation. *International Journal of Technology and Design Education* 9: 201–239.

Government of Canada. (2002). *A framework for environmental learning and sustainability in Canada.* Ottawa.

Homer Dixon, T. (2000). *The ingenuity gap.* Toronto, Random House.

Industry Canada. (2003). *Sustainable development strategy 2003–06.* Ottawa, Industry Canada.

Meadows, D., J. Randers, et al. (2004). *Limits to growth*. White River Junction Vermont, Chelsea Green.

Petrina, S. (2000). The Political Ecology of Design and Technology Education: An Inquiry into Methods. *International Journal of Technology and Design Education 10*: 207–237.

Petrina, S. (2000). The Politics of Technological Literacy. *International Journal of Technology and Design Education 10*: 181–206.

Petrina, S. and S. Dalley (2003). The Politics of curriculum reform in Canada: The case of technology education in British Columbia. *Canadian Journal of Science Mathematics and Technology Education* 3(1): 117-144.

Schor, J. B. (2004). *Born to buy*. Toronto, Scribner.

Speth, J. G. (2004). *Red sky at morning, America and the crisis of the global environment*. London, Yale University Press.

Statistics-Canada (2004). *Environment industry survey business sector 2002*. Report 16F0008XIE. Ottawa, Statistics Canada.

Statistics-Canada (2004). *Human activity and the environment: annual statistics 2004* 16-201-XIE. Ottawa.

United Nations. (2002). *Report of the world summit on sustainable development* Johannesburg, South Africa, 26 August- 4 September 2002, United Nations.

Wackernagel, M., N. B. Schulz, et al. (2002). Tracking the ecological overshoot of the human economy. *Proceedings of the National Academies of Science* 99(14): 9266–9271.

WWF, World Wildlife Fund, United Nations Environmental Program. UNEP, et al. (2004).*The living planet report*. Gland Switzerland.

P. JOHN WILLIAMS

14. TECHNOLOGY EDUCATION IN AUSTRALIA: TWENTY YEARS IN RETROSPECT

INTRODUCTION

The last 20 years of developments in Technology Education in Australia have arguably been the most significant period in its history. Prior to these 20 years, the genesis of technology education can be found in the institutions established in the early colonial centres to combat child delinquency, petty crime and to provide a trained workforce in the trades and in housekeeping. This early focus on skill development still remains in many schools. The transition from vocational to general education occurred partly after World War II through major curriculum revisions. Developmental focus on the technical curriculum seemed to correspond with periods of economic downturn, when the expectation became obvious that the technical curriculum was part of the solution to poor economic performance (A.Williams, 1993). These periods occurred in the 1890's, the 1950's and the 1980's. This latter period represents the beginning of this 20 year retrospect.

The year 1987 was key in the development of Technology Education in Australia. It was in this year that the Australian Education Council (AEC) began a series of initiatives that led to the publication in 1994 of nationally agreed curriculum statements and profiles related to eight compulsory learning areas, one of which was technology. In 1990 the *K-12 Technology Curriculum Map* (Australian Education Council) revealed a shift in emphasis in many schools toward broader conceptions of technology, gender equality, flexible outcomes and a variety of teaching and assessment strategies. The 1994 documents extended this trend.

The Australian states and territories are educationally and politically independent, so this period of cooperation to produce nationally agreed curriculum documents was remarkable, and the political climate has not been conducive to enable it to be repeated since. In fact soon after the publication of the curriculum statement in 1994, the political climate changed to the extent that the material that was developed was not adopted in all states.

The declaration of technology as a core learning area had profound implications. Firstly, up until this time, all subject areas in secondary schooling from which technology education developed were located within the elective areas of the curriculum. The implication had been that these subjects provided learning experiences relevant only for specific groups of students with particular interests or career destinations in mind. Indeed, some of these subjects were regarded by students and the community as relevant only to a particular gender. Secondly, in the case of primary education, technology had not generally been part of school

M.J. de Vries, I. Mottier (eds.), International Handbook of Technology Education, 183–196.

programs, and primary teachers had little experience to draw on to develop programs. The challenge for technology education was to determine the learning experiences that are essential for all students, and are unique to technology education or best undertaken within the learning area.

The most significant rationales for the development of technology as a discrete learning area were related to the technological nature of society and equity of opportunity for students. Australian culture was rapidly becoming highly technological, and all students needed to have the opportunities to develop, experience and critique a range of technologies as part of their core education. This rationale aligned with concerns for gender equity in technology education, with more flexible, open ended and collaborative approaches to delivery, and with a range of key competencies for all students.

A Statement on Technology for Australian Schools (Australian Education Council, 1994) set out what was regarded as the technology learning area. This included the place of technology in society, the need for all students to experience technology education and the form in which it should appear in the school curriculum. It outlined four strands for learning in technology education. These comprised Designing, Making and Appraising; Information; Materials; and Systems. These were regarded as interdependent and were intended to be developed sequentially through stages or levels in the compulsory years of schooling. This organization and its detail were significantly influenced by curriculum developments in the UK (Williams, 1994).

Prior to the 1990's, school curricula addressed technology in a very limited way. In the main, technology was referred to in elective or optional syllabuses. Most often students' perceptions of technology were developed from a very restricted range of learning experiences, for example, students might learn about the tools and machines used to work with timber. Invariably learning focused on an established body of technical 'know-how'. In some courses students learnt about designs that characterised past eras.

The current technology classroom activities have developed out of these traditions. At the primary school level technology education practices tend to have developed out of art and craft and science. Technology and Science still tend to be bracketed together for primary education as illustrated by government reports (ASTEC, 1997) and some learning area documentation.

At the secondary school level, technology education has tended to develop out of vocational studies such as Home Economics, Industrial Arts, Agriculture, and Business Education as well as other technical studies such as Computing, Information Technology, Media and Control Technology.

However, through the past decade curriculum have been introduced that address 'technology' in a more systematic or comprehensive way, and are grounded in a more general than vocational philosophy of education. These curriculum integrate the use of technology processes and encourage students to make value judgements and to be creative and innovative, thought few describe an accompanying body of knowledge . From entry to year 12, students are required to develop projects, practice management skills and engage in independent and group learning. These studies aim to develop students' qualities of flexibility, adaptability and enterprise.

Probably the most significant aspect of the change to technology education is the concept that as a learning area it contributes to all students' general education and therefore should be studied by all students in the compulsory years of schooling.

Since the publication of *A Statement on Technology for Australian Schools* (AEC, 1994) all the states and territories have established technology learning areas through the development of frameworks, curriculum and support material. Various titles have been adopted in different states (Technology Education, Technological and Applied Studies, Technology and Enterprise) but they contain similar elements. There is a significant degree of consistency in the definitions of technology used by education systems in Australia. Technology is defined broadly, and key common elements of the definitions include 'the application of knowledge and resources' and that it is used 'to extend human capabilities'. There is strong general agreement that technology involves a process, that is, there is an identifiable method used in the development of technology. This process is most commonly referred to as design, but it is not defined or described in detail. Similarly the relationship between the concepts or knowledge of technology and the processes of technology is not explored.

In the titles ascribed to subjects, technology is commonly linked with other concepts, for example 'materials, design and technology', 'science and technology', 'technology and enterprise'. This may suggest that existing notions or definitions of technology are inadequate to describe the scope of the intended learning, and this is an emerging area of the curriculum still in the process of definition.

While states have or are establishing clearer directions for technology education through curriculum frameworks, its implementation has been problematic. This is partly because there is a conflict between the curriculum, which is quite revolutionary in nature, and its implementation, which cannot be revolutionary but is developmental and must build on past practice. Teachers have to develop their understandings of technology education and implement new strategies over time. But the technology education curriculum does not incrementally develop from what has existed in schools in the past, it is revolutionary in both knowledge and associated pedagogy.

To some extent this problem has been exacerbated by the introduction of entry-level vocational education and training in the senior secondary years. Some teachers consider the introduction of industry-accredited vocational courses as justification for the maintenance of traditional vocationally oriented methodology and content in the compulsory years.

THE STATUS OF TECHNOLOGY EDUCATION

Many factors contribute to the status of technology education in schools. Links with other learning areas, its usefulness as a path to university study, vocational education and training, information technology, perceptions of influential groups and school priorities all influence the status of technology education. These factors do not clearly indicate high or low status. This section will examine the range of factors which contribute to the status of technology education.

The curricular position of technology education as equivalent with the other seven learning areas indicates an improved status in the 1990's. The 1989 *Hobart Declaration on Schooling* first established this curriculum sense of equivalence, later supported by the development of *A Statement on Technology for Australian Schools* and *Technology – A Curriculum Profile for Australian Schools* (Australian Education Council, 1994). Since then all states and territories have developed technology learning area frameworks and support material which are in various stages of implementation or revision.

Technology education was traditionally an 'elective' area in secondary schools and is a 'new' area in primary schools. Because of this it is often perceived as a less important learning area, and this perception has been slow to change. In addition there is little status in study in technology education for university, despite some encouraging trends which are discussed later in this paper.

Some differences seem to exist in schools regarding teachers perceptions of the place of technology education in the core curriculum. In a 2000 study (Williams, 2001) only 55% of technology teachers agreed that 'Technology is generally regarded by teachers in my school as an essential component of a student's general education', but 87% of school administrators and 84% of other teachers agreed with the statement. This difference in attitude also exists in perceptions of the status of technology education, with teachers of technology education rating the status of technology in their school much lower than other teachers and administrators. Parental support for core studies in technology is strong, with 91% believing that technology should be a compulsory area of study for both primary and secondary students as a component of their general education.

As discussed earlier, curriculum documents tend not to specify the development of a conceptual understanding of technology. This contrasts with areas such as science and the humanities, where this conceptual understanding is of prime importance. It can be argued that conceptual or higher order understanding is necessary if students are to transfer learning to new or unfamiliar contexts. In descriptions provided by education systems, the term technology is used as a convenient umbrella rather than a representation of a body of conceptual knowledge and understanding.

For secondary schools there is no clear definition or requirement for student technological literacy, and in primary schools it is accorded a lower status compared with the central importance of numeracy and language literacy. In their 1997 report, ASTEC proposed a broadening of the notion of literacy from a narrow focus on language literacy, to encompass other aspects such as technological literacy in the development of a broad concept of 'life functional literacy'. The current narrow focus on language literacy and numeracy in schools, reinforced by compulsory national testing, indicates that this notion has not gained general currency.

While there are few system level initiatives to develop the status of technology education, substantial numbers of schools have implemented their own initiatives. Leading school sites in technology education were selected throughout Australia (Williams, 2001) on the basis of the high status accorded to technology education at those sites. In many of the leading sites technology education was given a high status through one or more of the following:

1. Technology education had been set as a priority area in the school's strategic plan. For example, in one school it had been set as one of three priority areas for the past four years. As a result a substantial amount of equipment had been purchased and a considerable amount of professional development had been organised.

2. The Principal and other senior staff had a specific interest in technology education. For example, in some schools the Principal considered technology education of prime relevance to students and saw it as a medium for promoting outcomes-based education and integrating all the learning areas. The technology education leader supported these conceptions and took an active role in the strategic initiatives of the school.

3. The learning area had a supported technology leader with a paid allowance and a specific budget. For example, the allocation of an allowance and budget to a co-ordinator of technology education had allowed some schools resources to be expanded, professional development to be co-ordinated and an active implementation committee to be formed.

TECHNOLOGY EDUCATION IN PRIMARY SCHOOLS

The organized incorporation of technology education in the primary years of schooling is a recent phenomena in Australia and would not have existed 20 years ago.

In 1997 the Australian Science and Technology Council (ASTEC) reported on the teaching of science and technology in Australian primary schools. In that report, ASTEC noted a number of findings that it considered were likely to have a positive impact on technology education programs. These included the implementation of the new technology curricula, an increased level of interest in technology education by teachers, evidence that technology education can facilitate the general education of children, and recognition of the potential for science and technology education to be brought together in a complementary way.

ASTEC also noted concerns about the development of technology education in primary schools related to the quality of primary technology (and science) education. In terms of professional development, ASTEC noted that some good programs had been developed and that it was critical these professional development programs be sustained. The Prime Minister's Science, Engineering and Innovation Council (1999) also found that many primary teachers have outdated or insufficient technology teaching qualifications.

Despite the fact that technology is still a new area of study for many primary teachers, in 2000 90% of schools indicated that they taught technology in all grades (Williams, 2001). The emphasis of much of this technology was Information Technology, embedded in a range of subjects, rather than relating to broad technology education. School based decision making and curriculum planning mean that there is a variety of technology education occurring at a classroom level. Often the curriculum programs in this area are determined by individual interests and enthusiasm of the teachers and principals, and the educational priorities in particular schools.

In 1996 a limited evaluation of the NSW *Science and Technology K-6* syllabus was undertaken, finding that teachers allocated between 60 and 120 minutes per week to technology. However the majority of teachers were at the lower end of this range. The evaluation also found that:

- That the technology component of the Science and Technology Syllabus was not fully understood by teachers;
- Class programs tended to favour content relating to natural and physical science;
- Science and Technology is considered by the majority of teachers to have "mid-range" status in their school curriculum;
- Supply, storage and maintenance of consumable goods (batteries, corks etc) is considered a barrier to the full implementation of the syllabus;
- Four major factors appear to determine the selection of units of study and the extent of Science and Technology teaching: teacher understanding and confidence, student interest, the availability of resources, and content being taught in other Key Learning Areas.

In primary schools, technology education is generally delivered through an integrated approach with other learning areas, though there are some discrete technology programs. Few primary schools have specialist teaching facilities for areas of technology dealing with hard and soft materials, and as they purchase resources, tools and equipment, and students produce significant products, the facilities appear even more inadequate. The Australian Academy of Technological Sciences and Engineering study (Watts, 1998) concluded that the physical facilities for the teaching of technology were inadequate in primary schools, and the 1997 ASTEC study also concluded that resources were inadequate for teaching.

Many primary teachers are still coming to grips with the notion of technology education generally, and together with inadequate experience and training, lacked confidence and competence in teaching technology, as well as using basic hand and power tools with materials such as wood, metals, electronics and plastics. This is supported by the *Science and Technology in Primary Schools* report (ASTEC, 1997). As schools purchase such equipment there is a danger it will be underutilized and used either inefficiently or unsafely unless teachers are educated in its use.

The relationship between technology education generally and the area of Information Technology and computer studies is not clear, and the terminology tends to be interchangeable. In many primary schools there is a focus on computers but not on other areas of technology education.

TECHNOLOGY EDUCATION IN SECONDARY SCHOOLS

Technology Education is delivered through a range of technology related subjects in the secondary school including Home Economics, Technical Studies, Computing, Information Technology, Media, Industrial Arts, Design and Technology, Agriculture and Business Studies. In all states and territories, it is either a centrally mandated part of the junior secondary curriculum, or the majority of schools ensure students study some technology.

The pattern is generally that technology is compulsory in early secondary, and becomes an elective in later years. These elective subjects may work together, for example through a school organized technology learning area, to achieve the outcomes for technology education, or they may operate as independent subjects and share a line within the school timetable and so compete with each other for students. Such decisions are school based, and the trend is for individual technology subjects to cooperate more as a learning area. In no state or territory are technology subjects compulsory in years 11 and 12.

Because technology education, as it is taught in the classroom, has developed from the content and skills drawn from traditional subject areas such as Home Economics and Industrial Arts, in some schools it retains many of those characteristics. This is emphasised by the teachers of technology who still focus on the technical skills needed in a particular context (wood skills, textile skills etc) and do not always support a broader understanding of the innovative processes and design approach needed for students to understand how technological solutions are developed within society. So the type of technology education experienced by students in some schools is quite traditional and does not mirror the current definitions of technology education.

Since the adoption of technology as a learning area schools have slowly moved toward an organizational pattern that reflects the curriculum learning areas. In the case of technology this means one technology department at schools rather than, say, separate industrial arts and home economics departments. By 2001, 84% of schools coordinated technology education subjects as a learning area, and 16% coordinated the technology education subjects independently of each other. Conversely, the majority of schools (75%) assess student achievement in technology by individual subject, and 19% of schools assess achievement as a learning area. Putting this data together, the majority of schools (61%) coordinated technology education as a learning area and assess student achievement by individual subject.

There is some validity to this inconsistency in that schools tend to coordinate technology as a learning area, but assess individual subjects. Even though all the technology subjects may be working toward the same outcomes, student performance is contextual, and by measuring performance in a range of contexts, a more realistic picture of overall performance is possible.

An increasing number of schools are beginning to report to parents using state and territory based outcomes frameworks adapted from the nationally developed statement and profile in technology. This reporting information is not systematically collected, and not only do the broad outcomes and standards vary from state to state, but the specific outcomes used in reporting achievement vary both between systems and between schools. This is supported by the *Reporting on Student and School Achievement* report (Cuttance and Stokes, 2000). As state systems which have in the past used the national statement and profile develop their own state frameworks, the current diversity within technology will continue to expand. This represents a reversal of the trend which occurred around the mid 1990's, as the effect of the national statement and profile was to bring the states closer together in their conception of the area of technology.

VOCATIONAL EDUCATION AND TRAINING

'One of the most significant developments in Australian senior secondary education over the last few years has been the dramatic increase in the number of students involved in VET in schools' (MCEETYA, 1998, 31). The overall increase in the number of schools offering VET programs between 1997 and 1998 was 29%, by 2000 involving over 90% of all secondary schools in Australia (MCEETYA, 2000).

This rapid increase of vocational technology programs in the post compulsory years began with the introduction of various vocational education initiatives by the Commonwealth and state governments (Carmichael, 1992, Mayer, 1992), and also came about in response to school based initiatives to develop curriculum to meet the needs of the increasingly diverse post-compulsory student population. Many of these initiatives emerged from the technology area. The results were to introduce accredited vocational subjects from the National Modules scheme into the senior years of schooling, and to identify and include specific vocational competencies into existing senior school subjects. These initiatives have been coordinated through national organizations and through the implementation of National Training Modules, Registered Training Organizations and the Australian Qualifications Framework. This trend toward national consistency in VET offerings is continuing.

In contrast to this national consistency, the general technology offerings by schools up to year 10 are becoming more nationally diverse. The declaration of technology education as one of the eight learning areas in 1989 was accompanied by a rationale placing technology education firmly in the camp of general education; that is, it provided benefits to all students, not just those who were going to pursue a related technical vocation. The 1994 publication of the national

Statement on Technology for Australian Schools consolidated this rationale. For a short period after then, the states became more similar in their technology curriculum and frameworks. But the more recent reviews of state frameworks and the documents have resulted in more diversity. So there is an increasingly diverse compulsory technology education feeding into an increasingly centralized post compulsory vocational education. This will create difficulties in mapping progression and achievement for students in technology up to year 12.

The *MCEETYA Taskforce on Vocational Education and Training* (2000) recognized this potential barrier between compulsory and post-compulsory in calling for a re-conceptualization of vocational education in schools so it 'encompasses a broader range of initiatives and elements including expanded roles for community partnerships, the centrality of lifelong learning and generic skills (such as Key Competencies and enterprise skills and attributes), integrated career information and guidance services' (p. 4).

Many subject areas that are now included in the technology learning area at the secondary level have had a vocational orientation in the past, such as industrial arts, home economics and agriculture. These subjects tended to have a quasi-vocational status in that while they were seen as providing an orientation to various vocations, there was no explicit connection with industry, and no industrial accreditation.

The balance between vocational and general educational aims tends to be mirrored in the balance between the product and the process of technology, vocational aims being associated with concentration on the development of skills through a high quality outcome. The balance between these two sets of aims has implications for the range of technologies made available and the type and quality of equipment and materials provided in secondary schools. Vocational aims require students more access to a narrower range of more expensive 'industry standard' technology. General educational aims require students to experience a broader range of technologies but these do not have to be 'industry standard', and in many instances they can 'simulate' the technology.

Williams (1998) argued that vocational education was increasingly emphasising the importance of generic skills, such as teamwork and problem-solving (Mayer, 1992) as well as specific competencies for particular industries. At the same time that these changes were occurring, technology education was developing with an emphasis on remarkably similar goals in terms of generic skills. Williams argued that this apparent "confluence" of the goals of technology education and vocational education is problematic for technology education, given that technology education is intended to contribute to the general education of all students as a component of a liberal education. The problematic nature of the confluence is that there appears to be an increasing push for the specific industry competencies to be embedded within technology education programs. This is seen as likely to be antipathetic to the general educational goals of the area.

This confusion and tension between vocational and general technology education at post compulsory levels of secondary schooling was also recognized by Petrina (1999). The popular inclusion of vocational technology options at post compulsory levels of schooling, particularly when attempts have been made to offer the two approaches simultaneously, have necessitated a rationale for technology education as vocational education. The tension arises because of the elements of incompatibility in philosophy, pedagogy, processes and assessment between the two approaches.

Some technology teachers continue to use vocational rationales for their general technology teaching. In some instances this has been an impediment to moving toward new approaches to technology education which are more designerly and student centred.

The vocational component of technology education is strong, and the rapid growth of vocational technology programs has had a significant impact on schools, and this will continue. The links between the compulsory and post compulsory years of schooling, the general and vocational approach to technology education, are not strong, but there are some indications that these links are developing to focus both aspects on important generic skills. Vocational education is growing in importance as an educational route for an increasing number of students.

TECHNOLOGY TEACHER TRAINING

Up until 1988, primary and secondary teachers for Australian schools were trained at Colleges of Advanced Education. In this year the process of amalgamating these institutions began, some colleges combining and becoming new universities, others merging with existing universities.

The rationale for the training of teachers of technology education to become part of universities' responsibilities when this amalgamation took place was that those in the university technological faculties (Industrial Design, Engineering, etc.) could strengthen the content base of technology teacher education courses. The effective integration of teacher training into universities has only succeeded to a very limited extent as there seems to be a reticence on the part of university faculties to assume responsibility for the content of technology teacher education.

A survey of technology teacher education programs in Australia in 1996 (Williams) indicated that of the 38 universities in Australia, nine were identified as offering undergraduate technology teacher education programs. All these institutions offered a four year Bachelor of Education degree in technology education.

Since this survey was conducted in 1996, many institutions have moved away from this pattern, for example to a double degree structure or to graduate entry pre-service training courses. An additional development has been the demise of secondary undergraduate technology teacher education courses in four states, and an increase in post-graduate technology courses for both secondary and primary teacher trainees in all states except one. There is an increasing range of entry and exit points to training programs, developing links between universities and technical training institutions, and a number of courses have been designed for specific client groups.

A consideration for the introduction of post-graduate courses is that first degree students are suitably qualified, that is they have undertaken an initial degree relevant to the needs of technology education. This remains an issue for all states offering teacher training at the post-graduate levels, largely because of the breadth of technology offered in schools and the relative specialization of most initial degrees.

Four year undergraduate programs offer a range of specializations including design and technology, food technology, home economics, textile technology, engineering science, computing studies, business and technics. The study of content, curriculum and education is concurrent throughout all four years.

A more recent approach to training technology teachers, stimulated by the shortage of teachers, is the design of programs to suit specific groups of clients, sponsored by the state government as a way of ensuring and adequate supply of teachers. These courses vary from 1-2 years in length and include significant components of school based practice.

Another increasingly common trend is for university technology teacher training programs to make links with technical colleges for the provision of the skills-based machine and production oriented aspects of the course. The logic is that this is what the technical colleges specialize in for the training of apprentices and trades people, and as it is expensive to update and maintain equipment, this represents a sensible consolidation. A philosophical difference arises however as the technical college approach is competency based and generally teacher oriented, contrasted to the technology education approach which is generally outcomes based and student centered through a designerly approach to making. Some universities have rejected this liaison after trialing it for a number of years, others continue with a significant technical college component to their course.

For a number of reasons, technology teacher training programs are problematic for universities. Gibson and Barlow (2000) outlined the problems facing universities when they endeavour to provide a range of degree programs. Universities allocate Equivalent Full Time Student Units (EFTSUs) to their various programs based on the institution's academic profile negotiated annually with the federal government. This in turn determines the total Australian government funding that each university receives. Recently this source of funding has decreased over a number of years. As a result, universities are increasingly relying on non-government income sources, including financial endowments from private persons and industry, commercial enterprises, as well as an increasing willingness to enrol full fee paying students (local and international) to alleviate their budgetary constraints. Gibson and Barlow claimed that technology teacher education programs are not attractive to university administrators: they have suffered from low intake, they are perceived to be expensive, they provide limited opportunities for economies of scale through large lectures and they are less likely to attract fee-paying students than other courses.

There are still some primary teacher training programs at universities in Australia which do not provide any instruction in technology education, despite the establishment of technology as one of the core learning areas since 1989.

However, the majority of training programs offer at least one compulsory unit in technology education, and a number allow for specialization in the technology area by taking additional elective units. These specialized graduates often become technology resource teachers in a school or a region.

Teacher shortage

The shortage of technology teachers in Australia occurs in a context of low appeal of a career in teaching. 'Those with technological competence recognise better career prospects elsewhere. Graduates entering schools have available only limited term contracts and no clear career prospects. These realities compound and contribute to teacher discontent and a lack of public support' (Watts, 1998, p13).

While there is a current shortage of technology teachers available to meet this continuing demand, a number of state government employers have responded by actively investing in strategies aimed at alleviating the problem through specially developed Diplomas of Education, targeted retraining programs, student sponsorships, promotion of technology teaching in schools and recruiting from other states and overseas.

POST-COMPULSORY EDUCATION

Schooling is compulsory to age 15 (Year 10), so the last two years of secondary school are considered post-compulsory, despite an increasing emphasis and trend to keep people in school to Year 12. Traditionally Years 11-12 were only for those students who wanted to continue to university and so focussed on academic studies. One way of retaining students was to make the Year 11-12 studies more general, and a diverse range of vocational studies have been introduced into these years of schooling. Emphasis has been placed upon the provision of a range of pathways, not just leading to university but to further technical education and employment entry. Course design has been such that the pathways are flexible, in order to delay the determination of specific career paths for as long as possible.

A parallel recent development has been the broadening of those subjects that can be counted toward university entrance. All states have a system whereby specified subjects are examined in Year 12 and then the scores are combined to provide a ranking which is used for access into university courses. Popular and high status courses such as law and medicine have a high rank for minimum entry, and lower status courses such as teacher education have a lower rank. Very few technology related school subjects have traditionally been available for university entrance, even for technological university courses such as engineering, architecture or industrial design. This has changed over the past 10 years, and in some states as recently as 2005.

It is now generally the case that school technology subjects such as Engineering, Materials Design and Technology, Design and Technology and Information Systems can be used as university entrance subjects. For schools this means that students who perform well in technology during the compulsory years of schooling can continue with their technology studies, whereas in the past they would have left technology and focussed more on say, maths and science. It also means that universities can specify a broader range of prerequisites for specific courses. For example, rather than architecture relying on maths and physics prerequisites, it may be more appropriate to specify design and materials technology types of subjects.

PROFESSIONAL ASSOCIATIONS

Because technology education in schools has developed from a number of previously independent subjects, teachers professional associations are still organized along the lines of these subjects. For example, at the national level, organizations supporting technology teachers are Home Economics Institute of Australia, Australian Council for Education through Technology, Design in Education Council Australia, Australian Council for Computers in Education, Council of Australasian Media Education Organizations, Business Educators of Australia and National Association of Agricultural Educators. These organizations have traditionally supported secondary teachers, and while some are developing support for primary teachers, this is not their main focus. This national structure is reflected by the organizations in the states and territories. There is no support for both primary and secondary teachers which covers the breadth of the technology learning area.

This is an impediment for a number of reasons. Australia is a small country to have seven different educational systems (five states and two territories), and so there is a lot of repetition in the development of curriculum support materials and professional development. A single professional organization could develop significant economies of scale in these areas. In addition, the absence of such on organization effectively means there is no advocacy and representation for all technology teachers at the federal government and national organization level. There are no indications that this situation will change in the future.

REFERENCES

Australian Education Council. (1989). *Hobart declaration on schooling*. Australian Education Council.
Australian Education Council. (1991). *K-12 technology curriculum map*. Carlton: Curriculum Corporation.
Australian Education Council. (1994a). *A statement on technology for Australian schools*. Carlton: Curriculum Corporation.
Australian Education Council. (1994b). *Technology - A curriculum profile for Australian schools*. Carlton: Curriculum Corporation.
Australian Science, Technology and Engineering Council. (1997). *Foundations for Australia's future: Science and technology in primary schools*. Canberra: AGPS.
Carmichael, L. (1992). V*ocational certificate training system*: Report of the Employment Skills Formation Council. National Board of Employment Education and Training.
Cuttance, & Stokes. (2000). *Reporting on student and school achievement*, Canberra: DETYA.
De Vries, M.J., & Tamir, A. (Eds.). (1997). *Shaping concepts of technology: From philosophical perspectives to mental images*. Dordrecht, Netherlands: Kluwer Academic Publishers.
Gibson, J., & Barlow, J. (2000). *NSW technology teacher education: Y2K a time for optimism?* Paper presented at the Biennial National Conference of the Australian Council for Education through Technology, Canberra, ACT.

Mayer, E. (1992). *Putting general education to work: The key competencies.* Melbourne: The Australian Education Council and Ministers for Vocational Education, Employment and Training.

MCEETYA. (1999). *Adelaide declaration on national goals for schooling in the 21ˢᵗ century.* Carlton: Curriculum Corporation.

Ministerial Council on Education, Employment, Training and Youth Affairs. (1998). *Draft school teacher demand and supply primary and secondary.* Carlton South: MCEETYA.

Ministerial Council on Education, Employment, Training and Youth Affairs. (2000). *New pathways forlLearning.* Canberra: MCEETYA.

Petrina, S. (1994). Curriculum organization in technology education: A critique of six trends. *Journal of Industrial Teacher Education,* 31 (2), 44-69.

Prime Minister's Science, Engineering and Innovation Council. (1999c). *Ideas for innovation.* Canberra: Department of Industry, Science and Tourism.

Prime Minister's Science, Engineering and Innovation Council. (1999b). *Raising awareness of the importance of science and technology to Australia's future.* Canberra: Department of Industry, Science and Tourism.

Prime Minister's Science, Engineering and Innovation Council. (1999a). *Strengthening the nexus betweens Science and its applications.* Canberra: Department of Industry, Science and Tourism.

Watts, D. (1998). *A report on the readiness of Australian schools to meet the demands of Teaching the curriculum areas of science and technology in the compulsory years of schooling.* Perth, WA: University of Notre Dame, Australia.

Williams, A. (1993). *Rationale for technology education in NSW secondary schools.* Unpublished Masters Thesis, University of New England.

Williams, P.J. (1994). *Technology education in the United Kingdom and Australia: Some parallels.* Australian Council for Education through Technology Eleventh Biennial National Conference. Hobart, Australia.

Williams, J., & Williams, A. (Eds.). (1996). *Technology education for teachers.* Melbourne: MacMillan Education Australia Pty Ltd.

Williams, P.J. (1996). Survey of undergraduate secondary technology teacher training programs in Australia. *Australian Journal of Research in Technology and Design Education,* 4 (1), 11-15.

Williams, P.J. (1998). The Confluence of the goals of technology education and the needs of industry: An Australian case study with international application. *International Journal of Technology and Design Education,* 8 (1), 1-13.

Williams, P.J. (2001) *The teaching and learning of technology in Australian primary and secondary schools.* Department of Education, Science and Technology Working Report, Commonwealth of Australia, 299pp.

ALISTER JONES

15. THE DEVELOPING FIELD OF TECHNOLOGY EDUCATION IN NEW ZEALAND: THE LAST TWENTY YEARS

INTRODUCTION

In the last twenty years technology education in New Zealand has found a place in research, teacher education and classroom practice. This paper traces the development of technology education as a field of study in compulsory education over the last twenty years and explores the curriculum development in the 1990s, the emerging research field during that time as well as teacher pre and in-service development. Figure 1 outlines the key aspects of development of technology education in New Zealand and highlights key features of curriculum, research and teacher education and shows the links between these different aspects in a timeline from 1985 to 2005.

Year	Curriculum Development	Research	Teacher Education
1985	Traditional technology move to include design and social aspects	Technology as context to teach science, STS	Secondary school teacher education
	Curriculum Review		
	Charting the Course		
1990	New Zealand Curriculum Framework	PATT surveys	
	Technology Education Policy Development	LITE project (Teacher perceptions, student capability, classroom studies)	Masters degree courses
	Draft Curriculum	Masters and Doctoral research established (on-going)	
	Technology in NZ Curriculum	Teacher development research	
1995			Teacher development package developed

M.J. de Vries, I. Mottier (eds.), International Handbook of Technology Education, 197–211.

2000	Curriculum becomes compulsory for years 1-10 Development of national qualifications Curriculum Stocktake Revised curriculum structure	Research in assessment National School Sampling Study Classroom InSiTE project	Large scale national professional development Primary School teacher education courses begin
2005			GIF funding for senior secondary school

Figure 1: Timeline of developments in technology in New Zealand

DEVELOPMENT OF TECHNOLOGY FOR ALL IN THE CURRICULUM

New Zealand has had a long history of technical education in the senior primary and secondary school (Burns, 1992). A national school system was introduced in New Zealand in 1877 and technical education was introduced in 1890 with metal and woodwork for boys and cooking, needlework and/or laundry for girls being taught in the last two years of primary schooling (10-12 years). At the same time technical high schools were developed and tended to channel working class children into manual and trade employment. After 1945 common core subjects such as metal and woodwork and cooking and sewing were introduced in all high schools for third and fourth form students (13-15 years).

During the 1980's there were moves to include more design foci and the use of a range of materials. This saw the emergence of such subjects as workshop technology and graphics and design. During this time there was also attempts to break down the gender stereotyping by having girls and boys taking all technical/technology subjects in senior primary and junior high school, however by the senior high school these subjects tended to be gender specific (McKenzie, 1992). Also during the 1980's there was an increasing emphasis of technology in existing school subjects such as science (technology as applied science), social studies (technological determinism) and information technology (computers). Technology therefore as it has developed in past curricula encompassed a limited range of skills, processes and knowledge resulting from a narrow and gender specific perspective. As a consequence students have not had the broad experiences in technology that they need to successfully contribute to society.

Technology as a separate subject area emerged in the 1990 curriculum reforms. These curriculum reforms were influenced by the curriculum reviews undertaken in the 1980s. In 1984, a review of the curriculum for schools was undertaken (Department of Education, 1987). The public discussion and consultation was substantial - 21,500 submissions initially, and 10,000 submissions to the draft report (from a total population of approximately 3.4 million at the time). It recommended that there be a national common curriculum for all schools, from new entrants to form 5 (years 1-10), that it includes national curriculum principles, and knowledge, skills, attitudes and values. In 1990, a new government embarked on a project to revise the curriculum in primary and secondary schools, under the banner of 'the Achievement Initiative' (Ministry of Education, 1991). Many of these ideas where influenced by the curriculum reforms taking place in England and Wales in the early 1990s. The policies emphasised raising standards; levels of attainment and the notion of progression linked to accountability; and the contracting out of the development process (Bell, Jones and Carr, 1995). As part of an educational review process a Ministerial Task Group Reviewing Science and Technology Education was set up jointly by the Minister of Education and the Minister of Research, Science and Technology, in June 1991, and which reported in 1992 (Ministry of Research, Science and Technology, 1992). Some of the recommendations from the task group concerning technology education, were that: a technology curriculum be developed as an area in its own right; there be adequate teacher training and resourcing for technology education; technology curricula should not be imported from overseas; the inclusiveness of technology education be emphasised including, Maori input and the use of Maori language[1]. This report was endorsed by members of the business community, and by two Ministers of the Crown. In 1992, the Ministry of Education contracted the Centre for Science and Technology Education Research, University of Waikato to develop a policy framework for technology education in New Zealand. The contract required that: there be wide consultation; best practice be taken into account, nationally and internationally; it be consistent with other Government policies in education; it to take account of resources, teacher change, teacher development, qualifications frameworks, etc; and where possible give a range of options. The development of the policy had to fit within the structure of the New Zealand Curriculum framework, in terms of levels, strands and achievement aims and objectives. The policy decided the general aims of the curriculum, the technological areas, classroom and implementation directions as well as approaches to assessment.

---

[1] Maori are the indigenous people of New Zealand and under the Treaty of Waitangi (1840) were guaranteed exclusive and undisturbed rights in terms of preservation of land, fisheries, forest and language. Maori has been an official language in New Zealand (along with English) since 1987.

The general aims of technology education in *Technology in the New Zealand Curriculum* (Ministry of Education, 1995) were to develop:
- technological knowledge and understanding
- an understanding and awareness of the interrelationship between technology and society
- technological capability.

The three interrelated general aims provide a framework for developing expected learning outcomes, and make a valuable contribution to formulating a balanced curriculum for technology education. In the New Zealand technology curriculum the technological areas include: materials technology; information and communication technology; electronics and control technology; biotechnology; structures and mechanisms; process and production technology; and food technology. The individual objectives of the technology curriculum over 8 levels arise from the general aims of technology education.

The draft curriculum statement was trialed in schools during 1994. This provided teachers and others to respond to the draft statement. The responses generally indicated that teachers and professional technologists were supportive of the general structure and philosophy of the document. However, there was a need to reduce the number of objectives and strands given the number of other curriculum documents that teachers were dealing with. There was general consensus that the strands should reflect directly the three general aims of the technology curriculum: technological knowledge and understanding, technological capability and technology and society. The reduction in strands did in no way change the underlying philosophy but in fact strengthened the notion of technological practice as one of the conceptual bases of the curriculum. Other contexts were added and the number of learning experiences was reduced but an attempt was made to make these more holistic in nature. The final statement was released in October 1995. The curriculum was fully implemented by schools in February 1999. During the time between the release of the final statement in 1995 and implementation in 1999 teacher professional development programmes were been undertaken.

In 2001 a curriculum stocktake was undertaking with reviews of the curricula, international evaluations and teachers experiences of the curricula in practice. The current technology curriculum is currently being reviewed and it is proposed that the new organising strands of the technology curriculum be the *nature of technology, technological knowledge* and *technological practice*. The *nature of technology* strand focuses on students developing an understanding of the key characteristics of technology as a field of human endeavour. The *technological knowledge* strand focuses on students developing technological knowledge that underpins devices, systems/processes, and procedures. The *technological practice* strand focuses on supporting students undertaking technological practice and examining the practice of others. A programme developing student technological literacy provides experiences to develop understandings within each strand. This literacy is enhanced through exploring and understanding the inter-relationship of the strands.

CURRICULUM IN PRACTICE

To develop an understanding of the curriculum in practice The National School Sampling Study (NSSS) provided an opportunity for teachers who had been involved in implementing technology in the New Zealand curriculum to share their experiences (Jones, Harlow, and Cowie, 2004). The primary purpose of the study was to seek feedback from teachers about the effectiveness of the curriculum in practice. The key aspects investigated included: background and experience of teachers, general issues related to implementation, practice, support, the curriculum documents, impact and compliance issues. The structure of the National School Sampling Study encompasses national focus groups, questionnaires and case studies. This section describes the results of a national study to investigate teachers' experiences in the implementation of the technology curriculum in New Zealand schools from years 1-13. This investigation of the implementation of the technology curriculum is part of a larger study being undertaken nationally in all curriculum areas (National Schools Sampling Study) to explore how effective the curriculum is in practice and how the results can inform future developments. National focus groups, questionnaires and case studies were used to explore how the curriculum is being implemented. The questionnaires were distributed to over 10% of New Zealand schools. There are about 2900 schools in New Zealand and 269 sent returns in late 2001.

Overall, the results provide a broad sweep of information about teachers' experiences, and the general impression is that most teachers are reasonably positive about teaching from the technology curriculum statement. However, there are variations between teachers in different kinds of schools and within school types, and especially between primary and secondary school teachers. In order to find out how useful teachers had found the technology curriculum statement the questions asked of teachers were framed around the structure of the statement, covering areas such as the structure of the curriculum, the support and professional development for technology teachers, assessment and reporting issues and strategies for curriculum implementation. There was a general degree of satisfaction with the curriculum statement in that only one third of teachers (33%) wanted to make changes. The largest group who wanted to make changes to the structure/organization of the curriculum statement was senior secondary school (year 11–13) teachers (50%). The most popular changes would be 'making it more simple to understand' and 'including more and better developed learning and assessment examples'. The technology curriculum statement has been of most help in planning, gaining an overview of the progression of key technological ideas, achieving consistent understanding of the curriculum levels and in assessing student achievement. Approximately half of all teachers sometimes found the curriculum statement helpful in gaining an overview of the progression of key ideas.

Although 70% of teachers found the curriculum statement to be always or sometimes helpful in assessing achievement, many reported having difficulties with assessment in technology. The most popular way of assessing student learning in technology was the use of 'practical tasks'. Large classes, the 'time' factor, and establishing level accuracy, were also issues, but only noted by less than 20%. Secondary school teachers were more concerned with the amount of paperwork required than teachers in other schools and were influenced by qualification requirements. At the primary level teachers were concerned about finding appropriate forms of assessment for the junior years and felt that they needed more guidance, both in planning and in assessment. More work needs to be undertaken in the area of assessment in technology.

With the introduction of the technology curriculum, an extensive programme of professional development was offered to teachers. In addition the Ministry of Education has published various resources to assist teachers in their implementation of the technology curriculum. Nearly three-quarters of the teachers (73%) had received professional development in technology. 'Other teachers in the school' had been the most useful source of knowledge to almost 50% of teachers – particularly secondary school teachers. For 75% of teachers professional development had been helpful and 28% had found it had given them a depth of knowledge and ideas so that they could plan and implement the technology curriculum. Professional development had helped many teachers to gain confidence in teaching technology. Across all school types two thirds of teachers expressed a medium level of confidence in teaching technology and one-fifth a high level of confidence. Teachers were most interested in receiving future professional development in the specific technological areas. Information on planning and teaching skills was requested and they were also interested in knowing more about progression, assessment and reporting achievement.

According to 88% of teachers, all students up to and including year 10 in their school studied technology. The majority of teachers considered that the technology curriculum should be compulsory for all students to the end of year 10, as it provided students with important skills. Over 60% of schools were integrating technology with other learning areas. This was particularly evident in primary schools (71%), where teachers teach all curriculum areas. They tended to integrate technology into languages and science. Secondary school technology teachers taught technology in blocks or modules or as a new subject with its own timetable slots. Teachers detailed a wide range of approaches that had been successful in their teaching of technology. These included: choosing topics of relevance to students; practical, hands-on learning activities; a 'problem-solving approach'; and group or co-operative learning approaches. Teachers tended to favour a student-centred approach to teaching technology.

Materials technology and food technology were reported to be the most widely taught technological areas in New Zealand schools. All other technological areas were being taught in schools, with biotechnology the least widely taught. Primary school teachers covered all the technological areas in their teaching. Fewer teachers in intermediate/middle schools taught electronics and control technology, and food technology perhaps because specialist technology teachers often covered these areas. At secondary school level, biotechnology seemed to be the least frequently covered. Overall it appears that apart from the traditional technological areas of food and materials technology, secondary school schools have not developed courses in other technological areas to the same extent as in primary schools.

The general impression was that technology was being implemented across all school types and at all levels. However, on looking more closely at the three main school systems, primary, intermediate and secondary school, it was clear that the challenges of the curriculum at each level were different. Teachers were asked to list the three major challenges they had faced in implementing the technology curriculum:

- The prime concern of teachers was the difficulty of resourcing the equipment needed to implement the technology curriculum (50%);
- What was termed a 'crowded curriculum' was found to be a major challenge for 32% of all teachers, in particular the primary teachers;
- Teachers expressed the need for up-skilling or professional development in technology education (22%);
- Understanding the curriculum was one of the major challenges for 22% of all teachers.

Primary school teachers reported a moderate level of confidence (70%) in teaching technology and appeared to be well on the way to providing technological activities for their pupils in many of the technological areas. They asked for more support, in the form of practical ideas and nearly 60% of primary teachers said that a major challenge was the difficulty they had with resourcing and equipment. Their second major concern (32%) was how to fit technology into an overcrowded curriculum. As teachers who teach all areas of the national curriculum, primary teachers reported overcoming this to a certain extent by integrating technology with other subject areas. Although many secondary school teachers have new facilities in which to work, they have had difficulties with establishing technology in their schools either because of timetable constraints, management decisions or lack of enthusiasm on the part of former home economics and wood/metal teachers. Fifty-three percent of secondary school grade 9-12 teachers placed more emphasis on technological capability than the other strands. Concerns about the level of student knowledge and skill to be able to cope with requirements of the curriculum were expressed by 31% of secondary school teachers. Biotechnology was the only technological area that secondary school schools did not cover so well. Secondary school teachers most often used products, practical tasks, observation and school exemplars in the assessment of technology.

The findings from the study offer interesting insights into how teachers have implemented this part of the New Zealand curriculum framework. There was a general degree of satisfaction with the curriculum statement that had been most helpful to teachers in their planning, gaining an overview of key technological ideas, and achieving consistent understanding of the curriculum levels. Teachers were using the curriculum statement to guide them in their assessment of student achievement, but primary teachers in particular expressed a need for more guidance. Secondary school teachers were grappling with the introduction of new national qualification requirements. Technology teachers have had to adapt more than in any other curriculum area to new ways of teaching. They have found the subject challenging yet have taken technology in their stride, and believe in the value of the subject for their students. The technology curriculum has clearly established itself in the culture of New Zealand schools. Assessment and progression are key issues for the future that were identified by the teachers in this study, this is consistent with research agendas in the field which point out that this is a significant area of study if the field of technology in schools is to progress (Jones and Moreland, 2003)

TECHNOLOGY EDUCATION RESEARCH

In the last twenty years research in New Zealand in technology education has increased significantly. In the 1980's the research focused on using technology to enhance the learning of science e.g. using technological applications to teach science (Jones and Kirk, 1990). With a policy move in the late 1980's early 1990's to include a broad notion of technology in the curriculum, research was commissioned by the New Zealand Ministry of Education. This included research on student attitudes to technology based on the PATT questionnaires (Burns, 1992) and the Learning in Technology Education (LITE) research projects. The LITE projects (1992-1994) were carried out to inform both the curriculum and professional development in the implementation of the technology curriculum (Jones, Mather and Carr, 1995). The early LITE research focused on teachers' perceptions of technology and found the way in which teachers' existing subcultures influenced they way they might be prepared to implement the technology curriculum (Jones and Carr, 1992). The classroom investigations explored the way in which students carried out technological activities in the classroom. The classroom culture and student expectations appeared to strongly influence the way in which students carried out their technological activities (Jones, Mather and Carr, 1995). The final phase of the project explored effective characteristics of professional development for teachers in technology (Jones and Compton, 1998). This early research brought the focus onto the teacher and the learner. This time frame 1990-1995 also saw the emergence of Masters and PhD research in the area of technology education as the area developed prominence in both schools and tertiary education.

The focus of research from 1996-1998 was one teacher development as the full implementation of the curriculum loomed. However during this time there was no directly government-funded research as the resources were for professional development. However, some of the major professional development programmes built on teacher development research and some of the professional development programmes built in a research/evaluative component (for example Jones and Compton, 1998 and Compton and Jones, 1998).

In 1998 there was a shift to focus much more on assessment, both formative and summative (Compton and Harwood, 2003, Moreland and Jones, 2000, Jones and Moreland, 2003). This focus moved the research much more back into the classroom. This focus resulted in moving the research area forward in four interrelated areas:

- Learning in technology for teachers
- Learning in technology for students
- Assessment in technology
- Progression in learning technology

A greater emphasis on researching teachers' teaching technology was undertaken. Teacher conceptualisation of technology and technology education is a complex issue and requires an understanding of the many factors that influence it. Some factors researchers noted as having a large impact on how willing teachers were to change their own concepts of technology and technology education included the perceived need for change, background experience, subject sub-culture, level of support given to teachers during any change process, and personal disposition towards dealing with implications of these changes (Jones, 1997). Classroom based research from 1992-1997 (Jones, 1999) showed that the strategies developed by the teachers in their classrooms when implementing technological activities were often positioned within that particular teacher's teaching and subject sub-culture. Teachers entering areas of uncertainty in their planned activities often reverted to their traditional teaching and subject sub-culture. For a new curriculum area such as technology, this presents particular challenges for teachers as they search to construct a coherent, technological content base and appropriate assessment practices (Moreland and Jones, 2000). Classroom observation and teacher interviews over seven years suggest that technological knowledge, an understanding of technological practice, and an appropriate conceptualisation of technology and technology education, are important in order to teach in the learning area of technology education. However, much more research is required in this area to understand and develop the appropriate teacher knowledges for teaching in the technology classroom.

Technology is an activity that involves not just the social context, but also the physical context, with thinking being associated with and structured by the objects and tools of action. This means research in student learning has to consider not just the conceptual and procedural understanding alone but also the way technological tools and objects influence and interact with student thinking and doing. Research began looking at student learning in classrooms began in 1993 but greater emphasis on researching students' learning in technology education, including ways in which this learning can be enhanced is required. This highlights the need for the identification of appropriate concepts and processes for school technology, students' existing knowledge of these and ways in which student learning in these might be enhanced. This requires much fuller investigation and is beginning as part of a longitudinal study to be undertaken over the next three years in primary school classrooms (Compton, 2004; Jones, Cowie and Moreland, 2004). In classroom technology there is a need for multi-dimensional data and for those using the information to study and understand its structure and its terminology. Assessment judgements become all the more difficult to make in a new subject area such as technology, where there is a lack of a shared subculture on the nature of the subject, insufficient accumulated practical classroom experience and a limited assessment structure. Assessment strategies in technology need to be research and developed along these lines highlighted above. Research in assessment in technology and teacher pedagogical content technology has become well established in last few years (for example Compton and Harwood, in press; Jones and Moreland, 2004)

Extensive classroom research between 1998-2000 by the research team from the Centre for Science and Technology Education Research, University of Waikato, led to a collection of a substantial data set (Moreland and Jones, 2000). This included: 700 hours of classroom observation; 1500 pieces of student work – including student and teacher assessment; formal and informal student interviews; 100 formal teacher interviews; 400 informal teacher interviews; information from teacher workshops; and 50 lesson plans and lesson outlines. The data set contains work from students in Years 1 to 8 and from all technological areas with the work showing students undertaking technology tasks characteristic of everyday classroom technology. A reanalysis of a 3% national sample of student work from years 4 and 8 from the National Educational Monitoring Project in technology was also undertaken. This information may help to provide a model of progression in learning technology. Progression in learning in technology is reflected in the following categories:

- the nature of technology;
- dimensions of student technological practice;
- generic conceptual, procedural, societal and technical aspects and;
- specific conceptual, procedural, societal and technical aspects.

In comparing data between the year groups several trends are emerging. Compared with Year 4 students Year 8 students are more likely to consider a greater number and more functional alternatives; conflicting demands; and relationships between variables and the end user. They are more able to identify and operationalise a greater range of task variables. They demonstrate a greater use of technological language. Though hardly surprising, the trends assist us to understand what students can do and allow us to interact with students in more effective ways. Understanding capabilities students bring to tasks allows us to think about fast-forwarding particular aspects. Compton and Harwood (2004) showed that findings from research undertaken in 2001 research allowed for the identification of key features of components of practice. The three components of practice established were brief development, planning for practice, and outcome development and evaluation.

In summary, the research in New Zealand has shown that to enhance and sustain learning in technology there needs to be a focus on teacher knowledge of specific and detailed technological learning outcomes in conjunction with appropriate pedagogical approaches. Of particular importance was the use of a well-developed framework to focus the teachers' attention on the conceptual, procedural, societal and technical aspects of student learning in technology. However this is only the beginning and much more work over a sustained period needs to be developed. Although this research has a positive impact in the classroom much more research needs to be carried out on the development of models of progression and ways to enhance interactions with students in technology. If we are to move technology education forward as a significant area of learning for all students then there needs to be a much stronger focus on research in classrooms rather than the previous research effort.

PRE AND IN-SERVICE TEACHER EDUCATION

As teacher education institutions began to grapple with the introduction of technology education courses into teacher programmes the Ministry of Education was undertaking national professional development programmes. For the implementation of technology the Ministry of Education provided approximately $NZ22 million for professional development purposes. These national programmes had been informed by two teacher professional development programmes developed under contract from the Ministry of Education by the Centre for Science and Technology Education Research (1995-1997). These initial programmes were the National Facilitator Training Programme, and the Technology Teacher Development Resource Package (For full details of these programmes and the evaluation see Jones and Compton, 1998 and Compton and Jones, 1988). These teacher development programmes took into account past national and international research in teacher development, as well as recent technology education baseline research carried out in New Zealand schools (Jones, Mather and Carr, 1995).

Technology Education forms a part of all pre-service education for all primary school teachers. It is compulsory since technology is an essential learning area of the New Zealand Curriculum Framework with most institutions teaching technology education after it was fully implemented in 1999. However there are differences in emphasis depending on the structure of the institution. Teacher education takes a variety of forms within the Colleges of Education and Universities and there are a number of pathways. The Bachelor of Teaching is a three-year degree that prepares students for teaching in primary, intermediate or middle schools. This programme can be delivered at a distance through web-based media from a number of institutions. The first graduates educated in this way from this media graduated in 2000. The Graduate Diploma of Teaching (Primary) is a one-year programme for University graduates wishing to teach primary, intermediate or middle school students. For secondary school teacher education there are currently two pathways. There is the one-year Graduate Diploma of Teaching (Secondary) programme for graduates to teach in areas of their initial degree specialization, and the Bachelor of Teaching (Secondary), which is a conjoint degree programme. In this last programme the student studies for a degree in a relevant disciple as well as study in the teacher education programme. There are also Bachelor of Teaching (Honours) programmes that allow for students to gain greater depth and specialisation in various aspects of teaching.

The general structure of a primary teacher education course in technology is firstly to explore concepts of technology and technology education. In the course material the students are introduced to a number of different design concepts as well as the history of design and technology. The societal and values aspects of technology are highlighted for the students. There is an emphasis on design and the process of undertaking a technological project to develop an understanding both of technology and also to become aware of issues that children in schools might have to deal with as they learn technology. Through engagement in technology students are also made aware of issues that they may face in the classroom in terms of ways to teach technology, such as problem solving, group work, and resources. Early in the courses students are introduced to undertaking their own technological projects. In the short time that is available for the compulsory curriculum areas the emphasis in the courses has been to develop students understanding of the nature of technology and then make them aware of the characteristics of different technological areas. Although there are seven technological areas because of the limited time available the areas of Structures and Mechanisms and Materials are usually highlighted. These are also the most commonly taught areas in primary schools. The students are introduced to technical aspects, such as health and safety, drawing and construction techniques. Students are introduced to the curriculum in terms of its philosophy, strands, achievement objectives and examples of unit plans developed by other teachers to show the link between the curriculum and ways of planning. There is significant emphasis on planning for technology in the classroom. Thinking about scenarios through to curriculum objectives and then to specific learning outcomes. During this time the students are also introduced to ways of managing technology in the primary classroom. Assessment is another significant area that is introduced to the students, particularly in terms of both formative and summative assessment.

The graduate course development has been a significant one since the majority of teachers who are currently teaching technology trained without any formal technology education courses. The first course in technology education at the graduate level started in 1993 at the University of Waikato. With the release of the draft Technology in the New Zealand Curriculum in late 1993 there were a larger number of teachers studying the course in 1994. The structure of these courses will be discussed in comparison with those at the undergraduate level. Since 1995 one other university has developed a masters technology education programme and a College of Education developed a Technology education masters course at the later date. Two Universities (Massey University and The University of Waikato) developed master's programmes in technology education. From the initial face to face classes taught during semester time technology education now has been taught in distance mode, summer school and more recently there has been the development of fully web-based courses that are asynchronous and can be delivered internationally. As well as developing courses in technology education, that is courses with content related to the nature of technology, learning in technology, technology curriculum and issues such as teacher development and assessment, other courses were developed which emphasised the content area of technology such as technological knowledge, technological innovation, technology and society etc. At this graduate level the courses have traditionally been designed to assist practicing teachers develop knowledge to teach technology in the classroom.

In technology education graduate courses there is considerable emphasis on the nature of technology and technology education. This part of the course examines the history and philosophy of technology, the nature of technological knowledge, technological development in society etc. The courses then tend to examine learning theories associated with learning in technology and in particular current research in learning in technology such as technological problem solving, approaches to design, student conceptual understanding etc. An analysis of technology curriculum internationally and nationally is usually undertaken as well as a study of the historical development of the area of technology education. The graduate courses in technology education also consider such issues as professional development, gender and ethnicity, assessment, etc. The other graduate content area courses in technology are much more wider in range and are aligned to the expertise of the provider. These courses are design to develop the content areas associated with technology such as technology innovation and development, designing, manufacture, electronics, food technology. These courses are often taught by staff from the technology or engineering departments in the Universities.

CONCLUSION

This paper has attempted to briefly outline the development of technology education as a field of endeavour over the last 20 years. In twenty years technology education has moved from a subject limited to technical skills for a few students to a subject concerned with technological literacy for all students. Technology Education has become established in the rhetoric and practice of the classroom from year 1-13. However there is a range of both practice and time spent on technology education in the classroom (Jones, Harlow and Cowie, 2004). Technology is being squeezed in a curriculum that is being influenced strongly by literacy and numeracy initiatives in the primary school and new qualifications in the secondary school. Research on teachers introducing technology in their classrooms would show that these teachers had very high levels of pedagogical knowledge and were highly effective practitioners (Jones and Moreland, 2004). It has also been shown that these teachers can become highly effective technology teachers with appropriate teacher professional development. Overall, technology is becoming part of the school curriculum and teacher education at the pre-service level is beginning to contribute to this. The curriculum is currently under-going some changes to better reflect our understanding of both technology and learning in technology. There will be greater emphasis placed on the nature of technology and technological knowledge. Although these aspects are in the existing curriculum greater attention will be drawn to them.

In terms of research we have seen not only a greater amount of research but also a shift from defining the subject, teachers and student perceptions, through to professional development of teachers and now a much greater focus on learners and learning. This evident in an increase in classroom based research, including assessment and progression. Although there has been research carried out by research teams there has been an associated increase in graduate research being undertaken nationally. Technology education research and practice has emerged as being a significant area of the curriculum but still has someway to go to be seen in the same light as other well-established subjects such as science and social studies.

Although it may appear from Figure 1 that curriculum development, research and teacher education have in some ways proceeded separately there have been direct links between these three aspects. The policy work for technology education was informed by extensive international literature reviews and also the original Learning in Technology Education Research project. The literature searches highlighted the nature of technology and technology education as well as issues related to curriculum development in other countries. New Zealand was fortunate in this regard to build on the experiences of others. The research examined teacher and student perceptions and conducted classroom studies of student technological problem solving. The research also informed issues such as implementation strategies, that is, taking into account teacher subcultures, student perceptions and teacher development priorities. The teacher development strategies were also informed by the early research and formed the basis of the development of national facilitator training and teacher development packages. The evaluation of these programmes as well as the LITE research informed the development courses for pre service and as well courses at the graduate level. The Curriculum Stocktake was informed by the National School Sampling Study and this contributed to a number of initiatives such as revisions to the curriculum, increased initiatives such as Growth and Innovation Fund money for the senior secondary school as well increased research and development in the area of biotechnology. The research in assessment has influenced teacher education programmes as well as on-going resource development. Recent classroom research (from 2000) is informing the current revisions of the technology curriculum statement, particularly in terms of the nature of technology and technological knowledge.

In conclusion, technology education has become part of the curriculum for all students in New Zealand and is a compulsory component of primary pre-service teacher education. National school qualifications have been developed and pathways to tertiary education are becoming established. Technology education in schools continues to compete for space with other curriculum areas. The research field continues to grow with increased number of researchers, both individually and in larger teams.

REFERENCES

Bell, B., Jones A., and Carr, M. (1995) The development of the recent national New Zealand science curriculum. *Studies in Science Education* 26, 73-105

Burns, J., (1992) Technology - What is it, and what do our students think of it? *The NZ Principal*, 6 (3), 22-25.

Compton, V.J. (2004) So – What is technological knowledge? Developing a framework for technology education in New Zealand. 3rd biennial international conference on technology education research. 9-11 December 2004, Queensland, Australia.

Compton, V., and Jones, A., (1998) Reflecting on teacher development in technology education: Implications for future programmes. *International Journal of Technology and Design Education.* 8, 2, 151-166

Compton, V. and Harwood, C. (2003) Enhancing technological practice: An assessment framework for technology education in New Zealand. *International Journal of Design and Technology Education* Vol 13, #1, 1-26.

Compton, V.J. and Harwood, C.D. (In Press) Progression in technology education in New Zealand: components of practice as a way forward. Paper accepted for publication in *International Journal of Design and Technology Education*

Department of Education, (1987) *The curriculum review.* Report of the committee to review the curriculum for schools. Wellington: Government Printer.

Jones, A., (1997) Recent research in student learning of technological concepts and processes. *International Journal of technology and design education* Vol 7, No. 1-2 p 83-96.

Jones A (1999) The influence of teachers' Subcultures on curriculum innovation. In Loughran J, *Researching Teaching*. London, Falmer Press

Jones, A., and Carr, M., (1992) Teachers' perceptions of technology education - implications for curriculum innovation. *Research in Science Education,* 22 230-239

Jones, A., and Compton, V., (1998) Towards a model for teacher development in technology education: from research to practice. *International Journal of Technology and Design Education.* Vol 8, 1, 51-65.

Jones, A Harlow A and Cowie B (2004) New Zealand teachers' experiences in implementing the technology curriculum *International Journal of Technology and Design Education,* 14, 101-119

Jones A. and Kirk C. (1990). Introducing technological applications into the physics classroom. Help or hindrance to learning? *International Journal of Science Education.* 12, 5, 481-490.

Jones A and Moreland J (2003) Developing classroom-focused research in technology education. *Canadian Journal of Science, Mathematics and Technology Education* 51-66.

Jones, A., Mather V., and Carr, M., (1995) *Issues in the practice of technology education. Vol 3*: Centre for Science and Mathematics Education Research, University of Waikato.

McKenzie, D., (1992) The technical curriculum: Second class knowledge, In McCulloch G., (Ed) *The school curriculum in New Zealand: History, theory, policy and practice.* Palmerston North: Dunmore Press.

Ministry of Education, (1991) The achievement initiative. *Education Gazette*, 70 (7), 1-2, 16 April.

Ministry of Education, (1995) *Technology in the New Zealand curriculum.* Wellington: Learning Media

Ministry of Research, Science and Technology (1992) *Charting the course: The report of the ministerial task group into science and technology education.* Wellington: Government Printer.

Moreland, J and Jones, A. (2000) Emerging assessment practices in an emergent curriculum: Implications for technology. *International Journal of Technology and Design Education.* 10: 283-305.

KEN VOLK

16. THE RHETORIC AND REALITY OF TECHNOLOGY EDUCATION IN HONG KONG

"If you have the power of [rhetoric], you will have... the trainer your slave, and the money-maker of whom you talk will be found to gather treasures, not for himself, but for you who are able to speak and to persuade the multitude." (Plato, 380 BCE)

Politicians, government agencies and education authorities have long recognized and skillfully used rhetoric to present their positions. In so doing, they attempt to influence and convince the public that their proposals, actions or maintenance of status-quo are for the public's collective good and well-being. Hong Kong is no different from most other countries, with rhetorical statements espoused over the years on the need for technology education. While terminology and rationales have changed over time, the message remains essentially the same – that an educated citizenry equipped with the technological capability, understanding and awareness is required in order to meet the economic and social challenges ahead.

This paper will review selected Hong Kong position papers and reports regarding technology education, and in particular the secondary school subject of Design & Technology (D&T), arguing that the rhetoric contained therein often did not match the reality of public perception, educational commitment and/or financial backing. In this sense, rhetoric about technology education resulted in D&T programs that remained marginal in schools or not existing at all. Extrapolated from this, is that despite recent calls for technology education to now be included as one of eight required Key Learning Areas for all Hong Kong primary and secondary students, it is most likely doomed to the same fate of the past unless this new rhetoric is backed by adequate funds, mandates and public acceptance.

RHETORIC AND REALITY - THE EARLY YEARS

For as long as there has been formal education, there have been well-intentioned groups making recommendations for reform. These recommendations generally have several common aspects: those with power prescribe changes for others without power, and the changes usually apply to all teachers and students within a system (Tobin, 2002). For those with power and postulating change, rhetoric is an important device for determining the degree of public acceptance and success. Some may call it an "art" (Aristotle, 350 BCE; Hood, 2000; McPhail, 1996; Merriam-Webster, 1997), while others consider it more of a "skill" (Billig, 1987; Cockcroft and Cockcroft, 1992). Both descriptors can have positive connotations,

M.J. de Vries, I. Mottier (eds.), International Handbook of Technology Education, 213–226.

with rhetorical prose presented in a beautiful and quality manner, or with potential negative connotations of being able to manipulate and/or being superficial.

Whether an art or skill, rhetoric involves the use of written or spoken language. For school subjects in Hong Kong that relate to technology education, over the years there have been several important government position papers published and/or public comments made. These rhetorical statements have addressed various aspects on the need for technology education, as well as matters relating to the specific curriculum. Terminology relating to various aspects of technology education have changed somewhat since the statements were made (i.e., craft, technical education, manual training, design & technology), as have the scope and content of the subject. However, what has not changed is the rhetoric for the need for such subjects in schools.

The beginning of technology education in Hong Kong can be considered starting in the mid-1800's, with boys being taught carpentry, bookbinding and shoemaking at a Roman Catholic mission house (Waters, 2002). For official government-initiated education programs, a junior technical school was established in 1932 that featured a four-year course designed as pre-apprenticeship training. After World War II and the rapid industrialization Hong Kong was witnessing, there was an awareness of the dependency on sophisticated technology and calls for an expansion of technical education to meet workforce needs (Sweeting, 2004). Since these calls were from marginal (non-power) sectors that included small-scale and labor-intensive enterprises, nothing was done - that is until the Chinese Manufacturing Association offered financial help for the government to develop a Technical College in 1955, the forerunner of the current Hong Kong Polytechnic University.

Regarding the more-generic technology education subject of Design & Technology (D&T), which is the current name for the secondary school subject in Hong Kong that provides a wide-range of hands-on activities using tools, materials and technical approaches, the antecedents of the subject started in the mid-1950s. At that time, it was common to find lower secondary technical schools (S1-S3) offering manual training or handwork courses in bookbinding, carpentry, metalwork, pottery, leatherwork, paperwork and carving (Fung, 2002). However, not all "academic" grammar schools actually offered these subjects.

By the late 1950s, with much happening in the field of education, especially due to political, economic, and demographic pressures, there were many "false starts" and mistakes made by education policy makers (Sweeting, p.155). One was the short-lived "secondary modern schools" initiative that instituted shorter courses for students that found the largely academic subjects in grammar schools to be irrelevant. In fact, the modern schools were actually vocational in nature and included subjects such as technical drawing, woodworking and metalworking for boys. As these schools "tended to be less generously provisioned with qualified staff and suitable equipment… they were soon dismissed in the minds of many parents as a refuge for failing students and poor teachers" (p155). After four years, these schools disappeared in name, and were converted into technical or prevocational schools.

By the mid-1960s, it was recommended that as a standard specification for all secondary schools, special rooms in woodworking, metalworking and housecraft should be included (Education Commission, 1963). The degree to which these rooms were actually equipped is debatable, but there was some compliance, perhaps 50 percent of schools - enough for the Commission to make several recommendations. One of which was to have all schools expand these courses to upper secondary grades, enabling students to take Certificate of Education (CE) examinations at the end of S5. The Commission stated:

Efforts to introduce manual training to School Certificate standard into the secondary school curriculum have so far proved unsuccessful... This is considered a serious deficiency and it is recommended that the special rooms for woodworking, metalwork and housecraft... should be used to provide full School Certificate courses for some pupils in these subjects. (p. 93)

Despite recommendations by the Education Commission for more students to participate in S4-5 programs, there was little improvement over the years. As seen in Table 1, although the total number of CE candidates for these subjects increased, as a percentage of the total number of students taking examinations, any improvement was short-lived.

Subject	1963	1967	1973
Metalwork	103 (1.6%)	358 (1.9%)	486 (1.2%)
Woodwork	55 (0.9%)	265 (1.4%)	260 (0.7%)
Total No. of Candidates For All Exams	6,334	18,793	39,658

Table 1 School Certificate Candidature for Technical Subjects: Number (percent of total)

RHETORIC AND REALITY - THE 1970S THROUGH 1990S

As noted by Sweeting in his historical review of education in Hong Kong, "the proliferation of policy papers and of education-related pressure groups made this period [1970s-1980s] distinctive in Hong Kong's history of education, contributing to an atmosphere in which mass seemed more important than quality, though neither the papers nor the pressure groups were themselves massive in size" (p. 237). He further suggested that "although some of the policy documents in earlier times turned out to be paper tigers, many of them in these years served as kites, flown by the Government to ascertain the strength and direction of public opinion" (p. 239).

Perhaps the major policy paper that came out during this time that was related to technology- type subjects was the 26-page *Secondary Education in Hong Kong During the Next Decade* (Hong Kong Government, 1974). This *White Paper* was tabled and passed by the Legislative Council after considerable public debate of the earlier *Green Paper*. [Note: the term "Green Paper" was changed by the early 1980s to "Consultation Documents" and "White Paper" changed to "Policy

Paper"]. This *White Paper* proposed universal secondary education for all students up to S3, and expanding the goals set forth nine years earlier in another *White Paper* (Hong Kong Government, 1965) on universal primary education. The 1974 *White Paper* was also strong in its rhetoric about the need for technology education when it stated: "in junior secondary forms [Secondary 1-3], all pupils should follow the same general curriculum, of which 25% and 30% would be allocated to practical and technical subjects" (p.4). The paper expected that "the junior secondary curriculum will be designed to foster a liking for practical subjects" (p. 4). It further suggested "practical subjects [defined as woodwork, metalwork, integrated woodwork, metalwork and design, practical electricity, technical drawing, home economics, typing and commercial studies] will be included in the common curriculum of the junior secondary course, as speedily as facilities in school permit (p. 6).

The rhetoric on the need for this emphasis was apparent in that "the Government attaches considerable importance to a build-up of technical education at the secondary level in line with Hong Kong's future needs" (p.6). However, in softening this stance, and respecting the reality and quasi-independence of schools, the paper also suggested "...it will be left up to the discretion of individual schools to *increase* [emphasis added] the proportion of time devoted to them" (p .4).

The *Guide* produced by the Curriculum Development Committee (1975) describing the planning and implementation of the new secondary education program was also timid in the timetable and compliance for including subjects such as D&T. They softened the importance and need for D&T by stating "because of the present lack of appropriate resources it is neither possible nor desirable for schools to implement the common-core curriculum in its entirety next year" (p. 4). They further suggested "the curriculum has therefore been designed as a target towards which schools are expected to move" (p. 4). As such, the recommendations made in the *White Paper* about practical subjects were reduced to a "kite", with schools left to their own to make the decisions about curriculum matters.

The lack of rigorous guidelines, mandated or enforcement resulted in schools decreasing the time for some subjects, or determining which practical and technical subjects should (would) be offered at all. According to Eric Fung, Technology Subject Officer at the Hong Kong Examinations and Assessment Authority (personal communication, December 2, 2004), there was at that time, approximately 100 percent compliance with the offering of practical subjects, although not necessarily encompassing a complete range. For instance, only home economics, art and music might have been available in a school. Schools could also continue to offer woodworking or metalworking, even if new "D&T" facilities were placed in schools (Curriculum Development Committee, 1975).

Furthermore, practical subjects most often were allocated only two periods a week – a lot less than recommended. Complicating this was the interpretation by schools that the subject of physical education was also being included as one of the practical subjects (Curriculum Development Committee, 1975; Hong Kong Government, 1981). Later studies commissioned by the Government found grammar schools, which contained over 95 percent of the school population, averaged between 15 percent and 20 percent of the total instructional time for practical and physical education subjects, far less than the recommended 25-30 percent for just practical subjects (Hong Kong Board of Education, 1997).

By 1975, the subject of Design & Technology was slowly being introduced in secondary schools (Fung, 2002) and was "clearly related to their increasing importance within the economy" (Sweeting, 2004, p. 243). Borrowed from the curriculum developed in England, enthusiasm for this new subject was relatively high, given *White Paper* assurances for technical curriculum and facility support. In actuality, the enthusiasm for the potential of D&T soon waned, as traditional approaches of wood craft and metal working continued in most schools.

It was the release of the *Design & Technology Syllabus* in 1983 that confidently proclaimed the syllabus "proposes a major development in the materials-based subjects -woodwork and metalwork... and a move away from work narrowly concerned with the appreciation of manual skills" (Curriculum Development Committee, 1983, p.5). Notwithstanding this claim, basic skills obtained through the use of hand tools to saw, plane, drill and fasten continued to be heavily emphasized, reflecting the facilities that existed or were still being planned.

Maintaining this emphasis, if a school had programs at the Certificate of Education level (S4-5), students could take either the CE examination for D&T wood bias (English version), D&T metal bias (English version), Woodworking (Chinese version), or Metalworking (Chinese version). Since the Chinese version of the D&T CE examination was not even offered until 1990, many schools found the English-medium examinations difficult for those few students opting for CE level studies in this "non-academic" area. For this reason, the Chinese versions of woodwork and/or metalwork were more appealing to the students and continued to be offered. In fact, the Government position on CE subject selection by students expected this differentiation, and noted that it was "suitable... some students would have a greater aptitude for practical studies, while others would be more inclined towards academic education" (Education Commission, 1984, p. 10). Figure 1 shows the lackluster trend of D&T as a subject for CE level examinations after its introduction with project work in 1977 (Hong Kong Examinations Authority, 1982; Fung, 2002).

The problem of competing and overlapping subject content, as well as student options for D&T CE study were noted in a study conducted by Chow (1996). He found that pupils, parents and even school authorities viewed the subject as having no great value. Parents associated the subject with traditional skill training, and when their children had the opportunity to select elective subjects in Secondary 4, parents suggested or forced their children to select other subjects such as science or art. Technical subjects such as technical drawing or engineering science were perceived as being more academic and were thus more popular and successful in recruiting students than D&T. With approximately 250,000 students in Secondary 1-3 at that time, few continued studying D&T beyond this grade as an elective.

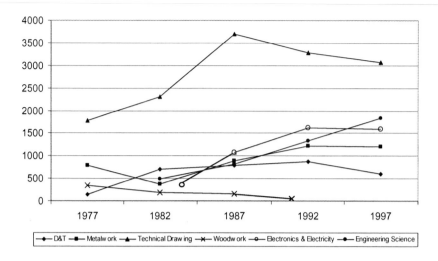

Figure 1Certificate of Examination Candidates
Note: 1977: First D&T Exam; 1983: First Engineering Science Exam; 1991: Last Woodworking Exam

Facilities also did not change significantly from the earlier woodworking and metalworking programs. As a result, they continued to reflect the bias in the end-of-course test and potential CE examinations. For instance, even up to the mid 1990s, the standard accommodation for D&T facilities contained two rooms, usually connected by a common passage used either for the artisan in charge or for storage. Each room was officially designated as a "D&T workshop" with a "wood bias" and "metal bias" (Education Department, 1995) and with the total size to be 325 square meters. The standard furniture and equipment list also reflected this bias, as witnessed by the headers of "wood hand tools", "wood machinery", "metal hand tools", and "metal machinery". With class sizes expected to average around 20 students, the list required the provision of 20 chisels of each various size, as well as 20 marking gauges, 20 knives, 20 mallets, 20 planes, 20 coping saws, 20 goggles, etc. – suggesting, and to some extent validating the continued repetitive and prescriptive exercises used in most programs. Thus, even the rhetoric contained in the syllabus to move away from the manual skills was not matching the reality of facilities being designed, the equipment supplied, or the activities by students undertaken in most D&T programs.

Perhaps the largest event that would impact the calls to implement and/or for the continued existence of practical subjects such as Design & Technology in secondary schools was the introduction of computers. The impact of this new technology was never imagined in earlier policy statements calling for the core practical curriculum. However, in 1982, the subject of Computer Studies was introduced in 30 pilot schools and by 1986 all secondary schools in Hong Kong offered the subject. Financial backing from the government was also very generous, such as the establishment of a HK$4 million (US$500,000) Computer Education Centre to train teachers and provide resources (Sweeting, 2004).

One major requirement necessary in order to accommodate this new subject in existing schools was the physical setting of the computer lab, with an obvious choice often being one of the D&T labs. With D&T facilities regularly located on the first floor of a school because of material and equipment considerations, a converted D&T lab not only provided ample space and electrical power requirements, it provided a premiere location by which to showcase new (and more-respected) technology education. The pressures for resources needed to equip and maintain these new computer facilities also tended to put pressure on D&T. Computer Studies was seen as a necessary subject for all students, at the expense of other less-respected subjects. In an already crowded curriculum and school day for students, the reduction of time or options for D&T was being felt. The required practical-technical "pie" was now being sliced in different proportions, with Computer Studies commanding the largest piece being offered and served to students.

Finally, another influence on the success, implementation and development of technology education subjects such as D&T was the timetable being set for new educational initiatives before the Handover to China in 1997. Lee and Bray (1995) commented on how these deadlines affected reform. They noted "the closer the year 1997 approaches, the deadline effects become stronger and stronger" (p.370). According to the authors, initiatives were either quickly being introduced with unrealistic implementation schedules, not introduced because of an uncertain future, or not adequately funded due to potential change in policy direction. In this regard, despite the rhetoric to integrate a wider range of materials, processes and subjects in D&T (Curriculum Development Institute, 1996), changes were largely negligible – that is up until after the Handover to China in 1997.

RHETORIC AND REALITY - AFTER THE HANDOVER

In his first *Policy Address* as Chief Executive of the Hong Kong Special Administrative Region, Mr. Tung Chee-hwa outlined several initiatives, including an increased emphasis on language skills and a Quality Education Fund (QEF) to encourage innovation and self-motivated reform in primary and secondary schools (Tung, 1997). For Design & Technology programs, these initiatives were to have different impacts. Language policy insisted on mother tongue instruction in all except for those in 100 secondary schools allowed to continue teaching in English. For D&T in English-medium schools, instruction regularly did not follow this policy, as the difficulty explaining technical terms and the limited language skills of D&T teachers resulted in mixed code teaching. The QEF turned out to be successful for only a few D&T programs, with computer hardware and software for CAD the most common award from successful proposals submitted by teachers.

The *Policy Address* and subsequent *Learning for Life, Learning Through Life: Reform Proposals for the Education System in Hong Kong* (Education Commission, 2000) also included rhetoric on the need and benefit of information technology as a required feature in schools. As Chief Executive Tung (1997) stated, we need to "equip our teachers with the necessary IT skills; to apply computer-assisted teaching and learning across the curriculum; and to place students in an environment where they can use this technology as part of their daily activities and grow up to use it creatively" (para. 46). Exacerbating the existing situation whereby schools were removing D&T labs in order to place computers, this official call for more IT sanctioned this move. Critical of this fixation with policies that promoted the use of IT, Sweeting (2004) suggested policy makers "supposed that new opportunities created especially by information technology and the 'knowledge-based economy' made earlier experiences in educational policy and practice more or less irrelevant" (p. 526). Bringing proposals such as *Learning for Life* to fruition required the use of public relations techniques for stylish publications and fanfare kickoff press conferences. This "top-down" communication to the citizens of Hong Kong was combined with "an assumption by administrators that information technology could cure most, if not all, problems" (Sweeting, 2004, p. 527).

The *Learning for Life* document also went into great detail as to what the problems and solutions were in order for students to learn more independently. Concern about excessive examinations, monotonous teaching and a lack of creativity in students were cited throughout the document. In broad terms, the Education Commission stated "our priority should be accorded to enabling our students to enjoy learning, enhancing their effectiveness in communication and developing their creativity and sense of commitment" (2000, p. 30). In regard to this challenge, many reform proposals were announced in the document. Two most relevant to technology education were the suggestion for a new S4-S5 subject called Integrated Science and Technology and for a required S6 and S7 subject called Liberal Studies, which would have an optional module on Science, Technology and Social Studies which students could select. Four years later, less than 40 of the more than 450 secondary schools have introduced Integrated Science and Technology. Liberal Studies is still being debated.

POSITIVE DEVELOPMENTS REGARDING TECHNOLOGY EDUCATION

Perhaps the single most important document in recent years with the potential to influence technology education was the release of the *Learning to Learn* (Curriculum Development Council, 2000) document that specifically identified eight Key Learning Areas for all students to study. Included was a Technology Education Key Learning Area (TEKLA) that was required for all primary and lower secondary grade students. The TEKLA broadly defined "technology" as "the purposeful application of knowledge, skills and experience in using resources to create products or systems to meet human needs" (p. 2). Yet, in describing how this was to be accomplished in primary or secondary grades, the document fell short in specifics. The accompanying *Technology Education Key Learning Area Curriculum Guide* (Curriculum Development Council, 2002) was also lacking in detail. Rife with rhetoric about technology being "an influential factor in the social and economic development of our [Hong Kong] society", the TEKLA was seen as being "essential…to the improvement of everyday living, and the social and economic development" (p. 5). With materials and structures, operations and manufacturing, and systems and control identified as three of the six learning elements of technology education, it seemed apparent the subject of D&T would naturally play an important role in having students meet the goals outlined in the TEKLA. However, in a typical fashion of placating individual schools and the public, the *Guide* softened its stance by insisting, "schools could choose to offer different TE subjects (i.e., D&T, Computers, Home Economics, Business Studies, etc) based on factors such as the mission and background of the school and the learning needs of the students" (p. 43). In his way, status-quo was protected and computer-centered subjects would suffice for being technology education.

In contrast, the public strongly supported the broad study of technology in schools. In a recent telephone survey conducted with over 750 randomly-selected adults, more than two-thirds agreed with Curriculum Development Council's more-encompassing definition of technology and that it should be included in the school curriculum (Volk, 2004). The results from questions asked about technology pointed out the public's own limited knowledge and misconceptions - further illustrating the need for technology education in schools. For example, when asked if they could explain how a flashlight works, 70 percent of the respondents said "No". When asked whether a microwave oven heats food from the outside to the inside, 55 percent answered "Yes".

Despite the rhetoric about technology education and the valuable experiences students can have, the sad reality is that very few schools actually implement the subject in a meaningful and sustained way. Primary schools may bury the content in the amorphous subject called General Studies, which would then share part of the 12-15 percent suggested time allocated along with Science and Personal, Social and Humanities Education. With limited resources, time and teacher training, most primary students receive just a cursory treatment of Technology education.

In secondary schools, D&T remains marginal. Although some improvements have made the subject more "legitimate". The first Pupils' Attitudes Toward Technology study (Volk and Yip, 1999) conducted in 1997 on over 3,500 Secondary 3 students showed significant differences between boys' and girls' attitudes toward technology. Following the PATT-HK study, the Equal Opportunities Commission reminded schools that the Sex Discrimination Ordinance made it unlawful to discriminate against a student in the way it affords him/her access to any benefits, facilities or services. Slowly, schools began to have girls participate in D&T, as well as boys in Home Economics. This action went a long way in starting to reduce gender stereotypes and making D&T a legitimate subject for all students.

After a few years of this new arrangement and opportunity for girls, the Pupils' Attitudes Toward Technology study was repeated (Volk, Yip and Lo, 2003). This time, some of the significant differences in attitudes between boys and girls had disappeared. Table 2 shows the changes from the 1997 PATT-HK and 2003 PATT2-HK studies.

Characteristics	Interest in Technology	Role Pattern	Technology is Difficult	Consequences of Technology	School Curriculum	Career Aspiration
1997 PATT-HK						
Boy (1882)	2.45	2.62	2.73	2.36	2.56	2.55
Girl (1477)	2.74	2.59	2.77	2.44	2.72	2.74
Significance	**	**	**	**	**	**
2003 PATT2-HK						
Boy (1502)	2.57	2.72	2.81	2.43	2.51	2.62
Girl (1374)	2.80	2.69	2.81	2.49	2.61	2.77
Significance	**			**	**	**

Table II T-test on Student Characteristics

While it is possible to assume changes in society during this time and/or other outside factors influenced this change, the new study seemed to indicate D&T was actually playing a role in promoting students' positive attitudes toward technology. The impact of these changes on students' future education and career goals is obvious.

Although the benefits and positive changes seem to be occurring with girls now taking Design & Technology, today only about 60 percent of the lower secondary schools offer the subject. Without all secondary schools providing D&T-type subjects, a form of discrimination still exists, with some students denied educational experiences solely due to a school's prerogative. The time appropriated for those schools with D&T has also been reduced, since the addition of girls into the programs doubled the number of students a teacher must see, but now in one-half the time. The TEKLA Curriculum Guide (Curriculum Development Council, 2002) recommended between 8-15 percent of total time allocated to TE. Yet, a report on how schools were actually implementing the reform found that for TE subjects in lower secondary grades (of which computers is contained), showed that the lesson time ranged from 5.1 to 10.0 percent of the total time, with 8.3 being average (Education and Manpower Bureau, 2004).

Even with school administrators' continued assumption that "computers" are the same as "technology education", with over 95 percent of secondary students now having computers at home, one could argue schools' continued emphasis on basic computer skills and applications may not be as relevant, necessary or appealing to students. Finally, the interest in the subject as a Certificate in Education exam has also declined by 15 percent from 1997 to 2003 (Examination and Assessment Authority, 2004), placing pressure on the continuation of the subject at that level.

THE FUTURE

Although there have been many position papers and policy statements over the years about the need for Hong Kong students to study and experience technology, perhaps the current Key Learning Area reform effort has the greatest potential for actually realizing this goal. Proposals being discussed for further changes in the secondary school structure such as reducing the current seven years of school to six, and reducing the emphasis on examinations will also necessitate a review of the total school curriculum, with perhaps many schools needing to change (Curriculum Development Institute, 2004). However, how this will actually affect technology education remains uncertain.

To reach the goals and recommendations set forth in the Technology Education KLA, Hong Kong's primary schools must encourage more subject integration and eliminate restrictions placed on learning through set time-on-task scheduling. This obviously challenges the current practice of having subject specialist teachers in primary grades and scheduling subjects to standard bell schedules. Teachers that can weave examples of technology into maths, science, history and languages will be much more successful at providing authentic, creative and meaningful learning experiences for their students. This would suggest that pre-service teacher must have technology education as part of their professional preparation.

For all lower secondary schools, they should have facilities and programs in Design & Technology in order for all students to have opportunities and experiences. In fact, with the "millennium school design" now standard for all new secondary schools, one large 325 square meter D&T workshop is still included (Education and Manpower Branch, 1997), although quite often, the space is left unequipped other than as a common office area for staff. Lower secondary students in schools with D&T could progress from somewhat structured technology and design activities in order to become familiar with tools, materials and processes, followed by problems that are more open-ended and challenging.

The scheduling for Design & Technology (as well as other cultural subjects) will also need to be re-examined, as the current practice is for students to take such subjects once every 6 day-cycle for 90 minutes. This scheduling for administrative convenience is at the expense of consistency, continuity and maintaining student enthusiasm. A better arrangement would be in a concentrated block of time, over several weeks so that students could rotate from one cultural subject to the next. This would help reduce problems associated with students having to focus attention on too many subjects and would greatly simplify teachers' lives. Attention also needs to be paid to the recommended time suggested for TE subjects and that schools should be held accountable that the time, content and activities suggested in the *TEKLA Curriculum Guide* are followed (Curriculum Development Council, 2002).

In senior secondary grades, the proposed new Liberal Studies core subject may appear to be a step in the right direction. In this subject, there are three areas of study: Self & Personal Development; Society & Culture, and Science; Technology and the Environment. Within the latter area, there are three compulsory parts, Diseases and Health; Information Technology & Society; and Pollution & the Environment. Students then select two out of a four electives on Biotechnology, Space Exploration, Transportation, and Energy. However, the lack of schools that actually have quality D&T-type facilities and the limited number of trained teachers make it doubtful students will be able participate in anything more than superficial lectures and discussions about technology. Furthermore, without all students having prior hands-on technology education experiences in lower secondary grades, most "independent learning" about technology in Liberal Studies will likely result in outcomes that are paper reports accompanied by PowerPoint presentations.

Finally, a feature of the new senior secondary curriculum beyond the core curriculum of Chinese, English, Mathematics and Liberal Studies, will have students select two to three electives from approximately 20 subjects (Curriculum Development Institute, 2004). Subjects include among others, Chemistry, Biology, Physics, Music, Physical Education, and a new subject called Design and Applied Technology (DAT). This new subject will combine features of subjects such as Graphical Communications, D&T (S4-5), and electronics, resulting in their elimination. The rhetoric and rationale for DAT is typical, suggesting it will "significantly enhance the competitiveness of our products and services", as well as " help... build Hong Kong into a centre for design and creative industries" (p. 244). However grand the intentions of this subject are, they must again meet the reality of school practice. There is no requirement for schools to offer each elective, and even if the elective is offered, with more academically-attractive options available such as mathematics and science, there is little to assume DAT will be selected by students or suggested by their parents.

CONCLUSION

Given past rhetoric and limited practices, existing economic and administrative constraints, coupled with the skewed perception by many schools of what constitutes technology, the reality is technology education subjects such as Design & Technology will most likely remain marginal in schools. Nevertheless, the growth and development of technology in Hong Kong will continue to impact all students' lives, and the current rhetoric about the importance of all students learning about technology will remain just that.

REFERENCES

Aristotle (350 BCE). *Rhetoric*. (W. R. Roberts, Trans.). Available on-line from: http://classics.mit.edu/Aristotle/rhetoric.html (The MIT Internet Classics).

Billig, M. (1987). *Arguing and thinking: A rhetorical approach to social psychology*. Cambridge: Cambridge University Press.

Chow S.C (1996). *A study of the declining candidature for design & technology at the certificate of education level in Hong Kong*. Unpublished Master's Dissertation, University of Wolverhampton.

Cockcroft, R. & Cockcroft, S. (1992). *Persuading people: An introduction to rhetoric.* London: Macmillan.

Curriculum Development Committee, (1975). *A preliminary guide to the curriculum for junior secondary forms.* Hong Kong: Government Press.

Curriculum Development Committee, (1983). *Syllabus for design and technology: Forms I-III.* Hong Kong: Government Press.

Curriculum Development Council. (2000). *Learning to learn: Technology Education Key Learning Area.* Hong Kong: Printing Department.

Curriculum Development Council. (2002). *Technology education key learning area curriculum guide.* Hong Kong: Government Printer.

Curriculum Development Institute. (1996). *Guidelines on the teaching of design & technology.* Hong Kong: Author.

Curriculum Development Institute. (2004). *Reforming the academic structure for senior secondary education and higher education.* Hong Kong: Author.

Education and Manpower Branch. (1997). *Schedule of accommodation for 30-classroom secondary school. (SS30, 12-97).* Hong Kong: Building Section Department.

Education and Manpower Bureau. (2004). *Report of survey on the school curriculum reform and implementation of key learning area curricula in schools 2003.* Hong Kong: Author.

Education Commission. (1963). *Report of education commission.* Hong Kong: Government Printer.

Education Commission. (1984). *Education commission report no. 1.* Hong Kong: Government Press.

Education Commission. (2000). *Learning for life, learning through life: Reform proposals for the education system in Hong Kong.* Hong Kong: Printing Department.

Education Department. (1995). *Approved schedule of accommodation for new standard design secondary school. (Approved code: SS26).* Hong Kong: Author.

Fung, E. (2002). Development of technology subjects in secondary schools in Hong Kong. *Hong Kong examinations and assessment authority 25th anniversary commemorative publication.* (pp. 63-66). Hong Kong: Examinations and Assessment Authority.

Hong Kong Board of Education. (1997). *Report on review of 9-year compulsory education.* Hong Kong: Government Printer.

Hong Kong Examinations and Assessment Authority (2004). *HKCEE exam statistics.* Available on line from: http://eant01.hkeaa.edu.hk/hkea/new_look_home.asp.

Hong Kong Examinations Authority. (1982). *Annual report.* Hong Kong: Government Printer.

Hong Kong Government. (1965).*Education Policy (White Paper).* Hong Kong: Government Printer.

Hong Kong Government. (1974). *Secondary Education in Hong Kong During the Next Decade (White Paper).* Hong Kong: Government Printer.

Hong Kong Government. (1981). *The Hong Kong education system.* Hong Kong: Government Printer.

Hood, C. (2000). *The art of the state: Culture, rhetoric, and public management.* Oxford: Oxford University Press.

Lee, W. & Bray, M. (1995). *Education: Evolving patterns and challenges.* In J. Cheng & S. Lo (Eds.). From Colony to SAR: Hong Kong's Challenges Ahead. (pp. 357-378). Hong Kong: The Chinese University Press.

McPhail, M. (1996). *Zen and the art of rhetoric: An inquiry into coherence.* New York: State University Press.

Merriam-Webster Dictionary (1997). Springfield, MA: Merriam-Webster.

Plato (380 BCE). *Gorgias.* (B. Jowett, Trans.). Available on-line from: http://classics.mit.edu/Plato/gorgias.html (The MIT Internet Classics).

Sweeting, A. (2004). *Education in Hong Kong, 1941-2001: Visions and revisions.* Hong Kong: Hong Kong University Press.

Tobin, K. (2002). Beyond the bold rhetoric of reform: (Re)learning to teach science appropriately. In W. Roth & J. Desautels (Eds.). *Science Education as/for sociopolitical action.* (pp. 126-150). New York: Peter Lang.

Tung, C.H. (1997). *Policy address.* Available on-line from: http://www.policyaddress.gov.hk/pa97/english/paindex.htm

Volk, K.S. & Yip, W. M. (1999). Gender and technology in Hong Kong: A study of pupils' attitudes toward technology. *International Journal of Technology and Design Education.* 9, 57-71. Dordrecht, The Netherlands: Kluwer Academic Publishers.

Volk, K.S. (2004). *What Hong Kong people think about technology*. Manuscript submitted for publication.

Volk, K.S., Yip, W. M & Lo, T.K., (2003). Hong Kong pupils' attitudes toward technology: The impact of design & technology programs. *Journal of Technology Education*. 15(1). 48-63. Blacksburg, VA: Virginia Polytechnic University.

Waters, D. (2002, April). A brief history of technical education in Hong Kong – With special reference to the Polytechnic University. *Profile*. Available on-line from: http://production.mic.polyu.edu.hk/~cpa/profile/02apr/index.html.

TOSHIKI MATSUDA

17. THE JAPANESE WORD "GIJUTSU": SHOULD IT MEAN "SKILLS" OR "TECHNOLOGY"?

INTRODUCTION

This article examines technology education in the past two decades in Japan. My major field of research is not technology education but educational technology and informatics education. However, I have worked on projects related to technology education; for example, I have been engaged in research on teacher education in mathematics and science for over 20 years at the Tokyo Institute of Technology, and I have studied science and technology education with teachers at the technical high school attached to our Institute. I participated as a curriculum specialist in the workgroups of the latest National Course of Studies revision conducted by the Ministry of Education, Culture, Sports, Science and Technology (MEXT), and was involved in the establishment of "Information Study" as a new subject area for high school students, as well as in the revision of the "Industrial Arts" course for lower secondary school students.

The present article is concerned with information technology and teacher education. These were the most important issues in the recent revision of the technology education curriculum. The purpose of reviewing and discussing the recent changes is to elucidate what reforms will be needed for the future. In so doing it is appropriate to give attention to the technology that has effected such changes in society, and to focus on teachers, who will be responsible for future educational change.

2. CHANGES IN TECHNOLOGY EDUCATION IN THE JAPANESE NATIONAL CURRICULUM

The National Course of Studies has been revised twice in the last two decades, in 1989 and 1998. As a result of these revisions, technology education in Japanese schools has changed as follows:

In the first revision, it was changed from a system in which boys separately studied mainly "Industrial Arts" while girls studied mainly "Homemaking", to a system in which boys and girls study the same syllabus in both "Industrial Arts" and "Homemaking", together in one classroom. This changed the role of technology education in lower secondary schools from vocational education to literacy education in technology. Further, two subjects were now taught in the same amount of time as one under the previous curriculum, so that the amount of time given to technology education was halved. As a result, of the traditional

M.J. de Vries, I. Mottier (eds.), International Handbook of Technology Education, 227–240.
© *2006 Sense Publishers. All rights reserved.*

categories within "Industrial Arts", such as "woodwork", "metalwork", "electricity", "machining", and "cultivation", only "woodwork" was now offered to seventh graders and "electricity" to eighth graders, whereas in the previous curriculum boys had taken four of the categories, while the remainder and "information technology", which was newly added at that time, became optional in the ninth grade. In addition, some aspects of technology education were included in a new subject "Home Life Techniques", established as a subject areas of "Home Economics", which became compulsory for boys in upper secondary schools, whereas "Industrial Arts" had been the only subject area which included technology education in elementary and secondary schools before the revision. Few schools, however, chose the new subject, because few teachers could teach it, and there were three alternatives which could be chosen from "Home Economics".

Table 1: Changes in hours of schooling for each subject area in the three most recent versions of the national curriculum

	1977			1989			1998		
	7th grade	8th grade	9th grade	7th grade	8th grade	9th grade	7th grade	8th grade	9th grade
Japanese Language	175	140	140	175	140	140	140	105	105
Social Studies	140	140	105	140	140	70-105	105	105	85
Mathematics	105	140	140	105	140	140	105	105	105
Science	105	105	140	105	105	105-140	105	105	80
Music	70	70	35	70	35-70	35	45	35	35
Fine Arts	70	70	35	70	35-70	35	45	35	35
Health and Physical Education	105	105	105	105	105	105-140	90	90	90
Industrial Arts and/or Home Economics	70	70	105	70	70	70-105	70	70	35
Foreign Language	–	–	–	–	–	–	105	105	105
Moral Education	35	35	35	35	35	35	35	35	35
Special Activities	70	70	70	35-70	35-70	35-70	35	35	35
Optional Subjects (hours for Foreign Language)	105 (105)	105 (105)	140 (105)	105-140 (105-140)	105-210 (105-140)	140-280 (105-140)	0-30	50-85	105-165
Period for Integrated Study	–	–	–	–	–	–	70-100	70-105	70-130
Total	1050	1050	1050	1050	1050	1050	980	980	980

* One school "hour" is normally fifty minutes.
** "Foreign Language" was included in "Optional Subjects" in the curricula of both 1978 and 1989. School hours assigned to "Foreign Language" are shown in brackets.
*** In the curriculum of 1998, students must take more than one optional subject in the eighth grade and more than two in the ninth grade.

In the second revision, in 1998, teaching hours in every subject area decreased, as is shown in Table 1, as a result of Saturday becoming a school holiday. For "Industrial Arts" and "Homemaking", the total number of school hours was reduced from 210 hours to 175 hours. Moreover, "Industrial Arts" was reorganized to consist of two categories: "Manufacturing (Monozukuri in Japanese)", which corresponded to the five traditional categories of "Industrial Arts", and "Information Technology", which was a new category added from the former revision. At the same time, "Information Technology" became compulsory, emphasizing its importance in modern society. Thus the advent of information technology has been central to the changes in "Industrial Arts" of these two decades. Some consider that "Information Technology" is not appropriately included in "Industrial Arts". However, if it is accepted as an element in technology education, the revision of 1998 becomes epoch-making in the history not only of technology education, but of school education itself in Japan, in that "Information Study" is the only new compulsory subject area at upper secondary level to be added to the National Course of Studies introduced in Japan after World War II. This reform was also responsible for creating the connection of technology education for all students from "Industrial Arts" in lower secondary to "Information Study" in upper secondary schools.

Technology education in Japan occurs as vocational and professional education, as well as in general education, and is taught in the subject area of "Industry / Manufacturing." If we interpret the word "technology" broadly, technology education should also include "Agriculture", "Marine Products Industry" and so on. However, I will not address changes in these subject areas in detail in this article.

3. TRENDS IN TECHNOLOGY EDUCATION AS REVEALED BY JAPANESE TEXTBOOKS

In the previous section, the changes in technology education in Japan over the last two decades were reviewed in terms of the revisions in the National Course of Studies. In this section, I will examine the changes in actual lesson contents through an analysis of the contents of textbooks. In Japan, each textbook company produces a textbook, which must be authorized by the MEXT, after checking to ensure that it satisfies the guidelines of the National Course of Studies, for use in schools. Supplementary teaching materials on the market, which are not officially approved, are also often used in teaching. The analysis of textbooks is useful for inferring changes in the aims, contents, activities, and style of typical and ideal school lessons, though they are different from real lessons as I will describe in section 4.

In Japan, only two "Industrial Arts and Home Economics" textbooks are published, by different textbook companies, and each company has a similar share of the market.

Because textbooks are not revised for at least four years, there are only four editions of the textbooks used during the previous and the present National Course of Studies. Of those four, I chose two from the same publisher for the present analysis. One was published in 1993, the first edition based on the revised National Course of Studies announced in 1989, and the other will be published in 2006 as the second edition based on the revision of 1998. Textbooks of the 1980s were not obtainable, but their contents can be readily inferred from a tendency to be described below. As mentioned in section 2, only the structure of the course, and not the contents, was revised in 1989.

Table 2 outlines the two textbooks. For the 1993 edition, the syllabus for "Information Technology", which was then a newly established optional area, is given, in addition to those for "woodwork" and "electricity", in the compulsory area. It has become compulsory in the 2006 edition. For the 2006 edition, for all syllabuses (except "cultivation") a distinction between compulsory and optional is shown, to make clear which had become optional by 2006. "Cultivation" is shown for neither edition because it was always optional and the election rate was quite low.

For Table 2, see the end of this chapter.

3.1 Trends in the Traditional Contents of "Industrial Arts" – "Monodukuri"

The first trend observable in Table 2 is that the categories of Industrial Arts in the 2006 edition are integrated while each category in the 1993 edition is kept separate. This difference reflects a loss of categories due to the reduction in teaching hours and the introduction of "Information Technology" as a compulsory category. There was the further change in objective to studying the "Industrial Arts" from the point of view of their usefulness in real life rather than just the technical skills. Figure 1 shows the ancestry of "Industrial Arts". In its inception it was influenced by "Arts and Craftwork" and "Vocation", and its main contents in the 1993 edition was the acquisition of the fundamental knowledge and skills needed to become, for example, carpenters and furniture upholsterers in "woodwork", or electrical engineers in "electricity". By contrast, in the 2006 edition, the concentration is on design, and instruction in "woodwork" and "metalwork" is combined (sections 1.2, 1.3, and 1.4). Metals and plastics, in addition to wood, are now included in the materials used to make products. Since many household goods are made from metals and plastics, learning about those materials will allow students to make things out of materials at hand and to repair household goods. Similarly, the design of a circuit and making electrical products in "electricity" in the 1993 text become optional in the 2006 version (section 1.6), while using electricity safely and efficiently and how to repair electrical appliances are compulsory (section 1.5). These changes suggest a focus on the knowledge and skills necessary for ordinary persons to cope with the products of technology in everyday life.

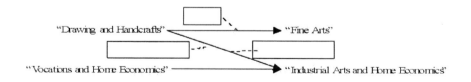

Figure 1: Ancestry of "Industrial Arts" from the National Course of Studies of 1958

Similarly, in the 2006 edition, the sections "1.1 Technology and life" and "1.8 Directions in future technology", which relate technology to changes in daily life and society, emphasize the viewpoint of the user rather than the developer or maker. Superficially, these contents might appear similar to sections 1.1, 1.6, 2.1, and 2.6 of the 1993 edition. In reality, their main concern is with the effect of technological progress on users' needs and lifestyle, to which is added a moral emphasis on the necessity, beyond individual convenience, of choosing desirable technology from the point of view of saving resources and the environment.

A further change in the 2006 edition is a trend toward problem-solving activities, and there is more concern with ways of thinking and collecting information to support such activities. For example, learning activities to investigate useful technology and making use of it by oneself is emphasized in section 1.2 of the 2006 edition. This means ability of problem solving is emphasized. I think this is because technology is making progress day by day and pupils should have the ability to solve problems by learning.

Only section 1.5 of the 2006 edition is against the trend emphasizing the needs of users, and deals with machines and tools for production. While section 2.3 of the 1993 edition mainly deals with home electrical appliances, this topic becomes optional in section 1.6 of the 2006 edition.

The 1998 revision of the National Course of Studies sought to reduce the repetition of material in different subject areas. For example, the basics of electricity are now taught at the end of the seventh grade, and "motion and energy" in the second half of the eighth grade, in "Science", before being encountered in "Industrial Arts", but were taught after "Industrial Arts" in the 1989 version of the National Course of Studies.

3.2 The Trend in "Information Technology"

In the 1998 revision of the National Course of Studies, "Information Technology" became compulsory. Its contents increased especially in "2.2 Elements and operations of a computer" and "2.4 Making use of information networks", and material on the influence and role of information technology in our society increased moderately. The reason for the increase in section 2.4 is related to the spread of computers in the home. In Japan, because of the need for thousands of Japanese characters, it takes time to master the entry of data to a computer. This has been a barrier to ordinary persons learning to enter and process information by themselves.

However, computers became more familiar and acquired more use at home after various services had been provided on the Internet making it easier to exchange data, aided by the reduction of fees due to the opening up of the telecommunications market. Now, cellular phones are in widespread use as telecommunication terminals. Many lower secondary school students have access, and this exposes them to various risks from information networks. There is also concern about security and file management because of increased use of networks and multi-user operating systems. Furthermore, it is considered desirable that people have the skills to choose the best solution among various alternatives for a given purpose and situation, emphasizing the flexibility of computers as a problem-solving tool.

Nevertheless, in "2.3 Making use of computers" in the 2006 edition, the kinds of software explained are almost identical with those in "3.3 Using software applications" in the 1993 edition. However, while in the 1993 edition each software package was treated independently, in the 2006 edition, the emphasis is on methods and ways of solving problems, such as decomposing and identifying the information necessary for a target product or solution, employing suitable software, and unifying or reconstructing the output. A significant change is that programming using the language BASIC, which was given emphasis in the 1997 editions, has become optional in the 2006 editions. To summarize, as in the case of "Industrial Arts", change is directed at the needs of users rather than developers in the later syllabus of "Information Technology".

3.3 The Influence of the Increasing Ratio of Students Entering Higher Education

Another reason that affected the revision of "Industrial Arts" was the increase of the ratio of lower secondary students continuing on to upper secondary schools and that of upper secondary students continuing on to institutions of higher education. The proportion of lower secondary students entering upper secondary schools in 1955 was about 50%. It increased steadily to reach 90% by 1975, and is currently over 97%. Moreover, the ratio of students in vocational high schools was about 40% in 1970, but is now less than 25%. The proportion of students going on to institutions of higher education had reached about 50% by 1978. There followed a ten-year period in which the percentage did not change, but an increase began again in about 1987, and the rate has now reached about 73% (MEXT 2004). This trend means that the point at which students decide on their future occupations comes later. If technology education focuses on vocational education at lower secondary school level, it then becomes difficult to motivate students' interest in technology. Under the present National Course of Studies, career education in lower secondary schools was introduced in "Periods for Integrated Study", and provides students with the chance to investigate occupations, experience the workplace, and so on.

4. "GIJUTSU" IN JAPANESE: IS IT THE SAME AS "TECHNOLOGY"?

If Japanese people are asked which subject areas come under technology education, a variety of answers will be received. These differences originate essentially in differences in the understanding of the term "technology", for which the Japanese word is "GIJUTSU".

A review of some recent versions of the National Course of Studies shows the word "GIJUTSU" used in the sense of "skills" or "techniques". For example, among the objectives of "Industrial Arts" was "to give students mastery of GIJUTSU (= skills) required in daily life and foster creativities and practical attitudes to enrich their lives". Technology education in this sense was already provided in "Drawing and Handcrafts" in both elementary and lower secondary schools, before "Industrial Arts" was established in the latter as described above.

Nevertheless, when the National Course of Studies was revised in 1989, a new objective, "to give an understanding of the relationship between life and GIJUTSU (= technology) in the home and society" was added, implying the introduction of new aspects of technology education. The use of the word GIJUTSU (= technology) here stresses its objective and intellectual aspects, its concepts, ideas, and methods of designing artifacts and systems; that is to say, it emphasizes the engineering mind. "Technology" in this sense was also introduced into "Science" in the 1989 revision with the inclusion of the phrase "to understand the relationship between the progress of science and technology and changes in our way of life."

The reason why "GIJUTSU (=technology)" has been understood to mean skills can be found in its origin as a Japanese word. The English word "technology" is composed of the Greek "techne (= art)" and "logos (=knowledge)". Therefore, it connotes the discipline of the arts (in the broadest sense). The Japanese word "GIJUTSU" is composed of "GI (=WAZA)" and "JUTSU", and both "WAZA" and "JUTSU" have the meaning of art or technique in English. Therefore, "GIJUTSU" education simply means training in skills. In Japan, the word "KOUGAKU" is the word for the discipline of the arts. However, since the meaning of the word "KOU" is "processing", "KOUGAKU" corresponds more closely to the English word "engineering". Thus, Japanese people gave it the connotation of manufacturing technology, whereas in fact "technology" is a larger concept than "engineering", as is clear from the existence of the term "engineering technology" in English.

The meaning people give to the word "technology" is likely to be influenced by what is taught as "technology" in technology education, and how technology education teachers understand the meaning of "technology" and convey it to students is probably also very influential. As described above, the meaning of "GIJUTSU" in the National Course of Studies and its textbooks has changed over time from skills to technology. However, it is not clear that teachers are aware of the nature of this change, because lessons of "Industrial Arts" we can see in many schools are different from the ideal one described in section 3. The stereotypical form of real lessons is that parents purchase work kits, students assemble them and bring the artifacts home, in return for the money, just to throw them away as garbage because they are not useful in many cases. This means there are many teachers who do not make use of textbooks in their classes. They have not had an interest in the changing demands for "GIJUTSU" education; therefore, their style of teaching has not changed to a large extent for a long period of time.

In considering the future of technology education in Japan, we must reflect on the meaning of the word "GIJUTSU (= technology)" and interpret it to students. Further, whether we emphasize technological skills or intellectual understanding as the goal of technology education is bound to be a source of controversy. It should also be decided whether we wish to teach practical skills that are accessible to most people, or rather, concentrate on imbuing attitudes and behaviors of exercising the democratic means to reflect their opinions on how to use technology. Parents and teachers, including university professors, should take such questions seriously, and ensure that children, who will one day be parents, understand the meaning they are giving to technology. However, many teachers think that controversy is dangerous to their status, and avoid confronting such issues.

The present status of technology education in Japan demonstrates the harmful effect of reneging on such discussions. In the National Course of Studies, subjects are classified as either "main" or "other" subjects. The main subjects are "Japanese", "Social Studies", "Mathematics", "Science", and "English", while "Industrial Arts" is in the category of "other" subjects. Most students recognize the main subjects as important because they must pass the entrance examinations in these subjects to go on to higher education; whereas they consider the school hours devoted to other subjects as a time to relax and enjoy school life. In some private schools, extra school hours are assigned to the main subjects by cutting down the hours of the other subjects, because of parental ambitions to enter their children in one of the famous universities.

However, this approach is not necessarily successful in creating a regard for these subjects. According to a survey by the National Institute for Educational Policy Research (NIER 2003), the rates for seventh graders, who agreed to "I like learning mathematics" and "I understand lessons in mathematics", were approximately 45% and 50%, respectively, and the rates for the same questions for "science" were 55% and 50%. Moreover, according to the NIER survey in 2004, the rates for twelfth graders, who agreed to "it is important to learn mathematics even if it is not required in entrance examinations," "it is useful to learn mathematics for use in daily and social life", and "I want a job in which I will use mathematics", were 40%, 33%, and 12%, and the rates for the same questions for "science" were 30%, 30%, and 18%. Thus, the strategy of using examinations as a motivator for studying means that students fail to appreciate the subjects themselves. This outcome was pointed out in "White papers on science and technology" as long ago as 1993. It was shown that the level of interest of persons in their twenties in science and technology topics and news was markedly lower than that for other age groups. Further, as the number of children of school age decreases, competition in entrance examinations is no longer a strong source of motivation for students. Therefore I suggest that subjects should be classified as main or other subjects depending on whether they are useful for the solving of problems in the real world. I am convinced that technology education should be a main subject in that it promotes understanding of the tremendous influence technology has on our society.

5. TECHNOLOGY EDUCATION IN THE FUTURE:
LEARNING FROM DISCUSSIONS OF TEACHING INFORMATION TECHNOLOGY

Fortunately, there was no choice but to discuss why the study of information technology is needed when the question of the new subject area of "Information Study" was raised. The justification for the establishment of "Information Study" was finally agreed to be, to provide students with the following abilities in the utilization of information for practical problem solving in daily life and society.

1. The practical ability to make use of information in problem solving and communication, with the knowledge to decide when or not to use information technology, without being misled by its seeming usefulness.

2. Understanding the appropriateness of methods for making use of information and information technology adequately, based on their properties.

3. Developing attitudes sympathetic to taking part in the creation of a desirable information society with an understanding of the roles of information and information technology and their influences on our society.

It is notable that the operational skills for computer use were not included in these objectives. Of course, this does not imply that learning to operate computers is unnecessary, but rather stresses that the focus of the teaching is not on mastering the skills involved in operating computers, but on understanding the respective roles of technology and human beings, and what should be learned about technology.

Based on this discussion so far, I insist that we should cope with the following two issues in order to ensure that "GIJUTSU" education in Japan, which emphasizes the acquisition of skills, will become technology education as it originally meant.

Firstly, we must change the system and curriculum of teacher education. As I have stated previously in this article, although the National Course of Studies and textbooks are revised, if the consciousness of teachers remains unchanged, the technology education in schools will remain almost unchanged. In Japan, it is said that the number of retiring teachers will increase and many new teachers will be employed in the next decade. Moreover, the council of the MEXT has been working on how to improve the quality of teachers. Thus, we should not ignore this opportunity to reform the teacher licensing system and teacher training system for technology education.

Secondly, we should select an innovative idea to be the core of technology education reform. Such an idea must be a basic concept that unifies "Monozukuri" and "Information Technology." Hereafter, I will describe my idea that was created during the process of developing the informatics education curriculum.

The curriculum for "Information Study" was never a single person's conception, but the philosophical basis of my views comes from two papers, "Study of the Information Industry" and "Civilization from Information Technology", by Tadao Umesao, a Japanese cultural anthropologist. The former, written in 1963, argued that we should see the mass media, movie productions, schools, and religious groups as information industries, if we define the word "information" as "all the sign series transmitted between human beings." To this he later added a supplement extending the meaning of information as follows: "Information is not necessarily sent by anyone. Everything in the world is information just as it is. It is a matter for each individual as to whether he/she can invoke it as information or not." He claimed that most of the industries that trade by adding attraction to the basic products themselves, such as travel agencies, leisure industries, restaurants, fashion brands etc., should be regarded as information industries. In the second article, written in 1988, he discussed the idea that changes in civilization result from the advancement of information technology. The point of his discussion was that information technologies should be seen as tools for managing information, and information is central to the understanding of our thoughts, behaviors, and many aspects of society. Therefore, the main concern of "Information Study" is information itself. In order to utilize information, to make our lives richer and safer and society better, we need to learn how to use information technology appropriately.

From my experience of establishing a new subject area, we need to examine and reorganize the contents of technology education. For example, there are three aspects that explain the phenomena of the world – material, energy, and information. It could be helpful to explain the development of technology from these three angles, and to discuss ideas on transforming materials, energy, or information more efficiently and effectively. The concept of "transformation" is an important perspective for systematically understanding technology; in addition, it is an important factor in supporting the way-of-thinking which brings about the innovation of technology. In cognitive psychology, developing an idea that brings an end to a deadlock is called "discernment", while solving a problem creatively is called "discernment problem solving". "Discernment" requires a change in the way of thinking; therefore, it is necessary to transform the representation of a problem situation and address the problem from various viewpoints. Specifically, if we replace the word "technology power" with "problem-solving power", it is important for technology education to teach students how to transform their ways of thinking and how to represent problem situations. For example, a simulation can be interpreted as one way to solve a problem by changing a phenomenon in the material or energy world into a phenomenon in the information world. Remote control technology can be interpreted as a method for transforming a phenomenon in the physical world into a phenomenon in the information world, and for transmitting, processing, and again transforming a phenomenon into a phenomenon in the physical world. From this perspective, the contents of "Monodukuri", which addresses the transformation of materials or energy, and "information technology", which addresses the transformation of information, must be integrated in future technology education, although they are currently separated, as has been shown previously.

Furthermore, the idea of "transformation" is related to ideas in mathematics and science. In order to transform and process coded data as we choose, it is necessary to use either advanced mathematics or the combination of simple mathematics and information technology. In order to transform materials and energy into information, it is necessary to use scientific laws. For example, you can determine the height of a building by measuring the length of a rope hanging down from the top, as well as by measuring the time or the kinetic energy of an object that falls to the ground from the top of the building. You could also determine it by comparing the length of the shadow of a one-meter stick with that of the building. Thus, if you possess the scientific knowledge that under certain conditions length can be transformed to speed, kinetic energy, or time you can easily solve the problem of measuring a phenomenon that cannot be measured directly. I think that it is possible to motivate children to learn mathematics and science by connecting the purpose of studying these subjects with technology (= problem solving). Therefore, we should not withhold technology education within a narrow frame in order to conserve its uniqueness. We should try to broaden it and think that it is ideal that various subject areas are related to technology education. This is identical to informatics education that is being carried out in several subject areas. Such actions will not reduce the required number of specialists in technology education, because the discipline of science is essentially different from that of technology. Namely, science is concerned with discovering the laws of nature while technology is concerned with creating the future. It is necessary to provide science education and technology education for children with either interests in science or with interests in technology as they grow up.

Table 2(a). Contents of Textbooks: 1993 edition (left-hand side) and 2006 edition (right-hand side)

1.Woodwork (50 pages)
1.1.Woods and our life (2 pages)
1)Woods in our houses /
 Uses of woods [fuel, chemical products, wood products]
1.2.Features of woods (12 pages)
1)Cutting and examining woods
2)Making a simple wood product /
 Summarizing features of woods [comparing with metals and plastics]
3)Kinds of woods and tissue of woods
4)Properties of woods
 [deformation, properties to heat and sound, strength]
5)Examples of wood products
6)Houses and woody musical instruments / Kinds of wood materials
1.3.Designing wood products (10 pages)
1)Planning / Flow of woodworking
2)Considering functions [shape, size, usability], structure, and materials
3)Choosing production methods /Varieties of methods to joint wood parts
4)Summarizing a plan / Preparing to work
 [Making a parts table and a process chart]
5)Examples of product concept
1.4.Technical drawings (8 pages)
1)Cabinet projection drawing / isometric drawing
2)Orthographic projection drawing
3)Kinds of dimension line / Writing Size
4)Process of technical drawing
1.5.Making woodwork products(16 pages)
1)Scribing
2)Sawing
3)Auto sawing machine and auto plaining machine
4)Plaining (4 pages)
5)Work process of tenon and mortise
6)Jointing wood parts and painting (4 pages)
1.6.Efficient use of woods (2 pages)
2.Electricity (38 pages)
2.1.Electricity in our life (2 pages)
1)What will be happened by blackout? / Process of electric power
 supply and consumption / Uses of electric power [light, heat, kinetic
 power, electronic signal]
2.2.Electric circuit (12 pages)
1)Electric circuits and their schematics
2)Making a simple circuit tester and an extension cable /
 Summarizing properties of electricity
3)Usage of a circuit tester (4 pages)
4)Power sources and loads [DC and AC, Ohm's law, Power] / Switches
5)Electric cords / Cord assembly
2.3.Mechanism of electric appliances and method of maintenance them
 (10 pages)
1)Mechanism of electric appliances [Iron, Desk stand, Washing machine,
 Radio]
2)Test of electric appliances / materials [conductor, resistor, insulator,
 semi-conductor]
3)Examples of electric appliances
 [kotatsu, light, wind fun, radio] (6 pages)
2.4.Electric appliances and in-door wiring (4 pages)
1)Power board / preventing electric shock
2)Rating of electric cords and parts / Safty use of electric appliances
2.5.Design and assembly of an electric circuit (8 pages)
1)Functions and usage of electronics parts
2)Amplifier effects of a transistor / Process of circuit design
3)Examples of electronic circuits and their assembly (4 pages)
2.6.Efficient use of electric power and progress of electric engineering
 technology (2 pages)

| 4.Metalwork | 5.Machining | 6.Cultivation |

1.Technology and "Monodukuri" (86 pages)
1.1.Technology and our life (6 pages)
1)Influence of technology advancement on our life [rice cooking,
 washing, preserving foods, communication]
2)Technology advancement in the use of energy
3)Enjoying "Monodukuri" [Examples of products for practicing]
1.2.Design of Products (20 pages)
1)Outline of "Monodukuri" [from design to production]
2)Investigation of products in our life and tools in an assembly
 room
3)Planning (method for collecting, creating, and evaluating ideas)
4)Choosing materials (properties suitable for purposes and functions)
5)Features of woods, metals, plastics, and so on. (6 pages)
6)Making products stronger and improving usability
 [Consider shape, size, structure, and functions]
7)Investigating and choosing production methods
 [Examples of jointing and bending methods]
8)Summarizing and drawing a plan
1.3.Technical drawings (10 pages)
1)Cabinet projection drawing / isometric drawing / writing size
2)CAD / Orthographic projection drawing
3)Examples of product concept (6 pages)
1.4.Making products(26 pages)
1)Outline of producing
2)Preparing to work [Making a parts table and a process chart]
3)Scribing
4)Sawing and cutting (4 pages)
5)[plaining / filing and making holes / bending and twisting off /
 checking , making tenon and mortise, lathe turning] process of
 parts (8 pages)
6)Assembly of parts (4 pages)
7)Painting
8)Casting of plastics and metals/ Maintenance for using longterm
1.5.Mechanism of machines and tools and methods to maintain
 them (16 pages)
1)Scenes of maintenance works
 [airplane, car, escalator, bus, and bicycle]
2)Investigation of [common] parts in machines and tools
3)Investigation of mechanism for conveying kinetic power[rotation]
4)Investigation of mechanism for using electricity
 [DC and AC, Ohm's law, Power]
5)Electric circuits and their schematics / Circuit tester
6)Accident prevention [leak current, Rating]
7)Check Methods for safety use of machines and tools
8)Safety use of electric appliances / Assembling a table tap
1.6.Direction of technology progress (8 pages)
1)Technology and ecology
 [recycle, efficient use of energy, technology for ecology]
2)Examples of recycle use/ecological use of technology in our life
3)Examples of study on technology in our life [ecology and
 technology / technology for welfare and universal design]
1.6.Transformation and making use of energy (22 pages)
1)Process of electric power supply and consumption
2)Transformation and making use of electric energy (4 pages)
3)Functions and use of semi-conductor parts
4)Mechanisms for conveying motions
 [gear, cam, link, belt, chain] (4 pages)
5)Making a product which applies energy transformation
6)Examples of product
 [Several types of lights, machine model] (4 pages)
7)Let's take part in a robot contest
8)Methods to save energy in our life
1.7.Cultivation (20 pages)

Table 2(b). Contents of Textbooks: 1993 edition (left-hand side) and 2006 edition (right-hand side)

1993 edition	2006 edition
3.Information Technology (34 pages)	2.Information Technology (54 pages)
3.1.Information technology in our life (2)	2.1.Information technology in our life (4 pages)
1)Several types of computers /	1)Examples of information system in our life
An example of information system [Weather report]	(Bus location system)
3.2.Computer operation and elements of a computer (4 pages)	2)Examples of change by IT [Accounting system by abacus, CD,
1)Operations of computers [Power on/off, keyboard operation]	and POS / appliance with computer]
2)Elements and functions of a computer	2.2.Elements and operations of a computer (14pages)
3.3.Using application software (16 pages)	1)Several types of computers
1)Software and Hardware / Choosing software according to purposes	[PC, PDA, handy phone, game machine, ATM]
2)Document processing software (4 pages)	2)Elements and functions of a computer
3)Graphic software (3 pages)	3)Hardware and software
4)Database software (3 pages)	[Why a computer system is consists of hardware and software?]
5)Spreadsheet software and compatibility of data (4 pages)	4)Operations of computers [Power on/off, log on/off, start up and
3.4.Programing (8 pages)	exit software, mouse operation]
1)Making a simple program [BASIC] (6 pages)	5)Keyboard operation [input and delete, translate from alphabet
2)Making a program including graphic commands	to Japanese character, print out]
3.5.Influence of information technology toward our life (4 pages)	6)Saving and managing files
1)Progress of information technology and its use [network, CAD, AI]	[directory, security, varieties of memory storage]
2)Effects and problems of IT in our life	7)Comparison of specification among computers
[POS, VDT, security, copyright]	2.3.Making use of computers (16 pages)
	1)Process of problem solving by making use of information
	2)Choosing software suitable to each type of information
	3)Graphic software (4 pages)
	4)Spreadsheet software
	5)Document processing software
	6)Database software
	7)Examples of exercises [name card, nameplate, calendar]
	2.4.Making use of information networks (12 pages)
	1)The Internet / Services on the Internet
	2)Mechanism of WWW
	3)Collecting information from the Internet
	[Web information retrieval system]
	4)E-mail system / Comparison of properties among
	communication systems
	5)Safety use of communication system
	[manner to use the Internet, copyright]
	6)Security, netiquette, computer virus, net shopping
	2.7.Self-responsibility in information society (8 pages)
	1)Aims to learn information technology
	2)Preventing illegal use, recycle use of computers, VDT
	3)Examples of investigation on information society (4 pages)

2.5.Multimedia (16 pages)
1)Definition of multimedia
2)Process to create multimedia contents
3)Making parts of multimedia contents
[images, animations, soounds, movies] (6 pages)
4)Editing multimedia contents from parts
5)Examples of multimedia contents [presentation, CG]
6)Universal design of web pages

2.6.Programing and Controling (16 pages)
1)Examples of automated controling
[Automated rice cooker, automated washing machine]
2)Roles of programs
3)Making a simple program (4 pages)
4)Concept of self controling system [4 pages]
5)An example of self controling system [Sensor car]
6)GPS

239

REFERENCES

Ishida, H., Chuuma, T., Abe, A., and Shibukawa, S., (1993) (eds) *New Industrial Arts and Homemaking*, Tokyo-shoseki, Tokyo, Japan.

Kato, K. Nagano, K, Shibukawa, S., and Watanabe, S., (2006) (Eds) *New Industrial Arts and Homemaking*, Tokyo-shoseki, Tokyo, Japan, (in press).

MEXT (2004) *Japan's Education at a Glance*, http://www.mext.go.jp/b_menu/shuppan/toukei/04042301/002.pdf (in Japanese).

MEXT (1998) *The National Course of Studies for Lower Secondary Schools*, http://www.mext.go.jp/b_menu/shuppan/sonota/990301c.htm (in Japanese).

MEXT (1989) *The National Course of Studies for Lower Secondary Schools*, http://www.mext.go.jp/b_menu/shuppan/sonota/890303.htm (in Japanese).

MEXT (1977) *the National Course of Studies for Lower Secondary Schools*, MEXT, Tokyo, Japan.

National Institute for Educational Policy Research (2003) *Reports on Comprehensive Evaluation of the Learning Proficiency of School Students: Primary schools and Lower Secondary Schools*, http://www.nier.go.jp/kaihatsu/katei_h13/top.htm (in Japanese).

National Institute for Educational Policy Research (2004) *Reports on Comprehensive Evaluation of the Learning Proficiency of School Students: Upper Secondary Schools*, http://www.nier.go.jp/kaihatsu/katei_h14/index.htm (in Japanese)

Umesao, T. (1963) *Study of Information Industry*, Tyuuou-kouron, 605, 46-58 (in Japanese).

Umesao, T. (1988) *Civilization from Information Technology*, Tyuuou-kouron, 1231, 152-172, Tyuuou-kouron (in Japanese)

SUMIYOSHI MITA, TOSHIKI MATSUDA, JUN IWAKI AND
TAKAHISA FURUTA

18. A CHANGE OF INDUSTRIAL TECHNOLOGY EDUCATION CURRICULUM AND DEVELOPMENT OF A DESIGN LEARNING SUPPORT SYSTEM FOR TECHNOLOGY EDUCATION

INTRODUCTION

The Upper Secondary Education Curriculum was reformed in July 1998 (The Curriculum Council, 1998). Upper secondary schools are being reconstituted. Furthermore, Specialized Courses are being drastically reconstituted.

So far, although industrial technology education has pursued the training of a corps of technicians who can work practically in industrial fields, that educational framework is being reformulated. New courses that combine several courses are being reconstituted: Manufacturing, Agriculture, Business, Home Economics, and Information study. New educational methods, new subjects, and new teaching methods corresponding to them are under development.

Until now, teaching methods that are appropriate for science education and those appropriate to technology education have existed, but a teaching method that relates technology with science is an important new teaching method.

The new curriculum is intended to help students acquire basic knowledge thoroughly along with problem-solving abilities. The new required subject of "Problem-Solving Study" was established in vocational education courses during curriculum reform in 1989. The "Period for Integrated Study" was established for elementary schools and lower and upper secondary schools in the curriculum reforms of 1998. It is aimed at helping students develop the capability and ability to discover problems individually and to solve those problems properly. As background for this, it is assumed that students' knowledge and skills acquired in individual classes will be mutually related and deepened through activities such as problem-solving.

Vocational education has allowed students to acquire problem-solving abilities through experimentation and practice. The main learning activity for solving problems is "design" in technology education. It is difficult to teach a design method to students. A typical design example is presented for students in usual design learning. Then students refer to it and solve the design subject. "Design" through this teaching method is actually a "copy" of the design example. Consequently, students often learn from a passive stance.

Many teaching materials using IT have already been developed to support learning. It is extremely important to combine and mesh virtual information with actual experiences in technology education. This study is intended to show how to

M.J. de Vries, I. Mottier (eds.), International Handbook of Technology Education, 241–252.

introduce learning with actual experience into learning information using IT. This study specifically explores a way to teach students that corresponds to learning contents and students' understanding, and explores what kind of information must be presented for students to learn: text, photographs, movies, graphs, simulations using physical models, inductive teaching materials based on experiments, and deductive teaching materials that present analyses based on fundamental theories. This paper describes educational change and development of teaching materials in the Specialized Course of upper secondary education.

CURRICULUM CHANGE IN UPPER SECONDARY EDUCATION

We specifically address upper secondary education. Upper secondary education is intended to help students appreciate the meanings of their own lives, develop their minds, and form the ability to choose a career and deepen their understanding of society. Depending upon students' interests, upper secondary education provides them opportunities to learn basic knowledge in the specialties of their choices and encourages them to further develop individuality and independence. Education is expected to help students develop the ability to anticipate social changes and to cope with them flexibly. It is important that a student's academic ability is assessed according to whether or not the student has acquired a "zest for living" concomitant with the ability to learn and think independently.

School education positively conducts its activities by emphasizing the importance of motivating students to learn individually and by helping them develop abilities to learn, reason, judge, express themselves accurately, discover and solve problems, acquire basic creativity, and act independently in response to social changes. These goals require the promotion of such educational activities as hands-on learning activities, problem-solving activities, and activities to teach how to research and how to learn. Therefore, at upper secondary schools, elective subjects occupy the greater part of the curriculum; common subjects are fewer.

The national curriculum standards have been specified clearly and made more flexible so that individual schools are able to show ingenuity in developing unique educational activities to make the school distinctive. Specifically, respective schools are able to produce their own curricula in accordance with actual community situations, schools, and students. In addition, the number of elective subjects has been increased and the "Period for Integrated Study" has been established to further promote each school's unique educational activities.

The total number of credits required to complete upper secondary school education was reduced to 74 credits from the current 80 credits. The standard weekly credit hours for a full-time student have been reduced to 30 credit hours from the current 32 credit hours. (1 credit hour = 50 min/wk × 35 wk)

TECHNOLOGICAL EDUCATION IN THE GENERAL EDUCATION COURSE

In response to the information-oriented society, a new required subject area of "Information Study" was established in the General Education Course Curriculum.

Upper secondary schools established a new general subject area, "Information Study", as a required area. It aims at helping students develop the ability to independently choose, process and send information appropriately using such information devices as computers and information communication networks.

Three subjects are established under the subject area of "Information Study". One is "Information A" presenting the use of computers and information communication networks. Another is "Information B" that promotes scientific understanding of the functions and mechanisms of a computer. One more is "Information C", which describes the role and influence of information communication networks in society. Students can choose one from among them. The only subject related to technology that students of the General Course learn is "Information Study".

THE EDUCATIONAL AIM OF THE INDUSTRY COURSE

Now, society and the economy are changing rapidly: change of industrial structure and working structure, the advance of science and technology, the information-oriented society, internationalization, and the aging society that is occurring along with the declining birth rate. Considering these social changes, the society of the future will require specialists who can think, judge, and act independently, and who can acquire professional knowledge and skills. Therefore, it is expected that the Specialized Course of the upper secondary education help students acquire basic technical knowledge and skills necessary to work as specialists in the future.

Industrial technology education of the upper secondary school has changed corresponding to the curriculum reform of 1996. Upper secondary schools for industrial technology education had been placed on the vocational education with agricultural education and commercial education, but their courses have changed to emphasize specialized education courses for training "Specialists".

Educational aims of the Industry Course are the following.

1. Industrial technology education helps students acquire basic knowledge and skills of various industrial fields and understand their significance and function in industry within society.

2. Industrial technology education helps students acquire creative abilities and practical behavior to develop society through solving various problems of industrial technology independently and rationally while considering our environment.

Industrial technology education helps students acquire basics thoroughly. Great emphasis is placed on experiments and practice in industrial technology education.

Learning through experimentation and practice is important for motivating students' will to learn and developing students' problem-solving abilities. These learning activities, which emphasize experience, must comprise the learning core in the Specialized Course of upper secondary education.

In the Specialized Course, the total number of credits required for the specialized subject areas/subjects was reduced to 25 credits from the current 30 credits. The required subjects common to every subject area are two: one comprises very basic content, whereas the other is "task-based research" for cultivating problem-solving ability. The former is "Basics of Industrial Technology", which promotes students' interest in various industries and understanding the social role of industries through practice and experimentation. The latter is "Problem-Solving", which fosters deep understanding of the knowledge and technology, while teaching the ability for solving problems.

CHANGES OF LEARNING CREDITS IN THE INDUSTRIAL COURSE OF UPPER SECONDARY EDUCATION

The Upper Secondary Education Curriculum was reformed in 1960, 1970, 1989 and 1999. The goal of education and the number of learning credits were changed through reformation of curricula. Until the 1970s, industrial technology education was intended to train technicians who were able to work practically in industrial fields, but since the 1980s, industrial technology education has been educating students to master the bases of industrial technology.

The total number of credits required for the specialized subject areas/subjects that were determined as the national curriculum were reduced: the minimum numbers of required credits were 35 credits (1960), 30 credits (1979), and 25 credits (1999).

In the 1970s, students mastered subjects of about 110 credits: specialized subjects of about 50 credits, and general subjects of about 60 credits.

In the 1980s, the number of total credits that students needed to master was about 96 credits: specialized subjects of about 42–43 credits and general subjects of about 54 credits. Moreover, two subjects of "Basics for Industry" and "Mathematics for Industry" were set up as the common required subjects. The number of their total credits was about 7 credits.

In the 1990s, the number of total credits that students mastered were about 91 credits: specialized subjects of 36–37 credits and general subjects of about 54 credits. "Basics of Information Technology and "Problem Solving" were set up, except for the above two common subjects; the number of total credits of common subjects was 11–12 credits.

At present, although the number of mean credits of specialized subjects is about 40 credits, that number is decreasing.

CHANGES IN UPPER SECONDARY EDUCATION

Recently, students who proceed from the Specialized Course to the university have increased. From this viewpoint, technical education of the upper secondary school needs to be connected with continuous learning in institutions of higher education and work.

Percentage distribution of upper secondary school students by the type of course is the following.

General Education Course: 72.9%
Specialized Education Course: 22.1%
  Agriculture: 2.8%, Industry: 8.8%, Commerce: 8.1%, Fisheries: 0.3%
  Home economics: 1.7%, Nursing: 0.4%
Integrated education: 2.3%
Other: 2.7%

At present, 75% of the upper secondary school students go to the General Course; 25% of them continue in Industry, Commerce, Agriculture, Home Economics, and Nursing Courses. 50% of the upper secondary school students proceed to universities and junior colleges. In addition, 20% of the Industry Course students proceed to universities; 25% of them proceed to college.

ESTABLISHMENT OF A NEW COURSE

Reconstitution of upper secondary education has been precipitated by the decrease in the population of 18-year-olds: 1994 – 1,860,000; 2004 – 1,410,000; 2014 – 1,180,000.

New courses have combined and reconstituted several courses: Manufacturing, Agriculture, Business, Home Economics and Information study. As one of them, a course based science and technology education is being established. Its educational program presumes that students learn in advanced educational institutions of universities and colleges. Development of a new educational method and a new subject and a teaching method corresponding to it are anticipated.

In the curriculum of the Specialized Course, 30–40% of the number of total credits (about 90 credits) is the number of credits for professional education; the number of credits for science and mathematics education is about 10 credits. Consequently, it is difficult to produce an educational program that maintains a close relation between science education and professional education.

DEVELOPMENT OF DESIGN LEARNING SUPPORT SYSTEM FOR TECHNOLOGY EDUCATION

We have been developing two packages of teaching materials based on the close relation between science and technology for cultivating basic abilities and problem solving abilities. One of them includes teaching materials for creating an ultra-micro wind turbine. The other includes teaching materials for designing a model car.

DEVELOPMENT OF TEACHING MATERIALS FOR CREATING AN ULTRA-MICRO WIND TURBINE

We developed a multimedia learning support system of ultra micro-wind turbines. This system consists of teaching materials concerning fundamental knowledge and theory of wind turbines and the database. Ultra-micro-wind

245

turbines of 220-mm diameter are produced from paper. The database is produced based on experimental values of their performance (Mita, Nomura and Matsuda, 2002). In addition, a software program for predicting wind turbine performance was developed based on this database (Mita, Namiki, Nomura, Matsuda, 2003). The software program, written in Visual Basic (Microsoft Corp.), was produced based on the database. If the blade area, the fitting angle, and the wind turbine shape are determined and these buttons are clicked on this software program's interface screen, the wind turbines' performance-predictive result is displayed.

EVALUATION OF TEACHING MATERIALS FOR CREATING A WIND TURBINE

The teaching program shown below is planned for evaluating the teaching materials for creating a wind turbine: the teaching material concerning fundamental knowledge and theory, the database and the software program. The total time required for completing this program was about 100 min.

1. instruction of a brief review concerning the wind turbine and of the method for making the prototype wind turbine The problem-solving subject: Can you devise blades for producing wind turbines that can lift a weight in a short time?;
2. students learn fundamental knowledge and theory of wind turbines through teaching materials;
3. students produce their wind turbines;
4. students design their wind turbines while accessing data of the database. In addition, students predict their wind turbines' performance as designed through determination of the area, fitting angle, and blade shape;
5. students evaluate their wind turbines' performance;
6. a questionnaire survey is conducted with students as respondents.

Nine fourth grade students (19 years old) at our college were selected as subjects. Each student operated one computer. Questionnaire items queried students as to the relative utility of respective materials: the teaching material concerning fundamental knowledge and theory, the database, and the software program. Questionnaire responses were the following.

Q1. Is the wind turbine teaching material useful for producing wind turbines? (9 respondents)

Answer/Number: Very useful/9, Useful/0, Nothing/0, Not useful/0, Very unuseful//0

Q2. Is the wind turbine database useful for producing wind turbines? (9 respondents)

Answer/Number: Very useful/4, Useful/3, Nothing/1, Not useful/1, Very unuseful//0

Q3. Is the software program for predicting the performance of wind turbines useful for producing wind turbines? (9 respondents)

Answer/Number: Very useful/4, Useful/2, Nothing/3, Not useful/0, Very unuseful/0

Summary: We emphasize which teaching material, the actual data of the database or the data predicted by the software program, was most helpful for supporting wind turbine manufacturing; then we investigated their effectiveness. The results clarified that students feel that the teaching material is very useful. Students referred to actual data and results predicted through the software program before producing wind turbines. These students' learning activities demonstrate that the database and software program are useful in combination with the teaching materials.

DEVELOPMENT OF TEACHING MATERIALS FOR DESIGNING A MODEL CAR

Students are interested in automobiles: their mechanisms and driving them. They need to learn much knowledge and conduct experiments regarding technology for designing an automobile. Transmission of mechanical power was taken up as a main design subject. The car model, which can raise a 150-g mass, is a concrete design subject. This design subject includes knowledge of dynamics and technology: force, moment of force, friction, center of gravity, motors, and gears. Text information concerning basic knowledge and theory, image information concerning the design subject and elements, analysis models based on dynamics, experiments concerning dynamics and simulation based on dynamics are all developed as teaching materials. These teaching materials are produced using a simulation and gaming system developed by Dr. Matsuda.

CONTENTS OF TEACHING MATERIALS FOR DESIGNING A MODEL CAR

This design learning support system consists of the following contents.
1. Problems and Evaluation:
   Problem and concept map of gravity, tension and friction
   Problem and concept map of gravity and moment of force
   Students solve problems and concept maps of the design subject; students' answers are evaluated by a learning support system.
2. Design:
   Design subject: Let's design a car model that can raise a mass of 150 g.
   Specifications of motors and gear reduction
   Design of a mechanical power transmission:
   Choice of a motor, Design of a reduction gear, Traction force of a model car
   Design of a center of gravity and friction force
3. Method:
   Method for assembling a model car, Method of performance test
   Method of measuring a center of gravity

4. Learning Contents and Analytical Models:
   Gear trains and its output torque
   Analytical Model of friction force acting between the tire and road
   Analytical Model of force acting on a car model
   Analytical Model of force transmission in the gear train
5. Design Check Sheet:
   Motor performance: Output torque and electric current
   Gears and a gearbox: Number of teeth and transmission ratio
   Driving force of driving wheels or traction force of the model car
   Judgment: Is the driving force stronger than 150 gW or not?
   Model car mass, Gravity center of the model car
   Reaction force acting on driving wheels, Frictional force acted on driving wheels
   Judgment: Is the frictional force stronger than 150 gW or not?

In the teaching materials about wind turbines, students only learned various teaching materials prepared by an instructor. In the design support system of a model car, students can choose teaching materials independently. Moreover, students can learn based on the result of evaluation from this system.

SCRIPT OF THE TEACHING MATERIAL FOR DESIGNING A MODEL CAR

Students solve the design subject through the following script.
1st Stage: The design subject is presented for students.
2nd Stage: Students solve basic problems related to the design subject.
Answer and judgment: Right answer →1st Stage→3rd Stage; Mistakes→Retrial
3rd Stage: Students confirm the specifications of parts used for producing the model car. Then they learn gears and gear reduction and solve basic problems of gears.
Answer and judgment: Right answer →1st Stage→4th Stage; Mistakes→Retrial
4th Stage: Students determine the required traction force of the model car and the frictional force acting on the driving wheels.
Answer and judgment: Right answer →1st Stage→5th Stage; Mistakes→Retrial
5th Stage: Students grapple with the design subject.
Judgment: Design completion →1st Stage→6th Stage
Students can not design the design subject.→1st Stage→They select among learning materials individually and learn basic design skills.
→Retrial
6th Stage: Students check their own design sheet.
Judgment: Design completion →1st Stage→7th Stage
Students misconceive the design subject.→1st Stage→They select among learning materials individually and learn the basic skills of design.→Retrial
7th Stage: Students assemble the model car and test its performance.
Judgment: Design completion, the car model can raise the weight. →End.

The car model can not raise the weight.→1st Stage or 5th Stage→
They select among the learning materials individually and learn the basic skills of design, or Redesign→Retrial
Learning materials: The above-mentioned contents of teaching materials: 2, 3, and 4.

Information regarding dynamics and technology that is necessary for solving the design subject is presented to students corresponding to the evaluation results. Again, knowledge, learning information through experiments, and analytic models are presented to students corresponding to the evaluation results. Students solve the design subject through these learning processes.

EVALUATION OF THE TEACHING MATERIAL FOR DESIGNING A MODEL CAR

We assumed that students who learn through this design learning support system are third grade students who learn mechanical engineering at Technical High Schools and at Colleges of Technology. Therefore, we infer that students have mastered the bases of dynamics necessary to solve this design subject.
The teaching program shown below is planned for evaluating this design learning support system on designing a model car.
1. Students grapple with the basic problems of dynamics: balance of force and moment of force.
2. Students design a model car based on the design learning support system.
3. Students complete the design sheet of a model car.
4. Students evaluate their design sheet by themselves based on the design check sheet.
5. Students assemble their own model car and evaluate its performance.

Four fourth grade students (19 years old) and five fifth grade students (20 years old) at our college were selected as subjects. Each student operated one computer. The learning process of each student is analyzed based on the log in the design learning support system. The utility of this system is evaluated through questionnaire responses.

EVALUATION OF THE LEARNING PROCESS

Analysis of the log in the design learning support system shows that all students learned about the reduction gear first. Next, they grappled with designing the model car and checked the design sheet based on the design check sheet of this system. At that moment, students noticed that it was necessary to calculate the center of gravity of the model car and the frictional force acting between tires and the road surface.
Students chose some teaching materials prepared in this design learning support system and learned them independently. They calculated the center of gravity and the load distribution of the front and back wheels of the car model.

From analyzing students' learning processes, the required time for design, design checking and performance tests, the learning content chosen by students, and the required time to learn them were clarified. Results of the number of students who grappled with the design and learning, and the mean required time for those tasks are shown in the following.

Design Start

Determination of the required traction force of the model car and the frictional force acting on the driving wheels: 9 students / 5.6 min

Determination of friction coefficient: 9 students / 7.1 min

Design of the transmission of rotational motion by gears: 9 students / 8.9 min

Learning about spur gears: 9 students / 2.5 min

Learning about the transmission of rotational motion by gears: 9 students / 4.8 min

Learning about the transmission of torque by gears: 7 students / 8.3 min

Learning about the gear train: 5 students / 14.7 min

Learning about motor performance: 3 students / 6.8 min

Learning about design of the required traction force: 6 students / 11.2 min

Learning through experimentation on raising a weight: 4 students / 3.7 min

Learning about force transmission from the motor to a tire: 4 students / 22.5 min

Check of the design sheet: designing the frictional force acting on the drive wheels: 9

students / 16.8 min

Learning about forces acting upon the model car: 1 students / 14.1 min

Learning about calculating the center of gravity: 4 students / 8.0 min

Learning about the reason for putting a weight on the model car: 5 students / 5.1 min

Learning about calculating the friction force acting between a tire and a road surface: 5 students / 22.2 min

Assembly and Performance Testing: 9 students / 4.8 min

The mean total time required for solving this design subject was 107 min

Summary: Students used all learning materials and completed the design subject. They used both the inductive teaching materials based on experiments and the deductive teaching materials through analysis based on fundamental theories. This fact emphasizes that various kinds of teaching materials must be prepared for students to choose and to be able to learn in the design learning support system.

EVALUATION OF THE UTILITY AS THE DESIGN LEARNING SUPPORT SYSTEM

A questionnaire survey is conducted with students as respondents. Its results are shown in the following.

Q1. Was this design subject easy? (8 respondents)

Answer/Number: Very easy/0, Easy/2, Appropriate/0, Difficult/2, Very difficult//0

Q2. What do you think about grappling with a design subject like this subject before the traditional machine design subject? (8 respondents)

Answer/Number: Very useful/3, Useful/5, Nothing/0, Not useful/0, Very unuseful//0

Q3. What do you think about grappling with a subject like this subject at the same time as dynamic learning? (8 respondents)

Answer/Number: Very useful/5, Useful/2, Nothing/1, Not useful/0, Very unuseful/0

Q4. What do you think about introducing a subject like this into a class of third-grade students who had learned about fundamental physics and machine design? (8 respondents)

Answer/Number: Very useful/2, Useful/5, Nothing/1, Not useful/0, Very unuseful/0

Q5. Did you understand the following learning contents deeply through learning this teaching material? (8 respondents)

Balance of forces: Yes/5, Nothing/2, No/1

Friction: Yes/6, Nothing/2, No/0

Moment of force: Yes/6, Nothing/1, No/1

Center of gravity: Yes/5, Nothing/3, No/0

Transmission of rotational motion by gears: Yes/6, Nothing/2, No/0

Q6. Was the following learning information useful to solve this design subject?

1.Experiments: Measuring the friction coefficient, Performance test of the model car, Experiment for raising a weight using a gear box. (7 respondents)

Answer/Number: Very useful/5, Useful/1, Nothing/1, Not useful/0, Very unuseful//0

2. Explanation based on real objects: Gear box and reduction, Diameter of pitch circle, Number of teeth and a module on spur gears, Transmission ratio of a gear train, Transmission of torque by a gear train (7 respondents)

Answer/Number: Very useful/3, Useful/3, Nothing/1, Not useful/0, Very unuseful//0

3. Deductive learning information based on experimental results: An experiment of measuring the center of gravity (7 respondents)

Answer/Number: Very useful/5, Useful/1, Nothing/1, Not useful/0, Very unuseful//0

4. Learning information based on the dynamic analysis: Analytical Model of friction force acting between a tire and a road, Analytical Model of force acting on a car model, Analytical Model of force transmission in the gear train (7 respondents)

Answer/Number: Very useful/3, Useful/3, Nothing/1, Not useful/0, Very unuseful//0

Students' opinions:

· It is useful to understand the learning content through actually producing a self-designed model.

· It is useful to understand learning contents deeply through actual observation and consideration.

· It is pleasant to learn through designing and production.

· I recognized that it is difficult to design something.

• I hope that learning activities of design and production are introduced into actual classes.
• I was able to understand how dynamics and the basics of machine design are actually applied.
Summary: The questionnaire results clarified the following.
• The degree of difficulty as a design subject is appropriate.
• This design learning support system is appropriate from the viewpoint of physics education.
• This design subject is appropriate as a subject that students must grasp before an actual design subject.
• It is necessary that various kinds of teaching materials be prepared for students to choose and learn in the design learning support system.

CONCLUSION

This report described curriculum reform and changes of Specialized Course education in upper secondary schools. In addition, development of teaching materials that are closely related to science and technology for corresponding to those changes was described.

Industrial technology education in Japan has been changing drastically. Its educational aim has changed from training "Technicians" to training "Specialists"; the number of total credits of specialized subjects concerning technology has decreased. Moreover, great emphasis has been placed on education that encourages students to acquire basic abilities and problem-solving abilities.

We have developed two learning support systems to foster students' basic abilities and problem-solving abilities. These systems were developed from the viewpoint of the close relation between science and technology. Results of practice using the developed learning support system clarified that the learning support system is useful for teaching basic knowledge. Nevertheless, it remains unclear whether the actual data and facts based on experiences and the analytical model based on scientific theories are effective in the technology learning process.

Therefore, we will continue to improve the learning support system and study the teaching-learning process of industrial technology education.

REFERENCES

S.Mita, T.Nomura, T.Matsuda (2002): *Multimedia learning support system concerning creating wind turbines*, PATT-12 Proceedings, 27-33.
S.Mita, K.Namiki, T.Nomura, T.Matsuda (2003): *Development of software program for predicting the performance of ultra-micro wind turbine for educational use*, Proceedings of the 34th Annual Conference of the International Simulation and Gaming Association Research, 971-980.
The Curriculum Council (July 29, 1998), Synopsis of the Report: "National Curriculum Standards Reform for Kindergarten, Elementary School, Lower and Upper Secondary School and Schools for the Visually Disabled, the Hearing-Impaired and the Otherwise Disabled"

DAVID BARLEX

19. THE CENTRALITY OF DESIGNING – AN EMERGING REALISATION FROM THREE CURRICULUM PROJECTS

INTRODUCTION

Kimbell and Perry (2001) have presented a powerful case for the significance of designing within the design & technology curriculum yet although design activity is implicit in design & technology national curriculum for England (Department for Education and Employment, Qualifications and Curriculum Authority 1999) the words design or designing are not used in the unique contribution statement which justifies the inclusion of the subject in that curriculum. This paper describes the role of designing within the design & technology curriculum in England from the perspective of three curriculum projects over 15 years: a) the Nuffield Design & Technology Project which developed a pedagogy to enable pupils to be successful at designing and making simple products, b) the Young Foresight Project which developed a pedagogy to enable pupils to tackle conceptual design and c) the Electronics In Schools Project that enables teachers to consider progression in the construction of a design based technology curriculum involving electronics. Finally the paper discusses the role of designing within a design & technology curriculum in which both designing and making occur and argues that it is engaging in design that is the key to the unique contribution that can be made by design & technology to the education of all young people.

PEDAGOGY TO SUPPORT DESIGNING AND MAKING

The Nuffield Secondary Design & Technology began in 1990 as design & technology was introduced as a new subject into the National Curriculum in England (Department of Education and Science / Welsh Office 1990). By 1995 the Project had developed pedagogy in response to the demands of designing and making that formed the core of this design & technology curriculum. The pedagogy consisted of three types of learning activity. Resource Tasks, short often practical activities that taught specific skills, knowledge and understanding likely to be useful in tackling a designing and making activity; Capability Tasks, longer more open designing and making activities; and Case Studies, true stories about design & technology in the world outside school to enable pupils to put their studies into a wider context. Through a careful combination of these types of learning activity across a number of years a teacher could construct a learning experience that was broad, balanced, covered the required programme of study and met the requirements of continuity and progression. A suite of publications were

M.J. de Vries, I. Mottier (eds.), International Handbook of Technology Education, 253–259.

developed to support teachers in using this pedagogy: a Resource Task File (Barlex, 1995a), a Capability Task File (Barlex, 1995b), a Study Guide (Barlex, 1995c) containing both advice to the pupil and an extensive set of case studies, a Student's Book (Barlex 1995d) which defined the content with which pupils should be familiar and a Teacher's Guide (1995e) to provide advice in using the materials. As is the case with much curriculum development, the content of these works derived largely from listening to teachers, limited piloting and the Project Director's intuition, but an analysis of the content (Barlex and Welch 2001) shows that the materials leant heavily on the work of the Assessment of Performance Unit for Design & Technology (Kimbell, Stables, Wheeler Wosniak & Kelly,1991) and had considerable resonance with the work of Welch et al on the behaviour of naïve that is, pupil designers (Welch, Barlex & Lim, 2000). There is little doubt that the pedagogy developed by the Nuffield Project was new to many teachers. To the delight of those associated with the Project the revision of the National Curriculum for design & technology in 1995 included key features from the work of the Project – focused practical tasks (i.e. Resource Tasks) and designing and making assignments, DMAs (i.e. Capability Tasks).

A questionnaire survey to probe the use made of the Nuffield publications (Givens & Barlex 2001) revealed the following. The most widely used were the Student's Book and the Resource Tasks. It may be relevant that both were easy for teachers to use selectively without necessarily changing their practice. However, the task structures were used nearly as much as the tasks themselves, but as frameworks for schools' own in-house materials. The task structures embody the pedagogy behind the materials ('the Nuffield Approach') through, for example, detailing activities (Resource Tasks and Case Studies) that will prepare pupils for a Capability Task and indicating value considerations and links to other subjects. When teachers adopted the task structures but not necessarily their content, were they, in fact, adopting the pedagogy and applying it to their pre-selected content? Becher (1971) relates how teachers adopted the content offered by a curriculum innovation but retained their existing (didactic) teaching methods. The findings appeared to show some teachers responding to accessible structures in the opposite way, i.e. adopting the pedagogy from a curriculum innovation while retaining content from their established practice. Although some teachers used the Nuffield approach in ways that would enable pupils to design what they were going to make and then make what they had designed this was not a National picture and the Office for Standards in Education consistently reported that skills in designing lagged behind those in making (Office for Standards in Education 1998 & 2000). Atkinson (2000) has noted that the assessment structure militates against the development of higher order thinking skills associated with designing.

Particularly interesting features of the Student's Book are the chooser charts, which were developed deliberately to support pupil autonomy in making design decisions and solving emergent problems. The book contains 12 such charts which summarise areas of content in such a way that pupils can use the content to make decisions either unaided or with minimal support from their teacher. An able pupil can use such charts to make decisions, which he or she can then justify to the teacher. For a less able pupil the teacher can ask questions, which engages the pupil with the content of the chart, so leading the pupil to make their own decisions. Of course the best way to use such a chart involves annotating the chart with possible choices by drawing circles, adding ticks or crosses and notes. To promote such use of these charts they are available as free downloads at www.secondarydandt.org the Nuffield Secondary Design & Technology Project website.

PEDAGOGY TO SUPPORT CONCEPTUAL DESIGN

Insisting that pupils should always make what you have designed can undermine pupils' autonomy especially if they have limited making skills. The Young Foresight project deliberately avoids this difficulty by requiring pupils to work collaboratively in designing but NOT making products and services for the future utilising new technologies as a starting point (Barlex, 2000). To facilitate this activity pupils are required to work as groups in which all members contribute to generating, developing and communicating design ideas. Importantly pupils are required to develop their own design briefs and mentors from industry work in a variety of ways to support pupils designing for the future. And pupils are required to present and justify their ideas to peers, their teacher and mentor, and to audiences at conferences on innovation.

Some of the products and services devised by groups of Year 9 pupils in response to the challenge of utilising the stress sensitive conductor QTC (Quantum Tunnelling Composite) include the following:
- Clothing that change colour as you dance
- Car tyres that sense their internal pressure
- An epileptic fit detector
- A self-weighing suitcase
- An arthritis treatment device
- Keep fit apparatus
- Depth sensitive submersible
- Internal heart beat monitor

These ideas show the use of imagination, the pursuit of purpose, originality and value – the four features of creativity identified by the report all our futures: Creativity, culture & education (Robinson 1999). If the pupils had been required to make what they were designing it is extremely unlikely that they would have shown this level of creativity. Indeed, designing without making, gives pupils the opportunity for conceptual design.

Through her evaluation of the Young Foresight Project Patricia Murphy identified two broad categories of teacher pedagogy (Murphy in Barlex 2003). First there was the pedagogy that was hegemonic:
- Learners are passive receivers of information

- They are not motivated to learn
- Can only learn if knowledge was presented 'pre-digested' by the teacher
- The teacher has sole authority for the curriculum and learning outcomes
- The teacher has to provide tasks which are based on instruction and school focused
- Any problems with learning rest with the learner, not the teacher i.e. a deficit view of pupils limited by their innate abilities

Second there was the pedagogy that was strongly aligned to the situated view of learning:

- Intellectual abilities are socially and culturally developed
- Tasks need to be culturally authentic
- Prior knowledge and cultural perspectives shape new learning
- Learners construct rather than receive meaning
- Pupils share responsibility for learning with teachers
- Pupils are motivated by dilemmas to which they are emotionally committed

Those teachers with the first pedagogy taught in ways that were at odds with the Young Foresight programme. They struggled to implement the programme and undermined its aims. Pupils' participation was marginalized and there were few opportunities for pupils' learning. Pupils were not motivated by the experience.

Those teachers with the second pedagogy were able to be highly effective in implementing the programme. There was significant learning and pupils in these teachers' classes were enthused and motivated by their experience of the programme.

ELABORATING DESIGN DECISIONS

The Electronics in Schools (EIS) Project involved collaboration between a government agency – the Department for Trade and Industry, a curriculum developer David Barlex acting as curriculum adviser, a researcher Patricia Murphy at the Open University, and SETPOINTs – organisations charged with providing support for STEM (science, technology, engineering and mathematics) in the school curriculum. (See www.setnet.org.uk for further information). In an effort to promote the teaching of electronics in schools the DTI funded seven SETPOINTs to explore ways in which teachers could receive in service training that would lead to an increased teaching of electronics in design & technology courses. Initially the professional development made available by the SETPOINTs consisted almost exclusively of providing subject knowledge. Under the influence of the curriculum adviser the training sessions were revised to include a consideration of pedagogy and how to introduce change in the participant's schools. The nature of the in-service programme and its impact on the design & technology curriculum, teachers and pupils in participating schools was evaluated as the programme was taking place by Patricia Murphy and her team at the Open University. Her evaluation report is available from the EIS Project website. www.electronicsinschools.com /about_eis/index.asp

The evaluation notes the positive effect of providing teachers with the opportunity to engage themselves in the sort of activity that their pupils will be doing, designing and making assignments, and a design decision audit tool that allows teachers to analyse these tasks from two perspectives (i) the opportunities for pupils' learning and (ii) cultural authenticity. The audit can be carried out using five key areas of design decision: conceptual (overall purpose of the design, the sort of product that it will be), technical (how the design will work), aesthetic (what the design will look like), constructional (how the design will be put together) and marketing (who the design is for, where it will be used, how it will be sold). This interdependence of the areas is an important feature of design decisions. A change of decision within one area will affect some if not all of design decisions that are made within the others. Usually the teacher identifies the sort of product the pupils will be designing and making. This makes it very difficult for pupils to engage in conceptual design. But even if the type of product is identified for the pupils there are still many opportunities for making design decisions in the other areas. Consider the designing and making of a puppet theatre and puppets. The pupils can make decisions about who will use the puppets and what for (marketing decisions), what sort of puppets would be appropriate, the sort of theatre such puppets would need, the nature of props and scenery plus any special effects that might accompany the performance. These decisions will encompass a host of technical, aesthetic and constructional design decisions.

DESIGNING – A CENTRAL FEATURE FOR TECHNOLOGY EDUCATION FOR ALL IN THE FUTURE

A pupil designing speculates about what might be. These speculations are developed, modelled, evaluated for fitness of purpose, realised as a prototype, and evaluated further against intention and impact. The design problem interacts with the design solution, elements of both the problem and the solution only becoming apparent as the solution is developed in response to the problem.

An intriguing way of looking at this problem – solution interaction is to consider the designing as a learning activity in which the designer is learning about the design that he/she is conceiving through successive iterations that give increasing clarity to the design proposal and its worth (Sim & Duffy 2004). The designer is learning about what he/she is creating as he/she creates it. From a pedagogic viewpoint this is fascinating – it is the pupil who has the knowledge and expertise in this situation, only he/she knows about his/her design. The teacher's role is one of enabling that learning to progress according to the pupils design intentions. This is very different from the traditional role of the teacher which is to help the pupil learn about that which the teacher already knows.

One of the problems facing the teaching of designing is the peculiar nature of the subject matter of design. Design has no special subject matter of its own apart from what the designer conceives it to be. The subject matter of design is potentially universal in scope because design thinking may be applied to any area of human experience. But in the process of application, the designer must discover or invent a particular subject out of the problems and issues of specific circumstances. It is possible to tackle this dilemma in schools to some extent by considering 'knowledge of the problem', which can be acquired by pupils through investigation and research and 'knowledge for the solution', which can be identified to (say) between 50% and 75% for a particular set of solutions and hence taught in a traditional way.

The Nuffield Project has developed a broad pedagogy which deals with this dilemma – Resource Tasks which support the acquisition of 'knowledge for the solution' leading to a Capability Task (a designing and making task) in which pupils identify 'knowledge of the problem' and work towards a solution acquiring any more 'knowledge for the solution' that they might need. Case Studies provide background information relevant to 'knowledge of the problem'. It is highly likely that resolving the task will require knowledge and understanding from other subjects hence designing is a powerful means of crossing and breaking down subject boundaries. Furthermore, the Nuffield Project has developed pedagogic devices that overcome pupils' lack of 'knowledge for the solution.

The Young Foresight Project revealed that it is not always necessary to design AND make and that pupils can develop a wider appreciation of and ability in designing if sometimes they can design without having to consider making. The Young Foresight Project has also indicated that positioning designing at the core of a technology curriculum will be highly challenging for some teachers. It has been argued that teacher's implicit beliefs inform their prevailing pedagogy (Dow 2003, 2004). Teachers whose implicit theories of learning are governed by notions of transmission of knowledge and control of learning will find it hard to create the type of structures which will encourage designing, however the importance of this is espoused. Implicit theories appear to play a significant role in the way teachers choose to teach. Revealing and confronting these theories is neither easy nor comfortable but it would appear that it should become an essential part of both initial teacher training and subsequent professional development if designing is going to be significant in technology education.

The EIS Project has shown that it is possible to audit a curriculum composed of designing and making assignments according to the demands of design decisions and so give designing, as opposed to making, the high priority required to ensure that the activity is cognitively demanding without demotivating pupils.

Hence I argue that the role of making though important is not central to technology education. Manufacturing technologies capable of generating complex 3D forms both solid and hollow are already finding their way into some schools and it is likely that these will be available for the domestic market before long (Massachusetts Institute of Technology, September 2003). The issue is not whether a pupil can make what they have designed but whether it is worth making. This is not to devalue making. It will be essential for pupils to handle materials, to use both hand tool and machine tools as part of their making experience in order to design appropriately with particular materials. But this making should be in deference to the act of designing. It is designing that will develop pupils high level cognitive skills through which they will be able to handle uncertainty, seek out relevant knowledge, solve problems, make and justify decisions and communicate effectively. These are qualities that will serve young people well whatever career path they choose.

REFERENCES

Atkinson, S. (2000), 'Does the need for high levels of performance curtail the development of creativity in design and technology project work?' *International Journal of Technology and Design Education*, 10 (3), 255-281.

Barlex, D. (1995a). *Nuffield design and technology, resource task file*. Harlow: Longman.

Barlex, D. (1995b). *Nuffield design and technology, capability task file*. Harlow: Longman.

Barlex, D. (1995c). *Nuffield Design and Technology Study Guide*. Harlow: Longman.

Barlex, D. (1995d). *Nuffield design and technology student's book*. Harlow: Longman.

Barlex, D. (1995e). *Nuffield design and technology teacher's guide*. Harlow: Longman.

Barlex, D: (2000). *Young Foresight: Handbook for teachers and mentors*. London: Software Production Enterprises.

Barlex, D., & Welch, M. (2001). Educational research and curriculum development: The case for synergy. *Journal of Design and Technology Education*, 6(1), 29-39.

Barlex, D. (2003). *Creativity in crisis? Design & technology at KS3 and KS4*. Wellesbourne, UK: Design and Technology Association.

Becher , A. (1971). The Dissemination and implementation of educational innovation, *Annual Meeting of the British Association for the Advancement of Science, Section L*, September 1971 (unpublished).

Department for Education and Employment, Qualifications and Curriculum Authority (1999) *Design and technology: The national curriculum for England*, HMSO, London, England.

Department of Education and Science / Welsh Office. (1990). *Technology in the national curriculum*, DES, London.

Dow, W. (2003). Technology students' views of Intelligence and the implications for classroom practice. In E. W. L. Norman & D. Spendlove (Eds.), *DATA International Research Conference 2003* (pp. 29-33). Wellesbourne, UK: Design and Technology Association.

Dow, W. (2004). The role of implicit theories in the development of creative classrooms. In E. W. L. Norman, D. Spendlove, P. Grover, & A. Mitchell (Eds.), *DATA International Research Conference 2004* (pp. 61-66). Wellesbourne, UK: Design and Technology Association.

Givens, N., & Barlex, D. (2001). The role of published materials in curriculum development and implementation for secondary school design and technology in England and Wales. *The International Journal of Technology and Design Education*, 11, 137-161. [Co-author]

Kimbell, R., & Perry, D. (2001). *Design and technology in the knowledge economy*. London: Engineering Council.

Kimbell, R., Stables, K., Wheeler, T., Wosniak, A., & Kelly, V. (1991). *The assessment of performance in design and technology: Final report*. London: Schools Examination and Assessment Council.

Office for Standards in Education. (1998). *Secondary education-a review of secondary schools in England 1993-1997*, OFSTED, *London*.

Office for Standards in Education.: (2000). *Ofsted subject reports secondary design and technology, 1999 – 2000*, The Stationary Office, London, UK.

Robinson, K. (1999). *All our futures: Creativity, culture & education*. London: Department for Education and Employment.

Massachusetts Institute of Technology.(September 2003), *Technology Review*, MIT's Magazine of Innovation, MIT, Massachusetts, USA.

Welch, M., Barlex, D., & Lim, H. S. (2000). Sketching: Friend or foe to the novice designer. *International Journal of Technology and Design Education*, 10, 125-148.

TONY LAWLER

20. 'I THINK THEREFORE I DESIGN' (WHEN DESCARTES MET BRONOWSKI)

Reflections on the last 20 years of 'designing' and projections into the future.

The nature of this paper as an attempt at some kind of reflective account, will lean on personal experiences, events and research and writings of the time. Inevitably it will be somewhat anecdotal, yet I would hope not lacking in rigour.
In the 'Ascent of Man'(1973) Bronowski outlined those qualities which distinguish us as a species from other animals and the qualities that have helped us succeed. Those qualities, I propose, have strong similarities to what we now call designing.

Man is distinguished from other animals by his imaginative gifts. He makes plans, inventions, new discoveries, by putting different talents together; and his discoveries become more subtle and penetrating, as he learns to combine his talents in more complex and intimate ways.
Bronowski 1973 page 20

Descartes notion of the view of the human condition being a 'subjective view' of reality means that these views of betterment which define designing are individually based. In the process of doubting everything, even his own existence, Descartes concluded that proof of his existence was that he was thinking. How could a non-existent being think? The fact that he was thinking proved to him that he existed-

'Cogito ergo sum'- I think therefore I am

and from that point on it allowed him to be more conclusive other things he had doubted, including God. The existence, within humans of a 'belief', in the case of designing 'that things can be better' is one of the ideas that links the two philosophies of Descartes and Bronowski.
And, that our individual perceptions of 'reality' will form our views of how we view the notions of change in our lives (for the better).
My rather playful notion of the coming together of two great thinkers represents an attempt to see designing as a defining capability in humans. Descartes definition with its emphasis on an individual's understandings of themselves and their world

M.J. de Vries, I. Mottier (eds.), International Handbook of Technology Education, 261–271.

and Bronowski's ideas of humans' pursuit of 'betterment' are central to my argument.

Prior to 1985 the idea of design and designing [in that in many contexts they are used interchangeably, Walker J.A. (1989)] emerged from an activity which was implicit within professional activities. Architects and engineers, for example, did it but often didn't recognise designing as a part of their work. Designing became a recognised generic activity which could have a methodology of its own and could be seen 'within' a range of professional activities. Alongside this recognition came the acceptance of a methodology by which design could be managed. The chart in figure 1 below shows the correlations of views which were evolving around the same time of methodologies in architecture, engineering, education and psychology.

Figure from Lawler. Idater 1999

Asimow 1962 (Engineering)	RIBA Architects 1965	Psychology of problem solving	Linear Model of Design and Technology (education)
Stage 1 Feasibility finding a set of feasible concepts	1. Inception 2. Feasibility	Preparation	
Stage 2 Preliminary Design Selection and development of the best concept	3. Outline proposals 4. Scheme design	Incubation	Identify problem research
Stage 3 Detailed design An engineering description of the concept	5. Detail design	Illumination	generate ideas select and detail
Stage 4 Planning Evaluating and altering the concept to suit the requirements of production distribution, consumption and product retirement	6. Production information 7. Bills of quantities 8. Tender action 9. Project planning 10. Operation on site 11. Completion 12. Feedback	Verification	make solution evaluate

Columns reproduced from J.C.Jones (1980)   Column reproduced from Lawson (1990)   Column reproduced from Kimbell et al (1991)

Figure 1

262

From the history of technology education (Penfold 1988,Rutland 1997) what I see as the tensions in education for designing are:

1. The desire to enhance the fulfilment of the individual;
2. The requirement of citizens to serve the needs of society. (a social, cultural, and economic construct)

(Penfold 1988) describes two primary school teachers from London visiting Sweden in 1844 for a summer school (no small feat) and bringing back with them ideas[1] of human fulfilment through activity, which they introduced to their slum school children. At the same time the moves by the Guilds and Education Boards aimed to ensure that all girls could study food and sewing, so that they could feed and clothe their families and be more employable as servants (Rutland1997). The boys, on the other hand, learned metalcrafts, woodwork and engineering drawing so that they could maintain their homes and become employable (in the industrialising world) (Penfold 1988). The contrast between the value positions behind the introduction of Sloyd on the one hand and the more functional skills teaching on the other, express these tensions.

Technology education in schools in the UK in 1985

In describing schools and the position of designing in 1985 in the UK I have focussed particularly on the examination systems. Prior to 1970 there were essentially two components of the examinations for 16 year olds, a written examination and a skills based practical test. In 1970 under George Hicks, the then chief examiner for London University GCE O level, the board introduced a 'pre-practical' element into their examination. This was the beginning of a designed element in the activity being 'embedded' into the curriculum. The pre-practical part of the examination -

'required candidates to work from a tightly constructed design brief and design and make a part-product... Kimbell (1997) page 6

For pupils of 16 years of age there were two levels of examination set and administered by different bodies; the GCE (General Certificate of Education) for the more able, and CSE (Certificate of Secondary Education) for the rest. Teachers were involved in the writing and moderation of both sets of examinations. Teachers would choose the examination most suitable for themselves and their pupils. The examinations were moderated to be of the appropriate standards such that a grade 1 for CSE was equivalent to a grade C at GCE. Whilst this may seem now a potentially chaotic situation it did provide opportunities for curriculum innovation to be directly rewarded an example of this comes from a school with a particularly innovative curriculum (Stantonbury Campus) who abandoned all GCE examinations preferring instead to write and administer special CSE examinations particularly for their school. Subject boundaries were no longer a problem and pupils were given credit directly for what they could do.

There was also innovation at A level for example Oxford A level Design which enabled a direct focus in on the generic activity of designing. Pupils were encouraged to work to design in ways which produced the most appropriate outcomes for their notions of 'betterment'. I myself marked submissions which included: the design of a television programme; a racing bicycle; and a booklet for parents of children with muscular dystrophy, in the same school with the same teacher.

Alongside this there were also numerous examples of syllabi which involved the reproduction of rote learned facts and processes - only a small development from their 19th century precedents.

Even earlier in the 1980's the Design and Craft Education Project at Keele University, directed by Professor John Eggleston developed the idea of designing as a process. Recognising the role that examinations had in curriculum development, the process was embedded within a CSE level examination established in 1970 entitled 'A Course of Study in Design'. As the course booklet explained it had an innovative approach to notions of content and assessment.

'It is not therefore possible to itemise a syllabus for practical work under headings of specific knowledge or motor skills because these may vary according to the individual needs of candidates and the requirements of different design problems'
NWSEB 1970 North West Secondary Examination Board page 2

In the UK in 1985 we had no agreed National Curriculum but having established a curriculum area called Craft Design and Technology a National Criteria for CDT examinations were agreed. Within these the aspects of pupils being assessed on individual and original pieces of course-work was well accepted. There was no doubt that pupils were required to design and make things. What was conducted by particular teachers in any single school was as a result of what they felt was 'appropriate' for their pupils. This view of appropriateness was often governed by the ability of those pupils to pass the terminal examination taken at 16 years of age. At that time there were around 10 examining boards each marketing a range of examinations. Exam boards in the UK are profit making businesses.

The difficulties of compatibility and reliability with such a diverse system, plus the speed of curriculum development, led to the amalgamation of the two levels of examination and a standardised set of GCSE General Criteria established by the Secondary Examinations Council (a government QUANGO,[2)] All examinations had to follow these criteria. The subsequent examinations areas were then re-named Craft Design and Technology, with sub titles for materials disciplines e.g. Woodwork, Metalwork, and Design Communication. All had to include notions of designing. These examinations retained aspects of the previous system including, a timed practical test, an exhibition of practical designed and made work (coursework) and a (traditional) written examination. Further evidence of the acceptance of the activity of designing was that at that time Art examinations were also renamed, Art and Design. The idea of pupils being required to exercise an element of designing expressed in individual and different outcomes was embedded within the marking criteria of examinations in both these areas of the curriculum.

The APU Design and Technology Project, commissioned by the Department for Education and Science reported in 1991, for the first time described capability across a range of pupils and subject areas of the curriculum. Significant in its approach was the emphasis that capability was an active measure. It was not based on a 'knowledge' base but on capability as a result of 'doing' designing and technologising.

From the earliest work in this field, there has been general agreement on certain basic tenets of Design and Technology. It is an active *study involving the* purposeful *pursuit of* a task *to some form of* resolution *that results in* improvement *(for someone) in the made world.*
Kimbell et al 1991

With the introduction of the National Curriculum in 1990 came a further definition of that which pupils should achieve in all areas of schooling. Attainment was classified as to Levels (how good pupils were) and Attainment Targets were established for the 4 major divisions: Key Stages 1 and 2 for primary schooling; Key Stage 3 for mid secondary schooling; Key Stage 4 up to the end of secondary compulsory schooling. These corresponded to 5 to 7; 7 to 11; 11 to 14; 14 to 16 years of age. At the same point the curriculum areas were regrouped and were called 'Design and Technology'. The new 'subject' now included the CDT subjects, Textiles and Home Economics, renamed Food Technology. Thus for the first time what had always been seen as similar disciplines were collected together under the same banner. Furthermore within the National Curriculum Order, there was a compulsory entitlement for all pupils from 5 to 16 years of age to Design and Technology. Some might say a dream of 'designing for all' come true.

But has this been the case? In my experience this entitlement has not resulted in a greater exposure of more pupils to designing for two reasons: the exam system and OFSTED inspections, in short an overemphasis on accountability.

The number of examining boards in England has reduced to nominally 3. The costs to administer the examinations, crucial to the boards' economic survival, have had an influence on assessment procedures. A linear process of designing has been translated piecemeal into the assessment rubric for the examination. Despite the findings of the APU report, teachers have translated and installed this model throughout the Design and Technology Curriculum. The resultant emphasis on filling in the 'right' pieces of paper at the 'right' stage seems to dominate schemes of work at all levels. The practical coursework which had become an assessed component of all exams under the CDT banner, rather than being previously marked by teachers and then moderated on site, now is submitted to the examining board, in a more standardised (and transportable) format. This has resulted in a greater emphasis on recording of the process of the work and less on the made outcomes. This change has often led to pupils giving excessive priority to the presentation of their work, rather than focussing on the content of that being presented. This often resulted in what Mike Ive, former chief HMI for Design and Technology, referred to as 'nice nonsense'.

Also in order to assess the effectiveness of schools nationally, a regime of inspection is carried out. OFSTED (Office for Standards in Education) seeks to ensure and drive up the quality of education. It cannot be questioned that OFSTED inspections and the National Curriculum have clarified and driven up standards. OFSTED reports however make scant reference to ideas of designing and creativity (Kimbell 2000) [3] The emphasis on 'tracking' students alongside Programmes of Study has seemingly taken the energy that teachers used to give to ensuring that pupils are stretched to engage in designing to produce varied and exciting outcomes has, in my view, been reduced to what in many cases is a series of 'focussed practical tasks'[4]. So this, in my view, has led to a position that whilst embedded within the curriculum, there are no means by which to assess pupil capability using terms such as creativity or designing abilities.

This key sentence in the National Curriculum for Design and Technology document

'It (Design and Technology) enables them (the pupils) to understand how to think and intervene creatively to improve the world' QCA, 1999: 122,

was applauded for its inclusion by Kimbell (20000 in his millennium conference keynote entitled Creativity in Crisis, is also seen as a 'hollow promise' at a time when creativity is in 'crisis' in our schools. And if creativity is in crisis, by association so is designing.

Commercial and Governmental Perceptions

In 1985 the UK and the developed world were still a part of an industrial continua where origination and manufacture were in most cases in the same country or continent. The ideas of the contribution that the activity of designing could make were well established within the process of production. It was how things were made. The emergent idea of Design Management was finding a level of acceptance. Ideas of 'Total Design' (Hollins and Pugh 1991) where the idea of design and designing could have an influence on the management of manufacturing and service industries were emerging. The increasing proliferation of computing and the subsequent access to and speed of transfer of information announced the dawn of the 'information age'. The natural and seeming congenital fear of business people to the concept of 'risk' was being confronted by the idea that 'risk' was essential, perpetual and speedy development was necessary in order to survive. Van Stamm(2003) Hollins and Hollins (1999) Cagan and Vogel (2002) have gained recognition by suggesting how 'design thinking' can help business in dealing with the risky business of being innovative.

Governmentally in the case of the UK and influenced by Hutton's 1995 The State We're In' (1995) advised by DEMOS (Seltzer and Bentley1999) and prompted by demographic changes in manufacturing, have recognised such ideas as 'stakeholder capitalism'[5] These have led through concepts of individual workers and their development, to constructs of 'national wealth' being that of the summation of the capabilities of society. The skills that such a society has is effectively what we have to sell and with what we will succeed in the future. Political mantra 'education education education' within Prime Minister Tony Blair's campaign speeches, are both altruistic and logical if such an argument is followed. Thus returning to my views that one of design and technology education's roles is as a provider of the 'workforce of the next generation', it would not be surprising for such ideas to surface in the present educational climate.

Philosophical, Marketing and Sociological constructs. (Strange bedfellows) Interestingly the links between marketing and philosophy over the last 15 years tell very similar stories, though maybe not for the same reasons. Both have moved to an increasing emphasis onto the individual and their view of their world.

Marketing

In 1985 the emphasis in marketing was around the marketplace as a mass of amorphous consumers. Markets were stratified approximately into socio-economic bandings based on the job people did and how much they earned. The use of standardised testing as descriptors of capability, were accepted widely. Questions by post modernist scientists and philosophers as to the validity of such views have led to recognition of the viewpoint of the individual. Phenomenological psychology is *as* concerned for the behaviour of, for example, the 'rat in the maze', as it is to how the rat 'feels' about the situation. Market researchers have moved through redefining consumer groups in terms of their lifestyles (e.g. sustainers, aspirers) to designers and market researchers alike (IDEO reported by Van Stamm 2003 page 123) focussing, through using anthropologists, on carefully targeted consumers. These researchers are concerned with tracking and recording the decisions of the selected individual, both at the point of purchase and during the life-cycle of its products and services.[6] So that their designs can be more relevant to the 'particular' consumer, and through this to more generalisable markets.

Philosophy in parallel

Descartes' 'Cogito ergo sum' which for him confirmed through the existence of thinking and confirmation that he existed, has been translated as 'I think therefore I am'. Interestingly this statement, in a world of science and philosophy which has come to doubt absolute rules, in favour of those of the individual, has certain resonances. Philosophers' ideas such as those of Sartre and existentialism, through to Lefevbre and Baktin's move increasingly to doubt the generalised theory and to value the ordinary, everyday and individualised experience (Baktin's prosaic) as having 'real' validity.

[7]The ideas of Barthes(1993) in his analysis of literature questioned the position of the author with regard to the reader - preferring to see it as a dialogue not a delivered edict, when interpreted into communications and products of all kinds has seen the notional 'conversation' between products and users as important. De Certo explores notions of reality and illusion for the individual, the 'illusion' of an object or situation, as interpreted by the individual, being just as important as its 'true' meaning. To take all of this back to a more concrete example- the humble training shoe has now taken on values and meanings far beyond its original 'function'. The 'dream' or image that the object carries, becomes its meaning, and that meaning is embodied in its logo. So much so that marketeers have moved towards seeing 'branding' as the essence of their trade. This matches the philosophers' concerns with meanings and realities for the individual.

And what of Bronowski?

Bronowski's notion of the qualities that have enabled us as a species to develop, describe ideas embedded within the activity of designing which imply 'betterment'; the desire to realise new things; the task of using what talents we have but of developing others by doing this; the desire to create. All these can be seen clearly in the context of designing.

Descartes on the other hand, through doubting everything, looks at the unique and personal way that each of us moves towards a way of describing our own existence.

So that when Descartes met Bronowski, their imagined conversation was around the activity to achieve betterment, and how this related to the individual's perception of it, and how the individual would achieve a better world for themselves and others.

The move towards individualised views of designing, have for me come from the following:

Starting from Gardner's notions of multiple intelligences, these were used positively to identify possible and differing ways of designing. For example, certain individuals will work predominantly in one intelligence, but also that dominant intelligence can be used to support other intelligences which may therefore expand the range of possible ideas of 'betterment' for the designer.

Myers Briggs' ideas, developed from Jung's work, allowed ways of seeing the continuum between sensing and intuition and thinking and feeling which were linked to designing by Durling (1996).

Riding's (1992) explorations of 'cognitive styles, and more recently Atkinson's (2005) work in the context of Design and Technology reveals tendencies in their test groups towards certain 'styles' of information processing and their correlation to success.

Neuro Linguistic Programming, (O'Connor and McDermott 1996)[8] which is based firmly in the individual's interpretation of their own situation, and rather than styles of operation looks at levels of abstraction and reflection.

The work around metacognition by Metcalf (1992) is echoed in aspects of writings about creativity by Koestler (1964). In the context of designing, the implications for the developing of a culture of self understanding, reflection on what has been Schon(1987)and projection as to what could be give a further dimension to the understanding of designing. My previous (Lawler 2003) work combines many of these ideas significantly in the interest of exploring descriptors of individual's designing capability. It differs from previous works in that they often have sought to diagnose and pigeon-hole individuals into groups for the purpose of analysis.

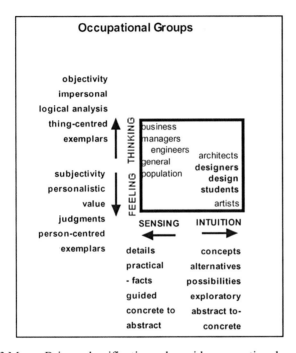

Figure 2 Myers Briggs classifications alongside occupational groupings

My work seeks to allow personal insights into individual preferences, which give access into other styles of designing. The implication being that designing involves a combination styles and capabilities.

So where are we now?

I see us at a point where the innovation wave is firmly established and with associated values to commerce and society, yet within Design and Technology in the UK, the recognition of the importance of the activity of designing has waned. Apart from a few warning voices, academics, teachers and pupils are more concerned with delivering skills and knowledge effectively to achieve the best result (in tests and examinations). The whole system seems to have moved via concerns for accountability, away from designing and back towards a curriculum of 20 years ago. In order to be able to surf the wave we must prepare ourselves for what is to come. The recent project by the Technology Education Research Unit TERU Kimbell et al 2004 commission by The Department for Education and Skills, has been effectively to cooperate with the examining boards to explore ways of 'putting the designing back into the curriculum'. Effecting change that allows value to be given in the assessment instrument will be a motivator to refocus curriculum interest. From the report of the National Advisory Committee on Creative and Cultural Education (1999), it was evident that other curriculum areas had fewer problems with the recognition and assessment of creativity. My own work with 'designing styles' shows that it is possible to make pupils and teachers fluent with their own and their pupil's ways of designing and technologising (Lawler and Howlett 2002), allowing them to get better at it quicker. If we are to accept this challenge it is important that we work towards common agreements as to the importance of designing and creativity within our discipline and actively explore ways to encourage , record and assess these capabilities in our students. Rather than seeing them as difficult to assess in the individual, and pretending therefore they have no relevance. The future for the area of Pupils and Technology Teaching , for me indicates us having to re-embrace designing, and re-integrate them into our teaching. Remembering that as a species it has been that ability- to think and postulate how we can and do make improvements to our situation as we see it, that have been the key to our survival so far.

We think therefore we design.

ENDNOTES

1 A doctrine called Sloyd which used the idea of teaching through practical activity developed initially in Finland

2 Quango - quasi non governmental organisation

3 Keynote speech to Millennium Conference reported in DATA Journal Autumn 2000 Volume 5 number 3 where from three Ofsted reports, nominally 60.000 words, the word creativity was used just once and management 86 times.

4 Because student project work involves both the acquisition of skills and the application of skills in the production of outcomes, a recommended strategy in the National Curriculum was that of having short skills based tasks (focussed practical tasks) and larger and more open ended tasks (Design and Make Projects)

5 the collective responsibilities of those engaged in working with each other: the worker's responsibility to the employer; the employer's responsibility to the worker and their development)

6 All of the concepts of philosophy are from Gardiner (2000)

7 Sometimes referred to as ethnography and by Van Stamm (2003) as 'emphatic design' page 123

8 Neuro linguistic programming -a technique developed as a combination of linguistics, psychiatry and hypnosis

REFERENCES

Atkinson, S. (2005) A study of preferred information processing style and its relationship to gender and achievement in the context of Design and Technology Project work *Design and Technology*

Education An International Journal, 10 Number 1 pages 26-42 Design and Technology Association UK.

Barthes, R. (1993) *Barthes a reader ed. S. Sontag.* Vintage, Random House UK Ltd.

Cagan and Vogel (2002) *Creating breakthrough products.* Financial Times Prentice Hall.Upper Saddle River NJ.USA

Durling, D. Cross, N. and Johnson, J. (1996) *Personality and learning preferences of students in design related disciplines,* IDATER 96: International conference on design and technology educational research and curriculum development. Loughborough, UK: Loughborough University of Technology ed. Smith, J. S. Loughborough University

Gardiner, M. E. (2000) *Critiques of everyday life.* Routledge London UK

Gardne, H.(1983) *Frames of mind ; the theory of multiple intelligences.* Fontana Press. London.

Hollins, W. and Hollins, G. (1999) *Over the horizon- planning products today for success tomorrow.* Wiley Chichester UK

Hollins and Pugh (1991) *'Total design' managing the design process in the service sector* Pitman, London

Hutton, W. (1995) *The state we're in.* Jonathan Cape Great Britain

Kimbell (1997) *Assessing technology.* Open University Press

Koestler A. (1964) *The act of creation,* Hutchinson & Co (Picador edition 1975) London.

Lawler, T. (1999) IDATER99 Ed. Smith J. and Norman E. *Examining gender effects of design and technology project work by comparing strategies for presenting and managing pupils work.* pages 22 – 31 Loughborough University UK

Lawler & Howlett (2003) Designing styles - *A new way of looking at design and technology learning and teaching.* DATA International research Conference 2003 Ed. Norman E.W.L. and Spendlove D. Design and Technology Association. UK pages 63 – 68.

Lawler, T. (2004) *Exploring descriptors of the act of designing.* Submission for MPhil London University.

O'Connor, J. and McDermott, I.(1996) *Principles of neuro linguistic programming,* Thorsons California USA

May, R. (1961) *Existential psychology.* In R. May ed. Existential Psychology. New York. Random House pp 11-51

Metcalf (1992) *Dynamic metacognitive monitoring during problem solving.* In Metacognition :Core readings Nelson. T. ed. (1992) Allyn and Baker MA. pages 196-214

National Advisory Committee on Creative and Cultural Education (1999) Robinson K. ed Department for Education and Employment. UK.

Penfold, J. (1988) *Craft design and technology, past, present and future.* Trentham Books

Riding, R.J.(1992) *Tests for cognitive Style.* Learning and Training Technology. Birmingham, England

Rutland, M. (1997) *Teaching food technology in secondary school,* page 3, Fulton Publishers

Schon D.A. (1987) *Educating the reflective practitioner- towards a new design for teaching and learning in the professions.* Josey Bass. California)

Seltzer, A. & Bentley, T. (1999) *The creative age, knowledge and skills for the new economy.* DEMOS. London

Van Stamm, B.(2003) *Managing innovation, design and creativity.* Wiley. Chichester UK

Walker, J.A. (1989) *Design history and the history of design.* Pluto Press. London. (1999)

MARION RUTLAND

21. THE INCLUSION OF FOOD TECHNOLOGY AS AN ASPECT OF TECHNOLOGY EDUCATION IN THE ENGLISH SCHOOL CURRICULUM

A critical review

THE RATIONALE FOR THE INTRODUCTION OF FOOD INTO THE ENGLISH SCHOOL CURRICULUM

The British Museum contains a record of a cookery school in London dated 1740, indicating that the study of food was originally available for ladies with private means from the upper classes. A number of eighteenth century educational writers referred to the importance of girls or young ladies from wealthy families learning how to cook (Yoxall, 1965), and throughout the nineteenth century specialist high class private cookery schools provided for the upper classes. However, the origins of food in the English school curriculum were more philanthropic or utilitarian and are linked to providing training for low paid employment. The teaching of food can be traced directly to the elementary state system for the lower working classes of the 1840s when domestic economy was introduced to improve basic living standards (DES, 1978). The emphasis in the elementary schools was not on high-class cookery skills, but on teaching girls the skills of plain cookery that could be used to feed their families. This was considered to be necessary because of the separation of home from the workplace and the movement of people to the overcrowded, poor living conditions of the new centres of factory industry in towns (Sillitoe, 1966). It was thought that the teaching of what was then know as domestic economy, would help girls develop an understanding of nutrition and the management of their family's resources (Arnold, 1908).

Health

Links between the teaching of food and health were reinforced during the South African Boer War 1899 - 1902, when it was found that the vast majority of the men who volunteered were physically unfit as a result, it was suggested, of a poor diet. The Hadow Report (Board of Education, 1926) reiterated the theme, justifying the teaching of food in terms of its value in promoting good health and efficient management to raise basic standard living standards. The study of food should be part of domestic subjects, the new title, and taught to girls as preparation for their future household duties adult life.

M.J. de Vries, I. Mottier (eds.), International Handbook of Technology Education, 273–284.

Vocational training

A second economic reason for the original introduction of food into the elementary state school system was concerned with vocational training for low paid employment, for example servants (Dyhouse, 1977). The teaching of food has a long history of links with industry, though originally this has been limited to preparing the working classes for menial, low paid employment (Whyld, 1983). In the eighteenth century Charity Schools provided training in crafts for future employment and the 'School of Industry' opened in 1799 in Kendal, Cumbria taught bakery for a this reason. The need to produce a skilled workforce in the UK led to an increased emphasis on vocational training in state education. Schools with a technical bias were created in the early years of the twentieth century where senior classes of elementary pupils were given a 'practical' bias to their curriculum, for example 'cookery', though it was emphasised that this should not prejudice general education.

Low status and association with the less able

However, in selective grammar school for more academically able girls, food was taught through domestic science with more emphasis on nutrition and science, with the most able guided towards academic subjects such as Latin and foreign languages. Similarly, in the post war era of 1945 secondary modern schools for the less academically able offered a curriculum with a practical bias for girls with a vocational slant towards catering and the food trades as a preparation for adult life (DES, 1963; Geen, Jenkins and Daniels, 1988). However, both these occupations were relatively low paid and considered low status. Creese (1965) described two main divisions in food related careers, a commercial path for the less able based on household management or catering in a large institution and another from course in domestic science leading to teaching or advising women how to run their own homes efficiently.

Gender

Food preparation, as with other household duties, has a long association with females, and this factor has had a strong traditional influence on the way in which food has been taught in the school system. Educationalists in the nineteenth and early twentieth centuries considered that boys required a different kind of education to girls with domestic subjects for girls and technical instruction or craft design technology (CDT) for boys. Both subjects, the precursors of design and technology (D&T) as we know it today, owe their introduction into the school curriculum to that philosophy. It was thought that girls should be taught how to feed and look after their families and boys how to earn their living outside the home. Domestic subjects were considered essential to prepare girls to be wives and mothers and 1885 saw the beginning of technical instruction or manual to prepare boys for the world of work outside the home to create a skilled workforce (Penfold, 1988; Attar, 1990; Newton, 1990; Eggleston, 1996). The range of roles undertaken by women during two World Wars of 1914-18 and 1939- 1945, when the men were away fighting, had little effect on attitudes. After the Second World War the rationale for the teaching of food to girls was the need to restore the health of a nation after a period of austerity and to rebuild family life.

Changing social attitudes

Such social attitudes and values were increasingly challenged by educationalists and feminists in the post-war era, where it was recognised that radical changes in the structure and life style of the population and the role of women would continue to have many repercussions on the education system (Crowther Report, DES,1959). Yet, despite these the Newsom Report (DES,1963) looking at the education of pupils aged thirteen to sixteen of average or less than average ability still referred to the need for provision of workshop crafts for boys and domestic crafts for girls. The Sex Discrimination Act (1975) in the UK was a landmark in the provision of a common education for girls and boys, as it made sexual discrimination unlawful in schools and required equality of access to the all areas of the curriculum. A direct result was the need for head teachers to make both 'craft' areas of the curriculum available for boys and girls. This resulted in equality of access but in management terms there was the issue of teaching time available and the introduction in many schools of 'circus' type lower secondary timetable where pupils followed short courses in the entire craft subjects.

Leading up to the introduction of the National Curriculum (DES, 1990), food teachers continued to strive to overcome food teaching's association with the issues of gender, status and the teaching of the less able. Prior to the introduction of the National Curriculum attempts were made to encourage a gender-free approach to the teaching of food, now known as home economics, more attractive to males. Brown (1985) describing his experiences gaining a BSc in Home Economics, included remarks from fellow school pupils regarding 'woman's' work. He felt it would be difficult for a man to become a teacher of home economics because of the traditional view that it should be taught to girls by females. After graduation, it took him some time to find employment as he felt that he was confronting both female and male stereotyping in a female dominated sector of society (Brown, 1988). It was increasingly argued that because of social changes, there was no valid reason to teach a subject that was created as a girls' subject to prepare girls for preconceived traditional female roles in the home (Attar, 1990).

THE INTRODUCTION OF THE NATIONAL CURRICULUM

Although, before the introduction of the National Curriculum in 1990 the term 'technology' had not appeared previously on most school timetables, it was not a new subject. The document 'The Curriculum from 5-16' (DES, 1985) included technology as an area of experience and learning and a particular form of problem solving concerned with bringing about change, of designing in order to effect control. The introduction of National Curriculum Technology (DES, 1990) was a landmark in that it was a compulsory subject for all pupils aged 5-16 focusing on the design process of designing and making and including the traditional practical, craft subjects of CDT and home economics. Though it was recognised by some that the skills and processes used in food, were common to other technological areas this was not a widely held view (Wandsworth, 1986). In food the learning style emphasised using domestic equipment for practical and investigative activities to prepare meals for the family (DES, 1985). On the other hand, the guidance published for CDT (DES, 1987) emphasised designing practical solutions and creative problem solving activities for boys and girls. As a result CDT teachers were more able to relate to the central philosophy of the design process in the Technology National Curriculum document when it arrived because the CDT guidance was closer to its requirements (Newton, 1990).

Many secondary food teachers were confused and alienated by the terminology used in the National Curriculum Technology Orders (DES, 1990). In the original Technology Orders there was a D&T and an Information Technology (IT) component, but these were later given their own Orders (DFE, 1995a, DFE, 1995b). Though, food was named as a material for designing and making for pupils aged 5 - 16 years, the programmes of study cited few examples related directly to food. Many food teachers felt 'de-skilled' when they considered the implications of the D&T component of the original Orders (Atherton, 1990, p50). Terms unfamiliar to food teachers were used, such as designing, artefacts, systems, environments and mechanisms which was not assisted by the noticeable absence of food specialists advising on the National Curriculum D&T Working Party (DES, 1988). In addition it was now expected that food should be taught as part of D&T not only for secondary pupils but also for children aged 5-11 years, though how this was to be achieved was unclear.

In National Curriculum D&T, as with other materials, the teaching of food technology, as it was now known, required a change of emphasis from the domestic to commercial production (DFE, 1992). The food industry in the UK was then, and continues to be, a large, influential body with the potential for a range of food related high status careers across the gender and ability range. This was a fundamental change from the purely 'domestic cookery' low status image that has for so long influenced the teaching of food within schools. Rigour is demanded in knowledge and application of nutrition and food science and an understanding of the processes involved in product development. There is an emphasis on sensory food evaluation in a methodical, analytical manner and understanding how food can be used creatively to produce a variety of high quality products to suit the needs of a target market of consumers. Food technology now includes knowledge and understanding of the properties of foods, and involves the ability to select and use the appropriate tools and materials to explore these properties for developing food products. There is a need to use designing skills, many of which are generic to other materials used in D&T, together with the appropriate knowledge, understanding and making skills for creative problem solving to design and develop food products for a target market (Rutland, 1997).

For example, when pupils follow a recipe out of a book and just make, copy what other people have designed and made with no thoughts of their own, they are engaged in rote, mechanistic learning without any understanding of the concepts and knowledge underpinning the activity. Such pupil are not designing, being creative, thinking and making decisions: they are only *making*. Food technology requires pupils to be creative, to design and make their own food products based on a sound knowledge of the working properties of foods. A sample brief might be based in the context of a school requiring pupils to develop a low cost, high-energy product for marketing at the lunch bar. Ideas for a range of food products using different ingredients and skills would be generated, made and evaluated for their suitability against the brief. One food product is then chosen for further development, a specification written and a prototype produced. Consideration would be given to suitable packaging and labelling but not necessarily made, though this has potential for working with graphics colleagues in an integrated project. There is a constant process of investigation, exploring possible solutions and ideas, modifying, evaluating, developing a prototype and evaluating against the original brief. This type of food work is not based on the mechanistic, rote learning of skills, but requires 'thought in action' (Kimbell et al, 1991, p21).

Implementation of food technology in the National Curriculum

In the early 1990's there was a growing consensus, lead by the National Association for Teachers of Home Economics (NATHE), that a new direction for the teaching of food could be found through food technology in the newly introduced National Curriculum Technology (DES, 1990). It was argued that this provided the best opportunities for the future of food teaching in schools as it was an approach that accommodated changing attitudes and values concerned with gender, status and its association with the less able. Food teachers could no longer afford to ignore the pressures of social and economic events, as despite the 'whole' family focus the field has been populated largely by women and had directed its message to a female audience. It was even suggested by some that food teachers were generally politically weak, resistant to change and tended to avoid the political arena of the school staff-room (Lawson, 1993). There was not a general call for the abolition of food but for increased flexibility to find a new direction for the teaching of the subject. There was genuine concern that if food teachers failed to acknowledge that food technology could be successfully taught as part of D&T, there was a danger of loosing the subject area from the school curriculum (Rutland, 1997).

Alternative views for food teaching

Food teachers have traditionally valued the link between food and society and the Orders (DES, 1990) implied that this would be lost with the move from a focus on the 'family' towards industry. In the early 1990s' there were food teachers who believed that food should be delivered through the cross curricular themes, for example health education and personal and social education. However at that stage the cross-curricular themes were not examined and did not carry a high profile. A range of curriculum patterns and management practices occur in schools to this day to address personal, health and social education and each can cause problems.

Taught outside the core and foundation subjects they can lack co-ordination, become fragmented and be of low status to the pupils. If food is taught in tutorial classes by the form tutor, there will be a lack of specialist knowledge of food and the teaching will be theory based without any practical activity. The essence of pupils learning how to 'make' with food would be lost. Today citizenship, including personal and social education, is a compulsory subject in the English curriculum and there are specialist teachers of citizenship, however, their curriculum brief is very much broader than just teaching food. Never the less, it is important to remember the contribution of food technology to the cross-curricular social, economic, cultural and environmental values.

In the early 1990s there were other problems for the food technology teachers, when within the community of D&T there was evidence of disagreement over the subject areas that should be part of Technology. Smithers and Robinson (1992, p15) thought that 'being able to cook, use a computer and word processor to fill in forms are affected by technology but are not necessarily part of it'. That cooking, for example, should be given its own slot in the curriculum. A comment indicating that little has changed regarding perceptions of the educationally value of teaching food. It was still seen by many as using equipment, learning 'how to cook' and little else. There was no appreciation of the wider value of food technology teaching to promote human well being (Geen, 1992), indicating fundamental differences between how people define or interpret the term technology.

Industrial focus

However, it would be unjust to say that food technology teachers did not take up the challenge. Despite a general lack of in-service training to support their work teachers made every effort to make the necessary changes, though government guidance was provided and a range of teaching materials developed. The change of emphasis from domestic to industry was supported by the production of a range of teaching materials including paper-based resources, videos and CDs. Secondary pupils learnt about health, safety and quality procedures such as hazard analysis critical control points (HACCP), industrial equipment and the manufacturing processes. The industry focus was introduced into the new Food Technology General Certificate of Secondary Education (GCSE) and post sixteen external national examinations, so influencing the food curriculum for pupils aged 14- 16 years.

The emphasis on industry in food teaching has had a positive impact, as it is generally perceived that the status of food has improved. Yet, teachers' concerns were highlighted in a recent national research study, supported by the Design and Technology Association (DATA), investigating teachers' perceptions of changes in food-related subjects. Questionnaires were sent to a sample of four hundred food technology teachers and were followed by interviews with thirty food technology teachers and ten key D&T informants. The study explored teacher's perceptions of the change from a domestic to an industrial focus in food education in England and Wales (Belby, 2005). It indicated that the majority of the food technology teachers in the study had reservations about the emphasis on 'industrial practices'. One of the findings was that the teachers perceived that this was at the expense of developing the practical skills required for food preparation and nutritional knowledge and understanding, factors considered necessary to guide pupils and adults in wise food choices and a healthy life style. It was considered that there was a lack of clarity for the aims of food technology and few of the teachers, though they wished food technology to remain in D&T, were clear about the value of teaching young people about the food industry. It was concluded that there is an over emphasis on industrial food production and a more critical view of the food industry, for example the impact of highly processed foods on children's health, should be encouraged as there is still scope to teach domestic food preparation.

The use of computer aided design and computer aided manufacture (CAD/CAM) has a high profile in D&T and plays an important role in manufacturing in the food industry, but its actual application in the classroom in food teaching is limited. A range of software, including spreadsheets and databases can be used very successfully in food technology, so a more effective approach might be to encourage the use of CAD/CAM in other material area of D&T and develop integrated curriculum projects that include, for example, food technology.

Today, there is growing concern by the public and the government that adults, and particularly children, are not considering the impact of unhealthy eating on themselves in the future. For example, eating 'junk' ready made foods produced by the food industry lacking in proteins and high in fat, sugar and starch at the expense of fresh fruit and vegetables. The government publication 'Healthy Schools, Active Minds: a Healthy Living Blue Print (DfES, 2004) is intended to encourage children to eat sensibly, stay physically active and maintain good levels of personal health. In food technology pupils could consider issues such as the genetic modification of foods and the use of chemically and physically modified starches in the foods the general public eat. It is interesting to note that the links between health and food teaching continue, as they did in the 19th Century, to be important though the issues current today may be different. Today the healthy issues include obesity, diet and cancer, food poisoning, heart disease, hypertension, under nutrition and the nutritional content of meals served to children in schools. Food technology teaching in schools has a major and important role in highlighting and addressing such issues.

Training food technology teachers

The introduction of food technology the National Curriculum for D&T meant that the term 'home economics' was outdated as a title. Over night experienced home economists had to take on a new title and new teachers entering the profession described themselves as D&T teachers with a food technology specialism. Before the introduction of the National Curriculum the most common route to join the profession for food teachers, as for CDT, was through four-year courses B Ed Home Economics courses combining a relevant subject degree with a teaching qualification and providing immediate entry to teaching. The majority of students on BSc Home Economics courses, that included a one year industrial placement, went into posts within the food and retail industry or welfare, social services with some completing a one year post graduate certificate in education (PGCE) as an entry into teaching (Rutland, 1984).

During 1997-8 The Association of Teachers of Home Economics and Technology (NATHE) became acutely aware a national shortage of food technology teachers, as schools wanted to recruit teachers able to teach the new Food Technology GCSE courses introduced in 1996 for pupils aged sixteen. In the spring of 1998 NATHE conducted a national survey of higher education institutions, as it was thought that the shortage of food technology teacher was due to a lack of food related degree courses as preparation for teaching. The results indicated that the range of food courses available for pupils leaving school at eighteen years had actually increased, as had the variety of possible careers. The content of many food courses had a strong industrial and business basis. Food degrees were predominately BSc courses and included a high element of food science, food product development, microbiology, nutrition, ICT and communication. There were only two courses that included 'home economics' in their title, but 'consumer studies' was frequently used. There was no shortage of relevant food related degree courses but there were no longer any four year food BA or BSc degree course that included qualified teacher status (QTS) and not all PGCE D&T courses were recruiting food technology specialists (Rutland, 1999; Rutland, 2001).

The degree courses are very appropriate to the content of food technology in schools but there is a disappointing lack of graduates entering the teaching profession due to for a number of reasons. Firstly, a lack of understanding by the public of the changes that had taken place in the teaching of food, secondly very good career opportunities in the food industry and finally, a shortage of ITE institutions that trained food technology teachers. Circumstance that are still relevant today, resulting in the removal by some schools of food technology from their curriculum because of their inability to recruit food technology teachers.

Teaching food technology in primary schools

A positive outcome for the compulsory inclusion within D&T of food technology for primary children aged 5- 11 years, is that essential knowledge of the importance of food for health and basic personal health and hygiene rules are taught to young children. Prior to 1990 D&T food activities were generally limited to 'fun' sessions taught by volunteer parents. In the early 1990s primary teachers lacked in-depth knowledge and were concerned about how to manage the teaching of food safely in a typical primary classroom environment. However, there is evidence that primary teachers have successfully overcome these difficulties using a variety of curriculum materials and resources (Rutland and Barlex, 2000; Barlex and Rutland, 2003b). In addition, food technology is generally taught as part of primary initial teacher education (ITE) D&T courses to support school experience classroom practice resulting in an increased confidence by primary teachers. Primary practice presents ideal opportunities to link the teaching of food to other areas of the curriculum including science and the humanities.

Designing with food

As with other areas of D&T, one of the key issues for food technology teachers in the early days of the National Curriculum was the emphasis on 'designing' and its interpretation by some teachers as a paper based activity and the subsequent loss of practical food based activities. Inspection findings (Ofsted, 1998, 2000) have reported consistently since the introduction of D&T into the National Curriculum in England that designing skills lag behind making skills. That in some schools there is insufficient attention to the processes of designing, particularly for pupils aged 11- 14 years where their experience of D&T is merely a sequence of short focused practical tasks with no opportunity to apply their own ideas in a longer design task (Ofsted, 2002). A government funded research project explored this issue with one year PGCE D&T course and it emerged that the trainees teaching food technology experienced difficulty and expressed particular concern over designing with food (Barlex and Rutland, 2003a; Barlex and Rutland 2004)

A second, on going, government funded research study at the same ITE provider is building on the previous findings with a group of sixteen trainees with food technology as a first or second area of expertise, within a cohort of thirty one-year postgraduate D&T trainees. Six food technology trainees are being studied in depth, three with food technology as a first specialiam and three with food technology as a second specialism. A series of intervention activities focusing on 'designing' are carried out during the course and the preliminary findings indicate that initially trainees with food as a first specialism have the greatest difficulty as the language and approach is unfamiliar. The concepts and techniques of researching, investigating, making and modifying a range of products using a variety of skills and knowledge before developing a final product is new to them. They tend to think designing is essentially a paper based, 2D drawing activity, for example food package, and do not at first value the use of generic design techniques.

A typical school food technology project for pupils aged 11-14 years in the UK covers eight one-hour sessions and how the other 'design based' sessions are planned and taught is crucial. Otherwise there is likely to be a lack of practical work and the development of 'skills', a predominance of written work with one product made and remade over a number of lessons. In home economics there would have been a series of practical and theory sessions around a unifying theme, for example a vegetarian. It has been noted in the study that trainees with food technology as a second specialist are more able to transfer their understanding of designing from, for example, product design. They understand the concept of a design brief and use a range of design based activities, for example mood, image boards, brainstorming ideas, presenting ideas through sketches and trying out a range of ideas before working on a final design. It is intended to explore how the food technology trainees teach designing in food through classroom observation, their teaching practice file, an analysis of interviews after the curriculum interventions and at the end of each teaching experience.

CONCLUSIONS

The paper identified the three key issues of an associated with the less able, low status in the curriculum and gender for the teaching of food before the introduction of the National Curriculum in 1990. Despite changes of name and dedication of the teachers over the years these issues continued to dominate the teaching of food. The introduction of the D&T National Curriculum with the inclusion of food technology for primary and secondary pupils has impacted on how food is taught in schools. On the positive side, the status and associated gender issues have steadily improved. Food technology is more likely to be studied to a higher level by the full ability and gender range and it is taught to young children. The knowledge content is rigorous and requires pupils to combine 'thinking and doing' with an ability to make informed decisions. The learning style is based on problem solving and no longer focuses on rote learning and despite problems in the early 1990s and difficulties recruiting food technology teachers it continues to be popular for pupils aged 14- 16 years. In the GCSE Examination entry for summer 2003 food technology was the second highest entry with twenty five percent of the total D&T entry (DATA, 2004).

However, there are causes for concern including the need to train more food technology teachers. Secondly, there is a perception by some teachers that the emphasis on industrial practices, including knowledge of equipment and processes in the food industry has been to the detriment of pupils gaining knowledge, understanding and skills in food preparation and factors related to healthy living. Thirdly, the curriculum requirement for the use of CAD/CAM in food technology is another cause for concern, as is the continued difficulty of some food technology teachers to relate to the language, terminology and concept of designing with food. Ways of addressing these issues are urgently required, including discussions with examination boards to review how 'industrial practices' in food technology can be realistically addressed without the loss of the teaching of domestic food preparation. In conclusion, a food technology curriculum that emphasises its contribution towards the future health of the pupils would be a positive way forward.

REFERENCES

Arnold, M. (1908) *Reports on elementary schools, 1852 -1883,* London: HMSO.

Attar, D. (1990) *Wasting girls' time,* London: Virgo Press.

Atherton, M. (1990) Technology and home economics....so far so good. In *Modus* Vol. 8 No 2, 50-52.

Barlex, D., Rutland, M. (2003a) *A small-scale preliminary pilot to explore the use of Mode 2 research to develop a possible solution to the problem of introducing one-year PGCE design and technology trainees to design methods that are relevant to the teaching of designing in the secondary school, DATA-* International Research Conference, 'Design Matters', Warwick, UK, 2nd – 3rd July, 2003, pp13- 21.

Barlex, D., Rutland, M. (2003b) Developing the teaching of food technology in primary schools in England through curriculum development and initial teacher education *In International Journal of Technology and Design Education* Vol. 13, No 2, pp 171-192.

Board of Education (1926) *The education of the adolescent* chaired by Hadow, London: HMSO.

Belby, G. (2005) *Teachers' perceptions of changes in food-related subjects: A study of historical roots and future directions* An unpublished PhD Thesis, The University of Sheffield.

Brown, S. (1985) Good morning ladies In *Modus*, Vol. 3, No 8, pp 288-289.

Brown, S. (1988) Sticking at it In *Modus* Vol. 6, No 6, pp 224-225.

Crease, B. (1965) *Careers in catering and domestic science*, London: The Bodley Head.

DATA (2004) Examination results and statistics: Summer 2003 In *data news Jan 2004*, Wellesbourne, DATA, p12

DES (1959) *15-18 A report of the central advisory council for education (England)* chaired by Crowther, London: HMSO.

DES (1963) *Half our futures a report of the central advisory council for education (England)* chaired by Newsom, London: HMSO

DES (1978) *Curriculum 11-16*, London: HMSO.

DES (1985) *Home economics from 5 to 16 - Curriculum matters 5*, London: HMSO.

DES (1987) *Craft, design and technology from 5 to 16*, London: HMSO

DES (1988) *National curriculum design and technology working party: Interim report*, London, HMSO

DES (1990) *Technology in the national curriculum*, London: HMSO.

DFE (1992) *Technology for ages 5 to 16. Proposals of the secretary of state for education*, London: HMSO

DFE (1995a) *Design and technology in the national curriculum*, London: HMSO.

DFE (1995b) *Information technology in the national curriculum*, London: HMSO

DfES (2004) *Healthy schools, active minds: A healthy living blue print*, London: DfES

Dyhouse, C. (1977) 'Good wives and little mothers: social anxieties and the schoolgirl's curriculum 1890-1920' In *Oxford Review of Education*, Vol. 3, No 1, 22.

Eggleston, J. (1996) *Teaching design and technology: Second edition* Buckingham: Open University Press.

Geen, A., Jenkins, H. and Daniels C. (1988) *Home economics: Teaching for the future,* Cambridge: Hobsons.

Geen, A (1992) Opportunities for home economics - Education and training for the 21st century In *Modus* Vol. 10, No 2.

Kimbell, R., Stables, K., Wheeler, T., Wosniak, A. and Kelly, V. (1991) *The assessment of performance in design and technology*, London; School Examinations and Assessment Council.

Newton, D. (1990) Does the home economist have a place in national curriculum technology? In *Design and Technology Teaching,* Vol. 23, No 1, 23.

Office for Standards in Education (Ofsted) (1998) S*econdary education 1993-97: A review of secondary schools in England*, London: HMSO.

Office for Standards in Education (Ofsted) (2000), *Ofsted subject reports secondary design and technology, 1999 – 2000*, London: HMSO.

Office for Standards in Education (Ofsted) (2002) *Design and technology in secondary schools Ofsted subject reports series 2001-02*, London: HMSO.

Penfold, J. (1988) *Craft, design and technology: Past present and future*, Hanley, Stoke-on-Trent: Trentham Books.

Rutland, M. (1984) *Vocational opportunities available to students of home economics,* Unpublished B. Ed. Dissertation, University of Wales.

Rutland, M. (1997) *Teaching food technology in secondary schools*, London: David Fulton Publishers.

Rutland, M. (1999) *Teaching food and textiles technology in secondary schools: Routes through higher education* The International Conference on Design and Technology Educational Research and Curriculum Development *(IDATER 99)* Loughborough University of Technology, pp 170 - 176.

Rutland, M., Barlex, D. (2000) *Teaching food technology in the primary classroom*, Design and Technology Millennium Conference, Institute of Education, London, April 2000, pp167-171.

Rutland, M. (2001) Teacher recruitment in design and technology: Food technology in *The Journal of Design and Technology Education*, Vol. No 2, pp 101 -108.

Sillitoe, H. (1966) *A History of the teaching of Domestic Subjects*, London: Methuen.

Smithers, A., Robinson, P. (1992*) Technology in the national curriculum: Getting it right, London*: The Engineering Council.

Wadsworth, N. (1986) 'This subject suffers sexist images. It's literature and resources are riddled with them' in *ILEA Contact,* December, 8-9.

Whyld, J. (1983) *Sexism in the secondary curriculum,* London: Harper and Row.

Yoxall, A. (1965) *A history of the teaching of domestic economy,* Bath: Cedric Chivers.

FRANK BANKS AND ROBERT MCCORMICK

22. A CASE STUDY OF THE INTER-RELATIONSHIP BETWEEN SCIENCE AND TECHNOLOGY: ENGLAND 1984-2004

INTRODUCTION

Politicians often refer to Science and Technology as an epistemological unit. In the early 1980s, the UK Thatcher Government generously financed a Technical and Vocational Education Initiative (TVEI) which tried to explicitly bring together the two curriculum areas of Science and Technology.[1] Indeed, despite the school politics that has surrounded the teaching of the two subject areas, which stresses the differences, there are some clear similarities. Both subjects opened up the group of pupils who would take the subject (science moved from being a specialist subject just for those going on to do it at higher levels, Technology had to appeal to the academically 'able' as well as the traditional group of 'non-academic' pupils), both make much of 'hands-on' learning; both claim to promote problem solving and other 'processes'; both try to explicitly link school tasks to useful learning for every day life and the needs of the work-place.

Our framework of analysis is illustrated graphically (Figure 1).[2] We consider both science and technology developments in England over the last twenty years, both separately and together through their common features, by considering three strands:

- Curriculum rationale (the *specified curriculum* as found in national curriculum documents, which, in England, has statutory significance);
- teacher knowledge (focusing on the *enacted curriculum*, i.e. what they bring to bear to plan and implement their teaching);
- pupil learning (focusing on the *experienced curriculum*, i.e. how both of the above are interpreted and made sense of by pupils).

Through our research at the Open University in both science and technology school lessons, we explore common issues and consider what each subject can learn from the other.[3] We hope that the case of England will highlight issues for consideration in other countries.

---

[1] There have of course been a number of moves to link these two, most notoriously the failed attempts at applied science (see McCormick, 1990; McCulloch, Jenkins & Layton, 1985).
[2] This framework was developed for an Open University course E836 *Learning, Curriculum and Assessment*.
[3] We would like to acknowledge our debt to the teachers and colleagues who have been involved in the research upon which we draw, and whose contributions have helped form our views.

M.J. de Vries, I. Mottier (eds.), International Handbook of Technology Education, 285–311.

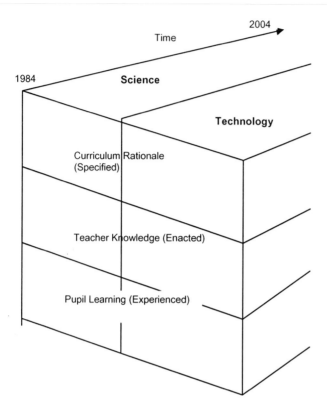

Figure 1. Analysis Framework

THE SPECIFIED CURRICULUM

The following statements are from the current National Curriculum in England published in 1999:

The importance of science

Science stimulates and excites pupils' curiosity about phenomena and events in the world around them. It also satisfies this curiosity with knowledge. Because science links direct practical experience with ideas, it can engage learners at many levels. Scientific method is about developing and evaluating explanations through experimental evidence and modelling. This is a spur to critical and creative thought. Through science, pupils understand how major scientific ideas contribute to technological change — impacting on industry, business and medicine and improving quality of life. Pupils recognise the cultural significance of science and trace its worldwide development. They learn to question and discuss science-based issues that may affect their own lives, the direction of society and the future of the world.

The importance of design and technology

Design and technology prepares pupils to participate in tomorrow's rapidly changing technologies. They learn to think and intervene creatively to improve quality of life. The subject calls for pupils to become autonomous and creative problem solvers, as individuals and members of a team. They must looks for needs, wants and opportunities and respond to them by developing a range of ideas and making products and systems. They combine practical skills with an understanding of aesthetics, social and environmental issues, function and industrial practices. As they do so, they reflect on and evaluate present and past design and technology, its uses and effects. Through design and technology, all pupils can become discriminating and informed users of products, and become innovators. (DfES/QCA, 1999)

These two statements lay out what has been the culmination of a change process in the school curricula of science and technology (in England 'Design and Technology') over the last twenty years, namely the rationale for the designation of the two subjects as required areas of study during the years of compulsory schooling, 5-16. In 2005 the requirement for all pupils to study technology is restricted, and Design and Technology (D&T) is now only an obligatory subject between the ages of 5-14 years. Science, however, is still a requirement for all pupils up to 16 years of age. Over the last twenty years, what lessons can be drawn about making the two subjects compulsory for all pupils? What decisions were taken about what all should be able to 'know, understand and do' as a result of studying science and technology in the school curriculum and what was communicated to teachers, pupils and their parents?

Science led the way. Building on the curriculum initiatives of the 1960s following the 'Sputnik panic', by the 1980s most secondary schools required all pupils to learn science and, as most schools were becoming 'comprehensive' (non selective), there was a desire to widen the science curriculum to all pupils including those less academically gifted. For example, Nuffield Secondary Science became popular, as did Science at Work in the 1970s as curricula specifically designed for such students. Science in England was being accepted as a core area of study for all pupils on a similar footing to mathematics and (mother-tongue) English. Also in the early 1980s the nature of a science curriculum for all pupils – a science for citizenship or 'scientific literacy' was being debated. In particular, the importance of learning 'facts' in science was questioned and a case was made that the processes of the scientific method were much more important for all pupils. The government policy document Science 5-16 (DES,1985), that pre-dated the national curriculum, did not merely define what should be taught in terms of content such as 'electricity' or 'plants', but instead emphasised the importance of a process approach. Indeed, science curriculum innovation in the middle 1980s saw a large number of new courses such as 'Warwick Process Science' and 'Science in Process' for secondary schools. These focused, not on science concepts, but rather on processes such as observation, interpretation and classification — aspects critical to 'the scientific method'.

This mood was picked up in the developing primary science curriculum at that time. Although not totally accepted by some (for example, Jenkins, 1987), many in the teaching profession generally welcomed a move away from what was often considered as merely the memorising of poorly understood facts. In contrast, there emerged a generally common consensus that science might be more accessible to all pupils if it emphasised skills applicable to other areas of life both inside and outside school. The attention to 'doing' science — raising questions that could be answered by an investigation — became the corner-stone of the developing primary science and in 2005 is a core principle in new courses which pick up on perceived failures of the national curriculum (see below). For example, the question 'What is the best carrier bag?' would be turned into an investigation question such as 'Which carrier bag carries the greatest weight?' in what was considered a problem-solving approach. To answer such a question, so-called 'dependent and independent' variables were identified. Thus the importance of the procedural knowledge of science was developed. At this time (1980s), primary teachers (normally untrained in science) were concerned about the introduction of science into their day to day work. The rhetoric from those advocating that science should indeed be part of the primary curriculum was that the teachers could 'learn with the pupils'; it was argued that only the process was important, not the science facts or concepts that the teacher did or did not know.

At this time there was concern more generally in schools in England about what was needed as a preparation for adult life. Education for competency in the work-place and the need to be able to 'problem solve' was seen as essential. Those advocating a core place for both science and technology in the curriculum of all pupils used the fact that problem-solving lay at the heart of the subjects as a key part of the argument.[4] This gave a different slant to the procedural knowledge, with the implication that general problem-solving processes could be identified. As we shall argue later, however, this latter assumption was erroneous. Also, we shall see that problem-solving in science is different to that in technology. However, despite the push to introduce primary science in the 1970s (e.g. Science 5-13) little had been achieved and, in most schools, Primary science is a relatively recent development. Just twenty years ago, Harlen could write a book entitled *Primary Science: Taking the Plunge* (Harlen, 1985) reflecting the fact that little science was then being taught in primary schools.

There was something of a backlash to the 'process is all that is important' line and the debate became heated (see Millar & Driver, 1987; Millar, 1988; Screen, 1988; Wellington, 1988 & 1989; Woolnough, 1988). Some argued that, for

---

[4] See Murphy *et al.* (1995) for the tracing of this for technology and Garrett (1987) for science.

example, 'observation' in isolation for the sake of it was pointless - one had to apply the process to the understanding of science concepts.[5] This was also accompanied by research-led initiatives emphasising constructivist learning ideas, resulting in a concern for pupil conceptual development and the associated pedagogy. The purpose of the science curriculum as the acquisition of 'facts' was, however, very deep-rooted. The National Curriculum for Science was first published in 1988 and, although it had an area devoted to process issues, was largely a re-emphasis on teaching 'content' or conceptual knowledge. The balance had shifted again away from procedural knowledge, reinforced at all levels by national testing which, despite the rhetoric of a concern for understanding concepts, emphasised memory and did not include a practical element. In the rapid revisions of the science curriculum over the last 15 years, the push has been to cut back on the extent of content in the curriculum but the premier position of scientific method in the curriculum would never be repeated. Throughout the period we have the shift in concern and balance of procedural and conceptual knowledge, a theme which is reflected in different ways in technology as a curriculum subject.

Technology is a relative newcomer to the curriculum for all pupils from 5 to 16 years. The compulsory National Curriculum was introduced in 1990 and focused on Technology as a process concerning design. It had four attainment targets:

- Attainment target 1 – Identifying needs and opportunities
- Attainment target 2 – Generating a design
- Attainment target 3 – Planning and making
- Attainment target 4 – Evaluating

This process-based curriculum was difficult to implement for both secondary and primary schools. Primary teachers were unused to considering designing, although craft activities had long been a feature of primary school life. It was also suggested that a wide range of teachers become involved at secondary level to cover material areas such as food and textiles, and aspects of business studies as well as the more traditional materials of wood, metal and plastics. Few secondary teachers could bring practical experience of design in the way they did for skills and craft work.

After only two years, The Engineering Council produced a damning report by Smithers and Robinson which declared that 'Technology in the National Curriculum is a mess' (Smithers & Robinson, 1992, p 1). Their main criticism was that by defining technology solely through a process approach meant that almost all problem-solving activity could be considered as 'technology'

Defined on problem-solving alone, most activities become technology - writing this report, conducting a scientific experiment, finding one's way to a railway

---

[5] The concern for more refined views of 'scientific method' led to a number of projects: The Exploration of Science Project (Foulds, Gott & Mashiter, 1990), the Children's Leaning in Science Project (CLISP) Driver, and Oldham (1986) and the primary focused SPACE project (Liverpool University, 1994).

station. What is needed is some statement of technology's domain. (Smithers & Robinson, 1992, p 3).

The report made recommendations as to what should be considered the subject domain of technology and what should not, and for a better balance between process and content. It also tried to untangle the 'vocational' and 'basic skills' labels that some had attached to the new compulsory subject, and it advocated a consideration of the 'literature' of technology; looking at and learning from the products and artifacts that already exist which can inform designing and making. Subsequent developments tried to address these concerns. In 1995 a new version of the curriculum for England and Wales gave a clearer steer to what D&T was, and the main activities that should be employed:

Pupils should be given opportunities to develop their design & technology capability through:

Assignments in which they design and make products, focussing on different contexts and materials and making use of:

Resistant materials;

Compliant materials and/or food (DMAs- Design and Make Assignments).

Focused practical tasks (FPTs) in which they develop and practise particular skills and knowledge;

Activities in which they Investigate, Disassemble and Evaluate familiar products and Applications. (IDEAS)   (DFE/WO, 1995, p. 6)

This methodology strongly reflected the pedagogic model promoted by Nuffield Design and Technology (Barlex et al 1994).   There was a reduction to two attainment targets that had looked for progress in each part of a process, Designing and Making and, eventually, considering even this separation as unhelpful to, now, just one attainment target Design and Making. Although there is a better balance of knowledge, skills and elements of the design process, the current Attainment Target is still based around the design process, with pupils being expected to achieve the following at the penultimate level:

Pupils use a wide range of appropriate sources of information to develop ideas. They investigate form, function and production processes before communicating ideas, using a variety of media. They recognise the different needs of a range of users and develop fully realistic designs. They produce plans that predict the time needed to carry out the main stages of making products. They work with a range of tools, materials, equipment, components and processes, taking full account of their characteristics. They adapt their methods of manufacture to changing circumstances, providing a sound explanation for any change from the design proposal. They select appropriate techniques to evaluate how their products would perform when used and modify their products in the light of the evaluation to improve their performance. (QCA http://www.nc.uk.net/)

Unlike science, D&T has tended not to use concepts to organise content, and in areas where conceptual knowledge is important, for example, control and electronics, this can be a problem as we shall show later (McCormick, 1997 & 2004; Murphy et al, 2004).

D&T, although a required subject for all pupils under the 1990 national curriculum, was always under attack from those who could not see the justification for that position. The reasons for the animosity range from those who would put science and technology together as one curriculum domain (especially at primary school level) to those who, more prosaically, just considered the subject too expensive to deliver in terms of tools, equipment and materials. The response from the D&T lobby was to argue that the subject was important as it prepared 'pupils to participate in tomorrow's rapidly changing technologies' and so much was done to introduce new technologies such as CAD/CAM mainly at secondary level as a tool for the designing and making processes.

So, in both Science and technology, there has been debate over the last twenty years as to the balance that should exist in the specified curriculum in both subjects between procedural knowledge and conceptual knowledge. However, these debates have largely been within each subject community, independent of each other, and tend to emphasise the inevitable differences between the goals of each subject rather than the common ground between the subjects. What can be learned generally, and what can the two subjects learn from each other?

A key lesson to be learned by the rapid revisions of the specified curriculum of both science and technology in England over the last twenty years is that it is very difficult to impose a curriculum onto teachers. As will become evident, a top-down method of seeking to describe the curriculum in close detail without working with teachers, and those involved in pre-service and in-service teacher education, to develop a common understanding of purpose, leads to a mismatch between a teacher's 'personal subject construct' and what is prescribed to be taught. Teachers have a view about what their subject is about and, although they wish their pupils to do well in externally set examinations, when the specified curriculum moves independently of these held views teachers feel obliged to 'teach to the tests'. It is therefore imperative that the tests accurately reflect the intentions of the curriculum designers.[6]

As evidence of the state of science, in 2002, the Westminster Parliament Science and Technology Committee reported on *Science education from 14 to 19* and said the following as part of the document summary:

Science has been a core part of the education of all students up to age of 16 since the introduction of the National Curriculum in 1989. Most students take double science GCSE [the national examination syllabus] from 14 to 16. This course aims to provide a general science education for all and, at the same time, to inspire and prepare some for science post-16. It does neither of these well. It may not be possible for a single course to fulfil both these needs. Government is supporting a pilot that may be resolve these tensions, which is welcome but not enough. Existing GCSE courses should be changed and a wider range of options in science offered to students. [...]

---

[6] Kimbell (1997) gives an account of the failure of the government to produce tests in D&T that reflected what he and his colleagues thought were assessing what the curriculum was aiming for.

Current GCSE courses are overloaded with factual content, contain little contemporary science and have stultifying assessment arrangements. Coursework is boring and pointless. Teachers and students are frustrated by the lack of flexibility. Students lose any enthusiasm that they once had for science. Those that choose to continue with science post-16 often do so in spite of their experiences of GCSE rather than because of them. Primary responsibility should lie with the awarding bodies; the approach to assessment at GCSE discourages good science from being taught in schools. (House of Commons, 2002, p. 5)

The national assessment for D&T also has its critics:

teachers provide coaching which allows pupils to pass through the assessment hoops for D&T GCSE coursework at the expense of following the wider rationale of D&T learning objectives (OfSTED, 2000, p3)

....public examinations in D&T have, one the one hand, enabled many pupils to achieve success in terms of performance, whilst on the other hand, they have wasted valuable education opportunities for the development of high order thinking skills at a crucial stage in a pupil's education. (Atkinson, 2000, p277)

In response to these criticisms the science community has attempted to introduce courses which exploit the relevance of science to contemporary life. Courses being piloted in 2005 include 'Science for the 21st Century', which attempts to 'square the circle' of providing science literacy for all and a grounding in science basics for those who wish to study the subject further. D&T has for a long time taken refuge in the links to 'real life' and has tried to provide pupils with authentic tasks. However, as the quotations indicate, to make the real world manageable to pupils within the constraints of time and resources that schools impose on the participants sometime leads to an algorithmic approach to the processes – going through the motions in a mechanistic way -and merely showing a 'veneer of achievement' (McCormick *et al*, 1994)

The last twenty years has seen extremes in both science and technology education. Tasks in technology, such as building and testing various model bridges to destruction, at the one extreme, to lock-step production of a textile bag (to take home) where the only design decisions concern the decoration, at the other. In science, tasks have ranged from making twenty observations on a burning candle to open-ended investigations on conditions for plant growth to memorizing the names of the parts of a flower.

So the government's attempts to control what pupils learn by specifying in detail the curriculum has had limited success according to those charged with monitoring its impact. We turn now to consider wider lessons to be learned from how the curriculum is enacted by teachers.

THE ENACTED CURRICULUM

To explore the nature of the 'enacted' curriculum, we draw on classroom research we have conducted in both science and technology lessons. We highlight two aspects of our research which gives some insight into the problems teachers in England have faced in trying to enact the specified curriculum. The first considers the teaching of problem solving in science and technology, the second centers on teacher professional knowledge and in particular its implications for the teacher training curriculum. Both examples, however, highlight that the way that teachers enact the specified curriculum depends on their own professional knowledge.

TEACHER PROFESSIONAL KNOWLEDGE

In our observation of teaching it is evident that success or failure of lessons organised by teachers was often linked, not only to their college-based subject knowledge and their choice of pedagogic strategies, but also to their appreciation of how their subject is transformed into a school subject. In D&T, in particular, an appreciation of the way the subject in schools had been created by an amalgam of the requirements of a national curriculum, the personal history of the teachers who currently teach this 'new' subject and the contextual constraints of accommodation, materials and equipment conspire together to create a particular area of teacher knowledge. We call this 'school knowledge'. Working with colleagues in Finland, Canada, New Zealand and other areas of the UK we have seen that the key areas of teacher knowledge: Subject knowledge, Pedagogic knowledge and School knowledge can provide a framework for us to consider teacher expertise in a number of different national contexts (see Banks *et al*, 2004). However, as indicated above there is more to consider than what is required by the state and the teaching capability of the teacher. Lying at the heart of the dynamic process between the different aspects of teacher knowledge are the 'personal subject constructs' of the teacher, a complex amalgam of past knowledge, experiences of learning, a personal view of what constitutes 'good' teaching and how pupils learn, and belief in the purposes of the subject. This all underpins a teacher's professional knowledge and is as relevant for highly experienced teacher as it is for the novice. A student teacher needs to question his or her personal beliefs about their subject as they work out a rationale for their classroom practice. But so must those teachers who, although more expert, have experienced profound changes of what contributes 'school knowledge' during their career (as has happened with the introduction of the national curriculum in England), particularly when that knowledge is open to external scrutiny by Her Majesty's Inspectors of Schools.

EXAMPLE: SCIENCE TASKS AND TECHNOLOGICAL CONTEXTS

This example of the enacted curriculum draws on our work on the implementation of science tasks in the classroom (See McCormick *et al*, 1996; Murphy & McCormick 1997). Models of science investigation are depicted as problem-solving processes (e.g. Gott and Murphy, 1987). Although such models are not simplistic step-like processes, they are interpreted as such; just as design processes are in technology education. Primary teachers of science now often use planning sheets and indeed are advised to use them to support children's procedural decision making. These sheets identify stages in children's decision making and ask them to focus on specific features e.g. what shall I do to make it fair, what shall I measure, how shall I measure? This produces in the child's mind a notion that these questions and procedures are appropriate and useful across *all* problems.

In Secondary school science there is ritual that has grown out of what constitutes a 'tradition' of procedure in practical science. For example, it was common practice, and often remains so, to structure reports of experimental activity around *title, method, results* and *conclusion*. Shifts in this have been to include *hypothesis* as opposed to *title*, and 'What I did to make it fair' prior to the method section or directly following it in the report. In observations in classrooms, selected because of 'good' practice in science, pupils were found to be including a whole range of disparate procedures under 'fairness'. These included the setting up of the test of the independent variable as fairness was translated to mean 'sameness' hence 'I tested X then Y then Z', 'I did the same thing', was an aspect of fairness in the pupil's mind. The 'assessed practical' is an example of ritual in science being supported by the concern of teachers for pupils to do well in the external examination regime in England. Hooke's Law, the observation that within the elastic limit, extension of a stretched spring being proportional to the load applied, is a common practical investigation easily carried out and understood by 11 year old pupils. However, as this is a phenomenon which many 15 year old pupils can offer a hypothesis which can be investigated, for which results can be quickly and easily gathered and data graphically displayed, it is often repeated for assessment purposes. This is an example of the dead-hand of assessment criticized as 'boring and pointless' by the parliamentary committee in the quotation earlier.

The authenticity of science tasks can also be thwarted even when teachers attempt to introduce 'contexts' to make science learning meaningful and purposeful for pupils. A typical approach to this is to use an everyday scene to contextualise a science investigation. For example, an investigation was set up to find out how temperature affected the time taken for sugar to dissolve (Murphy *et al*, 1996). 'Dissolving' was the science concept that the teacher wanted to teach and made relevant through the context of a family scene drinking tea.

The reactions of a girl and boy were characteristically different. The girl integrated the context in formulating her response to the task. The boy ignored the context. He went straight to the task 'Find out how the time taken for sugar to dissolve depends on the temperature of the liquid' and wanted to test a range of temperatures including room temperature. The girl could see no point in testing cold water. As she commented "nobody drinks cold tea." Neither the boy who was working as her partner in the practical task nor the class teacher could understand the girl's perspective. She would not 'play the game' as would the boy and as the teacher intended. She saw no point in investigating anything that was outside the real-world English context of drinking hot tea! This 'ritual of science in the classroom', although for a different purpose, we have called 'school knowledge' in the novice teacher example above as this is the approach to science investigations implicit in what is set by examination boards. The girl's main problem was that her solution had to be applied in the context of tea drinking. Another pupil acting as a mediator tried to help Rennie keep her concern with the authenticity of the context but also to play the science game. "Say Martians came down Rennie, they might not know about drinking cold tea. They might *like* cold tea!" The girl felt supported by this but basically accepted defeat and carried out the (in her view) artificial task required by the teacher, at some considerable cost in her view of herself in relation to science and to the teacher.

This concern with the reality suggested by context can be also be confirmed by a further example which also illustrates the way that boys often react differently to girls (Murphy, 1988). For an investigation of the thermal properties of different textiles such as nylon, felt, cotton wool and a range of other similar materials, pupils were given a copper can, hot water, thermometers and a stop clock. The pupils were asked to find out which of the materials was the best insulator to make a jacket for a mountaineer. In a similar way to the sugar and tea example, the boys at once saw that what the game to be played was all about. They set about wrapping the various materials around the can full of hot water and plotted a range of comparative cooling curves. The girls' reaction to the context was different. Some wanted to make a small jacket to do a 'proper test' on it and spent a lot of time making such a model. Some other girls rejected at the outset cotton wool (the best insulator amongst the samples offered) as 'No one would make a mountaineer's jacket out of cotton wool!'

EXAMPLE: NOVICE TEACHERS IN TRAINING

This example illustrates the difficulty teachers have in bringing together the different types of professional knowledge when organising lessons. The theoretical framework underpinning this work was developed by one of the authors and colleagues in the Centre for Research and Development in Teacher Education at the Open University (see Moon and Banks 1996, Banks 1997) and has been explored with many technology teachers (see Banks & Barlex, 1999, Banks *et al.* 2004). Although the teachers in this example are both very new and still on a pre-service course this example illustrates rather starkly the dilemmas which still face more experienced teachers (as shown above). The example has implications not only for how we should conceptualise the teacher training curriculum and but also lessons to be learnt for better links across school science and technology. As we will see, despite very obvious overlaps in curriculum content, here there was little collaboration between the teachers of science and those of technology.

Although they are at the *beginning teaching* phase of their course to become D&T teachers, Alun and Geoff have already planned and begun to pair-teach a series of lessons for their placement school. The department was concerned that the existing school scheme of work offered to 11 year-olds did not yet include aspects of simple electronics. Although some discussions took place with members of the Science department, the student teachers were largely left to themselves to carry out this work. Using their own ideas and curriculum materials such as text books and electronic kits already in the school, the students decided to organise their teaching around the development of a face mask with flashing eyes. They found this a very difficult exercise, and as we will see, the face mask product was rather pushed out by other considerations. A particular lesson concerned the pupils investigating which materials were conductors and which insulators. To do this the student teachers employed a standard kit called *Locktronics,* but talked first about the circuit by drawing diagrams on the chalkboard.

SUBJECT KNOWLEDGE

The teachers' own understanding of simple electricity was sufficient, but lacked the flexible and sophisticated features to ensure that it was conveyed clearly (McDiarmid *et al.*, 1989). They understood electricity themselves, but were unsure of the depth and nature of the topic pertinent to this design and make task. For example: a description they gave of current flow also involved a confusing discussion of electron flow; a picture of a battery was combined (incorrectly) with a diagram of the electrical symbols. The rather unsatisfactory chalk-board illustration shown in Figure 2 was the result, which inadvertently corresponded to a classic 'clashing current' misconception of pupils (Shipstone, 1985).

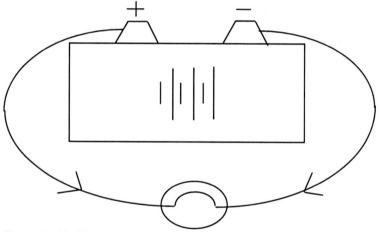

Figure 2: Chalkboard diagram

SCHOOL KNOWLEDGE

The purpose of the project was unclear in the minds of the beginning teachers. When describing the task they would sometimes see it as means to teach designing and making (a practical 'Design and Make Assignment'), however the functional aspects of wearing the mask were not thought through (e.g. the weight of the battery, its location, or how it would be supported). They also considered practical skills such as soldering as being central, but had not allowed enough time to develop such skills. In practice, the face mask became a means of 'selling' the lesson to the pupils – but that became secondary to the desire to teach aspects of conceptual knowledge about electric circuits. [7]

Geoff and Alun thought that an understanding of V=IR was important, but the science department staff had suggested that the use of such a difficult equation would not be taught and reinforced by them to these 11-year-old pupils. Although a D&T lesson, their desire to teach the *science* subject background, such as (in this lesson) conductors and insulators and the existence of electrons, cut down on the time for any designing and making. They were unclear if the overall purpose of the activity was designing, acquiring specific skills, or a 'seeing-is-believing' confirmation of scientific principles. Their prior selection of the subject knowledge they wished to teach was transposed into knowledge for teaching but, as their understanding of school technology was poor, it was without the necessary pedagogic rationale or appropriate teaching strategies.

PEDAGOGICAL KNOWLEDGE

Only Geoff had used the electronics kits before as a pupil, and both novice teachers were unfamiliar with the way they could be used in the classroom. The pupils had some difficulty in manipulating the components and interpreting the circuits the teachers had constructed on the boards. Making a simple series circuit with battery and bulb was difficult enough with the new kits, and introducing a break to accommodate different shaped rods of various materials in an experiment to classify 'conductors' and 'insulators' defeated almost all pupils.

As these beginning teachers were not able to enlist the experience of their mentor (whose own subject was business studies), they drew on their own embryonic pedagogical knowledge to formulate teaching activities for the project. They naturally used analogies to try to convey ideas about electrical flow.[8] For example, Geoff talked about how it is easier to walk around a hill, rather than walk over it, in an attempt to quickly cover the idea of a short circuit. As they considered knowledge of electrons an essential pre-requisite to an understanding of conductors and insulators, Alun showed the following real model and then talked about it using this chalk-board diagram (Figure 3).

The actual tube, shown to the pupils later, represented the wire and the ball bearings were the electrons. It is unclear what the pupils thought about the size of electrons and the need for a conductor for electron flow! Geoff and Alun wished to scaffold the learning of the pupils and they believed a hands-on approach was appropriate. However, they found it difficult to leave the pupils to experiment with the kits, and continually intervened to move them on because of time shortage. Too much was attempted too quickly and some pupils became confused then bored. The novice teachers did not have the pedagogical knowledge to know which aspects of electricity were difficult to convey.

---

[7] We have found this kind of problem with experienced teachers, where the context is used to 'deliver' some electronics (McCormick & Davidson, 1996).

[8] There is good evidence on the difficulty of many analogies (e.g. Dupin & Joshua,1989)

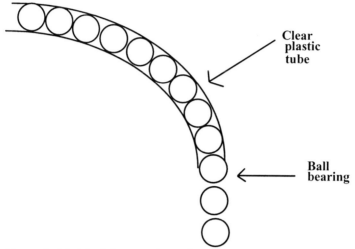

Figure 3: Model of electrons in a wire

PERSONAL SUBJECT CONSTRUCTS

Both Geoff and Alun have a personal subject construct molded by experience in industry, which strongly influences their direction and orientation to how and why pupils should learn Technology. They both also have views of how pupils learn and what constitutes 'good' teaching. They both see hands-on as being vital (although they get side-tracked by a view that detailed theoretical science concepts are an inevitable precursor to understanding of school technology) and wish to emphasise a link to marketing the face-mask product (although that aspect is not made explicit to the pupils).

Alun: I've a belief that everyone should follow Technology with a business and a legal aspect, i.e. unless you know how much it's gonna cost, it's pointless designing something [...] Can we make it? Far too often we find we design things which do not take into the remit [...] realistic targets. So I'd like to relate Technology to more...creative depth within the curriculum. (Interview)

We feel that the personal subject construct of teachers, such as articulated by Alun, has been a crucial factor influencing the way that teachers select the information from the specified curriculum, chose their teaching strategies and thereby affect pupil learning. Banks and Barlex (1999) support this view, arguing that, within the designing and making process there are features that will appeal in different degrees to a teacher according to the specialism and professional history of that teacher. The list below identifies such features and the often-articulated rationale for its significance. (see Table 1).

Table 1: possible elements of 'personal subject constructs'

• Aesthetics	The appearance is crucial. It says everything about the product.
• Communicating skills	Unless they communicate their ideas nothing will be accomplished.
• Design procedures	Without the procedural competence of design nothing can be achieved.
• Making skills	But if they can't make it it's a complete waste of time.
• Technical understanding	If it's not technically sound it just won't work.
• Values	Without an appreciation of the values implicit in the endeavour the whole exercise lacks worth

Ideally a balanced design and make assignment will call on each of these features if not in equal measure then certainly to a meaningful extent. But, if a teacher is strong in just one or two aspects, or believes that one is more significant than any of the others, the breadth and balance within the designing and making experience is lost. Many technology teachers were trained initially as craft teachers and their work has been generally criticised by the Office for Standards in Education.

.. .in general pupils' attainment in designing lags behind that in making. This is because pupils are either not introduced to a sufficiently wide range of designing strategies [...] or are not taught to use them effectively. Pupils are generally confident where work is closely directed by the teacher, but less so when working independently to their own plans, with little awareness of how their work will develop in the later stages of their projects. (OFSTED, 1998)

The above quotation points up one of the lessons to be learnt from the tradition in both science and technology for practical hands-on work. To make the tasks manageable in the classroom, economic on resources and generally successful in terms of teacher-intended outcomes, teachers tend to closely direct the activity of pupils.

We therefore have the situation where both science and technology teachers who adopt a general problem-solving approach to investigation and design run the risk of it being treated as rituals in the classroom. These rituals become associated with the science and technology classrooms and hence students' problem-solving strategies are more to do with this classroom culture, than with problem-solving in the domains of science and technology.

We now turn to consider what pupils are learning in science and technology lessons; how what is specified by government, mediated into tasks by teachers results in 'learning' by pupils.

THE EXPERIENCED CURRICULUM

A limited, but important manifestation of how the curriculum is experienced, in terms of the outcomes of pupil learning, are the scores that pupils achieve on tests and examinations. The international tests in science conducted in 1995, 1999 and 2003 (TIMSS 2004) indicate science assessment results for 14 year old pupils in each of the 25 countries which undertook the tests on these occasions. On that measure how do pupils in England perform? In the 2003 'league table' England came 6th with an average score of 544 behind (in rank order) Singapore (578), Taipei (571), South Korea (558), Hong Kong (556) and Japan. (552). Leaving aside the technicalities of the testing process, and what features of science it was testing (and the undersized sample for England), this can be seen as good news to the government and to its curriculum advisers. In terms of trends too, the average science score of pupils in England rose from 533 in 1995 and 538 in 1999. There are no similar international comparisons for Technology, and less consensus internationally about what constitutes the common features of school technology (Banks,1996), however other indicators exist which give clues about the difficulty of science and technology as subjects and pupils satisfaction with their learning experience, as we will shortly show.

A second indication of the experienced curriculum is the amount of participation in the subject, especially where pupils have a choice of what to study. In England the General Certificate in Secondary Education (GCSE), set by government-recognised examination boards, is taken by all pupils around the age of 16 years, and seen by many as the 'school leaving examination'. However, pupils choose (in conjunction with their teachers) what particular subjects to study for and, within specific subjects what course to take, all controlled by the framework of the national curriculum. Those wishing to study in higher education stay at school for two more years to take Advanced Level (A Level) examinations, and here we have an even sharper choice, which is likely to link to a pupil's future career. By considering the data of both science and technology GCSE candidates, and comparing them with A level candidates, one can make some rough conclusions about participation in further study of science and technology, when such study is no longer compulsory. Data exists for the years 1992 to 2001 from the Qualifications and Curriculum Authority provided by the GCSE awarding bodies in England, Wales and Northern Ireland, and are for candidates of all ages, although the majority were 16 at the time of the examinations. All D&T courses are included and the most common science GCSE 'Science Double Award', which includes aspects of all sciences and takes twice as much time to study as technology, counting as two 'subjects' (Table 2).

Table 2: Number of candidates entered for D&T and Science (Double Award GCSE)

Year	Total Candidates GCSE	Total Candidates D&T (inc. Short courses from 1997)	Total Candidates Science Double Award
1992	5028554	183606	621177
1993	4968634	154720	668272
1994	5029599	150353	810371
1995	5431625	414436	924462
1996	5525620	283974	937304
1997	5455665	269642	929523
1998	5398332	444330	948498
1999	5501193	465252	960870
2000	5514310	467931	980536
2001	5672767	475106	1001610

These data are the Joint Council's final results after any enquiries about the results have been completed.

Table 3: Number of candidates taking A level D&T and the Separate Science.

Year	Total A level Candidates	Total A level Candidates D&T (% GCSE in Year-2)	Total A level Candidates Biology (% GCSE in Year-2)	Total A level Candidates Chemistry (% GCSE in Year-2)	Total A level Candidates Physics (% GCSE in Year-2)
1992	731240	9572	48742	42697	41301
1993	734081	10934	47748	40975	38168
1994	732974	11046 (6%)	50851 (8%)	41231 (7%)	36147 (6%)
1995	730415	10659 (7%)	52255 (8%)	42293 (6%)	34802 (5%)
1996	740470	11057 (7%)	52053 (6%)	40418 (5%)	33033 (4%)
1997	777710	11572 (2%)	56706 (6%)	42262 (5%)	33243 (4%)
1998	790035	13220 (5%)	57436 (6%)	41893 (4%)	33769 (4%)
1999	787732	13739 (5%)	55810 (6%)	40920 (4%)	33548 (4%)
2000	774364	14650 (3%)	54650 (6%)	40261 (4%)	31794 (3%)
2001	770995	14909 (3%)	52382 (5%)	38702 (4%)	30802 (3%)

Table 2 illustrates the increasing popularity of Double Award Science over the years compared with the total candidates in the GCSE cohort. Similarly as D&T became established, the number sitting the examination rose steadily and on the face of it, that could be considered good news for curriculum planners. Both boys and girls are now obliged to study aspects of the physical sciences and of control technology for example. However, in both cases at GCSE there was a degree of obligation and that is no guarantee that when pupils have more choice they will later (e.g. at A level) opt to study science and technology in more depth.

Table 3 shows the number of candidates taking D&T and the separate sciences at A level. This is taken by people of around 18 years old who have opted to stay on in education after the compulsory years of schooling. The percentage figure shown in brackets from 1994 onwards is the fraction of the former GCSE subject cohort who passed the subject two years earlier (e.g. 1992), who went on to sit the corresponding examination at A level. Thus 6% of those who in 1992 passed GCSE in D&T went on to do A level in D&T; similarly 8% went on to do Biology at A level. Looking at the total number of A level examination candidates over the years, only D&T is rising in absolute terms. Biology goes up then down and both Chemistry and Physics have a generally downward trend. However, when one considers the fraction of the corresponding GCSE cohort who *could* have studied these subjects further at A level should they have wished to so, the trend since the introduction of compulsory study of science and technology has been that a smaller fraction wish to do so. Naturally looking at this quantitative data does not give a full picture. Not all schools offer D&T at Advanced level and Physics Teachers are often very difficult to recruit, so that even A level (and certainly Double Award Science) is sometimes taught by teachers without a Physics specialism. However, for whatever reason, the decline in the sciences and the reduction in the percentage wishing to study science and engineering in higher education is a concern to the government in England as it is in most of the western world.

The experience of science and technology within compulsory schooling is not increasing participation subsequently. As we have seen, the way that both science and D&T is transformed in schools by the pedagogy used, the need to cater for many pupils' needs at once, and the requirements of the assessment process all have an impact on the pupils' experiences of the two subjects. The final example gives some insights into *how* the learning is experienced.

EXAMPLE: PROBLEM SOLVING IN THE TECHNOLOGY CLASSROOM

We noted earlier that problem solving is often treated as a ritual. We and our colleagues have reported a body of empirical evidence that this ritual is the way designing as problem solving can be enacted by teachers, with a limiting experience for pupils (see McCormick & Davidson, 1996; McCormick, Murphy & Hennessy, 1994). This ritual we have already suggested was one of the results of the imposed curriculum. However, it also reflects the state of our knowledge about classroom problem solving that has found its way into teachers' knowledge such that it becomes part of their enactment of the curriculum. An example of this was evident in a case study of a teacher with 12-13 year-old pupils working on an electronic badge project based on a 'face' with LEDs for eyes. The teacher deliberately did not emphasise the design process; it was not one of his main aims, and he seemed to view designing as a logical approach rather than as a process that involved sub-processes to be taught and learnt:

...although I'd like them to understand and use the design process and I think it's quite a nice framework for them to fit things on to, I don't think there's a great need to be dogmatic about it and say you must learn it....the nature of projects leads them through the design process despite the teacher's bit, going through it with them in front of the class...(Teacher interview)

He appeared to see the 'logical approach' as a 'way of working', and in that sense the sub-processes were of little significance to him. For him the design process was very much in the background, not just in this project but in general:
I'm relying rather a lot on a subconscious level of going through things. Some of them won't do it, some will.

It resembles, therefore, a planning tool, and we had evidence of this ritual being used in other studies even when there was explicit teaching of the overall process as being made up of sub-process (McCormick & Davidson, 1996).

The particular view a teacher takes of the design process affects the way tasks are structured, the kinds of interventions that are made by the teacher, and the assessment of pupils' work. Not all of these will be consistent either with each other, or with the view espoused by a teacher, but collectively they will have a profound effect on the pupils' perceptions and activities (the experienced curriculum). But, whatever view is taken of designing, there is a tendency to see it as an algorithm to be applied in a variety of situations.

The teacher involved in an *electronic badge project* began it with the 'Situation' being presented:
A theme park has opened in [place] and it wants to advertise itself. It plans to sell cheap lapel badges based on cartoon characters in the park. To make these badges more interesting, a basic electronic circuit will make something happen on the badge.

This was set within the general title of 'Festivals', but the links to the 'Situation' were not discussed, and from then on no further reference was made to festivals. The teacher continued in the session by asking the pupils to define the 'Design brief' and draw up a spider diagram of 'Considerations' (a specification), tasks which all the pupils seemed familiar with. He did not, however, elaborate on the 'Situation' or the 'Design brief', nor invite pupils to discuss them in the context of the planned project.

The three pupils we followed (B, T and D) produced different design briefs that illustrated how the 'Situation' was interpreted by them. B & T interpreted it as a "button is pressed to light up the eyes", whereas D makes no such inference: "to design and make a clock badge". Their initial ideas of their personal 'briefs' lingered and influenced future tasks; for example, D continued to talk about a "clock face" for several lessons and abandoned the idea only when he realised that the electronics would not be like that of a watch. He also imagines that the battery would resemble that in a watch and was almost incredulous when the teacher showed a comparatively large conventional dry 9-volt battery that he (rightly) considered too heavy for a lapel badge. The teacher's discussion with D about this issue indicated that unlike D, he had not entered into the 'Situation' and 'Design brief' in a meaningful way, but only ritualistically - his ultimate answer to the problem was to "have a strong pin for the badge", a response D felt dissatisfied with.

Next the teacher gave several tasks relating to drawing the faces for the badge, which implicitly reflected the sub-processes of 'generating ideas', 'developing a chosen idea' and 'planning the making'. However, this was again done in a ritualistic way as the following indicates.

At the end of the first session pupils were asked, for homework, to create four cartoon faces as potential designs for the badge. No parameters were given other than that all four should fit into the design sheet and that pupils should be 'creative'. As with the 'Situation', 'Design brief' and 'Considerations', this step of producing four designs appeared to be a standard one and, again, was accepted without question by the pupils. However, in the next session pupils were asked to re-draw the faces so that they touch the sides of a fixed drawn square (70x70 mm). The reason for this was not made clear until a later session. Evidence from the pupils' folders indicates that pupils had to modify their designs in order to fit these new demands. For example, D had originally drawn a thin 'carrot' character, which he had to distort to make it fat enough for it to touch the sides of the square. The fact that the creation of several designs is perceived by pupils to be a ritual, is seen in D's comments to the teacher implying he had in fact already made a final choice while he is still completing the four drawings.

In our research we elaborated some of the strategies that pupils adopted in response to the various ways the teachers viewed and enacted the problem-solving process (Murphy and McCormick, 1997). These strategies certainly do not resemble the "algorithms" of problem solving that are so often taught.

The first strategy is what we characterised as *problem solving as dealing with classroom culture*. This occurs when students try to work out the rules the teacher sets in the classroom, and play to those rules. We saw the teacher setting out rules of the game in our examples of the 'enacted curriculum' above. Examples of pupils seeking this culture out is contrasted in the experience of two girls (Kathy and Alice) producing a mobile. Alice wanted to do something that clinks when the wind blows, and so had an idea of using metal. So, given a restricted choice of material, she chose to cut thick mild steel in the form of disks about two inches diameter. Because she played the rules of the classroom, Alice ended up with very sore hands, and took a long time; her endeavor resulted in a very inappropriate way of creating the effect she wanted. (But she did learn quite a lot about mild steel, as it turned out.)

Kathy had designed a moon and planets going around it, and wanted some kind of glinting material. When presented with the choice of material, Kathy in contrast to Alice, looked elsewhere and saw some aluminum (not available to the class) and asked to use this. The teacher agreed, and she cut this easily with tin snips. Kathy took this approach many times throughout the project. She broke the rules of the classroom, knowing what she could and couldn't get away with. She experienced different kinds of issues and problems from Alice, but she was avoiding many technological problems.

The second strategy is *problem solving as giving and finding a solution*, illustrated in a project involving a moisture sensor. The teacher in this study defined the task in terms of making a box in which to put the electronics (the transistor circuit, the bulb or the little speaker, switch, etc.). This had to be appropriate to the situation of detecting moisture or lack of it. He taught them to cut the material (styrene) in straight lines with a steel ruler and a knife because when he said "box", he had in mind a rectangular box. He also gave them a jig so that they could put the two edges together at right angles and run the solvent along to stick the two together. But some pupils wanted curved shaped boxes, which gave some of them at least three emergent problems. First they had to cut a curved shape, and pupils asked each other and the teacher how to cut the shape as the steel ruler method wouldn't work (the solution was to cut it slowly). Second, a curved profile on one part of the box required one side to bend to follow the profile, but the styrene they were given was too thick. The pupils asked the teacher who simply gave her a thinner gauge of styrene, without any discussion. Third, the pupil did not know how to support or hold the thinner styrene in place to apply the solvent, and so again asked the teacher. This time the teacher had to think and was obviously solving a problem himself, but again he gave the *results* of his thinking as a ready-made solution to the pupil and did not involve her in his problem solving. All she received was the solution without being involved in the problem solving. This continually being "given solutions" becomes a culture of the classroom at the expense of a 'problem-solving' culture.

In contrast, we found a teacher in a primary school, who worked with younger children (10- and 11-year-olds), who was able to create this *problem-solving culture* through interactions with students. When pupils came up with problems, the teacher asked questions about their problem, or posed alternative solutions (because sometimes students cannot cope with the questions or provide solutions). Pupils were given more than one solution, because the teacher was trying to engage students in the problem and the problem-solving process. Such a teacher has to set up a completely different culture in the classroom. It takes longer, and it is harder to do, but it is crucial to foster problem solving.

The final strategy is the *student collaboration model,* and that happens in a variety of ways (see Hennessy & Murphy [1999] for the literature on collaborative activity and Murphy & Hennessy [2001] for an analysis of examples of collaboration in technology). One way is through co-operation. In D&T in England pupils are usually set individual projects, so they may be working alongside each other on a table or a bench, and they can co-operate because they are doing similar things; they are not identical, but similar enough to help each other and share tasks.

The second form of collaboration involved pupils in dividing up the task: "You do this bit, I'll do that bit. You're good at that and I'm good at this." Some of the learning is lost in this approach. But at least it is a way of collaborating, because they have to put the two bits together at some stage, and that has an element of good collaborative problem solving. The final form of collaboration occurs when pupils have a shared task, and they can talk about it. This means the design of the task must *require* the students to collaborate. Designed correctly tasks should require solutions to a problem to be considered by all students through discussion and decision making.

These four strategies of problem solving in the technology classroom differ from the way problem solving is depicted in the national curriculum, and the way technology educators normally think about it. Without sensitivity to pupils' experience of problem solving the enacted curriculum will not have the required impact imagined by the teacher.

Problem solving in the science classroom has had no similar exploration, partly because the focus of any problem solving is on the development of conceptual knowledge not procedural knowledge (Murphy & McCormick, 1997). This gives some scope for science teachers to learn from technology teachers, even if it is only to be aware of how they set can up climates that encourage productive problem solving directed at important scientific approaches to problems.

EXAMPLE: KNOWLEDGE IN THE CLASSROOM

We indicated in our discussion of the specified curriculum that science education has been concerned with conceptual knowledge to a greater extent than in technology. Science educators, and many science teachers, recognise the learning issues involved in concept development (e.g. as illustrated in CLISP; see Note 3). Despite this concern there is evidence in technology classrooms that the science knowledge is inert, i.e. it cannot be used in the technological context. One technology teachers strategy is to enable this use is to teach knowledge on a 'need to know' basis, i.e. when it is needed within a project. This is problematic, and they under-rate the difficulties for pupils in learning and using knowledge, as we suggested was the case for the novice teachers Geoff and Alun in our first example.

One strategy is to design appropriate 'Focused Tasks' to cover the necessary conceptual knowledge requirements. However, teaching knowledge on a 'need to know' basis is an attractive alternative for a technology teacher in the situation where separate 'theory' lessons would destroy the motivation that the subject is able to engender in pupils. In addition, the knowledge demands are not always predictable, and hence have to be dealt with as required. If we consider the electronic badge project discussed in the problem-solving example above, then it is evident that the teacher would be faced with a variety of kinds of knowledge, much of which would not feature in the science curriculum for that year group, or at the very least contains different assumptions about starting points and progression of conceptual understanding. More to the point, science educators would be aware of the conceptual difficulties that pupils are likely to encounter, and in particular the importance of an awareness of alternative frameworks that pupils bring to the lessons. However, technology teachers are faced with a more complex situation than the carefully controlled science lesson, where the conceptual knowledge may be used to structure the tasks. Instead they will have the complexities of knowledge in action and an agenda of *technological knowledge* in addition to that of the scientific knowledge.

Levinson, Murphy & McCormick (1997) indicate such problems in a detailed study of 12-13 year-old pupils of the same age involved in a moisture senor project. This revealed that the science knowledge (in terms of what was learned in the science classroom) was not available for the pupils to use in their technology activity. In the science classroom the focus is on *explanations* of phenomena, not on its use. Thus, even though students could give an explanation of current flow in simple 'science circuit', they could not use it to design something nor to make a circuit work in a particular way.

All of the above knowledge relates to science concepts, but, as noted, to add to the complexity of pupils' understanding they also have to master technological concepts. In electronic circuits, and particularly where there is a design element, control system concepts are used and must be understood by pupils. At this level pupils are introduced to the idea of *input*, *process* and *output*, which in the case of the earlier electronic badge project translates into the light-dependent resistor (LDR) as *input*, the transistor (and associated resistors) as *process* and the LED as *output*. This match of system-level description and component-level (e.g. an LED) is not without its complications and arbitrariness (e.g. is the LED's protective resistor part of the output or the process?), and this became evident in the pupils' discussions we have researched (McCormick & Murphy, 1994). In the third session of the project the teacher asked the pupils to make the match of system descriptors and components having defined *input*, *process* and *output*. Pupils were able to use the circuit diagram, which had arrows into the LDR and out of the LED, giving a clue to the input and output respectively. Nevertheless it took even the most able pupils, some time to work this out, and more typically a pupil would insist, quite understandably, that the battery was the input. Indeed this is a legitimate idea, when *primary* and *secondary inputs* are considered (see McCormick, 2004). The teacher does deal with the idea of the 'transistor as a switch' i.e. as the *process* but not in any detail. In more recent work (Murphy *et al*, 2004), observing older pupils (14-15 year olds), we found pupils still having problems with these basic system concepts, and teachers with different approaches to the underlying control ideas (e.g. no distinction between open- and closed-loop control; some using the concept of 'feedback', some not).

The earlier problems with science concepts are at least well researched, and teaching strategies exist to deal with some of them, but in the realm of technological concepts we have much less understanding. Neither do we have much about the interaction of the different kinds of knowledge required in the technological task. So once again we have an area where we are unable as teachers to be aware of the experience of the curriculum for the pupil, without more understanding.

CONCLUSION

What lessons can be drawn from a consideration of science and technology education in England over the years 1984 to 2004? We have covered some issues in passing and here attempt to draw together what we consider are the crucial points. Although the framework we have adopted (Figure 1) helps us to focus on specific issues, its dimensions are naturally interlinked. Classrooms are social environments and the specified curriculum leads to what is enacted by teachers and what is experienced by pupils. Yet how pupils react to tasks set and how they learn modifies what teachers do and, particularly in the early years under consideration, leads to modification of what is specified.

The Specified Curriculum

- *It is very difficult to control the intended learning of pupils by an elaborate specification in law of what pupils should know.*

A curriculum specified as a legal document is open to challenge in the court if it is not carried out in schools. If teachers themselves are not part of the discussion on what science and technology in school should be, they will 'teach to the test' to cover themselves leading to pedagogies that have, for example, elements of 'ritual'. There will be a clash between their personal view of their subject and that specified by the state and classroom practice will go through a period of extremes until some commonly shared beliefs of what constitutes 'good' teaching emerge. In 2005, this concern to control centrally the work of teachers has not diminished. Following on nation-wide initiatives for numeracy and literacy, all teachers of science and of technology will be trained to improve the learning of 11-14year old – the so called Key Stage 3 Strategy (DfES, 2005). In countries such as Scotland where the curriculum is suggested by guidelines rather than legislation, development of the curriculum has been less hectic (see for example Dakers & Doherty, 2003)

The Enacted Curriculum

- *In an effort to direct the learning outcomes for all pupils and make the tasks manageable in the classroom, teachers tend to closely direct the activity of pupils.*

Through constraints of time and resources, teachers transfer their subject into 'School Knowledge' and pupils play the game of discovering what that is. Some pupils never quite understand the rules of the game and the relevance of the subject becomes lost to them; others pick up incidental aspects because teachers have either not made clear what is salient or their classroom culture produces effects at odds with their rhetoric.

The Experienced Curriculum

- *Requiring the study of the physical sciences and of technology does not lead to general satisfaction with the subjects and a desire to study it further.*
- *The way that pupils engage in problem solving in technology and in science depends on the view of designing and of investigating held by the teacher.*
- *Technology teachers have much to teach science teachers on the handling of processes and the science teachers much to teach technology teachers about the problems associated with acquiring conceptual knowledge.*

Our overwhelming conclusion, however, would be that science classrooms and particularly technology classrooms are under-researched. As new equipment such as ICT produces yet more pedagogic challenge and new professional development strategies focusing on its functionality attempted, very little is found out about their impact on the curriculum experienced by pupils. Despite considerable classroom-based work over the years 1984-2004 we feel we have merely scratched the surface.

REFERENCES

Atkinson, S. (2000), Does the need for higher levels of performance curtail the development of creativity in design and technology project work? *International Journal of technology and Design Education,* 10(3), 255-281.

Banks, F. (1996), Approaches and models in technology teachers education: An overview, *Journal of design and technology education* 1(3), 197-211.

Banks, F. (1997), *Assessing technology teacher professional knowledge.* Paper presented at the PATT-8 Conference, Scheveningen, The Netherlands, April.

Banks, F. & Barlex, D. (1999), No one forgets a good teacher! - What do 'good' technology teachers know?, *Journal of Design and Technology Education* 4(3), 223-229.

Banks, F., Barlex, D., Jarvinen, E-M, O'Sullivan, G., Owen-Jackson, G. & Rutland, M. (2004), DEPTH - Developing professional thinking for technology teachers: An international study, *International Journal of Technology and Design Education* 14(2), 141-157.

Barlex, D., Black, P & Harrison, G. (1994) *Nuffield design and technology: INSET guide*, Longman, Harlow.

Department of Education and Science [DES] (1985), *Science 5–16: A statement of policy*, HMSO, London.

Dakers, J. R. and Doherty, R. (2003) Technology education in T.G.K. Bryce and W.M.Humes (Eds) *Scottish Education, Second Edition Post-Devolution,* Edinburgh, Edinburgh University Press.

Department for Education and the Welsh Office (1995), *Technology in the national curriculum*, HMSO, London.

DfES/QCA (1999), *The national curriculum*, HMSO, London.

DfES (2005) *Key stage 3 national strategy,* http://www.standards.dfes.gov.uk/keystage3/ (accessed January 2005)

Dupin, J.J. & Joshua, S. (1989). Analogies and "Modelling analogies" in teaching: Some examples in basic electricity. *Science Education,* 73(2):207-224

Driver, R. & Oldham, V. (1986), A constructivist approach to curriculum development in science, *Studies in Science Education* 13, 105-122.

Foulds. K, Gott, R. & Mashiter, J. (1990), *Investigations in science*, Blackie, London.

Garrett, R. M. (1987),. Issues in science education: Problem-solving, creativity and originality,. *International Journal of Science Education,* 9 (2), 125-137

Gott, R. & Murphy, P. (1987), *Assessing investigations at ages 13 and 15,* Association for Science Education, Hatfield.

Harlen, W. (ed.) (1985), *Primary science: Taking the plunge*, Heinemann, London.

Hennessy, S. & Murphy, P. F. (1999), The potential for collaborative problem solving in D&T, *International Journal of Technology and Design Education* 9(1), 1-36.

House of Commons (2002), *The House of commons report: Science education for 14 to 19. volume 1:* Report and Proceedings of the Science and Technology Committee, HMSO, London.

Jenkins, E. (1987), Philosophical flaws, *Times Educational Supplement,* 2 January.

Kimbell, R. (1997), *Assessing technology*, Open University Press, Buckingham.

Levinson, R., Murphy, P. & McCormick, R. (1997), Science and technology concepts in a design and technology project: a pilot study, *Research in Science and Technological Education* 15(2), 235-255.

Liverpool University (1994), *SPACE Reports*, Liverpool University Press, Liverpool.

McCulloch, G., Jenkins, E. & Layton, D. (1985), *Technological revolution? The politics of school science and technology in England and Wales since 1945*, Falmer Press, Lewes.

McCormick, R. (1990), *The evolution of current practice in technology education.* Paper presented at the NATO Advanced Research Workshop: Integrating Advanced Technology into Technology Education, 8-12 October, Eindhoven, Netherlands.

McCormick, R. (1997), Conceptual and procedural knowledge, *International Journal of Technology and Design Education* 7(1-2), 141-159.

McCormick, R. (1999), Practical knowledge: a view from the snooker table. in R. McCormick & C. Paechter (eds), *Learning and knowledge* (pp. 112-135), Paul Chapman, London.

McCormick, R. (2004), Issues of learning and knowledge in technology education, *International Journal of Technology and Design* 14(1), 21-44.

McCormick, R. & Davidson, M. (1996), Problem solving and the tyranny of product outcomes, *Journal of Design and Technology Education* 1(3), 230-241.

McCormick, R. & Murphy, P. (1994), *Learning the processes in technology.* Paper presented at the British Educational Research Association Annual Conference, Oxford University, England, September.

McCormick, R., Murphy, P. & Davidson, M. (1994), *Design and technology as revelation and ritual* in J. S. Smith (ed.), *IDATER 94* – International Conference on Design and technology Educational Research and Curriculum Development (pp 38-42), University of Loughborough, Loughborough.

McCormick, R., Murphy, P. & Hennessy, S. (1994), *Problem-solving in design and technology: a case of situated learning?* A paper presented at the Annual Meeting of the American Education Research Association, New Orleans, Louisiana, April.

McCormick, R., Murphy, P., Hennessy, S. & Davidson, M. (1996), *Problem solving in science and technology education,* Paper presented to American Educational Research Association Annual Meeting, New York, 8-11 April.

McDiarmid, G., Ball, D. L., & Anderson, C. W. (1989), *Why staying one chapter ahead doesn't really work: subject-specific pedagogy* in M. C. Reynolds (ed.), Knowledge Base for the Beginning Teacher, Pergamon Press, Oxford.

Millar, R. & Driver, R. (1987), Beyond processes, *Studies in Science Education* 14, 33-62.

Millar, R. (1988), The pursuit of the impossible, *Physics education* 23(3), 156-159.

Moon, B. & Banks, F. (1996), *Secondary school teachers' development: Reconceptualising knowledge and pedagogy.* Paper at Association for Teacher Education in Europe (ATEE), Glasgow, September.

Murphy, P. (1988), Insights into pupils' responses to practical investigations from the APU, *Physics Education* 23, 330-336.

Murphy, P. & McCormick R. (1997), Problem solving in science and Technology Education, *Research in Science Education* 27(3), 461-481.

Murphy, P., Lunn, S. A., McCormick, R., Davidson, M. & Jones, H. (2004), *EiS Final evaluation report. evaluation of the promotion of electronics in schools regional pilot: Final report of the evaluation*, Open University, Milton Keynes.

Murphy, P., Scanlon, E. & Issroff, K. with Hodgson, B. & Whitelegg, E. (1996), Group work in primary science - emerging issues for learning and teaching, in K. Schnack (ed.), *Studies in Educational Theory and Curriculum*, Volume 14, Danish School of Educational Studies, Copenhagen.

Office for Standards in Education [OFSTED] (1998), *Secondary education 1993-97: A review of secondary schools in England*, The Stationary Office, London.

Office for Standards in Education [OFSTED] (2000), *OfSTED Subject reports secondary design and technology, 1999-2000,* The Stationary Office, London.

Qualifications and Curriculum Authority [QCA] (2005), *GCSE examination results 1992-2001* http://www.qca.org.uk/7255_2222.html (Accessed January 2005).

Screen, P. (1988), A case for a process approach: the Warwick experience, *Physics Education* 23(3), 146-149.

Shipstone, D. (1985), *Electricity in simple circuits,* in R. Driver, E. Guesene, & A. Tiberghien (eds.), Children's Ideas in Science (pp. 33-51), Open University Press, Milton Keynes.

Smithers, A. & Robinson, P. (1992), *Technology in the national curriculum: Getting it right,* The Engineering Council, London.

TIMSS (2004), *International student achievement in science*, TIMSS & PIRLS International Study Centre, Lynch School of Education, Boston College, Boston.

Wellington, J. (1988), Process and content in Physics education, *Physics Education* 23(3), 150-155.

Wellington, J. (ed.): 1989, *Skills and processes in science education: A critical analysis*, Routledge, London.

Woolnough, B. (1988), Whither process in science teaching? *Physics Education* 23 (3), 139-140.

KAY STABLES AND RICHARD KIMBELL

23. UNORTHODOX METHODOLOGIES: APPROACHES TO UNDERSTANDING DESIGN AND TECHNOLOGY

UNDERSTANDING D&T BEFORE APU

The decision in 1983 of the (then) Department for Education and Science's (DES) Assessment of Performance Unit (APU) to commission a major research project in the assessment of design and technological capability marked a watershed in the development of technology education. This was the first major initiative where the principal aim was to *find out* about capability and how to assess it, as opposed to developing and introducing new curriculum ideas. This is not to say that this project started with a blank canvas - a whole host of understandings had been developed through the profession grappling with both curriculum and assessment developments. Some of this was instigated and explored at the 'grass roots', other advances were spawned through major national initiatives sponsored, for example in England by Her Majesty's Inspectorate and by the Government funded Schools' Council and Design Council. Two particularly significant developments came through curriculum development projects introduced in the late 1960s: Project Technology, led by Geoffrey Harrison and the Design, Craft and Education Project (the 'Keele' Project) led by John Eggleston (Penfold 1988). Both projects worked closely with teachers to support and develop their practice and produced a range of resources to do this - magazines, text books, pamphlets and so on. The 'Keele' Project most importantly introduced (in 1967) the magazine 'Studies in Education and Craft', but while the articles in the early years illustrate a rich seedbed of shared ideas, as is illustrated in the 20th Anniversary 'best of' publication (Eggleston 1987), very few make reference to other literature or research and even fewer can be seen as ostensibly reporting on research. Further understandings were developed and shared through the various professional associations and a final set of understandings came through developments in national assessment systems. Again in the English context, of major significance was the Oxford 'A' level Design exam, with its criteria based on designing process and on descriptors of levels of attainment; the London 'O' level Design and Technology 'pre-practical' exam paper - a 'designing' exam prior to a formal making skills practical test; and, in 1985 guidance for the (then) new GCSE framework that focused assessment on 'what pupils know, understand and can do' (i.e. capability).

M.J. de Vries, I. Mottier (eds.), International Handbook of Technology Education, 313–330.
© *2006 Sense Publishers. All rights reserved.*

A related area of growth, that was stealing a march on d&t education, was that of design research, with the interests of the Design Methods movement in the 1960s (Jones 1970), the formation of the Design Research Society in 1967 and the introduction of the Design Studies Journal in 1979. This area had a direct impact on the birth and development of design education, and most notably the Design Education Unit at the Royal College of Art, the establishment of the National Association for Design Education (NADE) and the Design in General Education Project (Archer et al, 1979), all of which had a significant influence on a faction of teachers in the subjects that were precursors to d&t. And just as some were seeking understandings from the design profession, so others were seeking insight from the professional worlds of science and technology.

In virtually all of the above, the emphasis on research was either slim or non-existent and so, for the UK, the creation of the APU was significant as it provided the resources to create the first explicitly research-led development, enabling dedicated teams to undertake both fundamental and seminal work. The DES created the APU in 1975 to conduct surveys of performance initially in mathematics, English and science, predominantly at ages 11 and 15. A small number of additional surveys and reports were undertaken (in modern languages and aesthetics for example) and finally the single major survey in d&t. Leading to this survey was a working group (APU 1981) and a subsequent survey of d&t activities in the curriculum conducted by a team at the National Centre for School Technology, led by Geoffrey Harrison (APU 1983).

METHODOLOGIES DEVELOPED THROUGH APU D&T (1985-1991)

This early work provided the impetus for a full survey and the APU D&T project started in 1985. Its overarching brief was to monitor the design and technological capability of the nation's fifteen year olds (i.e. England, Wales and Northern Ireland). In keeping with previous APU projects, this was to be achieved by surveying a 2% sample of this population, which amounted to approximately 10,000 young people. Methodologically this presented a real challenge - nowhere else in the world had there been a similar research project in the growing area of technology education - either in scope or scale. There was no model from within the discipline for the team to refer to, which led us in the first instance to explore existing approaches in other educational disciplines, and in particular from previous APU projects. Particularly influential was research that focused on assessing *process* – especially APU research in language and in science investigations. Added to the immaturity of research in technology education was the immaturity (in research terms) of the project team - all of us experienced curriculum practitioners with strong understandings and beliefs about classroom practice in d&t, but who in research terms could, between us, muster one M.Phil. and 2 MA.s.

In order to address the brief - of monitoring capability, we had two overarching drivers: to develop understanding of capability we had to be able to *understand process* and to *assess performance*. As practitioners, the team established early on a commitment to the definition of d&t capability that had been developed through the earlier work of the working party and subsequent 1983 survey - that the capability was procedural. Further we developed a belief that to assess procedural capability assessments had to be conducted 'on task' in 'real' or 'authentic' settings. Methodologically this left us in very new research territory. While this was daunting, it did provide us with a clear, overarching criterion both to guide and defend our choice of research approach and, as it turned out, to develop the first of what could be seen as a growing repertoire of unorthodox methodologies. We prefigured our position on this in the opening statement to the final report of the APU D&T project.

There is no single, all-embracing approach to research in education. There are many approaches- indeed new approaches are constantly emerging as researchers tackle different kinds of problems and devise strategies to suit them. And so it is necessary not only to select the approach that is most suitable for any particular research undertaking, but also to demonstrate why it is more suitable than other approaches that might have been chosen. (Kimbell et al 1991:11)

In our quest to understand process in d&t we explored previous models and were frustrated by the stranglehold of linear and cyclical models that were more about managing the process than describing its reality. Through this project we sought to develop a different model that captured a more responsive and dynamic (if complex) conception of the process. We characterised the process as starting with a hazy idea that needs to be externally expressed in some way (drawings, writings, talking, modelling) in order that the idea can be seen more clearly and subsequently thought about more deeply to allow a further and more developed expression of the idea to be iterated. Figure 1 is how we illustrated the model in the final report of the APU d&t project (Kimbell et al 1991) and in writing about this some years later we summarised our model it in the following way.

The approach ... is built on a profoundly different model which views designing as an interaction between mind and hand (inside and outside the head) and the activity as being best described as iterative as ideas are bounced back and forth; formulated, tested against the hard reality of the world and then reformulated. We coined the phrase 'thought in action' to summarise the idea. (Stables and Kimbell, 2000:195-196)

To develop an appropriate assessment framework derived from the above model we did not turn to research methodologies, but to our own experiences of assessment as practitioners through which we believed that teachers could make reliable and valid overarching judgements about the quality of a given piece of work. This led us to a position where we saw the first and foremost assessment of a d&t project as being *holistic* - taking account of the total of what a learner was trying to achieve and the way they were going about it. From this we could analyse the work in more detail and make separate judgements about dimensions of the process - how effective was the evaluating, the generating of ideas, the planning and so on. Finally we could look in greater detail still to describe what the learners had done - what actions lay behind the quality of their evaluating. We created a three level assessment framework which allowed us to start with a holistic judgement - the 'big picture' of what had been achieved and then progressively dig deeper into the work as we increased the magnification through our questions and criteria. Within the framework we distinguished between those aspects where *judgements* were to be made (largely relating to procedural matters) and those where the questions allowed for a *cataloguing* (or mapping) of the terrain of the response, through simple yes/no answers (e.g. have they used colour? Yes/No). Building this level of detail allowed us to create a unique profile of each response - effectively 'fingerprinting' it. The framework and our approach within it are described in detail in project documentation (Kelly et al, 1987, Kimbell et al, 1991).

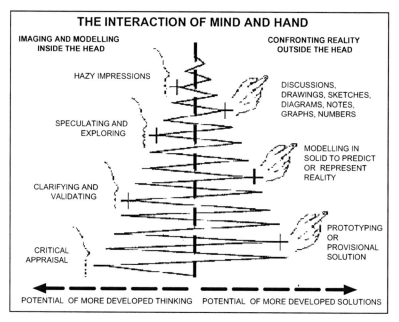

Figure 1: The APU model of interaction between mind and hand (Kimbell et al, 1991 p. 20)

In order to assess capability in the context of real activities two different approaches were taken. The first of these was simply to assess project work that was underway in schools through requirements in the (then) new GCSE coursework requirements. The second was to conduct a series of differently structured but standardised assessment activities through an approach that we have come to term the 'unpickled portfolio'. (Stables and Kimbell, 2000). For both approaches there were a similar set of methodological matters to be considered - how evidence was to be generated, how data was to be collected and how approaches were to be standardised across the survey population.

316

For the assessing of project work the basic evidence - the learners' project work - was generated through their individual responses to the briefs set by the GCSE examinations. The sheer challenge of monitoring project work that was going on over extended periods of time meant that the learners involved in this aspect of the survey were necessarily small in number - only 210 in the final count. Reporting was through illustrative case studies developed from the collection a whole range of evidence including photocopies and photographs of work, tape recordings and written notes of interviews, a detailed charting of the project work (deploying the assessment framework outlined above), the teacher's assessment, learner self assessment and school background data. As such this built very much on standard research methodologies adopted from elsewhere.

For the assessment activities we were on new ground - caused by the need to address both our determination to bring assessment to bear on authentic d&t activity and the sheer practicalities of conducting a survey involving 10,000 subjects. Our response to this was to develop a network of activities, structured through an unfolding response booklet and choreographed by an administrator's script that enabled learners to provide a rounded d&t response in a tight time frame of either 90 minutes (involving only paper and pencil) or 150 minutes (allowing also for 3D modelling and discussion of ideas), depending on the activity. The response booklet helped learners in both generating and collecting the evidence. The activity was standardised by the administrator's script, and through the provision of identical resources to all participating schools, including for each activity a short (7-9 minute) contextualising video programme to set the scene for the design task. The assessment was standardised by the assessment framework, accompanying rubric and assessed exemplars and by the careful training of the assessors. (see Kimbell et all 1991 for more detail)

In relation to the response booklet, there were a number of key innovations. The first and most obvious was the way in which the booklet unfolded. One of the constraints of the survey was that the learner's response had to be in some form of booklet and yet we didn't want to use a conventional booklet that involved turning pages and hence concealing the work already done. The activity was structured as a design task that was made up of a series of iterative (between 'thought' and 'action') steps. In response to our self imposed problem we designed a booklet that unfolded to progressively reveal the next step without concealing what had gone before. In addition to the way the booklet worked, there were a number of other key features that have become threads through future work:
- the use of 'red penning' - encouraging learners to evaluate their own work in an explicit fashion during the course of the activity;
- the use of everyday language such as 'put down' and 'jot down' as a way of not prescribing drawing or writing as a format for communication;
- the requirement for the learners to identify, at the close of the task, what they don't know but would need to find out if they were to take their design through to a finished outcome.

These features were all methodological tactics designed to make tangible the thoughts that lay behind the learners' actions - in order that the assessment could be made more reliably. As it turned out they also had a value to the learners - for example in providing the 'pause for thought'. On reflection, we are aware that the methodology was working at a number of levels - the unfolding booklet was an unconventional research tool in itself, and the collection of unconventional tactics it presented made it work for the learners as well as the assessors.

A final theme emerging from this first project relates to the way we presented data. It may be the very nature of our backgrounds in design, but from this first project onwards, we have sought to find graphic ways of presenting findings that makes them both clear and accessible. This has tended towards presenting data in 'non-standard', *quirky* ways. Our approach developed from the problem of dealing with large and complex data sets and, in outline terms our process was to collect and secure valid and reliable raw data and then to make pictures from the data to help us explore emerging patterns. The patterns in turn led to us creating pictures that allowed us to illustrate the patterns to others. There were a range of ways we went about this in the APU D&T project and we present just two examples here. The first is to do with the way the actual data is arranged. We had gathered performance data in relation to both gender and ability and wished to explore the difference in impact of the test structures in the survey. We had the absolute performance scores as a mean for each group, but wished to explore the difference between the groups. To do this we held the mid ability girls as a constant and arranged the data to show how much better or worse the high and low ability girls' performance was. We also arranged the data from the most open of our test structures (the 150 minute modelling activities) to the most tightly structured (a 90 minute paper and pencil test focused on evaluating products). The resulting chart is shown below and, in a very graphic fashion, illustrates quite clearly how the more tightly framed tests supported the performance of the lower ability girls.

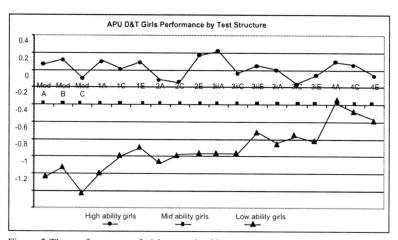

Figure 2 The performance of girls organised by test structure

The second example shows how we presented schematic pictures of performance, across the survey, in a visual way that showed patterns that would have been somewhat harder to detect from the basic data. Figure 3a shows basic data of average performance by girls and boys in each test. Figure 3b uses this data to show visually the overarching effect of the context of the test (in contexts of designing for people, environments or industry) and Figure 3c uses the data to show the way the test structure effect overlaid the context effect.

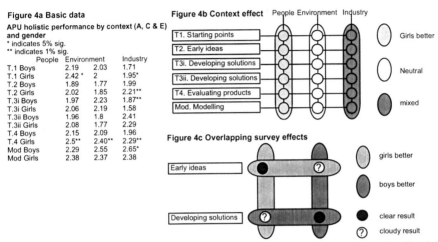

Figure 4a Basic data

APU holistic performance by context (A, C & E) and gender
* indicates 5% sig.
** indicates 1% sig.

	People	Environment	Industry
T.1 Boys	2.19	2.03	1.71
T.1 Girls	2.42 *	2	1.95*
T.2 Boys	1.89	1.77	1.99
T.2 Girls	2.02	1.85	2.21**
T.3i Boys	1.97	2.23	1.87**
T.3i Girls	2.06	2.19	1.58
T.3ii Boys	1.96	1.8	2.41
T.3ii Girls	2.08	1.77	2.29
T.4 Boys	2.15	2.09	1.96
T.4 Girls	2.5**	2.40**	2.29**
Mod Boys	2.29	2.55	2.65*
Mod Girls	2.38	2.37	2.38

Figure 4b Context effect

T1. Starting points
T2. Early ideas
T3i. Developing solutions
T3ii. Developing solutions
T4. Evaluating products
Mod. Modelling

Girls better
Neutral
mixed

Figure 4c Overlapping survey effects

Early ideas
Developing solutions

girls better
boys better
clear result
cloudy result

Figures 3a, Basic data from the APU d&t survey; 3b, Context effect and 3c Overlapping survey effects

Looking back over the research we have undertaken in TERU in the last twenty years we are conscious of a number of themes that have emerged, all of which to a greater or lesser extent can be seen in this first project:

• The *'by products'* from gathering *ephemeral* evidence (e.g. the assessment booklet was structured to gather the 'thinking' of the learners - and in doing so gave them the opportunity for a 'pause for thought')
• Approaches to assessment (e.g. 'fingerprinting' the responses through a combination of levels of valuing and describing within an overarching holistic judgement);
• The use of the *vernacular* in terminology (e.g. 'put down ideas' and 'jot down problems' rather than specifying 'write' or 'draw');
• The *quirky* ways of presenting findings (e.g. the effects of context and test structure on performance);
• Combining *qualitative* and *quantitative* data (e.g. the use of case studies for extended project work).

THE REPERTOIRE DEVELOPED BY TERU POST APU

From the end of the APU project to the present day, a further twenty projects have been undertaken by TERU. This paper will consider three further projects where distinctly different approaches were used and through which the themes identified above can be illustrated. The first of these, the *Understanding Technological Approaches* project (Kimbell, Stables and Green, 1994) developed an approach to observing and documenting the fine detail of actions undertaken in a range of d&t projects. The second, the *North West Province Technology Education Evaluation Project* (Kimbell and Stables, 1999), was the first curriculum evaluation project we undertook and illustrates both how we developed the APU 'unpickled portfolio' and also developed approaches to gathering opinion based data. The third, *Assessing Innovation* (Kimbell et al, 2004), took forward the assessment focus but with an emphasis on creativity and innovation. The following sections provide an outline of these projects and examples that exemplify methodological developments in relation to the above themes.

Understanding Technological Approaches (UTA) (1992-1994)

There were two fundamental areas of understanding that the APU D&T project did not provide insights into. The first was the fine detail of how learners engaged with *complete* d&t projects over time and the second was the extent to which capability varied between age groups. A subsequent project, the Understanding Technological Approaches (UTA) project (Kimbell et al 1994 & 1996) aimed to explore these areas by monitoring, minute by minute, the complete d&t projects of eighty learners spanning all age groups from five to sixteen. This demanded a methodological approach that allowed for close observation and analysis. We faced the problem of monitoring and recording the huge detail of a complete individual project – and monitoring more than one learner at a time. We had to establish what was important to observe and record and what to ignore. To do this we went into classrooms in pairs and through a process of observation and subsequent analysis devised categories that we considered meaningful in terms of understanding the activity and that allowed for recording the observations in a consistent and manageable fashion. The analysis resulted not just in the creation of the categories, but for each category a set of pre-coded data sub categories. Central to understanding d&t capability were the categories of d&t *intentions* and *manifestations*. This allowed us, for example, to explore the different ways in which learners approached the intention of developing an idea - did they do this by drawing, by talking to each other, by combining materials or in some other way? Through the development of the iterative model of designing in the APU d&t project we were clear that the dimensions identified in linear models of designing (e.g. generating ideas, making, evaluating) were better viewed as design intentions, rather than 'stages' in a fixed process, and that these could and would change in response to the needs in any particular design task, depending on the way in which the learner tackled it. By collecting this data across the length of a project we potentially would have proof-positive of our belief. Three further categories articulated were; learner engagement, teacher/learner interaction and focus of the project (i.e. technical, user or aesthetic). In addition we collected narrative data that provided a context through which to understand the coded data. Five minute time slots provided sufficient detail to capture the project in a meaningful way and enabled an individual observer to record data on four projects at a time. Figure 4 shows the structure, categories and sub categories of data collected.

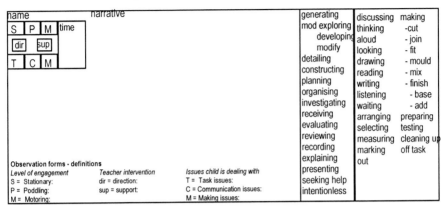

Figure 4 The observation schedule from the UTA project

UTA project: Combining qualitative and quantitative data

There were certain novelties in our approach. First we collected both quantitative (coded) and qualitative (narrative account) data. The narrative account was essential both to understand the context that the learner was operating in and also to verify and understand the coded data. The coded data varied from very objective data - particularly that which identified the manifestations where it was absolutely clear (for example) whether the learner was cutting material, measuring or writing, to quite subjective data - for example in identifying the design intention of the learner it sometimes required an element of inference on the part of the observer. At the time at which we were doing this, other researchers, within d&t education and also within the design profession, were exploring the related approach of 'protocol analysis'. That which equated most closely to our approach was research that of Rob Johnsey was undertaking with primary age children's d&t activity where he was applying a procedural analysis on a minute-by-minute analysis of video footage. (Johnsey, 2000). Amongst his conclusions was one that echoed our own findings.

The evidence from the behavioural charts suggests that when children are given a free hand to design and make, the making stimulates the designing and vice versa. It suggests that children do not plan everything at the beginning and then proceed but that planning runs in parallel with doing. Furthermore, it seems quite natural for children to change and add to the specifications they have for their product as they proceed. It is as though the half-completed product acts as a stimulus or modelling tool for new ideas. (Johnsey 2000: 20-21)

More explicit exploration of protocol analysis as a tool to understand designing was taking place in the world of Design Research. A major workshop in 1994 in Delft, took a rigorous, explicit technique of Protocol Analysis, wherein the participant designers spoke their thoughts 'out loud' throughout their designing. (Cross, Christians & Doorst, 1996) While the workshop was found to be of immense value, the authors reported that it was useful to capture certain aspects of activity in great detail, but that focusing entirely on what was communicated by out-loud thinking missed other forms of communicated evidence.

The adoption of protocol analysis as a research technique for design is an effort on the part of design methodologists to find a rigorous form for their empirical research. Protocol analysis is somewhere in the middle ground between the 'hard' experimental methods of the natural sciences and the 'weaker, purely observational methods of the social sciences. (Cross et al, 1996: 13-14)

The approach we had created for ourselves had certain similar characteristics, but perhaps (somewhat unwittingly) bridged the gap between the approaches of the natural and social sciences, particularly in the way we were collecting 'hard' quantitative and 'soft' qualitative data. Perhaps of most importance in our case was that we weren't seeking to bring a methodology from elsewhere to bear on what we were doing, but to create one that allowed us to gain insight into the processes learners (and their teachers) were employing. Seeking to collect both quantitative and qualitative data at the same time is more acceptable in 2005. Researchers who might previously have identified themselves with either a qualitative or quantitative research tradition are realising the valuable insights that can be gained by combing the two. In 1993, the approach was somewhat unorthodox and the richness that it enabled convinced us of the value of the combination.

UTA project: The use of the vernacular in terminology

A further novelty growing from the APU d&t project was the use of 'everyday' words to capture the spirit of our observations. Our need was for consistency in monitoring and recording data across the research team and everyday language proved a reliable way of sharing understanding. This appeared most notably in this project in the way in which we coded the learner's engagement - by identifying their activity level at any given time as 'stationary', 'poddling' or 'motoring'. These terms emerged early in the project as the team found how easily and reliably they could be used and, in analysis terms, how effective they were as discriminators of engagement and motivation. When disseminating the project we also came to realise the 'added value' of the use of these graphic, vernacular words terms that also helped teachers to share our understandings, despite being idiosyncratically English (the word 'poddling' has initially foxed international audiences).

UTA project: The quirky ways of presenting findings

As with the APU D&T project, we explored different ways of presenting findings in order to see the emerging patterns – and analysing the incidence of 'stationary', 'poddling' and 'motoring' provides a useful illustration of this approach. The problem we were addressing was how to compare the varied levels of engagement between age groups and also across the differing timespans of the projects, the shortest of which (with 5 year olds) was 3 hours, the longest (with 16 year olds) was 50 hours. To do this, we divided each project into five equal phases that allowed us to show variations in the 'big picture' of the project. Figure 5 shows our approach to this, providing a comparison of the average 'motoring' by learners in Key Stage (KS) 1 (5-7 year olds), KS2 (8-11 year olds), KS3 (12-14 year olds and KS4 (15-16 year olds). Following the 'motoring' line for the very young children their sheer enthusiasm and energy can be seen, and also the dip (probably in energy level) before building up to the crescendo of completing the project. This compares quite starkly with the pattern that emerged for the 11-14 year olds where a more prescriptive, linear pedagogic approach appears to have depressed engagement in the early 'paper work' stages, lifted it once they got their hands on materials and saw it begin to fade away as final evaluations were being required of them.

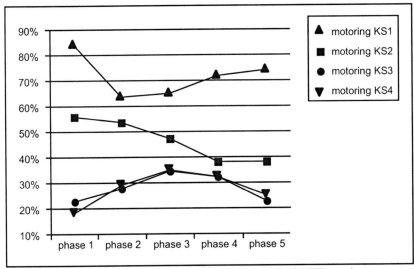

Figure 5 A comparison of 'motoring' across the key stages in the UTA project.

The North West Province Technology Education Project (NWPTEP) Evaluation (1998-1999)

This next project was an evaluation of a curriculum initiative undertaken in the North West Province of South Africa involving senior high school learners (16 year olds and above) from schools in both rural and urban communities. The initiative, funded by the UK Department for International Development (DFID), aimed to introduce a technology education curriculum into high schools and was part of the much larger 'Curriculum 2005' project. It implemented an approach that promoted mixed gender, participatory, collaborative group work, utilising a problem solving model of designing - an approach that was entirely new, both because technology education was new, and also because learning was more typically by rote, through teacher directed lessons.

NWPTEP: The 'by products' from gathering ephemeral evidence

The evaluation, also commissioned by DFID, looked at the impact of the project, the focus of which was not on what the learners knew, but what they did with what they knew - the quality of their *procedural* capability. To assess this we once more needed a tool that could be used 'on task' - to assess performance in an authentic way - and again utilised the 'unpickled portfolio' approach of the APU d&t project. However, the assessment needed to reflect the group work approach of the NWPTEP. To address this the APU structure was modified such that a mixed gender group of 6 learners worked together, with sub-tasks dividing the group into three pairs. Because the evaluation project was designed to measure the impact of the NWPTEP by comparing a whole cohort of learners who had experienced the project with one that hadn't, the assessment could measure the performance of the team of six learners as a whole, rather than individually. Our initial reaction was that this allowed us to avoid the thorny issue of assessing team work. However, when we trialed the activity it became apparent the test booklets provided a trail of evidence indicating how effectively the team had worked together. Thus in structuring the response booklets to support groupwork activity, we had inadvertently also captured evidence for assessment. This was a turn-around from our previous experience where, for example with the 'red penning' we had structured for assessment and inadvertently provided a format that supported the learner. We took advantage of this to use the evidence to develop criteria for assessing 'team working' within our assessment rubric.

NWPTEP: Combining qualitative and quantitative data

The NWPTEP provided so distinctive a shift in both curriculum and pedagogy that we wished to gain as much insight as we could from the learners themselves. To this end we conducted semi-structured group interviews, an activity evaluation questionnaire and an 'attitude to technology' questionnaire (derived from earlier PATT type research conducted by Dyrenfurth and Williams (Dyrenfurth 1995). This included inviting the learners to identify: the aspects of an activity that made it a 'technological' activity; what they believed technology to be; and the extent to which they agreed with a range of statements about 'technology in the world around us' and 'learning technology'.

The attitude questionnaire captured solely quantitative data but the activity evaluation collected both qualitative and quantitative, particularly in gender issues. Both questionnaires were coded such that we could connect up the responses of any one learner and this allowed a rich analysis of gendered responses showing, not least, how powerful the impact of the new technology curriculum had been on developing amongst both boys and girls very positive views about each other and, amongst the girls, a very strong sense of empowerment and self worth. Figure 6 shows examples of the range of ways this data was collected.

Assessing Innovation (2002-2004)

With the publication of the revised English National Curriculum in 2000

(NC2000), a Strategy Group for d&t was established to steer the subject through the following years. The group quickly became concerned about the lack of internal coherence between the 'vision' statement for d&t (as presented in NC2000), and the Programmes of Study and Attainment Target the document also provided. In particular the vision statement encapsulated the importance of creativity, innovation and teamwork whilst the Attainment Target was starkly bereft of any reference to, or recognition of, these factors. In addition, related problems were noted with current GCSE assessments - that GCSE project work had become formulaic and routinised – and that innovative learners were potentially being penalised by comparison with well organised, rule-following learners. For these reasons, the Strategy Group commissioned TERU to develop a system of assessment that would measure and reward creativity and innovation.

From the Activity Evaluation Questionnaire ...

ABOUT GIRLS AND BOYS WORKING TOGETHER

4. Was the partner you worked with today a boy or girl?

boy □ girl □

5. Do you think you worked well together?

very well □ well □ OK □ poor □

6. What are the best things about working with BOYS?

_____

_____

7. What are the best things about working with GIRLS?

_____

_____

From the Attitude Questionnaire ...

14. Girls think technology is difficult   o o o o

18. Technology is only for girls   o o o o

22. Boys and girls should learn about technology o o o o

35. Girls' attitudes to technology are different from those of boys o o o o

Figure 6 The gender explicit data collected from the Activity Evaluation and Attitude Questionnaires

To take on this challenge the team worked closely with both teachers and those developing and monitoring assessment for GCSE (the Qualification and Curriculum Authority and the Awarding Bodies). The project was structured through three overlapping phases: *creating descriptors* to inform the development of an assessment framework for creativity and innovation by analysing existing project work that was identified by the teachers as being either 'pedestrian' or 'innovative'; *creating evidence* by supporting teachers to develop two-day d&t projects aimed at facilitating creativity and innovation; and *creating assessment activities* focused on creativity and assessment, based on the 'unpickled portfolio' approach.

Assessing Innovation: The 'by products' from gathering ephemeral evidence

A resounding feature of the unpickled portfolio approach has been the capturing of evidence that might otherwise have been lost (such as the learner's evaluative thinking) and a 'by product' of this has been the way in which tactics employed to collect evidence have been genuinely supportive to the learner. In the Assessing Innovation project the most interesting and successful example of this came from addressing the problem of capturing evidence of 3D modelling of ideas. From the activities developed in Phase 2 it became apparent that if teachers were creating activities to explicitly support creativity and innovation, they encouraged the learners to engage in generative work early in the activity, often through 3D modeling using quick and accessible materials such as paper and card. This strategy was very productive but the question we faced was "how do we capture the evidence?"

The answer came through developments in digital technology - we structured into the activity (and the test booklet) a periodic taking of a digital photograph of the developing models which were printed and returned to the learners to stick into a growing 'photo storyline' in their response booklets. In doing so we gathered the (erstwhile) ephemeral evidence of the various personas a model had held in the course of its development. This served our purpose very well, but what we hadn't anticipated was that the learners found it a great impetus to their own thinking.

Assessing Innovation: The quirky ways of presenting findings

Having found that we could successfully capture evidence of the development of an idea through digital photographs we experienced the frustration that, although the photo stories allowed us to present the data visually as a set of images, we couldn't show the active growth of the modelling. Once more digital technology came to our aid by providing the facility to 'morph' the still images into a movie, presenting very clearly and powerfully, the evidence of innovation in a dynamic format.

Assessing Innovation: The use of the vernacular in terminology

Once again in this project we found ourselves building shared understandings both with the research team and with those we were working with in the broader d&t community, through the use of the vernacular. The first instance grew out of the exploration of descriptors where, in searching for the opposite ends on an innovation continuum we found ourselves using the words 'wow' and 'yawn'. These terms encapsulated an instant, agreed scale that we went on to use in developing criteria for the 'holistic' mark. Figure 7 shows the statements that characterise the four points on this continuum.

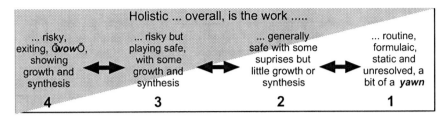

Figure 7 The 'holistic' wow <---> yawn continuum

REFLECTIONS ON THE APPROACHES WE DEVELOPED

The development of d&t prior to the APU survey depended in only a limited way on research - it was led predominantly by practitioners sharing ideas. While in many ways this was very positive, there is a danger that this situation provokes a cyclical, re-inventing-of-wheels approach. Richard Andrews identified this in his introduction to Eggleston's *Teaching and Learning Design and Technology: a guide to recent research and its applications* (Andrews 2000).

Internationally, the gap between research, policy and practice in public life has become a matter of concern. When professional practice - in nursing, education, local governance and other fields - is uninformed by research, it tends to reinvent itself in the light of a range of (often conflicting) principles. Research uninformed by practical considerations tends to be ignored by practitioners, however good it is academically. (Andrews, 2000: ix)

With the APU d&t project came the big opportunity for large scale, empirical research where methodologies were developed specifically to address the research issues identified. From this first project onwards, starting from issues rather than methodologies led us to develop approaches that didn't sit within any one methodological camp, to develop both quantitative and qualitative approaches. During the same twenty-year period, others, both in the UK and elsewhere were identifying research needs in the subject and also expressing concern at the limited way the emerging discipline area was being researched. In identifying how our own work relates to these concerns, certain key issues can be highlighted.

A strong thread of commentary has been developed by technology education academics in the USA, particularly calling for a move beyond the traditions of quantitative methodologies. Zuga (1994) - reviewing research in USA up to the early 1990s, found it to be narrowly and inwardly focused, with an emphasis on quantitative and descriptive research. Her view was that the predominance of this type of research marginalised qualitative and interpretative studies. Also she considered that too much focused on curriculum and that more was needed on technological literacy and 'instructional techniques'. Hoepfl (1997) also made a plea for more qualitative research in technology education that provided answers to significant and deep research questions. She pointed the finger at traditional views maintained in some universities, although she detected a change in attitude.

In the past, graduate students contemplating the use of qualitative inquiry were told that they would have to "sell" the idea to members of their research committees, who would probably view qualitative research as inferior to quantitative research. Fortunately, in most universities that belief has changed, to the point where qualitative research is the paradigm of choice in some schools. In spite of this growing acceptance, new researchers may still encounter difficulties in finding faculty advisors who are skilled in this type of research. (Hoepfl 1997: 61)

Petrina (1998) focused his concerns less on methodology, other than the need for more critical theory, and more on the need for a political and interdisciplinary approach to research, which he found to be largely missing in the technology education literature. In responding to Petrina, Lewis (1999) identified a range of types of research questions that technology education should be addressing - of particular interest in relation to the focus of much work in TERU this included questions relating to technological literacy; technology and creativity; gender in technology classrooms and curriculum change. He also echoed Hoepfl's concern with the need to move to more qualitative approaches to research and pre-figured Roberts opening address to IDATER 2000 in which Roberts (2000) made a strong case for greater involvement of teachers as researchers.

The key to how the field views research priorities in the future will depend on the willingness of researchers to range beyond the traditional positivistic paradigm toward phenomenological and critical modes. In particular, teachers would have to be encouraged to be researchers in their own right, or collaborators in research. (Lewis 1999: 51)

Lewis goes on to refer to Eisner's (1993) view that educational research has room for 'many mansions' and declares that

We in technology education must employ the paradigm that can best answer the questions we wish to have answered. If we stick to tried and true paradigms, the consequence is that certain key kinds of questions will not be asked or answered. (Lewis 1999: 52)

Lewis's plea accords well with our approach in developing an array of methodologies that can now be drawn on by others. These have included qualitative, interpretative approaches and have enabled us to grapple with fundamental questions about capability, learning, teaching and assessment. Within this we have, wherever possible, involved teachers as part of the research – addressing in part the issues raised by Phil Roberts. But reflecting on the above also critiques what we have not done. Have our methodologies contributed to the critical theory that Petrina makes a case for, enabling political, social and cultural agendas in technology education to be taken forward? How do we stand up to the concerns raised by Zuga around insularity? Have we shared our approaches beyond researching d&t, or properly taken account of innovative methodologies?

In truth we (and the majority of those involved in d&t or technology education) have not paid as much attention to these issues as they deserve. The repertoire that is now our legacy has been important in the development of the discipline. But now, new research questions, including those raised above need to be framed - and appropriate methodologies applied to addressing them - whether tried, tested and orthodox, or necessarily pushing at the edge of new and potentially unorthodox approaches. Finally, reflecting on the wisdom of Eisner.

'Because I am a conceptual pluralist, I believe it is important from an epistemological perspective for scholars to have available to them different methods for the study of education. Different methods make different forms of understanding possible. Hence, I am seeking neither a new hegemony nor a new orthodoxy, but rather the expansion of the utensils in our methodological pantry." Eisner, 1993: 54-55

REFERENCES

Andrews, R. (2000), Series editor's introduction in Eggleston, J., *Teaching and learning design and technology: A guide to recent research and its applications*, Continuum, London, UK.

Archer, B., Baynes, K. & Langdon, R. (1979), Design *in general education*, Royal College of Art, London UK.

Assessment of Performance Unit, (1981), *Understanding design and technology* APU/DES

Assessment of Performance Unit, (1983), *Report of the survey of design and technological activities in the school curriculum* National Centre for School Technology, Trent Polytechnic.

Cross, N., Christians, H. & Doorst, K., (1996), *Analysing design activity*, John Wiley & Sons, Chichester, UK.

Dyrenfurth M.J., (1995), *Initial Evaluation Report: RSA PROTEC Technology Education Pilot*, Missouri.

Eggleston, J., (1987), (Ed.) *The best of craft, design and technology: The 20th anniversary volume of studies in design education craft and technology* Trentham Books, Stoke on Trent, UK

Eisner, E. W., (1993), The emergence of new paradigms for educational research. *Art Education*, 46(6).

Hoepfl, M. C., (1997), Choosing qualitative research: A primer for technology education researchers, *Journal of Technology Education*, 9(1).

Johnsey, R., (2000), *Identifying designing and making skills and making cross-curricular links in the primary school*, in Eggleston, J., Teaching and Learning Design and Technology: a guide to recent research and its applications, Continuum, London, UK.

Jones, J. C., (1970), *Design Methods: Seeds of Human Futures*, John Wiley & Sons Ltd., Bath, UK

Kelly, A.V., Kimbell, R., Patterson, V.J., Saxton, J. & Stables, K., (1987), *Design and Technology: A Framework for Assessment*, HMSO London, UK.

Kimbell, R. A., Stables, K., Wheeler, A. D., Wozniak, A. V., Kelly A. V., (1991), *The assessment of performance in design and technology*, Schools Examinations and Assessment Council, HMSO, London, UK.

Kimbell, R., Stables, K. & Green, R., (1994), *Understanding technological approaches: Final project report to ESRC*, TERU, Goldsmiths, London, UK.

Kimbell, R., Stables, K. & Green, R., (1996), *Understanding practice in design and technology* Open University Press, Buckingham, UK.

Kimbell, R. & Stables, K., (1999), South *Africa: Technology education project: An evaluation report to department for international development (DFID)* pp 26 Goldsmiths College, London, UK.

Kimbell, R., Miller, S., Bain, J., Wright, R., Wheeler, T., (2004), *Assessing design innovation: A research and development project for the department for education and skills (DfES) and the qualification and curriculum authority (QCA)*, TERU, Goldsmiths, London, UK.

Lewis, T., 1999, Research in Technology Education— Some Areas of Need, *Journal of Technology Education*, 10(2).

Penfold J., (1988), *Craft, Design and technology: Past, present and future* Trentham Books, Stoke on Trent, UK.

Petrina, S., (1998), The politics of research in technology education: A critical content and discourse analysis of the Journal of Technology Education, Volumes 1-8. *Journal of Technology Education*, 10(1).

Roberts, P., (2000), *Aspects of Research concerning design education*, in (eds) Norman, E. W. L. & Roberts, P., Design and Technology Education Research and Curriculum Development: The emerging international research agenda, Loughborough University, UK.

Stables, K. & Kimbell, R., (2000), *The unpickled portfolio: pioneering performance assessment in design and technology* D&T International Millennium Conference: Learning from Experience: Modelling new futures, DATA, Wellesbourne, UK.

Zuga, K., (1994). *Implementing technology education: A review and synthesis of the research literature.* ERIC Document Reproduction Service No. ED 372 305.

JOHN DAKERS

24. TECHNOLOGY EDUCATION IN SCOTLAND: AN INVESTIGATION OF THE PAST TWENTY YEARS

INTRODUCTION

The evolution of technical education in Scottish schools over the last twenty years, I will argue, follows two contiguous rationales. The first, which has been engineered by policy makers, developed out of a post war curriculum which insisted that the concern of technical education should be the acquisition of a limited set of broadly based mastery skills, designed specifically to correspond with the perceived needs of industry at that time. As the nature of technology has changed over time, however, so too has the thinking behind, and the rationale for, a technical (technological) education. A new technology curriculum has consequently evolved. This incorporates at its heart, the overarching concept of "technological capability" defined as:

> "...understanding appropriate concepts and processes; the ability to apply knowledge and skills by thinking and acting confidently, imaginatively, creatively and with sensitivity; the ability to evaluate technological activities, artifacts and systems critically and constructively' (SCCC, 1996: 7).

Twenty years ago, therefore, it had become apparent to policy makers that radical changes were required to bring the technical curriculum into line with the rapid technological developments occurring at both national and international level.

The second rationale, which has been engineered by teachers, has exactly the same origins as the first. It has, however, essentially failed to evolve at all, and thus represents a technical educational in stasis. This second rationale, which follows the same time continuum as the first is, I will argue, the result of the poorly supported imposition of change through innovation embedded in the former model and the consequent resistance of teachers to this imposed change.

In this paper, I will explore the evolution of the technical curriculum in Scotland over the past twenty years. I will explore the development of policy and its application within the context of the classroom. Though a consideration of the tension that exists between policy and practice, moreover, I will reveal the twin rationales referred to above. But first, I will situate the field.

M.J. de Vries, I. Mottier (eds.), International Handbook of Technology Education, 331-346.

PRE 1984: THE ORIGINS OF TECHNICAL EDUCATION IN SCOTLAND

The industrial revolution regarded technology as a "system of mechanical and industrial arts" (Murphy and Potts, 2003. p3; Volti, 2001). It was during this period therefore that the term became closely associated with systems involving machine technology and the technological processes used in industry. Through this association, the concept of technology became inextricably linked to economic development as the engineering industry expanded. It is likely that the propinquity of technology with industrialisation served to establish the first chair of engineering in a British university; that university being Glasgow in Scotland (Ashby, 1959). Clearly, new techniques were required for the operation of these new industrial technologies, and a plentiful supply of workers, including manual workers, would have to be trained in order to operate and manage this (Dakers, 2005). In a major conference on technical education held in Edinburgh in 1868, this very issue was discussed and the following decision made:

"The time has arrived when it is desirable and necessary in the education of the people that the principals of science (and technology) (sic) should form an important element in the tuition of all classes of the community" (Conference, 1868)

A new industrially oriented world order sought a new 'technical' education which would serve the needs of these new and expanding industries at shop floor level as well as in more "elevated" positions.

Technical education in Scotland therefore has a long pedigree which was, and I will argue still is, considered to be the initial training ground of a future workforce for industry, particularly engineering. As far back as 1890, technical education was defined as "instruction which aims at communicating to the pupils knowledge and facilities which have a direct bearing upon some special occupation, industrial or commercial" (Cowper, 1970: 47 in Paterson, 2003: 90).

Around the same time, a strong movement towards the establishment of "working class" education grew up in Scotland. Funding from the government, and more particularly the trades unions, resulted in the provision of extra mural evening classes, or continuation classes as they were known. The *raison d'etre* behind this egalitarian philosophy was very much an intention to enhance "an intellectual understanding, not just technical dexterity" (Cowper, 1970: 115 in Paterson, 2003: 92). Indeed Heriot Watt College [forerunner to Heriot Watt University in Edinburgh], although offering vocational courses, at the same time made it explicit that it sought to attract students who wished to "...rise above the position of being mere machines performing certain mechanical and routine operations in order to acquire a fair knowledge of the fundamental laws underlying the science to which they owe their livelihood" (Cowper, 1970: 162 in Paterson, 2003: 92).

The post war curriculum in technical education, however, appeared to lose sight of this antecedent philosophy, concentrating instead on a vocational orientation with a continued emphasis on craft skills in subjects such as woodworking, metalworking, and craftwork in plastics and similar materials. Allied to these subjects were skills associated with the construction industry, notably brickwork, painting and decorating, plumbing and home electricity and car mechanics. Technical drawing and building drawing were incorporated to enhance the craft subjects whilst the principles of mechanical and electrical engineering gave a theoretical underpinning to technical subjects (Curriculum Paper 10, 1972). It is in this curriculum paper that technical education is linked most explicitly with the needs of industry - an industry which was, moreover, clearly regarded as being male-oriented.

> *"In support of modern industry we have seen during the last twenty years a substantial expansion of day further education for apprentice craftsmen and technicians and since the passing of the Industrial Training Act in 1964 a considerable expansion of industrial training and retraining for operatives, craftsmen, technicians and technologists. ... Clearly it will be an advantage if schools can produce a pupil with broad creative ability, with a flexible and adaptable attitude to industrial processes, with skills and knowledge which can be developed in several directions, and with a willingness and capability to be retrained several times during his working life"* (SED, 1972: 3). (My emphasis).

Technology education so defined, can therefore be concerned only with the acquisition of practical craft skills specifically related to the perceived needs of industry, and generally concerned with the provision of a manual workforce trained in service to those industries.

The fact that technical teachers from that time were recruited almost exclusively from trades backgrounds in industry (Dakers and Doherty, 2003), may also help to shed some light on the emphasis given in Curriculum Paper 10, to the development of a curriculum which stressed the acquisition of craft skills which were regarded as important in serving the needs of industry.

This instrumental form of technical education retained its 'industrial' orientation up until the last two decades, when it became apparent that the industrial base to which technical education had allied itself was no longer viable in what had become a technologically, rather than industrially mediated world. (Dakers, 2005)

1984: THE COMMITTEE ON TECHNOLOGY

The working party which had been constituted to deliver "Curriculum Paper 10" in 1972, was, apart from a few HMI and head teachers, almost exclusively made up of secondary school technical teachers.

In 1984, however, the constitution of the newly formed 'Committee on Technology' included one head teacher, a depute head teacher, a representative from the Scottish Education Department, a representative from the Scottish Curriculum Development Service, a major industrialist, an advisor from business subjects, a head of a physics department and significantly, only one representative from a school technical education perspective. Interestingly, another important addition was that of an adviser in Home Economics. It seems that policy in respect of the technical curriculum was to be re-defined by a wider representation who regarded technical education now to be much more than the development of industrially related psychomotor skills. This formed part of an even wider movement towards modernisation in which attempts were made to devise a curriculum more suited to the technological age of the late twentieth century.

"The deliberations of the Committee on Technology coincided with the tidal wave of curriculum change...in response to rapid technological developments and to political initiatives...on the introduction of new and more relevant courses" (COS, 1985: (i))

The Committee on Technology insisted that technical education should still be seen to serve the needs of industry. It also recognised, however, that the nature of industry had undergone important change. The hitherto solid "Industrial Revolution" was rapidly being overtaken by a "technological revolution" which was evolving at an exponential rate. Technical education, had to be seen to respond to this phenomenon, and was consequently reconstituted as Technology Education, where technology was defined as being:

"... concerned with the identification of some of the material needs of man (sic) and the endeavour to satisfy those needs of man (sic) and the endeavour to satisfy those needs by the application of science and the use of materials, resources and energy. It is concerned with solving problems where there is no right or wrong answer, only good or bad solutions to a problem. Technological behaviour requires activities that are creative and demanding, where laws and principles of science, the constraints of society and economics are applied to problems to satisfy human needs. Technological behaviour involves approaches and techniques, such as systems analysis, problem identification, decision making, planning, idea communication and solution evaluation, which are more that pure science or craft" (COS, 1985: 3-4).

This represented a paradigm shift in relation to both the content and delivery of technology education. A much broader conception of technology was now evident. Whereas previously, manual skill procurement had been developed through the transmission model, usually by way of demonstration, and the required manual skills had been assessed through the reproduction of prescribed artefacts, or through assignments which had essentially right or wrong answers, this new, broader model saw problem solving as playing a crucially important part in the

334

process. Under this model, there were no "right or wrong answers just good or bad solutions" (COS, 1985: 3). An emphasis was now therefore given to solving "real" problems rather than teacher based problems. The concept of the "design process" entered the field and took on a central role. Technological awareness was now regarded as essential for the formation of an educated democracy. Consideration was also to be given to working co-operatively with Home Economics. Opportunities for doing and learning about technology were to be considered under two headings: Technological activity and Technological awareness and appreciation (COS, 1985).

However, the links with serving the needs of industry still hung on tenaciously at the classroom delivery level, and this had the effect of reinforcing the academic/vocational divide. The distinction between technological activity and technological awareness and appreciation, moreover, together with an assessment system which put more stress on craft activity than it did on technological awareness, enabled teachers who were reluctant, or perhaps more appropriately, unable, to embrace the new technology curriculum, to subvert it back towards the old craft model.

Thus, while policy for technology education was motivated by a need for reform, teachers appeared to be in the business, for various reasons, of eschewing any new initiatives which threatened to move technical education away from the well established vocational "Industrial Arts" model which had served them so well during the post war years.

THE TRANSFORMATION OF TECHNICAL EDUCATION INTO TECHNOLOGY EDUCATION

The technical curriculum was transformed between 1984 and the early 1990's. Woodwork and metalwork were replaced with craft and design; technical or engineering drawing was replaced by graphic communications and engineering science or mechanics, was overtaken by a radically different new subject known as technological studies.

These new subject areas, once more, required a major shift in pedagogy - a movement away from the teacher led expert model, towards a more collaborative, facilitative and child centred approach. This model constituted a major rethinking of pedagogy across all areas of the curriculum. However, this new teaching style was completely antithetical to the style of teaching normally found in technical classrooms.

Support for teachers to help develop these changes varied in quality across different Local Authorities, especially for the very new subject technological studies. Unlike the other subjects, technological studies involved a number of new areas including "Pneumatics, Computer Numeric Control, Computer Aided Drawing, Electronic Systems, Electronic Control and Robotics" (Bain, 1999: 563). Whereas craft and design retained a large element of woodwork and metalwork, and graphic communications retained an element of technical drawing, Technological Studies was almost completely new. This necessitated the

335

implementation of very significant changes in both the content and delivery and the consequent difficulties encountered with the introduction of technological studies in fact, led to a significant downturn in its delivery in Scottish schools (HMI, 1999: 16).

Presentations of technological studies at Standard Grade (the examinations taken at age 16) across Scotland fell from 6,076 in 1994 to 3,649 in 1999. In the same period, however, craft and design increased by over 2,000 (Dakers and Doherty, 2003: 613). The problem in uptake of Technological studies is at its most serious around the West Coast of Scotland where, for example, schools presenting technological studies in Glasgow between 1998 and 2001, dropped by 50% (Dakers, 2000), and almost 90% in 2005. (Glasgow City Council Educational Services).

1987: INITIAL TEACHER EDUCATION IN TECHNOLOGY EDUCATION

As previously stated, prior to 1987, teachers of technology education at secondary school had been recruited from a background in industry and had studied for a Diploma in Technical Education. A large proportion of these teachers, many of whom had been teaching a very prescriptive and craft orientated technical curriculum for some time, found it particularly difficult to deal with the sweeping modernisations that were being implemented in the 1980's (Bain, 1999).

As part of the sweeping reforms of technological education, therefore, the Scottish Education Department decreed that teaching should now be an all-graduate profession. In 1987 the Universities of Glasgow and Edinburgh developed the first four-year degree courses in technology education. The hope was that these courses would help alleviate the worsening situation in technology education, particularly in relation to the delivery of technological studies. As is still evident each year, however, uptake of the subject continues to decline. Current research into Scottish student technology teachers' perceptions about technology education, moreover (Dow, forthcoming), suggests that student teachers have serious anxieties about teaching technological studies. This may be due in part to the fact that there is very limited access to the subject on school placements. There also, however, appears to be some evidence emerging that student teachers regard technology education as being more related to the teaching of practical skills than the teaching of technological awareness. Significantly, there is a perception among student teachers that more is learned about the teaching of technology on school placement than on university courses. The implication of this is that teachers of technology subjects, a significant number of whom still adhere to the old skills procurement model of technology education, will continue to have a strong influence on the mindset of student teachers. Dow's finding resonate strongly with research carried out in America by Hansen (in Hansen and Lovedahl, 2004), who found a dichotomy of opinion between teachers views as to the purpose of technology education. Teachers who considered themselves as teachers of technology education, thought technological awareness and appreciation was the purpose, whereas those who saw their role as teachers of technical subjects saw career preparation as the purpose.

1993: THE INTRODUCTION OF THE 5-14 ENVIRONMENTAL STUDIES CURRICULUM GUIDELINES.

The introduction of the 5-14 Environmental Studies curriculum guidelines heralded a significant change in the provision of technical education in Scotland from the earliest stage of primary to the end of the second year of secondary school. These guidelines incorporated social subjects, science subjects and significantly, for the first time at primary level, technology subjects. These were completely revised and updated in 2000.

The revised guidelines were introduced as a result of pressure from teachers who found the previous guidelines extremely difficult to follow. They were rewritten in conjunction with a primary school pack entitled "Primary Technology in Scottish Schools: Education for Technological Capability". These new study tasks, were the result of a joint project between Learning and Teaching Scotland and the Nuffield Foundation. This model for technology education delivery is supported by a corpus of research over the years. (Murphy, 1999; Barlex, 2000), and seeks to develop technological capability where "children are [seen to be] building a repertoire of design & technology problem-solving strategies whilst engaged in creative activity that makes sense to them and interests them (13). The concept of technological capability has its genesis in the SCCC position paper written in 1996.

1996 TO THE PRESENT: THE SCCC POSITION PAPER ON TECHNOLOGY EDUCATION IN SCOTTISH SCHOOLS

In 1996 the Scottish Consultative Committee on the Curriculum, in association with a wide ranging panel of consultants, (although significantly once again, only one technology teacher representative in the main review), published its seminal position paper on Technology Education in Scottish Schools. This paper outlined the four interconnected aspects of what was, and still is, the underpinning concept which now informs all aspects of technological education in Scotland, known as Technological Capability. This capability is acquired through the realisation of technological perspective, confidence, sensitivity and creativity, and forms the bedrock upon which all aspects of the modern technology curriculum stands.

The rationale for technology Education in this new model:

"...involves learning about the social and physical conditions that influence, or have influenced, the lives of individuals and communities and which shape, or have been shaped by, the actions, artefacts and institutions of successive generations. Acquiring, interpreting and using evidence and information about

the world they [pupils] live in is part of a sequence of discovery and rediscovery for every generation" (LTS, 2000: 3)

Once again it is apparent that the rationale for the technology curriculum has taken an ever more hermeneutic turn. Policy suggests that technology education should have less concern with the development of craft skills and a greater concern with both the interpretation of the made world, and a consideration of the impact of technologies on humans and the environment. Again, however, there is evidence to suggest that practice does not reflect policy. Teachers continue to show a reluctance to abandon the craft based model of technical education. In many Scottish schools evidence clearly indicates that for students in the first two years in secondary schools the curriculum followed is a craft orientated model where artefacts are fabricated on the basis of psychomotor skill development (Dakers, 2003). This continued emphasis on craft, therefore, belies the intention of policy for students to develop a technological capability which seeks to ensure that pupils will

"...be better equipped to live purposefully, productively, confidently and wisely in the world of today and tomorrow if they have been enabled to acquire and deploy a broadly based technological capability" (SCCC, 1996: 4).

THE PRIMARY TECHNOLOGY CURRICULUM.

The concept of technology education in primary schools in Scotland remained elusive until the early nineties. In 1991 primary education in Scotland underwent a systemic change with the introduction and implementation of the new 5-14 National curriculum guidelines programme as mentioned previously. This covered five areas: English, Mathematics, Environmental Studies (including History, Geography, Science and Technology), Expressive Arts (including Physical Education), and Religious and Moral Education. Environmental Studies, which included Technical education, was introduced in 1993. However, whilst teachers generally welcomed a structure to their curriculum and especially the detailed guidance which was offered, there were strong concerns about the ability of primary teachers to cope with the content and delivery of such a broad range of subject specific areas. This was particularly true in the case of the science and technology components (Pickard. 2003).

Prior to the introduction of 5-14 guidelines, the primary curriculum had been much more integrated and consequently holistic in its rationale. The Scottish Education Department's *Primary Education in Scotland (or The Primary Memorandum)* (SED, 1965), on which the primary curriculum was founded, had been considered quite revolutionary in its child-centred approach. The rationale had been grounded in the theory that children should be active in their own learning, that they had a natural curiosity about the world and most importantly, a natural desire to learn (Adams; Paterson. 2003). This move from a curriculum driven to a child-centred approach gave teachers a greater degree of autonomy in the teaching and learning process. This autonomy resulted in ensuring that the location of any form of technology education was the secondary sector where 'technical' education was very much about woodwork, metalwork and technical drawing, subjects which were considered to be beyond the capability of the primary schools to deliver (Dakers and Dow, 2004).

This model prevailed until the 1980's when a major survey into primary education was undertaken by the Scottish Council for Research in Education (SED, 1980). The findings of this survey suggested that, rather than the broad active curriculum proposed in the 1965 policy, in practice a very narrow curriculum had evolved. In particular, primary education was found to be delivering little or no science and technology. It was found, moreover, that contrary to the spirit of the Primary Memorandum, very little discovery learning and very little curricular integration was in fact in evidence (Adams, 2003). Another major concern related to the transfer from the primary to secondary stage where, particularly in relation to technology education:

"Significant weaknesses in primary-secondary liaison were identified with secondary teachers unable to appreciate the nature of work in primary and some primary teachers asking secondary teachers to tell them what to teach in upper primary leading to advice which was ill advised and which has had a restricting effect on the curriculum of the primary school" (Adams, 2003: 370).

The result of these findings was the creation of the 5-14 curriculum guidelines which were presented in a somewhat emollient fashion in the label 'guidelines'. This had the effect of concealing the intent of government to deliver a more centralised and prescriptive curriculum which would clear the way for the introduction of National testing. Although this emphasis on testing met with strong resistance nationally and was consequently never fully implemented (Paterson, 2003), there continues to be, notwithstanding, a strong emphasis on attainment at all stages of the curriculum. Each subject area, including technical, has a grading structure for reporting which is designed to ensure coherence, continuity and progression both within and between primary and secondary sectors. In reality, only in literacy and numeracy is this achieved. This emphasis (or lack of, in the case of technical) tends to drive the curriculum and has to a large extent, been responsible for the polarisation of the primary curriculum into separate subject domains, each with its own assessment arrangements. The effect of this has been to ensure that technical education, which has always been a controversial subject within primary schools, is perceived as a problematic subject area for primary teachers to deliver. This is further compounded by primary teachers' perceptions and confidence in relation to teaching the subject.

Recent research into primary teachers confidence in the delivery of technology education in Scotland (Dakers; Dakers and Dow, 2001; Dakers and Dow, 2004), for example, revealed some serious problems in this respect. A major problem lay in establishing a precise identity for technology education. This appears to elude most primary school teachers, and it might be argued, secondary school teachers also. Research carried out by Dakers and Dow (2001; 2004) found, for example, that primary teachers, and significantly, secondary teachers, were not familiar with the SCCC (1996) Position Paper which has been shown to form the bedrock of technology education in Scotland. Indeed most were unaware of its existence. There was, moreover, uncertainty on the part of primary teachers regarding the precise content of the secondary technology curriculum, with most being unable to even make a clear distinction between science and technology. Most had had no experience of technology education, either in their initial teacher education or in subsequent continued professional development. This reinforced findings by Eggleston, who further suggests that this is not confined to teachers, but that bewilderment over technological education is prevalent among parents, employers and the public at large. (Eggleston, 1994: 20).

This is not altogether surprising. As has been demonstrated, the rationale for technology education has changed considerably over the last twenty years. Traditionally it was predominantly craft based, non academic subject for boys only, prescriptive in its delivery, involved learning to operate industrial type machines, learning engineering based technical drawing and for the more able, mechanics. Girls on the other hand were taught domestic science. Boys were effectively being trained towards trades while girls were trained in the art of homemaking.

The ghost of this perception has faded but has not entirely disappeared. It is axiomatic that, for a significant proportion of both primary teachers, and secondary teachers of the subject, the old model still applies. The idea of the design and creativity paradigm, incorporating at its centre, the notion of technological capability, is not evident to them. This may go some way towards explaining the apparent fears, or at least anxieties, that many primary school teachers express towards this area of the curriculum. (Dakers, 2001)

If the 5 - 14 technology curriculum, incorporating the philosophy of "Technology Education in Scottish Schools" (HMI, 1999), which centres around the concept of technological capability, is to be delivered effectively, then primary teachers will require to undertake development in the pedagogical issues relating to technological capability. An insight into the aims and objectives, or philosophy of technology education and its delivery, is suggested as a requirement, preceding technological subject knowledge and methodology.

TRANSITION FROM PRIMARY TO SECONDARY

The problem of achieving curricular continuity for pupils in the transition from the primary to secondary sector is one which has exercised the minds of both educationalists and policy makers for many years. Although as early as 1931, the Hadow Report on Primary education clearly highlighted the importance of continuity within the education system, the emphasis of subsequent reports on the same theme (Plowden, 1967; Bullock, 1975) and the existence of a body of literature, including 5-14, all serve to emphasise the problems of transition (Dakers and Dow, 2004).

Several factors affecting the success of transition from primary to secondary school in relation to curricular continuity have traditionally been identified. These include: the existence of effective liaison procedures; a knowledge and understanding on the part of both sectors about the respective courses taught, programmes of work and teaching methods adopted; a willingness on the part of secondary teachers to value the work done in primary schools and to trust the primary teachers' judgements in terms of assessment, along with a willingness to use the information to provide a starting point appropriate for each individual pupil (Nicholls and Gardner, 1999). Secondary teachers must also have commitment to a curriculum which builds upon the knowledge, understanding and skills appropriate to their subject which pupils have already acquired.

Whilst these factors are clearly important in all areas of the curriculum, it is perhaps in the area of the Scottish technical curriculum that the least progress in affecting a successful transition has been made.

In terms of continuity, coherence and progression, the report "Achieving Success" (HMIa, 1997) which reviewed the provision in S1 and S2 in Scottish secondary schools identified a particular problem with those areas which were regarded as presenting particular challenges in relation to course design. In the area of technical education in particular, the ways in which the course had developed in secondary schools since its introduction in 1965 had resulted in difficulties in establishing continuity between the primary and secondary sectors. This was an issue which clearly needed to be addressed.

At secondary level, there were further problems. The third "Standards and Quality in Scottish Schools Report (HMIb, 1997) identified important weaknesses and unsatisfactory attainment levels in technology in over 65% of Scottish secondary schools. Clearly, despite the introduction of curricular guidelines, the problems associated with curricular discontinuity between the sectors remains an issue (Dakers and Dow, 2004).

In March 2002 a seminar was held on technology education in Scotland. A conclusion which arose from this was that the greatest and most urgent need in technology education was for support and guidance within the S1/S2 curriculum at secondary level (The first two years at secondary). It was also concluded that a stronger emphasis should be given to creativity and that stronger links with 'education for enterprise' should be established. The result of this initiative was the formation, in 2004, of the Technology Education and Enterprise in Scotland (TEES) project. This aimed primarily at the S1/S2 curriculum, although it also considers aspects relating to the transition from primary to secondary school. The rationale is to encourage pupils' development of knowledge, skills and attitudes in the context of technology and enterprise. Pupils will be expected to engage by learning through, learning about, and learning for enterprise education. The work builds on the success of the "Primary Technology in Scottish Schools" pack mentioned previously.

THE SECONDARY TECHNOLOGY CURRICULUM

The secondary technology curriculum has seen some major changes since 1984. The introduction of the 5-14 Environmental Studies course guidelines, which incorporate technology education, was intended to forge stronger links between the two sectors, as well as offering a more holistic technology education with an emphasis on technological capability. Thus, the first two years (age 12 to 14) of secondary schooling under this system requires that all children encounter technology education in which the single desired outcome listed, is that of developing technological capability (LTS, 2000). However, as reported by Her Majesty's Inspectorate (HMI, 1999), the secondary sector was seen, yet again, to continue to deliver a craft based curriculum, based upon a 'fresh start' approach at entry level. The rationale for this approach, as given by secondary technology teachers, was that they did not trust the work their primary colleagues were able to deliver in respect of technology education, and they needed to start developing the skills required for the Standard Grade examinations which would follow in four years time. (Dakers and Dow, 2001)

The Standard Grades follow a two year cycle (age 15 to 16) and follow on directly from the 5-14 programme. They supersede the antecedent 'ordinary grade' courses set in the early eighties, where the subject area of technical drawing evolved into graphic communication, integrated craft work became craft and design and engineering science or mechanics became technological studies.

In 1992 the Howie report on the upper level of secondary was published. This included a full analysis of the Scottish education system as it applies to the post sixteen age band. This report precipitated a radical overhaul of the higher school provision. The 'Higher Still Development Unit' was formed and they undertook many wide ranging consultations involving schools, colleges and employers. The result of these consultations was the introduction of a new set of courses for the upper secondary stages which were designed to be more inclusive and cater for all abilities.

The aim of the Higher Still framework was to make provision for groups of pupils who were not catered for by the former Scottish Higher examination system which had, what was considered to be a very narrow range of subjects on offer. The intention was to establish a coherent post-16 curriculum that provided routes for progression (Dakers and Doherty, 2003). Moreover, a new structure was developed whereby different entry levels would accommodate a much wider range of pupils. The levels ranged from 'Access' levels which were very basic courses, through Intermediate 1, then Intermediate 2, Higher and culminated in Advanced Higher. Students could enter at a level which best served their needs. Courses offered in technology education followed on from the Standard Grade subjects.

Since the start of the consultation process in 1996 further developments have occurred which have a direct bearing on the provision of technology education. The last few years has witnessed some Local Education Authorities replacing Standard Grade courses for Intermediate courses. The rationale for this is that they are considered to be a more modern equivalent, are thought to articulate more closely with the 5-14 programme, and allow students to enter at levels more suited to their ability from the earlier age of 14.

The subject of Craft and Design was considered to be out dated and the new subject "Product Design" was introduced in 2004 to replace it. This course is offered at Intermediate 2, Higher and Advanced higher and is designed to

"... help develop creative, flexible learners who are able to work autonomously, to achieve good quality, feasible proposals or outcomes through active experiences of product design. At its heart is creativity. The Course develops an ability to apply skills and knowledge in different situations — attributes which are becoming more and more valuable to individuals and organisations" (SQA, 2004: 4).

This course has much less emphasis on practical craftwork and has, as stated above, a very strong emphasis on the development of creativity. This has, however, caused a great deal of debate amongst the teaching fraternity. A very strong contingent of technology teachers are opposed to the lack of craft skills in this new course. (Evidenced from electronic technology education smart group discussion forums related to Higher Still development)

Another significant development for technology education arising out of the consultation process was the development of a new subject called Practical Craft Skills. The consultation, which included input from Further Education colleges and industry, and particularly technology teachers, revealed a need for a subject area which catered for students who, it was argued, might struggle with what was considered to be the more academic processes involved in design.

"This course will contribute to the knowledge, understanding and practical experience of candidates whose aspirations and abilities are towards practical work, or who are considering a career in an industry that involves practical activity in any capacity" (SQA, 1999: 5).

1999: THE INTRODUCTION OF PRACTICAL CRAFT SKILLS

Practical Craft Skills was introduced into the Scottish curriculum in 1999 at Intermediate 1 and Intermediate 2 level.

Practical Craft Skills is offered as part of the technology curriculum and currently, covers two areas; Woodworking Skills and Engineering Skills. It is important to establish at this point that the pedagogy underpinning the teaching of Practical Craft Skills has accommodated a quantum shift back to the pre 1984 model.

"There is no opportunity for proactive problem solving, as all decisions about artefact, dimensions, order of processes, and to a large extent materials are made for the pupils. Decision making is kept to an absolute minimum and

343

problem solving seems none existent at this particular level. The learning process is hierarchical, with the process of manufacture broken down into small, manageable steps" (Dow, 2005: In press).

Practical Craft Skills is perceived as filling a niche market for disaffected pupils, along with pupils who are regarded as less academically able; the children who would perhaps have left school in the past without any Standard Grade qualifications. A substantial number of technology teachers in Scotland feel that children are not able to deal with design, (perceived as being the academic element of Craft and Design), and are, as a consequence, opting for Practical Craft Skills (Dakers, 2003).

CONCLUSIONS

The past twenty years have seen major curriculum reforms in technology education at policy level. However, the resistance of teachers to the adoption of these changes remains and has remained constant over the years. Thus the two contiguous rationales remain. The continuation of a pedagogy that is founded upon behaviouristic ideologies, coupled with the determination of a significant proportion of teachers who doggedly persist with a craft skill based curriculum, and who refuse to engage with the concept of technological capability, seems set to continue to determine the shape of the technology education curriculum in Scottish schools.

In addition to this there are indications at post 5-14 level, that policy may be reverting to a more firmly entrenched industrial model. The Scottish Executive, for example, has given support to the recent introduction of "modern apprenticeships" in which sixteen year old school students are offered introductory apprenticeships in various trades. In a drive towards widening choice, moreover, the Scottish Executive is currently encouraging Further Education colleges to offer subjects which schools are unable to resource. These may in the future include courses in car mechanics and other engineering related skills which colleges are in a better placed to provide.

As long as Technology Education within the Scottish school curriculum persists in resisting the adoption of modern policy reforms, and continues to predominantly align itself with the notion that its purpose is the provision of a workforce suited to industries needs, it is likely, therefore to wither on the vine.

If on the other hand, it is to be recognized that design, innovation and creativity, realised through the development of technological capability, constitute the Technology Education bulwark, then the vocational paradigm must be removed from the citadel and the true purpose of Technology Education in a modern democracy restored. That purpose must be to help the formation of 'creative' citizens in a technologically mediated world by introducing them to a Technology Education environment which assesses, develops and encourages the essence of the child's creativity rather than the product of the child's labour. This will require a strong lead and adequate support from policy makers, more so than has previously been the case.

Dewey argued a convincing case for this over one hundred years ago.

"Its [technology education] right development will do more to make public education truly democratic than any other agency now under consideration. Its wrong treatment will as surely accentuate all undemocratic tendencies in our present situation, by fostering and strengthening class divisions in school and out...Those who believe the continued existence of what they are pleased to call the 'lower classes' or the 'labouring classes' would naturally rejoice to have schools in which these 'classes' would be segregated. And some employers of labour would doubtless rejoice to have schools, supported by public taxation, supply them with additional food for their mills...[Everyone else] should be united against every proposition, in whatever form advanced, to separate training of employees from training for citizenship, training of intelligence and character from training for narrow, industry efficiency" (Dewey in Apple and Beane, 1999. p50)

Perhaps it is finally time to listen.

REFERENCES

Adams, F. R. (2003). 5-14: *Origins, development and implementation.* In: (Eds.) T.G.K. Bryce and W.M. Humes. (2003). Scottish Education: Second Edition; Post Devolution. Edinburgh University Press. Edinburgh. 369-379.

Apple, M. W., Bean, J. A. (1999). *Democratic schools: Lessons from the chalk face.* Open University Press. Buckingham.

Ashby, E. (1959). *Technology and the academics:* An essay on universities and the scientific revolution. Macmillan & Co Ltd. London.

Bain, M. (1999). Technology education. In: (Eds.) T.G.K. Bryce and W.M. Humes. (1999). *Scottish Education: Second Edition.* Edinburgh University Press. Edinburgh. 562-567.

Barlex, D. (2000). Resources for technology education in Scottish primary schools. *Journal of Design and Technology Education,* 5(1), 45-46.

Bullock Report. (1975). *A language for life.* London. HMSO.

Conference. (1868). *Conference on technical education held at Edinburgh,* Friday, 20th March, 1868. Neil and Company, Edinburgh. (Publication held in University of Glasgow Special Collection, BG57c.17).

COS. (1985). *The place of technology in the secondary curriculum.* Final report of the CCCs Committee on Technology. Scottish Consultative Committee on the Curriculum. Dundee.

Dakers, J. (2000). Is technology in England different from technology in Scotland? In: (Ed.) Kimbell, R., *Design and Technology International Millennium* Conference Proceedings. Design and Technology Association. Warwickshire. pp 42-46.

Dakers, J. (2001). Primary teachers confidence in delivering technology education. In: (Eds) Benson, C., Martin, M., Till, W., *Third International Primary Design and Technology Conference Proceedings.* Birmingham. CRIPT. pp 50-54.

Dakers, J., Doherty, R. (2003). Technology education. In: (Eds.) T.G.K. Bryce and W.M. Humes. (2003). *Scottish Education: Second Edition*; Post Devolution. Edinburgh University Press. Edinburgh. 611-616.

Dakers, J., Dow, W. (2001). Attitudes of secondary teachers of technical subjects and home economics towards curricular continuity at the transition between primary 7 (11 years) and senior 1 (12 years). In: (Eds) Benson, C., Martin, M., Till, W., *Third International Primary Design and Technology Conference Proceedings*. Birmingham. CRIPT. pp 46-49.

Dakers, J. (2003*)* The introduction of practical craft skills into the Scottish technology curriculum: A new beginning or the beginning of the end. In: (Eds.) Norman, E. W. L., Spendlove, D. *DATA International Research and UK Education Conference Book*. pp 23-27.

Dakers, J. (2005). Technology education as solo activity or socially constructed learning. *International Journal of Technology and Design Education*. 15. pp 73-89.

Dakers, J., Dow. W. (2004). The problem with transition in technology education: A Scottish perspective. *The Journal of Design and Technology Education*. V9. N2. Summer 2004. pp 116-124.

Dow, W. (2005). Developing inclusive communities of learners in technology education: Practical craft skills – Facilitator or Hindrance. *International Journal of Technology and Design Education*. 15. pp 5-17.

Eggleston, J. (1994). What is design and technology education. In (Ed) Frank Banks. (1994) *Teaching technology*. Routledge. London.

Hansen, J. W., Lovedahl, G. G. (2004). Developing technology teachers: Questioning the industrial tool use model. *Journal of Technology Education* 15:2.
http://scholar.lib.vt.edu/ejournals/JTE/v15n2/hansen.html (accessed 22 February, 2005).

HMI. (1997a). *Achieving success*. A Report of the Review of Provisions in S1/S2 by HM Inspectors of Schools. SOED. Edinburgh.

HMI. (1997b). *Standards and quality in Scottish schools*. SOED. Edinburgh.

HMI. (1999). *Effective learning and teaching in Scottish secondary schools*: Technical Education. A report by HM Inspectors of Schools. Scottish Executive Education Department. Edinburgh.

LTS. (2000). *Environmental studies: Society, science and technology*. 5-14 National Guidelines. Learning and Teaching Scotland. Dundee.
www.sqa.org.uk (accessed 22 February 2005)

Murphy, A., Potts, J. (2003). *Culture and technology*. Palgrave MacMillan. New York.

Murphy, P. (1999). Evaluation of the Nuffield approach to primary design & technology
By Patricia Murphy in *Primary solutions in design & technology teacher's handbook*
David Barlex ISBN 1 898788 54 5 Nuffield Foundation & DATA 1999

Nicholls, G., Gardner, J. (1999). *Pupils in transition*. Routlege. London.

Paterson, L. (2003). Scottish education in the twentieth century. Edinburgh University Press. Edinburgh.

Patterson, L. (2003). *Scottish education in the twentieth century*. Edinburgh University Press. Edinburgh.

Pickard, W. (2003). The history of scottish education, 1980 to the present day. In: (Eds.) T.G.K. Bryce and W.M. Humes. (2003). *Scottish Education: Second Edition; Post Devolution*. Edinburgh University Press. Edinburgh. 229-238.

Plowden Report. (1967). *Children and their primary schools*. London. HMSO.

SCCC. (1996). *Technology education in Scottish schools*. A Statement of Position from Scottish CCC. Scottish Consultative Council on the Curriculum. Dundee.

SED. (1972). Curriculum Paper 10. *Technical education in secondary schools*. HMSO. Edinburgh.

SED. (1965). *Primary Education in Scotland*. Edinburgh. HMSO.

SED. (1980). *Learning and teaching in primary 4 and primary 7*. Edinburgh. Scottish Education Department

SQA. (2004). *Product design*: Intermediate 2. Scottish Qualifications Authority.
www.sqa.org.uk (accessed 22 February 2005)

SQA. (1999). *Woodworking skills: Intermediate 1*. Third Edition – published December 1999. www.sqa.org.uk (accessed 22 February 2005)

Volti, R. (2001) (Fourth Edition). *Society and technological change*. Worth Publishers. New York.

ROBERT A. DOHERTY AND BRIAN CANAVAN

25. MAPPING REFORM IN SCOTLAND'S TECHNOLOGY EDUCATION CURRICULUM: CHANGE AND CURRICULUM POLICY IN THE COMPULSORY SECTOR

In this paper we attempt to critically explore the changing technology education curriculum of Scotland's compulsory sector in the preceding twenty years. The first section of the paper sets out a framework for analysing such change drawing on the insights of policy studies. This analytical frame is developed with respect to such dimensions as historical antecedents, sociological perspectives, structural contexts and institutional and group actors. It also attempts to identify useful markers in analysing change within the technology education curriculum. The paper has a focus on 'technical education' as the main provider, in the Scottish context, of courses within the secondary technology curriculum. The paper gives a broad picture of what has changed, and using the framework above, seeks to examine the drivers and agents of change over this period. The final section of the paper sets out a critical appraisal of the status of technology education in Scotland's school curriculum and makes an attempt to look toward its future. In looking to the near and medium term future the paper considers tensions, opportunities and threats to technology education as it develops through the opening decade of the 21st century.

INTRODUCTION

The compulsory sector of Scottish education has, over the past twenty years, witnessed a process of curriculum drafting that has resulted in the establishment of a framework that covers the 3-18 age range. Within this framework, the sector has adopted a 'capability' stance in attempting to articulate the place of technology education in its curricular structures. Across all ages and stages, technology education has as its declared goal the development of technological capability defined in terms of: "...understanding appropriate concepts and processes; the ability to apply knowledge and skills by thinking and acting confidently, imaginatively, creatively and with sensitivity; the ability to evaluate technological activities, artefacts and systems critically and constructively" (SCCC, 1996).

In this paper we attempt to critically explore the changing technology education curriculum of Scotland's compulsory sector in the preceding twenty years. In using the term 'curriculum' we assume not just the content of official syllabuses of instructional subject matter, but embrace approaches to assessment, pedagogy and

M.J. de Vries, I. Mottier (eds.), International Handbook of Technology Education, 347–375.

organisation. We must also differentiate our exploration of technology education through the evolution of technical education, formerly technical subjects, from other aspects of technology education provided for within the curricular designs of Scotland's compulsory sector. Technical education can credibly claim to be the main contributor to courses that directly aim to produce technological capability. Historically, technical education in Scotland developed a continuum of knowledge, understanding and skills that could be described as fitting entirely within what has come to be defined as technology education. This range of learning both predates the introduction of technology as a principle of curriculum organisation and has, in turn, been shaped by its introduction.

SCOTLAND'S OFFICIAL CURRICULA

Technology education is more than technical education, but technical education is the major contributor, at the secondary level, of courses that directly seek to produce technological capability. It could be argued, in the Scottish context, that technical education is more than technology education with its inclusion of creative, aesthetic and social dimensions. This paper, therefore, focuses mainly on change in relation to technical education, but acknowledges the contribution made by other courses. At present, technology education is explicitly included in each of Scotland's curricular frameworks that together form a programme of learning covering the 3-18 age band.

PRESCHOOL

Curriculum guidelines for pre-school children published in 1999, (*A Curriculum Framework for Children 3-5* SCCC, 1999) explicitly included technology education:

> *"The children's environment is one in which technology is important in their everyday lives. As children use blocks, put on a warm jumper, look through a magnifying glass, clamber on to a climbing frame, use a computer or travel by train, they become aware of the everyday uses of technology in the home, in transport, in communication and in leisure."* (SCCC, 1999 :23)

In developing their knowledge and understanding of the world children should:

- *ask questions, experiment, design and make, and solve problems*
- *recognise patterns, shapes and colours in the world around them*
- *sort and categorise things into groups*
- *understand some properties of materials, for example soft/hard, smooth/*
- *become aware of everyday uses of technology and use these appropriately, clothing, fridge, bicycle.* (SCCC, 1999 :24)

THE 5-14 CURRICULUM

Following a period of reform in the late 1980's, technology education is an official dimension of the curriculum for all pupils in primary education and in the first two years of secondary. At present there are two main 'attainment outcomes' for technology education contained within the 5-14 curriculum; Knowledge and Understanding and Skills in Designing and Making, there is a third 'permeating' outcome; Developing Informed Attitudes. The present guidelines locate technology education within the 'Environmental Studies' (see Figure 1) aspect of the structure of the curriculum, along with science and social subjects.

Technology is a distinct form of creative activity where people interact with their environment to bring about change in response to needs, wants and opportunities. Technology is not new: it has always been profoundly influential in all human societies and impinges strongly on human relationships and on many aspects of social and economic development - locally, nationally and globally. It is an intrinsic part of all cultures, and reflects and shapes the values and beliefs of the wider cultural context - past, present and future. A broad, balanced and coherent experience of technology is an essential part of the curriculum of all pupils 5-14 and beyond. Pupils will be better equipped to live purposefully, productively, confidently and wisely if they have been enabled to acquire and deploy a broadly based technological capability. (L.T.S, 2000:5.16)

THE SECONDARY CURRICULUM

Scotland's secondary curriculum is a subject based curriculum. It is constructed around a modal arrangement that corresponds to a schema for the classification of knowledge developed by the philosopher P.H. Hirst. Hirst argued that forms of knowledge are, "complex ways of understanding knowledge which man has achieved" (Hirst,1965:122). Curricular modes have proved to be a very durable conceptualisation of Scotland's subject centred secondary curriculum, surviving a number of curricular reviews and continuing to form the framework for the middle and upper school curriculum. Subjects and courses are grouped under eight curricular modes (see Figure 1). Within this framework, pupils should be able to negotiate individual curricula that respect curricular principles of breadth, balance, coherence, progression, continuity, and elements of compulsion (see Table 1). An element of technology education is ensured, under this arrangement, by pupils being required to study a course under the mode, Technological Activities and Applications, or a combination of other courses with an auditable technological content.

Technological Activities and Applications, and Creative and Aesthetic Activities, are the two modes under which students can opt to study technical education courses. At present technical departments can choose to offer up to four courses, across two different modes, allowing pupils to study up to two technical subjects (within the curricular arrangements of a minority of schools, pupils can study three subjects) as part of their middle secondary curriculum (see table 2 for the relation of Intermediate and Standard Grade):

Technological Activities and Applications
- Standard Grade or Intermediate Technological Studies
- Standard Grade Craft and Design
- Standard Grade Graphic Communication
- Intermediate Practical Craft Skills

Creative and Aesthetic Activities
- Standard Grade Craft and Design
- Standard Grade Graphic Communication
- Intermediate Practical Craft Skills

POST-16 PROVISION

The same general modal arrangement that governs the middle secondary is applied (albeit, with more flexibility) to the curricula that are negotiated by individual pupils post-16. Under the same curricular modes as the middle years, technology education is present in the form of a range of courses leading to a national qualification (see Table 3).

Higher Grade is aimed particularly at students who have passed subjects at Standard Grade credit level, or who have successfully completed a subject at Intermediate 2. Highers are the qualifications normally needed for entry into university or college to study for degrees and Higher National courses (HNCs and HNDs). Advanced Highers are aimed particularly at students who have passed Highers and are usually taken in sixth year at school. They extend the skills and knowledge gained at Higher and can allow direct entry into the second year of some degree programmes. Technical departments can offer a range of post-16 courses including, Higher and Advanced Highers in Product Design, Graphic Communication and Technological Studies. In addition, technical departments provide a range of Intermediate courses at post-16 including a new course; Practical Craft Skills.

Recent developments in the Scottish system has seen effort expended on developing a coherent system of post compulsory education, and training, embracing the final two years of secondary education, further education and higher education (See Table 2). One key aspect of this initiative is the promotion of a Scottish Credit and Qualifications Framework. This framework seeks to promote a more coherent and flexible system for the awarding of qualifications and permitting progression across different sectors of learning. Technical and technology education would seem to be well placed in this climate with obvious links to vocational and further education.

Mode Minimum time over 2 years

Language and Communication	360
Mathematical Studies and Applications	200
Scientific Studies and Applications	160
Social and Environmental Studies	160
Technological Activities and Applications	**80**
Creative and Aesthetic Activities	**80**
Physical Education	80
Religious and Moral Education	80

Core 1200 hours

Table 1: Obligatory time allocations for each Mode in the 14-16 Curriculum.

Scottish Credit and Qualifications Framework

SCQF level	Schools	Schools and colleges	Colleges and universities	Workplace (Scottish Vocational Qualifications)
12			Doctorate	
11			Masters degree	SVQ 5
10			Honours degree	
9			Ordinary degree	
8			HND/Diploma of Higher Education	SVQ 4
7		Advanced Higher	HNC/Certificate of Higher Education	
6		Higher		SVQ 3
5	Standard Grade — Credit	Intermediate 2		SVQ 2
4	Standard Grade — General	Intermediate 1		SVQ 1
3	Standard Grade — Foundation	Access 3		
2		Access 2		
1		Access 1		

Table 2: The Scottish Credit and Qualifications Framework (SCQF) has been developed to help students, employers and the general public understand the full range and equivalences of Scottish qualifications.

351

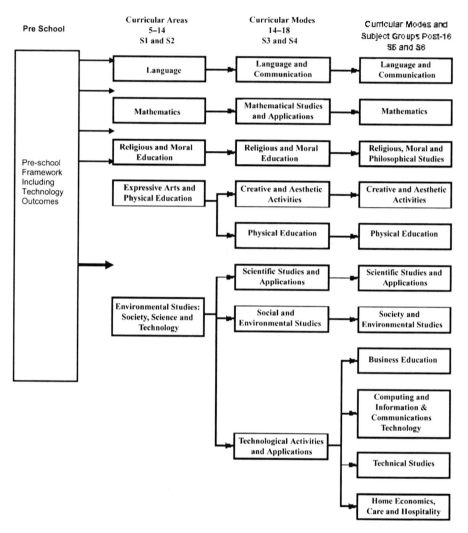

Figure 1: Diagram of Scotland's Curriculum Areas and Modes, Showing Progression within Technology Education from 5-18.

Standard Grades	National Courses/Units
	Advanced Higher
	Higher
Standard Grade — Credit	Intermediate 2
Standard Grade — General	Intermediate 1
Standard Grade — Foundation	Access 3
	Access 2
	Access 1

The 'New' National Qualifications, introduced from 1999.

Table 3: National Courses in the Post-16 Curriculum

SUBJECT	Technical Education: Standard Grade								
	1995	1996	1997	1998	1999	2000	2001	2002	2003
Craft and Design	12578	13413	13992	13613	13783	14032	15148	15219	15029
Graphic Communication	6670	7118	7543	7319	7860	7796	8780	9589	9944
Technological Studies	5978	5258	4897	4282	3649	3211	2739	2659	2244

SUBJECT	Technical Education: Higher (post 16)								
	1995	1996	1997	1998	1999	2000	2001	2002	2003
Craft and Design	2102	2428	2857	3010	3065	2593	2519	2606	2478
Graphic Communication	1888	2094	2290	2418	2423	2522	2808	3006	3071
Technological Studies	1146	1161	1106	951	964	847	1024	957	993

Table 4: Trends in presentations for National Examinations in Technical Subjects

SUBJECT	Entries by Gender at Standard Grade (Middle Secondary)				
	1999 Total	% Male	2003 Total	%Male	%Female
Craft and Design	10898	79	11426	76	24
Graphic Communication	5620	72	6854	69	31
Technological Studies	3370	92	2096	93	7

Table 5: Illustrative Statistics of Gender Balance in Middle Secondary Technical Subjects

FRAMEWORK

In looking to examine and develop a critical account of change, we begin by setting out a framework for analysing change, drawing mainly on the insights of policy studies. This analytical frame is developed with sensitivity to such dimensions as historical antecedents, sociological perspectives, structural contexts and institutional and group actors. Using this approach we try to identify useful markers that indicate change within Scotland's technical and technology education curriculum. This approach is underscored by a conception of change as contested and mediated through a political economy characterised by groups of actors interacting in patterns of hierarchically ordered relationships, differentiated by asymmetries of influence, intellectual climate and policy ambitions.

Exploring an area of activity, such as change in technology education, and looking to do more than catalogue, report or identify stages of evolution requires a perspective that provides a critical purchase. One dimension that recommends itself for inclusion in such an interrogatory frame is that of 'deep theories', or attempts to uncover the unexamined assumptions that have been assembled in marking off the object of our analysis, in this instance, technology education. The idea of 'hegemony', from the work of the Marxist theorist Antonio Gramcsi, is a central notion in his model of power. For Gramcsi (1971), the exercise of power by the ruling class was at its most pervasive in their domination of culture, their shaping of the very subjectivity of the subjugated to the extent that their subjugation is seen as unproblematic, as a natural relation of the very fabric of the social order. Another example is Foucault's (1970) notion of power/knowledge, exemplified in the application of disciplines as discursive structures whose power acts on the subject, regulating social life through the process of 'normalisation'. Or perhaps, in a less universal example of such theorisation, Bowles and Gintis' (1976) idea of the hidden curriculum. According to Bowles and Gintis, what children learn from the hidden curriculum is the lessons required by industrial capitalism. This is not in the form of the subject matter of the formal curriculum, but through the very experience of schooling, its structures, hierarchies and organisational form producing subservient workers motivated by external rewards, the fragmented subject curriculum corresponding to the subdivision of labour within Fordist production.

What we think of as technology education, its content, its limits, its central concepts, constructions, contrasts and oppositions have been created in a process that has depended on a range of assumptions, rationalities and forms of knowledge. A certain consciousness disposes us to work within the limits of what appears as the unproblematic and natural boundaries that establish the landscape we understand as technology education. In terms of a model of curricular change and evolution, this is perhaps the most difficult dimension to integrate, operating, as it does, at a submerged level, supplying the discursive, rational, logical climate that shapes and forms practice in technology education.

"Education has the characteristics it does because of the goals pursued by those who control it ... change occurs because new goals are pursued by those who have power to modify education's previous structural form, definition of instruction and relationship with society...education is fundamentally about what people have wanted of it and have been able to do to it" (Archer, 1984:p1-3).

Archer's idea of doing something to education by 'those' who can, informs our approach to change in technology education. Our analytical framework sits counter to a rationalist model that assumes the continual progress of a modernising project of technology education. It is predicated on a conception of curricular change as the outcome of struggles, at different levels, to assert an authoritative definition of technology education and to control the practices that represent its enactment. Change is also restrained by what has gone before; each layer of curricular development both builds on, and is constrained by an accumulation of curriculum history.

The form of technology and technical education present in Scotland's official and observable curricula is a result of its historical evolution through the national processes of educational policy development. In attempting to chart its present form it would seem appropriate to turn our attention to the policy making processes surrounding technology education. Within the scope of this paper we endeavour to outline something of the structures and the stakeholders who exercise control, influence and hold legal authority within the Scottish system and offer some initial comment on present arrangements. In conceptualising the policy process we make use of the insightful framework developed by Bowe, Ball and Gold (1992). Bowe and his colleagues suggest three contexts for policy production, organising the contexts in terms of: influence, policy text production and practice.

The context of influence is the main source of initiation in relation to policy making or change. What is crucial here is to appreciate the informal networks around members of the government and senior civil servants holding different areas of policy within their portfolio. It is in this socially mediated world of access, contact, and involvement that actors endeavour to promote their projects and agendas. This is a key area of policymaking; it is here that struggles over meaning and the promotion of ideas take place. Fundamentally, conceptions of the aims and nature of the education system are shaped within this context giving birth to new and evolving discourses of education.

The context of policy text production contextualises a second level of analysis. Policy texts embody policy. These may include; official documents, speeches, public engagements, statements, commentaries and guides, exemplar material, videos, CD-ROMs and websites. This context also contains a significant degree of positioning around meaning and influence within the process of publication and its dissemination. This is the level of making new thinking about education operational, creating an implemental form. The context of practice tries to capture something of the complexity and messy reality of policy implementation. Policy texts are open to 'interpretations' and as such, may be susceptible to diversion, subversion and resistance.

The mapping of national policy to group and institutional actors in the decision making process is important in understanding the present form of technology education. More importantly it also serves to locate sources of new thinking, innovation and change as well as the sites of conflict and a whole array of priorities and vested interests belonging to established stakeholder groups. It is important to note that each context can, and does, interact, exert influence and gain access to the others (Figure 2), but each level represents a distinctive set of activities within the policy process with differentiated influence deriving from legal authority and structural position.

In considering a political economy of technology education policy making it is possible to identify seven main institutions and group actors, the interaction and activities of which, constitute the process of defining, changing and controlling technology education. Together they form and populate the three levels of the model proposed by Bowie and his colleagues.

Scottish Executive Education Department (SEED): this is the national government department with a responsibility for education. This is the key context of influence and the locus of responsibility for decision making. Her Majesty's Inspectorate of Education (HMIE): this is an agency of government responsible for inspection, quality assurance and advising in relation to education. This is a very powerful group who straddle all three contexts and exert a strong hold on the context of influence. The Scottish Qualifications Authority (SQA): this is Scotland's only awarding body for qualifications below degree level. Developing courses is part of its official terms of reference; this grants the SQA a prime position in influencing the nature of curricular change. Learning and Teaching Scotland (LTS): is a non-departmental government sponsored advisory organisation; it is active in curriculum development, dissemination and project management; it is predominantly influential in the context of policy text production. Local authority Quality Advisers: this is a smaller group of local government officers responsible for advising schools and quality issues. The Technology Teachers Association (TTA, formerly known as the Technical Teachers Association): this is a voluntary professional organisation; it is at its most influential in lobbying and articulating responses in relation to official consultation and issues of contention. Practising Technical Teachers: have the possibility to take part in formal consultations, often at the level of a school response, and to have influence through involvement in the activities of SQA, LTS or TTA.

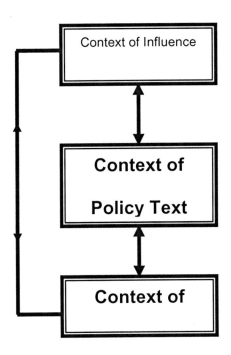

Figure 2: **Bowe, Ball and Gold (1992).**

THE CURRICULUM

A central arena for viewing change, and the object of much labour around change, is the technology education curriculum. In accounting for change, much of our analysis is centred on the official curriculum as a marker of change. However, in problematising change in the curriculum, other conceptions of the curriculum offer the potential to provide critical leverage in this task. Beyond the official curriculum, the course of study endorsed by a governing authority, we could consider the 'observed' and 'experienced' curriculum (Pollard and Triggs, 1997), along side the hidden curriculum. The observed curriculum points our attention to the difference between what is assumed in official curricula and what can be seen at the level of practice in the classroom. The curriculum-as-experience, focuses on the programme of study from the viewpoint of the learner's experience, and has a concern to understand something of the meaning that pupils take from this experience. The hidden curriculum, as noted above, directs our analysis to all the learning and messages that accrue to the learner beyond that of the formal ambitions of the education system. A recurring characteristic of the context of change in Scotland's technology curriculum has been reform of the wider official curriculum. Such projects have acted as an opportunity and driver of change in technology education and can be seen as occasioning periods of curriculum fluidity. In, for example, a parallel with the development of the national curriculum in England and Wales, periods of curricular fluidity allow for change as part of a broader curricular renegotiation as former curricular settlements give way to new arrangements.

The politics of educational change are threaded through by long running contests between opposing conceptualisations, ideas and priorities for education. One such fault line, transversing the history of technology education, and its predecessors, is the vocational-liberal divide. Different goals, ambitions and pedagogical approaches to technology education spring from different ideological positions on this continuum. At the risk of over generalisation, this continuum could be characterised, on one side, as arising from an unambiguous instrumentalism that locates technology education as preparation for a clearly defined progression into employment, and on the other, a more child-centred justification of technology education. This liberal approach argues that the study of technology is inherently valuable in its self, is an important aspect of contemporary culture, and that it has much to offer the intellectual development of all students (Banks 1994).

Another shaper and former of change within national systems of education could be explored under the banner of myth. Scotland has long maintained and cherished its own distinctive system of education, perhaps not as different in essence from its large southern neighbour as some would like to believe, but it is a system shaped and inextricably bound up with national fortunes. It is almost impossible to survey constructions of Scottish identity without unearthing notions of Scottish education interwoven in some configuration. Explanatory and legitimising mythology is to be found in even the most sophisticated and modern of societies. Myths elude tests of reality; they operate at a submerged subtextual level, seeping values, beliefs and orientations to action into human consciousness.

The myth of the 'American Dream', success being available to all through hard work and talent, has an equivalent in Scottish consciousness, the 'lad o'pairts' (McCrone, 1999). This 18th century characterisation is of course male, typically a son of the soil, lowly of birth, originating from an agrarian social order predating urbanisation. The young man has his talents recognised in the school of the parish, bequest of the protestant reformation, and is supported by those of means to attend one of the ancient universities and often to enter one of the great professions. The lad o'pairts is a myth of social mobility, an important expression and motif of the strong egalitarian strand to Scottish identity. The symbolism of the lad o'pairts illustrates the way in which Scottish education functioned as one of the locations bearing and sustaining resources of national identity.

The existence of myths provides a subterranean and powerful resource that can be put to work legitimising and persuading in favour of diverse agendas. The symbolism of the lad o'pairts has been laid claim to by the left and right, idealists and radicals alike. The place of educational mythology in the Scottish psyche has important implications for change and policy making. Reform perceived as injurious to Scottish education can rapidly be interpreted through national sensibilities as being synonymous with an assault on Scottish identity itself. This cultural context was to have a detectible impact on Conservative reforms to Scottish Education (1979-97) and in the posture and tone of New Labour north of the border following the 1997 election. The ancestry and pedigree of technical education is linked to its beginnings and fortune within the historical evolution of Scotland's education system and cannot be isolated from its place in a wider national narrative of education.

Teachers are a key set of group actors in the context of change in education. Making sense, in relation to change, of the role and impact of teachers in general and technical teachers in particular, suggests that any framework of analysis must accommodate the agency of practitioners. Sociological concepts and perspectives would seem to offer both a language, and range of theoretical approaches, that have a utility in accounting for this aspect of change. Ideas such as identity, professional self concept, role, status, governance and conflict would seem appropriate in attempting to describe and capture both the dynamic of this sector and teacher agency in relation to change.

MAPPING CHANGE

In limiting our review to a timeframe of the preceding twenty years we are prevented from attempting a detailed account of how technical education came to have the form it did at the beginning of the 1980's. In setting the context for our period of review we must limit our analysis to giving enough background to set the context for the following period. Key to this context, as to understanding many of the significant changes in technology education, are periods of change and reform that impacted across the whole Scottish education system. After the second world war, Scotland, in tandem with her large southern neighbour, sought social reconstruction through the extension of education and in particular the extension of secondary education. This reform was progressive in the sense that secondary level education was extended to all, but retrogressive in that it resulted in a two-tier provision of secondary education. Selection took place at age 11, directing a minority of children towards a senior secondary provision, with an academic curriculum, and allocating the majority to a junior secondary for a basic general education. It is here, within this general education sector, with its emphasis on a basic education, preparation for manual, unskilled and skilled employment, and character formation, the Scotland's technology curriculum has its modern origins.

"Although for most of the course the boy is rightly content to be a boy and to enter wholeheartedly into boyish activities, there comes a time when he feels that a man's work would become him better. At this stage, normally towards the end of the course, he examines from a new viewpoint all that the school has to offer, and is apt to assess it solely in terms of what use it will be for him in earning a living. He now needs the satisfaction of tackling workaday jobs and of carrying them out with the appropriate tradesman's tools. It is at this point that

359

the industrial aspects of Technical subjects make a considerable appeal to many boys." (Secondary Memorandum HMSO, 1955, p.231)

Significantly, for the development of technology education, by the mid 1960's Scotland's local government had been instructed by the central state to move to a comprehensive system of education, a directive that sat well with the spirit of the times and national sensibilities of the place of education in the national psyche. The move to comprehensive education, along with the raising of the school leaving age to 16, produced a confluence of factors that made deliberations on curriculum design, assessment and progression all the more pressing. By the early 1970s a range of certificated courses in technical subjects had become established in the emerging comprehensive sector. In addition to non-certificated general education classes, departments could offer up to five courses at national examination level (Ordinary Grade):

- Woodwork
- Metalwork
- Technical Drawing (conventional engineering drafting)
- Building Drawing (drafting in relation to civil engineering)
- Applied Mechanics (Newtonian mechanics as applied to engineering)

In 1972 the Scottish Education Department (SED) published Curriculum Paper 10, among its recommendations was that the title 'Technical Education' should be adopted in place of Technical Subjects and that the technical curriculum for the 14-16 stage should be reduced to three courses: discrete courses in Woodworking and Metalworking would be replace by one new course called Integrated Craftwork; Engineering Science was to replace Applied Mechanics; Technical Drawing would remain but Building Drawing was to be discontinued. The agenda for reform in relation to curriculum and assessment occasioned by the move to comprehensive education in the secondary sector continued to be felt during this period. In 1977 a report, *The Structure of the Curriculum in the Third and Fourth Years of the Scottish Secondary School* (the Munn Report, 1977) set out the modal framework (see Figure 1) for this stage of the curriculum made up of differentiated courses. A twin report on assessment (the Dunning Report, 1977) recommended 'assessment for all' as a principle. The recommendations of the Munn and Dunning committees was to set in motion, by the early 1980's, a reform of the middle school secondary curriculum (The Standard Grade Development Programme). This period of curriculum renegotiation created the context, in the following decade, for change to technical education's contribution to technology education in the Scottish system.

RETROSPECTIVE

In the period under consideration, from the early 1980's, until the present, technology education has undergone an almost continuous process of curricular change and revision. This process began in the middle secondary curriculum in the

1980's, moved to primary and lower secondary in the early 1990's, then re-emerged in a significant reform of the post-sixteen curricular framework in the late 1990's. Each programme of reform, while targeted at the national system as a whole, represented a period of fluidity in which settled forms of curricula could be reformed and recast.

Such a process of recasting took place in technical education during the reform of middle school arrangements in the 1980's. Under the Standard Grade development programme, pupils would study a compulsory core and choose additional subjects to complete their curriculum. Ensuring breadth and balance of study was attempted by restraining choice to a number of modes under which certain subjects could be selected for study. By the early 1990's technology education in the middle school emerged from this development with three distinct national courses at Standard Grade. Each of the courses can be interpreted to reveal both its continuities, and its distinctive differences with its preceding ordinary level national courses.

MERGING CRAFT AND DESIGN

Design first established a foothold in the secondary technical curriculum in the form of a less significant aspect of the Ordinary Grade course, Integrated Craftwork, first offered in 1979. The labours of a movement of individuals and organisations advocating design education (Design Council, 1980, Design Council Scottish Committee 1981) lead ultimately to integrated craftwork being developed into a new course; Standard Grade Craft and Design, launched in 1985. Courses in Craft and Design (C&D) encouraged pupils to understand and use the design process, to develop craft skills together with knowledge and understanding of related materials and processes. It has three assessable elements; Knowledge and Understanding; Designing; and Practical Abilities, notably the latter two elements are assessed internally by teaching staff and externally moderated. The establishment of this course initiated an almost automatic reform of post-sixteen provision through the production of a new national higher level course in C&D.

TECHNICAL AND VOCATIONAL EDUCATIONAL INITIATIVE

In the curricular history of technical education, the period from 1984 is marked by the impact of a vocational education imitative driven by the central state. The Technical and Vocational Educational Initiative (TVEI) began to make its presence felt in Scottish education around 1984. This was an initiative that originated in education system of England and Wales and was administered by the Department of Employment in London. This initiated what could be called a turf war, or the strategic organisation by the Scottish policy elite, to prevent the penetration of the London Based Manpower Services Commission across the border. The Commission was a significant extension of the Department of Employment. This context initiated a major reform to further education in Scotland, known as the Action Plan, the saw the creation of the Scottish Vocational Education Council

361

(SCOTVEC). Within the Scottish system, arrangements for TVEI operated at local authority level. Local Authorities became the mechanism for dispersing the not inconsiderable £100 million TVEI budget direct to schools making successful bids. This spurred a whole range of short courses and modules with technical and related content. Schools could bid for this money directly on the basis of offering technical or vocational aspects to the middle school curriculum. This source of funding boosted technical departments and in particular helped some schools with the start up costs of technological studies.

TECHNOLOGICAL STUDIES

Ordinary Grade Engineering Science was replaced by Standard Grade Technological Studies (TS) in 1988. The new course was very different from its predecessor that, historically, attracted small numbers of students. This was arguably the most fundamental curricular reform to the technical education curriculum, obvious in both the discontinuity with the content of its forerunners Applied Mechanics and Engineering Science, and in the approaches to teaching and learning encouraged in its inception. The content of Technological Studies (e.g. systems theory, mechanisms, electronics, pneumatics, computer control) together with its emphasis on the integration of technologies, coupled with an approach towards supporting learning that gave emphasis to project work, resource based learning and using technology in a problem solving context, all combine to characterise the distinctiveness of this development. Again, the establishment of this course initiated an almost automatic reform of post-sixteen provision through the production of a new national post-16 course in Higher Technological Studies.

GRAPHIC COMMUNICATION

In 1993 Ordinary Grade Technical Drawing was phased out, to be replace by Standard Grade Graphic Communication. The new course, Graphic Communication (GC) is concerned with the communication of graphical information in an engineering, technical or commercial context, the presentation of ideas and designs, knowledge of conventions and abilities in interpreting drawings and graphics. Students develop manual and computer based skills in drawing and graphic production. The course combines traditional elements of engineering drawing with illustration and presentation allowing some opportunities for creativity. The skills dimension of the course is assessed through a folio of pupil work assembled over the duration of the course. The folio is internally graded and externally moderated. The two other aspects of the course; knowledge and interpretation and drawing ability, are assessed externally by terminal examination.

THE 5-14 CURRICULUM

As the shape of the middle school technical curriculum changed over the 1980's the focus of policy makers shifted to the primary school curriculum and the first two years of secondary. This new reform project has its origins in a number of educational concerns over this sector of the curriculum, taken up as part of more ambitious political agenda in education by the Conservative Government of the time. This strong political dimension (mirroring events in England and Wales that would culminate in the establishment of a statutory national curriculum) sought to limit teacher autonomy, more explicitly define the curriculum, and introduce the prerequisites for a system of national assessment in primary and lower secondary. The 5-14 development programme was to culminate in a series of national guidelines covering curriculum content, assessment, organisation and structure. Not unexpectedly, during the development phase of this project, the curriculum became the subject of renegotiation and contestation as the new guidelines were formulated. Significantly, for technology education, it became established as part of the curriculum for all children in the primary stage and into the first two years of secondary education. Technology education is located within the 'Environmental Studies' sector of the 5-14 curriculum (see Figure 1).

As part of the environmental studies sector of the curriculum, technology education enjoys a formal presence in the primary school curriculum. Official advice encourages the arrangement of environmental studies education courses through the use of a nine-year plan that covers the entire primary period and the first two years of secondary. In the primary sector the use of 'topics', a long established, integrative, approach to this area of the curriculum, is encouraged. Over the course of primary education pupils would work on a number of topics at each stage (houses and homes, our bodies, exploring space, mini-enterprise), such topics may have a major focus on technology and a minor focus on science, or social subjects, or any combination of the three. The contention behind this argument is that over the 7 years of primary education there will be a balanced coverage across technology, science and social subjects. Environmental Studies will then continue to designate an area of learning after transition to the secondary school. This will take place in the first two years of secondary education through the coordinated study of courses provided by secondary departments of history, geography, modern studies, home economics, science and technical education.

HIGHER STILL

Higher Still was the title given to the ambitious reform of Scotland's post-16 curricular framework implemented in 1999. It mirrors in its agenda and context the work of the Dearing committee in England and Wales and anticipated the recent policy direction of the Department for Education and Science(Dearing, 1997, Tomlinson, 2004). It had as one of its central ambitions the goal of bridging the gap between the vocational and the academic, in search of the elusive notion of 'parity of esteem'. The range of courses available to departments of technical education has expanded as a result of the significant renegotiation of the official curriculum that took place during this reform. Prior to Higher Still, technical department could offer progression of study from each of the Standard Grades to Higher, and in the case of technological studies, to a further level of Sixth Year

Studies. In addition to this curricular strand, departments generally offered a parallel set of courses and modules of study that would be taken from a catalogue developed in further education (originally awarded by SCOTVEC, then the SQA from 1996). Such courses (typically: craft skill related; electronic assembly; engineering drafting) were vocational in nature and tended to reflect the interests of staff and the availability of resources. This parallel arrangement was to be replaced by the new national qualifications introduced under Higher Still.

During the development phase of Higher Still there was a movement, originating from within the management of the programme, to reduce the post-16 technical curriculum; generally thought to be difficult to sustain in small departments and making high demands of staff and resources. The idea of merging Graphic Communication and Craft and Design to form a new Higher and Advanced Higher course to sit alongside Technological Studies was proposed to teachers. In continuity with the past curricular history of technical education in relation to rationalisation, practitioners resisted this proposal. Eventually, the final form of Higher Still introduced a new course (Practical Craft Skills) at intermediate level, resulting in an expansion of the curricular options that departments could offer. It is worth noting that Higher Still has resulted in a new catalogue of national qualifications many of which can only be delivered in further education colleges.

MIDDLE SCHOOL

A significant development resulting from the reform of the post-16 curriculum can be seen in terms of 'back pressure', felt at the level of the middle school. The settled Standard Grade curriculum of middle secondary has been destabilised by the new courses introduced under Higher Still. In particular, change has been driven by a government decision to allow schools to offer the new intermediate courses in the middle stages of secondary alongside, or in place, of Standard Grade (see Table 3 for equivalences) together with the resulting search for coherence and progression in curriculum planning. This post-16 reform has impacted on the middle school provision of technical education; the most obvious impact has been the introduction of practical craft skills (a totally craft based course with continuous assessment) as an unintended competitor to Craft and Design. The most recent innovation is a new Product Design course at intermediate level, another potential competitor for Standard Grade Craft and Design. The menu of technical courses offered in middle school has, (four subjects provided through the option of seven different courses), become more differentiated across national provision as departments have opted to offer anything from one to four different subjects.

DISCUSSION

Change over the last twenty years in Scotland's technology and technical education provision has not fallen from on high or emerged complete from the social order. It has take one particular elaboration as apposed to another as the result of the interaction of a multitude of factors such as those discussed in the framework above. Mitcham (1994) classifies philosophies of technology as falling into one of two approaches, what he characterises as; an engineering tradition of philosophy of technology and a humanities tradition of philosophy of technology. In trying to take account of what we have referred to as 'deep theories' we conclude that Scotland's framing of technology education is profoundly engineering in nature. Broadly speaking, the engineering tradition assumes the centrality of technology in human culture and the humanities tradition and its exponents have approached technology from without, concerned to probe its moral and cultural boundaries. In its report, *The Place of Technology in the Secondary Curriculum* (1985:3), the Scottish Consultative Committee on the Curriculum defined engineering in the following terms:

"Engineering. The art of applying knowledge and experience of technology and scientific principles to satisfy some identified material need having regard to such factors as cost, safety, aesthetics and the effect on the environment."

Technology was defined in the same report in as being concerned with:

"...the identification of some of the material needs of man and the endeavour to satisfy those needs by the application of science and the use of materials, resources and energy. It is concerned with solving problems where there is no right or wrong answer, only good or bad solutions to a problem. Technological behaviour requires activities that are creative and demanding, where the laws and principles of science, the constraints of society and economics are applied to satisfy human needs. Technological behaviour involves approaches and techniques, such as systems of analysis, problem identification, decision making, planning, ideas communication and solution evaluation, which are more than pure science or craft."

It is not hard to argue that the two definitions above share considerable conceptual ground in common. The defining of technology, in the engineering tradition, echoes through the official curriculum texts of Scottish education. In defining technical education HMIE (1999) again reinforce this position drawing unambiguous upon an engineering philosophy. In addition, in the quotation below, there is a clearly located vocational element within HMIE's construction of technical education:

"The curriculum in technical education has developed in response to society's need for a technologically capable population that can make effective, responsible use of available resources in devising solutions to every-day technological problems. The national and international importance of scientific and technological capability has been emphasised in many quarters, not least in the White Paper, Realising our Potential: A Strategy for Science, Engineering and Technology (HMSO 1993):

The understanding and application of science are fundamental to the fortunes of modern nations. Science, technology and engineering are intimately linked with progress across the whole range of human endeavour; educational, intellectual, medical, environmental, social, economic and cultural.

The need to improve technological capability has been recognised as a priority as the United Kingdom seeks to maintain its manufacturing base and compete in global markets. An adequate supply of appropriately educated and trained personnel is an imperative for contemporary society." (HMIE, 1999)

This understanding has developed, in relation to time, in parallel with other systems (England and Wales, Australia) and has no significant differences in conceptualising technology education. Scotland's position is illustrated most clearly through its national position statement (SCCC 1996) on technology education and its adoption of a 'capability' stance. This construction of technology education, and its resulting practices, has formed the intellectual climate within which thinking about technology education takes place. This positioning of technology education as an organising principle of the curriculum has not been contentious. Technological capability, if anything, is absent from the vocabulary of practitioners. Technology and its relation to technical education, and other contributors of capability, is somewhat vague and perhaps lacking in a coherent commonly shared understanding that could contribute a firmer direction and purpose to curriculum design and planning.

In understanding change and questions of power and control such as posed by Archer and Bowie and his colleagues in the framework above, our attention is drawn to the political economy of educational change formed by the patterned interaction of the institutions and actors listed in the framework above. Raising awareness and gaining the attention of politicians and key civil servants at governmental level, within the Scottish Executive Education Department (SEED), is an important component of influence in attempting to highlight issues for reform or change. The channels of access both formal, and perhaps more importantly informal, are key dimensions of this context. The extent to which individuals, advisors, favoured organisations and networks have opportunity to exert influence, set the agenda or build a particular climate, is an important facet in understanding policy initiation and formation at this level.

There are a number of QANGOs and government agencies that dominate the context of policy text production and crucially, span the boundaries of contexts of influence and practice. Of significance here are the SQA, LTS and Her Majesty's Inspectorate of Education. By virtue of its structural position rather than design, the SQA casts a long shadow through its management and control of national courses and assessment. It has become a key player in developing and reviewing courses in Technical education and exerts a very significant influence on curriculum reform through its officers, working groups, panels and network of advisors and practitioners who work for it on a part-time basis. We would identify the HMIE and the SQA as the most influential actors in controlling the development and structure of technology education in the Scottish system. The role of practitioners is another interesting aspect of this context. Individual teachers can make representations to sites within the context of influence and publication, as can their professional body the Technology Teacher Association (TTA). Key sets of practitioners could be described as 'insiders'. Insiders may work for the SQA or LTS and sometimes both organisations; they are able to exert influence because of this position and also have the opportunity to influence other practitioners through the perception of their role as an actor within the process.

In advising, supporting implementation, attainment and teaching within national curricula guidelines and national courses, LTS is another organisation well positioned to influence reform, as well as current practice. The role of HMIE in the Scottish system was changed by national government in 2000. Until then this arm of government had provided both policy advice and quality assurance functions within education, after 2000 its policy function was officially removed. HMIE are still, however, very powerful players in policy reform. Attempting change in technology education in opposition to the views of HMIE is an undertaking with a very limited chance of success. Their current role as 'observers' on any significant committees and working groups within SQA or LTS as well as advising civil servants on education policy gives them very significant influence. This economy of decision making would suggest that control of technology education is centralised among a small group of actors who, no matter their ambitions for technology education, are constrained by the institutional and bureaucratic self-interest of their organisations.

In considering the secondary curriculum we would identify change in technical education as the outcome of a number of struggles over the meaning, content, and forms of knowledge and skills that should comprise the technical curriculum. We will explore this through considering a number of themes: the craft tradition, the drawing tradition, the introduction of design and (the turn to technology; e.g. electronics, pneumatics, mechanisms, systems approach and computer control) the new subject matter introduced by courses in Technological Studies (TS).

The craft tradition is the most established curricular element of technical curriculum dating back to the final stages of pre-war 5-14 schools and the earliest extensions of general secondary. It origins are clearly vocational, in an engineering context, and its place in the curriculum defended over time form a number of positions including the vocational and the liberal. Until the 1980's, the development of craft skills was a central consideration in courses of teacher education. The fortunes of the craft tradition have been, until recently, characterised by decline in relation to their place in the official curriculum. This retreat is detectable in a curricular history that records a reduction from two distinct courses, down to one, followed by a further reduction to make way for design, preceding their expulsion from the upper school curriculum. Under the Higher Still reform we have witnessed a resurgence of the craft tradition with the introduction of new courses in Practical Craft Skills. Among Scotland's practicing teachers today there is a divergence in the value attached to the craft tradition, but it retains strong support among sections of the profession.

The fortunes of the craft tradition can perhaps be explained in relation to the prevalent thinking within the decision making climate, in particular the need to modernise in response to the changing needs of industry at technician level, and pressures to escape the low status that was associated with craft work in the liberal curriculum. The ambitions of Higher Still, (coherence between school and further education, the bridging of the vocational-academic divide) created the conditions for a reassertion of this tradition resulting in the new national course in Practical Craft Skills available across the middle and upper school curriculum. In terms of students, courses with a craft dimension are still the most popular aspect of the technical curriculum (see Table 4).

Drafting has long been a constituent of technical education being cognate to the engineering origins of the craft tradition. It too has changed significantly during the last twenty years. Drawing entered this period as a smaller, if well established, aspect of the middle school curriculum. During curricular reform in the 1980's, Building Drawing was dropped from the curriculum leaving the more popular Engineering Drawing. In what is an interesting example of the economy of curriculum policy making, the idea to rationalise the technical curriculum from three into two subjects was floated from what we could described as the context of policy text production. Drawing was to be merged with Craft and Design to form a new subject to be offered alongside Standard Grade Technological Studies. This reform was defeated by the resistance of teachers, led by their professional association (TTA) in coalition with employers. The mobilisation of industry in support of the retention of Technical Drawing greatly enhanced the case being made by the TTA. Drawing was retained, the response of the then Scottish Examination Board was to update this course into what has became Graphic Communication.

This course clearly retained elements from its predecessors, but would now include new aspects such as CAD, CAG and graphical illustration and presentation techniques. Graphic Communication, which can be offered under two modes of the curriculum, can only be described in terms of being a success story (see Table 4, the trend in presentations is upwards and at Higher level it is becoming a dominant technical course). This course has also enjoyed the greatest success of any technical subject in approaching a gender balance (see Table 5). In terms of the future, the development of this course would seem to suggest a direction that would require a greater proportion of knowledge, skills and understanding being accrued through, and in relation to, computer based applications. One inhibition to this is the difficulties perceived by the SQA in relation to the arrangements for administering national assessment and the financial obligations on schools in relation to resources. The next stage in curriculum development seems apparent to practitioners, the use of contemporary software and computer based applications is attractive to pupils, but the administrative needs of national assessment and the resource implication for individual schools creates a disincentive for the SQA to action change. This situation exemplifies the political economy of curriculum policy in technology education within Scottish Education.

DESIGN

Since its success in establishing a beachhead in the technical curriculum through Standard Grade Craft and Design (1985), design has continued on a march toward an imperious position in the technical and technology curriculum. The extension of design is indicative of its secure acceptance among curriculum decision makers at the level of influence and text production. In a chronological harmony with the establishment of design in England and Wales, and internationally, design entered the Scottish technical curriculum. This reform was supported by group actors outside of education who were very successful in convincing government of its importance (Royal College Art, The Design Council, see McCormick 1994). Middle secondary courses in Art became Art and Design with a clear commitment to solving design problems and contributing to design education. During the 5-14 reform of primary and the first two years of secondary, skills in designing and making became an officially endorsed aspect of every child's curriculum.

Design's commanding place in the official curriculum is illustrated by its success in displacing craft in the post-16 curriculum. The most recent change to this provision is the replacement of Higher and Advanced Higher courses in Craft and Design with a new course; Product Design (as from 2004). In its original arrangements, Higher Craft and Design had a strong craft element; this was revised to reduce the craft element, accommodating a practical element in relation to modelling, a more minor aspect of the revised course. In this third incarnation as Product Design, there is a clear commitment to product design with little progression from the craft element present in the middle school course.

From the perspective of the Scotland's official curriculum technology education includes a strong design dimension. As part of a series of reports on effective learning and teaching in Scottish schools, HMIE published a report on technical education (SEED, 1999) it drew upon inspection evidence from 200 technical departments. This sheds some light at the level of the observed curriculum. Design education could be described, on the basis of this report, as having mixed fortunes. The design aspects of C&D are generally reported as being the most problematic by teachers and unpopular with sections of students. Learning and teaching about design is also reported as being in need of strengthening in the early years of secondary. Technology education could be described as the Cinderella subject of the 5-14 curriculum. It is the area identified as most problematic by primary teachers. Initial education courses for primary teachers, to date, allow little coverage of the technology curriculum in general and less for design.

Primary school technology has had to develop in the absence of an organic development by confident primary specialists and has tended to look for guidance to practice in the secondary sector. The secondary sector has tended to conceive a primary technology education that resembles the form of secondary, hampered in turn by the difficulty of the secondary sector in bring together coherently its own strands and traditions. There have been a number of initiatives to address perceived weakness in the technology curriculum in the 5-14 context. This includes national exemplar materials and a new project (launched in 2004) managed by LTS aimed at supporting technology education in the first two years of secondary schools. Another noteworthy development is the 'association' of Technical education with new initiatives around 'enterprise' education, both as a means of accessing funding for development and increase the currency of Technical education. The transition between primary and secondary technology education is consistently identified by HMIE as requiring improvement.

Arguably the most innovative curricular reform to technical education can be seen in the introduction of Technological Studies. The new content of Technological Studies, together with its emphasis on the integration of technologies, coupled with an approach towards supporting learning that give emphasis to project work, resource based learning and using technology in a problem solving context, all combine to mark the distinctiveness of this course from anything that had gone before. From its launch in 1988, the number of presentations for this course grew, in part assisted by funding made available through the Technical and Vocational Education Initiative. Presentations at Standard Grade in 1994 were running at 6076, however, significantly, by 2003 presentations had fallen to 2244. The decline of Technological Studies cannot be explained by reference to a single causal factor, but a number of contributing elements can identified (see Dakers and Doherty 2000). At the time of its launch, this new course was seen by curriculum decision makers as destined to become a new modern strand of a reduced Technical curriculum.

In comparison to the other course available to technical departments, the number of students opting to study Technological Studies has remained less than a quarter of C&D and around a quarter of GC and the trend is downward (see Table 4). Technological Studies was given a relaunch in 1999, the first cohort completing the new course in 2003. As part of its redesign, there was a move away from project and resource based learning approaches towards a more didactic approach coupled with a change in differentiation and entry requirements. The course is now available only to pupils capable of working at a Credit or General level, effectively asserting that this is a course for the more academic. The success of this strategy in halting the decline of Technological Studies will be a focus of future interest.

There is a historical perception, arising from its curricular history, that technical education is an area of the curriculum more suited to the education and vocational possibilities of boys. Technical education in Scotland is characterised by a significant gender imbalance in favour of males. Access to technical education was organised around gender in the newly emerging comprehensive system of the late 1960's. It was as recent as 1972 that equal access to this area of the curriculum became official policy (Scottish Education Department, Curriculum Paper 10). Today all pupils study in technical departments in the first two years of secondary as part of the environmental studies curriculum of 5-14. In middle secondary, pupils have an element of choice, and here some progress has been made towards more of a gender balance; particularly in GC and to a lesser extent, C&D (see table 5). Technological studies has failed to attract a significant portion of female students and this is one of the factors in explaining its decline in the same way as it accounts for a proportion of the growth in student numbers studying Graphics and courses in C&D. Patterns of gender balance within the post-16 curriculum are consistent with the picture of the middle secondary stage described above. Interestingly there has been a significant upward trend in the number of females applying to become teachers of technical education.

Scotland's technical teachers are, in demographic terms, top loaded in favour of the over 40's. It seems defensible to loosely conceptualise teacher attitudes in relation to the dominant educational climate prevalent during the period of their initial teacher education. This 'socialisation' maps to the nature of the curriculum at particular times, the nature of courses that comprise the technical curriculum, and associated pedagogical and organisational norms. Again this is a general observation, contradicted by teachers who are exceptions and enthuse about new curricular content and arrangements that played no part in their initial preparation for practice. There is evidence (see Canavan and Doherty 2001) to suggest that there is a relation between length of time in service, perceptions and curricular preferences. Practicing teachers can be disaggregated by differing loyalties and preferences for the different traditions and courses within technical education.

Historically the majority of technical teachers entered the profession with a background in industry. They would study for a diploma in Technical Subjects, (latterly Technical Education), the length of study required varied depending on experience and qualifications. This context created a strong reinforcement for the craft and engineering aspects of technical education. In line with the introduction of the new curriculum content of Technological Studies, and the establishment of teaching as an all-graduate profession, a number of new degree programmes (1987) and post graduate qualifications were established nationally to provide the initial education of technical teachers. This reform has altered the context of teacher socialisation and raises the question of changing attitudes, values and curricular preferences resulting form the new programmes. This question would seem to deserve further investigation. The provision of teachers able to deliver courses in Technological Study was a major influence in shaping the nature of such new courses, informed in part by an assumption that there would be a rationalisation within the more established technical subjects in deference to this new technological direction. This rationalisation failed to materialise principally due to a combination of practitioner resistance, political lobbying and the mobilisation of industrial supporters. Recently design has come to play a more significant role in the curriculum of initial teacher education.

Status, within the profession, and in general, has been an issue for technical teachers. Coming from what has been perceived within the liberal curriculum as the lowly status origin of practical work together with the strong industrial and vocational elements of technical curricular history endowed technical teachers with a more lowly status in the first two thirds of the 20th century. One reason why Technological Studies was promoted by a section of the profession was in relation to what was described as its 'academic rigour', positioning it as a rival to more established subjects such as physics. This could be read in terms of a concern for status. The new graduate teachers together with the new content of Technological

Studies and the widespread use of ICT within the technical curriculum have all helped to raise the esteem of technical teaching as we enter the new millennium.

There has been a tendency to appropriate, monopolise the 'technology' word by technical practitioners and technical teacher educators and academics. In a middle secondary curriculum, in which competition for pupils operates between subjects, the title 'technology' can be perceived has having a higher brand value than 'technical', with its antecedents in lower status general, vocationally oriented, education. This has contributed to tensions over identity within technical education. Positioning technical education as synonymous with technology, coming from a curricular area with traditions that predate the introduction of technology has perhaps lead to some confusion in discussions of curricular issues and debate within the profession.

FUTURE PROSPECTS

One of the recurring features of reform around national courses in technical education is resistance by practitioners to a reduction in curriculum breadth. This has resulted in a wide range of discrete courses that contribute to the development of technological capability. One consequence of this breadth is a demanding range of knowledge and skills required by teachers. The cost of technical education tends to be one of the most expensive aspects of the curriculum in relation to consumables and the maintenance of equipment. Scotland has moved to a more devolved form of financial management at the level of the individual school. In such a climate, school managers are always alert for the possibility of economies, thus creating a pressure of technical departments to rationalise the range of courses they offer. This climate seems set to continue if not intensify.

One of the challenges presented to technical teacher educators is the breadth and range of knowledge, understanding and skills required by teachers of technical education. This is a direct consequence of its broad curriculum, exacerbated by further expansion under Higher Still. Within Higher Education, changes to degree programmes tend to take time to implement, with the resulting lag time in teacher education programmes becoming a concern for some technology educators. In terms of the economy of curricular decision making, changes in the curriculum occur at relatively short notice with the resulting difficulties of keeping initial teacher education programmes up to date. Postgraduate courses of technical teacher education struggle to find candidates with an appropriate first-degree entry profile. In such programmes, time is a severe restriction; educators have the challenge of preparing teachers to teach this wide curriculum in one academic year.

The future of courses in Technological Studies is a concern at this juncture. The next five to ten years will be decisive in answering questions about how significant a contribution to technical education this course will make. The content of Technological Studies is relevant and contemporary and would be a loss if this course did not survive. The teaching of technology (e.g. systems theory, mechanisms, electronics, pneumatics, computer control, together with its emphasis on the integration of technologies) in the lower secondary is an area of weakness.

There is a tendency for craft, graphics, and design to dominate, more often in discreet packages as opposed to integrated projects. This can in part be explained by a lack of progression acting as a disincentive; many departments do not offer courses in middle school or as part of post-16 provision.

The teaching of drafting, CAD and illustration, and presentation within Graphics Communication courses will require to be updated to keep pace with the expansion in processing power and the development of new software and peripheral items. This will have to be undertaken in tension with the needs of national systems of assessment. The movement towards 3D modelling is a case in point, it highlights the separation of graphics courses from design and computer aided manufacture, this could be seen as a weakness in current arrangements. There is a very real enthusiasm to teach and promote learning through the use of ICT. In relation to lower secondary, practitioners often report inadequate access to computer clusters as a difficulty. Technical education, and its curriculum content, is very well positioned to offer an embedded ICT curriculum in lower school. In some schools departments provide a whole school course for lower secondary to meet the requirements of the 5-14 curriculum. Access to computing resources will be an important issue in the future development of technical education in Scotland. The use of ICT by practitioners is a strength, this can be built on for the future, and it chimes well with governmental concerns with ICT literacy.

A recent restructuring of teachers' pay, conditions and the promoted post structure may in the longer term pose a threat to technical education, in particular within smaller schools. The new arrangements have introduced a flatter management structure and in future there will be fewer teachers in middle management positions. This means more faculty arrangements (where one teacher from a subject department will have overall responsibility for a number of departments in a faculty, i.e. art, technical and home economics) the loss of a subject specialist as department principal raises concerns over curriculum leadership. Recruitment of teachers is also an area of future concern. At present there are shortages in some of the more remote areas of Scotland, the demographic profile of teachers in service is top loaded and entry into teacher education courses has remained static. Potentially this issue could have a very significant affect on the future capacity of schools to offer a technical curriculum. The existence of The Technology Teachers Association, an organic, practitioner lead professional association is another indicator of the health of technical education in Scotland. This creates a relatively autonomous forum outside of the established economy of decision making where questions and concerns from practice can be debated and courses of action decided.

The balancing of technical education's different traditions and their competing claims for space in a crowed curriculum is an issue that will require work and negotiation in the near future. The balance, breadth and integration of the craft, design, graphics and technology elements needs to be more coherent and manageable at the level of the observed curriculum. A more unified and coherent weaving together of divergent aspects of curriculum content would perhaps bring a beneficial focus to the aims and ambitions of technical education and its contribution to technological capability. The broad range of course options that can be used by departments to construct a curriculum, as well as being demanding and challenging, is also a strength. It allows individual departments to respond to the needs and preferences of their own pupils taking account of the location and social context of their school. Added to this, the comparative strength of pupil uptake of technical courses in the middle school curriculum, and its positioning in two modes of curricular options, must be seen as a positive and successful marker of technical education's progress.

The established nature of technology education in the official curricular position statements of Scotland's education system is perhaps the most reassuring aspect of its present condition. Officially, and conceptually, technology education has won space in a crowed and pressurised curriculum. Maintaining and enhancing its contribution to the education of Scotland's young people in a complex and changing educational landscape is the task that awaits in the near and medium future.

The Authors would like to express their gratitude to John Cavanagh and Bill Geddes for their thoughtful reading and incisive and helpful comments on earlier drafts of this paper.

REFERENCES

Archer, M. (1979) *The social origins of educational systems*, London, Sage.

Banks, F. (1994) What is a liberal education, in Banks, F. (Ed) *Teaching technology*. London: Routledge

Bowe, R., Ball, S. J., & Gold, A. (1992). *Reforming education and changing schools: Case studies in policy sociology*. London: Routledge.

Bowles, S. and Gintis, H. (1976) *Schooling in capitalist America,* London: Routledge and Kegan Paul.

Bowles, S. and Gintis, H. (1976) *Schooling in capitalist America: Educational reform and the contradictions of economic life*, London: Routledge & Kegan Paul.

Canavan, B. and Doherty, R. (2002) Technical education within Scotland's technology curriculum: A review of structure, Policy and Stakeholder Perceptions. In Dakers, J., de Vries, M. J. (2003). (Eds.) *PATT-13 Pupils attitudes towards technology*. International Conference on Design and Technology Education Research Proceedings.

Dakers, J. and Doherty, R. A., (2002). Technology education, In: *Scottish Education*. Bryce, T. & Humes, W. (Eds): Edinburgh University Press.

Dearing, R. (1997) *Higher education in the learning society*. Report of the National Committee / National Committee of Inquiry into Higher Education. London: NCIHE

Design Council (1980) Design education at secondary school level, London: The Design Council.

Design Council Scottish Committee (1981), *Design education and training in Scotland : A report from the Scottish education advisory committee of the design council*. Glasgow : Design Council Scotland.

Foucault, M. (1970) *The order of things: An archaeology of the human sciences*. New York: Vintage Books.

Gramcsi, A. (1971) *Selections from the prison notebooks*, Hoare, Q. and Nowell Smith, G (Eds and trans). London: Lawrence and Wishart.

Gramsci, A. (1971) *Selections from the prison notebooks*, London: Lawrence and Wishart.

Hirst, P. H. (1965) Liberal education and the nature of knowledge, in Archambault. R. D. (Ed) *Philosophical analysis and education*. London: Routledge and Kegan Paul.

L T S (2000) *Environmental studies: society, science and technology*, Learning and Teaching Scotland 2000.

Mc Crone, D. (1999) *Culture, nationalism and Scottish education: Homogeneity; and diversity*, in Bryce, T.G.K. and Humes, W. M. Eds Scottish Education, Edinburgh: Edinburgh University Press.

Pollard, A. and Triggs, P. (1997) *Reflective teaching in secondary education: A handbook for schools and colleges.* London : Cassell.

SCCC (1985) *The place of technology in the secondary curriculum,* the Scottish Consultative Committee on the Curriculum.

SCCC (1996) *Technology education in Scottish schools: A statement of position, learning and teaching Scotland*, the Scottish Consultative Committee on the Curriculum.

SCCC, (1999) *A curriculum framework for children 3-5,* Learning and teaching Scotland.

SEED (1999) Effective learning and teaching in Scottish secondary schools: Technical education : Edinburgh, SEED.

Tomlinson, M. (2004) *14-19 Curriculum and qualifications reform: Final report of the working group on 14-19 reform.* October 2004 DfES: Publications

DIDIER VAN DE VELDE AND PETER HANTSON

26. FROM DUALISM TOWARDS AN EMPHASIS ON TALENT: AN OVERVIEW OF CURRICULUM DEVELOPMENT IN FLANDERS

EARLY DEVELOPMENT OF THE GENERAL TECHNOLOGY CURRICULUM AND PRACTICE IN FLANDERS.

The first experiment in general technology education[1] arose in 1972. Main activity was the analysis of products and systems out of daily life: analysis of used materials, used production techniques, use of different systems, applied scientific concepts. Technological processes like designing, making, distributing ... were not explored[2].

The introduction of general technology in grades 7 and 8 in the beginning of the eighties was accompanied by an initiative to reform secondary schooling in Flanders: this new concept, VSO[3], intended a more democratic, participative, comprehensive approach. Still, in Flanders, most secondary schools had a profile coupled with general OR technical/vocational education. The result was an early streaming of children when they made the switch from primary to secondary school. A greater emphasis on orientation in the VSO-system went well together with the introduction of general technology. It softened the strict neo-humanistic separation between general and technical education.

The new curriculum of general technology in 1981 introduced the concept "technological process". Contexts were 'technology at home, energy, food, clothing, communication, hygiene, care, sales, and administration'.
Teachers were responsible for the concrete workout of this curriculum framework. A poor support of teachers and their experience with vocational technology and home-economics resulted in a lot of 'easy' making-tasks.

A separate curriculum for pupils with low cognitive capabilities, the B-stream, took shape. Until now, the curriculum for this group of pupils hasn't changed that much. It can be seen as relatively successful. Pupils can orientate themselves towards a choice of study by making tasks related to a rich variety of technical domains/sectors such as building, wood, metal, textile, food, electricity, horticulture, ...

---

[1] In Flanders general technology in secondary school is called "technologische opvoeding".
[2] Van Hecke, W. *Hints for teaching technology (Tob niet over top, een vingerwijzing voor technologische opvoeding)* (brochure). Zoersel, 1988.
[3] VSO= vernieuwd secundair onderwijs (new secondary education)

M.J. de Vries, I. Mottier (eds.), International Handbook of Technology Education, 377–386.

During a few years, the more comprehensive VSO model competed with the traditional education system and at the end of the '80 a compromise-education system arose: "het éénheidstype"[4] (unified secondary schooling-system).

In 1988, as a response, a new general technology curriculum appeared. All pupils received 2 hours/week (or more) of general technology in grades 7 and 8. Themes are: communication technology, electrical circuits, information technology (grade 7) and energy, technology at home and information technology (grade 8). From now on, the complete technological process had to be studied, and not only the making-process. The theme 'information technology' became very important. Problem solving with logic panels take 40% of the curriculum.

1997. The Flemish community described curriculum minimum goals[5] ("eindtermen") that were to be reached by all pupils, for general technology for grades 6 (primary school) and 8 (end of junior high school). Despite curriculum changes, the change in teaching practice in grades 7 & 8 remained limited: the minimum goals became situated in existing practice. In primary school, technology is introduced.

In 1999, the education inspection assessed the teaching practice for general technology in grades 7 and 8[6]. During grades 7&8, the pupils' natural interest for technology declined and the impact on choice of study was neglect table. Critical points were teaching conditions such as infrastructure and class group sizes, teacher education, a lack of coherent vision on general technology as a subject and unbalanced curricula.

2002: AN ACCELERATION OCCURS IN CURRICULUM DEVELOPMENT AND DISCUSSION.

In this year, the introduction of cross-curricular themes[7] with minimum goals for general technology education for grades 9-12 in general secondary education[8] is launched.

Also, a period of reflection and discussion begins: The role of competences in society becomes increasingly more important and this not only in economic life, organisations and companies but also in life-long learning, social and cultural emancipation. Inspired by a project from the Organisation for Economic Co-

---

[4] Flemish administration of education. *Statistics of education in Flanders*. Internet, Brussels 2005 (http://www.ond.vlaanderen.be/onderwijsstatistieken/)

[5] Decreet van 24 juli 1996 - tot bekrachtiging van de eindtermen en de ontwikkelingsdoelen van de eerste graad van het gewoon secundair onderwijs. *Belgisch staatsblad* 14/08/1996.

[6] Ministery of the Flemish community. Education department. *Onderwijsspiegel. Verslag over de toestand van het onderwijs, schooljaar 1999-2000*, p.69-72. Internet, Brussels,2004. (http://www.ond.vlaanderen.be/schooldirect/inspverslag/SO-TO.htm)

[7] Decreet van 18 januari 2002 - betreffende de eindtermen, de ontwikkelingsdoelen en de specifieke eindtermen in het voltijds gewoon en buitengewoon secundair onderwijs. Belgisch staatsblad 08/02/2002; err. B.S. 12-4-2002.
See also: Cross-curricular themes. Internet, Brussels, DVO, (http://www.ond.vlaanderen.be/dvo/publicaties/over_de_grenzen/OVER_DE_GRENZEN.pdf)

[8] General secondary education: algemeen secundair onderwijs (ASO)

operation and Development (OECD) for defining and selecting competences, (DeSeCo), a think-tank starts reflecting about the meaning of this for the Flemish context (Dunon and Van Driessche, 2001)[9].

Meanwhile, a commission representing the major actors in society describes an action plan[10] for the implementation of an integrated vision on learning and working. An important factor is the gap between the perceived status of secondary technical and vocational studies and the economic needs expressed by a shortage of applications for several technical occupations. Further key-elements of the plan are:

- the renewal of management in education organisations and schools;
- a reform of the educational system in an attempt to remove the social and appreciation barrier between "general", technical and vocational education;
- to facilitate a better choice of study by optimising the orientation of pupils, certainly in junior high school.

During 2003-2004, the corresponding taskforce 'a greater emphasis on talent' starts with experimental projects based on the conclusions of the commission.

The department for education development of the Flemish community starts a discussion on general technology teaching by means of a comparative international curriculum quick-scan "techniek voor iedereen" ("technology for everyone") (Moens, 2002)[11]. It suggests a more balanced framework based on the idea of technological literacy and defines context-areas as the basis for learning. Those contexts are health, food, energy, information and communication, transport, articles of use and building.

2003-2004.

The network of community schools[12] initiates a curriculum reform for general technology grades 7 and 8 based on the ideas of the study. The network of

---

[9] Dunon, R. & Van Driessche A. *Defining and selecting key-competencies in Flanders* (Definitie en selectie van (sleutel)competenties in Vlaanderen: een stand van zaken anno 2001.) Brussel, Ministery of the Flemisch community – Education department. 2001.

[10] Bossaerts, B. Denys, J. and Tegenbos, G. *Accent op talent. Een geïntegreerde visie op leren en werken.* Garant. Antwerpen. 2003. 130pp.
See also internet, Brussels, 2005
(http://www.ond.vlaanderen.be/schooldirect/BL0203/KBS_AccentTalent.htm
http://www.kbs-frb.be)

[11] Moens, G. *Technology for everyone: fundamentals for a transparent subject (Techniek voor iedereen Grondslagen voor een transparant vak Technologische Opvoeding).* Ministry of the Flemish community education department – Department for education development - studies and documents, Brussels. 2002. 55pp.

[12] School networks in Flanders: public schools and free schools. Public schools consist of a network of Flemish community schools (17%) and a network of schools associated with cities and provinces (16%). The largest group are the free schools (mainly Catholic, about 67%).

Catholic schools (VVKSO)[13] starts a think-tank and prepares gradual curriculum changes.

The minister of education appoints a coach for general technology teaching in Flanders. Several conferences for teachers take place (VVKSO, 2002; Arteveldehogeschool,2003; Popular science centre "Technopolis", 2004).

Teachers' and pupils' perception of the subject

At the end of the curriculum, pupils associate technology with electricity, electronics and mechanics. They see almost no links with human needs, economic, social and ecological impact of the subject. The natural interest for technology decreases through grades 7 and 8. Besides infrastructure and class group size, teachers criticize the curriculum for being too charged and for putting an overemphasis on information technology (Boolean logic, logic circuits, programmable controllers).

TEACHER EDUCATION

A large amount of teachers has never received a specific initial training[14] for general technology. Most of them were formerly active in teaching home-economics, vocational technology in textiles, mechanics .... An other group are the science teachers. The minimum qualification level is very low. When schools can't find good technology teachers, so to speak, even gym teachers can teach technology. As a result, the foundations of general technology are not very well known. Sometimes, lessons refer more to science or to vocational technology.

A GREATER EMPHASIS ON TALENT, ALSO IN GENERAL TECHNOLOGY EDUCATION: THE ORIËNTO PROJECT

At the end of 2004, the Arteveldehogeschool a university of professional education associated with Ghent university, disseminates a development called "OriënTO"[15] (Coulier, Hantson, Van de Velde, 2004), a product for gender sensitive orientation towards choice of study in grades 7 and 8. This development is financed by the European Social Fund and the Flemish community.

The main idea is based on structuring the reflection process of the pupils. This is stimulated by playing several interactive computer games and by conversations with teacher(s), parents, ...

---

[13] VVKSO: Verbond van het Vrij Katholiek Secundair Onderwijs (network of free Catholic secondary schools).

[14] Initial training: bachelor in education- secondary education option teaching general technology

[15] Coulier, C, Hantson, P. en Van de Velde, D. Oriento, *Gendersensitive oriëntation towards choice of study and occupation in general technology education (genderneutrale studie- en beroepskeuzeoriëntatie in technologische opvoeding).* Gent, Arteveldehogeschool. 2004. Internet (www.oriento.be).

- Pupils get to know more about:
  their 'technological intelligence' (defined as a combination of Gardner's multiple intelligences[16]);
- their "blue" and "pink" competences;
- the nature of work in our society;
- economic sectors, the nature of companies, professions and occupations;
- the role of professions and occupations linked with technological processes;
- history of work coupled with technology development;
- their view on socialisation processes, male and female role patterns linked to technological activities;
- their learning style by testing preference of approach in technological problem-solving;
- their interests and talents for developing key-competences in technology such as investigating and innovating systems, managing and executing processes.

The tool consists of an interactive cd-rom, a reflection-poster and a comic-book for pupils. For teachers, school management and other actors active in education, there are checklists to support a gender sensitive interaction in teaching, use of images, use of language.

Figure 1[17]: linking learning styles to key-competency areas in technological processes.

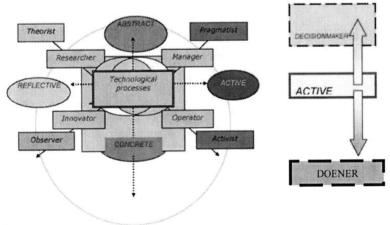

---

[16] Gardner, H. *Frames of mind*. Basic books. New York, 1983.
[17] Van de Velde, D. Hantson, P. and Coulier, R. 2004

Key-competence clusters in technological process steps				
Clusters / **Process steps**	**Researching**	**Innovating**	**Managing**	**Operating**
	Logical thinking, analysing, synthesising, reflecting, dealing with concepts	Creative thinking, observing, sensing, reflecting, dealing with variables	Planning, organising, structuring, managing, controlling	Making, performing, executing
Identification of needs Social, communicative, marketing and research competences	Analysing needs of individuals, groups, markets	Promoting, advertising, marketing, improving methodologies identification	Managing accounts Managing application of regulations	Questioning Promoting Receipting clients Administrating
Design Modelling, technological communication, creative competences	Analysing (subsystems): Researching properties of new materials, ... Researching technological possibilities of natural phenomena	Applying new techniques and materials in designs.	Controlling and optimising processes	Technical drawing Making models and prototypes, testing Executing work procedures
Production Process competences	Analysing processes and their aspect such as safety, healthy, environment, ergonomics, methods, tools, ...	Optimising processes (methods, tools, ...)	Planning, organising, following and maintaining processes (e.g. machines, stock, production, employees, ...)	Executing competences such as accuracy, punctuality, quality, order, attention for safety, environment, productivity,..
Distribution Installing, servicing, transporting, testing,...	Researching methods for distributing, logistics, conditioning, storage, use and maintaining, servicing, ...	Optimising systems for transport, distribution, storage, conditioning, servicing, ...	Planning, organising, following and maintaining processes such as distribution, logistics, service, ... and systems for conditioning, transport, storage, ...	Executable competences in logistics, service, flexibility, ...
Evaluation Analysing, reflecting, judging, consulting, improving, assessing....	Assessment of interaction between technology and customer, market, society... Researching technology assessment methodology. ...	Designing strategies for assessment of systems and processes based on existing assessment concepts	Planning and assessment of customer satisfaction and assessing the implementation of diverse regulations	Execution of given standards and procedures: - control - testing and measuring - data acquisition - analyse data

Fig. 2. Key-competence clusters in technological process steps. In every step there is teamwork needing social and emotional intelligence. Every step needs also competences in ICT. Every occupation/profession in technology demands a specific combination of competences.

The project includes a search for distinguishable key-competence fields as they can be observed in technological (sub)processes like identifying needs, designing, producing, distributing and servicing, assessing. This framework (Van de Velde and Hantson, 2004) serves to refine the look on pupils' technological interests: have they already been profiled as researchers, innovators, managers, operators? Which steps in the technological process have their interest? Do they feel something for the interaction technology-man-society or are they more product-oriented?

This framework helps to design a test comprising a series of meaningful technological problems where pupils must indicate their preferred way of solving. This test refers to authentic practices in technological processes as indicated in the framework (figure 2).

When defining clusters of key competencies in technology such as researching/gathering knowledge, innovating, managing and executing, a link with Kolb's learning styles[18] (Kolb and Fry, 1975) could be noticed. These relations are indicated in figure 1 (Van de Velde, Hantson and Coulier, 2004).

During grades 7 and 8, the tool should be discovered gradually through the curriculum development. As a result, pupils can progressively enrich their self-concept.

In every step there is teamwork needing social and emotional intelligence. Every step needs also competences in ICT. Every occupation/profession in technology demands a specific combination of competences.

RECENT DEBATE IN GENERAL TECHNOLOGY EDUCATION

Since 2002, when the curriculum was about to be revised, the following elements have been in the centre of the debate:

- active and constructive learning
- the choice of contexts
- charge of the curriculum: less is more?
- the structure of the curriculum
- discipline based subject with links to vocational technology and science or multidisciplinary and problem solving based learning subject.

ACTIVE AND CONSTRUCTIVE LEARNING

At this point, an agreement has been reached that future teaching practice must be more directed towards active and constructive learning. There is some debate on how to reach this goal: some want to activate pupils by putting more assignments for pupils in the current curriculum structure, others want to go further by replacing a content- oriented approach with a more project-based approach.

---

[18] Kolb. D. A. and Fry, R. *Toward an applied theory of experiential learning;*, in C. Cooper (ed.) *Theories of Group Process*, London: John Wiley. 1975.

CHOICE OF CONTEXTS

This debate is rather confusing because of the various interpretations of what a context stands for. Only a few participants in the debate see contexts as elements coming out of real life situations: e.g. as pieces of the designed world[19] or as domains in the life of children: technology at home, in school, in their free-time, in companies. The idea that a context should be linked with the structure of a traditional science or engineering subject is wide-spread.

Some actors want to broaden the range of contexts and want to add the contexts food and health. This options fits with the idea of transferring technology- specific key-competencies needing a range of different and authentic contexts. It also broadens the view of pupils on technology as a human-made world and gives more possibilities to appeal to girls' interests.

Advocates of the present practice argue that those contexts were part of the curriculum in the eighties and see this as a return to the past. They see the study of electricity, mechanics, information technology and machine controls, building, technical communication as a good base for learning technology.

Some actors justify the present overemphasis on information technology by arguing that it is a powerful context for developing logical thinking and problem solving. Recent research[20] even indicates that transfer of those capabilities to other contexts and daily life is not simple.

FROM CONTENT BASED TOWARDS PROCESS-BASED LEARNING: BRINGING STRUCTURE IN TEACHING TECHNOLOGY PROGRAMS.

The structure of the present curriculum consists of basic themes (technical drawing and communicating, electrical circuits, transmissions, information technology). During grade 7, pupils learn these "basics". Grade 8 intends a more project-based approach based on applying these basics. Problem is: the curriculum description shows little differentiation for both approaches and project/problem-based teaching practice is not common. Curriculum themes like technical communication develop spatial intelligence, but poor integration in other themes and limited contextualization makes learning not connected, situated and meaningful enough.

So the actual teaching practice is based on a logical and linear development of a theme derived from a particular technology such as electricity: the curriculum theme reflects the structure of the underlying scientific/engineering subject. As an example the theme 'electrical circuits' starts with exploring a simple circuit, learning the components of a simple circuit and their properties, learning the

---

[19] International Technology Education Association. *Standards for technological literacy: content for the study of technology*. Reston, VA: Author. 2000.

[20] De Corte, E. *On the Road to Transfer: New Perspectives on an Enduring Issue in Research and Practice*, International Journal of Educational Research 31. 1999.

properties of circuits with batteries, switches, loads, ... in series and in parallel. Such a theme often concludes with a "making-task" of a product with a function, in this example, based on electrical circuits.

This more content-based approach puts the structure and the conceptual knowledge of the underlying scientific/engineering subject in the centre.

At the same time, there is no attention for the specific profile of the several technological sub-processes, the kinds of procedural knowledge in technology such as identifying needs, investigating systems, designing, making, problem solving, assessing the impact of technology for the natural world. In most cases, pupils are trained to solve vaguely profiled technical problems following a unified 5-step heuristic process (identifying the problem/searching solutions/making the solution/testing/evaluating). This problem solving is based on very brief context descriptions.

The approach in technology education should be more project and process-based with pupils drawing on a rich range of learning styles. As also pointed out by Stevenson[21] and MCCormick[22], more attention for "connectedness of meaning" and "situatedness" is needed. So problem solving should be situated by means of rich and meaningful context descriptions. In order to achieve this, curricula should downsize the more context- and traditional subject-specific content.

Leaving the logical structure of the development of a subject as a supporting background generates a paradigm shift. This however will take some time for implementation into teaching practice. To enforce meaningful learning, more project/problem-based learning is necessary referring to authentic technological processes (procedural knowledge) and concepts of systems theory (conceptual knowledge). The traditional discipline-based subjects become a well structured tool-box for problem-solving inspired by real-life situations. Nevertheless, a mapping of subject-specific competence will be necessary in combining the advantages of both approaches. This more meaningful learning supports the discovery of pupils' talents and thereby the orientation process.

CONCLUSIONS

This chapter illustrates the importance and role of the 'more emphasis on talent' policy in Flanders in recent curriculum and teaching development. It is the Flemish approach in an attempt to change the attitude of pupils and parents towards a choice of study for technology. The underlying approach is key-competence-based learning, more attention for orientation towards choice of study in grades 5→8 and broadening pupils' horizon by means of more meaningful and more connected learning. Although the recent debate on curriculum reform is not

[21] Stevenson, J. *Developing technological knowledge*. International Journal of Technology and Design Education 14, 5–19, 2004.
[22] McCormick, R. *Issues of Learning and Knowledge in Technology education*. International Journal of Technology and Design Education 14, 21–44, 2004.

cleared out yet, it is to be expected that this policy of renewal will greatly influence future developments.

REFERENCES

Bossaerts, B. Denys, J. and Tegenbos, G. (2003) (ed.) *Emphasis on talent, an integrated vision on working and learning (Accent op talent. Een geïntegreerde visie op leren en werken).* Antwerpen. Garant. 130pp.

Coulier, C, Hantson, P. en Van de Velde, D. Oriento, (2004), *Gendersensitive orientation towards choice of study and occupation in general technology education (genderneutrale studie- en beroepskeuzeoriëntatie in technologische opvoeding).* Gent, Arteveldehogeschool. Internet www.oriento.be.

De Corte, E. (1999) On the road to transfer: new perspectives on an enduring issue in research and practice, *International Journal of Educational Research* 31.

Decreet van 24 juli 1996 - tot bekrachtiging van de eindtermen en de ontwikkelingsdoelen van de eerste graad van het gewoon secundair onderwijs. *Belgisch staatsblad* 14/08/1996.

Decreet van 18 januari 2002 - betreffende de eindtermen, de ontwikkelingsdoelen en de specifieke eindtermen in het voltijds gewoon en buitengewoon secundair onderwijs. *Belgisch staatsblad* 08/02/2002; err. B.S. 12-4-2002.

Dunon, R. and Van Driessche A. (2001) *Defining and selecting key-competencies in Flanders (Definitie en selectie van (sleutel)competenties in Vlaanderen: een stand van zaken anno 2001.)* Brussel, Ministry of the Flemish community – Education department.

Flemish administration of education. (2005) *Statistics of education in Flanders.* Internet, Brussels http://www.ond.vlaanderen.be/onderwijsstatistieken/.

Gardner, H. (1983) *Frames of mind.* New York, Basic books.

International Technology Education Association. (2000) *Standards for technological literacy: content for the study of technology.* Reston, VA: Author.

Kolb. D. A. and Fry, R. (1975) *Toward an applied theory of experiential learning*;, in C. Cooper (ed.) *Theories of Group Process*, London: John Wiley.

Ministry of the Flemish community. (2004) Education department. *Onderwijsspiegel. Verslag over de toestand van het onderwijs, schooljaar 1999-2000,* p.69-72. Internet, Brussels. http://www.ond.vlaanderen.be/schooldirect/inspverslag/SO-TO.htm.

McCormick, R. (2004) Issues of Learning and Knowledge in Technology education. *International Journal of Technology and Design Education* 14, 21–44.

Moens, G. (2002) *Technology for everyone: Fundamentals for a transparent subject (Techniek voor iedereen Grondslagen voor een transparant vak Technologische Opvoeding).* Ministry of the Flemish community education department – Department for education development - studies and documents, Brussels. 55pp.

Stevenson, J. (2004) Developing technological knowledge. *International Journal of Technology and Design Education* 14, 5–19.

Van Hecke, W. (1988) *Hints for teaching technology (Tob niet over top, een vingerwijzing voor technologische opvoeding)* (brochure). Zoersel.

JACQUES GINESTIÉ

27. ANALYSING TECHNOLOGY EDUCATION THROUGH CURRICULAR EVOLUTION AND INVESTIGATION THEMES

INTRODUCTION

Twenty years ago, a new concept emerged in our curriculum: introducing technology education (TE). From this point, we developed many projects which implemented this new subject area and which built progressively and meaningfully upon it. The aim of this paper is to present this evolution from the French viewpoint and to compare it with experiences in other countries.

We present this evolution through two perspectives: the curricular evolution and the place of investigation. Briefly, we can observe through the French national curriculum a phase of epistemological delimitation, followed by a phase of definition of activities, arriving, recently, at a phase of activities defined as applied sciences which have poor connections with the initial epistemological definition. Through these factual dimensions, we can analyze this evolution as the weakness of knowledge meaningfully expressed in the national curriculum, a weakness that reinforces the weakness of TE over other subjects such as mathematics, literature, foreign languages etc.

Many works have tried to analyze this particular approach but the audience for these has never really gone beyond the narrow sphere of TE investigators. A birthday (PATT) is an ideal occasion for opening perspectives and projecting ideas and the experience of exploring this issue has taught us that the position of TE is more a question of social positioning through knowledge than a question of purposed activities' interest.

CURRICULUM EVOLUTION IN FRANCE

The aim of this paper is to present some aspects of Technology Education in the French school. French schooling has two levels. Primary school starts at the age of three and lasts until the age of eleven. This phase comprises three cycles: the initial learning cycle (children three to five years old), the basic learning cycle (five to eight years), and the fundamental learning cycle (eight to eleven). Secondary school is divided into two main cycles: middle school (ages eleven to fifteen) and high school (fifteen to eighteen for general education or fifteen to nineteen for vocational training). Technology education was implemented at each of these two levels in the early eighties.

M.J. de Vries, I. Mottier (eds.), International Handbook of Technology Education, 387–397.

THE FIRST CURRICULUM
SOME ELEMENTS ABOUT THE GENERAL BACKGROUND

The main idea behind French schooling is the progressive elaboration of different school subjects. Understanding the world of children goes hand in hand with organizing that world into different knowledge areas, from the general view to the particular description given by the different subjects. "Technology education", like that of "science", "history", or "geography", appears as a school subject specific to the middle school level (Ginestié, 2001a).

The second idea behind French schooling is the concept of project pedagogy. The introduction of this pedagogy in the Eighties marked a departure from the traditional idea that the academic and dogmatic transmission of knowledge is the sole approach to teaching. Under pressure of a massive rise in number pupils in middle and high schools, project pedagogy was presented as a possible solution to meeting the needs of the diversity of pupils, addressing their individual needs, and developing pupil autonomy (Ginestié, 2002). It was in this context, in 1985, that technology education was introduced in France as a part of science and technology education in elementary schools, as a new subject for all pupils in middle schools and as an optional subject in high schools. We can note four stages in the organization of technology education between 1985 and today.

1985-1991: THE IMPLEMENTATION OF THE FIRST CURRICULUM

Technology education was conceived of as a new subject and took the place of MTE (manual and technical education) in terms of hours, classrooms, and teachers. The curriculum emphasized the industrial environment, leaving little room for home economics and craftsmanship (COPRET, 1984). It had two different elements that made these references clear. On the one hand, the general part of the course described the overall goals, context, and aims of technology education in France. The aims were in terms of pupils' attitudes towards technology (as related in many papers, e.g. de Vries, 1994; Jones, 1997; Compton & Jones, 1998; Gardner & Hill, 1999; Dugger, 2000) and in terms of the social and professional world of industrial production (this idea can also be found in many papers all over the world, e.g. Kantola et al., 1999). It offered a broad perspective to prepare pupils for professional training. At that time, the middle school became the intermediate cycle where pupils had to make their own personal plan for school, and technology education was responsible for indicating possible career choices. On the other hand, general goals were broken down into concepts and skills. This second element of the curriculum described the organization of concepts based on four domains of reference: mechanical construction, electrical construction, economics management and computer science. Clearly, the chosen references oriented technology education in the world of industry towards electro-mechanical production, to the exclusion of other possibilities (Ginestié, 2001b).

The main problem in introducing the TE curriculum has been to link the general aims to the specific fields (Sanders, 1999; Ginestié, 2004). These difficulties appeared with in-service teacher training programs. Earlier, the French Ministry of Education strongly affirmed the principle that TE was not a compendium of a little mechanics, a little electronics, and business management with different aspects of computer science as a binder. To link these subjects together, teachers have had to connect general aims and specific concepts into an overall pedagogical project (Ginestié, 2005). Many in-service teacher training programs develop this orientation rather than aiming simply for the acquisition of specific knowledge. The implementation of technology education has not been reduced to the simple substitution of cooking or handicraft lessons by lessons in mechanics, but the true construction of a "new world" (Ginestié, 2003). Many original curriculum experiments were conducted at the same time to develop new teaching approaches (differential pedagogy, autonomous work, cooperative work, personal projects, etc.) and to integrate the new references with industry, the market economy, and new labor organizations by taking into account the needs, design, production, marketing, use, and rationale of industrial methods. The major plan was to combine the pedagogical project with a theoretical industrial project method (IPM). We can note comparable initiatives in England and Wales at the same time (e.g. Hennessy & Murphy 1999).

THE CURRICULUM EVOLUTIONS
1992-1999: INTRODUCTION OF THE INDUSTRIAL PROJECT METHOD (IPM)

At the beginning of the Nineties, IPM appeared to be a good solution for implementing TE in the middle schools. Certainly, IPM has taken an overwhelmingly predominant place in TE, leaving no other alternatives for organizing technology education courses. This position was made official with different additions and modifications to the initial curriculum. The main decision to use IPM was taken in 1992 by the French Ministry of Education. This method allows for the simultaneous definition of content and organization of the teaching and learning process in TE. IPM provides content through the knowledge, support and technical language used and it provides method through the normal process arrangement by which one can go from idea to product. Everything was arranged so that each TE teacher plans and organizes a new project each year for each group of pupils. There are various practices around this IPM implementation but, commonly, all the teachers of one school elect the same project for the same school level (Ginestié, 2002). To understand the French school system, remember that the curricula are prescriptive curricula and therefore explain goals, activities and content; sometimes a teacher can be inspected by a pedagogical inspector who gives his assessment of the teacher's pedagogical practice.

1999-2004: THE SECOND CURRICULUM

Two points arose, however, that reduced the role of the project in TE. First, projects were mainly single production projects without any real progression from one year to the next. Second, the union of industrial science and technique exerted pressure on teachers to open up the curriculum to new technologies and new patterns of labor organization. We can also observe that the teachers' profile evolved considerably during this period, with a large increase in new graduates from the advanced technological universities. In accordance with the principles of the French teacher training system, these young teachers come mainly from very specialized studies (mechanical or electronic engineering) and they do not have an extensive background in all the technological dimensions of the project. The implementation of the new curriculum took four years, from 1996 until 1999. These changes attempted to organize the relationship between the respective roles of the project and the concepts. For the first three years of middle school, pupils have to make different modules of the whole project, but they do not have to make all of it. The teacher's task is to focus the attention of the pupils on specific points. During the last year, the pupils have to do a complete project (Ginestié, 2001c). The IPM is always a very strong frame of reference for TE in middle schools; the main ideas focus on the different socio-professional roles required to organize manage, execute, etc. the project, since the first task is to put a new product on the market. Through this, pupils can discover the different jobs, the corresponding qualifications and the training involved (Ginestié, 2002).

2005: AND SO LONG, ANOTHER CHANGE

There is currently a new phase of curriculum change. The Ministry of Education wants to promote pupils' individual choices regarding their future and, as a consequence, the study they have to do. We can observe a real reduction of TE as a general and cultural subject. The general aspects are more and more developed as applications of sciences; the general method is no longer the process of design and technology but more and more the process of observation and experimentation (as is found in science education). The principal knowledge, which was properly identified as technological knowledge, has been banished and the first draft of this new curriculum promotes links with scientific knowledge. The IPM is still a point of reference but it is now more an object of study than a method to use with pupils.

CONDITIONS OF STUDY IN TECHNOLOGY EDUCATION

As can be seen, the TE curriculum is unstable. This can be traced through the major changes that have occurred since the first curriculum arrangements. These changes are not linked with the technological evolution but are mainly due to a lack of understanding about the place of TE in the general system and to a misunderstanding about the aims of this subject and the knowledge taught. This lack of knowledge is patent when we observe the structure of the curriculum. This question of knowledge, moreover, is not so easy to solve.

Analysis of the conditions of study pertaining to TE's knowledge presupposes, in terms of questions for research, a strong agreement with two points:

1. there is some thing to study in technology education;
2. there would be multiple study conditions.

These two points are not in evidence. A majority opinion is that TE is simply a mix of handicraft activities and elements which highlight vocational training choices (Ginestié, 2000; Chatoney, 2003; Brandt-Pomares, 2003). In this case, all the knowledge comes from the sciences and TE is only a question of activities or applications. Clearly, this kind of view weakens the position of TE as a school subject and the recent French evolutions must be understood within this context. It is from the radically opposing viewpoint that we choose to work in our laboratory. The first orientation we choose is to understand the significance of the anthropological approach.

THE ANTHROPOLOGICAL APPROACH

The anthropological approach allows for the embedding of knowledge within theory and within the social field identified. The articulation between task and activity is incomplete if we do not speak about the manner of making. The technique employed by the person in realising the task is influenced both by context and personal factors. The articulation between the task and the technique defines a know-how that expresses the manner of realising a determined task type (Ginestié, 1995). To get off this private organization either to account for the activity, or to clarify the manner of making, presupposes the mediation of language.

Explicating the manner of making necessitates proceeding to an extraction of the individual praxis to elaborate a praxéological organisation, significant of the manner to realise the type of tasks and the context in which these tasks are registered. In fact, it concerns to give the senses in the typical articulation between tasks and techniques by elaborating a field of meaning in connection with a technology, perhaps with a theory. It is this elaboration of meanings on the practice that defines, in the anthropological perspective, knowledge. This approach allows rendering account organisations of knowledge as relationships between praxis, taken in the senses of the activity oriented to finality, and a field of significations that allows referring practice to a technology and/or to a theory (Ginestié, 2001c). The epistemological entry is interested in the nature of knowledge (well obviously in the evoked anthropological perspective above) and to the demarcation of a field of reference (Ginestié, 1997). Some articulations allow thinking these fields, objects to know that are fastened there and the manner of which they are or been able being, taken into account in the framework of a technology education:
The world of technical objects, their mode of existence and social organizations by and in order that these objects exist so as to register the technological education in the human and social activity field;
   The articulations between functioning, function, structure, form in the senses of a lighting of interdependences and the different manners to describe an object;
The articulation design, production, utilisation notably for marks given on process put at stake in each of terms, but equally, of a more global manner, either in a

specific approach on an object, or from an evolutionist viewpoint, in a perspective of an history of technical activities;

The articulation object, activity, language in an ergonomic inscription (from the thing to the object, the object to the tool, the tool to the instrument) as revealers of the bonds between gestures and techniques, techniques and technologies. The report to techniques is thought in this framework as a demarcation; the report to languages notices the elaboration of symbols (in a relationship meaning, meant) but equally tools to think the world of technical objects and to act in this world.

Well obviously, this qualification of fields is a bit coarse, it needs to be specified, notably if we want to be able to read existent curricular organisations, perhaps to propose evolution of these organizations. The curricular approach is one way to understand the knowledge's organizations for teaching purposes. The problem is not the transposition of praxis but the transposition of praxeological organizations. It is not difficult to ask to pupils making something, but it is difficult allowing them to construct the meaningful on what they make. Certainly, the important instability of our curriculum is based on this difficulty to elaborate this meaningful. Furthermore, the curricular entry is envisaged here as one of the stages of the didactic transposition process: that the placement in text of teaching objects in an prescriptive aimed that has to organize the teaching activity, to the breadth of the production of these teaching objects in the framework of the class to elaborate some objects of study for pupils, objects of study that are going to determine activities of pupils. This placement in text defines the matter to teach and induces the manner to teach it.

SCHOOL INSTITUTIONALIZATION

We can thus notice the specification and identification work that operates in this process of scholastic institutionalisation. School institution is characterized as the placement of interactions, surely tensions, between three poles: the pupil, the professor and the knowledge. As soon as we wish to describe these interactions, we are confronted with a problem of methodology, methodology that derives of course the framework in which place our study. Thus, analysing the conditions of the study is going to concern us in what the school institution puts to the study and the manner that's this study functions. This crossing of analysis rests on the articulation between task and activity:

The task is significant to the knowledge put at stake in the elaborated situation by the teacher in the framework that is fixed (curricular organizations, conditions of exercises, particular constraints, etc.);

The activity is significant to the work undertaken by the pupil to progress in the task that is appointed it by the teacher and representative of the knowledge's learning process.

It concerns to define a framework of analysis that allows looking the functioning of a teaching situation (Ginestié, 1992). The initial framework, elaborated by these analyses method, does not prejudge of:

- knowledge put at stake, their presence or not and their school form;

- organizations elaborated by the teacher so as to organize conditions of the study of this knowledge;
- activities developed by the pupil that are induced by the organization put in game for this study.

These two cross analyses, task and activity, characterize the interactions between three complementary existing logics but that can also appear as rival: the logic of subject, the logic of teaching and the logic of learning. The first one follows from knowledge organisation and requires an epistemological study; the second one takes in account the professional activity of the teacher considering his organisation, his style, his manner to do, the professional gestures he develops; the last one can be highlight by the learning theories, specifically the viewpoint of socio-constructivism theories. Many works have shown the incidence of these logics on the school situations and how they are inscribed in different references and different temporality. In fact, stressing these three logics in a school institution can be looked of different manners. But, for ourselves, we are really interested by what it happens in a class; specifically, we try to analyze the effects produced by this placement in tension (Ginestié, 1996).

On the one hand, this approach allows the identification of the organisational and structural elements that act and interact in the process of teaching-learning. In this perspective, the task appears as the preferential expression of the teaching's logic. It express simultaneously what is at stake, the context in which it is situated, what it is waited and what it is necessary that the pupil makes to achieve the task. In this senses, the task is a concentrated expression of a totality of values, models, elements of theories, knowledge that base the subject's references and that identify the teacher in a teaching population. The analysis of the task is therefore significant how curriculum is implemented, in the particular intimacy of a specific class. It is equally significant activities that it induced at pupils. It is also characteristic of the epistemological, curricular, didactical or pedagogical presupposition (Ginestié, Brandt-Pomares, 1998).

On the other hand, the passage to the real supposes to put in stake an analysis of the activity of the pupil. His perusal of the task, the manner he has to organize its activity and to orient its actions, what it takes in consideration and what it does not see even, allow characterising his learning process. In this perspective, we can notice difficulties that he meets, the manner whose he processes them, adopted strategies and the planning of his different actions (Ginestié, Andreucci, 1999). Reading activity through the description of the task allows proceeding pupil's activity with some precise characteristic elements of the task. We can value difficulties met by the pupil and identify which are relevant to the context (the formulation of the task, the organization of conditions of the study, the use of models, materials, etc.) and which notices obstacles to the learning (Amigues, Ginestié, 1991).

SCHOOL ORGANISATION AND PUPIL'S WORK

Organizations implemented at school, in the classroom and by the teacher have a direct influence on the work of the pupil and on the result of this work. Concerning the technology education (but it is not specific for these subject), it is important to specify and to define what is waited from the pupil, recourses he disposes to get there, the manner whose he gets there. Therefore, we have to understand the evaluation the nature of the goal, the manner to get there but also the breach of the goal; everything that allows to bring in front understanding about the process of knowledge's transmission-appropriation. From this point, we are not in a curricular approach that has for object to define contents of teaching and to determine goals to reach; we discuss goals fixed by the institution, their institutional pertinence, their coherence in a scholastic organization datum. Of course, the temptation is great to believe that we could have act on prescription as to reduce these gaps. The evolution of curriculum shows that this kind of actions is limited because it enters in social negotiations that the research can illuminate to defect to inspire them, even to affect them.

TASK ANALYSIS

Our entry by the situations is an analytic viewpoint to render real situations of classify or in a prospective perspective to think possible evolution. For that, the crossed analysis task-activity presents a good framework. The task's analyse gives some understanding about the placement in text (or the placement in word) of the object of study. This placement in text constitutes one of the last stages of the didactical transposition, stage in the course of which the teacher anticipates and executes the production of the object of study that it makes return in its class. Many indicators allow characterising some ingredients of the organisation that it counts to put in place:

- the nature of knowledge that he exhibits,
- the display of the result expected at the end of the sequence,
- the spatial and temporal organization type that he puts in act,
- the strategies that he gives to orchestrate the activity of pupils,
- the different levels of evaluation on which he counts to lean (evaluation his activity, the progress of his sequence, the activity of pupils, the breach of results),
- the devices of mediation and remediation that he envisages, etc.

Others indicators allow to notice explicit or implicit models that he uses for the organization of this production:

- model of the logic of pupil learning organized around acquisition of competence noticed to the breadth of significant observable behaviours versus a constructivist approach based on the elaboration of knowledge;
- model of the activity of pupils according to a logic of smooth away difficulties versus a logic of confrontation to obstacles;
- model of the teaching organisation according to a logic of guidance of the action of the pupil versus a logic of problem-solving;

- model of the organization of knowledge references that one can caricature in a binary alternative: in technology education, there is nothing to know versus there is only knowledge.

The construction of these models supposes the elaboration of a strong theoretical reference by which we can predict the appearance of the objects of study and how they become into school organisations. Of course, we front three different viability risks: one is an instant risk about what's happen with the course that is going to unfold here, at this hour, in this classroom, with this teacher and these pupils; second is a progression risk about what happen in the duration of the class, the articulation of the different sessions and their succession; third is durability risk about the permanency of a teaching at such level, in such class, in such context, according to evolution, development, interaction with the other subjects as a kind of general educational ecology.

ACTIVITY ANALYSIS

The activity analyse, as for it, tries to understand the logic of pupils in their evolution to achieve the task that is confided them and the manner of which they adapt conditions organised by the teacher. Retained indicators refer directly to theories of the apprenticeship, notably through:

- the strategy they adopt,
- the manner to organize their actions,
- the manner to notice and to anticipate difficulties and to overcome them or to avoid them,
- the manner to notice or not constraints imposed by the situation and to take into account them or no, etc.

Analysing the activity of pupils is a powerful tool that allows to notice, to qualify and to valorise gaps between what the teacher waits them, what they obtain really and the manner that they use to reach this result. It concerns, on the one hand, to give indicators of efficiency of a device concerning learning and, on the other hand, indicators on the manner to conceive plan. To adopt a criterion of efficiency of plan put in place by teachers is not easy. That supposes to place the question of the acquisition of knowledge by pupils to the heart of the educational act, what is not without consequences in TE.

This challenge is important if we want to reinforce the position and the role of the TE as a general education subject. Through our French experience, but also through some related experiences in different countries, we have change of period. The first time of innovation and implementation is definitively done. Many countries know a decrease period with disaffection for TE: decrease of budget, reduction of school time devoted to the subject. At the same time, more and more teams develop investigation in TE. May be, we have to diffuse the results of these investigations and to develop the support that we can provide to the teacher but also to the curriculum designers, this is our challenge to bring our contribution to TE.

REFERENCES

Amigues R., Ginestié J. (1991) Représentations et stratégies des élèves dans l'apprentissage d'un langage de commande : le GRAFCET. *Le travail humain*, Vol. 4, pp. 1-19.

Brandt-Pomares, P. (2003), *Les nouvelles technologies de l'information et de la communication dans les enseignements technologiques. De l'organisation des savoirs aux conditions d'étude : didactique de la consultation d'information*, Thèse de doctorat, Université de Provence, Aix-en-Provence.

Chatoney, M. (2003), *Construction du concept de matériau dans l'enseignement des sciences et technologie à l'école primaire : perspectives curriculaires et didactiques*, Thèse de doctorat, Université de Provence, Aix-en-Provence.

Compton, V. & Jones, A. (1998), Reflecting on teacher development in technology education: implications for Future Programs, *International Journal of Technology and Design Education*, n° 8 vol. 2, pp. 151-166.

COPRET (1984), *Proposition de la COPRET pour l'enseignement de la technologie au collège*, Ministère de l'Éducation Nationale, Paris.

De Vries: M. (1994), Technology education in Western Europe, in D. Layton (ed.), *Innovations in Science and Technology Education*, Vol. 5, UNESCO editions, Paris.

Dugger, W. (2000), Standards for technological literacy: Content for the study of technology, *Technology Teacher*, n° 59, vol. 5, pp. 8-13.

Gardner, P. & Hill, A-M.: 1999, Technology education in Ontario: Evolution, Achievements, Critiques and Challenges. Part 1: The Context', *International Journal of Technology and Design Education*, n° 9, vol. 2, pp. 103-136.

Ginestié J. (1992), *Contribution à la didactique des disciplines technologiques : acquisition et utilisation d'un langage d'automatisme*. Thèse de doctorat, Université de Provence, Aix-en-Provence.

Ginestié J. (1995), Knowledge or know-how: Overview about development of technology education. In Blandow D. & Wahl D., *Innovation and management in technology education*, Erfurt, WOCATE editions.

Ginestié J. (*1996*), Computer based control in technology education: Some questions about introducing and teaching. In Tamir A., *Report of the Jerusalem International Sciences and Technology Education Conference*, UNESCO, Jerusalem, section 3, pp. 21-29.

Ginestié J., Brandt-Pomares P. (1998), Distanced resources access in Technology education, In Kananoja T., Kantola J., Issakainen M., *The principles and practices of teaching Technology*, Jyväskylä, University of Jyväskylä editors, pp. 150-159.

Ginestié J., Andreucci C. (1999), Designing and building: how children do this. In Benson C., *Second international primary design and Technology conference: Celebrating good practices*, Birmingham, CRIPT-UCE editions, pp. 62-66.

Ginestié J. (2000), An integrated project with university, teacher training, school and enterprise, In Theuerkauf W., Dyrenfurth M., *Proceeds of the international conference in Braunschweig: Consequences and perspectives of a global approach on technology education*, Erfurt, WOCATE editions, CD-Rom publication.

Ginestié J. (2001a), Technology education in French primary school: Which direction for which goals? In Benson C., *Third international primary design and Technology conference: Quality in the making*, Birmingham, CRIPT-UCE editions, pp. 70-74.

Ginestié J. (2001b), Interés y perspectivas por una educación tecnológica para todos. In Benson C., De Vries M., Ginestié J., et al. *Educación tecnológica*, Santiago, Chili: LOM Ediciones, Fernando Mena Editor, pp. 19-30.

Ginestié J.: 2001c, Qué metodología, para qué educación tecnológica. In Benson C., De Vries M., Ginestié J., et al. *Educación tecnológica*, Santiago, Chili: LOM Ediciones, Fernando Mena Editor, pp. 55-82.

Ginestié J.: 2002, The industrial project method in French industry and in French school, *International Journal of Technology and Design Education*, vol. 12, n° 2, pp. 99-122.

Ginestié J. : 2003, Quelle place pour une éducation technologique pour tous ? Le complexe culturel à l'égard de la chose technique. In *Actes du colloque international La culture technique, un enjeu d'éducation*, Paris, novembre 2003.

Ginestié J. : 2004, Évaluer les élèves dans les formations initiales d'enseignants en éducation technologique. In *acte du colloque international Finalités et évaluations en éducation technologique*, Paris, mars 2004, AEET.

Ginestié J.: 2005 (à paraître), La formation des enseignants de l'enseignement technologique en regard des organisations curriculaires : aspects problématiques et questions de recherche. In Ginestié J. *Formation professionnelle des enseignants, au-delà des apparences, quelles différences ? Une étude internationale sur la formation des enseignants d'éducation technologique.* Santiago : Éditions Los Salesianos.

Hennessy, S. & Murphy, P.: 1999, The Potential for Collaborative Problem Solving in Design and Technology, *International Journal of Technology and Design Education* n° 9, vol. 1, pp. 1-36.

Jones, A.: 1997, Recent research in learning technological concepts and processes, *International Journal of Technology and Design Education*, n° 7, vol. 1-2, pp. 83-96.

Kantola, J., Nikkanen, P., Kari, J. & Kananoja, T.: 1999, *Through Eeucation into the world of work*, Institute for Educational Research, University of Jyvtskylâ, Jyviskylâ.

Sanders, M (1999), *Technology education In the middle level schools; Its role and purpose*, NASP Bulletin, No 83, Vol.608, 34-44.

PIERRE VERILLON AND COLETTE ANDREUCCI

28. ARTEFACTS AND COGNITIVE DEVELOPMENT: HOW DO PSYCHOGENETIC THEORIES OF INTELLIGENCE HELP IN UNDERSTANDING THE INFLUENCE OF TECHNICAL ENVIRONMENTS ON THE DEVELOPMENT OF THOUGHT?

TECHNOLOGY EDUCATION AND PUPILS' COGNITIVE DEVELOPMENT

Scholarly English language publications concerning technology education have considerably increased during the past years. However, as several recent reviews of literature have pointed out (De Miranda, 2004; Zuga, 2004), focus has essentially born on the design, development and assessment of curriculum. The prevailing approaches have left aside issues relating to the cognitive processes underlying student and teacher activity in the classroom. As a result, our knowledge of the singular nature and forms of cognition involved in the construction and transmission of technical knowledge and skills remains very scant. Some writers (Cajas 2000, Lewis 1999; Petrina, 1998, Zuga, 2004) link this deficiency to insufficient theoretical grounding and faulty problematics in research on technology education.

In France, the situation is quite similar. Studies in technology education have focused as elsewhere essentially on curriculum design and assessment. As A. Weill-Barais (1995), a psychologist of physics education, has stated:

"One can only observe the scarcity of research on how children access to technical objects... The specificity of technical objects generally goes unrecognised by developmental psychologists although it would warrant a psychogenetic approach. This lack of recognition leads to a situation where no manual or reader in psychology is available on the subject."

Technology education is a recent subject in the French national curriculum. Only since 1985 is it, for all pupils, a compulsory subject taught by specialized (trained technology) teachers during the four years of middle school. Prior to that date, precursory forms of technology education as a separate subject had existed on and off at different levels in the school system for the previous century. However these were optional and only concerned certain categories of pupils and were often taught by physics teachers. Thus, in France, until the permanent introduction of technology in the curriculum, only the pupils enrolled in technical and vocational branches of the education – often on account of their poor results in the academic subjects - were actually confronted during their schooling with technological

M.J. de Vries, I. Mottier (eds.), International Handbook of Technology Education, 399–416.

environments, activities and issues relating to industry, crafts and commerce. It is noteworthy that, today still, part of technology teacher training is carried out by technical and vocational education teachers and that most teacher trainees are former students of technical and vocational schools.

As regards the French research and development community in technology education, it is far from equalling in numbers and seniority those that have evolved around other school subjects. Even so, its existence actually predates the subject's entry into the curriculum. Curriculum design and testing was carried out as early as the 70's and eventually led to the founding of the LIRESPT (now LIREST), a university research lab that has now become prominent in technology curriculum studies. Likewise, at the National Institute for Pedagogical Research (INRP), a department dedicated to studies in technical and vocational education developed psychological and pedagogical approaches to teaching technological knowledge and skills. In particular, the learner's interaction with material and semiotic artefacts of the technical environment became a major topic of interest and research within the department in the 80's. Twenty years later, in continuity with these seminal interrogations and despite this department's dissolution, a theoretical and thematic line of work has been maintained and developed among a community now scattered inside and outside the institute. The aim of this paper is to give an account by two insiders of the conceptual change this community has both experienced and brought about in the approach of learning and development within technological settings. It describes how, drawing from theoretical and empirical evidence, research has led to a critical appraisal these two models and derived alternative propositions resting on their stronger points, such as Vygotsky's notion of mediated activity, and his conception of signs and tools as instruments as well as Piaget's vision of cognitive development as resulting from the child's active alteration of his (her) environment. Three examples will illustrate these alternative models: the first deals with some unsuspected effects of child-artefact interaction on the construction of the concept of volume, the second deals with tool use and the development of activity, the last with learning to read engineering drawings.

Some history

One of the unforeseen results of the advent of technology education in 1985 has been the emergence in French psychological research of a new field of study – instrumented activity in human–artefact interaction – and the development of a new theoretical paradigm, the instrumental theory (Rabardel, 1995; Vérillon & Rabardel, 1995) now developing in work psychology and ergonomics.

The story begins at the Département d'Etudes et de Recherche sur les Enseignement technologiques of INRP where two long-term INRP research programs headed by Pierre Rabardel and involving both INRP and university researchers were launched in 1984. The first program, entitled *"Made material objects as support for cognitive development in education"*, arose from the realization that technology education would introduce into the arena of learning activities objects sharply contrasting with the discursive and textual objects usually associated with other school subjects. Its aim was to investigate if - and how - interaction with made material objects[1], by reason of their material, finalized and functional nature, would affect cognition. The focus of the research agenda was clearly developmental: can pupils' dealings with artefacts within school organized settings, whether as objects of study or as means of action, influence their cognitive development and, if so, what are the determining conditions? The empirical work attempted to give evidence of cognitive change or growth resulting from situations in which pupils, in order to solve a problem or fulfil a task, had to design and/or build and/or use a material object.

The second research program, entitled *"Reading difficulties in engineering drawing"*, aimed at understanding the difficulties encountered by pupils in decoding engineering drawings, then considered a key skill in technical and vocational education. The dawning technology education was also expected to benefit from this program, as one of the objectives of new curriculum was to familiarize middle school pupils with engineering drawing. The work carried out within this program centred on analysing readers' errors and designing remedial material and tasks.

The predominance of Piagetian genetic constructivism

A remarkable point is that the conceptual frameworks summoned by the researchers involved in both these programs all derive from Piagetian constructivism, clearly dominant at the time in French educational psychology. In the early 80's, the works of Vygotsky and Bruner were just being translated and still practically unknown to researchers. Consequently, Piagetian constructivism seemed the most appropriate framework for investigating developmental processes.

Here are some significant empirical studies carried out under the first program:
- How do situations in which pupils build and use different types of weighing-machines influence their conception of weight/ length of beam ratio?
- How do spatial competencies evolve in woodworking activities involving tool use?
- How does everyday experience with familiar objects designed to vary in shape and size influence the child's construction of volume?
- How does pupils' experience of work with a lathe influence their conception of surface?

The hypotheses underlying these studies were clearly inspired by Piagetian theory. The assumption was that, in compliance with Piaget's model of cognitive equilibration (1975), the subjects' existing cognitive structures, when brought to bear on the specific structural and functional properties of made objects, would in the course of assimilation/accommodation bring about conceptual change. This was actually evidenced by some experiments: for example, pupils having been

---

[1] Fairly rapidly, through the group's interest in anthropological issues the phrase "made material object" (*objet matériel fabriqué*) was abandoned in favour of "artefact". See Rabardel (1995) for discussion.

involved in woodworking fared better in spatial tests than did those of a control group.

In the second program, again Piaget provided the theoretical framework for research. In conceptualising the cognitive processes underlying competency in reading engineering drawings, approaches based on Piaget's theory of the construction of the representation of space bore fruitful results. For example, many errors committed by students in reading tasks could be explained by their incapacity to grasp projective operations or to apply them when decoding the different orthographic views of an object. In a typical experiment, pupils were faced with oblique drawings of blocks of different shapes, of which they were also given top and front orthographic views. Their task was to draw a side view of each block. On analysis, many errors seemed to result from an impulse of students to conserve, and consequently reproduce, in their drawing of a side view some significant or outstanding feature of the front view. In keeping with Piagetian theory, which shows figurative thought to genetically precede operative thinking, these errors were attributed to students' use of figurative strategies whereas responses that showed evidence of mental coordination of the top and front views were considered as resulting from operative strategies (Vermersch P. & Weill-Fassina A., 1985).

Thus, genetic constructivism seemed to be, on the whole, a very satisfactory framework for the interpreting the evidence yielded by empirical work. However, some results did not entirely fit with theory thus revealing possible "anomalies" in the paradigm. If some instances of child-artefact interaction seemed to conform to the equilibration theory, other experiments were less conclusive. For example, exposure of children to telescopic, folding or inflatable objects in everyday contexts seemed to unbalance their construction of the invariance of volume. Likewise, progress in the geometrical modelling of the spatial aspects of turning, brought about by running a lathe, was shown to be due not to the subjects' interaction with the machine but to their gradual awareness of physical and spatial invariants in the course of their joint interaction both with the lathe and the work piece during the machining process. Similarly, concerning engineering drawing, Rabardel (1982) had already shown that some errors in reading tasks could also be induced by faulty comprehension of the object described by the drawing. Other errors (Vérillon & Rabardel, 1987) could be attributed to student's misconceptions as to how engineering drawing actually works (i.e., how the semiotic and geometrical solutions embodied in engineering drawing enable the production of accurate graphic descriptions of technical artefacts).

In the next section, we have a closer look at some of these studies.

THREE STUDIES IN PUPIL-ARTEFACT INTERACTION

Conceptualising volume

The first study (Andreucci, 1990) concerns an analysis of the difficulties met by children in acquiring the conservation (the invariance) of volume. Since Piaget, Inhelder and Szeminska's (1948) seminal studies of children's spontaneous geometry and their acquisition of physical quantities (1941), it is well known that the development of volume, as a physical and geometrical construct, comes very slowly and lately. Before 11 or 12 years, a child will not admit that a same piece of clay, rolled in a ball will occupy an equal amount of space as when rolled in a cylinder. Nor will he (she) predict that, immersed in a glass, it will raise the water to the same level. By contrast, the same child, using logical arguments which would apply also for this situation - identity, reversibility, compensation - will be quite sure of the invariance of the quantity of matter of that piece of clay (acquired around 8 years) and of its weight (around 10) when it undergoes the same transformations. Rather unsatisfyingly, Piaget explains this puzzling lag in the generalization of a logical structure to different notions as a horizontal "décalage" due to the specific resistance of the notion to assimilation within the structure. Other studies focusing on volume as a measure or quantifier of space have evidenced similar enduring difficulties in pupils' acquisition of the concept. Ricco, Vergnaud & Rouchier (1983) show that, at age 15, most pupils have trouble with the aspects linked to the trilinear aspect of volumic quantification. However, all these studies, focusing exclusively on a physics or mathematical approach of the conceptualisation of volume, have overlooked a possible source of difficulty - i.e., that the child's representations of volume linked to practical everyday interaction with three-dimensional artefacts might lead to conflict with scholarly notions.

A look at technical documents and catalogues shows that the measurements of artefacts are generally given in terms of overall dimensions rather than in terms of volume. The notions associated with the bulk (in French, *encombrement*) or amount of space occupied by an object are evidently close to that of volume, but their physical and mathematical characteristics remain nonetheless different.

Bulk is expressed in three dimensions but in contrast with volume, these dimensions cannot be combined, nor are they interchangeable, in the sense that an artefact generally has a definite orientation in space, linked to its functional properties. In stowing or packing an artefact, for example, each dimension is taken into account separately. The fact that in everyday life, bulk rather than volume is most often the practical concept for dealing with the spatial problems posed by artefacts can explain the difficulty of conceiving volumetric space as a product of three dimensions.

Moreover, bulk, as a sociological and technological characteristic of material artefacts, does not manifest the same invariance as volume. First, unlike plasticine or clay objects used by Piaget, most artefacts do not, for obvious functional reasons, easily undergo changes in shape without damage. When they do, it is generally because they have been designed in that intention (e.g.: telescopic, folding or inflatable objects). For instance, their utility being intermittent, they are designed so that, when not in use, they can be easily stowed or transported (e.g.: an umbrella, an ironing table or an air mattress). Also, bulkiness is a relative notion: it depends on relationships among other objects. Children will consider that objects imbedded in one another "take up less space room". Similarly they may consider that the space occupied by an object can vary, since it may or may not fit into a container according to the way it is introduced.

In studying the stowing techniques that children, aged between 5 and 12, use when asked to pack into a suitcase as many items as possible within a collection of everyday objects, we have shown that very early (around 7) they become aware that, as a result of design, the space occupied by artefacts is indeed a variable and relative characteristic. In ways not foreseen by Piaget, bulk or apparent volume, as a functional concept for thinking about objects in space (especially made objects), not only precedes the construction of volumetric concepts but, unknown to teachers and pupils, it may in fact become an impediment to this construction.

Interacting with devices for producing ruled surfaces

Another experiment (Verillon & Rabardel, 1995) consisted of asking a group of pupils, aged 10 to 15, to individually imagine ways of producing plane and revolution (cylindrical and conical) surfaces on pieces of wood. We were interested in seeing how the children, through the different technical processes they would suggest, would tackle both the underlying mechanical and spatial aspects of the material transformation.

The task was to transform a rectangular block of wood into a cylinder (or, inversely, a cylinder into a parallelepiped, or again a parallelepiped into a cone, etc.). In order to minimize language bias, the question actually asked was: "How would you make an object with this shape here from an object like that one there?" The objects (representing both the initial workpiece and the end-product), which the subjects they could handle at will, were in solid wood, approximately 100 x 30 x 30 mm.

In short, the transformation technique proposed by all the pupils consists in removing matter from the work piece. This is carried out in two phases: rough-cutting then finishing through abrasion. Each phase is associated with a particular class of instruments: knives, cutters and saws (even a power-saw!) for rough-cutting and files, abrasives, etc. for finishing.

As regards the management of the spatial aspects of the operation, the desired end shape seems, so to speak, projected by the subject on to the rough work piece. This projection, which is mental - though some children actually suggest drawing lines on the block - guides the step by step removal of matter from the work piece, until, through successive approximations, it "matches" the anticipated shape as near as possible.

404

The lack of particular constraints in the procedure to be used enabled the subjects to build and solve the problem in terms of tools, as well as technical and spatial schemes, which were familiar to them. Nevertheless, none of the pupils thought that the process that they suggested was the same as that used in industry to produce similar shapes. As expressed by one of them: "That's done with machines, otherwise it would take too much time ... and then, anyway, a machine is more accurate!"

We therefore followed up by asking them how they imagined such machines.

The relative diversity of the mechanized solutions suggested by the children contrasts with the procedure anticipated for manual manufacture, which is practically identical from one subject to another. Leaving aside one subject's initial proposal consisting of a sort of remote manipulating device capable of reproducing the manual procedure through a system of rods with terminal clamps, they may be grouped into three categories according to the technical solution anticipated to produce the desired transformation:

- moulding or deformation,
- removal of matter through abrasion,
- removal of matter by cutting.

The constraint of mechanizing their manufacturing process considerably transforms the task for the subjects. The main element at stake and the principal difficulty introduced by this constraint concerns the management of the spatial and temporal aspects of transformation. In the non-mechanized procedures, control of the amplitude and direction of the transforming action is provided by the hand holding the tool. Similarly, as regards the planning of action, the deviation from the anticipated final state is managed in a retroactive way, step by step, under the control of successive sightings, possibly facilitated by the reference marks drawn on the work piece. What characterizes the manual procedures is a lack of a general spatial coordination of action (which, for example, could take into account properties of axial symmetry or revolution). In our opinion, it is precisely because these procedures do not require any overall geometrization or synchronization of the transformation process that they are so readily proposed.

Conversely, the instruction to mechanize the process is interpreted as entailing attributing to the machine the management of the energetic, chronological and spatial aspects of the transformation – hence, the need to equip the device with the physical and geometrical operators capable of producing the desired shape in a direct and proactive way. The remote manipulator solution, which conserves retroactive adjustment and the ability to operate the removal of matter on a step-by-step basis, appears to be an attempt to get round this hard necessity. Finding an adequate design solution effectively requires addressing multiple and complementary problems concerning the physical aspects of the transformation, the spatial analysis of the desired final form, as well as, correlatively, the geometry of the generating organ, the locus of its successive positions, etc.

The devices imagined by the pupils - other than remote manipulators - demonstrate that this is reached through a geometric analysis (or breaking down) of the desired form and, at the same time, a corresponding dissociation of the means of its production. This joint dissociation of both the desired shape and its generating mechanism is carried out to a variable extent in the devices imagined by the children. Thus, moulding devices enable the shape to be conserved fully (i.e. without having to be broken down) within the geometry of the die, simply by reversing it. As one pupil asserts: "if you want to get that shape, the machine has to have the same shape". On the other hand, transformation by machining does not enable the desired shape to be conserved in the tool. Thus, devices driving abrasive strips in translation for the production of plane surfaces, while still partially conserving the anticipated form, are evidence of an analysis in terms of surface. Pushing geometric abstraction a step further, other systems using cutting edges and points, actuated by controlled movements, within different spatial arrangements, reveal their designer's capacity, at least "in action", to dissociate the initial shape into generator points or lines in liaison with revolution axes and directors.

The observation of these pupils' first acquaintance with a miniature lathe revealed similar processes. For most of the pupils, the idea of being able to produce a cylindrical surface using a single rectilinear longitudinal stroke only appears at a late stage. As a matter of fact, the sole idea of being able to remove matter from a piece of metal was in itself difficult to conceive for them: "metal is too hard!" Only after having tried different step by step strategies for "wearing away" or "cutting" metal along the work piece was it possible for them to become aware of certain invariant spatial properties of the lathe, imparted to it by its very design: for example, the fact that the distance between the tool and the rotational axis of the work piece remains invariant across action on the lathe's longitudinal handwheel.

This implies that the subject is able to decentre himself from his own actions so that he can resituate and coordinate them in an overall space. In effect, only the conscious discovery, or the discovery "in action" of the spatial characteristics underlying his procedures - often linked to their failure - enables the subject to recompose them and, for instance, to become aware of the relations of equivalence between a cutting edge of a given shape and a generator point with a suitable trajectory, or again between the iteration of elementary operations and their composed form.

Reading engineering drawing

The study of the child's development of what Piaget and Inhelder's (1947) termed "representative space" enabled decisive breakthroughs in the understanding of the errors made in reading engineering drawings. Expertise in reading drawings was seen as the ability to carry out the mental transformations – in Piagetian terms: "projective operations" – that enable the reader to mentally "visualize" what, in a view of an object, varies and what remains invariant as he modifies his point of view on that object. Different projective operations involved in reading were identified (Zougarri G. et al, 1984) and shown to be of unequal difficulty for learners. A diagnostic test and material for remedial training in these different operations were designed (Higelé, 1984).

However despite the undeniable value, both predictive and pragmatic, of these findings, there were some weaknesses in the approach. For example, in the reading experiments and in the remedial tasks, the objects depicted in the drawings – geometric blocks of differing shapes - were far from resembling the usual referents of engineering drawings, i.e. industrial artefacts. Similarly, the graphic mode used for their representation was quite distant from the actual graphic code and norms used in engineering drawing.

Studies carried out with real drawings and in functional contexts confirmed the importance of readers' mastery of spatial operative invariants. However they also revealed that certain spatial properties of the industrial artefacts depicted in engineering drawings are also invariants. The geometric characteristics of made objects are not – contrary to blocks – technologically neutral: the shape of an artefact is determined both by its functional properties (e.g. the thread of a screw, the wing of an airplane) and by constraints imposed by the means available to fabricate it (e.g. machine tools are limited in the shapes they can generate). The reader's knowledge of these regularities – his technological culture – was shown to influence his decoding of drawings (Rabardel, 1982; Bal et al, 1984). So alongside the need for spatial skills, reading drawings was seen as also requiring a technological acquaintance with the objects depicted. However, yet another dimension plays a part in student's reading difficulties: it is the extent to which they master the fairly complex code implemented in engineering drawing.

This code comprises several sub-systems or components (Rabardel, 1980). A descriptive component provides the underlying projective principles (i.e. orthogonal projection, oblique projection, etc.) that enable the production of views that conserve certain dimensional or geometric aspects of the depicted object. When coupled with a second component – the graphic system that furnishes the different line symbols used in drawing - material representations of the depicted object can be made. Finally, a third component, the conventional disposition of the different views in the 2-dimensional space of the drawing enables the reader to identify and mentally interconnect the different points of view on the depicted object in 3-dimensinal space. Suggestions for the explicit teaching of the semiotics of engineering drawing as well as of other graphic codes encountered in vocational and technology education were made (Vérillon & Rabardel, 1987; Andreucci et al, 1996)

ANOTHER LOOK AT GENETIC EPISTEMOLOGY

What the three above studies show is that, contrary to what would be expected within a classic Piagetian framework, the construction by a subject of the properties of made objects – whether they be material or symbolic - stems not solely from his (her) bilateral interaction with that object. In order to understand cognitive development resulting from human dealings with artefacts it is necessary take into account the subject's conceptual construction, jointly: of the artefact, of the reality on which it is brought to bear and of the resulting interaction between artefact and reality. In this section, we attempt to show why Piaget's constructivism may not be totally adequate in explaining human development in the made world and why it is necessary to appeal to other psychological theories.

The epistemic subject

It is first of all important to keep in mind that Piaget's constant aim was to reveal the mechanisms underlying "the child's construction of reality" (1937). His explicit project is to account for the development of what he termed the "epistemic subject" In this sense, his focus was on the genetic processes and mechanisms through which the human subject elaborates knowledge about the surrounding social and physical world. In our opinion, the aim of a genetic psychology of technique should, in contrast, be to focus on the "pragmatic subject". There is a need to describe and account for the mechanisms through which humans devise pragmatic projects and means aimed at conforming the world to their designs. In this perspective, action retains the decisive role it plays in constructivism (Inhelder, B., & Cellerier, G., 1992). However, it is no longer an action upon the environment aiming as with Piaget at eliciting its invariant properties. It is rather an action mobilizing knowledge concerning these stable and predictable patterns of the environment in order to put it to use advantageously. Technical action, through the design and use of artefacts, imparts artificial properties on the natural environment. In its search for beneficial and pragmatic effects, it strives to introduce novel invariant relationships among elements of existing reality. Which doesn't mean that no knowledge may be produced within the sphere of technique. On the contrary, Staudenmaïer (1985) argues that whenever technological development may be stemmed by lack of knowledge in a given field, "problematic data" is then generated to meet the specific demands of the design problem. Likewise, Perrin (1991) shows that artefact design is a major source of knowledge. However, he adds that the production of knowledge in technology differs from the scientific process of knowledge production in that it is only secondary and accessory to artefact production that remains "both the starting and end point of the design process". In this sense, we consider that what is needed is psychological insight into the design process equivalent to the insight brought by genetic epistemology into the knowing process.

Biologism

There is, in our opinion, another intrinsic limitation to applying the Piagetian model to interaction with the made world – a limitation that it shares with other approaches of cognition: it is its naturalistic point of view. It sees development as an epigenetic process: much as a biological organism develops through adaptation to its milieu, the epistemic subject is conceived as constructing his (her) cognitive structures by interacting with the environment. Initially, reality may resist assimilation and destabilize these structures but ultimately, through accommodation, they restructure thereby gaining stability and strength. A follower of Descartes and Kant regarding the philosophy of knowledge, Piaget seems to consider both his subject's environment and his (her) means of interaction with this environment as immune from social and historical influence. Language and artefacts, for example, have no particular status in his theory that might set them fundamentally apart from the world of physical or living objects. When investigating the construction of children's conceptions in mechanics, he may ask his subjects to comment the trajectory of a toy car on an inclined plane or that of a toy boat in a basin. However it is clear that these toys are used only because they are particularly convenient in demonstrating certain invariants of the physical world. Not surprisingly, might comment a technologist: the car wheels, the ship's rudder are artificial invariants, historically and socially brought about and transmitted. They shrewdly and profitably exploit the "laws of nature". In short they are artefacts, but this peculiarity is not taken into account by theory.

Dualism

One last problem raised by the Piagetian approach is its fundamentally dualistic conception of subject-environment interaction, which leads research to focus on dyadic relationships: subject-object, man-machine, student-teacher, student-curriculum, etc. The subject is always studied in his (her) face-to-face relationship with the world or a sub-set of the world. The idea of a mediated relationship is absent from this approach. This is consistent with the other aspects we have highlighted in this section: on the one hand, an exclusively constructivist and epistemic conception of development, and on the other, a biologist and a-historical view of human interaction with reality. Yet, as pointed out by French philosopher of technique, J. -P. Séris (1994), technique is inherently "interposition of mediations, be they instrumental (tools, machines, institutions) or methodical (manoeuvres, procedures, programs, processes)" (P. 48). In keeping with this analysis, a psychological theory striving to account for human cognitive functioning and development in technological settings should reserve a prominent status to mediation and mediational processes. In the following section, we sketch out some theoretical elements worked out during the last two decades that attempt to contribute to such a theory.

TOWARDS A THEORY OF INSTRUMENTS

Vygotsky is stated as having said " the central point of our psychology is mediation " (Wertsch, 1985). However mediation does not appear to have been a major concept in the psychological paradigms that dominated the second half of the 20th century. As Norman (1991) once pointed out, "despite the enormous impact of artefacts upon human cognition, most of our scientific understanding is of the [...] single, unaided individual, studied almost entirely within the university laboratory ". Unknowingly, some of the early work at INRP on interaction with made objects or with industrial graphics was liable to this criticism. But, as we have seen, the contradictions raised by empirical work soon showed the need for added reflection on the exact nature of artefacts. Readings in early 20th century psychological literature brought back into focus the issue of instruments and instrumented activity much researched in Europe before World War II (Rabadel & Vérillon, 1988). The instrumental nature of artefacts gradually imposed itself and it became obvious that interaction with artefacts could not be understood within a dyadic subject-object relationship. Of course, artefacts belong to the objective world but, as instruments, they necessarily intervene as "interfaces" between the subject and the world. In consequence, a triadic model of instrumented activity (Rabardel & Vérillon, 1985; Vérillon & Rabardel, 1995; Vérillon, 2000) was proposed (Fig. 1).

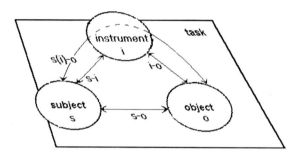

Fig. 1: The situated instrumented activity model

In contrast with the classic dyadic modelling of subject-object interaction, it underscores the multiple relationships that, in instrumented activity, bind together the subject, the instrument and the object towards which instrumented action is directed. It also indicates that instrumented activity is always grounded in – and hence conditioned by - situated tasks. Our study of pupils' first encounter with a lathe showed that the analysis of instrumented activity could not be limited to considering only direct subject-instrument interaction (s-i). The model shows it should also take into account direct subject-object interaction (s-o), as well as instrument-object interaction (i-o) and indirect subject-object interaction through the mediation of the instrument (s(i)-o).

Semiotic artefacts, such as engineering drawing, can also be seen as instruments (Vérillon & Rabardel, 1993; Andreucci et al, 1996). Just as for any artefact, their structural properties can be analysed functionally. For example, the semiotic and geometric properties of engineering drawing are not arbitrary. On the contrary, they are motivated by the type of information – essentially regarding shape and dimension – required in engineering tasks. As already mentioned, functional teaching of these properties is possible.

Vygotsky (1985a) termed instruments such as drawings and other symbolic artefacts "psychic instruments", in the sense that what they affect is not an object but one's own - or another person's – psyche, as shown in figure 2.

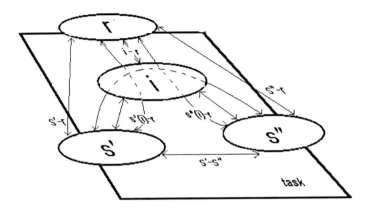

Fig. 2: Situated activity instrumented by a semiotic artefact

Modelling activity instrumented by semiotic artefacts is a bit more complex than modelling that instrumented by material instruments. The model represents communication as taking place between two subjects (s' and s'') by means of the semiotic instrument (i). Also, since semiotic instruments aim at modifying a receiver's information state or representations, a fourth element has been introduced: that about which there is information or representation - the referent (r). The referent is the object (or object class) to which refers the transmitter's instrumented action on the receiver. The model consequently shows the two-fold function of semiotic instruments: a signalling function resulting in the sensory and cognitive stimulation of the receiver and a referring function, which enables the subjects to relate the signal to an external object. A new set of relationships can be examined through this model. Instrument-referent relations (i-r) concern coding, that is the set of semiotic solutions that enable the transmission of information concerning the referent through signifiers (e.g. the specific graphic symbols in engineering drawing). Subject-referent relationships (s' (i)-r and s'' (i)-r) indicate a subject's relation to a referent object during coding and decoding. Direct s-r relationship points to knowledge, representations and actual, virtual or remembered perceptions that s' or s'' may have of the referent object.

411

Distinguishing artefacts and instruments

These models of instrumented activity can help understanding how and in what ways artefacts affect cognitive development. But first it is necessary to make a clear distinction between artefact and instrument. Artefacts are man-made material constructs. They are bodies of intentionally organized invariants designed to operate certain anticipated transformations of the human or material environment when put to use by a person. As such artefacts are only one component of instrumented action. The other component consists of the activity brought into play by the user of the artefact. Artefacts display both their function and their efficiency only through the operations of their user. Like words that have lost their meaning, tools of which the use has been lost can no longer become instruments even though they remain artefacts. In this sense, an artefact in order to qualify as an instrument requires the psychological and physical participation of a user. When in use, an artefact is caught up in a system of action schemes, representations, knowledge, intellectual and motor skills that alone actualises its function. In this sense, instruments are actually hybrid entities, part psychological and part artefactual (Rabardel, 1995).

Instrumental genesis

Artefacts become instruments for people through a process referred to by Rabardel as "instrumental genesis". As the above studies reveal, it can be a long and difficult process before a lathe or engineering drawing can become instruments. A look at the models shows why: many relationships have to develop in the course of instrumental genesis. Appropriation is a word that well describes this process. It indicates the two directions in which this process takes place: towards the self and towards outside reality.

In its first sense, appropriation indicates that the artefact has to be integrated within one's own cognitive structure – i.e. one's existing representations, available action schemes etc, which in general require adaptation. Often, socially formed utilization schemes exist which have to be learned from peers. This self-directed construction, which mainly concerns s-i relationships in our models, is termed "instrumentation". The second sense of the word indicates that the artefact has to be appropriated to outside context. Specific ends and functional properties - some not necessarily intended by design - are attributed to it by the user. This is termed "instrumentalization" and concerns mainly s (i)-o and i-o relationships and s' (i)-r, i-r, s' (i)-s" and i-s" relationships, for semiotic artefacts.

Instrumentation and instrumentalization both contribute mastering artefacts. As his (her) utilization schemes evolve, the user can observe the consequences on the artefact's behaviour and on artefact-object interaction. In return, his representations of the functional aspects of his mediated action (e.g. causal relationships involved in tool-object interaction) can cause him (her) to alter his (her) schemes. Our observations of pupils learning through discovery to man a lathe illustrate this interdependence between instrumentation and instrumentalization. Machining operations evolved gradually as certain technical characteristics were uncovered and taken into account by the pupils.

People's instruments develop at different rhythms and over different lengths of time. Consider the career of a professional pilot: the scope of his instrument – its "instrumental field" – both deepens and widens as he accumulates experience and incorporates continuous technological change. Instrumented technical activities can be seen to evolve along two lines of development, distinct although more or less linked: a line of operative development and a line of artefactual development. Operative development is tied to the extension of the transformations made possible by the integration of artefacts in a person's repertoire of means of action. As the artefact is put to use, novel effects appear, which in order to be repeated and controlled require the formation of new schemes. At the same time new properties (new invariants) are manifested causing the subject to modify or renew his (her) existing representations concerning the artefact, the reality on which it operates or the processes and transformations at hand. New objectives for artefact use can consequently be contemplated by the user, thus opening up possibility of renewed activity and mobiles. Operative development may take different forms:

- increased speed, power and discrimination of utilization schemes,
- scheme transfer from one artefact, or class of artefacts, to another,
- developing different schemes for an identical result,
- developing new schemes for original or extreme results...

Artefactual development is linked to the fact that artefact use is guided by the expectation of interesting effects that by design, if correctly manipulated, the artefact is supposed to produce. Thus in the course artefact use, the user is led to assign finalities and functional properties to the artefact. However, in each situated instance of use, because contextual conditions vary, the artefact is never engaged the same way, nor in ways always in conformity with its design. In a sense, each singular or novel use of an artefact redesigns it. This does not result in actual modification of the artefact, but the user's vision of the artefact, of its functional properties and of the effects it is liable to produce, changes. Think of someone using a spanner as a hammer. According to Rabardel (1995), through people's changing uses of artefacts, the design process continues well after their actual fabrication.

Operative and artefactual development cannot be conceived separately from what actually gives them significance: the subject's activity. For Vygotsky (1978), tool and symbol are brought into effect through the mediation of human activity. However this doesn't mean they submit passively to activity. Artifacts and activity influence each other in ways that leads the development of activity and of instrumental genesis to be closely associated, recalling Vygotsky's (1985b) concept of zone of proximal development. At first, an artefact (a lathe, for instance), not yet become an instrument, is for the subject but a mere promise of potential action, out of reach of his present possibilities. Yet, within reach are social models to be imitated and, on the artefact, perceptible characteristics - wheels, handles – that afford indication of possible operation. These generate a certain tension: new potential activity is envisioned, along with novel outcomes, and they trigger the appropriation process. With the beginning of instrumental genesis, activity starts to be realised. And as remarked Léontiev (1975): "realised activity is always more fertile and more genuine than the consciousness that anticipates it". Unexpected properties and possibilities become apparent and, consequently, visions change, new goals are set, schemes accommodate and new motives arise. Instrumented activity, enriched by its confrontation with reality, in return stimulates instrumental development. A circular movement of mutual development and renewal is initiated: developing activity demanding new operative and artefactual progress while these open up novel fields of action.

CONCLUSION

Empirical and theoretical work in psychology over the last 20 years at France's National Institute of Pedagogical Research has attempted to document the idea that cognition is not brought to bear on artefacts in the same way as it is on natural objects. Of course, like any constituent of the environment, artefacts confront cognition with a set of constraints it has to identify, understand and take into account. As such they partake in the resistance that the objective world opposes to human understanding and, in this sense, Piaget's "epistemic subject" can be seen as a model of how human understanding copes with this - indistinctly made or natural - world. Very much in the way of a scientist, he experiments and probes his environment in search of invariance and logical coherence. Quite understandably, it has proved very fruitful for the comprehension of learning in science education settings.

Yet artefacts also exert specific constraints related to their mediational and instrumental nature. These constraints pertain to their built-in functional and structural features as devices designed to produce transformations, and no longer just to their general physical characteristics, which are common to all material objects. One set of constraints is linked to the mental and material operations required of artefact users in order to effectively carry out, in a given context, a given transformation. These constraints account for some of the misconceptions concerning volume discussed in our first study: practical experience of certain artefacts focused users' attention on a number of their functional spatial characteristics in detriment of others, not functional in the context, yet useful for the conceptualisation of volume.

Another set of constraints pertains to the particular set of material transformations a given artefact is designed to enable. This type of constraints is the one with which the pupils of our second experiment were essentially coping as they pondered on ways of configurating and implementing mechanisms capable of generating different surfaces. In dealing with semiotic artefacts such as engineering drawing, as in our third study, pupils coped with similar, albeit semiotic, constraints. Their difficulties in reading were seen as resulting from the fact that they do not comprehend the functionality of these constraints.

Obviously, the "epistemic" framework is not pertinent here, in the sense that we are dealing with behaviour that is at once practical and mediated. In search of an alternative model, our present work seeks theoretical guidelines in both post-Piagetian Genevan authors and the vigotskian tradition. In the former, we find insight into what might be termed a theory of "pragmatic" cognition, in which action is not, as in Piaget's conception, orientated towards the production of knowledge, but in which, on the contrary, knowledge is activated and processed by the subject so as to elicit practical and utilitarian transformations of his environment. In the latter, we find the basis for a psychological model of instrumentation, that is a model of the cognitive process whereby artefacts, at first undifferentiated from other objects, progressively acquire instrumental value, are integrated into one's mental and physical interaction with the world and finally, in return modifies it. Addressing these two dimensions, the pragmatic and the instrumental, seems quite crucial if we are to better understand the early forms of cognition and development in technological contexts, as they appear in technology education.

REFERENCES

Andreucci, C. (1990). *Influence de la structure des matériels dans la genèse des activités de classification*. Rapport de recherche, INRP, 38 p.

Andreucci, C., Froment, J.P., & Verillon, P. (1996). Contribution à l'analyse des situations d'enseignement / apprentissage d'instruments sémiotiques de communication technique, *Aster*, 23, 185-215.

Bal, JJ., Rabardel P., & Vérillon, P. (1984). Présenter la géométrie du dessin technique. In *L'apprentissage de la géométrie du dessin technique: des constats d'échec et des moyens de réussite* (pp. 13-47). Collection Rapports de Recherche n°9. Paris: INRP.

Cajas, F. (2000). Research in technology education : What are we researching , A response to Theodore Lewis, *Journal of Technology Education*, 11(2), 61-69.

De Miranda, M. A. (2004). The grounding of a discipline: cognition, and instruction in technology education, *International Journal of Technology and Design Education*, 14, 61-77.

Higelé, P. (1985). L'apprentissage des opérations projectives. In *L'apprentissage de la géométrie du dessin technique* (pp. 117-162). Collection Rapports de Recherche n°9. Paris: INRP.

Inhelder, B., & Cellerier, G., Eds. (1992). *Le cheminement des découvertes de l'enfant*. Neuchâtel: Delachaux et Niestlé.

Leontiev, A. (1975). *Activité, conscience, personnalité*. Moscou : Editions du Progrès.

Lewis, T. (1999). Research in technology education. Some areas of need. *Journal of Technology Education*, 10, 2, 41- 59.

Norman, D. A. (1991). Cognitive artefacts. In CARROLL J. (Ed.), *Designing interaction*, (pp. 17-38). N.Y.: Cambridge university Press.

Perrin, J. (1991). Sciences de la nature et sciences de l'artificiel: deux processus différents de production de connaissances. In Perrin, J. (Ed.), *Construire une science des techniques* (pp. 381-397). Limonest: L'interdisciplinaire.

Petrina, S. (1998). The politics of research in technology education : A critical content and discourse analysis of the Journal of technology education, *Journal of Technology Education*, 10, (1), 27-57

Piaget, J. (1975). *L'équilibration des structures cognitives*. Paris: PUF.

Piaget, J., & Inhelder, B. (1941). *Le développement des quantités chez l'enfant*. Neuchâtel: Delachaux & Niestlé.

Piaget, J. (1937). *La construction du reel chez l'enfant*. Neuchatel : Delachaux et Niestlé.

Piaget, J., & Inhelder, B. (1947). *La représentation de l'espace chez l'enfant*. Paris: P.U.F.

Piaget, J., Inhelder, B., & Szeminska, A. (1948). *La géométrie spontanée de l'enfant*. Paris: PUF.

Rabardel, P. (1980). *Contribution à l'étude de la lecture du dessin technique.* Thèse de 3° cycle, Paris: E.H.E.S.S..

Rabardel, P. (1982). Influence des représentations préexistantes sur la lecture du dessin technique. *Le Travail Humain,* 2.

Rabardel, P. (1995). *Les hommes et les technologies.* Paris: Armand Colin.

Rabardel, P., & Vérillon, P. (1985). Relations aux objets et développement cognitif. In A. Giordan & J.L. Martinand (Eds). *Acte des septièmes journées internationales sur l'éducation scientifique.* Paris: LIRESPT, Université Paris VII, 189-196.

Rabardel, P., & Vérillon, P. (1988). Le statut de l'objet matériel fabriqué chez Piaget, Léontiev, Wallon et Vygotski. Unpublished paper, INRP.

Ricco, G., Vergnaud, G. & Rouchier, A. (1983). Représentation du volume et arithmétisation, entretiens individuels avec des élèves de 11 à 15 ans. *Recherches en didactiques des mathématiques,* 4/1, 27-69.

Séris, J. P. (1994). *La technique.* Paris: PUF.

Staudenmaïer, J. (1985). *Technology's storytellers.* Cambridge: MIT Press.

Vérillon, P., & Rabardel P. (1987). L'intériorisation du système projectif du dessin technique. In Rabardel, P., & Weill-Fassina, A. (Eds.), *Le Dessin Technique* (pp. 109-118). Paris: Hermès.

Vérillon, P., & Rabardel, P. (1993). De l'analyse des compétences à l'élaboration des contenus: contribution de la psychologie et de la sémiologie à la conception en ingénierie didactique. In Bessot, A., & Vérillon, P. (Eds.), *Espaces graphiques et graphismes d'espaces.* Grenoble: La Pensée Sauvage.

Vérillon, P., & Rabardel, P. (1995). Cognition and artefacts : a contribution to the study of thought in relation to instrumented activity. *European Journal of Psychology of Education,* X, (1), 77-101.

Vérillon, P. (2000). Instruments and cognition : Piaget and Vygotsky revisited in search of learning model for technology education. *The Journal of technology Studies,* 26 (1), 3-10.

Vermersch, P. & Weill-Fassina, A. (1985). Les registres de fonctionnement cognitif: application à l'étude des conduites de lecture et d'écriture du dessin technique élémentaire. *Le Travail Humain,* 48 (4), 331-340.

Vygotsky, L. S. (1930/1985a). La méthode instrumentale en psychologie.

Vygotsky, L. S. (1931/1978). *Mind and society.* Harvard University Press, Cambridge, Massachusetts.

Vygotsky, L. S. (1934/1985b). *Pensée et langage.* Paris : Editions sociales.

Weill-Barais, A. (1995). Genèse des rapports de l'enfant à l'objet technique. *Actes du 68° Congrès de l'AGIEM,* Metz.

Wertsch, J. V. (1985). La médiation sémiotique de la vie mentale; L.S. Vygotsky et M. M. Bakhtine. In Schneuwly, B., & Bronckart, J.P. (Eds.), *Vygotsky aujourd'hui* (pp. 39-47). Neufchâtel: Delachaux et Niestlé.

Zougarri, G., Weill-Fassina, A., & Vermersch, P. (1984). Performances et compétences d'élèves de LEP dans des épreuves de lecture de forme. In *L'apprentissage de la géométrie du dessin technique* (pp. 207-286). Collection Rapports de Recherche n°9. Paris: INRP.

Zuga, K.F. (2004). Improving technology education research on cognition. *International Journal of Technology and Design Education,* 14, 79-87.

GERD HOEPKEN

29. STAGES OF 30 YEARS OF TECHNOLOGY EDUCATION IN GERMANY

INTRODUCTION

Before the discussion about technology as a school subject of its own arouse, there were several preliminary stages which have to be mentioned, because they influenced the development of the subject. Preliminary stages were:

1. INDUSTRIAL PEDAGOGY: HANDICRAFT FOR BOYS (KNABENHANDFERTIGKEIT, APPR. SINCE 1886)

Fig. 1   Handicraft products

Since Industrialization has altered conditions of living, producing, and economics the children of industrial worker had to be educated to cope with the new conditions. To maintain arts capabilities in the industrial age, boys should have courses in processing card board, wood, and metal. Basic techniques were taught, but not inventing and planning. There were no special rooms in the schools and the classes had up to 90 students. So the techniques had to be learnt in the classroom with simple means. (fig. 1)[1]

---

[1] Sachs, p. 16

M.J. de Vries, I. Mottier (eds.), International Handbook of Technology Education, 417–427.

2. "REFORM PEDAGOGY" ARTS AND CRAFTS (REFORMPÄDAGOGIK, APPR. SINCE 1900) AND RESTAURATION OF "REFORM PEDAGOGY" ARTS AND CRAFTS (APPR. 1945 – 1965)

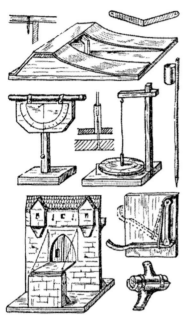

From several sources there came approaches to change handicraft to arts and crafts, to give the students more freedom to invent, design, and plan themselves – but not in technological ways. Technology was supposed to be utilitarian only and not really

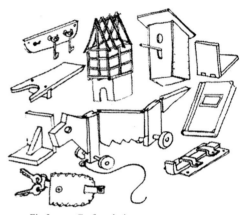

Fig 2   Products for other
school subjects

Fig 3   Craft techniques

educating, because humanistic education had to free of purposes including only arts and literature.

But arts and crafts could help to make pedagogical material to be used in other subjects. (fig. 2)[2] So it could help education. Also old craft techniques were supposed to be helpful in education. (fig. 3)[3]

Arts and crafts should set free the shaping and designing power of children. (fig. 4)[4]

---

[2] Sachs, p. 17
[3] Sachs, p. 17
[4] Sachs, p. 18

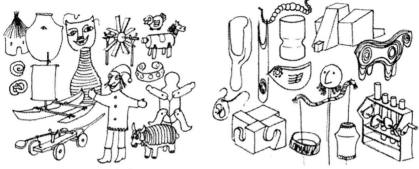

Fig. 4   Shaping and designing

3. DISCOVERING TECHNOLOGY AS A FIELD OF INTEREST FOR SCHOOLS

At the beginning of the sixties, there were calls for the changing of arts and crafts to include technology. The first was an attempt to address the problems young people had when they left school with 14 or 15 years. They did not cope with challenges of a changing working environment. 1964 the "German committee on the educational system" gave recommendations to change the lower secondary education and introduce a subject "Abeitslehre" (work/career education) including hands on work.

Fig. 6   Statics/dynamics

Fig. 5   Sculpture and functional shape

The second was a movement starting from college and university teachers of arts and crafts. They questioned the basics of and arts and crafts and urged a new orientation towards generating education to cope with a technological world. These teachers together with many other interested people conducted from 1966 to1977 six conferences on arts and crafts ("Werkpädagogische Kongresse"). Since nearly all participants came from arts and crafts, they had problems to structure the technology for educational purposes.

First examples look very much like before (fig. 5)[5], but within a short time, more technological topics were shown: statics/dynamics (fig. 6)[6], mechanisms (fig. 7)[7].

Fig. 7   „Mechanism"

Finding a suitable structure was still a problem for the technological laymen. Another problem was caused by efforts of the Arbeitslehre group. They tried to bring through politically influenced curricula. The federal states of Germany are independent in educational matters. So, wherever syllabi for technology education were established, their character depended on the state's government. In Germany we still have a wide variety of technology/Arbeitslehre curricula. Another source of ideas for technology education was the polytechnical education which was established in East Germany, the German Democratic Republic. Figure 8 shows these influences. The common problem for all approaches resulting from the different sources was that of the referential science. Engineering sciences are a so widely differentiated field that they cannot be used as a guideline for a generally educating subject technology. Polytechnical education (Wolffgramm) and some of the West German experts in technology education found a "general technology" which is a theory to reduce every technological process to the processing of matter, energy, and information. For the Arbeitslehre experts, technology can always be reduced to be a part of the labor process. For the multi aspect approach (fig. 8)[8], both approaches are part of its own theory, but not sufficient to explain technology with all its implications and consequences. An important part of the multi aspect approach is the splitting into "fields of action":

---

[5] Uschkereit/Mehrgardt/Sellin, p. 47
[6] Uschkereit/Mehrgardt/Sellin, p. 51
[7] Sellin/Wessels, p. 67
[8] Schmayl, p.14

420

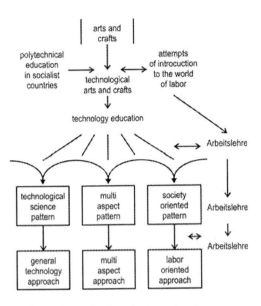

Fig. 8   Approaches in technology education

work and production, construction and building, supply and waste management, traffic and transportation, information and communication.

Today, most of the German curricula are structures after the multi aspect approach. One of the characteristics of it is a common set of teaching methods, which was completed and validated over the years. It comprises[9]:

Course of Instruction
This is a method to attain limited partial aims of technology education. It is restricted to teach knowledge and skills. Examples are: How to use a power drill, computation of a series resistor for a light emitting diode.

Design Activity
This method corresponds with an important technological action - designing. In the process of solving technological problems it emphasizes inventing, planning, designing and creating. Examples are: Designing a circuit board for an electronic circuit, Designing a time control (traffic light, flashing light, ...)

Making Activity
Manufacturing an object the pupils independently plan and organize the production process. Examples are: Manufacturing an electronic wiring, ...

Design and Making Activity
Design exercise and manufacturing can be combined. This is the original method of application of arts and crafts. It includes all stages of the planning and manufacturing process. But this means also, that only few exercises can be carried out during one term.

Technological Experiment
The technological experiment can provide unknown values, which are needed in the further course of the lesson. Examples are: Determining the adhesion of various adhesives, determining the life of batteries under different loads.

---

[9] Henseler/Hoepken, p. 53 ff.

421

Technological Analysis

In a technological analysis technological object or technical facts are examined concerning their components or factors. This can be done destructive or non destructive. Examples are: Disassembling an electric iron to see the components of a control loop (non destructive, the iron can be reassembled), opening the case of a power transistor (TO 3) (destructive).

Technological Exploration

This is a planned and purposeful investigation of institutions outside school. Examples are: Traffic light, machines in a factory or workshop.

Technological Assessment

Assessment and evaluation of technology is one of the most complex methods of technology education. It takes place after each manufacturing exercise to assess an evaluate the object made. The result can be used to evaluate the pupils standards. However technological assessment can also be a method of its own testing industrial products or even comparing types of power stations.

Project

The project is a method to enable students to solve complex tasks emerging form the reality of life. The project activities go from planning to practical realization. Characteristics of working in a project are orientation towards product and activity, interdisciplinarity, orientation towards students, reference to situation and society, joint organization of learning processes. A project requires the removal of separation between school subjects and of 45 minute lessons.

Case Study

In a case study, a real situation is the starting point for the learning process. After an exact analysis of the problem, several possible solutions are worked out in groups and a decision is made in the whole class. The result is compared with the real decision and assessed.

Expert Inquiry

Expert inquiry is a method aiming towards reality. An Expert is invited into the classroom to answer questions about a certain, limited issue. So the students get first hand knowledge, insight, and experience.

These teaching methods are embedded in a set of technological methods, which are used in technology and also must be represented in technology education.

methods of assigning and assessment	- developing alternative solutions and choice of solutions according to criteria of assessment - assessing consequences and danger using a technological system
anticipating methods	- choosing and assessing the appropriateness natural laws for achieving the object - anticipating a concrete solution by drawing or simulation - assessing the function of concrete solution by a real model, by drawing, by calculations based on natural laws, by experiment, .. - planning, organising and representing the course of the process
realising methods	- carrying out a process - controlling the course of a process - choosing and using appropriate objects, means and procedures
simplifying/ systematising methods	- abstract and symbolic representation of systems, subsystems and their combinations - splitting a complex system into single systems and subsystems easily to grasp - assigning relevant quantities to systems and subsystems - standardisation
analysing methods	- uncovering the natural laws, the system is basing on - explaining the mode of operation by following the causal connections between relevant quantities and subsystems - searching for errors and narrowing down errors by measuring relevant quantities at the interfaces of subsystems - determining specifics of object of operation, technological procedures and technological objects, assessing their appropriateness for a technological solution

Fig. 5   Methods of Technology[10]

4. TWO SCHLESWIG-HOLSTEIN EXAMPLES FOR TECHNOLOGY CURRICULA

Schleswig-Holstein is the most northern federal state of Germany. As one of the first states it got an elaborated technology curriculum in 1986. The following

---

[10] Henseler/Höpken, p. 41

overview (fig. 9)[11] shows the version for Realschule, one of the branches of lower secondary education. The next overview (fig. 10)[12] shows the 1997 curriculum for all braches of lower secondary education. A comparison of old and new curriculum shows that the new curriculum is less rigid. It gives more freedom to the teacher to teach the matters in different ages. To facilitate spreading the new curriculum, graphic representations were developed to show the intentions. The first presentation (fig. 11) shows the connections of the fields of action with the levels of technology education. The second representation (fig. 12) shows the interdependence of technological aspects with aspects affected by technology. Such a graphic representation was made for each teaching unit.

7	8	9	10
Work and Production			
- Designing and manufacturing a wooden object *Extensions:* - wood and wooden materials - technical drawing	- Designing and manufacturing an object from metal *Extensions:* - Standardisation of metallic materials and machine elements - Expanding the basics of technical drawing	- Manufacturing an object from plastic Labour divided in-dustrial production *Extensions:* - Estimation and orientation towards the market for product planning and sale - Ways of organising industr. production	- Casting in moulds - Machines in production processes/ From simple tools to modern automata *Extension:* - Facilities for enhancing efficiency in production
Transportation and Traffic			
- Solving technological problems of lifting and conveying	- Bicycle and moped, proven means of moving: analysis and repair, maintenance and care *Extension:* - Function and structure of selected machine elements	- Analysing and comparing transportation and traffic systems	- Technological development: From the carriage to modern motor cars *Extension:* - Constructing and analysing different kinds of gearing
Building and Built Environment			
- Building simple load bearing constructions *Extension:* - Comparing load bearing constructions	- Concrete as a building material. Experimenting and manufacturing simple objects	- Planning and realising a simple real building project	- Comparing conventional and industrial ways of building *Extensions:* - Unit construction systems - Heat protection and using solar energy in passive devices
Supply and Waste Management			
- Basic house equipment for supply and waste management *Extension:* - Heating systems	- Examples of technological facilities to protect the environment	- Development of energy technology/ Reinventing a energy technological plant *Extension:* - Electric energy, using energy in a comfortable way	- Constructing and testing simple facilities to exploit regenerative sources of energy
Information and Communication			
- Constructing, testing and comparing simple devices to transmit messages	- Planning and manufacturing simple devices to solve control problems *Extension:* - Different systems of control technology	- Automating technological processes with control technology *Extensions:* - Constructing and using basic digital circuits - Using computers for control tasks	- Using computers to solve specific technological problems

Figure 9   The 1986 Technology Curriculum, Overview

---

[11] http://www.unesco.org/education/ste/pdf_files/connect/Hopken.PDF, p. 4
[12] Ministerium für Bildung, p. 17 ff.

Socio-technolo-gical field of action				
Work and production	**Responsibility of man working with raw material in craftsman like production. Basic course: Communication in technology. 7. - 9. form**	**Development and employment of machines change place of work and vocation. Interdependence of man and machine in production. 7. - 9. form**	Industrial production of article for daily use and its impact on conditions of life. 8./9. form	
Transportation and traffic	**Bicycle technology and appropriate use of means of transport. 7. form**	**Car technology and its interactions with man and environment. 9. form**	Technology conceptions for environment conserving means of transport. 10. form/project	People develop technology (e.g. air craft engineering) and use it in different ways. 8. - 10. form
Construction - built environment	Former and present ways of constructing bridges- basic principles of static, selecting materials, impacts on man and environment. 7. form	People protect and secure themselves - safety systems of yesterday, today, and tomorrow. 7. - 8. form	**Dwelling in changing times - ecologically beneficial, human building and living together. 8. - 10. form/ project**	
Supply and waste management	Wrapping is a burden for environment - disposing and planning wrappings, avoiding refuse through abolishing, recycling relieves environment. 7. -9. form	Supplying and disposing garbage of a household under technological, ecological and economic aspects. 8. - 9- form	**Using energy efficiently and sustainable energies in households. 9./10. form**	Man as consumer - discriminating dealing with the supply of technical articles - analysing, testing, and purchasing products. 9. - 10 form
Information and communication	Basic electrical circuits and safety education. Basic course: Soldering. 7. form	**Impact of automation technology on man, working place and vocation. From hand control to computers 7. - 10 form**	Interchange of information, development and impacts. From the drum to wireless telephones. 8. - 10. form	bold: compulsory subject matters

Figure 10   The 1997 Schleswig-Holstein Technology Curriculum, Overview

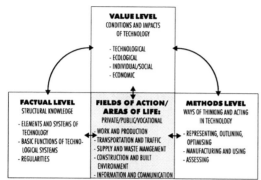

Figure 11   Pedagogical Structure of Technology Education[13]

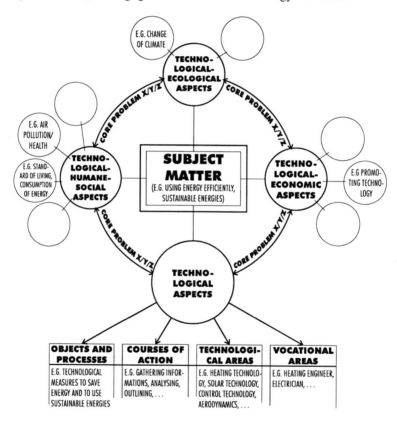

Figure 12   Interdependence of Subject Matter[14]

---

[13] Ministerium für Bildung, p. 23
[14] Ministerium für Bildung, p. 17

REFERENCES

Hoepken, G./Reich, G. (1981) *Elektrotechnik in der Sekundarstufe* I. Bad Salzdetfurth, Franzbecker.

Ministerium für Bildung, Wissenschaft, Forschung und Kultur des Landes Scheswig-Holstein (ed.): Lehrplan Technik. Kiel 1997.

Sachs, B. (1996) *Zur musisch-kunsterzieherischen Zwischenphase der Fachentwicklung vom Werken zu Technikunterricht.* In: tu 81, p. 15 – 21.

Schmayl, W. (1992) *Richtungen der Technikdidaktik.* In: tu 65, p- 5 – 15.

Sellin, H./Wessels, B. (1970) (ed.): *Beiträge zur Didaktik der technischen Bildung.* Weinheim/Berlin/Basel, Beltz.

Uschkereit, G./Mehrgardt, O./Sellin, H. (1968) (ed.): *Ansätze zur Werkdidaktik seit 1945.* Weinheim/Berlin, Beltz.

Uschkereit, G./Mehrgardt, O./Kaufmann, F. (1969) (ed.): *Werkunterricht als technische Bildung.* Weinheim/Berlin/Basel, Beltz.

Wilkening, F./Schmayl, W. (1984) *Technikunterricht.* Bad Heilbrunn, Klinkhardt.

Wolffgramm, H. (1978) *Allgemeine Technologie.* Leipzig, Fachbuchverlag.

DAVID PURCHASE

30. THE LAST TEN YEARS: CHANGE IN MALTA

THE SETTING.

Given its full meaning, Pupils Attitude Towards' Technology has not been the concern of Malta for the last 20 years. When the first conference was held, Malta was experiencing a success with the trade schools that students opted to go to after two or three years of secondary education. It was in 1995 that these few schools offered Technology Education. The programme for Technology Education was implemented in the trade schools through recommendations made to the Minister of Education in the report 'A Curricular Frame Work for the Proposed First Cycle of Studies at the Trade Schools' submitted in 1993. Paragraph 2.2.5 details that there would be a subject called Technology Education and that it would occupy eight 45 minute periods in a week of thirty five periods.

In a time line the year 2000 was a pivotal point in the development of Technology Education in Malta. The implementation of a new vocational education and training caused the Technology Education programme of the trade schools was transferred to the general secondary schools and the transfer of students of secondary school age to trade schools was stopped. Technology continued being an optional subject for students in their 4th and 5th year of study, having now five 45 minute periods a week. There was, initially, no move to offer the subject to younger students.

In December 1999 it was determined that Technology Education would be included in the National Minimum Curriculum. While a working group was established to determine particular aspects of the implementation of this subject, and later was to construct a curriculum, another group in the form of the Department for Technology in Education was created in 2002 and determined its own route. This work will examine the two routes in the light of the demands of the National Minimum Curriculum.

NATIONAL MINIMUM CURRICULUM

'Creating the Future Together: National Minimum Curriculum' (Ministry of Education, 1999) sets out the principles and objectives of the curriculum in Maltese schools. As such it is a rationale of what the teaching should accomplish rather than a description of the content of what should be taught. In the Preamble (pages 13&14) it is noted that 'Tomorrow's Schools' (1995) set the process in motion. In this document the implementation of Technology Education in the trade schools is

M.J. de Vries, I. Mottier (eds.), International Handbook of Technology Education, 429–436.

commented on and it is suggested that there was a need to rethink the notion of curriculum to provide space for the opportunities the subject offers (pp. 49-50). *Technology education should, ideally, provide students with the thinking tools they require for the future and should be introduced forthwith." (Tomorrow's Schools:50)*

'Creating the Future Together' distinguishes fifteen principles. It is in this section that the most substantive statement is made about Technology Education. Under the principle of relevance to life, it is stated:

Technology is a unique aspect of human life-experience. It forms part of our country's cultural heritage as do literature, science and art. For this reason, technology should be studied as an integral part of the education system. The teaching of design and technology in schools ensures that today's pupils are suitably prepared to live and work in a technological world. This is fulfilled through the teaching of technical awareness, design methodologies, and the application of problem-solving skills to real life problems. The teaching of design and technology stimulates both intellectual and creative skills and develops the personal qualities necessary to ensure that a project is successfully developed from the conceptual stage through to the creation of the final product.(page 33)

This is the fourth principle. In the section it is preceded by a paragraph saying that students need to see a relevant link between what they learn and their own experiences and that the learning should help them throughout their life. Within the context of Technology Education, it is also worth examining Principle 2, Respect for Diversity, which states:

… to standardise knowledge, with the focus on being on content rather than learning outcomes, numerous students feel marginalised by the system, viewing it as irrelevant to their needs. (page 30)

Fourteen objectives for the curriculum are detailed. Each objective is recorded under the sub-headings of knowledge/ information, skills and attitudes. Objective 12 details these under the overall heading of 'Greater Awareness of the Role of Science and Technology in Everyday Life' (pages 65, 66). These pages, shown in appendix, mention technology (or words based on technology) 13 times, whilst science (or words based on science) is mentioned 26 times. While eight statements deal only with science, no statement deals only with technology.

This section of the objectives of the curriculum clearly refers to scientific knowledge and scientific language without the recognition of technological knowledge and language. While the document gives no lead as to the contributors, it must be pointed out that at the time it was assembled there was no Education Officer, Assistant Director or Director of the Education Division with experience in Technology Education. The Faculty of Education was represented by a philosopher and a curriculum development specialist.

WORKING GROUP

The publication of 'Creating the Future Together' lead to working groups being established to work on 18 different themes in the national minimum curriculum. Of these, only three were subject (discipline) related: Science in the primary school, Co-ordinated Science in the secondary school and Technology Education. For Technology Education the working group comprised of two lectures from the Faculty of Education (myself included), two instructors from the trade school programme, a head of a trade school, a church school teacher (with previous knowledge of the programme in England) and a science specialist from the independent sector. The brief for each of the working groups was toward the implementation of their specific topic, not the content. Thus the report of the working group (chairperson: D Purchase) on the theme Technology Education is very sparse on what should constitute the subject. In recognition of what the trade schools had already been attempting to develop and deliver the following is stated:

The whole emphasis of the Working Group is that Technology Education must be considered a new subject to the curriculum. This is not to downgrade the efforts of the Trade Schools, nor to diminish the programmes that seem set to be transferred to the general secondary school. It is to recognise the changes necessary to create a 5 to 16 curriculum subject that will terminate in a SEC level examination.(Giordmaina, ed., 2000: 134)

[SEC: the school leaving examination set by the Matriculation and Secondary Examination Support Unit of the University of Malta. SEC is equivalent to the English General Certificate of Secondary Education (GCSE)]

With this recognition the working group were claiming the ability to focus on what would be rather than to focus on changing what was. In approaching this they recommended that the Technology Education programme to be implemented should, by utilising a design-and-make approach, follow a course of study that centred on the domains of production, energy & power, communication, control and biotechnology and that the study should be a core study for all pupils. The group also recorded their attachment to the curriculum objectives of values, holistic development, respect for (and allowance for) diversity, stimulation of analytical, critical and creative thinking skills (ibid:134 and to Technology Education being the right of all students (ibid:133).

CURRICULUM CONSTRUCTION

At the end of the 2000, the working group was commissioned to construct a subject curriculum for Technology Education in the secondary phase which was completed by March 2001. This curriculum was constructed around the domains the group had recommended in their report, with a design and make approach to the teaching and learning being emphasised. It included the expectation that students in forms 1 to 3 would complete two projects for each of the domains of production, energy & power, control and biotechnology. In form 4 the expectation was for a minimum of three projects and in form 5 that the students would identify their own design and make assignments. Communication, it was expected, would be experienced in all projects and did include the use of ICT.

The group was joined in the later stages by a representative of the primary sector and a representative of the trade schools programme to ensure a synergy with the previous programme and the programme to be devised for the primary phase.

DEPARTMENT FOR TECHNOLOGY IN EDUCATION

The Department of Technology in Education, Education Division was created in 2002. While there is a lack of practical experience of delivering Technology Education in the senior members of this department, they have a team of support teachers, mainly instructors from the previous Technology programmes. The Design & Technology team is completed by three previously appointed subject coordinators. The new department has organised its group of support teachers to determine the nature of Technology Education in Malta. In doing so the new group opted for the route of resistant materials, electronics, food and textiles. The change in emphasis has also meant a change in title, and now the subject is called Design & Technology.

The newest format of Design & Technology in Malta can be seen most readily through the site at http://schoolnet.gov.mt/des_tech/ (click on 'What is D&T', click on 'Presentation'). This details that during the first two years of secondary education, pupils should complete four design and make tasks, one for each of resistant materials, electronics, food and textiles. In the next two years, with double the time allowed, the pupils should complete eight design and make tasks. The fifth and last year is stipulated for the Extended Project of the SEC examination.

EXAMINING THE CHANGES

The significant changes made by the new group to the recommendations of the working group have not resulted in the formulation of a new curriculum document. They have, however, submitted a draft syllabus to MATSEC as part of the process of providing such an examination.

The first significant change in the way materials and components are referred to. The curriculum lists materials and components as 'generic families' and the choice of which to use to the design and make aspect of the programme. In the syllabus the materials and components are separated according to the sections noted. The curriculum states:

As production implies making and as energy and power, control and biotechnology can only be visualised in three dimensional form, the interwoven nature of the study can only be achieved by a management that ensures the pupils move from design to making understanding the explicitness of a given topic (page 4).

In the syllabus the areas of study are expected to be examined separately, although all candidates would have to answer questions on each of the four areas (page 1).

Assessment provides another significant change. It must be remembered, however, that the syllabus will eventual be published by an examination board. The new group may well have had to respond to that influence. In the marking scheme for the Extended Project the marks to be awarded have been divided into three bands, one for design, one for making and one for evaluating. As it has been suggested that the syllabus would cover the work of the third, fourth and fifth form of secondary education, it is possible that this form of assessment would be used throughout that period of time.

The curriculum argued for holistic assessment. On page 15 it is stated that Technology Education is an holistic experience and that component parts of that experience should not be separated.

The subject content of the syllabus for resistant materials (pages 14 to 18) does not mention energy and power in any manner, yet this section contains the content for mechanisms. Power and power supply units are note in electronics (page 22) and this includes mention of 'solar type batteries' but no other alternative source of energy. Neither food nor textiles mention energy and power. Production is catered for by the inclusion of :

E) know the process involved in manufacturing
i   One off
ii Batch production
iii Mass production (page 14)

While this statement is transcribed from resistant materials, it is copied for both food and textiles. Biotechnology appears only in the section on food.

The concept of values is not presented in the syllabus, a concept that is embedded in the statements of design in the curriculum. Words such as select, judgements, apply and use, are used throughout the curriculum where as the syllabus has a greater dependence on words such as know and define. It can therefore be put that the curriculum tends toward propositional knowledge to a greater degree than the syllabus.

Since Technology Education started to appear in the curricula of different nations there has always been the question as to what constitutes that body of knowledge and understanding that we shall be teaching. In each locality decisions on the content have been made by groups of people organised to do so. These decisions cannot be unchangeable because of the dynamics of the whole school curriculum and the rapidity of technological change. In this case, no debate has ever been held to find expression of need for the changes that have been so briefly outlined. Prior to the change the subject coordinators had been engaged in the task of constructing syllabi from the curriculum. They recommended the establishment of a group of teachers to take the work further, with the group being determined according to the abilities in the domains of the curriculum. This recommendation was not acted upon and the work accomplished thus far was stopped.

It has been said during a syllabus panel meeting that the new pattern, following that of the English examination system was better suited to the needs of Malta. If that is so, the question that must finally be answered is why the syllabus does not more closely resemble that of the English examination boards.

IMPLEMENTATION

In 1995 seven trade schools started delivering Technology Education. In June 2000 that number was down to four. In September 2000 nine general secondary schools were equipped to offer the subject to 4th and 5th former, using the syllabus of the trade schools. In March 2005 there are fourteen general secondary schools offering the subject: that is fourteen out of a total number of fifty eight secondary phased schools in Malta. In 2002/03 eighty eight instructors and teachers successfully completed a Faculty of Education Certificate in Technology Education. In the schools many of these instructors are lightly loaded, some with ten or fewer periods in a thirty five period week.

It was recognised by the working group that there would need to be a financial investment in Technology Education. While it is shown that the investment is being made in terms of equipment, the continued implementation is delayed because many schools require building works to be accomplished. There is no outcry from the junior lyceums and church schools about the subject as, particularly for them, the examination has not been established.

REFLECTIONS ON THE MATTER OF STATUS

The original status enjoyed by Technology Education in Malta found a reflection in the status accorded to the trade schools. Through the years that followed that introduction the two main political parties of Malta confirmed and followed through with a belief that the subject was beneficial to our students. Educationalists of renown such as Professor Kenneth Wain and Professor Ronald Sultana, a philosopher and a sociologist respectively have connected their names to the need for the subject through 'Tomorrows Schools' and their actions as Deans of the Faculty of Education in helping to establish a Technical Design and Technology course.

A status of importance was confirmed when the working group for Technology Education was created and when the Education Division created the Department for Technology in Education and included Technology Education along with ICT in its responsibilities. A status of importance has been given by the fact that the Department is working to issue a call for tenders, through the Foundation for

434

Tomorrows Schools, for the purchase of around Lm500,00 (approximately Euro1,160,000).

There are, however, approximately 19,000 secondary aged pupils who cannot gain any advantage from the subject at this time. Approximately 4,500 have been given the option to study it. In no school does an entire cohort of students follow the Design & Technology programme. Ours is a selective and non-mixed education system and Design and Technology is still to be found in the lowest tier of the selection and in only two girls' schools of the same level.

CONCLUSION

Technology Education came to Malta in an attempt to revitalise the trade schools. The benefits of the subject were taken up through Tomorrows Teachers and Creating the Future Together. Why have all the pieces not fallen into place?

The most basic reason that can be ascertained is that the work of Design & Technology was established in the Department for Technology in Education after the work of the working group was completed. This was their first opportunity to make a major impact on the area. While the curriculum had been worked on to provide a syllabus structure, the new group had to ponder whether the curriculum would succeed or whether it should be replaced. That, in many ways, was of course their job. The choice was whether to risk the new structure or to turn to a more established system and use that to determine how to meet their needs.

What can be established from the two documents used is that the two groups took different routes in the matter of knowledge construction. Propositional knowledge and procedural knowledge both have a place in the building of technological knowledge. While the working group constructed their document around the application of knowledge to a purpose, the new group have used the route of acquiring knowledge more for the sake of the knowledge itself.

In my previous work as a teacher in England, the management structure was in place for the coming of the new subject in 1990. Advisors and inspectors were geared up to provide the courses and support that teachers required for the start of the new venture. In Malta that structure was missing. The recognition that Technology Education would be included in the National Minimum Curriculum should have been followed up with the appointment of a member of the Education Division to have responsibility for the area and to serve on the working group or a member of the working group should have been given the responsibility.

The curriculum constructed and submitted in March 2001 was compiled by Mr. D. Purchase, Mrs J. Camilleri, Mr. Saviour Frendo, Mr. George Rye, Mr. Emanuel Zahra and Fr. Salvino Vella. The co-opted members to ensure synergy were Mr. Philip Camilleri and Mr. Joseph Buttigieg. The document was never published although it is in the public domain having been given to instructors on the Certificate in Technology Education course and to student of B.Ed. Technical Design and Technology.

The draft syllabus presented to MATSEC is unpublished. It may be said to be in the public domain as it is being discussed by a panel comprised of representatives of the University, representatives of the church schools and the representatives of the Education Division.

REFERENCES

Ad Hoc Committee (1993) *A curricular frame work for the proposed first cycle of studies at the trade schools*, Ministry of Education

Consultative Committee (1995) *Tomorrow's schools: Developing effective learning on education cultures*, publisher unknown, ISBN 99909-74-00-4

Giordmaina, J., (2000) (ed) *National curriculum on its way: Proceedings of national conference June 2000*, Ministry of Education, Education Division & University of Malta

Ministry of Education (1999) *Creating the future together: National minimum curriculum*, Ministry of Education

TAPANI KANANOJA

31. TECHNOLOGY EDUCATION IN FINLAND

1 BEFORE 1970

'Technology' was mentioned in Finnish handicrafts education texts for the first time in 1861 (Cygnaeus 1861). The idea was 'to educate for work'. At the same time the systematic general education was introduced to the whole of Finland (1866). Technology was a proposed subject title for teacher education in handicrafts [originally 'slöjd', a subject term used at first by Cygnaeus (Allingbjerg 1983, 28) and adopted by the Swedes later on; Swedish being at that time the official language in Finland]. Up to 1970, education of the 13 – 15 –year old pupils was divided in academic and prevocational schools. In the non-academic schools practical technological education covered about 50 % of the weekly periods.

2 FROM 1970 TO 1985

The Comprehensive school system was introduced in 1970. Non-academic and academic junior secondary schools were amalgamated. It lowered the status of practical education. The term "Boys' Handicrafts" was changed to 'Technical Handicraft', later on 'Technical Work' (TW). This writer of this chapter was personally interested in technological education in other countries for research purposes. I was engaged in a research project on handicrafts education from 1969 to 1975 (Kananoja 1975; 1980 – see 1987). Over the years 1970 – 91 handicrafts education struggled to survive. The Government reduced funding, gave smaller machinery, etc., because the idea of the new school was 'general education', no longer vocational or prevocational. Teachers were unhappy with the comprehensive school reform (1970), where design and creativity were strongly emphasized. They were wary of new plans for technology education (TE) and feared the loss of status for – or even the existence of – TW in the possible new changes. Resistance was strongest among textile work teachers. TE was first tried in one (academic) higher secondary school in 1972 – 74 (Kananoja – Rajamäki 1974). TE was mentioned in the national teacher education proposals as a replacement for TW in 1973 (Kananoja 1973), and in TW curricular texts in 1976 (Kananoja, 1976). The reasons for trying to launch the term were practically the same as in other countries: to reform and modernise the old reproductive handicrafts education; to try to get academic credibility for the subject; and to follow general technological developments. Of course there were also efforts to adopt the subject developments presented by UNESCO and CCC (Council of Cultural Co-operation of Europe), and developments in the UK and US (Olson,

M.J. de Vries, I. Mottier (eds.), International Handbook of Technology Education, 437–448.

Eggleston, Harrison, etc.). One of the reasons was also to try to avoid the possible adoption of Norwegian art integrated handicrafts curriculum model. These efforts for reform began in 1971 in TW. Adoption of the TE in TW began with adopting ideas from the German 'Technik' education. The elementary machine and electrical education in Germany were interesting in 'Arbeitslehre' (Deutscher Ausschuss 1964) and in the new curriculum in Hamburg (Richtlinien und Lehrpläne 1974). Swedish ideas in 'Teknik' education (1962) were also appreciated. Efforts were also made to activate Science education in the new subject. For collaboration between Science and TE – from the point of view of TW representatives interested in TE – there was readiness and a great deal of progress made from the 1980s on. In-service training sessions, conferences and negotiations were organised, practical electronics construction for science teachers was disseminated, etc. Real collaboration did not succeed because the science and handicrafts teachers and some administrators did not support the scheme. Later on I also found that in the Netherlands some intelligent reforms in Crafts education had been in the pipeline. These reforms were supposed to be realized in 1983 (Netherlands 1980). The emphasis was more or less on the Nordic Sloyd type of education.

3 FROM 1985 UP TO NOW

A new curriculum was published in 1985. A lot of work was done to get 'the simple machines' from science (environmental studies) in TW at primary level, in order to support the elementary level Technology Education. That became true in the curriculum. Problems arose, however, because there was not enough time to organize satisfactory measures, textbooks, etc., to help teachers. According to a questionnaire 5 years afterwards only 30 % of the primary teachers implemented the ideas (Kananoja 1990b). TE curricula reforms were revived in an IIET (Institute International pour l'Education Technologique) Conference in Budapest in 1986. The Finnish research project had also covered pupils' attitudes, and meeting the IIET people encouraged a continuation of TE curricula reforms. In Budapest the first contact with the Jan Raat and the nascent PATT ideas were promising. In 1986 UNESCO had a TE symposium in Paris. It confirmed the necessity of TE. In 1987 the first PATT Conference was organized in Eindhoven. The Finnish research was handled as an article (Kananoja 1987) in the report (PATT 1987). PATT speeded up the interests for the TE. To meet same kind of thinking all over the world was a step forward to important contacts. A curriculum guide for TW was published (Kananoja 1988). Because of the eager participation of teachers in curriculum discussions the effort was to give more freedom and options to teachers. The guide emphasized industrial technology. This guide was well received by teachers. In 1989 an OECD meeting for SMT (Science, Maths, and Technology Education) took place in Florida. It was a comprehensive project ending with a final report (Black, Atkin 1996). Unfortunately the Finnish representative was a different one in every 3 – 5 meetings and so the continuity or impact was not as good as it could have been. So the meetings did not have so much impact on TE in Finland. Also the final report emphasized more 'S' and 'M' than 'T'. Maybe the national activities were also taken care of better by 'SM' than by 'T'. In 1990 a seminar for Nordic sloyd education was organised in Sweden by German and Swedish enthusiasts. I was 'defending' Uno Cygnaeus as 'Numero Uno' in the meeting (Kananoja 1990a). Otto Salomon was also put forward as the founder of Sloyd. After that we have organised some conferences on Finnish handicrafts or TE in Finland. In 1991 a preliminary curriculum proposal for TE was written (Kananoja 1991). In 1991 the 'National Board of General Education' was changed to be the 'National Board of Education. After that, since 13 years, TW has not had any representative in the Board, which is responsible for the curricula. In practice Science seems to take over for the TE; mandate for handicrafts is in hands of a textile work representative. In 1993 UNESCO organised 'Conference 2000+', where WOCATE was founded. That was another reason to feel oneself to be committed to TE. Unfortunately WOCATE seems to have disappeared; and the UNESCO ST Newsletter handles mostly Science (>www.unesco.org/education/educprog/ste/index.html>).

Basic PATT research has been carried out in Finland, the questionnaires translated and delivered to the teacher educators / researchers. However, the preliminary Finnish results were published only at an ITEA meeting in the US in 1992 (Kananoja 1992), handling also Zambian pupils' and teachers' attitudes. Some students both in Rauma, and later on, in Oulu teacher education departments in Finland have also written their Masters' theses on PATT research.

Rauma teacher training department under Turku University takes care of teacher education for TW. The program has not been changed much recently. There was an effort to get a full TW subject teacher program also in Oulu University; but because of resistance from Rauma it did not succeed. Instead of that Oulu (from 1996 on) had a primary teacher education program in 'TE orientated TW education', where TE had a 35 credit mandate. Oulu is the only university in the country with education and technology departments under the same roof, and could have been a good centre for a full program in TW and TE development. At the same time also a new teacher education law was published stating 35 cr. studies to give the competence as a second subject for a teacher of primary classes or other subjects.

Collaboration with science and mathematics education has been in the pipeline according to the international models. The TW representatives have been giving quite a lot TE ideas for science people: Being the pioneers in TE, writing 'the TE philosophy', organising discussions, translating the US Standards, etc. Since 1991 the teacher training institutes have launched various projects to develop TE in collaboration with science and mathematics (Parikka 2000). For example:

- The 'LUONTI' project at Helsinki University, where technology is part of science and mathematics (Lavonen 1996).
- 'TOTY' at Joensuu University for RD of computers in education; for example, using LEGO kits and developing technological thinking.
- Jyväskylä University has a large project for RD in TE.

- Jyväskylä has several ongoing projects in educational technology with connections with TE, and separate TE projects. Licentiate and doctoral studies will be pursued in these projects.
- Since 1995 Oulu University has been done TE as a 35 cr. course as collaboration of faculties of education and technology and other interest groups. In Oulu TE is defined broadly consisting of opportunities for emphasis on educational technology, science, mathematics and entrepreneurial skills. A proposal for a 'TE Center' was made in 1995, and the plans were put into action in 2000. European Community is supporting the regional project.
- In 1996 Jyväskylä University has emphasized teaching technology as a large part of the future educational plans.
- The National Board of Education organized a program called 'LUMA' for science and mathematics development in 1995 – 2000. The Ministry of Education continued the project in 2000 – 2002. Also handicraft education was supposed to be included in the project from 2001 on. The project was supervised in 2002 (Allen, Black, Wallin 2002). Some success and some continuing problems were found. TE was not represented in the responsible group in the country or in the evaluation.
- In 1996 'FATE', Finnish Association for research in Technology Education' was founded by persons working in Oulu and Rauma TTIs (Parikka, Kananoja, et al.). Its aim is to help to develop technology education and the professional skills of the teachers in field and in the Teacher education institutes. Members of this association are comprehensive school teachers, teacher trainers and researchers. A few international meetings have been organized
- In 1998 Jyväskylä started the 'LUOTEK' (S+T) project to coordinate the local RD.
- In 1999 Jyväskylä University funded the LUOTEK coordinator for three years.
- Rauma TTI has for a longer time had a project for technological literacy with emphasis on information technology.
- In Savonlinna the TTI has been developing studies in collaboration with the regional opera company and local industry for a project on technology and technical work development.
- Kajaani TTI started EU project 'KYTKE' in 1997 for developing entrepreneurial skills and TE. The project was the continuation of an older project for developing TE (1989). The idea was to create a pilot network of teachers from every municipality in the region for versatile industrial and economic development.

In about 1996 I was invited to be a member of a group of the Maths & Science teachers' association to work with 'FACTE', 'Finnish Academies of Technology', for TE. I had to join the club. So we wrote some articles (Kananoja & al. 2000a; 2000b), published a booklet for pupils and teachers about the necessity of TE ('Who needs Technology?' [FACTE 2003]), made initiatives to the Government,

Ministry of Education and the National Board on TE and translated the US Standards in Finnish (Kananoja & al. 2000c) and published them on the Internet. After that collaboration the status of S & M improved somewhat, these subjects got increases in weekly periods and a practical monopoly for the TE in schools. After that there have been no more calls for collaboration in 2004 – 05. Nevertheless, the work done was of benefit to TE.

TODAY

The last 'Basics for curriculum' was published in 2004. It was written under the leadership of the textile work (handicraft) representative of the National Board. It is not satisfactory for TW or for TE. Moreover, possibilities for options have been diminished. Fortunately the TW teachers in the schools write the school curricula. They are, however, also under the same fashionable national (global?) stress of interpreting TE as Science, Maths and Computers. The present title for 'technological subject' in the Finnish comprehensive school in grades 1 – 9 (age 7 – 15+) still is 'handicrafts education'; some of us say 'crafts education'. It is integrated (technical + textile) in grades 1 – 2. It should be integrated also at 3 – 9 but is in practice divided (from age 10 on) in 'technical work' and 'textile work'. This is because of the tradition, the existing workshops and teachers. In grades 1 – 7 handicrafts is obligatory, in grades 8 – 9 optional, in some schools also in other grades. Integration of TW and textile work has brought some new problems. Pupils' time allocation for technical work is about half from the previous one, and there are not enough periods for subject teachers in many schools any more, especially not at lower comprehensive. Technology education according to the 2004 curriculum is a cross-disciplinary topic, a 'thematic entity', in grades 1 – 12. It is taught in lower comprehensive school (primary, grades 1 – 6) by the class teachers, who practically all have short training in TW or textile work, in higher comprehensive (grades 7 – 9) by TW subject teachers or science teachers, and in higher secondary school (grades I – III) by science (or even social studies) teachers. Neither Handicrafts nor TW have any mandate at the academic higher secondary level; generally there is not so much integration with vocational studies. The national (broad, basic) curriculum text for the 'thematic entity' in TE in Comprehensive school is as follows:
[An unofficial translation]

Man and technology"

The aim of the thematic entity 'Man and technology' is to aid the pupil in understanding the human relationship to technology and to help to see the meaning of technology in our everyday life. Basic education must inculcate basic knowledge about technology, about its development and impacts; it must be a guide to rational options and discuss the connected ethical, moral and gender-equality problems. Education must develop an understanding of the basic functions of tools, equipment and machines and teach to use them.

Aims:

Pupils will learn to
- understand technology, its development in and impacts on different areas of life, different sectors of the society and environment
- use technology in responsible ways
- use computer hardware, software and networks for different purposes
- take the point on decisions concerning technology and evaluate the impacts of the decisions on technology of today on the future.

Central contents:
- technology in everyday life, in society and in the local industry
- development of technology and the connected factors in different cultures, different areas of life in different times
- development of technological ideas, modelling, evaluation and the life circle of the products
- use of computer technology and networks
- connected questions of ethics, morality, well-being and gender equality
- future society and technology." (National Board 2004.)

For upper Secondary (academic) schools the TE 'entity' is:

"Technology and society"

The starting point for the development of technology is the human need to improve the quality of life and make life easier in work and leisure time. The basis for technology is to know the laws of nature. Technology consists of knowledge and skills to design, manufacture and use technological products, processes and systems. Teaching will emphasize the interactive process of technology and the development of society.

The aim is that the student
- can use knowledge from different sciences when considering the development possibilities of technology
- understands and can evaluate human relation to modern technology and has the skill to assess the impacts of technology on the way of life, on society and on the condition of the natural environment
- can evaluate the aspects of ethics, economy, well-being and gender equality and consider the technological alternatives
- understands the interaction of technology and economy and can evaluate the impact of technology on contents of work and employment
- learns entrepreneurship and becomes familiar with the local working life.

The thematic entity must guide the student to think over the development of technology in relation to the social changes from the historical, present and future viewpoints. The student is guided to understand, use and manage technology. He/She must learn innovation and problem solving skills, which belong to the technological development work. He/She must learn to consider the values as the starting point for technology and its impacts. The dependence of the modern man from technology must be discussed as questions of individual, working life and leisure time. Especially the necessary and non-necessary technology must be considered from the viewpoint of the basic human needs. The student is challenged to take the point to the development of technology and to participate in decision making as an individual and as a member of the civic society.

The questions connected with the thematic entity will be concretised by familiarising pupils with technologies from different fields. These are, e.g., well-being and health, information and media, design and music, environmental protection, production of energy, traffic and agriculture and forestry". (National Board 2003.)

The last passages possibly have impacts from the US Standards. Fortunately the texts are not only emphasizing theoretical approaches; hands-on activities are possible, if teachers want that.

Younger TW teachers actually do TE in their work; they strive for gender equality, use computers and media, design, construct electronics, and do projects and Control Technology. The older teachers still are happy for their old industrial arts type of machine shops and reproductive crafts or handicrafts. Some schools have introduced TE as an option; some schools have a subject 'TW and technology'. In the Jyväskylä and Savonlinna teacher training departments that title is also used for students' courses. In Rauma department for TW teachers' training the English title in the Internet is 'TE teacher education'. Oulu program continues. – In Rauma and Oulu both resistance and support for the new subject title was found. Unfortunately contacts abroad have not been very strong from Rauma and Oulu handicraft and TW program permanent representatives – except the Nordic contacts. TW has recently lost a lot in period allocation and status. The problems at lower comprehensive level (primary) are the most serious, where the TW teachers' association has no interest and where Science has a mandate now. Technology should according to the education authorities now be realized mostly on terms of science.

There is a smaller group of activists working for the TE. An association called 'FATE', 'Finnish Association for research in Technology Education' (>www.teknologiakasvatus.fi>) has been founded in order to activate and support teachers, teacher educators and researchers. Jyväskylä University is the centre of the development now. Some meetings and conferences have been organised. Funding is problematic for such informal type of work of enthusiasts. FATE has been working now for 9 years. Today 'FATE' has a challenge to keep up the public and teachers' interest in order to be able to have a better status in the future. There is about 5 years time to make a better impact on the next curriculum. Working together with TW association is approximately in order. FATE has a member from TW –teachers' association in the Board. The TW association has supported FATE to organize small conferences during the yearly TW –meeting. Around the

Millennium the TW journal was quite actively marketing the new ideas for the subject. The TW –association has unfortunately interpreted its mission to be more union-type taking care of safety, salaries and re-unions for the higher comprehensive teachers than pedagogy or development of the subject in the whole comprehensive school as it could and should be.

In the beginning of the Millennium a government report about the needs of industrial manpower was published. The message was that there were needs for about 3.000 engineers in information technology (mostly NOKIA) and about 40.000 professionals for industry (mostly metal workers). That should naturally have had impacts on education. The report has been interpreted generally so that science and mathematics had a better status and more weekly periods, and there is no focus or development of technical work or TE. However, most of the Finnish industry understands the problems in TE and between S and T. Unfortunately also at the employers' union's central body the education relations are taken care of science people today.

4 DISCUSSION

The end result of the TE experiments in higher secondary (Kananoja – Rajamäki 1974) was that the local higher secondary and vocational education moved closer to each other. Today it is possible to do both in a combined study programme, and also to have access to the universities through vocational studies.

David Layton sees the Finnish TE situation as 'another illustration of the recent introduction of technology as a component of general education' (Layton 1993, 14); comparing the developments in Finland, the US and the Netherlands. Layton describes 'the Finnish variant handicraft based and connected with TW'. It is true. The effort was, like in the UK and US, to replace handicrafts, industrial arts, engineering and technical drawing with the new title and approach. The TE movement seemed to be the only realistic theoretical effort in the area from the 1980s on. Layton continues: "This 'high-tech' and production-oriented version of technology education is in marked contrast to developments in several other countries where a greater emphasis is being placed on the process aspects of designing, making and appraising technological artefacts and systems, and on the cognitive development of pupils in ways which are unique to technology education."

That above is not exactly the whole truth. The main ideas were not just to follow the technological development in society and industry, but also to satisfy the individual civic needs for new technology. Finland began the reforming efforts in 1967 – 1970, when the only models for imitation were, in the beginning, from Sweden and Norway. The one-sided Sloyd emphasis in these countries was Design as 'Arts and Crafts'. We were not satisfied with that narrow approach but also wanted to have industrial education within. In Sweden there was another practical subject also, 'Teknik', which, however, was vocational, and we had not possibilities to realise that because of the tight education policy decisions.

444

During my responsibility as 'the leader of the reform' (1971 – 91) we got new ideas at first from German 'Technik' and then from the UK, US and The Netherlands. The application of the inputs has proceeded quite well with the younger technical work teachers. However, there are still problems, e.g. with the role of science education, which has 'found' TE later on and now keeps it as a monopoly.

The comments of Layton may be drawn from my one-sided descriptions of the Finnish system. I am sorry for that possibility. However, modernising technological education was the main purpose of the handicraft reforms from 1970 on. This approach was officially introduced in the curriculum in 1970 and is still there; and it is also connected with the old Cygnaeus tradition. The approach still is in the handicrafts tradition, more on making original objects for an individual than focusing on the Big Social Problems, e.g. the environmental problems, designing traffic junctions or checking airport noise levels – even if these also have been very interesting and successful projects in some countries.

Curricula usually have trends, which follow the international fashions. In 1980s and 1990s the Finnish national curricula in TW were quite broad and gave individual teachers a lot of possibilities to interpret them originally. It was a must, because there had been 13 different training programs for teachers. The subjects had no national tests. Freedom created an atmosphere for discussions in the schools. Also teacher education was developed and all teachers now have M.Ed. or M.S. and the programs are quite highly ranked by the best students. Today teachers' individuality has been limited and the national tests have come. Teachers do not like that so much (Juurikkala 2005). We will see if that all will have an effect on the next PISA.

I have been both happy and disappointed about the TE developments in Finland. Even if the development has not been as fast or as good as it could have been, some positive things have been happening. Best of these naturally has been the possibility in conferences to meet colleagues who have the same problems and to get new ideas. Another good thing has been the first footstep for TE in the Finnish curriculum. The subject title is there now, which was one of the primary needs. And all the development efforts have been a difficult but interesting time for us. Now the feeling is that the Younger Ones should show the way forward in Finland. We have about 10 doctors in TE, and some more in the pipeline. All these have grown from TW; from Science or textile work there is not so much; textiles have more than 10 doctors but only one on 'textile technology'; under the Science wings there are 2 – 3 who write or have been writing on TE. In our situation today it has been natural that the research efforts have been handling more or less the philosophical basis and the need for TE. What we older enthusiasts expect today is, on the one hand, experimental research and, on the other, development of practical activities in TE, public information and textbooks. These could solve some of the problems, especially at the lower comprehensive level, where the pupils' interests and options for higher comprehensive school are created and where the primary class teacher has too many subjects to take care of. Just at the last moment when writing this paper the latest issue of 'Primary teachers' journal' was published. Dr.

Rasinen had an article about the primary TE (Rasinen 2005). That kind of thing will surely speed up the process of reform!

I would personally like to see TW and TE collaboration – or even amalgamation – in Finland. According to the basics of Philosophy of Technology 'making artefacts' still is an aspect of technological and social progress.

'Cross-over' in music means efforts to combine different traditions. However, for example collaboration between the Beatles and Indian Ravi Shankar collapsed after some efforts. This may have a message. If we bring a curriculum from one culture to another, it may not work. TE needs to be constructed TE according to the local culture. It is, anyway, important for a teacher to know what is happening in other countries in the subject development. A teacher in Finland is also supposed to be a researcher.

'Cross-over' between theory and practice has been emphasized in TE. It has also been done in engineering studies. In Oulu University the first professor of electronics in the 1970s, Matti Otala, later on a CD-expert at Philips, had an idea that every engineering student should construct the gadget he/she was designing. The students went on strike and wanted to have assistants to do this. The professor did not give up, because he thought that learning only theories was not enough. Finally, every student began to construct their gadgets. And today Oulu University has a big Technology Center and NOKIA development labs. Moreover, in TE we should always practice what we teach, Hand-on experiences! With too much general and theoretical technological education we will lose the interest of the pupils. – After some hard experiences I have recently proposed a 'division of labour' instead of teachers' collaboration.

Jean Monnet, one of the Fathers of the European community has said: 'Without people nothing would be possible, without institutions nothing would be permanent.' Cross-over' also means to know other cultures (disciplines) in order to make an impact on the national and global decisions. Naturally that also means taking care of the leadership, with which we in Finland have had problems.

Innovations are seldom born in stable conditions. They also need tension, 'cultural friction', which is natural.

REFERENCES

Allen, A., Black, P., Wallin. H. (2002). *An evaluation report on the LUMA programme* prepared for the Ministry of Education. 48:202. Ministry of Education.

Allinbjerg, C. (1983). SLÖJD i Danmark 1883 – 1983. *Baggrund og vilkår. Aarhuus*: Dansk Skoleslöjds forlag.

Black, P., Atkin, M. (Ed.) (1996). *Changing the subject. Innovations in science, mathematics and technology education.* London and Paris: Routledge in association with OECD.

CCC. (1972). *The teaching of technology.* Strasbourg. (CCC/EGT (72) 14).

Cygnaeus, U. 1861. Letter.

Cygnaeus, U. 1866. *Law for the folk school*

Deutscher Ausschuss. 1964. *Empfehlungen und Gutachten des Deutschen Ausschuss* fuer das Erziehungs- und Bildungswesen. Folge 7/8. Stuttgart.

FACTE. (2003). *Who needs technology? (Kuka tarvitsee tekniikkaa?)* (In Finnish)

FATE. www.teknologiakasvatus.fi.

Juurikkala, J. (2005). *Article* in 'Primary Teacher'. Luokanopettaja 1/2005 (26.01.2005). (In Finnish)

Kananoja, T. (1987). *The influence of different kinds of organisation and contents of teaching technical work and textile work on pupils' dexterity, creativity and attitudes in some classes on the experimental comprehensive school.* In: Coenen-van den Bergh, R. 1987. (ed.) International conference for Pupils' Attitudes Towards Technology (PATT). University of Technology. Eindhoven, 286 – 318. (Litentiate Thesis. 1975; 1980. Turku University, Faculty of Education A: 72. Turku. In Finnish.)

Kananoja, T. (1976). POPS –opas 13b. (*Curriculum guide for technical work.*) The National Board of General Education. (In Finnish)

Kananoja, T. (1988). (Ed.) POPS –opas. (Curriculum guide for technical work.) The National Board of General Education. (In Finnish)

Kananoja, T. (1989). *Work, Skill and Technology: About activity education and education for work in general education.* Doctoral Dissertation. English summary. Publication Series B: 29. Turku University.

Kananoja, T. (1989). *Work, Skill and Technology: About activity education and education for work in general education.* Doctoral Dissertation. Publication Series C: 72. Turku University. (In Finnish)

Kananoja, T. (1990). *Uno Cygnaeus, der Vater des finnischen Volsschulwesens und seine Ideen zur Slöjd-Pedagogik.* In: Oberliesen, R., Wiemann. G. (Hrsg.) Internationale Berichte zur Geschichte von Arbeit ung Technik im Unterricht. Braunschweig: Internationaler Arbeitskreis Sonnenberg. (1990a)

Kananoja, T. (1990). *Realisation of environmental studies according to the 1985 curriculum.* The National Board of General Education. (In Finnish) (1990b)

Kananoja, T. (1991). *MEMO* for Technology Education. Report of a specialist Committee. The National Board of General Education.

Kananoja, T. (1992). PATT: Finland – Zambia. In: Bame, E.A., Dugger, W.E. Jr. (Ed.). *A Global Technology Education Perspective.* ITEA-PATT International Conference. Reston, Va., 295 – 311.

Kananoja, T., & al. (2000). *Technological education in general education schools in Finland.* FACTE. Helsinki: Edita. (2000a)

Kananoja T., & al. (2000). *Technology education in general education schools in other countries.* FACTE. Helsinki: Edita. (2000b)

Kananoja, T., & al. (2000). *The US standards for technological literacy* (www.teknologiakasvatus.fi - > Tekstejä) (In Finnish) (2000c)

Kananoja, T., Rajamäki, S. (1974). *Report on an experiment on technology in the higher secondary school in Kotka.* The national Board of General Education. (In Finnish)

Lavonen, J. (1996). LUONTI. *Science education project* in Helsinki University. Conference Brochure at JISTEC, Israel.

Layton, D. (1993). *Technology's challenge to science education.* In: Woolnough, B. (Ed.) Developing science and technology education. Department of Educational Studies, University of Oxford. Suffolk: Open University Press.

National Board. (2003). *Technology and society.* In: Basics for Curriculum for Higher Secondary School.

National Board. (2004). *Man and technology.* In: Basics for Curriculum for Comprehensive School, 20 – 21.

Netherlands: A new subject in general secondary schools in the Netherlands. In: Practical Education and School Crafts. *1980. (Ed.) The Journal of The Educational Institute of Design, Craft and Technology.* Kogan Page/Educational Institute of Design, Craft and Technology, 32 - 37. Originally published Mäkel, N. (Ed.) 1970. 'Education and the arts'. Government Printing and Publishing Office. The Hague.

Parikka, M. (2000). *MEMO* on initiatives on Technology Education. Jyväskylä university. (In Finnish).

PATT. 1987. *Conference Papers.* Eindhoven.

Rasinen, A. (2005). *Luokanopettajilla ratkaiseva rooli käsityönopetuksessa. (Primary class teachers have a decisive role in handicrafts education. Article in 'Primary Teacher').* Luokanopettaja 1/2005 (26.01.2005), 40 – 41. (In Finnish)

447

Richtlinien und Lehrpläne. 1974. *Behörde fuer Schule, Jugend und Berufsbildung.* Freie und Hansestadt Hamburg. Regensburg: Georg Zwickenpflug.

Unesco. (2003). 2000+ Conference Papers.

Unesco. Newsletter on STE. www.unesco.org/education/educprog/ste/index.html.

AKI RASINEN, PASI IKONEN AND TIMO RISSANEN

32. ARE GIRLS EQUAL IN TECHNOLOGY EDUCATION?

INTRODUCTION

Finnish technology education dates back to 1866 when craft education was accepted to be one of the compulsory subjects in the school curriculum. Uno Cygnaeus, founder of Finnish general education, considered "technological" contents an important part of craft education. Cygnaeus emphasized dexterity, design and aesthetics but also consideration, innovation and creativity. (Kantola 1997, p. 18)

There have been many pedagogical and administrative changes in general education since Cygnaeus' times, but one remarkable change took place in the beginning of the1970's when the parallel school system (folk school and gymnasium) was abolished and the comprehensive school was introduced in the country. A significant reform was introduced in teacher education in 1979. Since then all comprehensive school (grades 1 to 9) teachers, both class teachers and subject teachers, have been trained up to master's level.

In this article, we will discuss the changes in Finnish technology education since 1970 from the point of view of changes in curriculum, particularly from the gender point of view, but also considering pedagogy, teacher education, society, and the concept of learning.

TECHNOLOGY EDUCATION AND CRAFT EDUCATION

Handicraft teaching and technology teaching have seldom been compared in research literature. Comparisons are mainly made between technology, science and mathematics. The reason for this is obviously that, for instance, in England and the United States handicraft education has developed into technology education. According to Alamäki (1999, p. 37), technology education has evolved from craft education in many countries. He also argues that, due to technology education still being in the evolution process, many approaches from crafting to applied science are being used in technology. Järvinen (2004a p. 45 and 2004 b p. 8) claims that technology education cannot be monopolized by either craft or science education because it involves mathematics, science, arts, handicrafts and genuine innovative problem solving.

Kantola (1997) and Parikka (1998) define technology as an umbrella concept for handicraft education. Anttila (1993), Peltonen (1988) and Suojanen (1993), on the contrary, regard handicraft education as an umbrella concept for technology education. Alamäki (1999, p. 14), then, explains that 'käsityö' (craft or handicraft)

M.J. de Vries, I. Mottier (eds.), International Handbook of Technology Education, 449–461.

is the official name and overall term for a subject group that consists of the school subjects 'tekninen työ' (technical work) and 'tekstiilityö' (textile work). "Käsityö in the Finnish educational context has no direct English equivalent but implies a combination of crafts, design and technology education." (ibid. 1999, p. 173.) He also notes that "the contents and processes of the Finnish 'tekninen työ' correspond to the international view of technology education". He goes on by saying that in many Finnish publications (e.g. Alamäki 1998a; 1998b; 1999; Alamäki & Suomala 1998; Kankare 1997) the English equivalent of the term 'tekninen työ' is technology education. (ibid. 1999, p. 14.) By merely changing the title of the subject there is no change in learning. What matters is the contents of teaching. Therefore, the objectives and contents of craft education have to be discussed and altered towards technology education.

Experts in craft education and technology education, whether Finnish or foreign, agree on particularly one view. Both groups see that an essential part of learning is the creative planning and production process (Anttila 1993, Hill & Lutherd 1999, Eggleston 1994, Lindfors 1992, Peltonen 1988, Suojanen 1993, Yli-Piipari 1991). Kojonkoski-Rännäli (1998, p. 368) distinguishes, mainly following Bunge (1985, p. 220), the handicraft production activity and the technological production activity. According to her, hands-on methods are used in handicraft, whereas in technology, methods of modern technology are used.

In this article thinking and use of the brain is considered to lead all work done by hand. Technology is seen as "logos" of "techné", where technology is not restricted to modern technology, but is seen from a wide perspective - from traditional to modern.

THE 1970 FRAMEWORK CURRICULUM AND THE 1970 CURRICULUM

Girls and boys should not be separated during craft lessons (Peruskoulun opetussuunnitelmakomitean mietintö I, 1970 p. 49, Peruskoulun opetussuunnitelmakomitean mietintö II, 1970p. 338)

In 1970, the Ministry of Education published two memoranda to guide teachers in transferring from the old parallel school system to the comprehensive school system. The 1970 Framework curriculum (Peruskoulun opetussuunnitelmakomitean mietintö I, 1970) gave the rationale and philosophy, aims and objectives, information needed to implement and develop the curriculum, different methods, information about learning materials, information about differentiation, evaluation, extra mural activities, counselling, organizing the work and co-operation between the school and homes for the schools. The 1970 Curriculum stated the attainment targets and contents for different school subjects and in craft education listed grade by grade the techniques (i.e. measuring, marking, sawing etc.), materials (i.e. planks, metal rod, plastics etc.), and objectives (mainly different techniques) with some ideas for different projects. It also gave information on different working, learning and teaching methods, evaluation and integration. Craft education was divided into two sub-areas:

technical craft and textile craft. The document emphasized that the division should no longer be according to one's sex, but both girls and boys should study textile craft and technical craft. All pupils were supposed to study the same programme from grade one to three, then choose one of the two subject areas for grades four to seven. During the spring term (January – May) grade six pupils were supposed to change the subject area. (Peruskoulun opetussuunnitelmakomitean mietintö II, 1970). However, boys mainly went for technical craft classes and girls for textile craft classes. Girls were more open-minded in their choices than boys were. Technology as a concept is not to be found in the 1970 Curriculum. In turn, the concept of technique is to be found under the title "technical craft". One of the general objectives in technical craft studies was to become acquainted with technical domains. The pupils' own designprocess was regarded as important and the contents of, for instance, machinery and electronics can be seen to be of a technological nature. The 1970 Curriculum and Framework Curriculum documents is a very radical, educationally professional, ambitious and future oriented.

THE FRAMEWORK CURRICULUM FOR COMPREHENSIVE SCHOOLS 1985

Both sexes should study technical work and textile work (Peruskoulun opetussuunnitelman perusteet, 1985 p. 206)

Since the 1970 Curriculum document there has not been a national curriculum in Finland. The documents since then have been framework curricula, and the municipalities and schools have planned their own curricula following the national framework. The reasons for this are decentralization of the educational management, reform in teacher education, and need to plan the curriculum to fit the local circumstances. In the 1980's the inspection system was also abolished. Inspectors' posts at national and regional level were changed to instructors' and supervisors' posts. Their role was not to check if the teachers had done their job, but to assist and help teachers in planning, developing, and organizing in-service education for teachers. Schools and municipalities were guided to develop their own curriculum following the national framework curriculum. Teachers were highly educated and they were considered to be able to develop their own curricula.

In 1985, after 15 years experience of the comprehensive school- system, a Framework Curriculum for Comprehensive Schools (Peruskoulun opetussuunnitelman perusteet 1985) was published by the National Board of Education. The document introduced six general objectives, one of which is gender equality. Enhancing equality at school means offering the same possibilities for both boys and girls (ibid. 1985, p. 13). There are references to the discussions in parliament about promoting gender equality. According to the law, the schools should promote equality between sexes. The National Board of Education leaves it to the municipalities to decide how to organize craft education. However, from grade one to grade three all pupils should study both textile work and technical work, from grade four to six part of the studies are common to all pupils but part is

451

either technical or textile work. At grade seven technical work and textile work are common subjects to all pupils. However, if the municipalities want they can, on top of the common studies, differentiate teaching into technical or textile work. (ibid. pp. 206 – 207).

For the first time also the concept of technology was introduced - but not defined. However, the concept is to be found only under "Craft, technical work and textile work". Technology is the starting point of technical abilities, planning, and implementing (ibid. p. 206). During technical work lessons pupils should also learn to manage technology (ibid. p. 208).

In the curriculum the sector on craft, technical work and textile work introduces first the general objectives and gives information on how teaching should be organized. After this, the objectives of technical work and textile work are introduced together with contents grade by grade. The contents are mainly different techniques (i.e. cutting, sawing, soldering etc.). There is also information on how to differentiate the curriculum in different municipalities, how to evaluate, and what the opportunities for integration are. Although the general objectives are to develop problem solving and planning skills, the specific objectives are a mere list of different techniques (ibid. pp. 208 – 213). The approach in the curriculum can be characterized as behaviouristic. It has been written from teachers' point of view rather than from pupils' point of view. Such expressions as "pupils will be taught to turn wood" and similar are used (ibid. pp. 208 – 213). In practice, many schools continued to differentiate pupils after grade three in either textile or technical work groups. The groups were in most cases formed according to sex. Pupils were probably offered a chance for a short change of three to six weeks to study the other subject area of craft.

THE FRAMEWORK CURRICULUM FOR COMPREHENSIVE SCHOOLS 1994

"Craft, technical work and textile work form an entity at primary and junior secondary level which is meant for all pupils regardless of sex." (Peruskoulun opetussuunnitelman perusteet 1994, p. 104)

For the first time in the history of the curriculum development of Finnish general education schools, technology is clearly mentioned in the general objectives of the curriculum. For the comprehensive school the national guidelines state that the technical development of society makes it necessary for all citizens to have a new kind of readiness to use technical applications and to be able to exert an influence on the direction of technical development. Furthermore, it states that students without regard to sex must have the chance to acquaint themselves with technology and to learn to understand and avail themselves of technology. What is particularly important is to take a critical look at the effects technology has on the interaction between humanity and nature, to be able to make use of the possibilities it offers and to understand their consequences. (Peruskoulun opetussuunnitelman perusteet 1994, pp. 11 - 12.) However, the document does not give any operational instructions on how to study technology.

Under chemistry, the concept technology is mentioned once: "pupils should be able to acquire such a terminology that they are able to discuss questions concerning nature, environment, and technology" (ibid. p. 86). Under craft, the technological objective is that pupils will acquire knowledge of the traditional and modern technological materials on their own, knowledge of tools and techniques that can be applied in daily life, further studies, jobs, and hobbies (ibid. p. 105 - 106). Despite the stated objective at the end of 1990's woodwork was mainly taught during technical work lessons in the Finnish primary schools. Electricity and electronics tasks, plastic work, and service and repair were taught to a certain extent. Lack of financial resources and ideas were regarded as the most significant obstacles to the development of technology education. (Alamäki 1999, p.136). In informal discussions between teachers and teacher educators, technical work education in schools has been said to mainly include copying and reproducing processes, such as the copying of wooden and metal items, not modern, design-oriented processes. (ibid. p.39) According to Kankare (1997, pp. 156 – 157 and pp.176 – 177) woodwork was mainly emphasized by the Finnish technical craft teachers, although most teachers did not want to divide the contents according to materials, but considered the subject area in an holistic manner. Also Sanders (2001, p. 50) has found in the USA that most technology education teachers still stick to traditional general technology education and woodwork courses.

Although "craft, technical work and textile work form an entity at primary and junior secondary level which is meant for all pupils regardless of sex" (Peruskoulun opetussuunnitelman perusteet 1994, p. 104) in addition to having partly common craft education for both boys and girls, the document allowed the schools to emphasize one of the two craft domains. This meant in practice that most schools continued dividing pupils into either textile work or technical work after grade three. This is the first document since 1970 where cross-curriculum subject areas are introduced. The1970 and 1985 curricula mention holistic teaching and integration but there are no clear cross-curricular titles.

FRAMEWORK CURRICULUM FOR COMPREHENSIVE EDUCATION 2004

The human being and technology – a new cross-curricular theme

For the first time in the history of Finnish general education curriculum planning the 2004 framework curriculum introduces a cross-curricular theme:
* *the human being and technology.*

The other six are:
* development of personal identity
* culture identity and internationality,
* communication and media skills,
* committed citizenship and entrepreneurship
* responsibility for the environment, well-being and sustainable future

- safety and traffic behavior (ibid. pp.36 – 41).

Under the title " the human being and technology" the meaning of technology in our everyday lives and dependency of human beings on modern technology should be studied. This theme will offer basic know-how of technology, the development of technology and the effects of technology, guide pupils to make reasonable choices and guides them to consider the ethic, moral and equality questions related to technology. Teaching should also improve the ability to understand how different devices, equipment, and machines work and how to use them.

The aims are as follows:

A pupil will learn
- to understand technology, the development of technology and its impacts on different fields of life, different sectors in society, and on the environment
- to use technology in a responsible and critical manner
- to use information technology equipment, programs and networks for different purposes
- to state one's opinion concerning technological choices, and to consider the effects of today's decisions about technology on the future

The core contents
- technology in everyday life, in society and in local trade and industry
- the development of technology and factors affecting the development in different cultures and different fields of life during different eras
- the development, modeling, and assessing of technological ideas and the life-span of a product
- the use of information and communication technology and information networks
- the ethical, moral, well-being, and equality concerns related to technology
- future society and technology

(ibid. p 40 - 41).

"Teaching will be conducted following the same contents for all pupils including contents from technical work and textile work." (grades 1 -4) (Perusopetuksen opetussuunnitelman perusteet 2004, p. 240)

"Teaching comprises contents of technical work and textile work for all pupils together, on top of this pupils can be given a chance to emphasize in their craft studies either technical work or textile work according to their interests and aptitudes." (grades 5 – 9)(ibid. p. 242)

In the framework curriculum, references to technological studies can be found only under science (particularly physics) and to a considerable extent under craft (particularly technical work). The subject groups in other subjects have not considered the cross-curricular theme " the human being and technology" in their text. However, the instructions from the National Board of Education are that the schools have to clearly indicate in their curricula how these cross-curricula themes are included in different school subjects and they have to be seen in the activities of the schools (ibid. p. 36). The framework curriculum does not give instructions how this should be done, this is left for the schools to decide and think about. By studying 50 Finnish municipal curricula (this will cover an average of 400 schools) one notes that often " the human being and technology"-cross-curricular theme is understood to be information and communication technology. This indicates that the theme has not been understood in its' broad sense, but in a very narrow manner.

Technology education objectives under craft education are as follows:

pupils
- familiarize themselves with everyday technology
- familiarize themselves with Finland's and to an appropriate extent also other nations' design, craft, and technology culture for building their own identity and their own design activities
- familiarize themselves with the know-how connected to traditional and modern technology which can be applied in daily life, further studies, in future jobs, and hobbies
- learn to state their stand on the development of technology and the meaning of it for the well-being of human beings, society and nature (ibid. 241 – 242)

If one compares the objectives to the contents of technical work and textile work, it is obvious that by studying only one sub-area all technological objectives can not be achieved. However, most municipalities (of the 50 municipal curricula studied) have decided (against the regulations of the framework curriculum) to differentiate pupils after grade four into technical work or textile work. The document suggests integration between different school subjects. It is based on a constructivist learning concept where the learner is active and target oriented. The objectives are stated from the learner's point of view, not as teacher's activities.

THE MYTH OF GIRLS' AND BOYS' JOBS

There has not been much research done on gender equality in technology education in general education schools. Haynie (1999, 2003) has conducted studies in gender issues in technology education in the USA. His interest has been in if women are accepted into the technology education professions. Sanders (2001 p. 41)) noted that despite some gains in diversity, "technology education is still taught by middle-aged white men". Haynie (2003 p. 29), for his part, asks the question:

Why? One can assume that if the subject is mainly taught by men, the pupils tend to think it belongs to "the masculine category" and are not willing to choose to study the subject. However, there has been a remarkable change in the number of girls choosing technology education in the USA since industrial arts was abolished and technology education introduced. Nearly half (46,2 %) of middle-school technology students in 1999 were female (Sanders 2001, p. 43). Out of all school levels one third of students were female in 1999 while the percentage of females enrolled in industrial arts classes was 2,1 % in 1963 and 16,8 % in 1979.

The fact that girls do not choose technical studies can be explained by the myth of men's and women's jobs. During the agricultural era women took care of homes, cooking, nursing, making clothes and tended the domestic animals. Men, in turn, made sledges, furniture, hunted and worked on the fields. During the industrial era men went to work in the factories while women remained at home to take care of cooking, nursing, cleaning, washing, mending the men's clothes... We no longer live in an agricultural or industrial era, but in an information or technological era where women are no longer working at home but outside the home. However, the myth of women's and men's jobs is still to be seen when one examines the statistics on how the different sexes are divided across different fields of study. Nowadays the number of female and male students from vocational institutions to universities in Finland is about equal, for example 52,3 % of university students in 1997 – 1998 were female students (Suomen virallinen tilasto 2003). Female students choose health oriented studies while male students choose technically oriented studies (ibid. 2003). The number of female students studying in technical and technological institutions at vocational, polytechnic and university levels in Finland is minimal compared to the number of male students studying technically oriented branches. A minor increase in enrolment of girls in technical universities has taken place in recent years, but the number of female students is still very modest. In vocational institutions, polytechnics, and universities the number of female students in technical fields in 2000 was less than 20 % (ibid. 2003).

Our school curriculum before 1970 has supported the division of duties into women's and men's work. While girls at school studied cookery and textile handicraft, boys were doing woodwork and metalwork. Since 1970 the Finnish school authority have realized that crafts curriculum did not treat the two sexes equally. Already the 1985 but particularly the 1994 Framework Curriculum (Peruskoulun opetussuunnitelman perusteet 1994) states clearly that "craft, technical work and textile work form an entity at primary and junior secondary level which is meant for all pupils regardless of sex" (p. 104). This type of thinking is supported by a memorandum of the working group on the renewal of basic education (Perusopetuksen uudistamistyöryhmän muistio 2001). This document states that "the contents of craft education for grades 5 – 7 should be mainly the same for boys and girls including elements from textile work, technical work and technology" (p. 31). Also the 2004 Framework Curriculum (Perusopetuksen opetussuunnitelman perusteet) emphasizes equal craft education for all pupils. However, the 1985, and 1994 framework curriculum expressed a possibility for an emphasis on one of the two subjects. Also, according to the 2004 framework curriculum, pupils can be given a chance in their craft studies to emphasize either technical work or textile work according to their interests and aptitudes.

More than ten years ago, a technology education experiment was launched at the University of Jyväskylä. One of the aims of this experiment was to develop the craft curriculum in the direction of technology education. The reasons behind this were the awareness of the development of craft education globally and the development of Finnish society from an agricultural via an industrial to a technological or an information society. (Rasinen 2003). According to Parikka (1998, p. 40) craft education has developed via education of techniques towards technology education. Kantola (1997, p. 181) also supports the idea of craft education developing towards technological education.

In spite of national regulations, experiences from other countries (see e.g. Rasinen 2000, pp. 43 – 83) and experiences from some schools in Finland (Autio 1997 pp. 120 - 123), and research findings (Autio 1997, pp. 235 - 240 and Rasinen 2000, p. 130) supporting the importance of offering girls equal possibilities to study technological contents, the tradition in crafts education in many schools is still that after grade three pupils have to drop one domain of general education (see e.g. Heinonen p. 76). From then on they will study only textile work or technical work. It is claimed that pupils have a choice. However, this does not seem to be a choice but an obligation to leave aside one important field of education. The choice is quite often made by teachers or parents, not by the pupils. Or, if the pupil decides, there is always social pressure when making one's choice. Because girls have traditionally taken textile work and boys technical work, it is difficult to make individual choices which deviate from the mainstream. According to Linda Gottfredson (2002), different choices are made more based on sex than interest. The dominant factor is primarily one's sex, secondly social suitability and thirdly what is nice to do. Why force pupils to choose? We do not ask them at grade three or five if from now on they would prefer geometry to arithmetic. Nor we do teach English, music, history… separately to girls and boys.

By choosing the learning contents in both branches of craft education in such a way that they are not gender biased allows girls and boys to study a similar curriculum at all levels. This is reality, for instance, in teacher education during basic courses (4 credit units). The number of female students specializing in technology education and technical work (15 credit units) at the University of Jyväskylä is increasing annually and is 40 % this year.

GIRLS' VERSUS BOYS' PERFORMANCE IN MATHEMATICS AND SCIENCE

Another myth explaining why girls do not choose technological careers has been that they do not manage as well as boys in mathematics and science in schools. Because of this they will not be able to pass examinations at technological universities. This myth has no basis in reality. The 2002 international PISA (Programme for International Student Assessment) -studies proved that there are no gender differences in mathematics performance amongst Finnish junior secondary school students at 15 years of age (Välijärvi, Linnakylä, Kupari, Reinikainen & Arffman, 2002, p. 22, 26, 39). Finland's performance in mathematical literacy also showed high equality. The standard deviation for student scores in mathematical literacy was the smallest among the OECD countries (ibid. 2002, p. 10). Also in scientific literacy Finland showed a high level (ibid. 2002, p 12). In scientific literacy the standard deviation was the second smallest (ibid. 2002, p 13). Both in mathematical literacy and scientific literacy Finland seems to have achieved a high level of performance and low disparities (ibid. 2002, p 14). In mathematical literacy, no differences were found between Finnish boys and girls. The same applies to science. "In scientific literacy Finland displayed no significant gender differences". (ibid. p. 39.)

The 2004 PISA study (Kupari, Välijärvi, Linnakylä, Reinikainen, Brunell, Leino, Sulkunen, Törnroos, Malin & Puhakka pp. 24 – 25.) found that the gender difference was relatively small. In mathematical literacy boys gained 548 points (mean value) and girls 541 (mean value) points. The difference of 7 points is, however, statistically significant. In the 2002 study the difference was only 1 point. Also the scientific literacy of the Finnish pupils can be characterized by high performance and equality. Although the standard deviation gives an impression that equality is being realized, the score gained by the girls was significantly better than the score gained by the boys. Also in 2000 (reported in 2002) the difference of the mean values was 6 points, but then it was not statistically significant. (ibid. pp. 26 – 28). These resluts do not support the myth of girls being less able to study in technological institutions. However, in senior secondary schools girls tend to choose fewer courses in mathematics and physics than boys do. When applying for technical universities high marks in mathematics and physics are recognized and valued by the universites. This partly explains why technical universities and technical polytechnics are male dominated.

DISCUSSION

There have been several attempts to interest girls in technical studies. Unfortunately, the campaigns have been aimed mainly at students at the secondary school stage. It seems that it is too late to start affecting attitudes at this age. The attitudes are formed at a much earlier stage of development of the individual.

Technology has to be studied by all pupils at all levels. As long as technology is a cross-curriculum theme, different subjects should consider how it should be studied. There should be continuous consultation between different subject areas and strong co-operation and, where it is advisable, integration should be applied. Technology education is mainly to be seen under the objectives and contents of craft education. Therefore, this subject area should take main responsibility for making sure that all pupils will study technology and co-ordinate the activities at school level. Different studies (e.g. Alamäki, 1999, Kankare, 1997 and Rasinen 2000) prove that to develop the subject area learning materials and in-service education have to be improved. In future, to guarantee more efficient learning, the subject area of "technology" should be introduced.

However, even today by following the approved framework curriculum, schools can offer equal technology education to all pupils regardless of sex. The contents of the studies have to be developed in such a way that they are not gender biased. What would our globe look like if female brains were actively developing technology?

REFERENCES

Alamäki, A. (1998a). *Technology education in Finland-Trends and issues.* Paper presented at the 60th Annual Conference of International Technology Education Association. Forth Worth, Texas, the United States. March 1998.

Alamäki, A. (1998b). *Technology education in elementary school-Why and how?* Paper presented at the 60th annual conference of International Technology Education Association. Forth Worth, Texas, the United States. March 1998.

Alamäki, A. (1999). *How to educate students for a technological future: technology education in early childhood and primary education.* Publications of the University of Turku, Annales Universitas Turkuensis. Series B: 233.

Alamäki, A. & Suomala, J. (1998). *Starting points for developing technology education in kindergarten.* Paper presented at the Conference of the American Educational Research Association, San Diego, California, April 1998.

Anttila, P. (1993). *Käsityön ja muotoilun perusteet.(Principles of handicrafts and forming.)* Porvoo: WSOY.

Autio, O. (1997). *Oppilaiden teknisten valmiuksien kehittyminen peruskoulussa. Tytöt ja pojat samansisältöisen käsityön opetuksen kokeilussa. (Development of students' technical abilities in Finnish comprehensive school. Boys and girls in an experiment of shared craft education.)* Helsingin yliopiston opettajankoulutuslaitos. Tutkimuksia 177. Helsinki: Hakapaino.

Bunge, M. (1985). *Treatise on basic philosophy.* Volume 7. Epistemology & Methodology III: Philosophy of science and technology. Part II. Life science, social science and technology. Boston: D. Reidel publishing company.

Eggleston, J. (1994). What is design and technology education? In F. Banks (ed.) *Teaching technology.* London: The Open University, 20 B 35.

Gottfredson, L. (2002). Gottfredson's theory of circumscription, compromise and self-creation. In Brown, D & associates (eds.) *Career choice and development.* San Francisco: Jossey-Bass, 85-148

Haynie, W. J. (1999). Cross-gender interaction in technology education: A survey. *Journal of Technology Education* 10 (2) Spring, 27 – 40.

Haynie, W, J. (2003). Gender issues in technology education: A quasi-ethnographic interview approach. *Journal of Technology Education* 15 (1) Fall, 16 - 30.

Heinonen, A. (2002). *Itseohjattu ja tutkiva opiskelu teknologiakasvatuksessa. Luokanopettajakoulutuksen teknologian kurssin kehittämistutkimus. (Self-directed and inquiring studying in technology education. Design research in technology education in class teacher education.)* University of Joensuu. Publications in education. N:o 79

Hill, B. & Lutherdt, M. (1999). *Structuring innovation-oriented approaches to teaching technology.* In T. Kananoja, J. Kantola & M. Issakainen (eds.) Development of technology education-Conference B98. University of Jyväskylä. Department of Teacher Education. The Principles and Practice of Teaching 33, 181-199

Järvinen, E – M. (2004a). *Näkökulmia teknologian opetukseen. (Some views in teaching of technology.)* Dimensio 3/2004, 44 – 45.

Järvinen, E – M & Karsikas, A. (2004b). *Mitkrokontrollereilla luovuutta perusopetukseen! (Creativity in basic teaching by microcontrollers!)* TEK – tekniikan akateemiset 8/2004, 36 – 37.

Kankare, P. (1997). *Teknologian lukutaidon toteutuskonteksti peruskoulun teknisessa tyossä. (The context of implementing technological literacy instruction in comprehensive school's technical work.)* Turun yliopiston julkaisusarja. Sarja C: 139.

Kantola, J. (1997). *Cygnaeuksen jäljillä käsityökasvatuksesta teknologiseen kasvatukseen. (In the footsteps of Cygnaeus: From handicraft teaching to technological education.)* Jyväskylän yliopisto. Jyväskylä studies in education, psychology and social research 133.

Kojonkoski-Rännäli, S. (1995). *Ajatus käsissämme. Käsityön merkityssisällön analyysi. (Thoughts in our hands. Analysis of the concept of handicrafts.)* Turun yliopiston julkaisusarja. Sarja C: 109.

Kupari, P., Välijärvi, J., Linnakylä, P., Reinikainen, P., Brunell, V., Leino, K., Sulkunen, S., Törnroos, J., Malin, A. & Puhakka E. (2004). *Nuoret osaajat. PISA 2003-tutkimuksen ensituloksia. (Young talents. Primary results of PISA 2003-research.)* Jyväskylä: Koulutuksen tutkimuslaitos. Jyväskylän yliopisto. Kopijyvä

Lattu, M. (2000). *The nature of Finnish technology education. Paper presented at the Technology Education* Seminar in Oulu, Finland, May 2000.

Lindfors, L. (1992). *Formgivning i slöjd. Ämnesteoretisk och slöjdpedagogisk orienteringsgrund med exempel från textilslöjdundervisning. (Forming in handicrafts. Orientation basis for subject orientation and handicraft pedagogy.)* Raporter från Pedagogiska fakulten vid Åbo Akademi nr 1 1992.

Marsh, C. J. (1997). *Planning, management and ideology: Key concepts for understanding curriculum 2.* London: The Falmer Press.

Parikka, M. (1998). *Teknologiakompetenssi; Teknologiakasvatuksen uudistamishaasteita peruskoulussa ja lukiossa. (Technological competence; Challenges of reforming technology education in the Finnish comprehensive and upper secondary school.)* Jyväskylän yliopisto. Jyväskylä studies in education, psychology and social research 141.

Parikka, M., Rasinen, A. & Kantola, J. (2000). *Kohti teknologiakasvatuksen teoriaa. Teknologiakasvatuskokeilu 1992 - 2000: Raportti 3. (Towards the Theory of Technology Education. The Technology Education Experiment 1992 - 2000: Report 3.)* Jyvaskylan yliopisto. Opettajankoulutuslaitos. Tutkimuksia 69.

Peltonen, J. (1988). *Käsityökasvatuksen perusteet. Koulukäsityön ja sen opetuksen teoria ja empiirinen tutkimus peruskoulun yläasteen teknisen työn oppisisällöistä ja opetuksesta. (Principles of handicraft education. Theory of school crafts and how it is taught, and an empirical study of the contents and teaching of technical work in the upper classes of comprehensive schools.)* Turun yliopisto. Kasvatustieteiden tiedekunta. Julkaisusarja A: 1332.

Peltonen, J. (2002). Structural questions for the future from the viewpoint of subject teacher education of the crafts education. In J.Kantola & T. Kananoja (eds.) *Looking at the future: technical work in the context of technology education.* University of Jyvaskyla. Department of teacher education. Research 76.

Peruskoulun opetussuunnitelmakomitean mietintö I. (1970). *Opetussuunnitelman perusteet. (Memorandum. Foundations of the comprehensive school curriculum.)* Komiteamietintö 1970: A 4OPS 1970 I ja II. Helsinki: Valtion painatuskeskus.

Peruskoulun opetussuunnitelmakomitean mietintö I. (1970). Oppiaineiden opetussuunnitelmat. (1970). *(Memorandum. Curricula of different subjects.)* Komiteamietintö 1970: A 4OPS 1970 I ja II. Helsinki: Valtion painatuskeskus.

Peruskoulun opetussuunnitelman perusteet (1985). *(Foundations of the comprehensive school curriculum.)* Kouluhalitus. Helsinki:.Valtion painatuskeskus.

Peruskoulun opetussuunnitelman perusteet (1994). *(Foundations of the comprehensive school curriculum.)* Opetushallitus. Helsinki: Painatuskeskus.

Perusopetuksen opetussuunnitelman perusteet (2004). *(The Framework curriculum of comprehensive schools.)* Opetushallitus. Vammala: Vammalan kirjapaino.

Perusopetuksen uudistamistyöryhmän muistio. (2001). *(A memo of a working group on renewing the basic education)* Opetusministeriön työryhmien muistioita 11:2001. Opetusministeriö. (Ministry of Education.) Helsinki.

Rasinen, A. (2000). *Developing technology education. In search of curriculum elements for Finnish general education schools.* Jyväskylän yliopisto. Jyväskylä studies in education, psychology and social research 171.

Rasinen, A. (2003). *Is technology education for healthy, young, urban men only?* Paper presented in UNESCO Conference on Intercultural Education. Jyväskylä, Finland June 2003.Published on CD-ROM. Jyväskylä: Koulutuksen tutkimuslaitos.

Sanders, M. (2001). New paradigm or old wine? The status of technology education practice in the United States. *Journal of technology Education*. 12 (2) Spring. 35 – 55.

Suojanen, U. (1993). *Käsityökasvatuksen perusteet. (Principles of handicraft education.)* Porvoo: WSOY.

Suomen virallinen tilasto. Tilastokeskus. *Naiset ja miehet numeroina. Koulutus. (Men and women in numbers.)* Available: http://www.stat.fi/tk/he/tasaarvo_koulutus.html (17th February, 2003).

Välijärvi, J., Linnakylä, P., Kupari, P., Reinikainen, P. & Arffman, I. (2002). The Finnish success in PISA - and some reasons behind it. PISA 2000 OECD PISA. Available: URL: http://www.jyu.fi/ktl/pisa/publication1.pdf (12th November, 2002).

HANA NOVÁKOVÁ

33. INNOVATION OF THE CONCEPT AND CONTENT OF TECHNOLOGY EDUCATION IN THE CZECH REPUBLIC IN CONTEXT WITH THEIR DEVELOPMENT IN THE COUNTRIES OF CENTRAL EUROPE

1. BACKGROUND

Technology education as an organic part of general education on basic schools and upper secondary schools (gymnasium) have during the last fifteen years gone through significant concept and content changes which have been conditioned particularly by massive application of ICT in all the spheres of human activity, but also by significant changes of the whole political-social frame and by the preparation of these countries for entry into the European Union which has taken place on May, 2004. The aim of the most effective integration of the concept of technology education and its concept orientation in advanced countries of the European Union with the application of all the positives from national traditions of the schools systems in individual countries of Central Europe has been gradually reflected into the concept and content changes which have occurred from the nineties of the last century till the present.

The trends of reform of the school system as a whole and innovation of technology education in the countries of Central Europe – in the Czech Republic, in the Slovak Republic, in Poland and Hungary have generally a common denominator even though the methods of their realization differ according to the specific conditions of individual countries.

2. THE CZECH REPUBLIC

Technology education has a two-hundred year tradition in our country even though the name and concept of the subject was quite different. We would like to mention a fact that the Austrian-Hungarian monarchy has on our schools implemented hand works as an obligatory subject on our basic schools (with a different content for boys and girls) concepted as a preparation for future life and oriented only to practical part of teaching. It is not our aim to be concerned in detail with the historical development of the subject which has as a rule gone through innovations. We would like to specify the changes which have occurred

M.J. de Vries, I. Mottier (eds.),International Handbook of Technology Education, 463–475.

during the course of the last 20 years. The principle of technology education was applied on our nine-year basic schools from the half of the fifties of the last century to the year of 1991. This principle was understood as a system applied in the whole educational process, i.e. this means in all subjects with regard to their specification. Its centre was in the relevant subject – <u>Work Teaching</u> with time appropriation of 1 hour per week from the 1st to the 5th grade, and 2 hours per week from the 6th to the 9th grade. The aim of this obligatory subject which has in the curriculum for the 8th and 9th grade included different topics for boys and girls, was to equip the pupils in the sphere of technical theory as well as practical part of the subject with basic knowledge and practical skills from the sphere of technology (from work with paper, cardboard, paper-board, wood, metal to the basic electro-engineering works and simple assembly and disassembly works in the highest classes of basic schools), and plant-growing. The girls also got acquainted with the bases of house-keeping. The schools proceeded in accordance with centrally approved curricula in which it was possible to uses 20% of teaching time for updating of topics in accordance with the conditions of the school. This subject of which the content has been during the years innovated on a systematic basis, should have contributed to conscious professional orientation of pupils to further studies and future career choice and to support functional connection of school with life in a wider context. Many technology free activities of interest as for example radio-technicians, modelers, breeders of small animals, realized at schools as well as in many special facilities – for example Houses of Children and Youths, have followed this subject in the system of technology education. It is necessary to remind of the fact that many production plants have financially supported schools and created suitable conditions for teaching of this subject.

Teachers – leavers of five-year studies on Faculties of Education were commissioned with the subject of work teaching.

The center of technology education on <u>upper secondary schools</u> was in an obligatory subject of Bases of Technical Preparation with time appropriation of 2 hours per week in the 1st and 2nd grade, 4 hours per week in the 3rd grade and 6 hours per week in the 4th grade. This subject which was of a technological character in the first two grades, was in the 3rd and 4th grade specialized according to the interests of the students to various technical spheres as for example machinery, electro-engineering, construction, computer technology, agriculture, technical chemistry, etc. One of its parts was also formed by practice in production plants. In the theoretical and practical part of the subject taught by engineers – leavers of Universities of Technology, the pupils got acquainted with the basic principles of technology, with its application in practice. In specialized studies in the last two grades they adapted the bases of the relevant technology subject. This enabled them to acquire technical qualification on the basis of successful passing through graduation examination of general technology subject and subjects of technology preparation. They applied this qualification at the entry to job of technical-economic offices. A particular role was played by technology subjects on upper secondary schools in the conscious choice of further studies, due to the reason that a larger number of percent of leavers of this secondary school proceeded in their studies on various technology fields on universities. Many production plants, research institutions and other facilities significantly participated in teaching of these subjects on upper secondary schools.

The reform of the school system in the CR which was realized from the beginning of the nineties was reflected into the concept and content of technology education. One of the characteristic features of the gradually implemented reform of the school system in our country was among others the development of frame educational programmes providing the schools with greater freedom in the realization of curricula with regard to the interests of the pupils and students and to the conditions of concrete schools. Experts have during the course of the last decade developed frame educational programmes which together with educational standards specify new tasks and aims of technology education in basic schools. Its center lies in the subject called Practical Activities. The frame educational programme lays in the new concept an emphasis upon technical knowledge and practical activities connected with school and out-of-school life and with the ability of pupils to apply the acquired pieces of knowledge and experience in various situations of the present as well as future life. The new concept of this subject is expressed in competencies, as for example ability of orientation on the labour market, application of free activities, rational use of energy sources and protection of environment, etc. These competencies are connected with applications to the sphere of economic life, legal relations in new social-economic conditions, to the application of information technologies and influence of mass-media, etc.

The frame educational programmes define a set of competencies in the subject of Work Activities so the pupil particularly gets to know the following:

- to apply the acquired working skills and simple activities in everyday life.
- to solve simple work tasks with suitable selection of materials, instruments and tools with the application of the corresponding technologies,
- to select the most suitable progress of works,
- to work with information including ICT and with other technology means,
- to organize and to plan his/her working activity with the observation of the principles of hygiene and safety at work, and technological discipline,
- to evaluate the result of his/her working activity from the aspect of quality, functionality, economy and social importance,
- to design, organize and control processes of work on the basis of acquired information on technologies and organization of works,
- to work in teams according to his/her abilities,
- to quickly adapt to the changed working conditions at work,
- to fulfill the imposed duties and obligations,
- to communicate with co-workers, to find compromising solutions with the aim to effect the quality of common work,
- to express his/her opinion, to independently make decisions, to be responsible for his/her decisions, to meet with opinions of the others.

Practical Activities are taught on lower basic schools (grades 1 to 5) 1 hour per week in total as the minimum number of hours in the third grades during the course of 5 years (the total number of 99 lessons on the lower level). This number of hours can, however, be extended of optional subjects of technology character. There is a much larger number of lessons of Practical Activities on special schools which pay greater attention to the development of practical skills. The minimum number of hours is on the higher level of basic schools (grades 6 to 9) 1 hour per week during a four-year study. The school director has the possibility to distribute teaching of this subject in the model of 1-1-1-1-, or 1-0-1-2-, or 0-2-2-0-, etc. The center of topics in the 6th to 9th grade is oriented to the following fields of topics:

- work with computer,
- work with technical materials,
- plant-growing,
- assembly and disassembly works,
- electro-engineering around us,
- preparation of meals,
- operation and maintenance of households,
- man and the world of work.

The pupils in the 7th to 9th grade can deepen their technological knowledge and skills in the offered wide palette of optional subjects with time appropriation of the total number of 6 hours (during the course of 3 years), that means 2 hours per week in each grade. Let's mention (out of optional subjects) for example the subject of Informatics, Technical Drawing, Technical Activities, Bases of Economics and Accounting, etc.

Technological literacy enabling the pupils to acquire significant information from the sphere of work performance and helping them in conscious decision making on their further studies or further professional orientation is being gradually developed in subjects included into the new concept of the system of technology education.

The system of technology education is oriented to the fulfillment of educational standards which concretely define the requirements which should be fulfilled by the pupils in concrete grades or on concrete school levels. The standards are formulated as a set of knowledge, skills and habits in relation to the planned content of education in the relevant teaching subjects. The function of educational standards can be specified as follows:

- of motivation (of simulation of self-regulation)
- prognostic (self-selective, differentiating)
- of verification and regulation
- of information and cooperation.

It is necessary to mention that the new concept of the system of technology education on basic schools in the CR has been reflected into the new concept of preparation of teachers on the Faculties of Education. During the course of the five-year magisterial studies (in combination with other subjects) the future teachers choose the study of the relevant subjects as for example: Introduction into Information Technology, Technology and Ecology, Introduction into Technology Education, Materials and Technology, Principles and Systems in Technology, Electro-Engineering, Graphical Communication in Technology, Operational Systems, Principles and Systems of Machines and Equipment, Database and Information Systems, Practice from Material and Technology, etc.

Evaluation of subjects of technology character on basic schools by the students themselves as well as by the parents is positive. The teachers, however, request a larger number of teaching hours which are necessary for the development of working skills and habits.

Basic innovation changes in technology education have occurred during the last 15 years on upper secondary schools (gymnasium) which offers four-year studies in the 1st to 4th grade.

The system of technology education is applied in generally educational subjects with regard to their specification particularly in science and in special subject of Informatics and Computer Technology (obligatory) with time appropriation of 2 hours per week in the 1st grade. The aim of this subject is to get the students acquainted with the basic terms of informatics and computer technology and to provide theoretical knowledge and practical skills necessary for work with information and equipment of computer technology. Moreover to the extending and deepening of the students´ literacy in this sphere, this subject is oriented by its content to practice, to the development of their algorithmic thinking and leads them to systematical approach to problem solving. The aim is to teach the students to work with Internet not only as a source of information but also as a mean of presentation of results of activity of an individual and institution.

The topics is in this subject particularly oriented to the significance of informatics for each individual as well as for the development of the whole society, to computers as an instrument at work with information, to Internet and computer networks, text editors, to text processing, presentation technologies, table calculators, database systems as well as to the bases of algorithmization, to drawing with the support of computer, to the creation of www pages, etc.

The frame curricula make up-dating of topics possible according to the conditions of school and interest of students. When working with Internet it is possible to connect to international projects of which aim is the exchange of information between schools. The students also get shareware and freeware from Internet.

The school has moreover to the obligatory subject of Informatics and Computer Technology also the possibility to include within optional subjects even other subjects within technology education with time appropriation of 2 hours per week in the 2nd, 3rd an 4th grade. The school develops curricula for these optional subjects on its own.

Significant decrease of the number of hours paid to special subjects included into the system of technology education occurred during the last years in our republic due to the reason that upper secondary schools have been understood as a preparation for further studies on various types of universities. Intensive technical preparation of students of upper secondary schools realized on these schools to the nineties made for its students possible to immediately after graduation examination (if they don't continue in their studies) to enter employment on the basis of acquired acknowledged qualification to medium-technical jobs, i.e. according to technical orientation of the students on the upper secondary schools.. Unfortunately, it is a fact that in market economy there are thousands of upper secondary school leavers on the labour market who have only a small chance to find an adequate job without their preliminary technical preparation, and they are for many months on unemployment benefit. In this connection it is necessary to mention that the rate of unemployment in the CR forms an average amount of 10%, this percentage rate significantly differs in individual regions. However, in case of detail analysis of the structure of the unemployed according to the acquired education we have found out that fresh school leavers make about 20% out of the total number of unemployed. This says, that in the future it shall be necessary to solve the innovation of education on upper secondary schools by the preparation of its school leavers by the intensification of technology education for a more effective inclusion of jobs immediately after their graduation.

3. THE SLOVAK REPUBLIC

The development of the school system as well as technology education in the Slovak Republic was analogous with the Czech Republic due to the reason that both of the above mentioned countries formed till the beginning of 1993 and for more than 70 years part of the Czechoslovak Republic. The unified curricula for technology education were binding for basic schools in the whole Czechoslovak Republic.

After many innovations of the subject similarly called Work Teaching as in the CR, the concept and content of this subject has been particularly changed in the Slovak Republic. These changes have come into effect in school year 1997/98.

The topics of the subject of Work Teaching was in the 1st and 2nd grade of basic schools integrated in the present concept into the subject of Arts and Crafts and part of plant-growing was integrated into Elementary Teaching.

The Work Teaching is a separate subject included in the 3rd and 4th grade in an extent of 1 hour per week, and includes part of technical work and plant-growing works. On the contrary to the CR, there is a four-year lower level of basic school in the SR. The aim of realization of the new concept of Work Teaching on the lower level is the acquisition of technical literacy, knowledge, skills and working habits as well as the acquisition of basic pieces of knowledge about technology, about its utilization in households, in the school system, in the health care system and in other fields.

An innovated subject of Technology Education has been implemented in the 5th to 9th grades of basic schools from 1997. The following aspects formed the bases for the curricula development:

- Steep development of science and technique and particularly information technologies are conditioned by educational aims of Technology Education.
- The present trend of development of technology education in the world.
- Pedagogical-psychological special characteristics of pupils as to their age.
- Interests of the pupils, connection with other subjects (interdisciplinary relations).

The new concept of this subject has been significantly reflected in the curriculum development itself. The topics is in the curriculum divided into two parts:

- The basic part representing 30-40% of time appropriation of the subject. This topic enables basic orientation of the pupils and is obligatory in its whole extent.
- The alternative part enables the orientation of the process of knowledge to problems in which the pupils are interested. The alternative topics makes the bridging-over of the present material and technical school possible, and to apply conditions of schools for manual activities.

The time appropriation for technology education is in the 5th to 9th grade one hour per week with the possibility of teaching it for 2 hours once per 14 days.

The concept of the new subject of Technology Education should particularly develop technical thinking of the pupils and creativity in the work of teachers and pupils.

The topics of the subject of Technology Education is oriented in the 5th to 9th grade to the following fields of topics:

- Man and technology.
- Technical materials, raw materials, production, energy, communication in technology.
- Electric energy, simple electrical circuits, electrical appliances.
- Simple machines, conversions, transfer of powers and movement.
- Means of mechanization.
- Operations and instruments for the technical materials processing.
- Elements of household installations.
- Electro-assembly works. Electronic automation and regulation elements.
- Minor maintenance works in households.
- Technical electronics.
- Technical, economic, ecological and aesthetical evaluation of investments into households.
- Alternative topics and independent works.

Many optional and non-obligatory subjects follow the obligatory subject of Technology Education in an extent of 1 to 2 hours per week. The pupils can choose from the subjects of technology character the following: work with computer, household keeping, graphical processing of materials. Various technically oriented free activities also contribute to the support of Technology Education. These are for example the Basis of Electrical Engineering, Work with Computer, Maintenance of Bicycles and Motor-bikes, etc.

If we evaluate interests of the pupils in subject of technological character, we can state that most of them have a positive relation to these, they like to work with materials, to produce objects and often present their products at exhibits.

The contribution of Technology Education is also evaluated by parents particularly from the aspect of preparation of pupils for future choice of career and their successful application on the labour market. The teachers positively evaluate the contribution of technology education from the aspect of support of communication and mutual cooperation between the pupils.

The pre-gradual teachers training for technology education is in the SR realized by the two following forms:

- 1st level within bachelor's studies which lasts for 3 years.
- 2nd level within magisterial studies which takes 2 years (the studies can be of one subject or in combination with second subject of teaching qualification – these studies last five years in total).

Even though there is the possibility of acquiring the relevant technology qualification the subject of Technology Education is taught only by 42% of teachers with teaching qualification.

The subject of Technical Work was taught on upper secondary schools from the beginning of the nineties of the last century according to the same curricula as in the Czech Republic. However, there is absolute lack of this subject on this type of schools at the present. Experts, however, criticize this situation and they recommend implementing an obligatory subject of technology character in the first two grades on these schools in an extent of 2 hours per week.

4. POLAND

Significant concept and content changes in Technology Education occurred at general schools the same as in the Czech Republic and the Slovak Republic.

The subject of technology character was at the beginning of the nineties included as an obligatory subject in all the 8th grades of basic schools. In advance of reform of the school system which took place in Poland in the nineties, the time appropriation for the subject of Technology Education was 1 hour per week in the 1st to 4th grade, with the possibility to link-up two teaching lessons once per 14 days. The time appropriation in the 5th to 8th grade was 2 hours per week. The aim of the subject which was common for boys and girls, was to get the pupils acquainted with the bases of culture of work, to acquire the bases of technology in theory and in practice. The topics oriented to various materials, wood and metal processing, household keeping and maintenance of its technical equipment, to the bases of graphical art and the utilization of technology information etc. should have with the use of activating forms of teaching as work of pupils in teams and solution of technological problems, led to the fact that the basic school leavers are prepared to understand the scientific and technological progress and its initiating into national economy. This should help in the preparation of young people to successfully enter life after they complete their studies.

The obligatory subject of technology character was included <u>on upper secondary school</u> (lyceum) as obligatory in the 1st and 2nd grade of the lyceum. Its content was the same for boys and girls. The aim of this subject was to get the students acquainted with the following topics:

1. Culture and history of technology
2. Bases of technology:
   - Technology at home
   - Technology at work
   - Communication technology
3. The tasks and exemplary practice:
   - Drawing tasks
   - Assembly tasks
   - Production tasks
   - Designing tasks
4. Vocational guidance

The student could in the 3rd and 4th grade of the Polish lyceum continue in deepening of technological literacy in optional subjects oriented for example to operating of computers, cutting materials, sewing and knitting, electrical and electronic engineering, agricultural technology, building and construction, architecture, etc.

Innovation changes in the concept and content of Technology Education have taken place during the course of the years to the start of reform of the school system in Poland in 1999. Particular limitation of time appropriation of subjects within Technology Education has occurred in Poland after the implementation of the school reform the same as in other countries of Central Europe. This subject is being taught from the 4th grade of basic school and is taught in the 5th and 6th grade in an extent of 2 hours per week. That means that Technology Education is taught on basic schools as an obligatory subject in three consequent years and the teachers have the possibility to choose work according to various curricula.

The main aim of Technology Education in the new concept is to let the pupils acquire technological knowledge necessary for everyday life. Its primary task is to let the pupils acquire the basic obligatory knowledge and skills of technology out of the following fields of topics:

1. Environment analysis from the technological point of view.

2. Technological documentation tests and economic calculation
3. Various materials, their features and application.
4. Technologies and basic tools useful in the pupils´ environment.
5. Machines and installations.

Poland has on the contrary to the CR and SR continued in teaching of obligatory subject of technology character on upper secondary schools (lyceum) in three grades in an extent of 2 hours per week. Regarding the steep development of science and technology its tasks and aims are specified at a more general level as follows:

1. To teach the habit of evaluation one's own abilities to choose a school, career, and one's own vocational activity.
2. Development of the ability to read technical and economical information which can be found in instructions, manuals, technical literature, everyday press, computer programmes, etc.
3. To teach creative solving of technological problems connected with safe handling of technical equipment in everyday life.
4. To show the technology creators influence on the civilization development.
5. To indicate safety rules of cycling, motorbike riding, how to behave as a pedestrian and how to use different means of transport.

The Polish educationalists remind of the fact that on the basis of results (reached till the present) in teaching of technology lessons on lyceum these should improve the technological skills which form the foundation for further Technology Education.

5. HUNGARY

Technology Education has a long tradition in Hungary. The original pre-war concept has been based upon the Scandinavian concept of "Slojd" developed by Finnish educationalist Udo Cygnaens. The subject of Technology Education was till the nineties of the last century obligatory for pupils aged 6 to 16, i.e. in an extent of 1 to 2 hours per week. The schools had the possibility to work according to centrally valid curricula, i.e. according to curricula of Technology A or Technology B.

The aim of the centrally developed curricula for Technology Education was to provide the pupils with basic technological knowledge and skills, and to cultivate in them the ability to apply these in practice. The fields of topics of Technology Education were oriented to the following:

- Materials and their processing (30 – 40% out of the total volume of topics).
- Construction (10 – 15% out of the total volume of topics).
- Assembling (10 – 15% out of the total volume of topics).
- Industrial products (0-15% out of the total volume of topics).

- Technical communication, Transport or Traffic.
- Computer Technology.

School working on the basis of curricula of Technology Education B had the possibility to alternate the fields of topics with topics oriented to agriculture, to housekeeping, etc.

Technology Education was on <u>upper secondary schools</u> (four-year gymnasium) included in an extent of 1 to 2 hours per week in the 1st and 2nd grade (students aged from 14 to 16 years). The topics was particularly oriented to the understanding of mutual relations in technology and was oriented to conscious choice of future studies and career.

The Hungarian educationalists remind of the fact that teaching of technology in its original concept was on some schools reduced to mere compulsory problem solving and that is why they did not realize its real potentials. Technology education was considered to be a place of getting practical information and not a way of forming attitudes.

The school reform in Hungary which started in the nineties of the last century has also brought new concept of Technology Education.

The new National Core Curriculum for Technology Education developed by groups of experts follows from the following aims:

- The aim is to prepare the pupils and students for activities where they are aware of their environment, and to provide a framework for the acquisition of basic technical culture. The tasks within this area are primarily aimed at the practical solution of problem situations taken from everyday life which extend the pupils´ and students´ knowledge of the relationship of natural, social and artificial environment surrounding them.

The new concept of the subjects takes into account its inclusion in all the grades of <u>basic schools</u> (grades 1 to 8). Technology Education on <u>upper secondary schools</u> (gymnasium) include the following fields of topics:

1. The necessity of work and technology, their significance and role, usefulness and hazards in human life; the notion of sustainable development.

    1.1 The artificial environment
    1.2 The role of technology and the solution of technical problems arising from human needs
    1.3 The relationship between humans, society, nature and technology
    1.4 The use of the environment, life in the environment.

2. Knowledge of documents (object, books, network documents)

3. The process of creation. Elements of the practical problem recognition and problem solving process.

3.1 Problem recognition

3.2 Planning

3.3 Execution (objects, principle of models, structure and agrotechnical solutions, household and hygiene solutions)

3.4 Evaluation of activities and their results.

The topic of individual fields of subject (thematic fields) is specified in the curricula according to individual levels of basic schools and upper secondary schools and creates logical system of Technology Education in Hungarian schools which lay great emphasis upon the development of literacy of youths in the sphere of ICT.

6. CONCLUSIONS

If we evaluate the development of technology education in the Czech Republic and in the neighbouring countries during the course of the last 15 to 20 years we can state the following:

- The system of technology education has together with the changes of political, social and economic character in progress, met with significant changes as a consequence of school reforms.
- The development of science and technology and particularly the application of ICT in all the spheres of national economy and the whole society has significantly influenced the concept of technology education. The application of ICT has been included into the content of the topics at various levels according to the age of the pupils the same as the innovation of the topics from the wide sphere of technology.
- The aspect of compatibility of the concept of the subject of Technology Education with analogous subjects in the countries of West Europe was also observed in the development of the new curricula for Technology Education, due to the reason that the countries of Central Europe have become the members of the European Union on May 1st, 2004.
- The new concept of technology education emphasizes the new activating approaches in teaching as a solution of technical problems, work of the pupils in teams, system of module teaching, the use of Internet etc. which support their education to independent and creative work.
- The innovated Technology Education in the countries of Central Europe has according to the educationalists as well as the parents brought some negatives as for example the decrease of time appropriation for this subject which eliminates space for the development of working skills. Partial or total absence of subjects of technological character on upper secondary schools (students aged from 14 to 18 years) is understood as a significant shortage not only from the aspect of education but also from the aspect of limitation of direct entry of youths to the labour market immediately after their graduation, due to the

reason that if they do not continue in their studies on universities or on three-year higher technical schools, they do not have the bases of technical preparation and they become unemployed.

By way of conclusion, it is necessary to remind of the fact that innovation of Technology Education in its whole broadness is a long-term process. The results of research and verification of this subject in school practice contribute to the parallel improvement of its concept, content as well as of teaching strategies with the aim to prepare young people for work and life in a democratic society.

REFERENCES

Mošna, F., Battisová, E., (2003): *Educational sphere of man and the world of work* in Frame Educational Programme Proposed for Compulsory Education in the Czech Republic, The Charle's University, Prague

Nováková, H., (editor), Kiss, S., Uždzicki, K. et al, (1993): *Priority components of general education in the potential future countries of the European community* in the European Context with the View to the Technology Education (in the International Pilot Project WAER).

Nováková, H. , (editor), Kiss, S., Uždzicki, K. et al (2003): *The development of new approaches in technology and vocational education in the countries in transition – The countries central Europe and South Africa* (in the International Pilot Project WAER).

Teaching Documents for Basic Schools (1999), Fortuna, Prague

Teaching Documents for Upper Secondary Schools (1999), Fortuna, Prague

Vargová, M. (2004): *Development of technology education in the Slovak Republic during the last 15 years* (study materials, manuscript), Faculty of Pedagogy, Nitra

MOSHE BARAK

34. ENGINEERING AND EXCELLENCE: AN OLD-NEW AGENDA FOR TECHNOLOGY EDUCATION IN ISRAELI HIGH SCHOOLS

INTRODUCTION

In an era of socio-economic changes and educational reforms, as is currently prevailing in Israel, there is ongoing pressure on the educational system in general, and technology education in particular, to re-examine their objectives, methods and achievements. Educational professionals and decision-makers have raised questions regarding the aims of technology education, its contribution to preparing high school graduates for successful integration into today's complex and dynamic society, promoting excellence and reducing socio-economic gaps.

In Israel, as in several other countries, the roots of technology education of about 30 years ago have been in arts and crafts studies for young children, and vocational education for high school pupils. The most important change in teaching technology in primary and junior high schools took place in the mid 1990s, when an integrated program entitled "Science and Technology" for these schooling levels replaced the separate programs for science and technology previously in use. The current programs for primary and junior high schools represent a moderate version of the Science-Technology-Society (STS) approach (Yager, 1996) and comprise specific technological topics, such as design, systems and communications. Adopting the integrated curriculum for science and technology in primary and junior high schools has increased cooperation between experts in science education and technology education, encouraged combined projects for curriculum development, and fostered joint programs for teachers' pre-service and in-service training. Consequently, this reform in the curriculum has increased the community of scholars who are interested in questions such as: What is science? What is technology? What are the relationships between science and technology in the curriculum (Gardner, 1994)? Although the extensive efforts in developing new curricula and training teachers for the new program nationwide helped in breaking down walls between science teachers and technology teachers, the majority of teachers continue to stick to their areas of specialization. Consequently, the degree of teaching technological subjects in the combined curriculum in practice depends, largely on the background of the teachers in each school.

Technology studies in high schools are elective; they are taken by about 50% of the pupils having a wide range of scholastic achievements and from diverse socio-

M.J. de Vries, I. Mottier (eds.), International Handbook of Technology Education, 477–486.

economic backgrounds. The Israeli high school system is unique in that the majority of pupils study in comprehensive high schools, and not in separate schools for general education or in vocational schools as was customary until the late 1960s. Under the title of technology education, very talented pupils study advanced engineering-related subjects such as electronics and computers; lesser achieving pupils learn subjects such as electricity, mechanics or architectural drafting. Crafts, like woodwork or metalwork, are found less and less in Israeli high schools. All of the pupils study general subjects, such as mathematics and languages, and take matriculation exams at different levels in the all the subjects they study, including those related to technology.

In light of the growing public and professional criticism regarding the achievements of Israeli education, the government established a national committee, called the National Task Force for the Advancement of Israel's Education (NTAIE, 2004), which examined the entire structure and achievements of K-12 education. This committee recommended a major reform in K-12 education that involved, for instance, eliminating junior high schools, reorganizing high school studies and matriculation exams, and modifying teacher training frameworks. Towards implementing this reform, now would be the right time to ask the following questions again: What are the objectives of teaching technology to high school pupils? How could technology education respond to the expectations and needs of pupils having a wide range of scholastic achievements? To what extent do technology studies impart the essential knowledge and skills to pupils to help them integrate into modern life? This paper aims to address these questions in light of the processes taking place in the Israeli educational system at the beginning of the 21st century.

TECHNOLOGY EDUCATION AND EXCELLENCE

As technology education in Israel serves a very heterogeneous population, one of the most important missions faced by scholars in technology education is to attract high-achieving pupils to major in technology studies in high school, the final stage before entering a higher education framework. The class of pupils taking an elective subject such as technology in high school determines the status of this subject in the eyes of the pupils, the parents, the educators and the decision-makers. Therefore, having a layer of very competent pupils studying technology in high school is critical for strengthening the discipline in the long run and for ensuring its status as a central component of K-12 education.

Since Israeli high schools are very demanding and most of the high-achieving pupils major in mathematics, and often in science, the question arises as to why a competent pupil would study technology education. To answer this question in part, let us briefly review the processes that have characterized electronics studies, one of the 'engines' of technology education in Israel, over the past two decades. In the early 1980s, one of the peak periods in the development of the electronics and computer industries, many talented pupils opted to study electronics in high school. Coming from industry, many teachers brought to schools a spirit of enthusiasm and inventiveness, working with their pupils on the design and construction of advanced technological systems, such as mini-robots and other types of electro-mechanical machines. Schools all over the country used to hold final-year ceremonies and exhibitions of pupil projects aimed primarily at younger children, candidates for registering in the same school, and their parents. In the early 1990s, the projects were eliminated almost entirely from the lab work and the matriculation exams due to a reform in the curriculum that placed more emphasis on theoretical studies and standardized lab experiments. Later, many talented pupils expressed disappointment in their electronics studies, and a decrease in the demand for electronics studies by competent pupils was observed (Barak, 2002). In the late 1990s, schools, with the support of the mainstay of education, reinstated the preparation of mini-projects in electronic studies during the 10th and 11th grades, and final projects as part of matriculation exams taken in the 12th grade. Consequently, the number of pupils preparing final projects in electronics nationwide increased from under 50 in 1999 to over 1,000 in 2004. This "back-to-projects" phenomenon gained rapid success since it had been initiated by the teachers rather than as the result of a top-down decision and had responded to needs from the field. This case demonstrates that competent pupils frequently study technology education because they hope to be involved in the design and construction of sophisticated systems and artifacts that trigger their imagination, fulfill their dreams and realize their ambitions. Project-based learning has gained increased attention not only in electronics studies but also in other areas of science and technology education in Israel. Computer-based projects in technology are increasingly becoming a major tool for catching the attention of competent students to technology education, as will be described below in more detail.

TECHNOLOGY EDUCATION AND ENGINEERING

Underlining engineering as the main paradigm for technology education has numerous advantages for the future of technology education Israel, for several reasons.

Firstly, engineering is the natural learning environment for technology education at high school, since pupils expect that technology studies will take place in a sophisticated laboratory equipped with modern instrumentation. Educators recognize that the era of building simple technological models using pieces of cardboard, wood or plastic is behind us. Even the use of building block sets like Lego or Fisher-Technick, as is common in many technological labs, is significant for today's technology studies when these systems comprise electronic components, like motors and sensors, and are interfaced to computers. High school pupils use professional instrumentation for their technological projects as a means for the design, construction and testing of electronic circuits, software packages for the design and simulation of electro-mechanical systems and industrial programmable controllers (PLCs). Having engineering-based laboratories in school is important not only for facilitating pupils' work or enabling them to design more sophisticated systems. Through being involved in an authentic engineering world, a pupil is likely to become a member in a community of professionals, feel confident to request help from practitioners, and learn to use books, catalogs and on-line databases targeted at engineers and scientists. Many high schools in Israel share well-equipped technological labs with technical colleges located on the same campus.

Secondly, the alignment of technology education with engineering is natural for the training of technology teachers. One of the main aspects of the reform in the Israeli educational system expected shortly (NTAIE, 2004) is the requirement that every teacher completes a full academic degree (B.Sc. or B.A.) in his/her field of specialization, such as mathematics, physics or electrical engineering. The B.Ed. degree, currently provided by academic colleges of education, will be eliminated. In addition to completing a bachelor's degree in engineering or science, a teacher will have to study an existing program towards an "Academic Teaching Certificate," which consists of courses in education, psychology and teaching methods. As there are neither faculties for technology nor a bachelor's degree in technology, it is obvious that in the upcoming years, the vast majority of new technology teachers will be engineering graduates.

Thirdly, pupils, parents and decision-makers understand the term engineering much better than the term technology (Liao, 2000; Hacker, 2000). Israeli society greatly appreciates engineering, which is often associated with an academic education and a higher socio-economic status. The high-tech industry is very central to the economy, and engineering faculties in universities are often highly esteemed and among the most difficult gain admission to. Although technology education is not aimed solely at preparing pupils for higher studies in engineering, many people hope that studying technology will develop pupils' learning and thinking skills in the areas of science and technology, and help them to decide more knowledgeably about their future.

WHAT KIND OF ENGINEERING?

Although it is felt that the term technology is broader than the term engineering, it is useless to seek exact definitions for each of these terms or determine how they differ from one another. Definitions of these terms in dictionaries, encyclopedias or professional books frequently overlap each other. For example, according to *Encyclopedia Britannica* (2005):

- **Technology** is the "Application of knowledge to the practical aims of human life or to changing and manipulating the human environment. Technology includes the use of materials, tools, techniques, and sources of power to make life easier or more pleasant and work more productive."
- **Engineering** is the "Professional art of applying science to the optimum conversion of the resources of nature to the uses of humankind."

Many countries, for example the United States, Britain, Canada, Australia, New Zealand and Israel, comprise standards for technology education elements in their curriculum that relate directly to engineering, such as engineering design, energy and control, information and communications, system thinking, modeling and optimization. According to *Benchmarks for Science Literacy* (AAAS, 1993): "In its broadest sense, engineering consists of construing a problem and designing a solution for it. The basic method is to first devise a general approach and then work out the technical details of the construction of requisite objects or processes."

In Israel, pupils study general technological concepts such as design and control in primary and junior high schools in the compulsory "Science and Technology" program mentioned above. The technology education curriculum in high schools is arranged traditionally according to specific engineering fields. For example, electronics studies for the 11th and 12th grades comprise subjects such as analog and digital electronics, energy conversion, control and communication systems. Recently, more updated subjects, such as cellular and satellite communications, computer networks and the analysis of sound and pictures, are being introduced into the high school curriculum. Engineering indicates not only the use of mathematics and science for the design of technological systems, as do engineers, but also the use of the 'language' and tools used by engineers such as formulas, drawings, simulation software or programming tools. Thus, engineering provides a learning environment that is likely to support, rather than undermine, the development of pupils into creative designers and proficient problem-solvers.

EXCELLENCE, ENGINEERING AND ADVANCING LOW-ACHIEVING PUPILS

Emphasizing technology as an area for competent pupils and adopting engineering as the main paradigm for technology studies does not necessarily mean neglecting the low- to mid-achieving pupils. A number of studies in Israel (Barak, Yehiav and Mendelson, 1994; Barak and Doppelt, 1999) have shown that engineering-related technological studies might be a successful platform for raising pupils' self-esteem and motivation to learn, as well as fostering their learning skills. Since many people confuse the terms technology education and vocational education, technology studies for low-achieving pupils are often understood as being vocational education. Stevenson (2003) mentions several aspects frequently used in discussing the differences between technology education and vocational education: imparting general knowledge vs. specific knowledge, theoretical knowledge vs. practical/functional knowledge, conceptual understanding vs. proficiency in skills, creative abilities vs. reproductive abilities, intellectual skills vs. physical skills, preparation for life vs. preparation for work. Stevenson examines each of these dualities and shows that this type of differentiation between vocational education and technology education is questionable. For instance, the separation of theoretical and practical knowledge is at odds with the ways in which people learn; there seems to be little substantive basis for the cognitive separation of physical and intellectual skills, and it is increasingly problematic to impose a division between preparation for life and for work. Specifically, the low-achieving pupils might benefit from a rich, flexible and non-stigmatizing learning environment, which enables them to work individually or in teams on authentic projects, and in this way break out of the circle of failure and despair many of them experienced in conventional teaching frameworks. A recent study on the impact of projects in electricity and electronics on low- to mid-achieving pupils (Barak, 2004b) showed that pupils might gradually develop from being fully dependent on their teachers to becoming more autonomous learners and creative thinkers. Therefore, identifying technology with engineering and excellence is vital for providing an adequate education not only to high-achieving pupils, but also to pupils who start high school with relatively low achievements and motivation to learn or poor learning skills.

DEPARTURE FROM TRADITIONAL TEACHING-LEARNING TECHNOLOGY FRAMEWORKS

One of the most significant changes characterizing technology education in Israel in the past two decades is the departure from traditional teaching-learning technology frameworks. As previously mentioned, an integrated program for the study of science and technology in primary and junior high schools was introduced in the mid-1990s. This reform reduced the borders between the two areas and increased cooperation between experts and teachers from both fields. One example of this cooperation is the hot-air balloons program, in which high-achieving pupils in junior high schools studied physics and technology through the design and construction of electronically-controlled hot-air balloons (Barak and Raz, 2000). Frank (2004) presented an example of a pre-service training course for teachers aimed at establishing cooperation between science teachers and technology teachers around scientific-technological projects. Another example of strengthening links between the learning of science and technology is the "Physics and Industry" program that was initiated by physics teaching experts (Eylon, 2002). In this program, talented high school pupils work during one year on final projects supervised by scientists and engineers from advanced industries, and get credit for their projects as part of the matriculation exam in physics. According to Eylon, departing from the traditional frameworks of science and technology education, projects and joint high school-industry programs are likely to increase pupils' interest in the world of science and technology, develop their learning competencies, and provide them with a more realistic perception of the work of scientists and technologists. A third example is the program entitled "Integrated Technology," in which high school pupils study advanced courses in technology and science, and prepare a final project under the supervision of experts from academia or industry. These pupils get credit for their projects as part of the matriculation exam in technology.

A different aspect of the changes in learning technology in Israel has been the increasing participation of Israeli high school pupils in national and international contests for the design of sophisticated scientific-technological artifacts. For example, Israeli pupils are frequent participants in the Annual Trinity College Fire-Fighting Home Robot Contest (TCFFHRC, 2005). The goal of this contest is "to encourage inventors of all ages and levels of skill to develop an autonomous fire-fighting home robot that can find, and put out as quickly as possible, a fire in a model house." Since 1998, pupils from all over Israel have participated in the annual national contest, which precedes the international competition. The fact that Israeli pupils have frequently won top prizes in the international competition has attracted the attention of a variety of schools and fostered technological activities by pupils and educators who had previously not been involved in technology education (Verner and Hershko, 2003).

THE ROLE OF COMPUTERS AND INFORMATION TECHNOLOGIES IN TECHNOLOGY EDUCATION

One of the most significant changes that took place in technology education in Israel during the past two decades was the wide-spread use of computers and the Internet. In recent years, most technological laboratories have been equipped with computers connected permanently to the Internet. Accordingly, technology teachers and pupils have almost unlimited access to these means, and are often the most extensive users of computer technologies in their schools.

The educational literature has pinpointed many expectations regarding the contribution of computer technologies towards enhancing learning. For instance, Salomon (1998) mentioned four aspects of how intelligent technologies contribute to improved learning:

- Computers and communication systems are not only knowledge-transfer technologies but also knowledge-building technologies.
- Computer technologies are not knowledge-receiving technologies, but rather they facilitate the intellectual partnership between the learner and the sophisticated and intelligent tools (Pea, 1993).
- Computer technologies are not restricted to the individual learner, but rather they present opportunities for shared thinking and knowledge construction.
- Novel computer technologies do not constitute tools for structured teaching, but rather encourage open learning, and challenge the learner with enormous knowledge resources when confronting challenging problems.

In technology education, computers are not just a means for data collection, analysis or presentation, but often an integral part of the technological systems pupils design and build. Thus, integrating computers into technology education is likely to create a constructivist learning environment that promotes meaningful learning through knowledge construction, conversation, articulation, collaboration, authentication and reflection (Jonassen et al., 2000).

The most meaningful impact of computer technologies on learning technology has been in project work. Recently, the majority of projects pupils design and build comprise computerized control systems. For their projects, pupils use a variety of professional interfacing cards and means of data measurements, A/D conversion and power amplification. Barak (2004a) found that pupils working on computer-based projects tend to adopt flexible strategies, such as creating new ideas, risk-taking, improvisation, using trial-and-error methods for problem-solving, and rapid transition from one design to another. In contrast, pupils working on non-computerized projects are more likely to progress along a linear path: planning, constructing and troubleshooting. Moreover, pupils working on computer-based projects tend to cooperate and exchange ideas with their friends more than pupils working on hardware-based projects mainly because the development of software is more flexible and challenging. Actually, the broad use of computers in project work has put into practice the model suggested by Johnson (2002) aimed at creating "a powerful learning environment" by: (1) addressing individual differences, (2) motivating the pupil, (3) avoiding information overload, (4) creating a real-life context, (5) encouraging social interaction, (6) providing hands-on activities and (7) encouraging pupil reflection.

Yet, the mere use of computers in school does not ensure better learning. For instance, although Israeli pupils and teachers use computers and the Internet extensively, computerized means have not caused significant changes in the way theoretical topics are learned. Teachers and pupils still prefer conventional frontal lessons for learning theoretical topics, especially in the first stages of teaching new concepts (Barak, 2004b). At times, the use of simulation becomes a substitute for practical lab experiments, and the use of the Internet has become a cover-up for superficial learning.

CONCLUDING REMARKS

Resnick (2002) mentioned that there was much talk in the 1980s about the transition from an "industrial society" to an "information society." In the 1990s, people started talking about a "knowledge society." They began to realize that the key is not in the information itself but in how it is transformed into knowledge and how this knowledge is managed. For today, Resnick suggests the concept "creative society," since success in the future will be based not on how much we know but on our ability to think and act creatively.

It is widely accepted that one of the major goals of technology education is to develop pupils' intellectual competencies such as analytical thinking, creativity, problem-solving abilities and teamwork. This objective is not just rhetoric or a matter of educators' intentions, but rather the main desire of the pupils themselves. To achieve this goal, the following guidelines are suggested for technology education in the coming years:

- Involve pupils in the design and construction of advanced technological systems, emphasizing state-of-the-art technologies such as communications, robotics and biotechnology.
- Link technology studies to the advanced industries, academia and the community.
- Encourage teamwork of pupils, teachers and experts both inside and outside the schools.
- Strengthen ties between the study of technology, computers and the natural sciences.

An important challenge for scholars in technology education is to intensify the research of the influence of technology studies on developing pupils' intellectual competences, such as independent learning, teamwork and creative thinking.

REFERENCES

American Association for the Advancement of Science: (1993). *Benchmarks for science literacy, science for all,* American online, Chapter 3: The nature of technology. URL: http://www.project2061.org/tools/sfaaol/chap3.htm.

Annual Trinity College Fire-Fighting Home Robot Contest (TCFFHRC) (2005). URL: http://www.trincoll.edu/events/robot/welcome.asp.

Barak, M. (2002). Learning good electronics, or coping with challenging tasks? Priorities of excellent students, *Journal of Technology Education* 14(2), 20-34.

Barak, M. (2004a). From order to disorder: The role of computer-based electronics projects in fostering higher-order cognitive skills. *Computers & Education* (in press).

Barak, M. (2004b). Issues involved in attempting to develop independent learning in pupils working on technological projects. *Research in Science and Technological Education* 22(2), 171-183.

Barak, M & Doppelt, Y. (1999). Integrating the cognitive research trust (CoRT) program for creative thinking into a project-based technology curriculum. *Research in Science and Technological Education* 17(2), 139-151.

Barak, M. & Raz, E. (2000). Hot-air balloons: project-centered study as a bridge between science and technology education. *Science Education* 84 (1), 27-42.

Barak, M., Yehiav, R. & Mendelson, N. (1994). Advancement of low achievers within technology studies at high school. *Research in Science and Technological Education* 12(2), 175-186.

Encyclopedia Britannica online (2005). UTL: http://www.britannica.com/.

Eylon, B. S. (2002). Breaking the learning frameworks in teaching science and technology, the potential and problems. *Workshop for encouraging science and technology education, the National Israeli Academy for Science,* Jerusalem, 14-15 (in Hebrew).

Frank, M. (2004). Project-based technology in the science and technology curriculum: a teaching approach for developing technological literacy. *Paper presented at the National Association for Research in Science Teaching (NARST) Conference,* Vancouver BC, April, 1-4.

Gardner, P. (1994). Representations of the relationship between science and technology in the curriculum. *Studies in Science Education* 24, 29-47.

Hacker, M. (2000). The politics of technology education. *International Conference on Technology Education,* WOCATE & UNSECO, Braunschweig, Germany, September 25-27.

Johnson, S. D. (2002). A model for enhancing thinking through technology education, In: G. Graube, M. J. Dyrenfurth and W. E. Theuerkauf (eds.), *Technology Education, International Concepts and Perspectives.* New York: Peter Lang Press, 51-62

Jonassen, D., Peck, K. & Wilson, B. (2000). *Learning with technology: A constructivist approach.* Upper Saddle River, NJ: Prentice Hall.

Liao, T. L. (2000). Engineering-based paradigm for K-12 technology education, *International Conference on Technology Education,* WOCATE & UNSECO, Braunschweig, Germany, September 25-27.

National Task Force for the Advancement of Israel's Education (NTAIE) (2004). Jerusalem: Ministry of Education and Culture.

Pea, R. D. (1993). Practices of distributed intelligence and designs for education. In: G. Salomon (ed.), *Distributed cognition,* NY: Cambridge University Press, 47-48.

Resnick, M (2002). Rethinking Learning in the Digital Age, In: G. Kirkman, *The global information technology report: readiness for the networked world,* Oxford University Press, 32-37.

Salomon, G. (1998). Novel constructivist learning environments and novel technologies: Some issues to be considered. *Research Dialog in Learning and Instruction* 1(1) 3-12.

Stevenson, J. C. (2003). Examining cognitive bases for differentiating technology education and vocational education, In: G. Martin and H. Middleton (eds.), *Initiatives in technology education:*

comparative, proceedings of the American-Australian technology education forum. Brisbane: Centre for Technology, Education Research, 194-206.

Verner, I. & Hershko, E. (2003). School graduation project in robot design: a case study of team learning experiences and outcomes, *Journal of Technology Education* 14(3), 40-55.

Yager, R. E. (ed.) (1996). *Science/technology/society as reform in science education,* Albany, NY: State University of New York Press.

DOV KIPPERMAN

35. SCIENCE AND TECHNOLOGY LINKS IN ISRAELI SECONDARY SCHOOLS - DO WE HAVE A REASON TO CELEBRATE?

INTRODUCTION

"Communities of technology and science educators have been passing as two ships pass silently in the night without speaking to each other about their relationships." (Zuga, K. in Yager, 1996)

There is wide agreement in Israel that appropriate scientific and technological literacy should be provided to every boy and girl at all levels of their education.
Since 1996, technology and science curricula in Israeli junior high schools (grades 7-9) have been combined to form one mandatory curriculum subject: "Science and Technology". Although, to some extent, and in some schools, different kinds of relationships between science and technology teachers exist, the collaboration between science and technology on a state level is more wishful thinking than reality. In this paper I suggest that the lack of clear conceptual pedagogical frameworks within the curriculum has been one of the obstacles to effective integration/collaboration of science with technology. In order to cooperate effectively, science and technology educators have to speak to each other on the basis of agreed and well defined conceptual pedagogical frameworks. Such frameworks are essential for the implementation and diffusion of the "Science and Technology" curriculum. This paper starts with a review of the literature on different models of collaboration/integration, and goes on to describe the current situation in Israel with regards to the implementation of the national curriculum. Finally, a possible conceptual framework (curriculum organizer) for relationships between science and technology is suggested.

REVIEW OF LITERATURE

There has been much discussion about the relationship between teaching and learning in science and technology, resulting in a diversity of views. At one extreme, science and technology are regarded as separate and independent, whilst at the other end of the spectrum, they are seen as one integrated subject.
Some strongly support linking science and technology in education, arguing that this increases student motivation and enhances learning (Sage, 1993; Loepp. 1995; Laporte & Sanders, 1993; Sanders, 2000). This is also seen as a way to establish technology education as a vital addition to the public school curriculum (Linnell,

M.J. de Vries, I. Mottier (eds.), International Handbook of Technology Education, 487–497.

2003). Others provide a rationale for the separation and independence of the two subjects in the curriculum (De Vries, 1996; Williams, 2002; Barlex & Pitt, 2002), and question the advantages for technology education in combining them (Foster, 1994; Foster, 1995).

This review focuses on various models for integrating science and technology. STS (Science-Technology-Society) programs began to flourish in the early 80's as a new approach to science education (Yager, 1996; Aikenhead, 1994). These programs have been criticized with claims that they were mainly a new type of science education (Foster, 1995), and that the technology aspects were not represented properly (Layton, 1993).

Rubba (in Yager, 1996) suggested an explanation for the failure of integrating technology in science classes:- "one could not expect that science teachers without proper background and experience in technology would be able to implement an integrative approach".

Daugherty & Wicklein (1993) found that science and mathematic teachers had stereotyped perceptions about technology education. They recommended workshops for science and technology teachers to demonstrate the potential of technology education and to promote effective cooperation.

From the mid 80's technology educators began to explore and develop programs and curriculum materials that linked technology and science (Black & Harrison, 1985; De Beurs, 1998; Raudebaugh, 2000) and even integrated them with mathematics education (MST, 1996: IMaST, 1995; MSTe, 1999).

While some have described such programs as effective and successful (Gloeckner, 1991; Kain, 1993 in Loepp 1995), others reported that they did not find any significant contribution with regard to improving technology problem solving (Childress, 1996), or generally found differences to be insignificant (Dugger & Johnson, 1992; Dugger & Meier, 1994; Scarborough & White, 1994).

Sage (1992) proposed a Technology Led Model for collaboration, characterized by the relations between the technology activities and the scientific knowledge that is required as support in order to solve a problem. He defined three levels of support relations:

- essential and specific scientific knowledge that is needed in order to solve the problem;
- practical scientific knowledge that is related to the technology activity and might be relevant in order to solve the problem (can be taught in the science class);
- opportunities to develop extra scientific knowledge based in the relevancy and motivation (in science class).

The Mste Project (Hacker, 1999) described three models that schools across the state are using to integrate science, mathematics, and technology instruction.

Model 1   Individual teachers help students make explicit connections between what they learn in a particular M, S, or T class and what they are learning in other classes.

Model 2   Teachers work together to develop interdisciplinary units.

Model 3   A fully integrated approach. Students are either block -scheduled into three periods of mathematics, science, and technology or to an integrated course where teachers team- teach.

Barlex & Pitt (2000) describe three possible relationships between science and technology in education : co-ordination, collaboration and integration. Their report supports co-ordination and collaboration among the subjects but rejected integration.

Those who have supported linking the subjects have identified factors that significantly affect the success or failure of the multidisciplinary curriculum: a new constructivist teaching approach combined with authentic assessment methods (Loepp,1995), teacher and administration commitment to the integrative approach (Wicklein & Schell, 1995; Loepp,1995)or the ability to organize and coordinate the activities among teachers from the different subject areas. (Sanders, 1996).

Layton (in Sage,1992) claims that one of the difficulties in implementing collaboration is the dual roll of science, as an autonomous subject which has its own goals, and as a subject that serves technology as part of the collaboration.

On a broader level, few states have science and technology as a combined curricular subject – Israel (1996), Massachusetts (1999) and New York (Hacker, 1999). In Australia (New South Wales), science and technology is a single learning area in primary school and then separated in secondary education.

In short, the review shows that there is a potential to enhance learning, but difficulties in implementation accompanied with doubts on the contribution of integration continue to exist.

Technology Education in Israel – Rationale and Content

There is wide agreement in Israel that appropriate scientific and technological literacy should be developed in every student at all levels of education.

Since 1996 technology and science curricula in Israeli junior high school (grades 7-9) have been combined to form one mandatory subject: "Science and Technology". The rationale for the linkage is expressed as follows:

".... Collaboration between science and technology is essential because of the growing linkage between scientific subjects and relevant technologies and also because of the unclear borders between them."
(The Israeli National Curriculum for Science and Technology, 1996. p.5)

According to the new curriculum for junior high schools, 540 hours of instruction will be provided to all students in the following main subjects (table 1).

Although it has been established as a combined curriculum (Science and Technology), it is recommended that there should be different teachers who specialize in different subjects and who will collaborate within a teamwork structure. However, no clear conceptual pedagogical framework for such collaboration is specified in the national curriculum.

Table 1: Main subjects

Main Subjects	Hours : grade 7- 9
Materials: Structure, Function and Processes	105
Energy and Interaction	90
Technological Systems and Products	90
Information and Communication	30
Earth and Universe	45
Phenomena, Structures and Processes in Living Organisms (with special emphasis on the human body)	150
Ecological Systems	30
	540

On one hand, the curriculum emphasizes an inter-disciplinary approach:

> *"Teaching the subject matter according to this inter-disciplinary approach which characterizes the contemporary approach of science and technology teaching, will expose the student to science and technology aspects, and will introduce the social connections while emphasizing the combination between them".* (The Israeli National Curriculum for Science and Technology, 1996.p.6)

On the other hand, the relationships should be established while maintaining the knowledge structure of each subject matter (physics, biology, technology, etc,), and avoiding associative connections.

> *"Examining different teaching models that integrate science and technology reveals diverse existing possibilities of combining and integrating subjects..."*
> (The Israeli National Curriculum for Science and Technology, 1996.p.11)

> *"...it is worthy mentioning and emphasizing that the inter- disciplinary approach will be expressed in those cases in which the connections derive from the essence of the subject, while avoiding compulsory associative connections".*
> (The Israeli National Curriculum for Science and Technology, 1996.p.5)

Strangely here, "different teaching models", "diverse existing possibilities", and "avoiding compulsory associative connections", are not specified in the curriculum. In fact, it is left to each school to decide.

In order to understand the whole picture, two more points are worth mentioning:

1. differences in the status and in the attitude toward science and technology;
2. differences in academic background of science and technology teachers.

TEACHER TRAINING

Due to the new curriculum, a national in-service teacher training program was held in regional centers and academic Institutions.

The programs included: main subjects of the curriculum, instructional strategies, and project based learning and team working.

While most of the science teachers focused on the scientific subjects with which they were familiar, the technology teachers had to move from the craft/industrial art approach to learning new concepts such as design and systems. This was in order to establish and facilitate a new framework for technology education.

Bar Josef (2004) reports on the impact of such training programs on the teachers' practicum. Science teachers point to the following features as those which have had the most significant positive contribution:

- their perception of the links between science and technology;
- their perception of team working;
- their perception of their ability to teach technology.

Although the in-service training programs have a positive contribution on their ability to teach technological aspects (mainly design), they do not feel skilled enough to teach those aspects.

DEVELOPMENT OF CURRICULUM MATERIALS

Several Institutions were responsible for developing curriculum materials, according to the following guidelines:

"Examining different teaching models that integrate science and technology reveals diverse existing possibilities of combining and integrating subjects..."
(The Israeli National Curriculum for Science and Technology, 1996.p.11)

As the "different teaching models" and "diverse existing possibilities" were not specified, different approaches to the science–technology relationships were presented. Science oriented curriculum materials (mainly textbooks) emphasized the scientific world (scientific knowledge, inquiry methods and skills) while technology was presented mainly through measurement tools and systems that are essential for conducting a scientific inquiry. Some of these materials presented technological concepts such as design, but they did not encourage the actual "doing" aspects. This approach was embraced by science teachers.

Technological oriented materials (mainly textbooks) emphasized the design process and the system approach as primary concepts of technology, as well as the "doing" aspect of technology but lacked scientific segments (scientific knowledge and skills). This approach was embraced by technology teachers.

DIFFUSION

In the first four years of implementation, due to the massive in-service teacher training program and new curriculum materials that had been developed for all the main subjects, most of the technology teachers made the transition to teaching design and systems (see in table 1: Technological Systems and Products). The learning environment consisted of Project Based Learning using mainly LEGO for learning systems (figure 1) and "soft" materials for the design and make (figure 2).

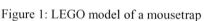

Figure 1: LEGO model of a mousetrap   Figure 2: Prototype of a chair with a drawer

In most schools, relationships between subjects were characterized by coordination; the technology teachers were responsible for teaching technological subjects (systems and products) while science teachers were responsible for scientific subjects (energy, living organisms, etc.). On this level the teachers were informed of what the others were teaching.

In some schools the relationships between science and technology were established around collaboration on one of the subjects, mainly on materials. Design, for example could be utilized in the selection of materials. The science teacher focused on teaching the structure of materials (the atomic model) whilst the technology teacher focused on design and the choice of materials within the framework of actually producing a model or a prototype.

Some schools organized the relationships between science and technology around social topics: waste, pollution or water problems in Israel. This appealed mainly to science teachers. Usually on this kind of project, the technological aspects were reduced to mentioning different available solutions (technology as applied science).

Several difficulties were encountered in Israel; some are similar to those mentioned in the literature review; others are unique to the Israel scene:

- no clear perception in the curriculum about the relationships and ways of linking science and technology;

- no required commitment of teachers and subject coordinators to coordinate/integrate/collaborate. Thus, links between science and technology emerged as school initiatives;
- lack of appropriate curriculum materials for collaboration/integration and insufficient scientific knowledge among the technology teachers appear to have had an impact on the integrating of science in classroom practice.

In the last four years, science and technology classes have been reduced from 6 to 3-4 hours per week. As a result, in many schools the technology education (as part of the unified curriculum) is in decline. In some schools technological subjects do not exist; in others, where technological subjects still exist, some of them are taught by science teachers. There is still a lack of a conceptual framework for collaboration/integration.

Frameworks for Relationships

How should schools integrate science and technology and still preserve the underlying concepts of each discipline?

Due to the principles in the national curriculum which promote collaboration on the one hand, and preservation of disciplinary subjects on the other hand, we suggest two parallel frameworks of relationships:

Framework 1: Connections within each discipline

Individual teachers in each discipline can help students make explicit connections between what they learn in a particular science or technology class and what they are learning in other classes (figure 3).

Figure 3: Explicit Connections

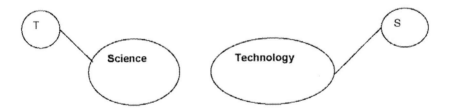

According to Barlex (2002) this kind of link has limited impact on class practice.

"Curriculum materials designed to encourage pupils to use science in design and technology lessons appear to have had a little impact on classroom practice. Curriculum materials designed to enable science teachers to use technological context to motivate students and improve learning appear to have had only limited uptake". (p. 6)

The description above presents the current situation in Israel. It certainly does not do justice to technology education in science classes and to science education

493

in technology classes, but it enables both disciplines to preserve and maintain their own disciplinary structure.

Framework 2: Collaboration/Integration among disciplines.

Collaboration means that teachers of each subject plan their curricula so that some, but not all, activities within each subject are designed to establish an effective relationships among the subjects (Barlex & Pitt, 2000).In practice, teachers from both disciplines collaborate through integrated projects. The projects focus on problem-solving in a social context (Krumholtz,1998). Each aspect of the project is led by a teacher who is the most skilled in a specific area.

The collaboration is based on a didactical model for collaboration between the disciplines, known as the STSS (Society-Technology- Science- Society) model.

Figure 4: The STSS- Model

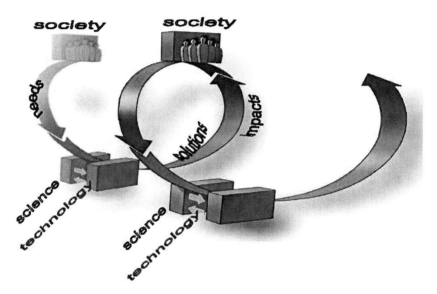

The STSS Model is supported by four elements:
- problem solving;
- the use of social, scientific and technological knowledge for problem solving and decision-making;
- the view that science and technology are two distinct but interacting disciplines;
- utilization of the gap between the needs of society and reality as a "driving force" for developments in science and technology.

This model can help science and technology teachers to collaborate and exploit their capabilities and strengths. Science teachers focus on science aspects of the projects while technology teachers focus on technology aspects of the projects. For example, starting with an issue in **society** such as "The noise around us" (Kipperman, 2003) leads to finding out about the nature of sound and noise through a set of learning activities that develop understanding of key science concepts (**science** teachers). Another stage involves using tools to record noise and analyze different existing systems that create noise and different existing systems to reduce noise (**technology** teachers). **Science** investigations lead to using this understanding as one of the resources to solve the problems created by noise by developing(designing) solutions (**technology** teachers) appropriate for particular contexts and evaluating the impacts on the society and the environment.

The following (table 2) is an example for collaboration among teachers (physics, biology, technology) in organizing lessons plan for teaching the unit.

Table 2 : lessons collaboration

Timeline	Technology Teacher	Science Teacher	Types of activities
	Introducing situations, Identifying needs & problems		
First week		x	Gathering information
Second & Third week	x		Gathering information
		x	Scientific inquiry
	x		Technology inquiry
		x	Scientific inquiry
Forth week	x		Brainstorming for solutions
		x	Further investigation according to the specific area
Fifth week	x		Make and evaluate the solution
	Presentations of projects		

This framework is similar to models that are presented in the literature review: (Sage, 1992; Raudebaugh, 2000). Based on evidence from the literature (Loepp, 1995; Laporte & Sanders, 1993), we believe that such a framework can facilitate meaningful collaboration which is based upon the capabilities and strengths of the teachers in each discipline.

Both frameworks as a whole will enable science and technology teachers to teach their subjects as an autonomous subject which has its own goals (framework 1), and to collaborate as two disciplines that serve society (framework 2).

DISCUSSION & SUMMARY

The science and technology curriculum in Israeli junior high schools (grades 7-9) are combined into one mandatory curriculum subject: "Science and Technology".

So…do we (in Israel) have a reason to celebrate (with regard to collaboration)?
On the one hand, the new combined curricula formed a corner stone. It served as a driving force to shift from craft and industrial arts to a technology education which emphasizes skills such as problem solving (design process) and system approach.

In addition, the linkage between science and technology in education has the potential for enhancing technology education as an integral component in the Israeli general curriculum.

On the other hand, the current situation is that collaboration between science and technology on a state level is more wishful thinking than reality. Technological aspects of the curriculum are not delivered properly within the collaboration, and do not do justice to the real relationship between science and technology.

It is clear that there is no one simple and general solution to the problems confronting those who attempt to establish productive relationship between school science and school technology. This paper focuses on the lack of clear conceptual frameworks within the curriculum as an obstacle to collaboration within one combined subject. Conceptual frameworks are essential for the implementation and diffusion of "Science and Technology". Therefore, the first step needed is a dialog between science and technology educators in order to be clear about the goals of the collaboration and establish agreeable conceptual frameworks that will serve as curricular organizers for interactions between science and technology teachers. The didactical frameworks for relationship presented in this paper have the potential to serve as one platform for productive collaboration.

REFERENCES

Aikenhead, G. (1994). *What is STS science teaching?* STS Education: International perspectives on reform (1994). Teachers College Press, New York. http://www.usask.ca/education/people/aiken head/sts05.htmhttp://www.usask.ca/education/people/aikenhead/sts05.htm.

Bar Yosef, N. (2004). *Professional development of science and technology teachers.* (Unpublished dissertation, in Hebrew).

Barlex, D. & Pitt, J. (2000). *Interaction – the relationship between science and design and technology in the secondary school curriculum.* Engineering Council.

Barlex, D. (2002). *The relationships between science and design & technology in the secondary school curriculum in England* http://www.iteawww.org/PATT12/Barlex.pdf .

Black, P. & Harrison, G. (1985). *In the place of confusion: Technology and science in the school curriculum.* The Nuffield- Chelsea Curriculum Trust and the National Centre for School Technology, Trent Polytechnic, (1985).

Childress, V. (1996). Do integrating technology, science and mathematics improve technology problem solving? A quasi- experiment *Journal of Technology Education.* Vol.8 (1) Fall 1996.

Cor de Beurs, (1998). *Technology 15+: Integrating technology in the Science curriculum of the upper level secondary education in the Netherlands.* International working seminar of scholars for technology education, 1998, p. 187-190.

Daugherty, M. and Wicklein, R. (1993). Mathematics, science and technology teacher's perceptions of technology Education. *Journal of Technology Education*. Vol 4 (2) Spring 1993.

De Vries, M. (1996). Technology education: beyond the "technology is applied science" paradigm. *Journal of Technology Education*. Vol. 8 no. 1 , 1996.

Dugger, J. & Johnson, d. (1992). A comparison of principles of technology and high school physics student achievement using a principles of technology achievement test. *Journal of Technology Education*. 4(1), 19-26.

Dugger, C. & Meier, L. (1994). A comparison of second-year principles of technology and high school physics student achievement using principles of technology achievement Tes. *Journal of Technology Education*, Volume 5 (2) Spring 1994. http://scholar.lib.vt.edu/ejournals/JTE/v5n2/contents.html.

Fosrer, P. (1994). Must we MST?. *Journal of Technology Education*. Vol 6 (1) Fall 1994.

Foster, P. (1995). *Integrating educational disciplines*. The Technology Teacher, 54(8), p.45.

Gloeckner, W. (1991).The integration of science, technology, and mathematics myth or dream? *Journal of Technology Education* Volume 2 (2) - Spring 1991. http://scholar.lib.vt.edu/ejournals/JTE/v2n2/tml/contents.html.

Hacker, M. (1999)- MSTe- *Integrating mathematics, science and technology in the elementary School*. http://www.hofstra.edu/pdf/mste_irg_part2.pdf.

IMaST, *Integrating mathematics, science and technology*, Center for Mathematics, Science, and Technology, Illinois State University, 1994.

Israeli Ministry of Education. (1996). *Science and technology curriculum for junior high schools*, Jerusalem, Israel. (In Hebrew).

Krumholtz, N. (1998), Simulating technology to foster learning. *The Journal of Technology Studies*, Volume xxiv, Number 1.

Kipperman, D. (2003). *The noise around us*. PATT Conference, Glasgo University, 2003. http://www.iteawww.org/PATT13/PATT13.pdf.

LaPorte, J. & Sanders, M. (1993). The T/S/M integrated project . *The Technology Teacher* 52(6) p. 17-22

Layton, D. (1993). *Technology's challenge to science education*. Open University Press.

Linnell, C. (2003). Focus on communication and collaboration: Suggestions for implementing changes in the 21st century. *The Journal of Technology Studies*, vol. 27(1).

Loepp, F. (1999). Models of curriculum integration, *The Journal of Technology Studies*, Fall, 1999. http://scholar.lib.vt.edu/ejournals/JOTS/Summer-Fall-1999/PDF/Loepp.pdf.

Massachusetts Department of Education, S*cience and technology/engineering curriculum*, August 2, 1999. http://www.doe.mass.edu/frameworks/scitech99/.

Raudebaugh, R.A. (2000). MWS&T – *Move with science and technology* The Design and Technology International .Millennium Conference 2000, London. P. 146-153.

Sage,J ,(1992). *Developing relationship between science and technology in secondary schools*. http://info.lboro.ac.uk/departments/cd/docs_dants/ideater/papers1992/sajej.html.

Sage, J. and Torben, S. (1993). *Linking the learning of mathematics, science and technology within key stage 4 of the national curriculum*. IDEATER Conference, Loughborough university,1993.

Sanders, M. (2000). *Integrating technology education across the curriculum*. http://www.iteawww.org/mbrsonly/TEmonographs/TEAcrossCurric.pdf.

Sanders, M. (2000). *A brief summary of technology education in the United States: A study of public school technology education programs*. Paper presented at the 62 Annual Conference of ITEA, Salt Lake City, Utah.

Scarborough, D. & Conard W. (1994). PHYS-MA-TECH: *An Integrated Partnership Journal of Technology Education*, Volume 5, Number 2 Spring 1994. http://scholar.lib.vt.edu/ejournals/JTE/v5n2/contents.html.

Williams, J. (2002). *Processes of science and technology: A rational for cooperation or separation*. http://www.iteawww.org/PATT12/Williams.pdf.

Wicklein, R. and Schell, W. (1995). Case studies of multidisciplinary approaches to integrating mathematics, science and technology education. *Journal of Technology Education* Volume 6, Spring,1995.

Yager, R. (1996). *Science-technology-society as reform in science*. New York Press,1996.

FRANCISCA ELTON

36. TECHNOLOGY EDUCATION IN CHILE AFTER NINE YEARS OF IMPLEMENTATION: FROM PAPER TO CLASSROOM

AN OVERVIEW OF THE STATE OF ARTS OF THE SUBJECT IN CHILE

Since 1996 technology education in Chile has had the same legal status in the curriculum of traditional subjects such as math, language or science. It is a vertical subject, compulsory during the first 10 years of schooling for all students and optional for students of 11 and 12 grades.

During the last curriculum reform, educational policy was decisive in introducing technology education as a compulsory and independent subject for all the educational system. There was a firm conviction that the subject should be part of the educational experience of every child in the country as a response to the need for entrepreneurial citizens able to take responsible decisions in the use, consumption and development of technology bearing in mind its personal, social and environmental impact.

However, there were no policies to ensure its implementation in the classroom such as inclusion of the subject in initial and in-service teacher training, development of relevant teaching materials and procedures for student assessment and research and monitoring of the implementation. This has had enormous costs with respect to the teachers motivations and performance, and on the quality of the student learning. Thus, despite the allocation of two/three weekly hours of technology education in all schools, the effective time used for the subject is less. Most teachers (1rst to 4th grades) use these hours for more math and language, handicrafts or other activities not related to the subject. The situation is different in the middle and upper school grades (5th to 10th) given that time allocated to technology (2 hours) is used for the subject, and most teachers plan their lessons based on the official syllabus. However, teachers' lack of knowledge of the subject makes their efforts meaningless. Although these teachers articulate the rhetoric about technology education, they do not comprehend the type of learning involved in the subject and they do not know how to go about teaching it.

Initially, the teaching of technology was left to arts and crafts teachers. There were two reasons for this. The first one, was that simultaneously with the introduction of technology education handicrafts as a subject was removed from the curriculum and its teachers were charged with the teaching of technology. The second reason had to do with the focus of the first version of the technology curriculum that represented a slightly upgraded version of the handicrafts subject. This enabled teachers to accept their new role without protesting the removal of

M.J. de Vries, I. Mottier (eds.), International Handbook of Technology Education, 499–503.

their old subject.   Most of the handicrafts teachers perceived technology education as a lease on life for their increasingly devalued subject in the context of the general education.

Until now, few teacher training institutions are including technology as a teacher specialization or investing in research and professional development in the field. Most are not willing to do so unless they see government policies oriented to ensure the implementation of technology at the classroom level.

Industry, on the other hand, sees in technology education a possibility of developing knowledge and skills related to entrepreneurship, innovation and participation. Although their experience dictates that there are advantages in developing these skills and capacities from a very early age, they have not stood up to ask for results of the implementation of the subject.

MAIN CONCERNS

The main concern at this point should be to know why we reached this point of stagnation within the development of technology education. It is obvious that one reason is that policy priorities are placed on other aspects of the curriculum. But I firmly think that the problem has more to do with the body of the subject. In order to achieve social and political support, it is necessary to share a solid vision on the following aspects:

1. As long as there is no strong consensus over the main contribution of the subject to a student's education, technological education it will not be a priority for society. International tests, such as PISA, TIMSS and PIRLS, assess student learning in math, sciences, social sciences, language and civics, on the basis that there is agreement about what forms of learning are valued in these subjects. Why is it difficult to identify the knowledge and skills that technology contributes to the students' education?   There may be two reasons for this: The first one is that there is not a body of knowledge that is exclusive to technology education. This would explain the variety of approaches that still coexist. A second reason is that in the process of defining technology education learning we mix two elements of importance: the main knowledge objectives and the concrete contents we use in order to achieve those objectives.   For example, in seeking to teach the identification of the components of an object as well as the contribution of each of them to the fulfillment of its purpose, learning about an electrical circuit is just one of the many forms through which that greater learning purpose can be achieved. The greater the variety of versions about what is the focus of technology education, the greater the difficulty to muster support for the subject from people at social, political and economic levels. Additionally, the accumulation of evidence to assess the impact of this learning's on students' later professional performance, as well as on the social and economic development of the country, becomes more difficult.

2. Assuming that we share a clear understanding over the main contribution of the subject, there is a need to understand how such learning is mobilized at different

school levels. In regard to the traditional subjects, there is collective knowledge about how each is to be learned. There are many curricular materials that specify routes to follow in order to achieve learning such as reading, writing, math operations, sciences, etc. And although they can have different positions, they move around a solidly constructed body of knowledge. Within technology education, there is not enough investigation to permit mapping the students learning progress with respect to the different contents strands that we evaluated. Not having this understanding about the subject makes it very hard for teachers to know how to help students to progress in subject knowledge and abilities, or even understand if they are really learning.

3. Teachers need to know how to recognize, from students work, how close or how far they are from achieving a given learning goal, and how to help them to move along. Some valuable work has been already done about this in other countries, specially for the processes involved in designing technology, but unless we have enough evidence collected from students work performance addressing the precise desired learning, it will be not sufficient to assess the students progress in the subject learnings.

4. Finally, if starting from today technological education disappears of the school curriculum, it would probably not be news. If mathematics or language were eliminated, every media would have it in the front pages, and surely the decision would encounter a tremendous social opposition. This is because a collective knowledge exists based on information that learning math is an essential part of a students education. This is not the case with technology education, which requires building social knowledge of the subject, although as it is now, the dispersion of focuses that we encounter can play against it.

A MODEL FOR TECHNOLOGY EDUCATION IN SERVICE TEACHER TRAINING

A model for a in-service teacher training Program could contribute in solving some of the problems sited above among teachers (A collective knowledge about the subject aims and contents; Knowledge about how to teach technology education; Awareness and comprehension of the learning students should acquire; Comprehension of how students learn concepts, abilities and understandings within technology education; Understanding of how the student learning progresses; Knowing what to look for when assessing student performance and how to report back to students and to the teaching plan; Knowledge of management and planning to promote enrichment of learning objectives in the class) was developed and conducted by F. Elton within the this curriculum unit of the Ministry of Education, and implemented as a pilot program with a fourth grade class during 2004 in conjunction with the University of Concepción, with 40 teachers and 1.600 students from seven schools, starting on April of 2005.

The model at issue privileges the construction of knowledge on the basis of teaching practice, by reflecting on the subject contents, the classroom experience and the evidence of the students work. It is also based on backing up teachers by academics. During the teacher training process, school leadership capacities to assure the continuity of technology education without external support are worked through mentors.

Program Structure

The Program is structured so that reflection over the practice serves as a platform to learn about Curriculum, Didactics and Evaluation. The working dynamics that are used for learning in each one of these topics has three components:
- knowledge acquisition on the subject (concepts, abilities and attitudes) and on teaching the subject
- reflection on the teaching practice on the basis of evidence from their own and their students classroom work (how technology education is learned, is taught and assessed), and
- teaching

Academic validation

The program permits teachers to obtain:
Accreditation from CPEIP[1] (192 hours)
Associate Degree on Technology Education (256 hours)
Bachelor degree as Teacher on Technology Education (448 hours)

In order to access the associate and bachelor degrees, the users must already count on a bachelors degree in education.

Block descriptions

Theory and reflection
A technology education content specialist and mentors work with teachers. Contents are worked based on reflection about the teaching practices. These are:
- Technology education curriculum analysis (curriculum)
- Technology Education Syllabus analysis and content learning: project development; technological system analysis; technology and society (curriculum)
- Analysis of the technology education teaching process based on classroom work evidence (didactics)
- Lesson planning (didactics)
- Student work analysis (evaluation)

---

[1] Unit from the Ministry of Education in charge of promoting and certifying in service teacher training.

Degree	Theory and reflection	Planning	Teaching	Thesis
Accreditation from CPEIP	8 Monthly hrs. Total: 64 hrs.	2 weekly hrs. Total: 64 hrs.	2 weekly hrs. Total: 64 hrs.	
Associate Degree 2 terms	8 Monthly hrs. Total: 64 hrs.	4 weekly hrs. Total: 128 hrs.	2 weekly hrs. Total: 64 hrs.	
Bachelor Degree 3 terms	4 weekly hrs. Total: 128 hrs.	4 weekly hrs. Total: 128 hrs.	2 weekly hrs. Total: 64 hrs.	4 weekly hrs. Total: 128 hrs.

Planning
Teachers work collaboratively with the assistance of the mentor. Activities are:
- Didactic material development for lessons (didactics)
- Assessment material development for lessons (assessment)

Teaching
2 hours a week in the classroom in technology education.

Thesis
Required only for obtaining the Bachelors degree
Investigation based thesis in any of the following areas: technology education curriculum development; didactics in technology education; student assessment in technology education.

CONCLUDING REMARKS

Technology education will be a struggle until there is a solid knowledge of its contribution to the curriculum, and awareness of people of its importance by showing them evidence of how this learning impacts on student performance in other subjects, in superior studies and their performance on the job.

It is also necessary to get teachers to reflect and learn about the subject contents and expectations based on classroom work. This can be done by bringing teachers and academics to work together towards these goals. The information that can be derived from this experience is essential for curriculum development and classroom implementation of the subject.

ANDREW STEVENS

37. TECHNOLOGY TEACHER EDUCATION IN SOUTH AFRICA

INTRODUCTION

Although twenty years is a long time in the relatively short global history of technology education, it is an even longer time in the educational history of a democratic South Africa. Twenty years ago, South Africa was in the midst of a state of political emergency and it would be five more long years before Nelson Mandela would be released and the process of nation-building could begin. Only last year, South Africa celebrated the tenth anniversary of its first democratic election. In the past ten years, South Africa has undergone fundamental transformation in many spheres, not least in the educational sphere. In order to present a coherent picture of the development and progress made in technology education, it is necessary to provide a brief account of its history.

APARTHEID EDUCATION

Prior to 1994, education in South Africa was organised on racial lines with separate schools, universities, teacher colleges and administration systems for each of the four main groups as defined by the apartheid state: namely black, white, coloured and Indian. (Note: Although it is offensive to use these racial labels, it is difficult to describe or understand South African education system without almost continual reference to them). To complicate maters further, there were four so-called 'independent homelands' within the borders of the country for four of the main black population groups, each having their own educational ministry and administration. Although the curricula in each of these systems was theoretically equal, the huge differential in state funding made a mockery of the apartheid state's claim of 'separate but equal' treatment for all races. In the resource heavy areas of the curriculum such as science laboratory work, home economics, woodwork and the other 'practical' subjects (which many see as the forerunners of technology education) very little provisioning was made in the black schools. This was particularly true in the rural schools where large proportions of black children were (and still are) educated. The result was that few schools in South Africa offered subjects with a 'practical' orientation: those that did were largely to be found in urban areas and were, to a large extent, reserved for white children only.

M.J. de Vries, I. Mottier (eds.), International Handbook of Technology Education, 505–514.

THE BEGINNINGS OF CHANGE

It is perhaps not surprising that it was an education issue which sparked the famous 'Soweto Uprising' in June 1976 which signalled the beginning of the end of apartheid. The fifteen years following 1976 were marked by almost continual unrest in many of South Africa's black schools which was met with considerable force by the state. Military vehicles were a common sight on school property in this period. One of the more considered responses of the state was a comprehensive investigation into education published as 'Provision of Education in the RSA' by the Human Sciences Research Council (HSRC, 1981). Although the main findings of the report were rejected by the government as being too radical, many of the recommendations were to find resonance in the legislation of the late apartheid state and even in the reform legislation of the post 1994 democratic government. As Kraak (2002) points out, the HSRC report attempted to shift the focus on formal education based on the traditional 'academic' arts and sciences curriculum towards a more 'appropriate' skills-based vocational curriculum, particularly for the majority of black school goers. Although it is doubtful that the radical proposals of the HSRC regarding the vocationalising of the curriculum would have been accepted by the black community, there is little doubt that a key shortcoming of the curriculum, namely its over- emphasis on academic forms of knowing and knowledge production had been identified.

THE INFLUENCE OF MARKET FORCES

In the eighties, a period characterised by widespread unrest in black education, the vocationally oriented ideas of the HSRC report began to take root in much of the official discourse of the time. In accordance with global trends, the language of the market became an increasingly dominant voice in SA education and market-driven analyses and policies began to gain ascendancy over the traditional race-based ideology of apartheid. The influential Walters Report of 1990 recommended significant changes to the curriculum, specifically recommending that subjects such as Hand- and Needlework, Basic Techniques, Technical Orientation and the Handwork subjects 'be recurriculated in their entirety with reference to the English 'Craft, Design and Technology' approach, but taking the South African context and South African needs into account." (DEC, 1990, p.123). The Education Renewal Strategy (ERS, 1991) made similar proposals to the Walters Report, recommending the introduction of a number of new compulsory subjects into the general formative curriculum (Gr 1-9). Amongst these were the new (to SA at least) subjects: Economics, Technology and Arts Education, the rationale being that these three subjects would provide education relevant to the needs of learners and society as well as contributing to the personpower requirements of the country. In the discussion document 'A curriculum model for education in South Africa' the following definition of technology appeared which indicates this economic/productivity rationale for the new subject:

Technology involves humankind's purposeful mastering and creative use of knowledge and skills with regard to products, processes and approaches so as better to control his environment. Technology comprises, inter alia, the utilisation of artefacts and processes by means of which labour productivity is increased. (DNE 1991).

It is clear that the proposals of the ERS were substantially influenced by the demands of the rapidly globalising knowledge economy in which flexibility, adaptability and the ability to respond to changing market circumstances are key skills. In this economy, as Castells points out:

It is the ability to retool and respond to rapidly changing market conditions that is highly valued. Only a formative general education can provide these capabilities through high levels of generalised yet unspecified skills which are in excess of those currently needed in the work place, but which in the future will be in great demand. (cited by Kraak, 2002, p83).

Since general formative education has been identified as providing such skills, and the ERS seems to have been aware of research pointing towards the dangers of vocationalising/specialising too early, it was careful not to propose too clear a differentiation between academic and vocational pathways in the compulsory phase of secondary education (i.e. Grades 1 to 9), but in the proposed post-compulsory phase, vocational education was to assume far greater significance. Although never implemented, these proposals by the apartheid government were to find strong echoes in the policies and legislation of the new democratic order.

THE NEW ORDER: CURRICULUM 2005

When the ANC convincingly swept to power in the first democratic elections in 1994, much was expected, particularly in the long neglected area of educational transformation. At the level of policy, Kraak (2002) identifies the following three pillars underpinning the new dispensation

- An integrated education and training system: The new government committed itself to eradicating the difference in status and privilege which a differentiated 'academic' vs. 'technical/vocational' system promoted. This has done much to boost the status of technology as a subject in schools, but it is still too early to judge how this will play out in further and higher education.
- A single qualifications structure. A new statutory body, the South African Qualifications Authority (SAQA) was established in 1995 to co-ordinate and manage the new National Qualifications Framework (NQF). This framework acts as a mechanism for linking the previously separate education and training fields together.
- A new curriculum framework. The new curriculum, named Curriculum 2005 (C2005) for the year in which implementation was to be

accomplished, is the first single curriculum for all South Africans. Education, for the first time, was to be compulsory for all learners for nine years, the newly named General Education and Training Band (GET). Thereafter would follow three years of Further Education and Training (FET) which would provide for more differentiated general, vocational and work-based education and training.

A feature of the new C2005 was the introduction of eight new compulsory 'learning areas' (replacing the label 'subjects' was an attempt at encouraging the integration of disparate 'disciplines'). These were Language, Literacy and Communication; Mathematics Literacy; Human and Social Sciences; Natural Sciences; Technology; Arts and Culture; Economics and Management Sciences; and Life Orientation. For the first time, Technology, in a form corresponding largely to the British Design and Technology model, was to be part of every learner's education to Grade 9. The guiding philosophy of C2005 was to be 'outcomes-based education', a somewhat controversial philosophy with strong links to the 'competency based' approaches which were current in the vocational and work-based training arenas. Underlying the whole educational system are twelve 'critical outcomes' which all learning programmes are presumed to encompass. These include problem solving, working co-operatively, time management, communication in various modes, using science and technology effectively, etc. The fact that the new technology learning area, itself a product of recent educational thinking, clearly incorporated most of these critical outcomes, was certainly one of the factors which prevented it from being removed from the curriculum when the curriculum was reviewed in the year 2000 (See Chisholm Report, later in this paper).

INTRODUCTION OF SPECIALISED AND VOCATIONAL EDUCATION

Another important feature of the new system with a bearing on technology education is the introduction, after the formative general education of the GET Band, of specialised education at the FET levels. It is here that the work of the previous government (the ERS and CUMSA) can be detected in that vastly expanded vocational education is envisaged. This phase of education transformation has been long delayed and there is still uncertainty about whether the proposed introductory date of January 2006 will be achieved. As far as technology is concerned, there is considerable confusion about *what* will be offered (the curricula for many of the new subjects in the technology field have yet to be finalised), *where* the subjects will be offered (there is confusion about the resource requirements for many of the new subjects) and *who* will offer the various subjects (there are very few, if any, teachers who have received training in the new subjects). At present, it is apparent that a general technology subject along the lines of the GET Technology will *not* be offered, in spite of strenuous protest by members of the Technology Association to Minister Asmal during the course of 2002/03. The rebuttal by the Minister (personal communication, 28 January 2003) and his department indicated their commitment to a narrow view of specialisation: they believed that aspects of GET Technology could be found in various of the new subjects which would be introduced in the new FET, namely Design, Computer Applications Technology, Mechanical Technology, Electrical Technology, Civil Technology, Engineering Graphics and Design, and Consumer Studies. All of these 'new' subjects are reformulations or aggregations of previous art, computer or technical subjects which appear to have retained a rather narrow focus. The argument that it is the holistic nature of a general technology subject with its emphasis on creative, flexible thinking, its combination of conceptual and procedural knowledge and its unique practical focus seems to have fallen on deaf ears. However, an informal group of teacher educators based at a number of universities is working on a curriculum for a general technology subject which it is hoped will convince the authorities. As we have long been accustomed to saying in South Africa: Aluta Continua!

THE INTRODUCTION OF TECHNOLOGY EDUCATION

Returning to the introduction of technology as a learning area in the GET Band, this was a process not without its problems as can be expected in a resource- poor country with no experience of technology in the curriculum. At this point, it is instructive to recall the rapidity of the changes that took place following the unbanning of the African National Congress (ANC) and the first democratic elections in 1994. Although there had been discussion around the introduction of technology into the South African curriculum prior to 1994 (see the ERS and CUMSA proposals) and there was some trialing of programmes in schools at this time, it was only after the elections and the establishment of a new non racial education system that such innovations could gain legitimacy. A National Task Team was appointed early in 1994 to spearhead the introduction of technology into the curriculum. This project, titled 'Technology 2005' (T2005), had the task of developing a national curriculum and trialing it in schools in all nine provinces from March 1994 to March 1997, a very tight time frame for such a novel innovation. Unfortunately, the difficult work of T2005 was overshadowed by the launch in March 1997 of Curriculum 2005: an event which was to transform, if not quite revolutionise, the policy and practise of education in South Africa. The massive task of rebuilding a national schools curriculum from the grassroots was one which stretched the educational resources of the country to the limit. The introduction of the new curriculum within the unrealistic time frames set by National Department of Education placed such strains on the system that Technology lost its novelty opportunity: all learning areas were in a very real sense 'new' and demanded the attention of all involved in education. The burden fell particularly heavily on the shoulders of the teachers (now called 'educators') who not only had to master a plethora of new terms and jargon, but also were expected to translate the new curriculum into implementable classroom activities.

Although the work of the T2005 project committee was extended for a further period, the teacher training aspect of the project was only completed in three of the nine provinces, namely Gauteng, KwaZulu Natal and the Western Cape. Even in these provinces according to Mouton et al (1999), the 'cascade' model, which had been envisaged as a means of extending training into a wider and wider network of schools, was a failure. It was not particularly surprising therefore that the Chisholm Commission, appointed by Minister Asmal in February 2000 to review the new C2005, recommended that the two newest learning areas of the GET, namely Technology Education and Economic and Management Sciences, be scrapped. That this recommendation was not accepted by the Heads of Education Committee (HEDCOM) was due, at least in part, to the enthusiastic following that Technology had built up in the short period following its introduction. The following quote from the extensive evaluation study (see Mouton et al 1999) done of the T2005 project indicates the extent of the enthusiasm with which Technology was being received:

Teachers' enthusiasm for and dedication to technology is one of the most consistent and impressive findings from this evaluation. **The positive attitude of teachers was fed, in part, by the enthusiasm of their learners.** *Most teachers indicated that they would like to continue technology. More than that, many seemed pleased to be able to break out of the old modes of teaching and reconceptualise their notions of what it means to be a teacher/facilitator.*

Technology was an introduction to OBE-style teaching for most teachers, who found this approach to be a positive experience, and one that often gained the attention and recognition of their peers. Most teachers thus commented that they had benefited both professionally and personally from their participation in the project. (Mouton et al 1999, p.157-8)

FACTORS CONSTRAINING THE DEVELOPMENT OF TECHNOLOGY

It would make an interesting study to understand what other factors lay behind the decision to retain Technology: clearly it was not the success of the teacher preparation programme which was, at an official level at least, only operational in two thirds of the provinces of the country. Apart from the work done in some provinces by the T2005 team, much of the early teacher education was done by non governmental organisations (NGOs) such as the ORT-STEP Institute who were active in some of the provinces. In addition, some of the former technical subject educators at universities and teacher training institutions, realising the limited future of their existing programmes, had begun to offer training programmes in the new Technology learning area. On the other hand, many teachers and teacher educators in the former technical and practical subjects did not make the necessary changes and opted for the various severance 'packages' that were being offered at that time. In this way much potentially valuable expertise was lost.

In summary, I would list the following factors as having a constraining influence on the development of technology in schools and in teacher education in particular:

- The transformation of the South African curriculum in the form of C2005 has made it difficult for the new learning area to attract the necessary attention and resources to establish itself in the curriculum and in schools.
- The loss of NGOs who performed a vital role in championing Technology and in providing teacher education programmes (although the latter role has to some extent been taken over by tertiary institutions).
- The ending of the T2005 project meant that Technology lost its most visible champion and its most direct channel of communication with the education authorities. This role is slowly being taken up by the emergence of teacher –led organisations such as the Technology Association (TA) and the South African Association for Science and Technology Education (SAASTE).
- The major upheavals and changes in the tertiary education landscape have dangerously destabilised teacher education programmes, the effects of which on the supply of MST teachers are predicted to be far-reaching.
- The focus on MST subjects towards the late 1990s has, ironically, not necessarily favoured Technology: although it is seldom that you hear the phrase 'science and technology' without the word technology, it is clear that for many it means at best the use of high technology devices and at worst only the use of computers. Indeed the perception that technology is synonymous with computers is a persistent one even in curriculum circles in South Africa and abroad as confirmed by a recent Gallup poll commissioned by the ITEA (ITEA, 2004). The wider conception of technology as an engagement with the technological processes of designing and making has yet to develop deep roots in our curriculum and in our society at large.
- Perhaps the largest constraint to the development of Technology as a learning area in schools is the fact that there is no general technology subject at tertiary level in South African institutions. The subjects which are closest are to be found in the Art, Design and Engineering fields, very few of whose graduates traditionally enter the teaching profession. The lack of a general technology subject in the FET Band exacerbates the situation and is an issue which the TA has attempted to address. I believe that the development of an FET curriculum for a general technology subject is essential if the visionary goals of technology education are to be fully realised. The motivating 'pull' which the presence of such a subject will have on the learning and teaching in the GET Band will be significant. The creation of such a curriculum may even inspire the development of similar tertiary interdisciplinary courses which will assist in alleviating the shortage of suitably qualified teacher trainees.

TEACHER EDUCATION IN SOUTH AFRICA

As has been mentioned above, teacher education in South Africa is in considerable flux at present owing to the closure of the majority (over a hundred) of teacher training colleges and the incorporation of the remaining twenty-seven under the authority of tertiary institutions. This radical process has been further complicated by the process of restructuring and merging of higher education institutions which is due to continue for the next few years until South Africa will have eleven universities, six technikons/universities of technology, four 'comprehensive' institutions (the result of mergers of universities with technikons) and two higher education institutes (based in the Northern Cape and Mpumalanga provinces which are the only provinces without tertiary institutions). Although the closure of many of the former colleges of education was widely seen as necessary (some of these were little more than glorified 'finishing schools', producing 'teachers' with minimal skills and little chance of employment), the restructuring process has continued the disruption of teacher training in ways which are difficult to quantify. At present, predictions about teacher shortages as a result of these transformations and the effects of HIV/AIDS fluctuate widely: some analysts such as Crouch and Perry forecast that we will need around 25 000 new teachers per year from 2005 (Crouch and Perry, 2003). The Western Cape Education Department has estimated that total current enrolment in teacher education has declined from 70 000 in 1994 to only 13 000 in 2003. (Vinjevold, 2002). This suggests that there will be fewer than 5 000 new entrants to the profession for the next few years. Nevertheless, in spite of these predictions, some provinces (e.g. the Eastern Cape) still operate 'closed bulletins' as a result of an apparent excess of unemployed teachers in the system. In this climate of confusion, many of our newly qualified young teachers are seeking employment overseas. What is clear however, is that there is a very great shortage of qualified teachers in the scarce subjects of mathematics, science and technology.

TECHNOLOGY TEACHER EDUCATION: A PRELIMINARY SURVEY

In an attempt to gain insight into the supply of qualified teachers of technology in South Africa, I undertook a survey of all the tertiary institutions in the country in 2002-2003. At that stage, the work was complicated by the rationalising and merging of institutions mentioned above and the survey will need to be repeated when the new landscape has finally emerged. Nevertheless, the following features of the landscape can be detected from the data:

- A majority of the tertiary institutions are offering teacher education in technology, but there are significant exceptions, such as some of the prestige universities which appear to be scaling down their teacher education programmes in favour of research.
- The teaching staff on technology education courses represents a mix of technical/vocational and academically trained personnel. This represents an opportunity for a rich tradition to emerge, provided opportunities are

created for collaboration and cross-fertilisation between institutions. A significant number of institutions employ part-time lecturers to deliver the courses. Some employ NGO 'partners' in a range of creative arrangements to provide education to teachers nearer their places of work.

- Some institutions offer only in-service programmes and some only pre-service programmes, but many offer both, attempting to respond to the critical shortages.
- Many of the programmes suffer from a severe shortage of staff, with a number of institutions operating 'one person bands'. There are very few institutions with more than three technology education staff members, thus limiting the opportunities for research and development of the field.
- There is a wide range of interpretation of what counts as relevant 'content' for teacher education in technology. Although the school curriculum clearly underpins much of the content of the various courses, there is a lot of variation both within the technology components of the courses and in the number and variety of ancillary courses (education theory, methodology etc) offered. This is an area for future research.
- There is a wide range in length and duration of course, even where equivalent qualifications are offered. Many institutions report that they are 'under orders' from educational managers to cut contact time to the bare minimum. This clearly has severe implications for course quality.
- Very few institutions have access to 'resource-rich' environments for technology education. Although computer facilities are fairly common, there are few institutions which have access to purposely designed workshop or studio environments. Many staff are ambivalent about such facilities, feeling that teachers should be prepared for the realities of a poorly resourced school environment. The result is that few programmes deepen the practical capability of teachers (this is particularly true of in-service courses).

A survey such as the above is merely a starting point for an analysis of the state of teacher preparation in technology in the country. Many important dimensions have not been addressed and await future research. For example:

- What are the numbers of teachers being trained at present and how many need to be trained in the years ahead, bearing in mind the predicted impact of HIV/AIDS?
- What is the nature of the courses being offered and how can mechanisms be established so that these are continually developed and improved?
- What is the impact of the courses on schooling and on the lives of school learners? Is the experience of technology enriching the lives of all school children, particularly those in disadvantaged circumstances?

CONCLUSION

The above list is not complete nor is it intended that the above should be used in a normative context: rather I hope to stimulate a debate around the provision of education and training of technology teachers in South Africa in order to strengthen the credibility of the learning area and to establish it more firmly in the educational landscape of the country. I believe that, as a result of the immense pressure teachers and teacher educators have been operating under in South Africa for the last decade, there has been limited opportunity for the reflexion which is necessary if we are to develop technology education so that it occupies its rightful place as one of the most significant innovations in the curriculum of the past twenty years.

REFERENCES

Crouch, L and Perry, H. (2003). In *Human resources development review 2003:* Chapter 21: Educators. Pretoria: HSRC. Available online at http://hrdwarehouse.hsrc.ac.za/hrd/chapter.jsp?chid=138.

Hartshorne, K. (1992). *Crisis and challenge: Black education 1910 – 1990.* Cape Town: Oxford University Press.

HSRC (1981). *Provision of education in the RSA.* Report of the main committee of the investigation into education. Pretoria:HSRC.

International Technology Education Association (2004). *ITEA Gallup poll on technological literacy.* Available online at http://www.nae.edu/nae/techlithome.nsf.

Kahn, M.J. and Volmink, J.D. (1997) *A position paper on technology education in South Africa.* Development Bank of South Africa: Johannesburg.

Kimbell, R. and Perry, D. (2001) *Design and technology in a knowledge economy.* London: Engineering Council.

Kraak, A. (2002). Discursive shifts and structural continuities in South African vocational education and training: 1981-1999. In P. Kallaway (Ed). *The history of education under apartheid, 1948 – 1994.* New York: Peter Lang.

Kraak, A. and Young, M. (2001) *Education in retrospect. Policy and implementation since 1990.* Pretoria: HSRC

Mouton, J., Tapp, J., Luthuli, D.and Rogan, J. (1999). *Technology 2005: A national implementation evaluation study.* Stellenbosch: CENIS.

National Education Policy Investigation. (1992) Teacher education. *Report of the NEPI teacher education research group.* Cape Town: Oxford/NECC.

South Africa. Department of Education (DoE). (2002). *Revised national curriculum statement grades R-9 (Schools).* Pretoria: Department of Education.

South Africa. Department of Education and Culture (DEC) (1990). *The evaluation and promotion of career education in South Africa.* Main Report of the committee chaired by Dr S.W.Walters. Pretoria: Government Printer.

South Africa. Department of National Education (DNE) (1991). *A curriculum model for education in South Africa.* Pretoria: Committee of Heads of Education Departments.

Stevens, A.(2003). *Getting technology into the FET.* Proceedings of the technology association conference, Cape Town, September 2003: Technology Association.

Technology 2005 (1996) *Draft national framework for curriculum development.*

Technology 2005. (undated) *Curriculum model for a preset teacher education course in technology.* Unpublished circular compiled by H.Johnstone, National task team co-ordinator

Vinjevold, P., quoted by Business Day, 29 September 2002. Web edition viewed at http://www.bday.co.za/bday/content/direct/1%2C3523%2C1095576-6096-0%2C00.html on 20 October 2004.

CALVIJN POTGIETER

38. LINKING THE PROBLEM, THE PROJECT AND THE DESIGN PROCESS

A RETROSPECTIVE VIEW ON INTRODUCING RURAL TEACHERS TO TECHNOLOGY EDUCATION

BACKGROUND

During 1995 a pilot project, the Technology 2005 Project, was initiated to introduce technology education into public schools in three of the nine provinces of South Africa on recommendation of the Heads of Education Departments Committee (Mouton, Tapp, Luthuli & Rogan 1999). It should, however, be mentioned that at that time a number of non governmental institutions had already been active in the field of technology education in South Africa. During the same period a new outcomes-based national curriculum (Curriculum 2005) was developed for the General Education and Training Band (up to Grade 9) in South Africa and introduced in 1997 after extensive world wide consultation (Department of Education 1997). For the first time, in public schools in South Africa, technology education was included in the national curriculum as a separate learning area (subject). During 2000 the curriculum was reviewed by the Review Committee on Curriculum 2005 (Chisholm 2000) and technology education was retained as a separate learning area in the Revised National Curriculum Statement which was adopted in 2002 (Department of Education 2002). In the Revised National Curriculum Statement the original seven specific outcomes for the Technology Learning Area were reduced and combined as the following three learning outcomes: Appreciate the interaction between technology, society and the environment; Develop and apply specific skills to solve technological problems; Understand the concepts used in technology and use them responsibly to solve technological problems.

Against this background it should be noted that the critical and developmental outcomes, as envisaged by the Revised National Curriculum Statement emphasise the notion of technological literacy (Department of Education 2002, p.11) especially for that part of the population at present locked in a Third World situation (Ankiewicz, Van Rensburg & Myburgh 2001, p.93). The notion of technological literacy links up with the general purpose of technology education to supply young people, as future citizens, with the necessary resources to live effectively and meaningfully in an increasingly complex technological world (Dugger & Yung 1995, p.4; Gilberti 1994, p.10; Savage 1993, p.41). To cater for the training needs of educators (teachers) (Hansen and Lovedahl, p30) in this

M.J. de Vries, I. Mottier (eds.), International Handbook of Technology Education, 515–532.

regard, higher education institutions in South Africa began to introduce in-service teacher training programmes in technology education.

PURPOSE OF THIS PAPER

During 2004 the standard process of a three-yearly programme evaluation and programme revision for the in-service technology education programmes offered in the School of Education at the University of South Africa was initiated. In this paper the experience gained over the past five years regarding a strategy used to introduce rural teachers to technology education is critically reflected on. The strategy to use simple practical projects (using readily available material and tools) to introduce teachers in rural areas to technology education has proven to be successful in general. However, it was felt that there was a need to address misconceptions and difficulties that the teachers experienced to link the problem, the practical project and the design process.

This retrospective analysis draws on the responses of approximately 500 teachers in a teaching practice workbook where inter alia problems had to be identified and explained. The critical reflection is done according to the following categories: the strategy in general, the specific strategy for the teaching practice sessions, the responses in the teaching practice workbooks and the experience of the presenters during practical sessions. As the first phase of this process the results pertaining to the teaching practice component of the in-service technology education programmes offered in the School of Education at the University of South Africa were revisited. This paper concentrates on one aspect of the in-service technology education programmes offered by the School of Education at the University of South Africa, namely the teaching practice component. In particular, the ability of teachers to link the problem, the project and the design process is revisited.

GENERAL STRATEGY

The programmes involved are in-service teacher training programmes aimed at introducing teachers to technology education. A mixed mode of presentation is used incorporating a distance education component, a compulsory one week practical course and a compulsory one week teaching practice session. The distance education tutorial matter is activity-based using the design process as foundation. A wide variety of activities related to technology education are included ranging from research and problem analysis through designing and making to portfolio and project activities. The practical course is project-based concentrating on the design process, simple projects, the use of available tools and the use of available or waste material. The teaching practice sessions (individual teachers at their own schools under the supervision of a senior teacher) also have design and projects as foundation but emphasise the development of learning programmes to be used in each teacher's particular circumstances. The main target group for these programmes are teachers in rural areas who are confronted with having to teach technology education for the first time. As part of an outreach programme to rural teachers an extract of three days from the practical workshop mentioned above is also presented on demand especially in remote rural areas where teachers have had very little exposure to technology education. The outreach programme is usually done on demand and in collaboration with the local educational authorities and also includes programmes aimed at mathematics, science and environmental education.

In the technology education curriculum of the Revised National Curriculum Statement a functional approach is adopted and the design process is described as a cycle including the following steps: *problems, needs and wants are identified and explained, a range of possible and relevant solutions are considered, an informed choice is made, a design is developed, solutions are realised according to the design, the realised solution is evaluated and the process is recorded and communicated* (Department of Education 2002:28; 1997: 85). During 2004 the education authorities in South Africa also proposed the inclusion, in the new curriculum for the Further Education and Training Band (grades 10 to 12), of *Design* as a separate subject (Department of Education 2004: 9).

For the purposes of the technology education programmes offered by the University of South Africa the above mentioned structure for the design process has been adapted slightly to include the following six basic steps:

- **analyse** the problem, need or want;
- **design** and develop alternative solutions;
- **plan** for the realisation of the optimum solution;
- **make** or manufacture a prototype of the optimum solution;
- **evaluate** the implementation of the design and prototype;
- **present** the information for report and/or marketing purposes.

In figure 1 the structure of the design process is depicted in more detail. The reciprocal link between the problem need or want and the design process is depicted by the two thick shaded arrows. The cyclical nature of the design process is depicted by the arrows linking the different steps. The dashed arrows indicate that continuous assessment is recommended during the design process as a whole and also during each individual step. This indicates that the design process as a whole or the individual steps should be repeated as many times as is necessary to ensure that the problem is solved or the need or want is satisfied. Although the design process is depicted as having a particular structure, it also includes a problem solving perspective and the notion that different permutations are possible by systematically choosing alternative paths and starting points depending on the situation in which it is applied (Williams 2004: 43)

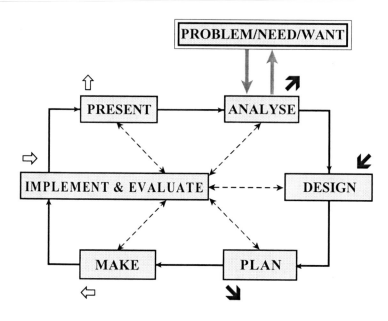

Figure 1. The design process

SPECIFIC STRATEGY REGARDING THE TEACHING PRACTICE SESSION

Although based on both design and projects, the main thrust of the strategy regarding the teaching practice component of the programmes mentioned in the general strategy is that the learning outcomes of the teachers (as learners during the teaching practice sessions) include that they should be able to:

- select appropriate projects to incorporate when developing learning programmes for their learners in the classroom;
- generate a problem/need/want scenario around a chosen project which their learners could use to apply the design process in the classroom during their learning programmes;
- apply the design process to the chosen project as part of their preparation to develop learning programmes for their learners in the classroom.

Against the background of the new outcomes-based national curriculum in South Africa, the emphasis that is placed on the design process and the required pedagogic knowledge (Seemann 2003: 30; Banks, Barlex, Owen-Jackson, Jarvinen, Rutland 2000: 23), a multi-faceted strategy is used to facilitate these learning outcomes. Inter alia, the teachers as learners are supplied with a theoretical background to the design process, examples of the different steps in the design process, a template to complete when applying the design process, a template to complete when developing their learning programmes, basic assembly instructions for a number of projects and a basic set of materials and tools to be used. For some of the projects no assembly instructions and/or materials are supplied in order to facilitate the outcomes-based approach, the use of waste materials and the application of the design process using different paths and starting points.

CRITICAL REFLECTION ON THE SUCCESS OF THE STRATEGIES USED

During the first phase of evaluation/revision process mentioned above it was confirmed that the emphasis which is placed on the design process and problem solving, corresponds to the guidelines of the education authorities in the new curriculum statements. Part of the brief of the evaluation/revision process is to ratify the importance assigned to the design process and problem solving in general and it was decided to, inter alia, peruse the proceedings of a number of recent PATT conferences. Confirmations of the importance of the design process and problem solving in technology education as found in the literature perused are briefly listed below. In an article analysing the technology education curricula of six countries Rasinen (2003: 46) indicates that, although the approaches vary, technological literacy, problem solving and the design process are considered to be important aspects in the curricula of all of the countries. In a paper discussing technological reasoning as the human side of technological innovation (including an empirical study in Finland) Alamäki (2000: 9) stresses the importance of designing, producing and using technology as part of technology education and in a paper based on a study in the USA Thomson (2004: 4) stresses the importance of problem solving strategies and the importance of the design/technology process. In a paper discussing the development of trainee teacher's ability to teach designing within secondary schools in England, Barlex and Rutland (2004: 1) emphasise the importance of design decisions. In a paper linking the technology education curricula of Malaysia and Taiwan, Jen and Huang (2000: 62) also stress the importance of technological literacy and the procedures involved in problem solving. Lee and Todd (2004: n.p.) in a paper aimed at clarifying the design task, stress that teachers should have knowledge of and should understand designing.

During the same period it was decided to retrieve the teaching practice workbooks from the archives and retrospectively analyse the extent to which they reflected the achievement of the three outcomes mentioned above. After an initial general assessment of the teaching practice workbooks it was found that in 85% of the workbooks appropriate projects were chosen, in 55% of the workbooks the problem/need/want scenarios generated were deemed viable and from an overall perspective 75% of the design process portfolios were completed sufficiently.

From these results the main aspect of concern that emerged was the ability of the teachers to achieve the second learning outcome mentioned above under the specific strategy regarding the teaching practice session: *generate a problem/need/want scenario around a chosen project which their learners could use to apply the design process in the classroom during their learning programmes.* This concern corresponds with experience gained during the facilitation of the practical course component where it was found that many students had misconceptions in this regard and experienced difficulties to link the problem, the practical project and the design process.

This concern is directly linked to the first step/phase of the design process. In particular it pertains to what is referred to as *identifying the actual problem, need or want* in the theoretical component. In the theoretical component the first step/phase of the design process is expanded as depicted in Figure 2.

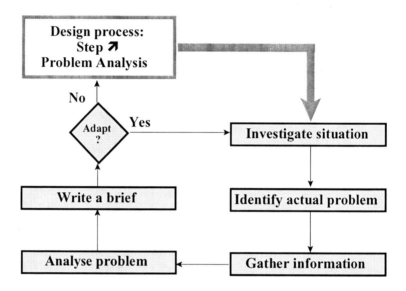

Figure 2 Problem analysis

The portion related to *identifying the actual problem, need or want* is explained, examples are given, related activities are set and it is summarised as having the following components:

- identify whether the problem, need or want is a perceived problem or an actual problem;
- for those problems which are identified as perceived problems, ascertain whether they can be translated into actual problems;
- for the actual problems mentioned above derive/identify the main problem, need or want associated with the actual problems;
- ascertain whether there are any other secondary problems, needs or wants which are associated with the primary problem, need or want;
- describe and clarify the actual problem, need or want by separating it from that which is secondary or only perceived.

Although the ratification (as part of the brief of the evaluation/revision process) of the importance assigned to this particular part of the assessment could be derived from the confirmations listed above it was decided to add a few confirmations directly related to the issue of the identification and description of the problem. In a paper addressing a methodology for infusing creative thinking into project-based learning from an American perspective Doppelt (2004: n.p.) indicates that recognizing the problem is an important part of the first stage of the six stages he suggests for a creative design process. Jones and Moreland (2000: 66) from a New Zealand perspective maintain that technological activity arises out of the identification of some human need or opportunity. In a paper about teaching decision making through a creative and co-operative technology education course, Autio and Lavonen (2004: 1) based in Finland, list the recognition of a problem as the first phase in creative problem solving.

PURPOSE OF THE ASSESSMENT OF THE TEACHING PRACTICE WORKBOOKS

The original evaluation of the teaching practice workbooks by peers only includes an overall assessment of the relevance of the facilitation and presentation of the learning programmes to the project portfolio. It does not include a separate assessment category specifically related to the different steps in the design process, in the project portfolio template included in the teaching practice workbook. The reason for this being that, although the peers that are used for the assessment are senior teachers, they are not necessarily technology education experts. In the template used by the teachers for the teaching practice workbook they are, however, expected to identify the actual problem and then describe the main problem derived from the actual problem and other problems related to the main problem.

The purpose of the assessment was thus stated as to retrospectively assess the problem descriptions in each teaching practice workbook with regard to:
a)   the relationship between the problem descriptions;
b)   the relationship between the problem descriptions and the project that was chosen and
c)   the relationship between the problem descriptions and the design that was chosen as the solution to the problem.

To be able to comment on the relationships as mentioned above it was decided to assess the following aspects in the teaching practice workbook:
- the relationship between the description of the actual problem and the project chosen;
- the relationship between the description of the actual problem and the final design;
- the relationship between the description of the actual problem and the description of the main problem derived from the actual problem;
- the relationship between the description of the main problem and the project chosen;
- the relationship between the description of the main problem and the final design;

- the relationship between the description of the main problem and the other problems related to the main problem.

RESULTS OF THE ASSESSMENT OF THE TEACHING PRACTICE WORKBOOKS

Of the 560 workbooks that were retrieved, 57 were not suitable for assessment (e.g. only partially completed or with missing pages) and thus a total of 503 were used in the assessment. The relationships mentioned above were assessed and rated as being either fully related or partially related or not related at all. During the assessment process mentioned above it was found that it was possible to also retrieve information as to whether the design that was chosen as the solution to the problem was either a model or an artefact and whether the workbook was completed either before or after the practical course was attended. It was anticipated that these aspects could perhaps have had an influence on results of the initial assessment of the teaching practice workbooks as mentioned above. Table 1 depicts the scores from the assessment as pertains to the whole group of 503 workbooks that were assessed. It was found that for the individual relationships scores of between 14.9% and 35.19% were recorded for the items being not related at all.

Table 1 Scores regarding relationships for the whole group (related = fully + partially related)

Whole group	Fully related		Partially related		Related		Not related	
N=503	%	score	%	score	%	score	%	score
Actual/Project	69.18	348	15.90	80	85.1	428	14.90	75
Actual/Design	66.20	333	14.91	75	81.1	408	18.90	95
Actual/Main	46.32	233	29.82	150	76.1	383	23.90	120
Main/Project	46.92	236	24.06	121	71.0	357	29.03	146
Main/Design	43.74	220	27.44	138	71.2	358	28.83	145
Main/Other	30.62	154	34.19	172	64.8	326	35.19	177
Average	50.50	254	24.39	122.7	74.9	377	25.12	126.3

As depicted in Figure 3 the averaged scores for the group as a whole indicate that in 50.50% of cases the items were related, in 24.39% of the cases the items were partially related and in 25.12% of the cases the items were not related at all.

Whole group

Averaged scores

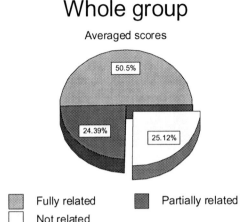

Fully related ☐ Partially related

☐ Not related

Figure 3 Averaged scores for whole group

Due to the retrospective nature of the assessment the statistical analysis of the results were limited to internal comparisons (obviously no control group existed). The statistical analysis of the scores for the different relations indicated a positive correlation in all cases ranging from a high correlation of 0.92 to a low correlation of 0.27. As depicted in Table 2 the correlation between the scores for the *Main/Other* relationship and the rest of the relationships was consistently lower than the correlations between the other relationships. For the other relationships the correlation between the scores recorded for the different relationships were consistently above 0.50.

Table 2 Correlations between the scores for the different relationships

Correlation	Actual/ Project	Actual/ Design	Actual/ Main	Main/ Project	Main/ Design	Main/ Other
Actual/Project	1					
Actual/Design	0.505757	1				
Actual/Main	0.856456	0.54441	1			
Main/Project	0.546722	0.765423	0.543671	1		
Main/Design	0.515231	0.775097	0.570665	0.924019	1	
Main/Other	0.268518	0.415325	0.325796	0.390504	0.436456	1

Table 3 depicts the scores from the assessment as pertains to the workbooks of the group who did the practical course before the teaching practice session. It was found that for the individual relationships, scores of between 12.37% and 28.18% were recorded for the items being not related at all.

Table 3 Scores for the group who did the practical course before the teaching practice session

Practical before Teaching Practice	Fully related		Partially related		Related		Not related	
N=291	%	score	%	score	%	score	%	score
Actual/Project	74.227	216	13.402	39	87.629	255	12.371	36
Actual/Design	78.007	227	6.5292	19	84.536	246	15.464	45
Actual/Main	58.763	171	25.430	74	84.192	245	15.808	46
Main/Project	64.605	188	18.213	53	82.818	241	17.182	50
Main/Design	65.292	190	15.808	46	81.100	236	18.900	55
Main/Other	41.581	121	30.241	88	71.821	209	28.179	82
Average	63.746	185.5	18.27	53.1667	82.016	238.67	17.984	52.333

Practical beforeTeaching Practice

Averaged scores

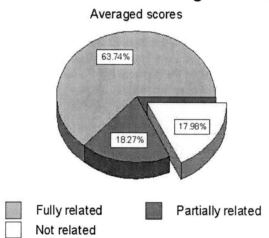

Fully related   Partially related

Not related

Figure 4 Averaged scores for the Practical before Teaching Practice group

As depicted in Figure 4 the averaged scores indicate that, for the group who did the practical course before the teaching practice session, in 63.74% of the cases the items were related, in 18.27% of the cases the items were partially related and in 17.98% of the cases the items were not related at all.

Table 4 depicts the scores from the assessment as pertains to the workbooks of the group who did the practical course after the teaching practice session. It was found that for the individual relationships scores of between 33.49% and 38.68% were recorded for the items being not related at all.

Table 4 Scores for the group who did the practical course after the teaching practice session

Practical after Teaching Practice	Fully related		Partially related		Related		Not related	
N=212	%	score	%	score	%	score	%	score
Actual/Project	41.981	89	19.340	41	61.32	130	38.68	82
Actual/Design	40.566	86	25.943	55	66.51	141	33.49	71
Actual/Main	28.302	60	35.377	75	63.68	135	36.32	77
Main/Project	23.113	49	39.623	84	62.74	133	37.26	79
Main/Design	21.226	45	41.981	89	63.21	134	36.79	78
Main/Other	25.943	55	37.264	79	63.21	134	36.79	78
Average	30.189	64	33.255	70.5	63.44	134.5	36.56	77.5

Practical afterTeaching Practice
Averaged scores

- Fully related
- Partially related
- Not related

Figure 5 Averaged scores for the Practical after Teaching Practice group

As depicted in Figure 5 the averaged scores indicate that, for the group who did the practical course after the teaching practice session, in 30.19% of the cases the items were related, in 33.26% of the cases the items were partially related and in 36.56% of the cases the items were not related at all.

It was also possible to separate the information for a group of 70 teachers who in 2004 received additional tuition (due to demands as specified by a particular sponsor) in the form of a second five-day practical course before they completed their teaching practice sessions. Table 5 depicts the scores from the assessment as pertains to the workbooks of this group. It was found that for the individual relationships scores of between 0.00% and 12.86% were recorded for the items being not related at all.

Table 5 Scores regarding relationships for the 2004 group of 70

2004 group	Fully related		Partially related		Related		Not related	
N=70	%	score	%	score	%	score	%	score
Actual/ Project	84.286	59	10.0000	7	94.286	66	5.7143	4
Actual/ Design	81.429	57	11.4286	8	92.857	65	7.1429	5
Actual/ Main	87.143	61	12.8571	9	100.00	70	0.000	0
Main/ Project	72.857	51	14.2857	10	87.143	61	12.857	9
Main/ Design	75.714	53	14.2857	10	90.000	63	10.000	7
Main/ Other	72.857	51	15.7143	11	88.571	62	11.429	8
Average	79.047	55.333	13.0952	9.166667	92.143	64.5	7.8571	5.5

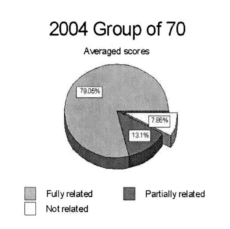

2004 Group of 70
Averaged scores

79.05%

7.86%

13.1%

Fully related Partially related
Not related

Figure 6 Averaged scores for the 2004 group of 70

As depicted in Figure 6 the averaged scores indicate that, for the 2004 group who received additional tuition in the form of a second five-day practical course before they completed their teaching practice sessions, in 79.05% of the cases the items were related, in 13.10% of the cases the items were partially related and in 7.86% of the cases the items were not related at all.

Table 6 depicts the scores from the assessment as pertains to the workbooks of the group who choose an artefact as the result of the design. It was found that for the individual relationships scores of between 12.32% and 26.51% were recorded for the items being not related at all.

Table 6 Scores for the group who choose an artefact as the result of the design

Artefact as result of design	Fully related		Partially related		Related		Not related	
N=381	%	score	%	score	%	score	%	score
Actual/ Project	70.341	268	17.323	66	87.66	334	12.34	47
Actual/ Design	64.567	246	20.735	79	85.30	325	14.70	56
Actual/ Main	49.344	188	32.021	122	81.36	310	18.64	71
Main/ Project	44.882	171	32.546	124	77.43	295	22.57	86
Main/ Design	45.932	175	31.759	121	77.69	296	22.31	85
Main/ Other	35.958	137	37.533	143	73.49	280	26.51	101
Average	51.837	197.5	28.653	109.167	80.49	306.7	19.51	74.33

As depicted in Figure 7 the averaged scores indicate that, for the group who choose an artefact as the result of the design, in 51.84% of the cases the items were related, in 28.65% of the cases the items were partially related and in 19.51% of the cases the items were not related at all.

Artefact as result

Averaged scores

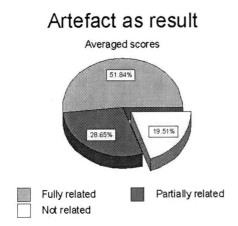

Figure 7 Averaged scores for the group with an artefact as the result of the design

Table 7 depicts the scores from the assessment as pertains to the workbooks of the group who choose a model as the result of the design. It was found that for the individual relationships scores of between 29.51% and 66.39% were recorded for the items being not related at all.

Table 7 Scores for the group who choose a model as the result of the design

Model as result of design	Fully related		Partially related		Related		Not related	
N=122	%	score	%	score	%	score	%	score
Actual/ Project	44.262	54	26.230	32	70.49	86	29.51	36
Actual/ Design	50.820	62	17.213	21	68.03	83	31.97	39
Actual/ Main	36.885	45	17.213	21	54.10	66	45.90	56
Main/ Project	36.066	44	13.115	16	49.18	60	50.82	62
Main/ Design	32.787	40	13.115	16	45.90	56	54.10	66
Main/ Other	16.393	20	17.213	21	33.61	41	66.39	81
Average	36.202	44.167	17.35	21.1667	53.55	65.33	46.45	56.67

Model as result

Averaged scores

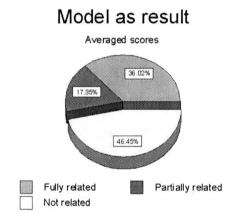

Fully related   Partially related
Not related

As depicted in Figure 8 the averaged scores indicate that, for the group who choose a model as the result of the design, in 36.20% of the cases the items were related, in 21.17% of the cases the items were partially related and in 46.45% of the cases the items were not related at all.

Figure 8 Averaged scores for the group with a model as the result of the design

FINDINGS AND CONCLUSIONS

Introduction

From the results of the initial general assessment of the teaching practice workbooks mentioned above it can be deduced that the strategies followed to a large extent enabled the teachers (as learners) to achieve two of the outcomes envisaged with the teaching practice sessions, namely that they are able to:

- select appropriate projects to incorporate when developing learning programmes for their learners in the classroom (85% of the 503 teachers achieved this outcome) and
- apply the design process to the chosen project as part of their preparation to develop learning programmes for their learners in the classroom (75% of the 503 teachers achieved this outcome).

However, only 55% of the 503 were able to achieve the outcome of being able to generate a viable problem/need/want scenario around a chosen project that their learners could use to apply the design process in the classroom during their learning programmes. This resulted in the retrospective assessment of how the problem analysis phase was completed in the teaching practice workbooks. For the purposes of this paper the conclusions are based only on the averaged scores as listed in the results and the scores for items rated as "fully related" and "partially related" were combined as "related".

Findings

In general when using the averaged scores it was found that the results for the group that attended the practical course before completing the teaching practice workbook, the 2004 group who attended an additional practical workshop and the group who chose an artefact as the result of the design were consistently higher than the results for the group that attended the practical course after completing the teaching practice workbook and the group who chose a model as the result of the design with a margin of approximately 20%.

Table 8 Comparison of the averaged scores for the different groups

	Related	Not related at all
2004 group of 70	92%	8%
Practical before teaching practice group	82%	18%
Group who chose an artefact as the result of the design	80%	20%
Whole group	75%	25%
Practical after teaching practice group	63%	37%
Group who chose a model as the result of the design	54%	46%

When comparing the results regarding the relationships between the problem descriptions it was found that for the relationship between the actual problem and the main problem (Actual/Main) the scores increased from 64% for the group who did the practical course after the teaching practice session to 76% for the group who did the practical course before the teaching practice session and then to 100% for the group who attended an additional practical course before the teaching practice session. When comparing the results regarding the relationships between the problem descriptions it was found that for the relationship between the main problem and other related problems (Main/Other) the scores increased from 63% for the group who did the practical course after the teaching practice session to 72% for the group who did the practical course before the teaching practice session and then to 86% for the group who attended an additional practical course before the teaching practice session

When comparing the results regarding the relationships between the problem descriptions and the project that was chosen it was found that for the relationship between the actual problem and the project chosen (Actual/Project) the scores increased from 61% for the group who did the practical course after the teaching practice session to 88% for the group who did the practical course before the teaching practice session and then to 94% for the group who attended an additional practical course before the teaching practice session.

When comparing the results regarding the relationships between the problem descriptions and the design that was chosen it was found that for the relationship between the actual problem and the design chosen (Actual/Design) the scores increased from 67% for the group who did the practical course after the teaching practice session to 84% for the group who did the practical course before the teaching practice session and then to 93% for the group who attended an additional practical course before the teaching practice session.

When comparing the results regarding the relationships between the problem descriptions and the project that was chosen it was found that for the relationship between the main problem and the project chosen (Main/Project) the scores increased from 63% for the group who did the practical course after the teaching practice session to 83% for the group who did the practical course before the teaching practice session and then to 87% for the group who attended an additional practical course before the teaching practice session.

When comparing the results regarding the relationships between the problem descriptions and the design that was chosen it was found that for the relationship between the main problem and the design chosen (Main/Design) the scores increased from 63% for the group who did the practical course after the teaching practice session to 81% for the group who did the practical course before the teaching practice session and then to 90% for the group who attended an additional practical course before the teaching practice session.

When retrospectively analysing the nature of the interventions during the practical courses it was found that although the teachers were exposed to group work during the normal practical course they had to repeatedly complete their own templates regarding the problem analysis phase which was then peer reviewed by another member of the group on a rotational basis. During the additional practical course the only difference was that the teachers also had to collectively formulate a common response regarding the problem analysis phase which was then peer reviewed by another group.

The results regarding the choice between an artefact and a model as the solution to the particular problems were significantly different. However, it was retrospectively decided that the difference could most probably be attributed to a misconception because the template used for the teaching practice workbooks does not include a section where this choice can be motivated.

Conclusions

From the results of the assessment and the findings it is concluded that exposure of the teachers (as learners) individually to only theory regarding the design process, descriptions of the steps to follow when analysing problems, needs and wants and examples of completed templates in this regard through distance education is not sufficient to enable them to generate viable problem/need/want scenarios around a chosen project which their learners could use to apply the design process in the classroom.

It is further concluded that to enable the teachers (as learners) to generate viable problem/need/want scenarios around a chosen project which their learners could use to apply the design process in the classroom they should be exposed to an instructional situation where they practice the formulation of problem descriptions for a variety of instances collaboratively with peers in a group setting where the collaborative efforts of the groups are peer reviewed by other groups. To a large extent this conclusion is corroborated by an empirical study conducted by Autio and Lavonen (2004) where they found that decision-making in the design process is learned more effectively through a co-operative creative problem solving process.

The general and specific strategies mentioned above should thus be adapted to make it possible for all the teachers to attend the practical course before completing the teaching practice session and to adapt the normal practical workshop to include the collaborative and group peer review aspects of the additional practical workshop.

REFERENCES

Alamäki, A. (2000), *Technological reasoning as a human side of technological innovation*, Proceedings PATT-10 Conference. Retrieved Jan 15, 2005 from http://www.iteawww.org/PATT10/PATT10.pdf.

Ankiewicz, P, Van Rensburg, S & Myburgh, C. (2001), Assessing the attitudinal technology profile of South African learners: A pilot study, *International Journal of Technology and Design Education* (11), 93-109.

Autio, O. & Lavonen, J. (2004), *Teaching decision making through a creative and co-operative technology education course*, Proceedings PATT-14 Conference. Retrieved Jan 15, 2005 from http://www.iteawww.org/PATT14/PATT14.pdf.

Banks, F., Barlex, D., Owen-Jackson, G. Rutland, M. & Järvinen, E. (2000), *Findings of an international teacher training research study: the DEPTH Project*, Proceedings PATT-10 Conference. Retrieved Jan 15, 2005 from http://www.iteawww.org/PATT10/PATT10.pdf.

Barlex, D & Rutland, M. (2004), *Developing trainee teachers' ability to teach designing within secondary school Design & Technology in England*, Proceedings PATT-14 Conference. Retrieved Jan 15, 2005 from http://www.iteawww.org/PATT14/PATT14.pdf.

Department of Education. (1997), *Curriculum 2005 - Specific outcomes, assessment criteria, range statements*, DET, Pretoria.

Department of Education. (2002), *Revised national curriculum statement grades R-9 (Schools)*, DET, Pretoria.

Department of Education. (2004), *National curriculum statement grades 10-12 (General)* Design, DET, Pretoria.

Chisholm, L. (2000), *A South African curriculum for the twenty first century* - Report of the Review Committee on Curriculum 2005, DET, Pretoria.

Doppelt, Y. (2004), *A methodology for infusing creative thinking into a project-based learning and its assessment process*, Proceedings PATT-14 Conference. Retrieved Jan 15, 2005 from http://www.iteawww.org/PATT14/PATT14.pdf.

Dugger, W. & Yung, J.E.: (1995), *Technology Education Today*, Phi Delta Kappa Educational Foundation, Bloomington.

Gilberti, A.F. (1994), *Technology education and societal change*, NASSP Bulletin 78(563), 10-20.

Hansen, J.W & Lovedahl, G.G. (2004), Developing technology teachers: Questioning the industrial tool use model, *Journal of Technology Education* 15(2), 20-32.

Jen, C.I. & Huang, C.J. (2000), *Application of the concepts of the smart schools of Malaysia to Taiwan's technology education*, Proceedings PATT-10 Conference. Retrieved Jan 15, 2005 from http://www.iteawww.org/PATT10/PATT10.pdf.

Jones, A. & Moreland, J. (2000), *From technology national curriculum statement through to sustaining classroom practice and enhancing student learning: The New Zealand experience*, Proceedings PATT-10 Conference. Retrieved Jan 15, 2005 from http://www.iteawww.org/PATT10/PATT10.pdf.

Lee, J. & Todd, R. (2004), *Clarifying the design task – developing a toolkit for teachers and Pupils*, Proceedings PATT-14 Conference. Retrieved Jan 15, 2005 from http://www.iteawww.org/PATT10/PATT10.pdf.

Mouton, J., Tapp, J., Luthuli, D. & Rogan, J. (1999), *Technology 2005 - A national implementation evaluation study*, DET, Pretoria.

Rasinen, A. (2003), An analysis of the technology education curriculum of six countries, *Journal of Technology Education* 15(1), 31-47.

Savage, E: (1993), *Technology education: Meeting the needs of a complex society*, NASSP Bulletin 77(554), 41-53.

Seemann, K. (2003), Basic principles in holistic technology education, *Journal of Technology Education* 14(2), 28-39.

Thomson, C. (2004), *What are the unique and essential characteristics of technology education in the primary school? A study based in the USA*, Proceedings PATT-14 Conference. Retrieved Jan 15, 2005 from http://www.iteawww.org/PATT14/PATT14.pdf

Williams, J. (2004), *Pupils' decision making in technology: Research, curriculum development and Assessment*, Proceedings PATT-14 Conference. Retrieved Jan 15, 2005 from http://www.iteawww.org/PATT14/PATT14.pdf

List of authors

Frank R.J. Banks
The Open University, Milton Keynes, UK
f.banks@open.ac.uk

Moshe Barak
Ben Gurion University of the Negve, Beer Sheva, Israel
mbarak@bgu.ac.il

David M. Barlex
Brunel University, London, UK
dbarlex@nuffieldfoundation.org

Brian Canavan
University of Glasgow, Glasgow, UK
b.canavan@elec.gla.ac.uk

Osnat Dagan
World ORT, London, UK
osnat.dagan@ort.org

John R. Dakers
University of Glasgow, Glasgow, UK
jdakers@educ.gla.ac.uk

Robert A. Doherty
University of Glasgow, Glasgow, UK
R.Doherty@educ.gla.ac.uk

William E. Dugger, Jr.
ITEA, Technology for All Americans Project, Blacksburg (VA) USA
duggerw@itea-tfaap.org

Leo J. Elshof
Acadia University, Wolfville (Nova Scotia), Canada
Leo.elshof@acadiau.ca

Francisca Elton
Ministry of Education, Santiago, Chile
felton@mineduc.cl

Daniel E. Engstrom
California University of Pennsylvania, California (PA), USA
engstrom@cup.edu

Jacques G. Ginestié
IUFM Aix-Marseille, Marseille, France
j.ginestie@aix-mrs.iufm.fr

George J. Haché
Memorial University of Newfoundland, St. John (Newfoundland), Canada
ghache@mun.ca

Peter Hantson
Arteveld hogeschool (Gent University), Gent, Belgium
peter.hantson@arteveldehs.be

Ann Marie Hill
Queen's University, Kingston (Ontario), Canada
hilla@educ.queensu.ca

Marie C. Hoepfl
Appalachian State University, Boone (NC), USA
hoepflmc@appstate.edu

Alister T. Jones
University of Waikato, Hamilton, New Zealand
a.jones@waikato.ac.nz

Tapani Kananoja
Riskutie 14C, Helsinki, Finland
tapani.kananoja@kolumbus.fi

Dov Kipperman
ORT Israel, Tel Aviv, Israel
dkipperm@ort.org.il

Tony Lawler
Goldsmiths University of London, London, UK
t.lawler@gold.ac.uk

Gene Martin
Technical Foundation of America, San Marcos (Texas), USA
Gm01@centurytel.net

Toshiki Matsuda
Tokyo Institute of Technology, Tokyo, Japan
matsuda@hum.titech.ac.jp

Robert McCormick
The Open University, Milton Keynes, UK

r.mccormick@open.ac.uk

Howard E. Middleton
Griffith University, Brisbane (Queensland), Australia
h.middleton@griffith.edu.au

Sumiyoshi Mita
Oyama National College of Technology, Ashikaga City, Japan
mita@oyama-ct.jp

Ilja P.A.M. Mottier
PATT Foundation, Leyden, Netherlands
imottier@freeler.nl

Hana Novakova
Pedag Program
Konevona 241, Prague, Czech Republic

Margarita Pavlova
Griffith University, Brisbane (Queensland), Australia
m.pavlova@griffith.edu.au

Calvijn Potgieter
University of South Africa, Pretoria, South Africa
potgic@unisa.ac.za

David Purchase
University of Malta, Msida, Malta
david.purchase@um.edu.mt

Aki Rasinen
University of Jyväskylä, Jyväskylä, Finland
rasinen@edu.jyu.fi

Philip A. Reed
Old Dominion University, Norfolk (VA), USA
preed@odu.edu

John M. Ritz
Old Dominion University, Norfolk (VA), USA
jritz@odu.edu

Marion G. Rutland
Roehampton University, Roehampton, UK
m.rutland@roehampton.ac.uk

535

Kay Stables
Goldsmiths University of London, London, UK
k.stables@gold.ac.uk

Kendall Starkweather
ITEA, Reston (VA), USA
itea@iris.org

Andrew W. Stevens
Rhodes University, Grahamstown, South Africa
A.Stevens@ru.ac.za

Didier H.V. Van de Velde
Arteveld hogeschool (Gent University), Gent, Belgium
Didiva@arteveldhs.be

Pierre Verillon
Institut National de Récherche Pédagogique, Marseille, France
Pierre.verillon@inrp.fr

Ken S. Volk
The Hong Kong Institute of Education, Tai Po, Hong Kong
kvolk@ied.edu.hk

Marc J. de Vries
PATT-Foundation/Eindhoven University of Technology, Eindhoven, Netherlands
m.j.d.vries@tm.tue.nl

P. John Williams
Edith Cowan University, Mt. Lawley (WA), Australia
p.j.williams@ecu.edu.au

536

Printed in the United Kingdom
by Lightning Source UK Ltd.
121092UK00001B/2